AFRICA

Maps and Charts by
Cathryn L. Lombardi and
John M. Hollingsworth

AF

Edited by

Phyllis M. Martin
and
Patrick O'Meara

RICA

Third Edition

Indiana University Press • *Bloomington and Indianapolis*
James Currey • *London*

This book is a publication of

Indiana University Press
601 North Morton Street
Bloomington, IN 47404-3797 USA

http://www.indiana.edu/~iupress

Telephone orders 800-842-6796
Fax orders 812-855-7931
Orders by e-mail iuporder@indiana.edu

In Britain this book is published by James Currey Publishers, 54B Thornhill Square,
Islington, London N1 1BE.

The paper used in this publication meets the minimum requirements of American National
Standard for Information Sciences—Permanence of Paper for Printed Library Materials,
ANSI Z39.48-1984.

Manufactured in the United States of America

Library of Congress Cataloging-in-Publication Data
Africa / edited by Phyllis M. Martin and Patrick O'Meara.—3rd ed.
 p. cm.
 Includes bibliographical references and index.
 ISBN 978-0-253-32916-5 (alk. paper).—
ISBN 978-0-253-20984-9 (pbk. : alk. paper).

 1. Africa. I. Martin, Phyllis. II. O'Meara, Patrick.
 DT3.A23   1995
 960—dc20   95-5772

 8 9 10 11 08 07

British Library Cataloging-in-Publication Data
A CIP catalog record for this book is available from the British Library.
ISBN 0-85255-230-0 (paper)

CONTENTS

Preface   xiii

I. Introduction

1. Africa: Problems and Perspectives
   Phyllis M. Martin and Patrick O'Meara   3
2. The Contemporary Map of Africa
   Michael L. McNulty   10

II. The African Past

3. Prehistoric Africa
   Kathy D. Schick   49
4. Aspects of Early African History
   John Lamphear and Toyin Falola   73
5. Islam and African Societies
   John H. Hanson   97
6. Africa and Europe before 1900
   Curtis A. Keim   115
7. The Colonial Era
   Sheldon Gellar   135
8. Decolonization, Independence, and the Failure of Politics
   Edmond J. Keller   156

III. Society and Culture

9. Social Organization in Africa
   John C. McCall   175
10. Economic Life in African Villages and Towns
    Mahir Şaul   190
11. African Systems of Thought
    Ivan Karp   211
12. African Art
    Patrick R. McNaughton and Diane Pelrine   223

13. African Music Performed
    Ruth M. Stone   257
14. Popular Culture in Urban Africa
    Dele Jegede   273
15. African Literature
    Eileen Julien   295
16. Social Change in Contemporary Africa
    Claire Robertson   313
17. Law and Society in Contemporary Africa
    Takyiwaa Manuh   330

IV. Economics and Politics

18. African Politics since Independence
    N. Brian Winchester   347
19. Economic Change in Contemporary Africa
    Sara Berry   359
20. The African Development Crisis
    Richard Stryker and Stephen N. Ndegwa   375
21. South Africa
    C. R. D. Halisi and Patrick O'Meara   395
    Africana Resources for Undergraduates: A Bibliographic Essay
    Nancy J. Schmidt   413

Index   435

MAPS

1. African Nations with Dates of Independence   xv
2. Location of Selected Ethnic Groups   xvi
3. The Countries of Africa   11
4. United States and Africa   12
5. Language Families of Modern Africa   14
6. Population Distribution of Africa   17
7. Major Production Areas   18
8. Capitals and Railways of Africa   19
9. Economic Islands in Africa   20
10. Major Physiographic Features   23
11. Physical Features of Africa   24
12. Average Annual Precipitation   25
13. The Climates of Africa   29
14. Vegetation Zones of Africa   30
15. Seasonal Migration of ITCZ—January   34
16. Seasonal Migration of ITCZ—July   35
17. Main Vegetation Areas and Some Prehistoric Sites   54
18. Major African States through the 19th Century   84
19. Eastern Africa   93
20. North Africa and the Sudan   103
21. Muslims in Africa Today   111
22. Europe and Africa, 15th–19th Centuries   118
23. European Rule in Africa, ca.1870   129
24. Colonial Africa—1914   137
25. Agriculture and Food Crops in Tropical Africa   204
26. The "African Homelands" under *Apartheid*   398

FIGURES

1. Average Annual Rainfall by Month   26
2. A Simplified Chart of Primate Evolution   51
3. A Chart Showing Possible Evolutionary Paths of Early Hominids and the Emergence of Early Stone Age Traditions   55
4. A Range of Oldowan Artifact Forms from Koobi Fora, Kenya   56
5. Tools   62
6. A Farming Household   196

PLATES

1. Farmers grazing cattle, Cameroon Republic   22
2. Tropical rain forest in the Cameroon Republic   27
3. Women planting vegetables, The Gambia   28
4. Planting millet, Chad   31
5. Seventeenth-century map of Africa   33
6. Goods being unloaded at Tema Harbor, Ghana   37
7. Transporting tropical hardwoods for export   38
8. Toureg and his family in the Sahel of West Africa   39
9. Testing for malaria in a health clinic   40
10. Olduvai Gorge, site of excavation of early humans   53
11. Excavation at Site 50, Koobi Fora, Kenya   57
12. Remains of Meroe, center of Kushitic civilization   68
13. A *griot* from The Gambia, with *kora* accompaniment   75
14. Ancient Niger river port of Mopti   83
15. Paramount chief and retinue arrive for a meeting, Togo   85
16. Seventeenth-century depiction of the court
    of the ruler of Loango   89
17. The ruins of Zimbabwe   90
18. Mosque in Jenne, Mali   100
19. *Dhows*, Arab sailing ships   105
20. The cattle and camel market at Kassala, Sudan   106
21. Drawing of Fort Jesus, the Portuguese castle of Mombasa   117
22. Diagram of a slave ship   119
23. Unloading surf boats at Accra Harbor   127
24. *Apartheid* sign excluding Africans from
    a park in South Africa   131
25. *District Officer on Tour,* an African carving   141
26. A judicial inquiry in British Cameroons   143
27. Dar-es-Salaam, 1954, colonial capital of Tanganyika   146
28. Coal mining, eastern Nigeria, 1956   152
29. Kwame Nkrumah, the first president of Ghana   158
30. Kenya achieves independence, December 1963   159
31. Political meeting near Cotonou, Dahomey (Benin), 1964   165

32. President Julius Nyerere addressing the United Nations
    General Assembly, 1985   167
33. Voter registration for Namibia's first free election, 1990   169
34. Women pounding millet, Burkina Faso   177
35. Woman sweeping her compound, Burkina Faso   178
36. Village of Cabrais, Togo   179
37. An ironsmith at work, Central African Republic   183
38. Young herder with cattle, Ethiopia   194
39. Women farmers, Tanzania   201
40. Outdoor market, Mopti, Mali   206
41. Yoruba divination tray, collected before 1650   231
42. Maasai woman with jewelry   231
43. Standing figure, Lulua   232
44. Power figure, Songye, Zaire   233
45. Komo mask, Bamana, Mali   234
46. Power figure, Kongo, Zaire   234
47. Commemorative head, Kingdom of Benin, Nigeria   235
48. Whistle, Pende, Zaire   235
49. Figure of a kneeling man, Nok culture, Nigeria   236
50. *Kente* cloth, Asante, Ghana   237
51. Men's looms   238
52. Women's loom   238
53. Fragmentary head, Ife, Nigeria   239
54. Figure of a king, Ife, Nigeria   240
55. Plaque depicting a king with attendants, Benin   241
56. Equestrian figure, Jenne culture   242
57. Afro-Portuguese saltcellar, Sherbo, Sierra Leone   242
58. Staff for Esu cult, Yoruba, Nigeria   243
59. Mask for the Sande society, Mende, Sierra Leone   244
60. Bird masquerade, Bamana, Mali   244
61. Reliquary figure, Kota, Gabon   245
62. The Golden Stool, Asante, Ghana   245
63. Chief sword-bearer to the Asantehene   246
64. Initiation mask, Bidjogo, Bissagos Islands, Guinea-Bissau 247
65. Staff, Kongo, Zaire   247
66. Figure for Bwami society, Lega, Zaire   248
67. Youth association masquerade, Bamana, Mali   249
68. Slit drum, Yaoundè, Cameroon   259
69. Royal drummers in chief's procession, Ghana   261
70. Trumpeters and drummers in
    Independence Day parade, Niger   263

71. Performing on an ivory horn, Liberia 264
72. Fulani *griot*, Ouagadougou, Burkina Faso 267
73. Influence of new technology on music, Liberia 269
74. Mural in local bar, Liberia 270
75. Member of Aladura sect, Nigeria 277
76. Aladura church sign, Nigeria 278
77. New Messenger Apostolic Church, Soweto, South Africa 279
78. *Coronation* (1983), an oil painting by Kenneth Ideh 291
79. Advertising, Lagos style 292
80. A Senegalese family in their home, Dakar, Senegal 315
81. Young boy riding a homemade wooden scooter 318
82. Outdoor nursery, Maputo, Mozambique 319
83. Science class, Teachers' Training College, Lagos, Nigeria 322
84. Women's sewing lessons,
    Damara, Central African Republic 323
85. A typical "shantytown" 325
86. Collecting water at a public fountain, Lomé, Togo 327
87. Young MPLA soldier, Luanda, Angola 352
88. Celebrating national independence, Namibia, 1990 356
89. A sewing room at a fiber factory in Ghana 362
90. Diamond mine, Namibia 364
91. Miners returning from their shift, Zimbabwe 365
92. General view of Kariba dam, Zambia/Zimbabwe 368
93. Famine victims, Ethiopia, 1984 379
94. Women displaced by war, Eritrea, 1993 380
95. Women building a road in Lesotho 384
96. Johannesburg, the largest city in South Africa 396
97. Kwazulu, one of South Africa's ten former "homelands" 399
98. Living quarters for African gold miners
    near Johannesburg 400
99. Funeral of anti-*apartheid* demonstrators,
    South Africa, 1985 405
100. Nelson Mandela with Thabo Mbeki
    and F. W. de Klerk, 1994 410

TABLES

1. Basic Information   xvii
2. Countries and Resources   15
3. Urbanization   41
4. Sub-Saharan Africa in Comparative Perspective   376

PREFACE

Twenty years ago we started working with the faculty of the African Studies Program at Indiana University on the first edition of *Africa*. We had come to realize that in order to advance our understanding of the continent and its people, we had to work not only within our own disciplines but also through interdisciplinary perspectives. Interaction with undergraduates in an introductory course and discussions with colleagues at other colleges and universities were instrumental in developing the first edition of *Africa* in 1976. The second edition represented a mid-1980s approach and reflected changes in Africa as well as new scholarly perspectives.

Given the size and diversity of the continent, this book does not attempt to provide a detailed account of social, political, economic, and historical development for all of Africa. Rather, this overview addresses significant themes that relate to the continent as a whole, such as the development of early humans, social transformations, colonialism, and cultural innovation; or it deals with themes which, although primarily concerned with specific regions and peoples, have far-ranging impact, such as Islam in the northern third of the continent, dramatic changes in South Africa, relationships with international funding agencies, economic decline, and political instability.

All of our contributors have lived and worked in different parts of Africa, but they vary in their individual interpretations, insights, and disciplinary perspectives. Each chapter is enlivened and informed by the personal experiences, the academic training, and, at times, the ideological perspectives of the writer. Comparisons and linkages can also be made between chapters. Gender issues are raised at many points in the book, for example, in the contributions by Şaul, Robertson, and Manuh. There are obvious connections between the McCall, Jegede, and Stone essays which demonstrate the vitality of popular culture. The lasting impact of colonial domination is evident in the contributions of Gellar, Keller, Berry, Julien, and Stryker and Ndegwa. The history of conflict in southern Africa is a theme that appears in chapters by Keim, Lamphear and Falola, and Halisi and O'Meara. There are many other cross-cutting themes that will become evident to teachers and students as they use the book.

Over the past forty years since African Studies came into its own as an area of academic study, there have been dramatic changes on the continent and in the ways scholars think about it. The writing of this preface has given us an opportunity to go back and review the scholarly emphasis of previous editions. In 1976, our contributors tended to emphasize the rich heritage of the African past and the limitless possibilities of the future. In the mid-1980s, when we wrote the preface to the second edition, we noted a new realism in scholarship. The achievements, creativity, and resilience of African societies and cultures over centuries were still very much recognized, but issues such as the roots of rural poverty, hunger, class differentiation, and the weakness of political institutions had to be confronted. In the second edition, new directions in research also required the inclusion of completely new chapters and revisions; for example, gender was fundamental in the analysis of social change, and the growth of African cities and accompanying transformations in urban lifestyles were recognized in a chapter on popular culture. A shift in emphasis in the arts toward performance and context was evident in the chapter on music. Political instability, military takeovers, and the prevalence of one-party regimes demanded a restatement of the chapter on African politics. A sense of crisis in many countries required the inclusion of a chapter on poverty, famine, and economic weakness.

The third edition, written at the end of the twentieth century, continues to address the range of issues that preoccupied contributors in the previous editions. Significant archaeological discoveries in recent years, changing perspectives on social and economic life in African towns and villages, and different approaches to the African arts and humanities, and the importance of law have necessitated new chapters. Democracy and civil society, the end of the Cold War, political transformation in South Africa, ecological deterioration, continuing decline in many areas, and local agricultural initiatives in others, as well as new ways of thinking and writing about these issues, have caused contributors to reconsider and revise other chapters.

The completion of this book would not have been possible without a great deal of help. We would like to acknowledge the students and colleagues in Africa, the United States, and Europe who have commented on previous editions and provided us with new insights and directions. We are grateful to Chris Gray for his research assistance with the text, maps, and charts. Once again, we particularly want to thank Sue Hanson of the African Studies Program for her invaluable assistance in preparing the manuscript. Not only is she careful and efficient, she is also patient and good-humored even under the severe duress caused by the editors. Finally, we are indebted to our contributors, for their essays have broadened our knowledge and enhanced our understanding of Africa.

Phyllis M. Martin
Patrick O'Meara
October 1994

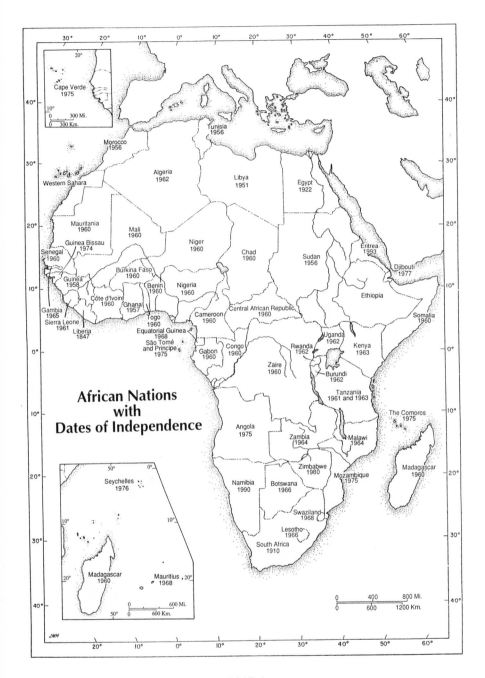

MAP 1

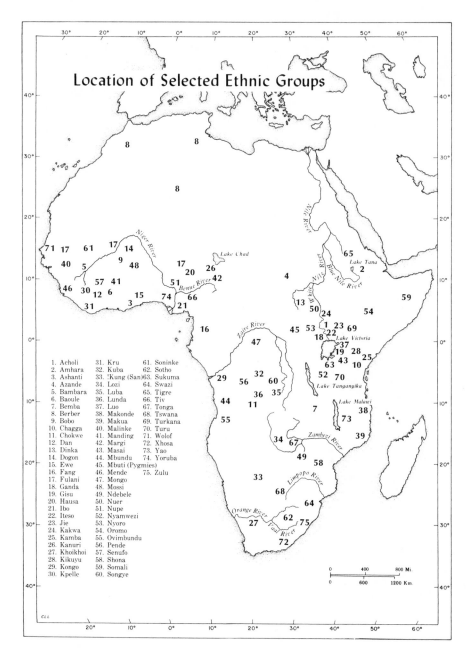

Location of Selected Ethnic Groups

1. Acholi	31. Kru	61. Soninke
2. Amhara	32. Kuba	62. Sotho
3. Ashanti	33. !Kung (San)	63. Sukuma
4. Azande	34. Lozi	64. Swazi
5. Bambara	35. Luba	65. Tigre
6. Baoule	36. Lunda	66. Tiv
7. Bemba	37. Luo	67. Tonga
8. Berber	38. Makonde	68. Tswana
9. Bobo	39. Makua	69. Turkana
10. Chagga	40. Malinke	70. Turu
11. Chokwe	41. Manding	71. Wolof
12. Dan	42. Margi	72. Xhosa
13. Dinka	43. Masai	73. Yao
14. Dogon	44. Mbundu	74. Yoruba
15. Ewe	45. Mbuti (Pygmies)	75. Zulu
16. Fang	46. Mende	
17. Fulani	47. Mongo	
18. Ganda	48. Mossi	
19. Gisu	49. Ndebele	
20. Hausa	50. Nuer	
21. Ibo	51. Nupe	
22. Iteso	52. Nyamwezi	
23. Jie	53. Nyoro	
24. Kakwa	54. Oromo	
25. Kamba	55. Ovimbundu	
26. Kanuri	56. Pende	
27. Khoikhoi	57. Senufo	
28. Kikuyu	58. Shona	
29. Kongo	59. Somali	
30. Kpelle	60. Songye	

MAP 2

TABLE 1
Basic Information

Country (Independence)	Former Name	Former Colonial Power	Capital (and former name)
Algeria (1962)	Algeria	France	Algiers
Angola (1975)	Angola	Portugal	Luanda
Benin (1960)	Dahomey	France	Porto-Novo/Cotonou
Botswana (1966)	Bechuanaland	Britain	Gaborone
Burkina Faso (1960)	Upper Volta	France	Ouagadougou
Burundi (1962)	Part of Ruanda-Urundi	Germany; Belgium, under League Mandate & UN Trust Territory	Bujumbura
Cameroon (1960)	French Cameroun, British Cameroons	Germany; France & Britain, UN Trust Territories	Yaoundé
Cape Verde (1975)	Cape Verde Islands	Portugal	Praia
Central African Republic (1960)	Ubangi-Shari	France	Bangui
Chad (1960)	Chad	France	Ndjamena (Fort-Lamy)
The Comoros (1975)	Comoro Islands	France	Moroni
Congo (1960)	Middle Congo	France	Brazzaville
Côte d'Ivoire (1960)	Ivory Coast	France	Yamoussoukro/Abidjan
Djibouti (1977)	French Somaliland; Afars & Issas	France	Djibouti
Egypt (1922)	United Arab Republic	Britain	Cairo
Equatorial Guinea (1968)	Spanish Guinea, Rio Muni (mainland) & Fernando Po	Spain	Malabo (Santa Isabel)
Eritrea (1993)	Eritrea & Ethiopia	Italy, Britain	Asmara
Ethiopia	Abyssinia	Independent (Italian occupation 1935–41)	Addis Ababa

Country	Former name	Colonial power	Capital
Gabon (1960)	Gabon	France	Libreville
The Gambia (1965)	The Gambia	Britain	Banjul (Bathurst)
Ghana (1957)	Gold Coast	Britain	Accra
Guinea (1958)	Guinea	France	Conakry
Guinea-Bissau (1974)	Portuguese Guinea	Portugal	Bissau
Kenya (1963)	Kenya	Britain	Nairobi
Lesotho (1966)	Basutoland	Britain	Maseru
Liberia (1847)	Liberia	Independent	Monrovia
Libya (1951)	Former colonies of Cyrenaica, Fezzan Tripolitainia	Italy; Britain & France, UN Trust Territory	Tripoli
Madagascar (1960)	Malagasy Republic	France	Antananarivo
Malawi (1960)	Nyasaland	Britain	Lilongwe
Mali (1960)	Soudan	France	Bamako
Mauritania (1960)	Mauritania	France	Nouakchott
Mauritius (1968)	Mauritius	Britain	Port Louis
Morocco (1956)	Morocco	France & Spain	Rabat
Mozambique (1975)	Mozambique	Portugal	Maputo (Lourenço Marques)
Namibia (1990)	South-West Africa	Germany; South Africa; League of Nations Mandate & UN Trust Territory	Windhoek
Niger (1960)	Niger	France	Niamey
Nigeria (1960)	Nigeria	Britain	Abuja
Réunion	Réunion	French département	Saint Denis
Rwanda (1962)	Part of Ruanda-Urundi	Germany; Belgium under League Mandate & UN Trust Territory	Kigali
São Tomé and Príncipe (1975)	São Tomé and Principe	Portugal	São Tomé
Senegal (1960)	Senegal	France	Dakar
Seychelles (1976)	Seychelles	France; Britain	Victoria
Sierra Leone (1961)	Sierra Leone	Britain	Freetown
Somalia (1960)	British & Italian Somalia(s)	Britain, Italy & UN Trust Territory	Mogadishu

TABLE 1 (continued)

Country (Independence)	Former Name	Former Colonial Power	Capital (and former name)
South Africa (1910)	South Africa	Britain	Pretoria/Cape Town/ Bloemfontein
Sudan (1956)	Anglo-Egyptian Sudan	Britain & Egypt	Khartoum
Swaziland (1968)	Swaziland	Britain	Mbabane
Tanzania (1961 & 1963, with unification in 1964)	Tanganyika & Zanzibar	Tanganyika: Germany; Britain under League Mandate & UN Trust Territory Zanzibar: Britain	Dar-es-Salaam
Togo (1960)	Togoland	Germany; France & Britain, League Mandate & UN Trust Territory	Lomé
Tunisia (1956)	Tunisia	France	Tunis
Uganda (1962)	Uganda	Britain	Kampala
Western Sahara *	Spanish Sahara	Spain	El Aaiún
Zaire (1960)	Belgian Congo; Congo-Léopoldville; Congo-Kinshasa	Belgium	Kinshasa (Léopoldville)
Zambia (1964)	Northern Rhodesia	Britain	Lusaka
Zimbabwe (1980)	Southern Rhodesia; Rhodesia	Britain	Harare (Salisbury)

* Disputed territory occupied by Morocco since 1979 following Spanish decolonization in 1976. A UN referendum called for in 1991 offering inhabitants a choice between independence or integration with Morocco had yet to be organized as of September 1994.

Introduction

I

Phyllis M. Martin and Patrick O'Meara
Africa: Problems and Perspectives

1

Within three short months in 1994, two dramatically different developments in Africa claimed world attention. In South Africa, after centuries of oppression and discrimination by a small white minority, the long-time African nationalist leader and political prisoner Nelson Mandela was inaugurated as president. The democratic election, which brought about black majority rule, triumphed over the destructive forces that had tried to exploit racial, class, and ethnic tensions. About the same time, in Central Africa, Rwanda was plunged into civil war, violence, and bloodshed on a massive scale. Hundreds of thousands died, millions fled to refugee camps, where they suffered from disease and starvation, and basic political, social, and economic institutions collapsed. Such extremes of human existence are most frequently portrayed on television, in popular magazines, and in reports and photographs, because they are considered the most newsworthy by the media.

Scholars and students have the different task of grappling with the complex realities that go beyond simplistic headlines. Those who study the continent in depth soon discover that political instability, economic stagnation, international marginalization, and health and ecological crises are only a part of what is actually happening in Africa today. While only a few countries can expect to have the promise and euphoria of South Africa, there is cause for optimism. In recent years ordinary people have expressed their discontent with one-party governments and military dictatorships and have reasserted demands for protection of basic human rights. In countries such as Malawi, Zambia, and Côte d'Ivoire there have been peaceful transitions to new leadership. Many countries have certainly suffered from devastating economic conditions because of drought and mismanagement, but some are exporters of minerals and petroleum, and local farmers have found ways to increase food production. While the realities of the African development crisis cannot be minimized, the ability of ordinary people to create new organizations when the state is unable to meet their needs must also be recognized. In addition, cultural vitality and inventiveness remain an important and animating presence in African daily life, as is evident in many of the chapters in this book.

Size, Diversity, and Division

The size and diversity of Africa are striking. It is more than three times the size of the continental United States and includes fifty-three countries and about 700 million people. Africans are divided not only by the boundaries of nation states but also by ethnic identities, class distinctions, urban and rural experiences, geographic barriers, and vast distances. Great diversity also exists between countries. Population varies widely; for example, Gabon has just over 1 million people, the size of many American cities, while Nigeria has 115 million. The Gambia is less than half the size of New Hampshire, while Sudan is almost four times the size of Texas (see table 2). Ways of life, even within the same country, vary dramatically. Some people may be employed in offices, work in skyscrapers, buy their clothes in department stores, drive automobiles, and own refrigerators and television sets; others may seldom visit cities, live in rural communities, walk miles in the dry season to fetch water, and grow their own food, which they cook over wood fires. At the same time, those who live in the cities may have numbers of their extended family living with them, seek out traditional healers when they are sick, and participate in centuries-old festivals, while those who live in rural areas may listen to transistor radios, buy Coca-Cola at local cafés, and welcome a daughter or son back from graduate studies overseas.

Some contemporary diversity is rooted in the past. All countries on the continent, except for Ethiopia and Liberia, experienced different forms of foreign domination and control under colonial rule, which lasted from about 1880 to the second half of this century (see table 1 and map 1). This experience created many levels of diversity. It caused new language and cultural divisions such as those between anglophone, francophone, and lusophone countries, and imposed norms and values which continue today even though colonialism has formally ended. Governments still have to grapple with profound problems which date from this colonial past. In almost all cases, colonial boundaries cut across particular ethnic groups, and very few countries, for example Swaziland and Lesotho, have only one dominant ethnic group. Most include within their boundaries many different peoples. Ethnic differences may be very real and rooted in the distant past, but often, "tribal" identity is not something fixed which has existed unchanged for centuries. Rather, ethnicity, in recent times, has been accentuated through the use of language, symbols, and history for political ends. Frequently, a sense of a shared identity has been "imagined" or used by leaders and their followers who compete with rival groups for scarce resources and political power. A good example of this comes from recent events in South Africa, where the Inkatha Freedom Party of Mangosuthu Buthelezi used elements from the Zulu past as a means of rallying followers during sensitive constitutional negotiations. In Rwanda and Burundi, where the two dominant groups, the Hutu and Tutsi, have been locked in a tragic conflict, the ethnic nature of the struggle seems not to be in doubt. However, a closer look also shows that the conflict in its modern form and the intense hostility between groups are very much based on class differences resulting from colonial policies and from a politicized ethnicity fanned by modern politicians. Even if the distinctions are new, they have a powerful hold on the imaginations of local people, whose grievances are largely the result of struggling to survive under harsh economic conditions.

During the Cold War, these divisions within or between countries were sometimes intensified when, for economic or strategic reasons, international superpowers intervened and intensified what were essentially local disputes. This was the case, for example, in the "civil war" which has raged in Angola since independence in 1975, where South Africa and the United States armed and aided the opposition while the Soviet Union sent Cubans and arms to bolster the government forces.

An apparent division between North Africa and the rest of the continent, often referred to as black Africa, sub-Saharan Africa, or tropical Africa, is seen as another point of diversity. There is some substance to this perception, since North Africans have been more heavily influenced by the forces of Islam in all aspects of life, political, social, and ideological. Historical and cultural influences and the use of Arabic have provided linkages between countries such as Mauritania, Morocco, Algeria, Tunisia, Libya, and Egypt, and to some extent Sudan and Somalia, and the Arab countries of the Middle East. Thus, the countries of North Africa are connected with each other and to peoples across the Red Sea and the Mediterranean as much as to the rest of the African continent. At the same time, the historical chapters in this book clearly show that for centuries there have also been direct and continuous linkages between North Africa and the rest of the continent, and that the division of the continent by the Sahara Desert can be overemphasized. A majority of the population of the whole northern third of the continent is Muslim, and the forces of Islam are strongly present elsewhere (see map 21). Trade, diplomacy, the transmission of skills and techniques across the continent from north to south and south to north are all evidence of continuing continent-wide interaction.

African governments have been well aware of the fragmented nature of the continent and of the need to cooperate, especially for economic reasons. For example, francophone territories joined in various supranational organizations such as OCAMM (Organization commune africaine, malgace et mauricienne) in an effort to promote cooperation. Likewise, ECOWAS (the Economic Community of West African States) was established in 1975 to bring together countries in West Africa for cooperative activities. During the civil war in Liberia, ECOWAS sent a peacekeeping force to help mediate the dispute. While national political systems range from radical to conservative, differences can be overcome in continent-wide or regional cooperation for specific common goals. The Southern African Development Coordination Conference (SADCC) was established in 1980 by nine nations in an effort to reduce their dependence on South Africa, particularly in the fields of transport and agriculture. When it was started, the organization included conservative Malawi and more radical states such as Zimbabwe and Angola. In 1994, with the coming of majority rule in South Africa, SADCC, now known as the Southern African Development Community (SADC), evolved into a regional cooperative organization with South Africa as a key member. The Organization of African Unity (OAU), which came into existence in 1963, embraces the entire continent and remains an important forum for the mediation of disputes and the achievement of common aspirations.

Thus, integrative forces and shared experiences derived from a deep awareness of a common past and a concern for solidarity over future objectives draw different African peoples and cultures together. Although strong divisions do exist and have been accentuated by the economic hardships and political problems of the last three decades, there are common goals that transcend divisions. Indeed, many leaders and ordinary people actively cooperate to achieve mutual cultural, social, political, and economic goals. Diversity, however, continues as a positive and intrinsic part of the rich, exciting, and multifaceted African experience.

Africa in World Perspective

Africa has never been cut off from the crosscurrents of world history. It was the source of the earliest human biological and cultural developments and the point from which some of the most essential elements of human society and growth were derived. Africans also borrowed from other continents for fundamental innovations in agriculture and material technology: food crops, such as corn (maize), manioc (cassava), and yams from the Americas and East Asia, and the knowledge of iron probably from the Middle East. As early as the first millennium A.D., Africans participated in a busy Indian Ocean trading system dealing with distant places in Arabia, India, Persia, and China, and they exported gold and other commodities across the Sahara Desert to Europe. The Middle East and Europe were also in contact with Africa, exchanging scholars and ideas with important centers of learning in the Arabic-speaking world. Thus, long before the better-known contacts between Europe and Africa that started in the fifteenth century, parts of Africa had interacted continuously with other world areas over centuries. Yet the emphasis in Western writings and popular thinking on the "discovery" of the continent by white explorers from Prince Henry the Navigator to David Livingstone in the nineteenth century contributed to the false impression that Africans had been isolated from the rest of the world.

With the beginnings of the transatlantic slave trade in the sixteenth century, Africa's interaction with the Americas became an important strand of world history. At least 11 million people were forcibly taken to the Caribbean, North America, and Latin America. In the course of the twentieth century, many African Americans have increasingly celebrated their ancestry, through incorporating African elements into their dress, food, and festivals, and by traveling to Africa. African American intellectuals are reinterpreting their history, and African beliefs and symbols are now a significant part of religious practices. Africans have clearly been as important in American multiculturalism as other immigrant groups such as the Poles, the Italians, the Irish, the Jews, and, more recently, Asians and Hispanics.

The interaction of Europe and Africa took on a new dimension at the end of the nineteenth century with the subjugation of the continent under white rule. From the African point of view, the colonial period meant land alienation, the exploitation of raw materials, forced labor, racism, political domination, and Christianity, as well as Western education and technology. Although colonialism lasted less than a century, the impact of this period has been considerable, as we have already noted in referring to African divisions and diversity. Associations between many African states and their former colonial rulers continue. The contacts, which are often termed "neocolonialism," are particularly strong between states that were once part of the French empire. France, for example, still sends personnel to staff armies and administer banks, and provides investment capital and economic assistance for most of its former colonies. To a lesser extent, Britain, Portugal, and Italy also continue their interests in countries they once ruled. For some, these ties are not always considered undesirable. African nations, of differing ideological persuasions, have chosen to retain such linkages and have received privileges and economic benefits. Others see this as a continuation of dependency.

In the mid-1980s the World Bank and the International Monetary Fund (IMF) emerged as the most significant external influences on the economic and political life of many African countries. IMF "conditionality" and demands for "structural adjustment" have required drastic changes in domestic monetary and fiscal policies and have frequently created severe strains on internal political stability and the viability of regimes. Critics of the IMF allege that conditionality has become tantamount to a new form of colonialism.

Traditional and Modern

The terms "traditional" and "modern" are frequently misused and can mask a clear understanding of the continent. The popular view regards traditional Africa not only as isolated from the outside world but also as static, and emphasizes an unchanging lifestyle and value system. Contrasted with this is the popular view of modern Africa as much more progressive and dynamic, due largely to the impetus of Western ideas and technology. Implicit in the concept of traditional and modern is the idea of evolution or progress over centuries. The traditional is seen as anachronistic and inadequate, inevitably to be superseded by the modern, and since the traditional is thought to be incapable of adapting to either internal or external forces, its decline is often seen as inevitable. A tendency to see a sharp dichotomy between the traditional and the modern portrays individuals who try to bridge the "gap" as caught between two worlds. Outsiders often mistakenly think that whole societies are under stress because of these conflicting pressures.

These terms, "traditional" and "modern," are clearly invalid and do not reflect reality if they are used to describe separable parts of individual or group experience; they are not absolute categories into which individuals, institutions, and societies can be neatly fitted. While the division of the African experience into such dichotomies is misleading, the terms continue in use as simple, convenient, almost unavoidable concepts which can provide an initial though limited understanding of the world. If they are to be used, however, they should not be seen as counterbalancing or opposing forces but rather as interdependent. They are a useful way of identifying relative differences in values and lifestyles, but they do need qualification and explanation.

Tradition implies time depth, the continuity of ideals, values, and institutions transmitted over generations; but the process also involves continuous borrowing, invention, rejection, and adaptation on all levels, individual, local, and regional. The emphasis is always on continuity *and* change for all societies, although change in traditional societies was less rapid than in the twentieth century. This increase in the rate of change has been a worldwide phenomenon, resulting from a period of radical technological growth in the Western world in particular. With the coming of colonialism to Africa, the impact of new forces and values was pronounced. In the colonial period, the first agents of change at the local level were traders, missionaries, and petty bureaucrats, soon to be followed by settlers and businessmen. Their interaction with Africans resulted in the introduction of new expectations and value systems which diminished the significance of local ties, emphasized the importance of the individual over the group, encouraged the development of universal norms, and led to an increased emphasis on status resulting from achievement rather than birth. New national political authorities, integration into regional, national, and world capitalist economies, and the introduction of services such as highly developed communication systems and formal Western education all contributed to this period of intensive change.

The terms "traditional" and "modern" are often used to differentiate between rural and urban societies in contemporary Africa. As we have already suggested, not only is this distinction too sharply drawn, it is erroneous; the connections and continuities between villages and towns remain pervasive and strong. Town life incorporates elements of the past and present, indigenous and foreign influences, and generates its own ideas, values, and institutions. This is true of cities that have existed for many centuries, such as Kano in northern Nigeria and Timbuktu in Mali, as well as for cities which were established in colonial times, such as Brazzaville in Congo and Lusaka in Zambia. Migrant laborers who go to the cities to work on temporary contracts return to village farms, families, and festivities and perhaps return to urban employment within a few months. They carry with them to the rural areas elements of city culture, such as tape recorders, pop music, the latest fashions, and new ideas. In the cities, workers and professionals, whether they are newcomers or whether their families have been townspeople for generations, retain in their values, in their social relations, and in their support networks influences from village life as they also embrace changes brought about by their urban milieu. Many permanent city dwellers own or at least have access to land in the countryside and will return there to visit relatives and to celebrate events such as marriages and funerals, or they may retire there in their old age.

Thus, concepts of traditional and modern break down when one begins to examine more closely aspects of African life, individual and institutional, local and national. In contemporary politics in many African countries, politicians recognize the significance and legitimacy both of chiefs whose authority is hereditary and of representatives who have been chosen by the people. Experience is integrated, fusing new and old influences, village and urban ideas and values according to situations, preferences, and needs.

Africa's diversity and integration, its continuous interaction with other parts of the world, and the complex notions of "traditional" and "modern" have been highlighted because they are crucial to an understanding of the continent and are recurring ideas throughout this book. There is a danger that such discussion may reduce these and other themes to a level of abstraction removed from the struggles, vitality, and excitement of daily life. Every day people and nations must make choices, solve problems, and create new options for the future.

Michael L. McNulty
The Contemporary Map of Africa

2 Few students or faculty in American universities would be able to name more than a handful of the African countries in map 3 (identified by number in table 2). The ability to accurately identify and locate such a large number of countries is not particularly important in itself. However, the inability to do so often reflects a more profound ignorance of the important events and processes affecting contemporary Africa. Ignorance of Africa is not a new phenomenon. A general lack of knowledge and frequent misunderstanding of the continent characterized European thought for centuries. In many of the early accounts and accompanying maps, scholars employed an ingenious cartographic device in an attempt to cover up gaps in their knowledge (see plate 5). This practice is characterized in a rhyme by Swift written in the early eighteenth century:

> So geographers in Afric maps
> With savage pictures fill the gaps
> And o'r unhabitable downs
> Placed elephants for want of towns.

In the 1960s and 1970s, the first decades of independence, there was a growing interest in studying Africa at the university and secondary school levels in the United States, although the popular image of Africa was still based on exotic pictures and concepts. The images of Africa presented in newspapers and television coverage emphasized the exotic, the "savage," and the romantic. This period was marked by a great deal of optimism and the promise of a bright new future for the emerging nations of Africa. More recently, environmental, political, and economic crises have shattered the early promise of African development; the popular image now is one of famine, natural and societal disasters, and political collapse. Headlines and cartoons reflect the continuing tradition of "filling the gaps" in our knowledge with familiar but often inaccurate or incomplete images. Students of contemporary Africa who are interested in moving beyond these stereotypes must seek out additional sources of information (see the extensive bibliography at the end of this book).

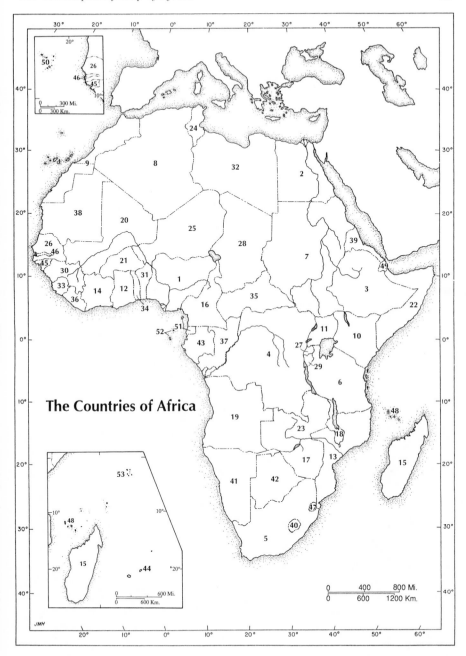

The Countries of Africa

MAP 3

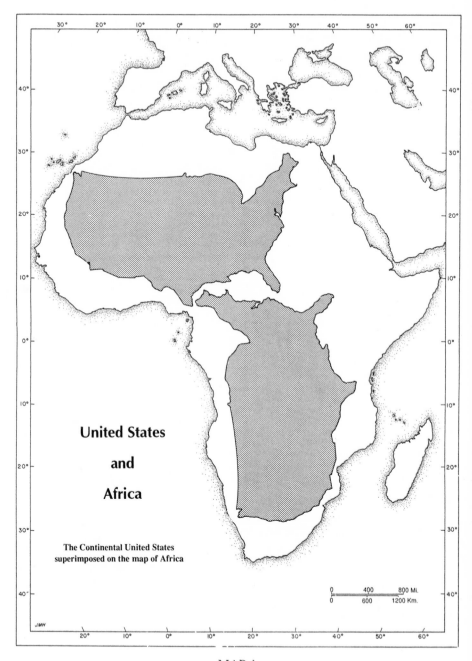

United States

and

Africa

The Continental United States
superimposed on the map of Africa

MAP 4

Africa is a continent of great contrast and diversity. Its vast size, more than three times the land area of the continental United States (see map 4), and its diversity make it difficult and at times misleading to generalize. Africa's diversity is reflected in the regional distribution of human and natural resources, in the nature of urban and rural environments, and in the contrasting lifestyles of a small but growing urban elite and the mass of small-scale farmers. It is also seen in the wide spectrum of social and political institutions. The languages spoken on the African continent can be grouped into four large linguistic families (see map 5); however, on a more particular level there are perhaps as many as a thousand languages, which are as distinct as English is from German. Contemporary Africa is influenced by indigenous, colonial, and national ideas. Despite this tremendous diversity, there are strong elements of commonality among and between the diverse peoples that make up the countries of Africa. This chapter attempts to identify and discuss the significance of these similarities and to provide a broad framework within which the problems of contemporary African development may be understood.

The Geographical Pattern of Development in Africa

At independence the countries of Africa constituted a significant part of what has been called the "commonwealth of poverty," made up of those countries of Africa and Asia that were just emerging from long years of colonial rule and economic exploitation. Today, the countries of Africa remain among the poorest and least developed in the world. Africa is the only continent to record negative growth in the past two decades, and many African countries are actually worse off today than they were twenty years ago. Yet, within this general pattern of underdevelopment there are conspicuous differences (see table 2). This is evident at the national level, but it is even more pronounced at the regional level and within specific countries. The distribution of population presented in map 6 reflects the high degree of regional diversity. Large areas of the continent are virtually uninhabited, while others, particularly urban centers, exhibit a high degree of concentration. Some of the highest population densities occur along the coast, most notably in West Africa, with occasional clusters further inland, as on the shores of Lake Victoria in East Africa. Comparison of population (map 6) with centers of major commercial production (represented in map 7) indicates the close relationship between the distribution of economic and human resources. While there are exceptions, it is clear that the distribution of population and the areas of major commercial production are very similar. A map of the distribution of railways in Africa (map 8) illustrates how the transportation networks focus on these same areas of population concentration and commercial production. Indeed, if individual elements of African development were superimposed on the map as though they were a series of transparencies, a growing and intensifying geographical pattern of inequality would be evident. This series of maps would highlight several prominent "development islands" surrounded by a large "sea" of underdevelopment (map 9). As has been noted:

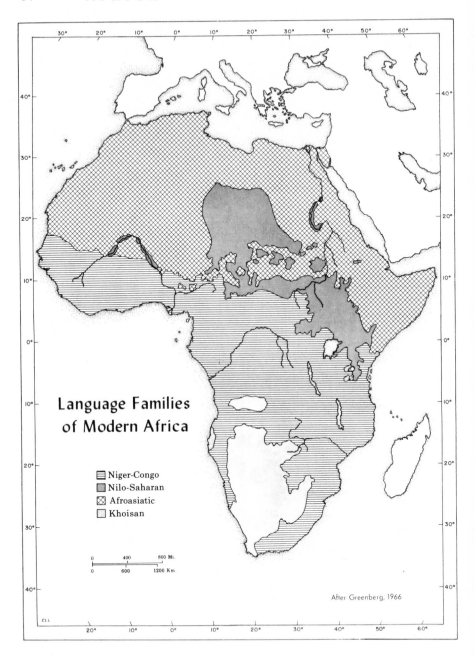

Language Families
of Modern Africa

▤ Niger-Congo
▦ Nilo-Saharan
▧ Afroasiatic
▢ Khoisan

| 0 | 400 | 800 Mi. |
| 0 | 600 | 1200 Km. |

After Greenberg, 1966

MAP 5

TABLE 2
Countries and Resources

No. (see map 3) Country	Population est.(1992) (thousands)[1]	Area (square miles)[2]	GNP (1992 current $) (billions)[3]	GNP ($) per capita (1992)[4]
1 Nigeria	115,660	356,669	32.94	320
2 Egypt	55,163	385,229	34.51	630
3 Ethiopia	53,110	436,349	6.20	110
4 Zaire	39,880	905,365	8.84	260
5 South Africa	39,820	471,445	106.01	2670
6 Tanzania	27,830	364,900	2.56	110
7 Sudan	26,660	967,500	10.10	400
8 Algeria	26,350	919,595	48.32	1830
9 Morocco*	26,320	274,461	27.21	1030
10 Kenya	25,700	224,081	8.45	330
11 Uganda	18,670	93,104	2.94	170
12 Ghana	15,960	92,100	7.06	450
13 Mozambique	15,730	308,641	1.03	60
14 Côte d'Ivoire	12,910	124,503	8.65	670
15 Madagascar	12,830	226,658	2.80	230
16 Cameroon	12,200	183,569	10.00	820
17 Zimbabwe	10,580	150,873	5.89	570
18 Malawi	10,360	45,747	1.89	210
19 Angola	10,020	481,354	6.01	620
20 Mali	9,820	478,841	2.73	300
21 Burkina Faso	9,490	105,870	2.90	290
22 Somalia	9,200	246,201	1.03	170
23 Zambia	8,640	290,586	2.58	290
24 Tunisia	8,400	63,170	14.61	1740
25 Niger	8,250	489,191	2.46	300
26 Senegal	7,740	75,955	6.12	780
27 Rwanda	7,530	10,169	1.81	250
28 Chad	5,960	495,800	1.26	220
29 Burundi	5,780	10,747	1.19	210
30 Guinea	5,600	94,926	3.10	510
31 Benin	5,050	43,484	2.05	410
32 Libya	4,870	679,359	22.97	5310
33 Sierra Leone	4,380	27,699	.72	170
34 Togo	3,760	21,925	1.57	400
35 Central African Republic	3,170	240,535	1.30	410
36 Liberia	2,580	37,743	1.05	450
37 Congo	2,370	132,047	2.50	1030
38 Mauritania	2,140	397,950	1.10	530
39 Eritrea	2,000	46,774	NA	NA
40 Lesotho	1,840	11,720	1.09	590

TABLE 2 (continued)

No. (see map 3) Country	Population est.(1992) (thousands)[1]	Area (square miles)[2]	GNP (1992 current $) (billions)[3]	GNP ($) per capita (1992)[4]
41 Namibia	1,530	318,261	2.50	1610
42 Botswana	1,370	224,711	3.79	2790
43 Gabon	1,240	103,347	5.34	4450
44 Mauritius	1,080	788	2.96	2700
45 Guinea-Bissau	943	13,948	.21	210
46 The Gambia	880	4,361	.36	390
47 Swaziland	820	6,704	.93	1080
48 The Comoros	580	863	.26	510
49 Djibouti	470	8,958	<u>.15</u>	<u>480</u>
50 CapeVerde	380	1,557	.33	850
51 Equatorial Guinea	370	10,830	.14	330
52 SãoTomé and Principe	<u>116</u>	372	.04	370
53 Seychelles	70	175	.37	5480

Figures underlined are for years other than those specified.

* International statistics for Morocco include the disputed territory of Western Sahara.

1. Sources: International Monetary Fund, *International Financial Statistics: July 1994* (Washington, D.C., 1994); *Africa South of the Sahara, 1994*, 23rd ed. (London: Europa Publications, 1994).

2. Source: *Africa South of the Sahara, 1994.*

3. Sources: *The World Bank Atlas, 1994* (Washington, D.C.: The World Bank, 1993) *Africa at a Glance, 1992: Facts and Figures* (Pretoria: Africa Institute of South Africa, 1992); *Africa South of the Sahara, 1994.*

4. Sources: *The World Bank Atlas, 1994*; *Africa at a Glance, 1992: Facts and Figures*; *Africa South of the Sahara, 1994.*

Development has so far taken place, and in all probability will continue to take place, within a framework of social and economic islands and their growing tributary areas which have already left an indelible imprint on the African continent. It is this common factor, this established pattern of advance, which is the key to the analysis so urgently needed. That pattern is, and in the foreseeable future will remain, essentially nodal; with social and economic growth focusing on a number of dominant centers and their expanding territorial spheres of influence.[1]

There has been remarkable stability in the geographical pattern of African development since at least the turn of the century. Areas which stand out today as major "development islands" would have appeared on a similar map drawn eighty years ago, although at the beginning of the twentieth century, commercial production

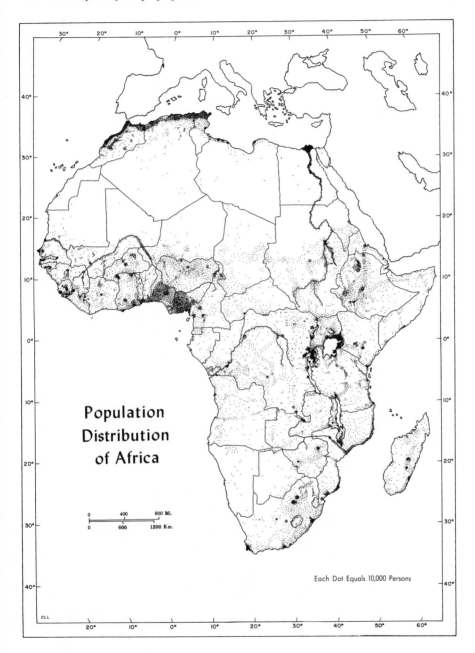

Population
Distribution
of Africa

Each Dot Equals 10,000 Persons

MAP 6

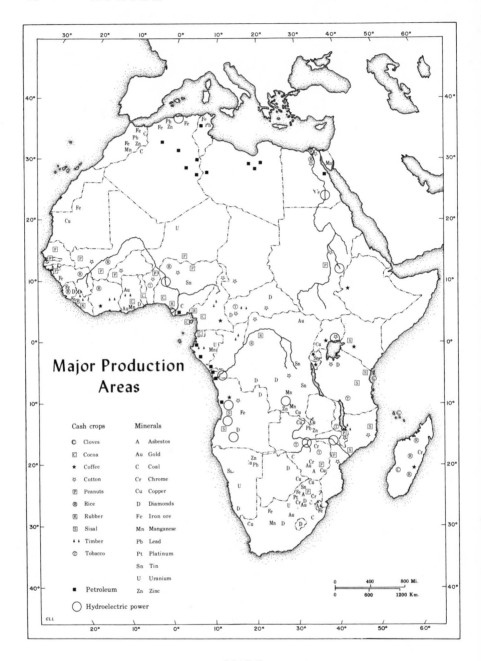

Major Production Areas

Cash crops

©	Cloves
©	Cocoa
★	Coffee
✿	Cotton
P	Peanuts
®	Rice
R	Rubber
S	Sisal
♠♠	Timber
T	Tobacco
■	Petroleum
◯	Hydroelectric power

Minerals

A	Asbestos
Au	Gold
C	Coal
Cr	Chrome
Cu	Copper
D	Diamonds
Fe	Iron ore
Mn	Manganese
Pb	Lead
Pt	Platinum
Sn	Tin
U	Uranium
Zn	Zinc

0   400   800 Mi.

0   600   1200 Km.

CLL

MAP 7

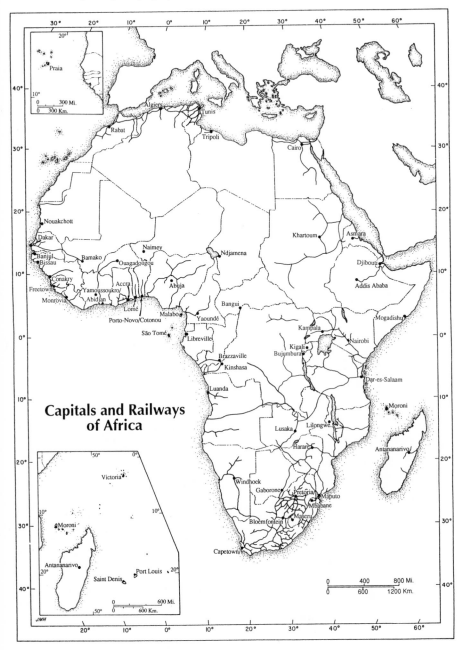

Capitals and Railways of Africa

MAP 8

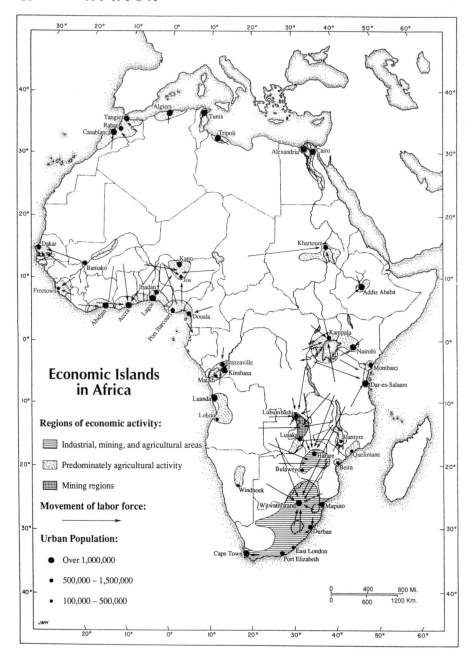

Economic Islands in Africa

Regions of economic activity:

Industrial, mining, and agricultural areas

Predominately agricultural activity

Mining regions

Movement of labor force:

Urban Population:

● Over 1,000,000

● 500,000 – 1,500,000

● 100,000 – 500,000

MAP 9

was even more highly concentrated. Essentially it was limited to a few areas along the coast, to some interior centers of mining, and to isolated patches of commercial agriculture, most notably in the highland regions of East Africa. Areas of major commercial production account for only about 4 percent of the total area of Africa, yet they include nearly all the urban population and more than three-quarters of the value of African products sold on world markets. Thus, much of Africa's wealth is concentrated in a relatively small part of the continent.

The influence of these "development islands," however, extends far beyond that limited area which they occupy. They have an important impact on surrounding regions, and by attracting migrant labor they provide linkages to rural areas often far removed from the actual sites of commercial production. Through commercial linkages and migration streams, these "islands" have a profound influence on local economies, social institutions, and cultures in even the most rural areas. Thus, although relatively few in number, the major areas of urban concentration and commercial production play an important role in articulating the overall pattern of African development. This phenomenon has remained relatively unchanged over the past eighty years, and the dominance of these centers in economic and political terms has been accelerating. What accounts for this highly unbalanced pattern of development? What processes have brought about an increasing concentration within relatively few areas? Why do these few "islands" contain most of the wealth, the highest standards of living, the greatest concentration of educated and skilled people? Why do these centers dominate the flow of goods, people, and ideas?

To understand the origin of these "development islands" and the reasons for their continued growth, we need to consider a number of important processes which have contributed to their continued existence. These include the initial distribution of natural resources and the elements of the natural environment; the historical pattern of development in precolonial Africa; the impact of colonial domination; and the efforts of the independent African countries to achieve higher levels of development.

The contemporary map may be characterized in terms of physical and activity patterns. Physical elements include those features such as towns, highways, dams, agricultural regions, and other features of the landscape which are physically present at particular locations. Activity patterns refer to the flow of goods, people, and information between and among the elements of the physical pattern. Together the physical and activity patterns define the geographic structure of contemporary Africa.

Elements of the Natural Environment

The unevenness of African development is often thought to result from the nature of the physical environment and the distribution of natural resources. Until recently, textbooks often overemphasized the importance of the physical environment. For example, climate and soil were presented as "obstacles" which made development difficult or impossible in certain areas of the continent. Although the physical

Plate 1. Farmers taking their cattle for grazing, Mokolo, Cameroon Republic.
Photo courtesy United Nations/Sean McCutcheon.

environment is important, it cannot be viewed as the only, or even the most important, reason for Africa's underdevelopment at the present time. Elements of the natural environment must be viewed within the context of particular periods of history and corresponding levels of technology. An assortment of isolated facts regarding the natural environment, the landscape, and the climate cannot give the reader a clear understanding of why or how such elements are significant. Nothing could be more tedious than learning that the mean annual temperature in Navrongo, Ghana, is 83 degrees and that the total precipitation is 43.1 inches per year. Such information is important only in relation to other factors.

Physiographic Features, Climatic Patterns, and Development

Africa is a large but rather compact continent. Its shoreline has few natural inlets or harbors. There is a notable absence of extensive coastal plains, and the land often rises to a plateau within a few miles of the shore. Indeed, Africa may be viewed as a large plateau area, broken up by a series of basins (map 10). While the consequences of this physiographic structure are numerous, two aspects have been discussed frequently by authors concerned with development in Africa. First, the smooth coastline (map 11) afforded little opportunity for gaining access to the interior for those Europeans who wanted to tap inland resources. In addition to lacking natural harbors, the coast was often inhospitable because of desert-like conditions or the

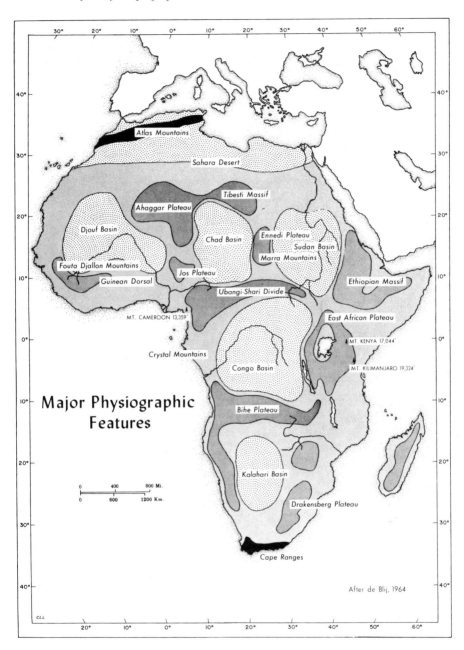

Major Physiographic Features

Atlas Mountains
Sahara Desert
Tibesti Massif
Ahaggar Plateau
Djouf Basin
Chad Basin
Ennedi Plateau
Sudan Basin
Marra Mountains
Fouta Djallon Mountains
Jos Plateau
Guinean Dorsal
Ubangi-Shari Divide
Ethiopian Massif
MT. CAMEROON 13,359'
East African Plateau
MT. KENYA 17,044'
Crystal Mountains
Congo Basin
MT. KILIMANJARO 19,324'
Bihe Plateau
Kalahari Basin
Drakensberg Plateau
Cape Ranges

After de Blij, 1964

CLL

MAP 10

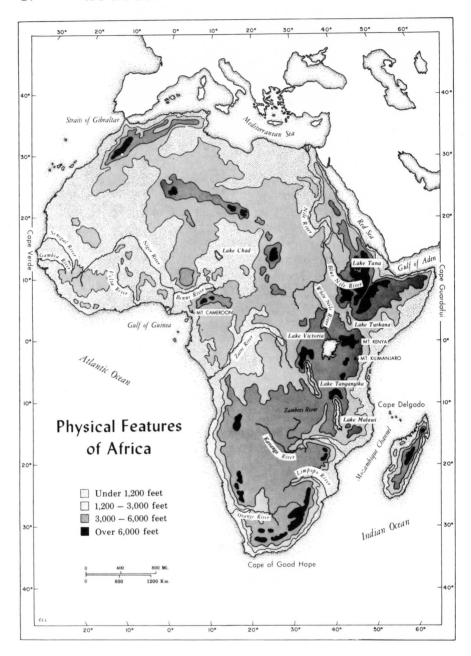

Physical Features
of Africa

☐ Under 1,200 feet
☐ 1,200 – 3,000 feet
▨ 3,000 – 6,000 feet
■ Over 6,000 feet

MAP 11

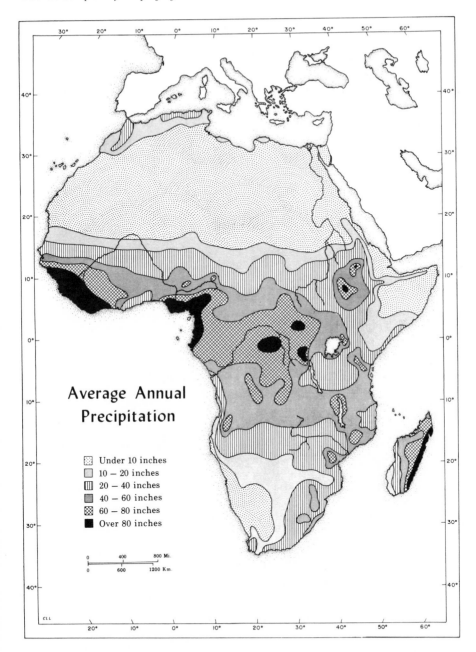

Average Annual
Precipitation

Under 10 inches
10 – 20 inches
20 – 40 inches
40 – 60 inches
60 – 80 inches
Over 80 inches

MAP 12

presence of lagoons and swamps at the mouths of major rivers. Secondly, the plateau-like structure also meant that rivers draining from the interior generally have a series of rapids which rendered navigation difficult or impossible and reduced the use of such rivers as avenues into the interior. Initially, these features limited contacts between peoples of the interior and European merchants, soldiers, and other agents who were attempting to penetrate Africa from the coast. Access from the north was also difficult, although never impossible, because of the vast expanse of the Sahara. Furthermore, the Nile, the only river connecting the Mediterranean coast with areas to the south, was a poor communication channel. It flowed through the Sudan basin, which was marked by extensive areas of floating vegetation, called sudd, that made early navigation difficult.

Another important feature of this physiographic structure is its effect upon precipitation. Particularly along the west coast, the prevailing onshore wind, carrying moist maritime air, rises over the plateau, resulting in a high level of precipitation (map 12). This heavy annual rainfall produces dense tropical forests, which further impede transport development from the coast. Rainfall is indeed a key factor in understanding the climatic conditions that contribute to Africa's development. It must be viewed in both seasonal and annual contexts. Seasonally, rainfall is distributed into wet and dry seasons, which correspond roughly with the temperate seasons of summer and winter. This means that in many parts of the continent virtually all rain, certainly all useful rain, falls during the five or six months of the wet season, while none or almost none falls during the dry season. This severely limits agricultural production, animal pasturing, and general human activity. It is this seasonal characteristic which makes the African climate so markedly different from that of

AVERAGE ANNUAL RAINFALL
BY MONTH

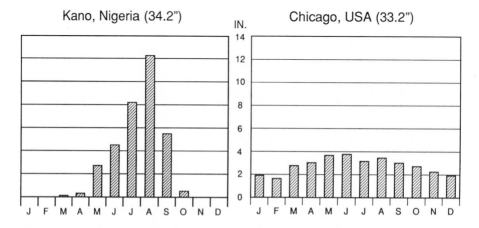

Figure 1. Average Annual Rainfall by Month

Plate 2. Tropical rain forest in the Cameroon Republic.
Photo courtesy United Nations/jt.

more temperate continents. For example, the city of Chicago has slightly less rainfall annually than does the West African city of Kano, but the Chicago rainfall is distributed relatively evenly throughout the year, while the Kano rainfall occurs in only six months (see figure 1). The contrast is remarkable: Kano looks like near-desert in comparison to Chicago. But the difference goes beyond mere appearances, for northern Illinois has much more productive farmland than does northern Nigeria.

Africa, because of its shape and location astride the equator, exhibits a classic climatic pattern which ranges from tropical climates near the equator to more temperate ones to the north and south. Of the total land area of some 11.7 million square miles, more than 9 million lie in the tropics, defined as between 23° 30′ north and 23° 30′ south latitudes. Despite its having been characterized as the most tropical of continents, Africa has relatively few areas of tropical rain forest; savannas constitute approximately one-third of tropical Africa; and approximately three-fifths of the continent, or two-fifths of tropical Africa, is desert or steppe (see map 13). The

Plate 3. Women planting vegetables, The Gambia.
Photo courtesy United Nations/A. Holbrook.

transition from one climatic type to another is usually gradual. In moving from the coast in West Africa toward the north, one encounters a series of ecological zones; the rain forest of the coast gives way to a mixed environment of savanna, trees, and grasses; gradually the trees become more scattered and grasslands predominate; finally, the grasslands merge into areas of steppe. The boundaries between these zones tend to shift as changes occur either in the amount and timing of rainfall or through the action of farmers as they remove trees from agricultural land and burn off the grasses to prepare their fields or to graze livestock. People play an important role in the ecology of Africa and have been a prime agent in changing the nature of the ecological zones.

Vegetational zones (see map 14) which reflect environmental conditions have cultural consequences as well, for different crops are suited to different environments. Societies located in savanna regions grow cereals as staples, principally sorghum, millet, and eleusine, and, since the fifteenth century, corn and manioc introduced from the New World, while societies in the forest area rely upon tuberous crops such as yams and taro. The choice of crops in itself may have deeper social implications, as in the division of labor among farmers along social class and gender lines.

The distribution of large domesticated animals is also related to water in the environment. The tsetse fly, which is a vector of parasitic infection in both humans and cattle, requires a very humid habitat and is generally limited to areas with more than forty inches of rainfall annually, though its seasonal distribution may vary. Areas

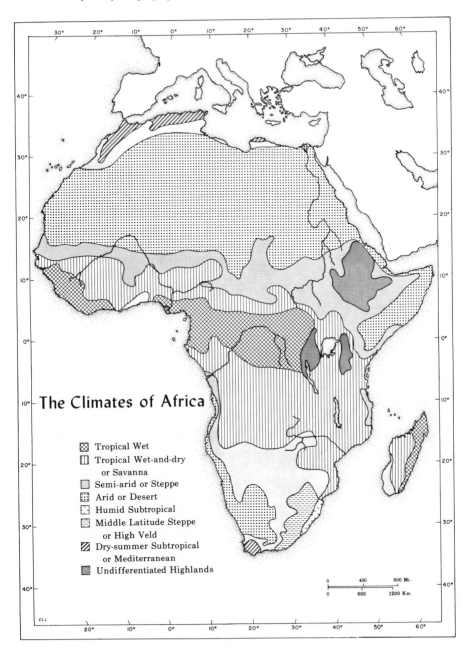

The Climates of Africa

⊠ Tropical Wet
▥ Tropical Wet-and-dry
  or Savanna
▦ Semi-arid or Steppe
▦ Arid or Desert
▨ Humid Subtropical
▦ Middle Latitude Steppe
  or High Veld
▨ Dry-summer Subtropical
  or Mediterranean
▨ Undifferentiated Highlands

MAP 13

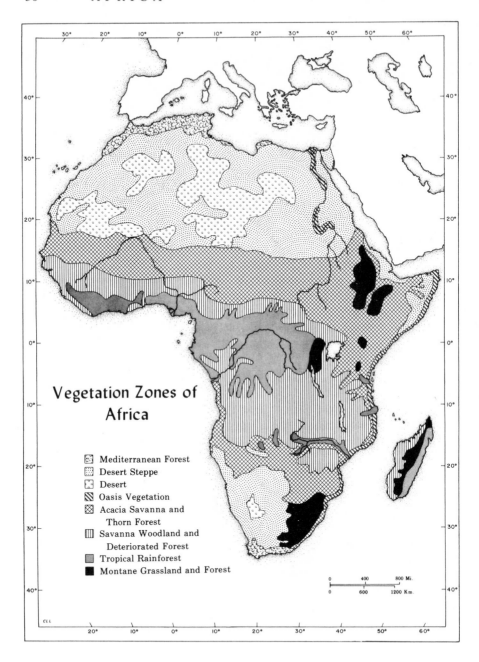

Vegetation Zones of Africa

- ▨ Mediterranean Forest
- ⬚ Desert Steppe
- ⬚ Desert
- ◩ Oasis Vegetation
- ⊠ Acacia Savanna and Thorn Forest
- ▥ Savanna Woodland and Deteriorated Forest
- ▨ Tropical Rainforest
- ■ Montane Grassland and Forest

MAP 14

Plate 4. Planting millet, Chad.
Photo courtesy United Nations/Carl Purcell.

inhabited by the tsetse are thus not suited for livestock such as horses and cattle. Consequently, in these areas there is no milk (except for goat's milk), there are no draft animals, and there is a limited supply of natural fertilizer. The fly does not affect smaller domestic animals such as chickens, sheep, and goats, or a rare dwarf breed of cow.

In some areas people have developed ingenious methods of agriculture to make the best use of the tropical soils and meager rainfall and to protect against deterioration of the land. In other areas, however, the increasing human and animal populations have had deleterious effects upon the landscape and have contributed to soil erosion and accelerated the pace of desertification.

The combined effects of inadequate rainfall and poor conservation methods have been dramatically evident in recent decades. During the early 1970s, the Sahelian region of West Africa, including parts of Chad, Niger, Mali, Burkina Faso, and Senegal, was brought to the world's attention when reports of widespread crop failure and prospects of massive starvation resulted in an international effort to provide some degree of relief to the people in the region. In late 1984, the world was shocked once again when the effects of the Ethiopian drought were brought into comfortable homes in the Western world by television crews transmitting dramatic and horrifying images of starvation and death. More recently, in the first years of this decade, drought and famine in the Horn of Africa took a terrible human toll as hundreds of thousands were affected. In each case it was said that the starvation and suffering were the results of a drought which had destroyed crops and upset the delicate ecological balance characteristic of daily life along the southern margins of the Sahara. This was true, but these events are only the most recent in a series of droughts affecting the area over a long period. Some scientists suggest that these events are evidence of a gradual climatic change which is causing the Sahara to extend southward. The Sahara is described as "creeping" inexorably, as if it were a malevolent creature.

But the problems of the Sahel and the Horn of Africa are not a matter of climate alone. The physical environment is not perverse enough to have conjured up these recent calamities. People and governments must bear a fair share of the burden of responsibility, through ill-advised agricultural policies, inappropriate farming and animal-husbandry practices, overgrazing, and increased soil erosion and destruction of indigenous agricultural systems that had achieved a delicate ecological balance through generations. Development policies of African governments, often designed, funded, and staffed by international donor agencies, all too frequently have exacerbated the problem through ill-advised action. For example, in response to drought conditions which were forcing local pastoralists to extend their search for pasture further south than normal, encroaching upon lands cultivated by sedentary communities, the government of one Sahelian state undertook a project to employ modern technology to sink boreholes to provide water to the pastoralists' herds. A carefully designed plan called for an optimal number of boreholes, strategically located and subject to specific rules governing access to the water. The sites of the boreholes quickly became overcrowded as formerly nomadic pastoralists converged on the newly opened sources of water. The numbers of livestock concentrated in the area surrounding the boreholes quickly surpassed maximum carrying capacity, local officials were ineffective in maintaining control over the pastoralists, and clashes between local people and those drawn from further afield escalated into interethnic conflict. The impact of the drought was thus much more severe than might otherwise have been the case. In Somalia, political strife and regional conflict in the last several years have also exacerbated the worsening climatic conditions and magnified the dimensions of the problem. Here is evidence of the way in which climatic fluctuation in relation to social and economic institutions can result in severe problems which contribute to the underdevelopment of a region.

Presently, the countries of the Sahel are among the poorest of the poor in Africa. They lie at the periphery of the area dominated by the major commercial center along the west coast. It is tempting to interpret this pattern of development and underdevelopment solely as a result of climatic differences. However, this has not always been the case in West Africa. For centuries, some of these same Sahelian areas were centers for African kingdoms and urban centers which dominated politics and commerce in West Africa (see chapters 3, 4, and 5). These kingdoms were at that time focal points of economic and political activity, while the southern coastal areas were at the periphery.

Thus the contemporary development pattern represents a complete and dramatic reversal of the spatial structure of West Africa. This cannot be explained solely by climatic change, but must be understood in terms of changing economic and political conditions as well. There is indeed some evidence that the climate in this area has

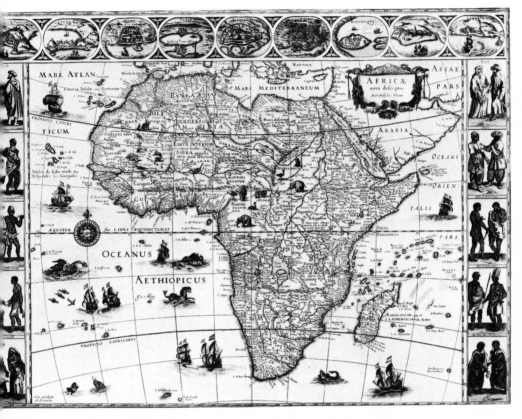

Plate 5. Seventeenth-century map of Africa from G. and I. Blaeu, *Atlas,* 1648.
Photo courtesy Lilly Library of Rare Books and Manuscripts, Indiana University.

been changing, and that conditions were less severe during the period when trans-Saharan trade was flourishing. But what dramatically altered the situation was the decline of the ancient kingdoms occasioned by political strife related to control of the trans-Saharan trade and to the impact of colonial penetration along the coast.

Understanding the nature of climatic variations together with the nature of social and economic institutions aids in interpreting many features in this West African region. The climatic differences between the northern and southern areas directly contribute to one of the most significant features of West African seasonal migration. Rainfall decreases as one moves from south to north in West Africa, with eighty inches or more annually along some parts of the coast and less than thirty-five inches in areas just a few hundred miles further inland. Aside from being drier, the northern areas of West Africa also have marked seasonality in the distribution of rainfall. West Africa is affected by the movement of the Intertropical Convergence Zone (ITCZ), which marks the boundary between a moist, maritime airmass and a drier, continental airmass (see maps 15 and 16). As the ITCZ moves north and south, it results in the

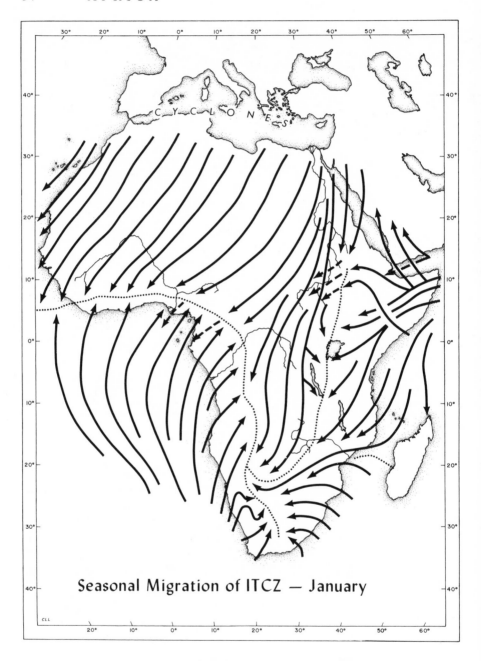

Seasonal Migration of ITCZ — January

MAP 15

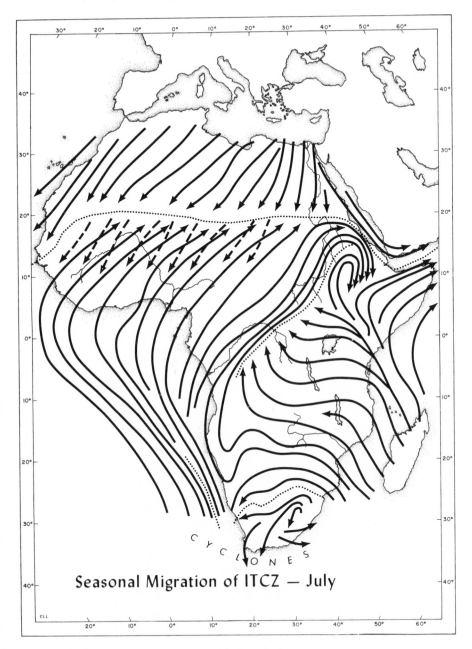

Seasonal Migration of ITCZ — July

MAP 16

highly seasonal distribution of rainfall, alternately characterized as the "rainy season" and the "dry season." Agricultural practices are related to the distribution of rainfall, and in the north, where the distinction between the seasons is most marked, little can be grown during the dry season. Because of the lack of adequate storage facilities, the dry season, referred to in some areas as the "hungry season," is a period of food shortage. During this time many northerners migrate to the south, where employment is sought on farms. Just before the rains return to the north, many of these men go back to prepare their fields for planting. The periodic absences of migrant labor also have significant implications for the division of labor between men and women. For extended periods of time the women in the northern villages have primary responsibility for the household. This seasonal pattern of migration is an important feature of West African life and has had a significant effect upon social and economic conditions in both the north and the south. The difference in climate, then, strongly affects the organization of economic and social life. Many other examples of this interrelationship between the natural environment and social and economic institutions could be provided to help explain certain important features of development in other parts of the continent (see chapters 10, 19, and 20).

Population, Politics, and the Environment

In seeking explanations for the continuing state of underdevelopment of Africa, we have argued that the environment cannot be seen as the sole, or even the most important, element. At the 1994 International Conference on Population and Development held in Cairo, Egypt, many experts argued that population, rather than environment, is the most serious cause of continuing poverty. This argument suggests that as long as population growth outstrips the growth of the economy, especially in countries so overly dependent on primary production, they will never escape from poverty. In fact, the continuing pressure of population growth on the resource base leads to environmental degradation and the reduction of the carrying capacity of the land. This suggests that African countries will never escape the poverty trap until they control the rate of population growth. Although Africa, owing to its vast size, has a relatively low population density, its population is growing at a faster rate than that of any other continent. Much of the population of the continent is clustered around the relatively few development islands discussed above (see map 6). Population migration, both voluntary and involuntary, is putting additional pressure on the areas with the most productive agricultural land and other natural resources. This is contributing to deforestation and desertification in the countryside and to the accelerating growth of Africa's cities (see table 3), which are fast becoming overburdened and incapable of providing even the most rudimentary of urban services. Few African governments have addressed this situation, and many continue to have pronatalist policies. Health conditions across the continent are uniformly poor, and rates of infant mortality and morbidity remain among the world's highest. Nonetheless, children under the age of fifteen constitute an estimated 45 percent of total population. Those who survive will

Plate 6. Goods being unloaded at Tema Harbor, Ghana.
Photo courtesy United Nations/PR/mh.

live out their most productive years in economies which are woefully unprepared to provide opportunities for education or employment. The consequences will have important political and social ramifications, such as local struggles over access to resources among increasingly desperate people, unrest among unemployed urban youth, and rising dissatisfaction with governments that appear unable or unwilling to provide basic security and services. In many countries the combined effect of prolonged drought, inappropriate and unsustainable agricultural practices, and civil strife has created in Africa one of the world's largest refugee populations. This vast tide of humanity moving across boundaries and crowding into camps and settlements has become an almost chronic condition in some regions of Africa. The combination of population, environmental degradation, and politics has recently contributed to civil unrest and bloody conflicts in several countries, including Somalia and Rwanda.

Environmental Elements and Health

The impact of environment is particularly evident in terms of health. The conditions of tropical Africa contribute to a host of health-related problems, which are aggravated by a lack of research, insufficient health facilities, and inadequate

Plate 7. Valuable tropical hardwoods being transported to the coast for export.
Photo courtesy United Nations/PJ/db.

resources to control or eradicate certain endemic diseases. Large areas of the continent are still affected by the tsetse fly, which carries trypanosomiasis. Commonly called sleeping sickness on account of the dramatic symptoms which precede death, this disease impairs the health of both humans and animals, for whom it is usually fatal. Malaria, despite current levels of medical technology, still adversely affects large segments of the population and results in a waste of human resources. These and a number of other environmentally related health factors seriously limit the full use of Africa's human and natural resources and affect the pattern of their development.

At the regional and local levels, this relationship between health and development may be seen in the occurrence of a disease known as river blindness or onchocerciasis. The disease formerly resulted in an incalculable loss of human resources every year; its victims suffer serious physical debilitation and eventual blindness. Twenty years ago in West Africa, one of the areas most affected, an estimated 1 million people suffered from the disease in the Volta basin alone. Onchocerciasis, which is spread by the small blackfly, was a major contributing factor in underpopulation of fertile areas in the river basins of West Africa. The blackfly survives in areas close to rivers and most seriously affects populations living near or on the riverbanks. The effects of this

Plate 8. Toureg and his family in the Sahel of West Africa.
Photo courtesy United Nations/Cida/w.

disease were clearly evident in the settlement pattern in affected regions. "Stemming the River of Darkness," a pamphlet describing the joint efforts of the United Nations, the World Bank, and seven West African countries to eradicate or control the disease, describes its effects:

> On the ground, the disease spreads in zones. The blackfly seeks the nearest source of blood. The closer a village is to a river where the blackfly breeds, the heavier the likely degree of infection. In addition, a small village runs a much greater risk than a town in a similar position. If there are only a few people, they are bitten more often. The human tragedy is coupled with an economic one. If you fly over the worst onchocerciasis regions, you see green, well-watered land that looks ideal for agriculture and animal raising. But you see little sign of man. When you do, it will be a deserted village, grass-roofing collapsed and mud walls crumbling. Along the White Volta alone, some 50 villages are abandoned.
>
> Having been forced to surrender their fertile land to the blackfly, people crowd on to the plateau, where uncertain rains and thin soils produce violent fluctuations in crop yields. Much of the plateau land should not be farmed at all, but retained as forest reserve. Soil exhaustion, and then erosion, often follow. These less-favored areas often lack roads, clinics, or even markets. Listless and undernourished communities drift along, vulnerable to disease and to the vagaries of weather. This the Governments are determined must end.[2]

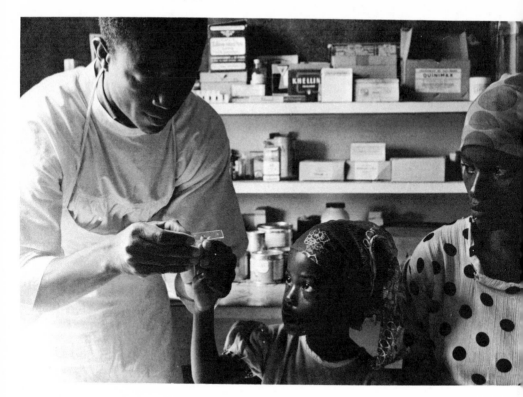

Plate 9. Testing for malaria in a health clinic.
Photo courtesy United Nations/BZ/ara.

In 1974 a massive effort by African governments and international donors was launched to control the blackfly. It was anticipated that this would reduce human suffering and aid in reclaiming vast areas of potentially fertile agricultural land, which would contribute to regional development. Twenty years later, the control program has been judged a success by most observers. River blindness is no longer the major health problem it was, and resettlement of river basins has indeed occurred. However, the anticipated economic impacts have not materialized as readily as predicted. Agricultural infrastructure in most resettled areas is inadequate, and lack of appropriate settlement and land-use policies has led to overpopulation and increased pressure on the land, leading to grave concerns about the sustainability of the economic activities initiated in the river basins.[3]

Problems of health and development are economic and political problems as well. How much of the national budget will be spent on health care? Where will resources be spent? On whose health problems will medical research concentrate? Where will the medical facilities be located? Should the government build a large urban hospital capable of "state-of-the-art" coronary surgery, or ten rural health clinics emphasizing primary health care and preventive medicine? Although the nature of the African

TABLE 3

Urbanization[1]

No. (see map 3)	Country	Urban population as % of total population		Population in capital city (thousands)		Population in capital city as % of	
						Urban 1990	Total 1990[4]
		1970	*1992*[2]	*1960*	*1990*[3]		
1	Nigeria	20	37	364.000	5.000[5]	23	8
2	Egypt	42	44	4.460	8.640	39	17
3	Ethiopia	9	13	470.000	1.880	30	4
4	Zaire	26	40	500.000	3.300	24	9
5	South Africa	48	50	425.000	1.008[6]	12	6
6	Tanzania	7	22	160.000	1.800	33	7
7	Sudan	16	23	350.000	1.800[7]	34	8
8	Algeria	40	54	870.000	3.380	23	12
9	Morocco	35	47	280.000	1.150	9	4
10	Kenya	10	25	230.000	1.700	26	6
11	Uganda	8	12	130.000	730.000	38	4
12	Ghana	29	35	400.000	1.630	22	7
13	Mozambique	6	30	180.000	1.470	38	10
14	Côte d'Ivoire	27	42	178.000	1.930[8]	45	18
15	Madagascar	14	25	250.000	770.000	24	6
16	Cameroon	20	42	80.000	880.000	17	7
17	Zimbabwe	17	30	170.000	1.060	31	9
18	Malawi	6	12	20.000	450.000	31	4
19	Angola	13	28	220.000	1.900	61	17
20	Mali	14	25	160.000	680.000	33	8
21	Burkina Faso	6	17	60.000	410.000	30	5
22	Somalia	20	25	90.000	760.000	38	9
23	Zambia	30	42	80.000	1.030	30	13
24	Tunisia	44	57	600.000	1.630	36	20
25	Niger	9	21	70.000	520.000	39	8
26	Senegal	33	41	360.000	1.480	51	20
27	Rwanda	3	6	30.000	290.000	77	4
28	Chad	12	34	80.000	760.000	41	13
29	Burundi	2	6	60.000	400.000	85	4
30	Guinea	14	27	130.000	1.470	87	23
31	Benin	18	40	70.000	250.000[9]	12	4
32	Libya	22	70	170.000	1.720	NA	64
33	Sierra Leone	18	34	120.000	610.000	52	17
34	Togo	13	29	80.000	510.000	50	14
35	Central African Republic	30	48	140.000	630.000	52	24
36	Liberia	22	45	100.000	520.000	57	26
37	Congo	33	42	120.000	600.000	68	28
38	Mauritania	14	50	30.000	600.000	83	39
39	Eritrea	NA	NA	NA	275.000[10]	NA	NA

TABLE 3 (continued)

No. (see map 3)	Country	Urban population as % of total population		Population in capital city (thousands)		Population in capital city as % of	
						Urban	Total
		1970	1992[2]	1960	1990[3]	1990	1990[4]
40	Lesotho	9	21	8.000	109.000	18	4
41	Namibia	19	29	36.000	115.000	36	10
42	Botswana	8	27	3.000	111.000	41	10
43	Gabon	26	47	27.000	350.000	57	26
44	Mauritius	42	41	107.000	140.000	36	15
45	Guinea-Bissau	15	21	26.000	109.000	36	7

Figures underlined are for years other than those specified.

1. Figures for countries with populations of more than 1 million.
2. Source: *World Development Report*, published for the World Bank (Oxford University Press, 1990-94).
3. Sources: *Africa at a Glance, 1992: Facts and Figures* (Pretoria: Africa Institute of South Africa, 1992); *Africa South of the Sahara, 1994*, 23rd ed. (London: Europa Publications, 1994).
4. Source: *World Development Report*, 1990-94.
5. Refers to former capital, Lagos.
6. Refers to administrative capital, Pretoria.
7. Refers to Khartoum and Omdurman.
8. Refers to Abidjan.
9. Refers to Porto Novo.
10. 1984 Ethiopian estimate for Asmara.

climate presents severe challenges to good health, many of the problems are exacerbated by inappropriate human action on account of inadequate education. A significant part of infant mortality rates in Africa, which are among the highest in the world, is related to poor sanitation and use of contaminated water. Inadequate attention to public health, an emphasis on curative rather than preventive medicine, and a distinct urban bias in the distribution of health facilities have characterized the policies of African governments. It will take enormous political will to reverse these patterns.

In the past decade, the world has become aware of a frighteningly fatal disease, AIDS, which threatens millions of lives and for which there is no known cure. The number of people infected by the HIV virus responsible for AIDS (Acquired Immune Deficiency Syndrome), according to the World Health Organization (WHO), has grown from an estimated 8 million worldwide in 1990 to an estimated 12 million only two years later. Of these 12 million, 62.5 percent are African—some 7.5 million people (including 1 million children). WHO estimates predict that the numbers will double or triple in just five years, and that as many as 30 million people worldwide, and nearly 25 million Africans, will be infected by the year 2000. Information and reporting on the incidence of AIDS in Africa is sparse, but available studies characterize it as an urban disease, occurring among sexually active heterosexual partners, and spreading rapidly. It is difficult to imagine how this serious health threat can be adequately addressed in countries where medical services are largely absent or, at best, unable to cope even with widespread malaria and water-borne diseases, which claim millions of lives annually. The response of African governments has been varied. Some governments, such as those of Botswana and Zimbabwe, have taken the disease seriously, while others have been slower to recognize the magnitude of the threat. Many local populations do not understand the nature of AIDS or its means of transmission. Lack of adequate public health information has hampered efforts to inform the public and deal effectively with the disease.

The Impact of Colonialism and Postcolonial Policies

The continued uneven pattern of development in Africa cannot be attributed to the physical environment alone. To fully understand contemporary patterns of development, it is necessary to examine the economic and political institutions which have determined how natural resources have been used. Why have some areas continued to be underdeveloped while others have experienced development? Why is development found on relatively few areas of the map while large areas continue to be neglected? It is important to recognize that the contemporary map of Africa reflects elements of physical and activity patterns of the past which still affect the present to some degree.

In many ways the contemporary map of Africa remains a colonial map. This is reflected in existing national boundaries, which bear little relation to natural divisions (mountains, rivers, etc.) or to indigenous concepts of space (ethnic areas, traditional kingdoms, etc.). Most of the present-day urban centers and transportation systems were designed with colonial objectives in mind. They were built to facilitate effective colonial administration and efficient economic exploitation. As part of an export-oriented, primary producing economy, they connected coastal areas and ports to important sources of raw materials and agricultural production but afforded little opportunity for internal circulation of goods or people. Until recently it was difficult at best, indeed nearly impossible, to travel overland along the coast in West Africa between neighboring countries. This colonial pattern of transportation has important implications for interregional economic exchange and severely hampers the realization of the often stated goals of closer African ties embodied in such organizations as the Organization of African Unity (OAU) and the Economic Community of West African States (ECOWAS).

Immediately following independence, African governments rushed to implement programs and projects aimed at increasing production, expanding basic services, and building essential physical infrastructure. Import-substitution strategies and promotion of exports were the central features of postcolonial development policy. Often encouraged by donor agencies and international financial institutions, ambitious programs were launched. The record of the past thirty years is generally considered to have been a failure. Many features of colonial institutions and practices persist, and basic elements in the postcolonial situation remain unchanged. Major exports are essentially the same as in 1960, heavily dependent on one or two primary products. Agriculture, minerals, and forest products still account for nearly 90 percent of Africa's foreign exchange earnings. Most countries are still overly specialized and dependent upon one or a few products. The map of physical infrastructure remains essentially the same in most countries, reproducing the colonial spatial structure. Can such spatial configurations, designed for essentially colonial ends, serve the purposes of now-independent African nations? As in so many other areas of economic and social life, there is a clear need for the decolonization of the map of Africa. But many African governments have failed in their attempts to develop their economies (see chapters 19 and 20). The map of Africa remains a physical manifestation of social, economic, and political policies and actions. In the future, new patterns of social order, political institutions, and economic institutions more consistent with the objectives of independence must be developed. Political, economic, and social reforms must be carried out, and the map of Africa must be redrawn; these are the challenges which now face the African people.

An African Challenge

Africa presents a challenge not only to Africans but to all who are concerned with economic and social development. The problems of Africa have been described in graphic detail by scholars, planners, journalists, novelists, and travelers. But how are these problems to be addressed? The level of material well-being on the continent has fallen in the past twenty years. Agricultural production has actually declined in recent years, and Africa, an overwhelmingly agricultural continent, now imports much of its food. Expert opinion differs as to the causes of and the potential cures for the African crisis. Just over a decade ago, two reports emphasized these differences. In 1980, the OAU published the Lagos Plan of Action, a statement by the African heads of governments. In 1981, the World Bank issued its report *Accelerated Development in Sub-Saharan Africa: An Agenda for Action*. These reports gave different emphasis to the factors contributing to the economic crisis on the continent, and offered contrasting prescriptions for the most desirable courses of action. Many of the debates contained in these documents continue today, but owing to political instability, many African countries have been unable to sustain any consistent policy of economic recovery. In the past decade, much attention has turned to the twin needs for political reform and economic restructuring. Although it may be too early to assess the ultimate impact of recent policies of structural adjustment and political reform, most observers agree that Africa has enormous potential. If the natural and human resources of the continent can be fully mobilized, its future development is assured. That mobilization, political, economic, and social, remains the greatest African challenge.

NOTES

I wish to acknowledge the assistance of Charles Abbott, Ph.D. candidate at the University of Iowa, in revising this chapter.

1. L. P. Green and T. J. D. Fair, *Development in Africa* (Johannesburg: Witwatersrand University Press, 1962), p. 11.
2. United Nations, Development Programme, *Stemming the River of Darkness: The International Campaign against River Blindness* (New York, 1974?), 20 pp.
3. Della McMillan, "Diversification and Successful Settlement in the River Blindness Control Zone of West Africa," *Human Organization* 52, no. 3 (1993).

SUGGESTIONS FOR FURTHER READING

Adelman, Howard, and John Sorenson, eds. *African Refugees: Development Aid and Repatriation.* Boulder, Colo.: Westview Press; North York: York Lanes Press, 1994.
Clough, Michael, *Free at Last?: U.S. Policy toward Africa and the End of the Cold War.* New York: Council on Foreign Relations Press, 1992.
Mortimore, Michael J. *Adapting to Drought: Farmers, Famines, and Desertification in West Africa.* Cambridge (UK) and New York: Cambridge University Press, 1989.
Rhodes, Steven L. "Rethinking Desertification: What Do We Know and What Have We Learned?" *World Development* 19 (Sept. 1991): 1137–43.
United Nations Development Programme [UNDP]. *Human Development Report, 1994.* Oxford and New York: Oxford University Press for UNDP, 1994.
The World Bank. *Sub-Saharan Africa: From Crisis to Sustainable Growth.* Washington, D.C., 1989.
Young, Crawford. "The African Colonial State and Its Political Legacy." In *The Precarious Balance: State and Society in Africa*, ed. Donald Rothchild and Naomi Chazan, pp. 25–66. African Modernization and Development Series, ed. Paul Lovejoy. Boulder, Colo., and London: Westview Press, 1988.
___. "The Heritage of Colonialism." In *Africa in World Politics*, ed. John W. Harbeson and Donald Rothchild, pp. 19–38. Boulder, Colo., and London: Westview Press, 1991.

The African Past

II

Kathy D. Schick
Prehistoric Africa

3 Of all the earth's continents, Africa provides the longest, deepest record of the human past. Several million years ago in Africa, a group of primates diverged from the rest of the apes and set forth on a distinctive evolutionary pathway involving bipedal or upright walking. This was an important evolutionary event for all people, as humans represent the only living descendants of this primate line. The first several million years of evolutionary development of this protohuman lineage also appear to have taken place in Africa, before our ancestors broke through critical geographic and ecological barriers and started a gradual spread throughout the rest of the world. In addition, both fossil and genetic evidence indicate that it may well have been in Africa that modern forms of humans, with a brain and body essentially similar to our own, first emerged, subsequently spreading through the rest of the world in more recent migrations, perhaps within a few hundred thousand years. Thus Africa is often referred to as the cradle for all humankind, but it should also be seen as its nurturing ground. It has served not only as a place of origin but also as the setting for critical stages of human evolutionary development over a long period of time.

The more recent phases of African prehistory are more specifically related to the continent itself. The archaeological record documents the development of different regional groups of people, technological trends in different areas or among different groups, the evolution of new ways of life, population migrations and expansions, a web of increasing contacts between different African groups as well as with outsiders, and the development of distinct regional or local cultural styles. The archaeological record, combined with modern linguistic evidence, studies of biological variation in Africa, and prehistoric and historic evidence of domesticated plants and animals, can help connect prehistory with the historic periods of modern African peoples. The long and complex prehistoric record extends far beyond the reach of written historical records or oral traditions and has helped shape the ethnic identity of modern African peoples.

Overview of Major Developments in African Prehistory

The prehistory of Africa can usefully be divided into several major phases, with each succeeding one of shorter duration as the pace of cultural change quickened over time. After more than 60 million years of primate evolution, elements of which are recorded at fossil localities in various parts of the world, there is solid evidence in East Africa, dating from more than 4 million years ago, of upright-walking ancestors who had split away from the rest of the apes. By approximately 2.5 million years ago, we see these ancestors in interesting new behavior patterns as they began to make stone tools, ushering in what is known as the Stone Age.

Changes seen in the Stone Age archaeological record were relatively slow during the Earlier Stone Age. More rapid change and great regional diversification in tools, behavior patterns, and cultural styles were not visible until the later phases of the Stone Age, mostly during the Middle and Later Stone Age, beginning approximately 100,000 to 150,000 years ago. Throughout the Stone Age, protohuman and then fully human populations subsisted primarily upon wild foods procured through gathering, hunting, and probably even scavenging.

Beginning approximately 5000 to 6000 B.C., new ways of life began to emerge in many parts of Africa with the introduction of food production in the form of agriculture and herding. This subsistence change involved the adoption of a number of domesticated species introduced from outside the continent, particularly from the Near East, but also involved the indigenous domestication of some local species, particularly various plants. The archaeological record shows the step-by-step spread of many of these domesticates from one part of Africa to another. With food production as the basis for subsistence, some African societies developed relatively large populations organized in sedentary villages.

Iron technology was introduced into Africa within the first millenium B.C. from the Mediterranean or Indian Ocean region near where it was first discovered, and gradually spread from northern Africa to the northern reaches of sub-Saharan Africa, particularly West Africa, where ironworking was widespread by the first century A.D. Many ironworking centers developed large populations organized as chiefdoms or kingdoms, several of which displayed classic attributes of civilizations, including hierarchical social stratification, complex division of labor, craft specialization, well-developed artistic traditions, long-distance trade, and even campaigns of conquest. It appears that the spread of food production and ironworking to central and southern Africa occurred mostly within the past two thousand years, apparently during a major expansion of Bantu-speaking peoples.

Evolutionary Background

The evolutionary history of the primates, the mammalian order to which humans belong and which also includes apes, monkeys, and prosimians, extends back approximately 70 to 80 million years ago. Starting about 65 million years ago, early

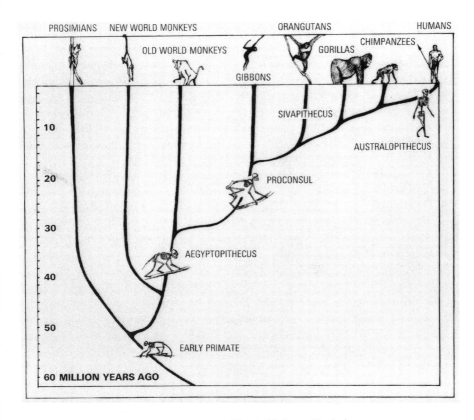

Figure 2. A Simplified Chart of Primate Evolution

primates begin to show several trends, such as an enlarged brain, an emphasis on visual perception rather than a sense of smell, and grasping hands that tended to have nails rather than claws. During the next several tens of millions of years, these primates radiated throughout much of North America, Europe, Asia, and into South America and Africa. In each of these areas the primates spread, adapting and radiating into diverse niches. Early apes and Old World monkeys appeared in Africa by 23 million years ago and later spread into Eurasia. At first the apes flourished and diversified, but as the climate cooled and forests dwindled, monkeys started becoming more common and diverse than the apes. Some apes survived, however, and continued to adapt to the changing environments. From these eventually emerged the group showing the distinctive hallmark of human ancestry, upright or bipedal walking. Members of this group are often called "hominids" or members of the biological family Hominidae, which includes humans and their fossil ancestors who share a common evolutionary pathway since our lineage split from the rest of the apes between 4 and 8 million years ago. (See figure 2.)

The first fossil evidence of hominids anywhere in the world appears about 4 million years ago in East Africa. Not only did East Africa's habitats favor early hominid evolution, but its geological environment permitted rapid burial and preservation of the evolutionary record. The East African Rift Valley system, a trough of faults in the earth's crust coursing from the Red Sea area of Ethiopia southward through East Africa, has produced a complex of subsiding basins threaded with lakes and streams. It is in these basins that the fossil and archaeological evidence left behind by early hominids has been preserved, buried in sediments laid by the ancient rivers and lakes. More recent faulting has uplifted portions of this record, allowing modern streams and erosion to cut through the ancient sedimentary layers and yield some of this buried information for discovery.

There is only one living species in the hominid family, ourselves—*Homo sapiens sapiens.* Over the past 4 million years, however, the fossil record reveals a number of other hominid forms, particularly during the first 3 million years of hominid evolution, and some of these coexisted. The earliest upright-walking hominids found so far are usually assigned to the species *Australopithecus afarensis* (meaning "southern ape-man from the Afar"). They are found in the Rift Valley between about 3 and 4 million years ago in the Afar region of Ethiopia and at Laetoli in Tanzania. While its skull is apelike in many ways, many features of the skeleton show profound changes in the hip, legs, feet, and spine indicating an adaptation for upright walking. In addition, remarkable sets of fossilized footprints found at Laetoli reveal, among the imprints of hundreds of other animals, those made by the feet of three hominids apparently walking together. Thus far, fossils of *Australopithecus afarensis* have been found only in East Africa. (See Figure 3.)

Between 3 and 2 million years ago, new species of small-brained hominids called *Australopithecus africanus* ("southern ape-man from Africa") appear in the fossil record in South African limestone caves. During this period in East Africa, a very different hominid form appears, however, also with a small brain (from 400 to 550 cubic centimeters, compared to the modern human average of about 1,350 cubic centimeters) but distinguished by massive jaws and teeth. This form, called *Australopithecus aethiopicus,* represents a hominid species believed to be adapted to eating very tough, low-quality foodstuffs. This small-brained, large-jawed hominid is the earliest known species of a major hominid group known as the "robust australopithecines," with later representatives found in East and South Africa between 1 and 2 million years ago.

For at least 1 million years, these robust australopithecines coexisted with a larger-brained hominid lineage assigned to our genus, *Homo.* The first definite evidence of this new species, *Homo habilis,* with a brain size of about 600 to 750 cubic centimeters (about half the size of modern humans), is found at least 2 million years ago in East and South Africa. Some believe that early in its evolution the *Homo* lineage may have split into more than one species. By at least 1.7 million years ago, a new hominid form appears in the fossil record, with a large body and a brain even larger than *Homo habilis.* This new form, called *Homo erectus,* had a brain size ranging from 850 to 1,100 cubic centimeters (or roughly two-thirds to three-quarters the size of modern humans), but had a very thick skull with big brow ridges, a sloping

Plate 10. Olduvai Gorge, near the Kenya-Tanzania border,
site of excavation of early humans.
Photo courtesy Boyce Rensberger.

forehead, and jutting jaws. First found in East Africa and South Africa, *Homo erectus* then spread to northern Africa and into Eurasia, a significant expansion beyond that seen in the australopithecines or earlier *Homo*.

Aside from these fossil hominid finds, other critical prehistoric evidence appears in East Africa starting about 2.5 million years ago: deliberately manufactured stone tools. The earliest archaeological sites with simple stone artifacts are found in Ethiopia and northern Kenya.

The Earlier Stone Age

The Earlier Stone Age in Africa is generally divided into two major phases, the *Oldowan* and the *Acheulean*. The Oldowan stone tool industry is named after the famous site of Olduvai Gorge in Tanzania, where decades ago Mary and Louis Leakey discovered early stone tools and hominid fossils buried deeply in sediments in an ancient lake basin (see map 17). These sediments have been uplifted and sliced through by erosion in recent times, exposing the ancient archaeological sites. These discoveries established for the scientific world and the general public an incredible depth to the human prehistoric record in Africa.

Starting about 2 million years ago in East and South Africa, many sites appear which contain simple Oldowan artifacts (meaning "manufactured by humans"), and

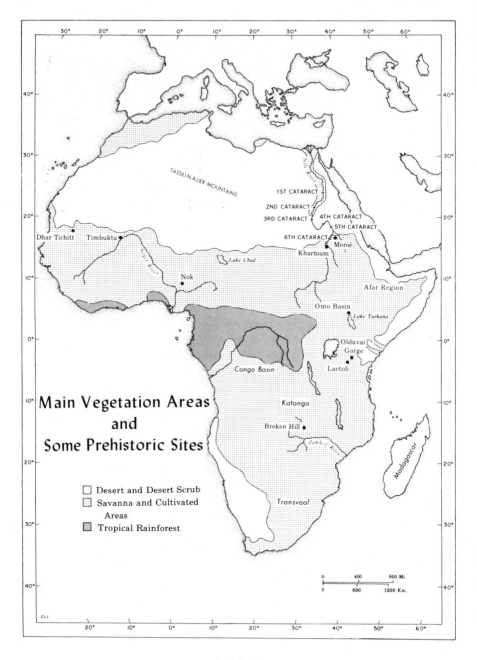

Main Vegetation Areas
and
Some Prehistoric Sites

☐ Desert and Desert Scrub
▒ Savanna and Cultivated
    Areas
▓ Tropical Rainforest

MAP 17

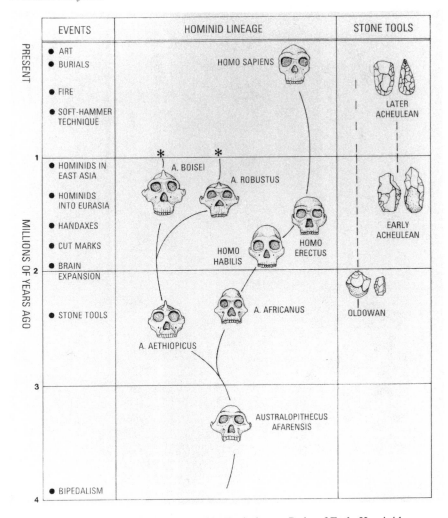

Figure 3. A Chart Showing Possible Evolutionary Paths of Early Hominids
and the Emergence of Early Stone Age Traditions

usually broken animal bones as well. Oldowan technology consists of cobbles and chunks of rock from which pieces have been removed by deliberate percussive blows. The major kinds of stone tools at Oldowan sites consist of "cores," the parent pieces of rock from which pieces were removed and the stone fragments or "flakes" detached. Traditionally, archaeologists have classified Oldowan cores into various types based upon some supposed function, such as "choppers" or "scrapers," or their morphology, such as "discoids." It now appears that such arbitrary categories do not necessarily represent shapes deliberately imposed by their makers, as toolmaking experiments show that all Oldowan core types can be produced simply by random

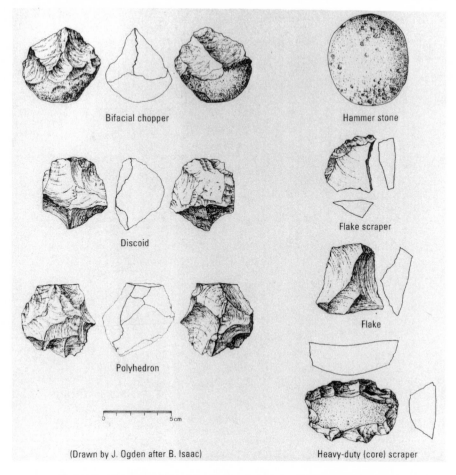

Bifacial chopper

Hammer stone

Discoid

Flake scraper

Polyhedron

Flake

0   5 cm

(Drawn by J. Ogden after B. Isaac)

Heavy-duty (core) scraper

Figure 4. A Range of Oldowan Artifact Forms from Koobi Fora, Kenya

flaking. Thus, the variety of core forms found at Oldowan sites likely do not represent specific tool types produced for particular purposes. Rather, the shape of each may result as an incidental by-product of flaking stone to produce the real tools, the sharp flakes.

Experiments with stone tools have shown that even the simplest of them could be useful, particularly for cutting operations: sharp cutting edges do not generally occur in nature but can be produced in seconds through flaking stone. Thus, stone toolmaking constituted a critical behavioral shift in early hominid populations, one in which acquired or learned toolmaking behaviors gave them important advantages beyond their natural biological abilities. In particular, it would have given them ready access to animal resources, as a simple Oldowan flake is capable of cutting through even the thickest animal hide. This is of great importance, as many early Oldowan sites have large quantities of animal bones and bone fragments together with the stone tools.

Plate 11. Excavation at Site 50, Koobi Fora, Kenya, c. 1.5 million years ago.
Photo courtesy Kathy Schick.

Some bones bear cut marks made with stone flakes as well as bash marks made with stone hammers, indicating removal of meat and joints from carcasses and procurement of marrow from long bones. Current opinion favors a scavenging hypothesis for the acquisition of animal remains by these early hominids, particularly from larger animals, with hominids beginning to compete successfully with carnivores for carcasses of dead animals, using their stone tools to gain quick and easy access to parts of the animals. At some sites in East Africa, large concentrations of Oldowan cores and flakes are found. This suggests that Oldowan hominids were consistently carrying stone tools with them and repeatedly using some site locations, probably for favorable shade, water, or food resources they offered.

Thus, the adaptive significance of Oldowan technology would appear to lie in how these simple but effective tools enabled early hominids to move into a new dietary niche. They allowed ready access to animal resources which these early hominids were ill equipped to obtain through purely biological means. Moreover, it appears to have set forth an adaptive trend that stressed a heightened use of technology and reliance on intelligent, learned behavior at a level never before developed in the animal world, a trend that within approximately 2 to 2.5 million years led to the evolution of large-brained modern humans.

The next major phase of the Early Stone Age, the Acheulean technological tradition, first appears in East Africa approximately 1.5 million years ago. Acheulean technology is distinguished by relatively large tools such as handaxes, cleavers, and picks. These are sometimes called "bifaces," as their manufacture often entails flaking on both sides or faces of a large flake or a large, relatively flat cobble. As opposed to the opportunistic flaking and widely ranging core forms seen in Oldowan technology, Acheulean bifaces were deliberately shaped, usually through a rather skilled procedure of flaking. Experiments in using Acheulean handaxes and cleavers show that they are extremely well suited for heavy-duty butchery, or defleshing and dismembering large animals, as the butt end serves as a "built-in" handle, and the sharp working edges and end serve as an effective cutting tool. It is, of course, possible that they were used in other tasks such as woodworking, but the deliberate shaping of the edges and tips of these tools indicates that cutting was a primary purpose for many of them. (See figure 5.)

An extraordinary aspect of the Acheulean technological tradition is its extreme longevity: Acheulean tools continue to be found for about 1.5 million years, or until 150,000 to 200,000 years ago. The Acheulean is thus the longest cultural and technological tradition ever maintained and spans significant biological evolution in hominids. The earlier phases of the Acheulean are associated with the hominid form that appears in Africa close to the start of this technological tradition, *Homo erectus.* The later Acheulean sites are found during the time of a more evolved hominid form, often referred to as archaic *Homo sapiens,* that appears about 500,000 years ago. Considerable workmanship is evident in many Acheulean tools, particularly by about 1 million years ago, as hominids were able to produce finely shaped tool forms. In late Acheulean sites another novel technological development is often seen, called the prepared-core or Levallois technology, in which cores were carefully preshaped in order to strike off flakes of predetermined size and shape. Levallois technology involves precision control of flaking similar to that seen in the skillful shaping of Acheulean handaxes.

Acheulean technology eventually became widespread over most of the continent except within the dense forests of equatorial Africa. A significant expansion of hominid habitat is seen at some sites, such as Gadeb in Ethiopia, where hominids adapted to an environment about 2,300 meters above sea level. It also appears that the first major successful migrations outside of Africa into Eurasia were made during the Acheulean period. Interestingly, sites containing only Oldowan-type technology coexist in Africa throughout the Acheulean period and may represent other subsistence or food-processing activities in other parts of the environment or during other seasons.

The relative importance of hunting and scavenging to the subsistence of the Acheulean toolmakers is not yet known, particularly whether they successfully hunted big game. In view of the apparent butchery tools they were making in great numbers and the quantities of animal bones found with these, it appears that meat resources played a significant role in their diet. The subsistence strategy of the Acheulean hominids would appear to have been quite successful in view of their geographic and environmental spread within and outside of Africa. Although there are signs of fire at sites during this period, there is no definitive evidence for its controlled use.

The Middle Stone Age

The next major phase of the Stone Age has been referred to over much of Africa as the Middle Stone Age, or in North Africa and the Sahara as the Middle Paleolithic. This period started in most regions between 100,000 and 200,000 years ago and lasted until 40,000 to 20,000 years ago. During this period there is evidence of further geographic and ecological expansion within Africa and more detailed information on changing subsistence behaviors. A number of researchers argue that hominids with modern human morphology first emerged in Africa during this time period and subsequently spread to the rest of the world.

The precise nature of the transition from Acheulean to Middle Stone Age technologies remains somewhat obscure, partially because of a gap between Acheulean and Middle Stone Age layers at many sites. Evidence at some sites indicates a period of environmental deterioration during which settlement patterns may have been severely disrupted. Technologies during the Middle Stone Age show some major changes from Acheulean industries. Flake tools became more common and more systematically made, often with finely made tools fashioned into recurring, standardized forms. The overall trend seen in Africa, Europe, and Asia toward more standardized flake tool industries may indicate widespread diffusion of this technological development. Refined bifacial stone points became common over much of Africa and are often thinned or stemmed at the base. This was apparently to aid in hafting or mounting them on a spear shaft and represents a genuine advance in technology for hunting, offense, and defense. During the Middle Stone Age, for the first time, very distinct regional tool styles or traditions appeared and regional technological sequences emerged.

Some sites show progressive or precocious technological trends, such as stone industries in some regions based upon long, narrow flakes or blades, or others in southern Africa in which blades were shaped into small geometric shapes. These presage patterns that become widespread over much of the continent in the Later Stone Age. Other regions show a large tool tradition different from the preceding Acheulean, such as the Sangoan and Lupemban core-axe industries of equatorial Africa, which mark the first successful adaptation to more closed forest zones. These are characterized by large, thick bifacial tools believed to be woodworking axes. Another example of a regional industry, the Aterian, is distinguished by stemmed or tanged points and scrapers at sites found across much of the Sahara and North Africa before aridity began to set in 30,000 to 40,000 years ago. Presumably mounted on spears, Aterian points are thought to have been important elements of a hunting tool kit in this now desiccated region. Meanwhile, sites nearer the North African coast or in the Nile Valley contain tools similar to those found in the Near East during this period.

There is better evidence for subsistence patterns in the Middle Stone Age than for earlier times. Successful hunting is suggested by the widespread appearance of spear points, and animal bones found at many sites give further signs of hunting patterns. At some sites a mass hunting technique seems evident, such as a mass kill of an animal herd by driving them over a cliff or into a trap. Evidence for hunting of dangerous animals such as wild pigs and buffalo is relatively rare, though, and often seems to have targeted younger animals of such species. The apparent inability of Middle Stone Age peoples to hunt adults of more aggressive species is thought to be related to the risks of close-quarter hunting with spears. Judging from the bones found at Middle Stone Age sites, hunting appears to have concentrated on very young and very old animals, although scavenging of older animals could also have contributed to subsistence.

There are also other developments in subsistence patterns seen at some Middle Stone Age sites, such as the use of sea animals and the collection of shellfish. Fishing, however, appears relatively uncommon. Overall, it appears that Middle Stone Age peoples were more successful hunters than their Early Stone Age predecessors but were less sophisticated in exploiting seasonal resources than were later peoples. A few sites also show some other interesting shifts in behavior patterns, such as the use of ochers and other natural pigments (though whether for rock art, painting the body or tools, or whatever, is not known), grinding stones (likely for processing foods or grinding pigments), and possibly bone harpoons. Quantities of ash and carbonized material at many Middle Stone Age sites suggest that humans had successfully mastered controlled use of fire. Thick and extensive ash layers perhaps indicate meat drying or accidental combustion of bedding or other materials, or they could represent actual hearth areas. Many sites are found in caves or rock shelters, but a few sites contain possible evidence of structures. At such "base camps," groups apparently congregated regularly and conducted a variety of activities. There is also evidence of special work areas for activities such as stone quarrying or toolmaking. Middle Stone Age sites generally show gradational changes from earlier Stone Age behavior and subsistence patterns but also show hints of some more modern behaviors.

The Origins of Modern Humans

Over the past several years, strong arguments have been made for the origin of modern human morphology in Africa during Middle Stone Age times and the subsequent spread of this new physical form to the rest of the world. These claims have generally relied on two major sources of evidence: hominid fossils in the prehistoric record and genetic data from modern human populations.

At a number of sites from late in the Earlier Stone Age, early evidence of "transitional" *Homo sapiens* has been uncovered. These consist of hominids with a cranial capacity approaching that of modern humans but with other distinctly nonmodern features such as thick skulls or heavy brow ridges. Then, between 50,000 and 100,000 years ago, fossils appear that many argue show distinctly modern human morphology. This would indicate an early appearance of modern skeletal features in Africa at a time when more archaic-featured, Neanderthal-like forms existed in Eurasia. While there is some evidence for early appearance of modern forms in the Near East in this period, many argue that the bulk of fossil evidence for the emergence of modern humans appears to come from Africa. Interestingly, the archaeological record does not show good evidence for an abrupt or widespread shift in human behavior to coincide with this physical evolutionary change. Rather, as discussed below, more fully modern behavior patterns do not prevail in the archaeological record until later in time, within the past 40,000 years during Later Stone Age times.

In addition to the skeletal evidence for the origin of modern humans, genetic similarities and differences among modern populations can reveal evidence for the time and place of a common "root" population ancestral to all modern human groups. Both nuclear DNA and mitochondrial DNA, the latter found in structures in our cells and inherited from our mothers, have been used to explore genetic similarities and differences among populations that might reveal ancestral relationships. It has been argued that such studies indicate that all humans today share a common ancestral population within the past few hundred thousand years or so. Moreover, such studies appear to point toward Africa as the geographic location of this ancestral population, which need not have had fully modern morphology. In fact, from the fossil evidence found so far between 100,000 and 500,000 years ago, it is very likely that it still retained archaic features. Some claim that this ancestral population began splitting up into geographic variants starting 50,000 or more years ago, perhaps coinciding with major migrations throughout and outside of Africa.

The Later Stone Age

Over much of sub-Saharan Africa, the Later Stone Age refers to the final stage of a period during which a hunting-gathering subsistence was combined with reliance on stone technology. In northern Africa, despite ties with sub-Saharan Africa and indigenous innovations, major links with the Near East continued, and this period is often referred to as the Late or Upper Paleolithic. Biological remains show widespread appearance of fully modern humans within Africa, Europe, and Asia. Regional cultural diversification becomes even more pronounced, with smaller subregions having their own styles in tool kits, subsistence patterns, and artwork. In addition, the pace of change accelerated over time. Although different tool industries do not necessarily represent distinct cultural entities, the variability observed over time and space may reflect aspects of developing sociopolitical entities.

A prominent technological change is the development and spread of what is often called "microlithic" technology, or stone tool industries based upon the manufacture of small blades for use as tool elements. In many regions, stone tools became quite small in Later Stone Age times, as they were made primarily as components or bits that were fitted into handles to make the final tool form. An important application of these tools was in the emergent use of the bow and arrow, in which razor-sharp microliths were mounted on the end of an arrow shaft. This trend toward the use of microlithic technology represents a significant innovation in tool manufacture, as it stressed systematic production of standardized tool parts eminently replaceable in case they broke or became dull. Many Later Stone Age peoples shifted to the use of

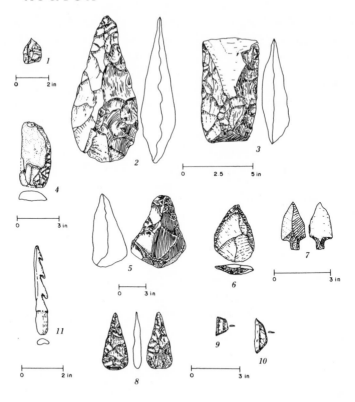

Tools: *1. Oldowan core;   2. Acheulean handaxe;   3. Acheulean cleaver;   4. scraper (Acheulean and Middle Stone Age);   5. core axe (Middle Stone Age);   6. Mousterian point (Middle Paleolithic of North Africa);   7. Aterian point (Middle Stone Age of North Africa);   8. Stillbay point (Middle Stone Age);   9–10. geometric microliths (Later Stone Age);   11. bone harpoon (Later Stone Age)*

Figure 5

such microlithic technologies, although the shift appears to have taken place at different times, as early as 30,000 to 40,000 years ago in some areas but as late as 20,000 to 10,000 years ago in others. The end of the Later Stone Age is generally marked by a shift from hunting and gathering to food production through agriculture and herding, usually involving larger, more complex settlements. Among some societies, this economic and social transition is seen relatively early, starting at least 7,000 to 8,000 years ago. Others retained a lifestyle based primarily on hunting and gathering for a longer period, sometimes until the modern era.

Rock art is another feature of the Later Stone Age in some parts of the continent. Between 10,000 and 2,000 years ago, Later Stone Age peoples in East Africa were apparently producing naturalistic, usually monochrome, representations of animals and stylized ones of humans on the walls of some caves and rock shelters. The earliest dated rock art in southern Africa is in Namibia, where naturalistic representations of animals were painted at least 28,000 years ago. Southern African rock art found on the walls of shallow caves and rock outcrops consists of fairly naturalistic representations of animals and people, but also includes some stylized or geometric designs. A rock art tradition appears to have continued here until the last few centuries and in fact documents the arrival of domesticated animals and European colonists in the region. Most is thought to have been made by Later Stone Age peoples within the past few thousand years. Curiously, the animals most frequently represented do not reflect their importance in the prehistoric diet: for example, the eland is favored in the paintings but rarely shows up in food debris at sites. This has potential relevance, as the eland has an important place in the belief systems of the San, the surviving hunter-gatherers of southern Africa. In fact, ethnographic parallels have been drawn between some elements of rock art and features of San rituals such as the trance dance, and many believe that Later Stone Age rock art in southern Africa may have had an important role in the ritual systems of its makers.

Subsistence strategies appear to have become much more efficient. There are many signs of intensified use of many resources, such as those found in lakes and the ocean, and some peoples practiced focused, intensive exploitation of particular foods. For instance, between 20,000 and 15,000 years ago, a number of groups along the Nile were concentrating on fishing and intensive hunting. Elsewhere in Egypt, some sites show intensive use of tubers as early as 18,000 years ago, and others were collecting large quantities of wild cereals between 15,000 and 11,000 years ago. In addition, people appear to have made significant improvements in their hunting abilities. This was probably associated with advances in hunting technology, such as use of the bow and arrow. They consistently hunted large plains animals, including dangerous species such as the buffalo. In historic times, Later Stone Age peoples were known to enhance their hunting effectiveness with the use of toxic poisons on their arrow tips, but it is not known when this innovation was introduced. The common presence of grinding stones likely represents an improvement in processing of foods such as grass grains and tubers. Apparent digging stick weights also suggest improved use of underground food sources.

Other distinct trends in the Later Stone Age include the widespread appearance of well-made bone tools, and also body ornaments such as pendants and beads of shells, bone, and ostrich eggshells. Pigments such as ocher became popular and may have been used for personal decoration as well as painting rock shelters and graves. Burials became relatively common in some regions, and grave goods often included items of personal decoration.

Thus, in the Later Stone Age, all regions of Africa were successfully occupied by a large number of societies of people who looked like modern humans. Their behavior also appears fully modern in terms of its complexity and ingenuity and the development of aesthetics and symbolic behavior. In some parts of Africa, particularly the more arid southern parts of the continent, a hunting-and-gathering way of life and associated technologies persisted until historic times. In most areas, however, Later Stone Age industries and the hunting-gathering lifestyle of their makers were replaced by new technologies and a new way of life based upon food production. This occurred first in the northern part of the continent, where transitions toward food production began between 5,000 and 7,000 years ago, and developed somewhat later in Central and eastern Africa. Finally, the prehistoric record also documents this change in most of southern Africa, with the spread of iron-using food-producers who apparently replaced or absorbed stone-using hunter-gatherers, except for some restricted populations in more arid regions poorly suited for agriculture.

The Origins and Spread of Food Production

The story of the prehistoric development of food production is a complex one. It involved indigenous subsistence changes that began to occur in many regions of Africa in Later Stone Age times; influences from outside the continent, especially the introduction of important domesticated plant and animal species from the Near East; long-term experimentation in subsistence that incorporated local domesticates into farming traditions; and a complicated web of interaction and population expansions from one region of Africa to another. Each region followed its own course, depending upon many factors: local climate and terrain, wild plants and animals available, contacts with other peoples within and outside Africa, population density, strength of cultural traditions, the distribution of insect pests and disease, and the particular exploitation of plants and animals by societies in any one region. Nevertheless, food production developed and spread throughout most of the continent and eventually supported the complex cultures of Iron Age times.

As noted above, between 10,000 and 20,000 years ago, diverse Later Stone Age populations in Africa began intensively exploiting specific plants and animals available to them in their respective regions. Hunting often focused on a few or even one species, and wild plant gathering sometimes centered on particular plant types such as tubers or grasses. In northeast Africa, sickle blades used to harvest grasses as well as grinding stones that may have been used to process the grain are found at some sites by at least 10,000 years ago. Although peoples in the Nile Valley were intensively exploiting wild cereals and other plants between 10,000 and 15,000 years ago, no evidence indicates that this practice led at that time to true domestication or alteration of the wild plant species.

Domestication eventually entails long-term management of the breeding of a species until some of its characteristics become altered from the wild state. Ultimately some of these are brought more in line with human needs, such as cereals with larger seeds or stronger stalks to resist dispersal by the wind, or smaller, more docile cattle with less dangerous horns, more meat, or greater milk yield. The earliest stages of domestication are difficult to detect, however, and not all experiments in managing wild species ultimately succeeded in truly domesticating them. For instance, Egyptians appear to have managed the reproduction of a number of wild animal species, such as gazelles, hyenas, oryx, and perhaps giraffes, without finally domesticating them. In Africa, as elsewhere in the world where plants and animals came into early domestication, this process seems to have been preceded by a long period of intensive exploitation of wild species during which human populations would have been learning their qualities, habits and habitats, and patterns of growth and reproduction.

A number of African populations during the Later Stone Age appear to have readily adopted domesticates while also domesticating some locally available plants. Major indigenous cultigens include African yams, African rice, bulrush millet, finger millet, sorghum, and oil palm. Centers of early domestication of such plants necessarily were within the distribution zones of their wild progenitors. Other plants, such as wheat and barley, appear to have been imported from western Asia, where they were domesticated in the Near East a few thousand years earlier than their first appearance in Africa. The resulting amalgam of cultivated plant foods differed from one region to another in Africa and also changed over time with the spread of people and domesticates. This received another important overlay within the past several hundred years with the introduction of plants from South Asia, including bananas and coconuts, and then corn and manioc from the New World. Meanwhile, African domesticates such as sorghum, finger millet, and bulrush millet spread to Asia, perhaps starting as early as 1000 B.C., where they became very important and sometimes even central elements in the diets of large populations.

The major domesticated animals in Africa are species imported from western Asia, where they were originally domesticated. These species include sheep, goats, cattle, and, important in more arid areas of northern and eastern Africa, the camel. The wild ancestors of domesticated sheep and goats are not found prehistorically in Africa, nor are ancestral cattle indigenous to sub-Saharan Africa. There is some evidence, however, that experiments in domesticating wild cattle did occur in northern Africa, and these local forms may have contributed to some domesticated breeds. The donkey and the cat appear to have been domesticated in Egypt. It has been suggested that the influx of fully domesticated animal species from western Asia may have cut short many early animal-domestication experiments in Africa.

There are a number of centers of early food production in Africa. An important one appears to have been in the Sahara Desert region, which after the end of the last glaciation entered a period of higher rainfall and lower evaporation that lasted from about 10,000 to 6,000 years ago. During this period the Sahara supported good-sized populations in settlements around lakes, ponds, and rivers interspersed throughout plains that, although sparsely vegetated, had a Mediterranean climate and were considerably better watered than today. Relying on intensive fishing, hunting, and plant food collecting, some of these settlements appear to have supported year-round, sedentary populations. Some peoples between 6500 and 8500 B.C. seem to have developed the use of pottery, a common feature among sedentary food-producers and some intensive hunter-gatherers with a very rich resource base.

By about 7000 B.C. in the Egyptian Western Desert, well before evidence of food production in the Nile Valley, peoples with microlithic tools and living in settlements around ponds were using domesticated barley and domesticated local cattle. At about the same time, domesticated Asian "imports"—sheep or goats—also appear within the region. During this period there is evidence for significant structures, such as houses with stone foundations. By 4000 to 5000 B.C., other sites further west in the Sahara also show sheep or goats and domesticated cattle, many grindstones, and possible plant domestication. In this period, sometimes referred to as the "Sahara Neolithic," microlithic industries are augmented by many grindstones, pottery, and, more rarely, ground stone axes. Many Saharan rock paintings believed to date to this period depict early domesticated animals as well as tethered giraffes. Starting after 2000 B.C., depictions of newly imported horses and camels and the milking of cows also appear in paintings.

In the Nile Valley, intensive use of tubers and wild grasses such as barley continued for thousands of years along with fishing, hunting, and perhaps management of wild animal herds. This appears to have supported significant settlements between 10,000 B.C. and 6000 B.C., some occupied year-round. But large-scale village farming does not seem to appear in the Nile region until about 5000 B.C., when Egyptians supplemented hunting and fishing with many domesticated species, including a full spectrum of domesticates from southwest Asia: wheat, barley, and flax, as well as goats, sheep, cattle, and pigs. At some places where this subsistence supported large populations and fostered craft specialization, societies formed the socioeconomic foundation for the pre-Dynastic Nile Valley Cultures starting about 4000 B.C. which in turn developed into the Egyptian Dynastic Cultures starting about 3100 B.C.

To the south in Sudan starting after 5000 B.C., hunters and fishers with microlithic tools along the Nile began to use large quantities of local plants such as sorghum and finger millet, which are not demonstrably domesticated, and kept domesticated cattle, sheep, and goats. These peoples developed large and complex settlements, used pottery, and sometimes built substantial house structures. In northern Sudan the influence of Egypt was greater, and wheat, barley, and some Egyptian trade goods appear over time.

Between about 6000 and 5000 B.C., domesticated sheep and goats and pottery appear to have been rapidly adopted by local cultures across coastal North Africa, and herding appears to have rapidly replaced hunting. The physical human type found at such North African sites may be ancestral to modern Berber populations. Gradual desiccation of the Sahara after 4000 B.C. appears to have spurred dispersal of populations south and west into wetter regions, where they adapted their food producing to new environments. Domesticated cattle appear to have spread south of the Sahara by 3000 to 4000 B.C. and supplemented local hunting and fishing subsistence. Winter-rainfall wheat and barley were not suited to equatorial summer rainfall, so societies in the Sahel zone south of the desert appear to have turned to domestication of indigenous wild plants such as sorghum and bulrush millet. Other important domesticates in West Africa include the African yam, originating in the forest fringes, and African rice, probably in some of the large river valleys such as the Niger and Benue.

Starting between 5000 and 4000 B.C., pottery and ground stone axes and hoes were added to microlithic tool industries at many sites in West Africa. Pottery generally reflects increasingly sedentary populations, and ground stone tools seem to indicate forest clearance, woodworking, and digging. In addition, intensive use of plant resources is further indicated by tools with sickle gloss, a silica-rich sheen that develops through cutting grasses. In Congo and Zaire, pottery, ground stone tools, and oil palm nuts appear some thousands of years later, within a few hundred years B.C.

In the highlands of Ethiopia, several indigenous plants came into unique domestication in the highlands but were not significantly dispersed elsewhere. These include the cereal teff, which is still a staple of modern Ethiopia, as well as the edible-oil plant noog and the starch-rich plant ensete. Finger millet was domesticated either in Ethiopia or in Uganda. In addition to these indigenous domesticates, Ethiopia also appears to have adopted imported species such as wheat, barley, cattle, goats, and sheep within the last few millennia B.C.

Domestic cattle, sheep, and goats and pottery had spread to microlithic cultures in northern Kenya between 3000 and 2500 B.C. Domestic herds were adopted by fishers near Lake Turkana as well as inland hunters, who also began to use camels. A settled herding adaptation appears to have been maintained until climatic deterioration during the past thousand years favored a nomadic pastoralist way of life still practiced by some local groups. Herding appears to have become established in southern Kenya and Tanzania between 2000 and 1000 B.C., and subsequently appears to have involved more than one cultural group, as multiple styles are evident in pottery, burials, and other traits. Linguistic studies indicate that these early herders may have spoken Southern Cushitic languages rather than the Bantu and Nilotic languages present in this region today.

Further spread of herding and agriculture to the south beyond northern Tanzania seems to have been blocked for nearly two millennia. Suggested explanations have sometimes attributed this to the extremely successful hunter-gatherer adaptation and cultural conservatism of the Khoisan-speaking peoples apparently occupying much of southern Africa. It was not until much later that peoples with iron tools and weapons spread into southern Africa and brought herding and farming with them, a subsistence that soon came to dominate the region. With the development and spread of food production throughout Africa, an overall increase in the size and complexity of settlements is seen. Many of these food producers achieved a sufficient size, population density, and stable resource base to support the complex, centralized societies that arose in many parts of the continent during Iron Age times.

Iron Age Developments

During the last few millennia B.C., many societies based on agriculture in Africa and Eurasia rapidly developed great complexities. Many became increasingly large and less insular, specialized crafts and arts flourished, thriving trade emerged, power was consolidated, and populations grew, sometimes spurring phases of conquest and consolidation. It was in this context that complex societies developed within the past five thousand years, including, in northeast Africa, the ancient kingdoms of the Egyptian Nile, Meroe in Nubia, and Axum in the Ethiopian horn; in West Africa the kingdoms and states of Ghana, Mali, Songhai, Asante, Ife, and Benin; and in southern Africa the large commercial center responsible for the Great Zimbabwe and many other stone-built trading centers (see map 18).

Societies undergoing such changes in Africa, as in Europe and Asia, were thrust

Plate 12. Remains of Meroe, center of Kushitic civilization.
Photo courtesy Ruth Hidore.

increasingly into a web of interaction and influence. Developments in one region were often affected by other societies in Africa and elsewhere, in technologies, foods, religions, and trade. In many parts of Africa and increasingly so over time, prehistory began to give way to historic times, as accounts of many local developments became incorporated into written documents of the widening literate world. Much information about African societies during this period, especially their settlement and subsistence patterns, is accessible primarily through archaeological evidence. These events occurred within the time period in Africa often referred to as the Iron Age, when iron came into common use, a development that is taken up in the next chapter.

The technology of making tools out of copper and bronze developed in western Asia before 3000 B.C. but never developed a foothold in Africa except in some northern regions, possibly as it was overtaken by the spread of iron technology. After the fall of the Hittites about 1200 B.C., the complex iron-smelting technology they had developed began to spread rapidly throughout the Near East, around the Mediterranean, through Europe, and into Africa. The superior strength and efficiency of iron tools and weapons as well as the wide distribution of iron ore favored this rapid spread. Iron technology appears to have entered North Africa with Phoenician colonists and traders by the eighth century B.C. It appears among peoples in West Africa by the fourth century B.C., where it is associated with the early Iron Age Nok cultures in Nigeria, famous for the large terra-cotta heads they fashioned (see chapter 12). Over the ensuing centuries, more sites throughout much of West Africa show evidence of using and working iron.

Large trade networks began to develop during this period in northern Africa, with Phoenicians developing centers in the western Mediterranean, trading pottery, glass, and metals with Saharan populations in return for salt, ivory, and slaves. These colonies also fostered the growth of Berber kingdoms, with whom they traded. Emerging Greek civilization exerted its influence from colonies established in the eastern Mediterranean by the seventh century B.C. The Romans then established their presence by the third century B.C. after their defeat of the Phoenicians at Carthage.

Before iron technology reached Egypt, the unification of Upper and Lower Egypt about 3100 B.C. had begun a long succession of dynasties. By 2000 B.C. Egyptians had extended their control southward into the northern part of Nubia (northern Sudan), a land they called Kush. Over the next several hundred years, Egyptians lost control of this area to the Kushites, regained it, and then lost it once more in the ninth century B.C., when Kush reestablished itself as an independent kingdom. In the next century Kush went on to conquer Upper Egypt and subsequently Lower Egypt, but then lost the latter to invading iron-wielding Assyrians by 671 B.C. After the Egyptians destroyed their capital in the next century, the Kushites established a new capital further upstream in a more wooded region of the Nile at Meroe. Here, separated from Egypt by arid reaches of the Nile Valley, this city-state flourished for centuries, cultivating millet and sorghum and keeping cattle and the recently introduced horse. Using the abundant local wood for smelting, Meroe developed a large ironworking industry and traded with other peoples of the Sudan and, through Red Sea ports, with peoples further abroad. Most iron produced, in fact, appears to have been traded away: iron furnaces abound, but iron implements at Meroe are few. Meroe's decline may be due in part to environmental causes such as overgrazing and deforestation as well as intrusion of an outside force, the rise of the Axumite kingdom.

During the first millennium B.C., Semitic-speaking peoples immigrated from southern Arabia into the Ethiopian highlands, where they developed settlements that seem to have slowly incorporated the local Cushitic-speaking agriculturalists. They introduced iron technology and urban living into Tigre and Eritrea in the fifth century B.C. and by the first century A.D. had established an extensive state reaching across much of Ethiopia and Sudan. This mercantile empire, the Axumite kingdom, controlled trade through the Red Sea from its port capital at Adulis and produced monumental architecture including great stelae and tombs. The Axumite kingdom appears to have conquered Meroe in the fourth century A.D. and centuries later to have gone into decline itself after Arabs took over the Red Sea trade in the seventh century. While the Axumite kingdom was flourishing, some societies in Ethiopia continued village-based food production and a microlithic-based tool tradition without significant intrusion of iron until just a few centuries ago. Such parallel trends were also maintained in other regions of Africa.

In the centuries following the Assyrian invasion, Egypt came increasingly under the influence of the Greeks and then the control of the spreading Macedonian empire. Finally, Roman conquest was accomplished by 30 B.C. It was through the Roman Empire that Christianity moved into northern Africa, spreading by the fourth century into Ethiopia and Nubia. In these regions Christian culture flourished for centuries among villagers pursuing irrigation agriculture, even after the expansion of Muslim

Arabs throughout northern Africa largely cut them off from more northern centers of Christianity. The early development of Christianity in much of northern Africa was interrupted when the Arab invasion in the seventh century A.D. brought in Islam, which rapidly took hold over much of North Africa, especially to the west of Egypt. Through the Arabs, who with their camel caravans were vying with the Berbers for trade across North Africa and southward beyond the desert, Islam also spread to much of sub-Saharan Africa, particularly into West Africa.

After Arab trade caravans began to reach West Africa, the developing trade networks began to involve many of the local Iron Age societies, enhancing the development of large urban communities and the centralization of political power in the West African kingdoms that regulated and controlled this trade. First these trade networks involved the peoples settled in the savanna regions to the south of the Sahara. By the mid-eighth century A.D. there is evidence of the rise of the wealthy and powerful state of Ghana. Situated in the region of southern Mauritania and south-western Mali, Ghana apparently played a critical role in regulating trade, particularly between the gold-producing area in Guinea and the camel caravan traders that ranged across the Sahara. Islam seems to have made a major entrance into West Africa with these trade contacts. The state of Mali took over the control of much of this trade in the twelfth and thirteenth centuries and entered a stage of expansion of its empire, extending its control over a substantial area of West Africa until it was eclipsed in the sixteenth century by the Muslim state, the Songhai empire.

Coastal peoples also asserted their power and gained some control in the lucrative West African trade. In Nigeria, where the Benin kingdom started to emerge by about the twelfth century, its center had developed into a very large, wealthy, and powerful city by the time it was first visited by the Portuguese in the late fifteenth century. The Benin kingdom flourished for centuries, largely on control of trade, and also developed in its royal court a well-known tradition of lost-wax casting in brass and bronze and of fine sculpture in ivory. Ife, the center of the powerful Yoruba kingdom in southwestern Nigeria from the eleventh to the seventeenth centuries, also shows the development of fine artistic traditions in terra-cotta that show affinities to the Nok human figurines, as well as lost-wax castings in a bronze-like copper alloy that some claim to be associated with Benin castings.

During the first millennium A.D. some Nilotic speakers may have brought iron into the highlands of East Africa, but many Nilotic and Cushitic speakers continued their herding, farming, and fishing without the use of iron. A rapid spread of technology further south began in the middle of the last millennium B.C. From archaeological, human biological, and linguistic evidence, it is believed that this represents a major migration of iron-using Bantu-speakers of the Niger-Congo language subgroup into Central and eastern Africa (see map 5). Linguistic evidence traces the initial source area of these peoples to the region of western Cameroon and eastern Nigeria. This appears to have led to a rapid dispersal of these people throughout much of southern Africa between about the second and the fourth centuries A.D.

Over the ensuing centuries in southern Africa, the archaeological record shows larger, more permanent villages and more complex mixed farming. Concentration of wealth and power and other social complexities are sometimes suggested by the evidence, such as large homesteads with large cattle herds, the appearance of crafts (sometimes including clay cattle figurines), or accumulation of trade goods such as gold, glass beads, or ivory. In Zimbabwe an important trading and, presumably, political center was established by at least the tenth century A.D. at the site known as the Great Zimbabwe (see chapter 4). Active in the trade of gold to the coast and the import of goods such as pottery and glass from China and Asia, the Great Zimbabwe appears to have been a central site among a number of such stone-built centers in southern Africa. It flourished and grew for several centuries until approximately 1450 A.D., when the opening of mines further north appears to have influenced a northward shift in the trading routes.

In many areas, once food-producers appeared, evidence of stone-tool-using hunter-gatherers became rare or disappeared. In others regions, such as Zimbabwe, Malawi, and eastern Zambia, stone-tool hunter-gatherers maintained presence in the region and limited contact with the food-producers throughout the first millennium A.D. Over time, however, hunter-gatherer populations diminished in extent, until by the period of European contact they were restricted to more arid regions of southern and, to a lesser extent, eastern Africa. While relying heavily on hunting and gathering, they also appear at times to have incorporated domestic animals, especially sheep, in their subsistence, particularly in southwestern Africa. The precise nature of the various relationships and interactions that prevailed between the iron-using food-producers and the stone-tool-using hunter-gatherers is a subject of considerable interest among many archaeologists today.

Conclusion

This brief overview of the past few million years has presented a broad outline of major events and trends in the very long period of African prehistory. Historical records can deal only with a fraction of the time period accessible through archaeological investigation, and sometimes they favor certain aspects of society, such as politics, over others, such as subsistence and technology. Prehistoric archaeology offers a great time depth and other valuable perspectives on the long-term formation of populations, their subsistence patterns, their technologies, and their social achievements. These were the essential foundations for developments in the early history of the continent.

SUGGESTIONS FOR FURTHER READING

Clark, J. Desmond. *The Prehistory of Africa*. London: Thames and Hudson, 1970.
Clark, J. Desmond, ed. *The Cambridge History of Africa*. Vol. 1: *From the Earliest Times to c. 500 B.C.* Cambridge: Cambridge University Press, 1982.
Ehret, Christopher, and Merrick Posnansky. *The Archaeological and Linguistic Reconstruction of African History*. Berkeley: University of California Press, 1982.
Fage, J. D., ed. *The Cambridge History of Africa*. Vol. 2: *From c. 500 B.C. to A.D. 1050.* Cambridge: Cambridge University Press, 1978.

Harlan, Jack; Jan M. J. deWet; and Ann B. L. Stemler, eds. *Origins of African Plant Domestication*. The Hague: Mouton, 1976.

Klein, Richard G. *The Human Career: Human Biological and Cultural Origins*. Chicago: University of Chicago Press, 1989.

Phillipson, David W. *African Archaeology*. 2nd ed. Cambridge: Cambridge University Press, 1993.

Schick, Kathy D., and Nicholas Toth. *Making Silent Stones Speak: Human Evolution and the Dawn of Technology*. New York: Simon and Schuster, 1993.

John Lamphear and Toyin Falola
Aspects of Early African History

4 The study of Africa has grown at an impressive pace since the Second World War. Old myths of a "dark continent" without history until the coming of Europeans are no longer retold with credibility. From the earliest time, adaptation, creativity, innovation, change, and continuity have characterized African history. In what follows we explore some of these elements, focusing on a number of important events and issues. We begin by discussing the various methods used by historians of Africa before examining some of the main themes of early history which those methods have brought to light.

Sources of Precolonial African History

While most African peoples do not have a literate tradition, not all of Africa was devoid of written sources before the early twentieth century. In some areas, a literate tradition of great antiquity exists. Indeed, one of the earliest forms of literacy in the world, the hieroglyphic writing of ancient Egypt, was invented in Africa by Africans by about 3000 B.C. These ancient accounts give a vivid and intimate picture of this great African civilization during the nearly three millennia of its existence. South of Egypt, the Kushitic civilization, focused on the ancient city of Meroe, had its own form of writing five centuries or more before the birth of Christ, and in neighboring Ethiopia, Ge'ez, the classical language of ancient Axum, was being expressed in written form by the fourth century A.D.

Other literate traditions were brought to Africa by outsiders. In Mediterranean Africa, literacy in a variety of languages, including Greek, Latin, and Arabic, dates back many centuries. Literacy in Arabic also penetrated to the western Sudanic belt, where important centers of learning, such as Timbuktu and Jenne, existed during the fifteenth and sixteenth centuries. The same tradition was also found in the Swahili city-states of the East African coast. Later, with the arrival of Europeans along the coast of sub-Saharan Africa in the fifteenth century, came the written accounts of

Portuguese, Dutch, English, French, and other visitors. With the end of the nineteenth century and the imposition of European colonial rule, a veritable flood of written documents began to appear. Arabic and European written sources have enabled historians to reconstruct the past of some parts of Africa from the eighth century A.D. Neither is without its limitations. Arabic sources devoted more attention to religion and criticized "pagan" societies, and many were not firsthand accounts. With respect to European accounts, most of them before the nineteenth century were largely confined to the communities along the coast, the informants upon whom they relied were not always reliable, and they were written with an air of superiority and arrogance.

Many parts of Africa remained essentially without written sources before the colonial period, however, and in these areas oral history becomes indispensable in gaining a glimpse of the African past. As with any historical source, oral tradition must be understood to represent only a limited reality. It must be carefully analyzed, always within the wider cultural context of the society producing it, to decode the messages it contains.

Different African societies have different kinds of traditions. In some, especially those which were politically centralized and had powerful hereditary dynasties, selected individuals were entrusted with the memorization, recitation, and passing on of oral history from one generation to the next. The *griots* of West Africa were such men, and they often accompanied their recitations with the music of stringed instruments. In these centralized states with professional court historians, great care was taken to ensure that the traditions were recited in a precise, verbatim way. Such traditions have been termed "fixed" texts.

In other societies, including those without centralized political systems based on hereditary rule, oral traditions tended to be "free" texts. Here the traditions were not the concern of any professional class but could be rendered by any member of society, though most often by the elders. Unlike the fixed texts, these free texts were not recited verbatim from one telling to the next. Frequently the personality of the individual telling them would be reflected to some degree in the manner in which they were told.

Oral traditions can also be analyzed on different "levels" and from different perspectives. Most African peoples conceive of the past as being vibrantly linked with the present. Revered customs and traditions find validity in the present by being associated in oral tradition with important personages of the past, who, for the most part, are mythological. Such traditions often serve as mechanisms of social control and can be interpreted from what is termed a "functionalist" perspective. In African kingdoms, for example, the fixed texts of the *griots* often reflect the "official version" of a particular event. These exist mainly to underscore and support the legitimacy of the royal dynasty. In such cases, an oral historian might go about determining the "functionalist" nature of these fixed recitations by carefully collecting and analyzing the parallel traditions of "commoner" clans, which usually provide a very different version from that of the "official" royal tradition.

Other oral traditions sometimes embody fundamental sociocultural concerns of a given society and can be interpreted from what is called a "structuralist" perspective. Among many of the decentralized pastoral peoples of eastern Africa, for instance,

Plate 13. Nyama Suso, a *griot* from The Gambia,
reciting with *kora* accompaniment.
Photo courtesy Roderick Knight.

traditions frequently depict the formation of a particular society in terms of young men taking livestock off to dry-season pastures, then never returning to the parent community. Such traditions help to foster a sense of group cohesion, the lack of which can often be a problem in these highly egalitarian, mobile communities. The traditions can thus be seen to contain an important structuralist message about the significance of group solidarity and unity. At the same time they identify, in a more positive sense, the pioneering role which younger men often did play in the migrations of pastoral people.

With most African societies, it is possible to discern three distinct chronological periods in their oral history. There is first a remote early epoch when the world was "created" and the particular society was "formed." This is followed by an intervening middle period in which the society coalesced, interacted with other communities, and perhaps experienced migrations, conflicts, or famines. The most recent period extends back two or three generations, into the time just before the living experience of the community's oldest surviving members.

The "origin" traditions of the earliest period can be especially difficult to interpret, as they tend to derive from a mode of expression inherently dissimilar to that of written documents. Such traditions often contain what has been termed a "central cliché": that is, they compress what is in reality highly complex into a deceptively simple statement. Frequently the "cliché" also serves as a kind of mnemonic device about which to weave specific historical information. Unlike a written source, where variations in the recounting of a given event often imply manipulation or "faulty transmission," the differences in accounts in oral tradition often contain the most valuable clues for historians.[1] Traditions relating to this period are sometimes highly truncated or embellished versions combining two or more quite separate traditions. Frequently, too, time tends to be "telescoped" in such a way that events happening over a considerable span of time are expressed as having taken place all at once.

One common way to approach this middle period is to concentrate on those traditions which deal with the individual historical experience of a particular clan or smaller kinship group. These "local" or "family" traditions are known only by the specific group to which they pertain, and in general they tend to be more reliable and a better source of historical information than the "general" traditions known throughout the entire community. Those widely known traditions are often of the "pleasing story" variety, related in some instances to folktales, and are told more to entertain than to instruct.

Another concern of the historian working with oral tradition is to establish a chronology for the events described. This is especially important since many peoples in Africa and in other parts of the world do not share the Western concept of linear time. Some people, for instance, have a cyclical notion of time in which alternate generations are seen to replace one another quite literally. In the centralized states, traditions are frequently told with regard to the reign of a particular ruler. Here the historian must try to assemble a reliable king list and determine the approximate lengths of the reigns of individual rulers. Several formulas for determining the lengths of dynastic generations in various African kingdoms have been painstakingly worked out by historians.

With the decentralized societies, there are neither king lists nor deep genealogical memories to aid the historian. Fortunately, many of these societies do have age-set systems, and historical events often are told with regard to a particular named set. By very carefully analyzing the dynamics of these systems and collecting lists of remembered sets, the time spanned by individual sets can be gauged and the historian gains some reliable chronological pegs by which events can be approximately dated.

When historians conduct research in neighboring societies, they frequently find that the same event is described in the oral history of each. Working independently, they try to determine a date for the event through their own chronological reconstruction, and then compare their work with that of their colleagues as a check on the reliability of that reconstruction. If a tradition makes reference to a natural phenomenon, such as an eclipse, or if it refers to an event also recorded in a written source, it sometimes becomes possible to establish a precise date. Beyond this, oral historians always try to corroborate the information derived from traditions against evidence gleaned by scholars of other disciplines, such as archaeology or linguistics.

Such evidence becomes increasingly important in reconstructing something of the African past in the long epochs before the period recalled by oral tradition. In general, oral tradition does not have a chronological depth of more than a couple of centuries, and often it is much less. There are exceptions to this. For example, the Sundiata epic, still widely recited by West African *griots*, includes a detailed account of the battle of Karina, fought in about 1235 A.D. Oral traditions from East Africa have been at least indirectly responsible for the discovery of archaeological sites some two thousand years old.

Nevertheless, one must rely mainly on the "tools" provided by other disciplines to recapture a glimpse of Africa's history before about 1700. Archaeology, for example, can provide valuable insights into early material culture. The nature of an early society's economy, its technology, and something of its artistic development can often be understood through archaeological studies. By the use of a process such as the radiocarbon dating method, it is possible to date with some accuracy artifacts from as much as 60,000 years ago. Archaeology has made it possible for us to establish the antiquity of human habitation, of the knowledge of iron, and of agriculture in many parts of Africa. There are limitations. For instance, it is not always possible to establish definite links between a civilization known exclusively through the archaeological record and later civilizations about which something is known through oral or written historical sources or through linguistic evidence. The most serious problem today is finance: archaeological research is expensive, and very little sponsorship is being provided, especially in Africa itself.

Linguistics is another discipline to which the historian of Africa can turn for help. Using such methods as lexicostatistics and glottochronology, linguists can analyze the vocabulary, grammatical forms, and sound changes of a given language to achieve an understanding of its evolution. Sometimes developments that took place even thousands of years ago become discernible. In some cases, contacts between two different linguistic groups are clearly indicated. Where such linguistic evidence can be compared with the existing archaeological record, and these are found to be mutually corroborative, both disciplines become even more important to historians. Great care must be exercised in such comparisons, and historians must be careful not to draw overly hasty inferences from incomplete or only partially corroborative data. Archaeology cannot tell anything about the language of a particular culture, except, of course, where writing existed, as in ancient Egypt; and, conversely, the inferences drawn by linguists about the material culture of a given language group at a particular time in its history require definite archaeological confirmation.

Another discipline which has been extensively employed by historians is anthropology. By helping the historian to understand the values, institutions, and ideas of a society, anthropology becomes a vital tool in the historical analysis of oral tradition. It can instruct the historian in concepts of time, the dynamics of political institutions, the nature of kinship and other social groups, and the whole complex process of social change. The historian must understand all of these in order to interpret and use oral tradition satisfactorily and effectively.

Other disciplines, such as botany and genetics, can also make useful contributions to historical reconstruction. The former, for example, can measure pollen counts in the ground to reveal long-term climatic change and provide data on plant domestication. The latter may discern the genetic development of both humans and domestic animals.

Traditions of Origin and State Formation

Every ethnic group has legends on the beginning of its history, usually about how ancestors arrived in their present area. Many of the legends talk of culture heroes (e.g., the Oduduwa among the Yoruba or Bayajida among the Hausa) who migrated from somewhere else to the present abode. In some Yoruba and Kanuri legends, both Oduduwa and Dhi Yazan were migrants from the Middle East. There are legends that do not talk about migrations but simply say that the present-day abode is the original homeland and the place from which humankind evolved. For instance, there are Igbo Nri legends that do not believe in external migrations.

Traditions of migrations are the most common and perhaps the most useful in understanding a great deal of African history. Migration stories make it possible to identify the emergence of dynasties and the impact of external influences on indigenous populations. Migrations often entail interactions between different groups of people from which new modes of cultural expression and, eventually, a new sociopolitical entity would be born. The emergence of different cultures and food-producing societies and the widespread use of metallurgy have been attributed to large-scale internal migrations within the continent. The movement of human beings from one place to another greatly facilitated the spread of ideas and technology and contributed to the development of new societies. An investigation of migrations and the formation of African societies also sheds light upon other aspects of the African historical heritage. While a hallmark of African civilizations is their stunning cultural pluralism and tremendous diversity, there is also a basic traditional continuity that provides, simultaneously, a surprising degree of similarity between even widely separated societies.

Yet another common element in the traditions and process of state formation is the role of environment. Indeed, it is impossible to study African history in isolation from its environment. In the first place, the environment permitted certain human efforts such as animal domestication and farming. Second, in the process of settlement, Africans had to act as agents to change the environment, for instance, by migrating in search of new land and other resources. Also, great environmental changes might derive from human activities; for instance, the deterioration of some parts of the Sahel to desert occurred because of overgrazing and intense cultivation. The vegetation of the forest-grassland margin saw changes attributable to annual bush fires. Third, there are always locational advantages, such as with the Sahara, which served as the link between the north and the west, or the Atlantic Ocean, which was to bring Europeans. Lastly, uneven population distribution in the continent is partly a function of resource availability.

With evidence and interpretations from oral tradition and other sources, it is becoming increasingly possible to identify factors in the formation and development of African communities. These factors include leadership, environmental adaptation, plant and animal domestication, external borrowings, migrations, and political and economic stability. At this point the chapter will explore the interplay among those various factors in several selected historical examples drawn from different regions of Africa. The availability of source materials determines which issues and which places will be investigated, and a primary consideration will be the emergence of states and their institutions.

North and Northeast Africa

This region has yielded rich evidence concerning historical evolution, ancient civilization, and the interaction of Africa with the rest of the world. So profound is the history of Egypt, Kush, and Axum that they have become part of the most enduring legacies of world civilization. To some extent, the interpretation of the achievements of the region has become part of the great historical debates on such issues as the contributions of different races, the foundation of universal philosophical thought, and the impact of Africa on the West. In recent times, part of the debate defines the emergent political thought of Afrocentricity, which argues that the root of contemporary civilization can be traced to ancient black civilizations and that many ideas which have derived from blacks have gone unacknowledged in the formation and development of ancient civilizations such as those of Egypt and Greece.

As to the antiquity of this region, there can be no doubt. As was noted in the previous chapter, the Nile Valley is one of the earliest centers of food production. Some strains of wild barley were cultivated in Egypt and Nubia by 10,000, and perhaps as early as 15,000, years ago. By 6000 B.C., millet and sorghum were being harvested in the Khartoum area of the Upper Nile. The region became increasingly dependent on the Nile's fertile banks, and between 5000 and 4000 B.C., farming communities which could control the annual flood of the river and build irrigation systems were flourishing. By 3500 B.C., two kingdoms of Upper and Lower Egypt had emerged. Ca. 3100 B.C., King Menes (or Narmer) of Upper Egypt was able to conquer the delta part of Lower Egypt and established Ancient Egypt's first "dynasty." King Menes's achievement was remarkable: his unification of Egypt began the history of Ancient Egypt, a 3,000-year-long civilization which became the most enduring in the history of Africa, and indeed in all human history.

Ancient Egypt was governed by the "pharaohs," divine kings with great powers. The pharaohs were many, and can be grouped into thirty dynasties, from 3100 B.C. to 332 B.C. Some dynasties were weak, others strong, but Egypt retained a strong centralized authority. The pharaohs relied on a large bureaucracy to govern and obtained resources from peasants to support their administrations and opulent lifestyles.

The basis of the economy was farming. The predominantly rural population produced wheat, barley, flax, and other products, but the bulk of their surplus went to the kings. Trade with neighbors was also important: Egypt exported grain and gold and imported many other commodities, including ebony, ivory, timber, chariot horses, ostrich feathers, precious stones, metals, and incense.

In addition to its government and economy, Ancient Egypt was noted for such other achievements as the development of hieroglyphics, mathematics, and astronomy. It made highly important contributions to architecture, art, medicine, and religion. Even now onlookers are dazzled by the grandeur of Egyptian pyramids, monuments, jewelry, pottery, and other artifacts.

After 1100 B.C., however, Ancient Egypt began to experience great turmoil. It was troubled by attacks from the north and from across the desert to the west. By 1050 Nubia and other subject areas were able to free themselves. Waves of invaders, including Assyrians, Nubians, Persians, and Romans, swept in, and by about 30 B.C. Egypt had permanently lost its independence.

South of Egypt in the Upper Nile, the Nubians had been under Egyptian domination until about 1000 B.C., when they were able to establish the independent kingdom of Kush. Kush successfully invaded Egypt in about 730 B.C. and governed for at least sixty years before finally withdrawing, first to Napata and later to Meroe, where a distinctive culture emerged. The Nubians were able to shed many Egyptian practices, replacing them with local cultural features, such as the Meroitic language and script, new gods and shrines, new art forms, and pyramids. Meroe was rich in timber and iron, useful in building a good agriculture and defense, and it engaged in far-flung regional trade. But in about A.D. 300 Meroe declined, and the kingdom came to an end, in part because of the disruption of its agriculture and trade caused by an Axumite invasion, in about A.D. 350.

Axum, a thriving civilization in the Horn of Africa, had converted to Christianity by the time of its invasion of Meroe, partly as a result of Greco-Roman influences. Subsequently, several Nubian successor states to Meroe also adopted it as their state religion, and Alexandria in Egypt became one of the most important centers of Christian theology anywhere in the ancient world. By A.D. 640 another important world faith, Islam, was expanding rapidly from the Arabian peninsula. Arab invaders conquered most of northern Africa by A.D. 711, bringing the entire region firmly into the Islamic world.

West Africa

Between 5000 B.C. and 2000 B.C., the steady desiccation of the Sahara began to force populations of cultivators and herdsmen to flee their hostile conditions. Some of these took refuge in the Sudanic grasslands of western Africa below the desert's southern periphery, and new cultural centers began to develop. The establishment of these communities took place well before the chronological range of oral tradition, and long before the appearance of any written record in this area, so it is necessary to turn to archaeology for some glimpse of the process.

At Daima and other locations in northern Nigeria, excavations have shown that pastoral societies, with perhaps some grain agriculture, flourished as early as the first millennium B.C. To the west, at Dhar Tichitt in Mauritania, there is evidence of an even earlier food-producing society where a population herding domestic animals lived in stone villages by 1200 B.C. Within two centuries these people had begun to cultivate millet, and their population increased substantially. By 800 B.C. they had reached their peak, with even greater numbers settled in large, well-constructed towns. Perhaps they had commercial contacts with the Garamantes of the Fezzan region of Libya, or with some other trading people who used wheeled chariots to cross the Sahara. By three centuries later, however, this thriving population was gone, forced by continued desiccation to migrate to more fertile areas further south.

Archaeological evidence indicates that some form of state system, linked to the agricultural economy of the inhabitants, existed in these large stone towns. Indeed, the impact of food production on the development of any society is tremendous. A food-producing population, especially one engaged in agriculture, has to become more sedentary than a food-gathering population, so that farmers can remain close to their fields. As agricultural technology develops and production intensifies, farmers often begin to produce more food than their own families can consume. This surplus not only brings about dramatic and rapid population explosions, but also enables some of the population to become involved in non-food-producing activities. Such people can devote their energies to religious, political, or military activities, or they can become full-time artisans or traders. Such specialization and the expansion of populations ultimately lead to a clustering of sedentary agricultural communities.

Archaeological findings indicate that this process probably occurred in the Sudanic regions, as the food-producing revolution introduced by Saharan migrants triggered rapid population increases, the development of nonagricultural specialization, and the roots of urbanization. It was probably the need for some overall regulation of the agricultural cycle which occasioned the appearance of political centralization. Additional stimuli, in the form of pressures from hardy Saharan pastoralists, who represented the last populations to be driven from the steady encroachment of the desert, probably intensified the process, which was also aided by long-distance commercial contacts. At any rate, it is safe to conclude that the roots of political centralization in sub-Saharan Africa extend at least into the first millennium B.C.

The steady movements of people southward from the expanding desert appear to have continued into the first millennium A.D. From this point the archaeological record is augmented to some extent by West African oral traditions which vaguely recollect early migrations of certain clans from their places far to the north or northeast. As the food-producing revolution spread to the south, two groups in the West Central Sudan, the Mande-speakers of the Upper Niger and the Kanuric-speakers driven south by the desiccation north and west of Lake Chad, became the leading cultivators. It would seem that these and other groups of food producers transmitted ideas and techniques, rudimentary urbanization, and the beginnings of centralized government throughout a wide area. The growing Sudanic populations were probably further swelled by incoming Saharan pastoralists in search of new grazing lands and watering places. There was considerable interaction between the agricultural communities and others employed as mercenaries or military allies to check the encroachment of other pastoral bands following hard behind.

Another important factor in the development of the Sudanic communities was the introduction of iron technology. By the third century B.C., blacksmiths at Nok, a thriving civilization in central Nigeria, were smelting and working the metal, and within a few centuries the technology had become widespread throughout much of western Africa. Still another stimulus to the growth of states in the western Sudanic region was a strong economy, partly based on the trans-Saharan trade. By the end of the first millennium A.D., huge camel caravans were carrying cargoes of salt, collected in the north, across the Sahara to be exchanged for gold mined in the equatorial forests of West Africa to the south. Well before 1000 A.D., Nok and other societies were utilizing their iron technology to improve hunting and farming efficiency, increase their populations, and form large political units.

By perhaps as early as the fifth century A.D., the first of the great Sudanic states for which reasonably good historical evidence exists, Ghana, was formed. The picture of Ghana is far more complete than that of other early Sudanic civilizations, for the archaeological record and oral sources are augmented with the written accounts of visitors from North Africa from about the ninth century. The Soninke inhabitants of Ghana formed a powerful, complex kingdom, able to dominate vassal states in every direction. Located at the desert's edge, Ghana enjoyed a strategic position which allowed its rulers to control, as middlemen, the lucrative trans-Saharan trade in salt, gold, ivory, copper, and slaves, and they also derived a rich profit from taxing the intricate network of short- and middle-distance trade routes which spanned much of western Africa. The region was suitable for horses and camels, and the Ghanaian kings established large armies, built around a core of well-equipped cavalry, with which they maintained law and order throughout the sprawling territory under their control. In the eleventh century Ghana declined, and its capital was captured by the Soso. Several successor states appeared, of which the most influential was Mali.

Mali, a Mandinka kingdom further south of the desert's periphery, built its reputation on a strong economy, notably commerce and farming. Unlike Ghana, it used Islam to create social cohesion and transform its government. Thanks to its kings such as Mansa Musa, who undertook pilgrimages to Mecca, Mali became known internationally. With a formidable military machine and astute kings, during the thirteenth and fourteenth centuries Mali was able to expand and dominate western Sudan. At its peak, its boundaries extended to the sea in the west and the big bend in the River Niger to the east. Mali's demise came in the early fifteenth century when it was successfully attacked by Songhai.

The region around Lake Chad in central Sudan was at the heart of the Kanem-Bornu empire, in some respects the grandest and the most enduring of all the West African states. Its dynasty produced notables such as Mai Idris Alooma of the late sixteenth century who were able successfully to withstand external aggressions and internal dissensions. The largest states could boast populations in excess of 10 million people and controlled territories larger than all of western Europe. A host of

Plate 14. Ancient Niger river port of Mopti.
Photo courtesy United Nations/AP/AB.

smaller states—the Mossi kingdom, the Tukolor state, and the Hausa city-states, to name but a few—existed as well (see map 18).

With few exceptions, these Sudanic states, large and small, displayed remarkably similar political institutions. Their rulers were held in awe and entrusted with important religious functions, and their personal vigor was closely identified with the well-being of the state itself. They kept magnificent courts and appointed high officials of state, who frequently served as a council of ministers. In many cases, hereditary office did not exist outside the royal clan, and thus the danger of factionalism so prevalent in the federal structures of Europe and other parts of the world could be avoided. As time passed, administrative control became ever more refined and sophisticated, although powerful systems of checks and balances continued to limit the authority of the kings and kept it from becoming absolute. In all cases, taxes and tribute served as important sources of income for the royal courts, although typically such tributary wealth was routinely redistributed by the kings as a means of maintaining the loyalty of their followers and ensuring the well-being of all parts of the state.

To the extent that these states exerted control over vassal kingdoms, they can be termed "empires," but it must be emphasized that most of them maintained only loose imperial structures. In most cases, vassal states were allowed considerable autonomy.

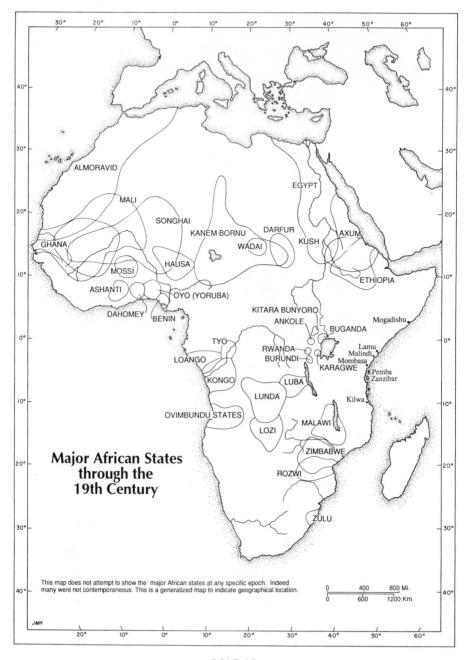

30° 20° 10° 0° 10° 20° 30° 40° 50° 60°

40°

30°

ALMORAVID

EGYPT

MALI

SONGHAI

20°

KANEM-BORNU   DARFUR   AXUM

GHANA   WADAI   KUSH

MOSSI   HAUSA

ASHANTI   ETHIOPIA

10°

OYO (YORUBA)

DAHOMEY   BENIN   KITARA BUNYORO

ANKOLE   BUGANDA   Mogadishu

TYO   Lamu

RWANDA   Malindi

LOANGO   BURUNDI   Mombasa

KONGO   KARAGWE   Pemba

LUBA   Zanzibar

LUNDA

Kilwa

OVIMBUNDU STATES   MALAWI

LOZI

**Major African States
through the
19th Century**   ZIMBABWE

ROZWI

ZULU

This map does not attempt to show the major African states at any specific epoch. Indeed
many were not contemporaneous. This is a generalized map to indicate geographical location.

0   400   800 Mi.

0   600   1200 Km.

JMH

20° 10° 0° 10° 20° 30° 40° 50° 60°

MAP 18

Plate 15. Paramount chief and retinue arrive for a meeting, Togo.
Photo courtesy United Nations/EE/jt.

As long as they paid tribute and taxes when called upon to do so, they were allowed to follow many of their own customs, speak their own languages, and practice their own religions. In fact, they were "enforced confederations."[2] In some cases, as with Ghana and Songhai, the loose-knit fabric of these empires would prove an important factor in their demise, together with the persistent problem of finding an effective system of royal succession.

In most states, the population was divided into two distinct strata. Each state had important urban centers which for their time were very large cities indeed. By as early as the eleventh century, the capital of Ghana had an estimated 30,000 inhabitants, while Gao, the largest city of Songhai, had nearly twice that many by a few centuries later. Apart from these townspeople, many of whom were engaged in commerce, cottage industries, or administration, there was a large rural population involved in agriculture. Especially with the introduction of the Islamic faith by northern traders into Sudanic regions from about the eleventh or twelfth centuries, there was a growing dichotomy between these two segments of the population. It was largely the urban dwellers who converted to Islam, while the rural folk, working the soil of their ancestors season after season, adhered to their traditional religions. After the collapse of Ghana in the late eleventh century, the rulers of the other great Sudanic civilizations adopted Islam as the state religion. Many of their cities became important centers of Islamic culture and learning. Such was the case, for example, with the Songhai cities of Jenne and Timbuktu, each of which boasted fine Islamic universities by the sixteenth century. Literacy in Arabic gave new sophistication and effectiveness to administrative machinery, and greater cohesion could be derived.

The farmers of the rural villages, on the other hand, who were more isolated from Islam and other outside forces, found satisfaction in the reaffirmation of traditional values and beliefs. Thus, the essence of Sudanic culture was expressed through an enduring resilience which enabled it to survive the shifting political structures and even the collapse of the great states which embraced it.

Most of these main features of the Sudanic civilizations, with the notable exception of the importance of Islam, were duplicated in the systems of other large states which developed in the forests to the south along West Africa's Guinea Coast: Benin, Oyo, Asante, and Dahomey, to name but a few. Here, too, powerful kings controlled trade and gathered taxes, while large towns developed into centers of commerce and manufacturing. Trade partnerships were established with the Sudanic states. In rural and urban areas alike, artists working in bronze, wood, ivory, clay, and stone produced spectacular works of art which were a visual manifestation of the constancy of enduring cultural traditions.

Central, Eastern, and Southern Africa

Bantu Africa, as the southern subcontinent often is called, demonstrates a most successful case of how human interactions can facilitate the rise of cultures (see also the previous chapter). Here the processes by which the great majority of Africans living south of the equator came to speak one or another of the closely related Bantu languages is examined. Implicit in these processes were important cultural interactions which led to the development of the rich, highly varied civilizations of "Bantu Africa." "Bantu" does not refer to any one language or people, but to the conglomeration of more than 450 languages in a family that traces its descent to "proto-Bantu" speech, in which the word *ntu* meant "person." The leading theories of Bantu origin and migration derive from linguistic reconstructions, sometimes supported by archaeological evidence.

From about the second millennium B.C., early Bantu-speaking communities were pressing slowly into the great equatorial forest of West Central Africa from their cradleland in the Benue-Cross region of what is now Nigeria and Cameroon. Evidence indicates that early economic life centered on the cultivation of root crops and fishing, activities well suited to the tropical forest environment. Except for a few goats, they apparently raised little livestock, and they had, as yet, no knowledge of iron technology.

By the next millennium, however, Bantu pioneers had arrived on the fringes of the forest and began to press into the open savanna grasslands beyond. In time, the expanding Bantu-speakers made contact with longer-established Africans who spoke other languages and possessed different cultures. Bantu expansions were usually not military conquests, but were more a subtle cultural intrusion and integration, involving the diffusion and assimilation of various social and economic institutions, as well as languages.

By as early as the sixth century B.C., ironworkers associated with a type of pottery called "Urewe Ware" had penetrated into the interlacustrine area of East Africa, perhaps up the Nile from the important ironmaking center at Meroe, in what is now the Sudan. These East African sites represent the earliest evidence of iron technology to be discovered thus far in sub-Saharan Africa. Having acquired the ironworking skill, Bantu agriculturists carried it with them as they ranged further from the forest margins and deeper into various parts of the southern subcontinent during the first millennium A.D.

By the fifth century A.D., Early Iron Age settlements of Bantu-speakers were dotted across much of Africa south of the equator. Archaeological evidence indicates that such settlements were compact and densely settled, but widely spaced. They tended to be located in the wetter areas of the savannas, along forest margins, and in the fertile bottomlands of river valleys. Their growth was facilitated by new food crops, some varieties of bananas and yams from Southeast Asia, introduced into Africa in the second century A.D. by Malayo-Polynesian sailors who settled on the island of Madagascar. The drier savanna lands interspersed between these better ecological zones were at first left vacant, and it was not until the Bantu-speakers were introduced to still other new forms of food production involving intensive pastoralism and dry-grain agriculture, hardy cereal crops which could be grown in all but the driest conditions, that they began to establish themselves in these less-favored regions. Those responsible for this pastoral tradition were Nilotic-speaking peoples, the vanguard of whom began pushing down the natural migration corridor of the Rift Valley by the early centuries A.D. from their homeland along the Upper Nile in what is now the Sudan.[3] Other evidence indicates that Cushitic-speaking peoples who had moved south from the southern fringes of what is now Ethiopia may have introduced the Bantu to dry cereal grains, new types of livestock, and the art of irrigation even earlier than this, and Central Sudanic-speaking migrants from the Sudan may have influenced them as well. In any case, by the beginning of the second millennium A.D., Bantu-speaking communities had rapidly begun to fill the drier regions, and a new and more sophisticated technological era, the Later Iron Age, had dawned in much of Bantu Africa.

Two key features of these Bantu "migrations" need to be emphasized at this point. First, these movements were, for the most part, carried out very slowly and over very short distances. Certainly it would be incorrect to envision a great horde of people moving together in a single migratory stream. Usually a small group of kin or a band of associates would undertake a particular move. From what can be derived from oral tradition, it is difficult to discern any definite pattern or even any given direction to the movements of such bands. It was as if "the whole drifted almost as unconsciously and as slowly as a glacier drifts from its mountain top."[4]

Undoubtedly, many incentives spurred on the migratory process. A Bantu-speaking community whose economy was based on shifting cultivation, for example, might be forced to expand to new agricultural lands as the soil of their old area became leached of nutrients or as population pressures developed. Where pastoralism was important, traditions sometimes portray young herdsmen driving animals into grazing lands beyond the range of their community's normal pattern of transhumance, thus effecting a short-distance migration. There were countless other reasons for migration: family quarrels, diseases, droughts, supernaturally caused misfortunes, succession and inheritance disputes, feuds, or even the sheer love of adventure—each could be sufficient for setting a group in motion.

A second feature that needs emphasis concerns the considerable interaction which went on between the Bantu-speakers and other African peoples inhabiting the subcontinent. The great majority of this interaction probably was peaceful: assimilation rather than extermination was the rule. Influences flowed in both directions. While Bantu speech usually predominated, it did not always do so in southern Africa, where the distinctive click sounds of San-speaking hunters were incorporated into several Bantu languages. If in some instances Bantu-speakers were responsible for introducing new political, economic, and technological concepts to non-Bantu-speakers, the reverse also happened. In the same way, many Bantu-speaking societies adopted patrilineal kinship organizations of various neighbors and in some parts of East Africa took over political organizations based on the age-grade systems of Cushitic- and Nilotic-speakers. Throughout their migrations, the Bantu-speakers proved themselves capable of adapting smoothly to new areas, new concepts, and new situations. The proof of this outstanding adaptability can be seen in the surprising variety now to be found among the diverse societies of Bantu Africa: from forest cultivators, to grain-producing empire builders, to politically decentralized pastoralists.

There are probably a number of reasons, depending on the time and the region in question, why Bantu speech has predominated in subequatorial Africa. In many parts of southern Africa, the Bantu-speakers were technologically far superior to the Khoisan hunters and pastoralists they encountered, especially after the advent of the Later Iron Age. Many of the Khoisan peoples were probably quickly assimilated by the Bantu, though others, especially some bands of hunters, preserved their language and their economy and established symbiotic relationships, valuable to both peoples, in which the assimilation process took place much more slowly. In other instances, where the technology of the Bantu was matched or even surpassed by those with whom they interacted, other factors were at work. Some observers have seen in the original matrilineal kinship system of the Bantu-speakers a means for the wide expansion of Bantu lineages during the early stages of the migrations. It has also been maintained that "Bantuization" was closely tied to urbanization. The Bantu usually lived in more compact settlements than did their more widely dispersed neighbors, who came into the Bantu towns to trade and eventually intermarried and began speaking Bantu languages. In other instances, the diffusion of Bantu speech seems to have been a facet of political processes. With the Lunda of the Upper Kasai, for

Plate 16. A seventeenth-century European depiction of the court of the
ruler of Loango, from O. Dapper, *Description de l'Afrique,* 1686.
Photo courtesy Lilly Library of Rare Books and Manuscripts, Indiana University.

example, a gradual process took place by which small groups of migrants pushed out
from the core area, setting up new Lunda-speaking chiefdoms further and further
afield.

The Lunda are but one example of many Bantu-speaking groups that developed
into large and complex centralized kingdoms, in some ways reminiscent of the states
of West Africa described above. In some instances, centralization probably stemmed
more or less directly from urbanization. Sometimes it may have been a more subtle
process in which political centralization developed only gradually from a preceding
period of ritual centralization. In other instances, the development of a more intensive
pastoral focus, which could significantly increase the possibility of economic accumulation, may have provided a stimulus to centralization. Thus, interactions between
pastoralists from the drier savannas with sedentary agriculturists of the more fertile
regions may have stimulated the formation of many kingdoms. By lending livestock
to the farmers, wealthy herdsmen might attract clients and begin to exert a degree of
political control, culminating in the evolution of large states in which the royal herds
became a major state industry.

One of the earliest centralized states to appear in Bantu Africa was Zimbabwe,
located in the area of the modern Central African nation of the same name. It is mainly
the archaeological record that provides a glimpse of this civilization. At the site of
Great Zimbabwe are stone ruins of impressive size and indicating considerable
technological expertise. By as early as the fourth century A.D., the people of this area
were skilled metalworkers, smelting iron and extracting gold from extensive mines.

Plate 17. The ruins of Zimbabwe.
Photo courtesy Department of Information, Zimbabwe.

Written accounts of traders at the busy Swahili ports of East Africa's coast refer to a thriving inland kingdom existing in the Zimbabwe area by the tenth century. Indeed, the very existence of these ports came to depend heavily on the flow of gold from this region, and they vied with one another to control its export to the Indian Ocean world. In a situation very similar to that of the West African commercial empires, Zimbabwe and, by the fifteenth century, its successor state, Monomotapa, derived considerable stimulus from this long-distance trade and were transformed into powerful and far-reaching empires.

Other great states, including the kingdoms of Kongo, Luba, and the Lozi, also developed in various parts of Central Africa, as did smaller chiefdoms, which sometimes formed themselves into looser confederacies, such as the Bemba union. In many instances, these states grew up in relative isolation from one another, although as time passed, thriving networks of regional trade, involving the exchange of local specializations such as salt, copper, iron, or livestock, bound them together commercially, sometimes over great distances. As in West Africa, powerful kings and chiefs derived rich incomes from taxes and tribute, and in their overall development, these Bantu states, and even many of their specific political institutions, bore a striking resemblance to their West African counterparts.

In southern Africa, large politically centralized states developed considerably later and in a somewhat different manner. In many parts of this area, apparently one of the last to be penetrated by pioneering agriculturists and herdsmen, ecological conditions were not as conducive to the same intense buildups of population as they were in the more fertile Central African grasslands. Consequently, transhumant pastoralism tended to play an even more important role than it did further north. Until the nineteenth century, these areas tended to be rather sparsely settled, and there was always room for further migration to alleviate localized demographic pressures. Here, then, the political process tended to be one of fission rather than imperial fusion, with the dominant political structure being that of the small, independent chiefdom. By the beginning of the nineteenth century, however, population pressures, at least in many parts of this area, had begun to grow. The situation was exacerbated by the appearance of another migration, which pushed into the region from the south: that of the land-hungry *trekboers,* descendants of the seventeenth-century Dutch settlers who had established themselves at Africa's southern tip (see chapter 6). With the previous peaceful migration thus curtailed, the Nguni-speaking Zulu sought a radical solution. Under the leadership of Shaka, one of Africa's true military geniuses and innovators, the Zulu transformed themselves into an efficient and powerful military empire. They accomplished this by mobilizing large armies that assimilated, crushed, or displaced vast numbers of other peoples. The process, known in southern Africa as the *mfecane* (a Zulu word meaning "time of troubles"), set off a series of chain reactions that had wide repercussions through much of East Central Africa, as far north as the area of modern Tanzania.

In much of East Africa, in ecological conditions similar to those in southern Africa, political organizations either tended to be decentralized or else took the form of small chiefdoms. Some of the societies, born of intimate and ongoing interactions between neighboring peoples, tended to be small-scale and transient. But such dynamic activity also frequently led to discernible, though flexible, cultural boundaries in which a definite sense of selfhood and ethnic identity could develop. Only in the more fertile interlacustrine region did large centralized states similar to those of the Sudanic region and Central Africa develop. But here the process of political consolidation was more complex. East Africa experienced not only the spread of Bantu-speaking peoples but also equally important immigrations of other peoples from the north. Nowhere in Africa is the historical process of interaction and assimilation between various peoples more vividly to be seen than in this region.

Such interactions were taking place long before the arrival of the first Bantu-speakers. The earliest discernible inhabitants of East Africa were several different groups of food gatherers, including some who spoke Khoisan languages. By as early as perhaps the third millennium B.C., immigrants from the north had begun to enter the region. Southern Cushitic-speakers from Ethiopia settled in the Rift Valley and in the adjacent highlands and plains of present-day Kenya and Tanzania. They were to be followed in the next millennium by Eastern Cushites from the same area. A third possible intrusion from the north was by Central Sudanic-speakers into Uganda, west of the Rift Cushites. The next group to enter the area were Southern Nilotic-speakers, ancestors of the Kalenjin-speaking groups, who may have been responsible for the introduction of a strong pastoral tradition into the southern subcontinent, as suggested above. The linguistic evidence indicates that these Southern Nilotes, pushing down the Rift, experienced close contacts with the previously settled Cushites, and considerable intermingling took place.

The Southern Nilotes were followed in turn by their linguistic cousins the Eastern Nilotes, who also came south along the Rift corridor in the early centuries A.D. The vanguard of this group were ancestors of the pastoral Maasai. In their wake followed other groups, including ancestral elements of such peoples as the Iteso, the Turkana, and the Jie. All these peoples tended to become increasingly oriented to nomadic pastoralism as they pushed south.

By this time, Bantu-speaking peoples had also begun to push into the eastern parts of East Africa. A complex process of interaction between the various northern immigrants and the Bantu began. In the process most of the Cushitic-speakers, as well as the hunting communities, were absorbed. In many cases, Bantu speech prevailed in the new societies born of this interaction, but in other cases the cultural, political, economic, and linguistic aspects of the non-Bantu endured. While there were certainly some instances of conflict between the various groups, for the most part these different migrations and assimilations again were carried out peacefully. Even the fundamental rivalry between agriculturists and pastoralists, a key feature of interactions in western and northern Africa, was absent in East Africa. Rather, agricultural and pastoral societies apparently coexisted (often with the farmers occupying the wetter highlands and the herders ranging the plains below) and entered into symbiotic relationships. When conflict did develop, it was usually between groups with the same economic outlook and often with the same linguistic affiliation.

The establishment of Bantu-speaking communities in the interlacustrine area was greatly facilitated by the introduction of Southeast Asian food crops, especially bananas, which thrive in wet climates. From this economic base emerged centralized states quite unlike the decentralized, egalitarian communities that developed throughout most of East Africa. The largest of these states, known as Kitara, was located in what is now southern Uganda, and the oral traditions of Bantu-speakers associated it with an early dynasty of god-kings, called the Abatembuzi. By the fourteenth century A.D., the traditions claim that the Abatembuzi were supplanted by a new dynasty, the Abachwezi, pastoralists from the north, whose original linguistic affiliation is unknown and who are today represented by the Tutsi of Rwanda and Burundi. The Abachwezi are credited with establishing a political hegemony over the Kitara region and with the construction of massive earthwork enclosures (see map 19).

The final major influx of migrants into East Africa was yet another group of Nilotic-speakers from the north, the Lwoo. Pushing into Uganda around 1450, the Lwoo Babito dynasty supplanted the Abachwezi. The coming of the Lwoo caused the disintegration of the sprawling Kitara state into a number of new yet still highly centralized kingdoms, such as Bunyoro and Buganda. Like the Abachwezi before them, the Babito kings quickly abandoned their Nilotic languages in favor of Bantu speech.

MAP 19

Elsewhere, the Lwoo established smaller and less strongly centralized states. In the north, for example, the Acholi were organized into small kingdoms and even smaller chiefdoms, while to the south, on the northeastern shores of Victoria Nyanza (Lake Victoria), the Ja-luo were politically decentralized. In both of these areas, the Lwoo experienced very close interactions with their neighbors, although there were periods of conflict as well. Once again, however, the process was by no means only in the one direction. Some Lwoo-speaking clans were absorbed by their neighbors, and several features of the Eastern Nilotic–speaking societies, notably their military and age-grade systems, were taken over by many of the Lwoo, once again demonstrating that migration in Africa was largely a gradual process of cultural, political, economic, and linguistic interaction.

Migrations in East Africa were still going on when the forces of European colonialism appeared in the late nineteenth century. Typically, these migrations were small-scale, short-distance moves by bands of pastoralists seeking new grazing lands or communities of farmers moving to new agricultural lands. Occasionally, though, they were on a larger scale. In the second half of the nineteenth century, many Maa-speaking peoples found their progress southward along the Rift Valley blocked by powerful neighbors and, turning back on themselves, engaged in a period of internecine conflict, known as the "Maasai Civil Wars." At the same time, in a dramatic expansion, the Turkana occupied the region where they now live in northwestern Kenya. Even here, though, the process involved complex interactions with and assimilations of outsiders, as alien populations "became Turkana" in the face of mounting ecological, demographic, and, to a lesser degree, military pressures. As was probably true of most African migrations, the process involved the "move-ment" of a cultural and linguistic system at least as much as it did the actual movement of human beings.

Patterns of Authority

There were two basic kinds of traditional political organizations: centralized states, with political authority vested in the hands of hereditary rulers, and more egalitarian decentralized communities, where political power was regulated by interactions between kinship groups, such as clans or lineages, or was maintained by a congregation of elders whose status was determined by their "rank" in an age-set system.

Political centralization is an ancient tradition in Africa. Archaeological evidence strongly indicates that centralization, while nurtured by commercial, religious, and cultural influences from outside Africa, was fundamentally an outgrowth of the African historical experience itself. The kingdoms mentioned above were central-ized. They tended to be large, well populated, economically diversified, and highly socially stratified. Leadership could be exercised by a select few with hereditary claims. Competition and conflicts were endemic as claimants to the throne or leading titles engaged in bitter struggles which could lead to serious fractionalization and the breakdown of the state. Judicial systems were always well established. Revenue collections were taken seriously to obtain resources to maintain power and privileged lifestyles.

Research also has proved that decentralized communities were far more complex and sophisticated than was originally supposed. Moreover, these communities often were marked by a stability far greater than that of the centralized states. Certainly, centralization did not necessarily imply any "superior" political or cultural develop-ment. In many decentralized societies, the lineage or clan formed the political units. Heads of lineages or clans exercised authority, although power tended to diffuse in such a way that many elders could cooperate to arrive at consensus. Judicial and religious authority was vested in the hands of certain people, suggesting specializa-tion of functions.

Some notable examples of decentralized societies were the San of the Kalahari Desert, the Igbo of Nigeria, the Nuer of the Sudan, and the Maasai of East Africa. Space does not permit full elaboration of these cases, but the Igbo example provides an illustration. The village was the largest unit of the Igbo political system, in contrast to a kingdom based on a large territory comprising hundreds of villages. An Igbo village was independent and autonomous, and would fight to defend its sovereignty. A village acquired a name, land, and territory, all recognized by its neighbors. There was a very strong belief in a common patrilineal descent. A village had a shrine to honor mother earth, a place of meeting which served as the main market, ritual, and political center. Every village was democratic, as decision making involved most of its elders.

In all African societies, women played dynamic and varied roles. Some centralized states had women rulers, and the "Queen Mother" was a highly important functionary in many others. Typically, women were essential in religious and economic affairs. In many instances it was they who were the healers, diviners, and priestesses, serving as vital intermediaries between their people and supernatural forces. Women dominated important areas of the economy, controlling many facets of agricultural production, the flow of commerce, and a wide variety of industries and crafts. It was women who milled flour, preserved food, built houses, manufactured clothing and ornaments, brewed beer, established markets, and composed songs, poetry, and stories of lasting appeal. And they controlled the income they derived from the sale of their surplus production.

Intergroup Relations and External Contacts

Small or large, centralized or decentralized, no African society was an island unto itself. Trade, warfare, diplomatic relations, migrations, and marriage constituted some of the basic elements of intergroup relations. There were no fixed boundaries to create permanent lines of human divide. Instead, cultural frontiers existed that allowed for profitable contacts among Africans.

Three main patterns of interactions are identifiable. First, there were extensive interactions at the regional level, involving members of the same ethnic or language group, or one group and its immediate neighbors. Second, there were interregional relations. The trans-Saharan trade was one notable case that united West and North Africa. Third, there were international relations, for example, the relations with Arabs, which facilitated the spread of Islam, and, after the fifteenth century, with Europeans. Languages, religions, skills, ideas, and goods were able to spread as a result of these contacts. All three patterns of interactions served to unite Africans and to connect their continent with the rest of the world.

NOTES

1. J. Miller, ed., *The African Past Speaks* (Folkestone: Wm. Dawson, 1980).
2. E. Jefferson Murphy, *History of African Civilizations* (New York: Thomas Y. Crowell Press, 1971, 1972), p. 93.
3. R. Oliver, "The Nilotic Contribution to Bantu Africa," in Ranier Vossen and Marianne Bechhaus-Gerst, eds., *Nilotic Studies* (Berlin: Dietrich Reimer Verlag, 1983), pp. 359–61.
4. Jan Vansina, "Traditions of Genesis," *Journal of African History*, 15, no.1 (1974): 319.

SUGGESTIONS FOR FURTHER READING

Ajayi, J. F. A., and M. Crowder, eds. *History of West Africa*, vol. 1. Harlow: Longman, 1985.

Davidson, Basil. *East and Central Africa to the Late Nineteenth Century*. London: Longman, 1968.

Connah, Graham. *African Civilizations*. New York: Cambridge University Press, 1987.

July, R. W. *A History of the African People*. 4th ed. Prospect Heights, Ill.: Waveland Press, 1992.

Kiernan, J.A., and B. A. Ogot, eds. *Zamani*. Nairobi: East African Publishing House and Longman, 1968.

Lamphear, John. *The Traditional History of the Jie of Uganda*. Oxford: The Clarendon Press, 1976.

Oliver, R. *The African Experience*, chapters 1–7. New York: Harper Collins, 1991.

Vansina, Jan. *Oral Tradition as History*. Madison: University of Wisconsin Press; London: James Currey, 1985.

John H. Hanson
Islam and African Societies

5 Today estimates suggest that one in three Africans is Muslim.[1]
Visitors often are impressed by the widespread public practice of a
common set of Islamic rituals, particularly in the northern, western, and eastern regions of the continent. However, this liturgical
conformity does not mean that Muslims follow identical social practices dictated by
Islam. Rather, Africa's richly textured social fabric includes a great variety of Islamic
motifs, produced by specific Muslim initiatives in particular contexts. This diversity
was evident from the time Islam was introduced. The Arab conquest of northern
Africa encouraged both conversions to Islam and the adoption of Arabic language
and identity, whereas south of the Sahara, Muslim merchants spread the faith through
peaceful means and most converts retained their languages and customs. In subsequent periods, the proselytization of Sufi mystics and the successes of reform
movements brought new patterns to some localities. Responses to the challenge of
European domination also varied among Muslims.

The Emergence of Islam as a World Religion

Islam is a religion with origins in the oases of seventh-century Arabia. The ideas
of the monotheistic religions, Judaism and Christianity, circulated in the region,
although at that time most Arabs remained faithful to the polytheistic traditions of
their ancestors. In Mecca, where Islam's prophet Muhammad was born, control of a
local shrine gave some families advantages in commercial transactions. Other
residents were not as fortunate, and rallied around the leadership of Muhammad,
whose spiritual search led him to question the old ways. Muhammad asserted that
God communicated divine revelations to him in Arabic; these messages eventually
were committed to writing and preserved in the Qur'an. The principal message was
that there was only one God, the Creator of the Heavens and the Earth, who wished
that humankind would follow God's will in this world and thereby earn a place in
Paradise. The revelations also stressed social justice and advocated specific changes

in the treatment of the poor, in relations between husbands and wives, in the practice of business, and so forth. Resistance from powerful Meccan families forced Muhammad to emigrate with his followers to Medina, another oasis, where he gained social recognition as both prophet and political leader in 622 A.D.[2] At Medina Muhammad received additional revelations, elaborated the rituals of the new faith, and gained a series of military and diplomatic victories which made him the political leader of central Arabia.

After Muhammad's death in A.D. 632, his closest companions decided that a *khalifa* or "deputy" ought to continue serving as political head of the Muslim community. Successive *khalifas* led Muslims in a *jihad* or military struggle in support of the faith. The Prophet Muhammad had acknowledged warfare as a religious act when he defended the Muslim community from its enemies at Mecca, but he cautioned against its use and spoke of the "greater *jihad*" as the personal struggle against sin. The *khalifas* or "caliphs" nonetheless focused on the military *jihad* and directed Arab armies in campaigns which secured regions of economic potential, first against the Persian and Byzantine empires in the Fertile Crescent, and then in lands beyond this southwestern Asian base. Arab Muslims thus became a ruling elite in an empire or "caliphate" extending from the Iberian Peninsula in the west to the edges of the Chinese empire in the east. Muslim rule in the caliphate spurred economic expansion and the creation of a world civilization which synthesized the cultures of many peoples from Europe, Asia, and Africa.

At first the Arab conquerors maintained Islam as the exclusive cult of the elite, but Muslim visionaries ultimately stressed the inclusive nature of God's revelations in the Qur'an. They drew inspiration from the passage that asserted that the community established by Muhammad at Medina was "the best community ever raised up for humankind" (Qur'an III: 110), and allowed converts to join its ranks. The numbers of converts were small in the initial centuries of the caliphate, but over time mass conversions made Islam the majority faith in much of southwestern Asia and northern Africa. Confronted by a growing number of converts, pious Muslims defined five basic "pillars" which expressed membership in the Muslim community: public profession of submission to God, giving of alms to the poor, praying at set times during the day, pilgrimage to the holy places in Arabia, and fasting during the Muslim month of Ramadan to re-enact Muhammad's quest for divine revelation. These pillars are part of the *sunna* or "path" blazed by Muhammad and the early disciples. The *sunna*, known through *hadith* or "reports" of Muhammad's life, constitutes an authoritative guide to behavior in accord with God's will. Non-Muslims sometimes confuse this attention to the details of Muhammad's practice with veneration of him as a deity; references to Islam as "Mohammadism" imply such an inaccurate view. Scholars of religion more precisely view this concern for correct behavior as a trait which Islam shares with other religions, such as Orthodox Judaism. Muslims believe that Muhammad was the last in a prophetic tradition inaugurated by Abraham and the other Jewish prophets. They thus allow Christians and Jews to retain their religious allegiances if they so choose, but encourage all to obey what they consider the last and most complete revelation received by Muhammad.

Muslims believe that the Qur'an is the literal word of God and that classical Arabic is a sacred language. From the tops of mosques, they are invited to pray five times a day by someone calling in Arabic. Inside, Muslims prostrate themselves before God as they repeat litanies in Arabic. The emphasis on the Qur'an finds expression in other domains. Children are often sent to religious schools where they memorize the Qur'an by heart. Artistic expressions also value calligraphic representations of verses from the Qur'an. Religious leadership is conferred upon the *ulama* or "learned ones," who are fluent in classical Arabic and interpret Islam's messages to each new generation. Over time the *ulama* came to establish a legal process to define correct action when the Qur'an was silent or ambiguous on particular issues. The result was the creation of the *sharia* or Muslim "way," often translated as "Islamic law." The formation of a legal tradition with fixed texts served to set parameters for acceptable social behavior, but historical circumstances have always pressed Muslims to reassess the meaning of the *sharia*. For example, most would agree that the *sharia* demands that Muslim women cover themselves, but they differ as to whether the act should take the form of veiling, wearing certain styles of clothing, or merely dressing modestly according to personal taste. Similarly, in sub-Saharan Africa, some *ulama* view traditional masks as unacceptable representations, whereas others tolerate them as expressions of local culture. The *sharia*, as with other aspects of Muslim life, is a process which the faithful understand to be a quest to obey God's will, rooted directly or indirectly in the sacred precedents in the Qur'an and the *sunna*.

Islam's Introduction to Africa

The introduction of Islam into Africa took two basic courses: one for northern Africa, where Arabs established themselves as a ruling elite and settled in garrisons throughout the region, and another for sub-Saharan Africa, where Muslim traders introduced Islam and resided in commercial enclaves. The pace and extent of conversion differed markedly in the two regions. Arab policies benefited Muslims and created incentives for conversion to Islam; within four centuries, mass conversions had produced Muslim majorities in northern Africa. In regions south of the Sahara, the initial converts tended to be local merchants involved in long-distance trade. In a few contexts, such as the city-states of eastern Africa, Muslims established islands of social power. Elsewhere Muslim traders depended upon the goodwill of local kings. Even when African rulers converted to Islam, they continued to cultivate traditional sources of authority. This coexistence gave African Muslims the opportunity to articulate Islam in a way that was relevant to Africans of many walks of life.

Conquest and Social Change in Northern Africa

Arabs conquered northern Africa in the first two centuries after Muhammad's death. Byzantine Egypt fell within a few years of the Arab invasion in A.D. 641. At that

Plate 18. Mosque in Jenne, Mali.
Photo courtesy United Nations/A. Rozberg.

time most Egyptians spoke Coptic (related to the language of the pharoahs) and belonged to the local Orthodox Christian church. Coptic church leaders responded to the Arab invasion by negotiating a peace which secured Arab recognition of Coptic Christianity in exchange for regular payment of taxes to Muslim rulers. Arab conquests farther west did not receive much local support and proceeded more slowly. The Arabs secured the coastal areas of Libya and the Maghrib ("the west" in Arabic), but in the mountains and arid lands to the south, local Berbers resisted Arab armies with some success. Conversions to Islam among both Berber and Coptic populations occurred centuries after Arab political victories. While many converts certainly were attracted to Islam as a new religion, social factors also played a role in the process. For example, after a series of revolts failed to force the Muslim state to lower taxes in Egypt, Copts began to convert because as Muslims they paid fewer taxes. In the Maghrib, Muslim garrisons on the frontier allowed Arabs and Berbers to exchange goods and ideas, leading eventually to the conversion of some Berber merchants and political leaders. By the eleventh century, Muslims were a majority in northern Africa.

The expansion of Islam was accompanied by Arabization, the adoption of the Arabic language and culture by Berbers and Copts. The transformation proceeded slowly and still is incomplete in some areas, such as in the Atlas Mountains of Morocco and Algeria, where many Berbers retain their language and separate identity. Military victories allowed an Arab ruling elite to construct a dominant culture rooted in their language and customs. Muslim decisions to make Arabic the official language also compelled Copts and Berbers working in the state bureaucracy to learn Arabic. The periodic migration of large numbers of Arab herders altered ethnic balances in some areas and encouraged Arabization as well. The increasing pace of conversion to Islam played a role, because converts usually adopted an Arab name to symbolize the switch in religious allegiance. Acting in combination, these factors altered the cultural geography of northern Africa. Indigenous influences nevertheless are apparent in many domains. For example, colloquialisms and differing pronunciations of consonants distinguish the Arabic dialects of northern Africa from those elsewhere in the Arab world.

Conversions to Islam altered relations between the state, religion, and society. In the early centuries, Islam was an Arab cult and northern Africa was incorporated into the caliphate based in Damascus and then Baghdad. As local populations converted, some rallied around alternate visions of Islam and challenged the social order. The Fatimids were perhaps the most dramatic example in the early centuries. They were Berber Shi'a, members of the dissident movement which challenged the succession of *khalifa* in favor of descendants from the Prophet's family. The Fatimids conquered regions of the Maghrib in the early tenth century, invaded Egypt in A.D. 969, and ruled from a capital at Cairo until A.D. 1171. The Fatimids never succeeded in convincing most northern Africans to become Shi'a, but they established a tradition of state support for Muslim religious institutions. The Ayyubids and the Mamluks, immediate successors to the Fatimids in Egypt, actively cultivated close relations with non-Shi'a *ulama*, in order both to diminish Shi'a influence and to give themselves legitimacy as rulers. Patronage eventually led to a system of state appointments of Muslim judges who interpreted the *sharia* for the state. The post-Fatimid era also saw expansion of state support for Muslim education, for example, the establishment of Azhar University in Cairo, which became one of the Muslim world's most prestigious educational institutions. In the Maghrib, especially in Morocco and Tunisia, post-Fatimid political regimes made similar moves to associate closely with religious leaders.

Imperial Muslim rule returned to much of northern Africa beginning in the sixteenth century in the form of the Ottoman Turkish empire, which used the cannon and other military innovations associated with the gunpowder revolution to control the eastern Mediterranean world. The Ottomans justified bringing independent Muslim states in northern Africa under imperial control because of their goal to unite all Muslims under one leader, the sultan based at Istanbul. Only Morocco escaped incorporation within the empire. Once in power, Ottoman governors retained and even expanded the links between the state and local *ulama*. They also used their northern African provinces as bases to harass the emerging maritime powers of western Europe. Beginning in the seventeenth century, even as the influence of the Ottoman sultan diminished over his African provinces, local Muslims continued the pattern of maritime harassment; to European sailors they were the infamous "Barbary pirates." On the mainland, Ottoman decline allowed *ulama* to increase their social power in relation to political authorities. Ottoman rule, even in its dissolution, reinforced the Muslim heritage of northern Africa.

Trade and Social Change in Sub-Saharan Africa

The commercial activities of Muslim merchants, not Arab military conquests, introduced the faith south of the Sahara Desert. Beyond the political boundaries of Islam, relations between Muslim merchants and host societies followed rules established by local rulers. African kings tried to confine Muslim traders to specific locales in order to tap the revenues associated with long-distance commerce. In this context, only a few Africans came into contact with Muslims. The initial converts were local merchants who shared a commercial ethos with foreign Muslims, and political elites who adopted the religion of their trading partners to solidify ties with them. Most residents of these states, however, remained faithful to the polytheistic beliefs of their ancestors. This enduring commitment to local traditions forced political elites to maintain non-Muslim symbols in court ceremonies in order to claim authority over all subjects. Tolerance of local customs became a hallmark of most African states in the savanna lands stretching just below the Sahara Desert, from the Atlantic Ocean to the Red Sea.[3]

These patterns are evident in the history of Ghana, Mali, and Songhai, a succession of empires which controlled access to West African gold between the ninth and the sixteenth centuries (see chapter 4). The rulers of Ghana confined foreign merchants to enclave settlements, and the first local converts were the Wangara, traders who transported gold to the enclaves. Only later did African rulers adopt Islam. The kings of Ghana converted after the rise of the Almoravids, Berbers who imposed their interpretations of Islam throughout the Sahara beginning in the eleventh century. The rulers of Mali, the empire which succeeded Ghana in the thirteenth and fourteenth centuries, seem to have made Islam a component of courtly culture from the beginning of their rule. Mansa Musa made the *hajj* to Mecca and drew international attention to the fidelity of Mali's rulers to the pillars of the faith. Even with this reputation for orthopraxy, Muslim travelers to Mali still complained about certain court rituals which they saw as unacceptable practices. The kings of Songhai, Mali's successor in the fifteenth and sixteenth centuries, also maintained Muslim traditions at their court and supported the rise of Timbuktu, the Muslim commercial town which served as a center of religious learning for West Africa.

From Timbuktu and other commercial centers, African merchants spread Islam in their commercial travels. They replicated the patterns of expansion associated with the initial years of Islam's expansion: they arrived as merchants, maintained the faith in commercial enclaves, and occasionally converted local rulers to Islam. African Muslims were adaptable, too, building reputations among local populations as healers and saints. Muslim scholars sometimes turned mastery of Arabic literacy into an expression of their ability to manipulate supernatural powers. For example, Muslim leaders inserted verses of the Qur'an into amulets or made potions from herbal mixes washed off writing boards; local populations sought such amulets and potions as protection against illness and future misfortune. The history of the Jakhanke people of West Africa illustrates this development. They were members of the Wangara trading diaspora who settled in Senegambia after the decline of the Mali

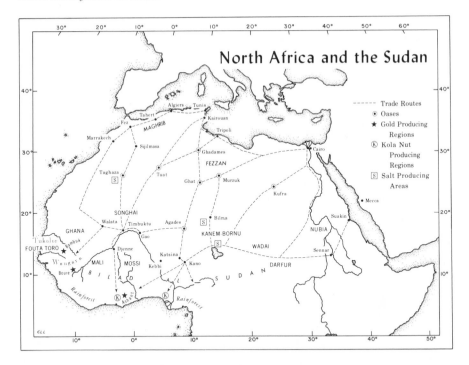

North Africa and the Sudan

MAP 20

empire. While some Jakhanke continued to engage in regional trade, the most famous were *ulama* who supplied non-Muslim kings with amulets. Although they usually did not convert local kings to Islam, Jakhanke leaders maintained the traditions of the faith within their own community and enhanced perceptions of Islam's spiritual efficacy in the general population.

An important variation in these patterns occurred along the eastern coast of Africa. Muslim commercial expansion in this region resulted in the formation of a Creole culture rooted on the African continent but influenced from southwestern Asia. Kiswahili, the language associated with this culture, symbolizes the interaction: it is a Bantu language with many loanwords from Arabic and other languages. Its name is derived from the Arabic word for coast, *sahel*, and points to the small coastal islands and their continental hinterland as the place for the fusion of cultures. Recent work by linguists, archaeologists, and historians suggests that Bantu-speaking fishing and farming lineages occupied the coast around A.D. 1000 in a purposeful migration from areas in today's Kenya.[4] The distinctive coastal environment, with its relatively fertile soils and adequate rainfalls in a region of general aridity, led the migrants to occupy the entire ecological niche, which in many areas does not extend more than a few miles from the coast. The fission of Swahili lineages over the course of the migration did not prevent coastal dwellers from maintaining trading contacts with settlements up and down the coast. The Swahili incorporated enclaves of seafaring Muslims from Arabia and Persia and plied the Indian Ocean in sailing vessels known as *dhows*. The Swahili eventually adopted their commercial values and religious beliefs and extended them throughout the coastal settlements. By the thirteenth century, Swahili merchants had moved down the coast and monopolized the international trade in gold mined on the Zimbabwean plateau in South Central Africa. The town of Kilwa was the coastal entrepôt for the Swahili gold trade. Ibn Battuta, a traveler who visited many Muslim towns, including Kilwa, noted that it was "amongst the most beautiful of cities and most elegantly built" and that its residents were virtuous and righteous Muslims.[5]

In northeastern Africa, Islam's expansion had elements of novelty, but largely followed patterns seen elsewhere in sub-Saharan Africa. The Nubian states of the Middle Nile Valley, alone among sub-Saharan regimes, engaged Arab armies during the early Muslim conquests. Nubian resistance prevented Arabs from expanding up the Nile and set a boundary close to the current divide between Egypt and the Sudan. Despite this proximity to Egypt, conversions to Islam followed the gradual expansion associated with other regions of sub-Saharan Africa. The coastal settlements along the Red Sea and Somali coast largely mirrored the Swahili experience: Arab traders converted local merchants and helped support their consolidation of power in coastal towns. The interior regions of northeastern Africa tended toward the example of the West African empires: the Nubian states in the early period and Dar Fur and Sinnar in the seventeenth and eighteenth centuries pursued comparable strategies of administering long-distance trade, confining Muslim traders to enclaves, and adding Islamic symbols to synthetic court traditions. In some areas of northeast Africa, Arabization also occurred. As in the Maghrib, Arabization still is far from complete in this region.

Western European maritime expansion influenced areas of Muslim sub-Saharan Africa beginning in the fifteenth century. At this time Portuguese sailors pioneered a sea route to Asia, circumnavigating Africa. When the Portuguese arrived in the Indian Ocean, they intervened militarily to secure access to existing trade networks. They attacked Kilwa and other towns along the Swahili coast with the cannon on their ships, and forced the Swahili to relinquish control of the export gold trade. Ottoman influence in northeastern Africa prevented much Portuguese intervention north of the Kenyan coast. One exception was the Christian state in the Ethiopian highlands, where the Portuguese sent envoys and missionaries. The Ottomans promoted a military *jihad* against the Ethiopian state, which gained African leadership in the person of Ahmad ibn Ibrahim of Adal, often referred to as "Ahmad the Left-Handed." Ahmad rallied support from fellow Muslims, and Ethiopian Christians avoided complete defeat only when Ahmad ibn Ibrahim died and left the Muslim armies leaderless and divided. Although the *jihad* was lost, the Muslim campaigns helped to precipitate the decentralization of the Christian state in the highlands. Thereafter, local Muslim merchants extended their networks into the highlands, sold weapons to rival leaders, and bought war captives produced by the disorder. At the same time, they converted some local merchants and rulers to Islam.

Plate 19. Arab sailing ships, called *dhows,* are used by traders
across the Indian Ocean.
Photo courtesy Ministry of Information and Broadcasting, Kenya.

The history of Muslim-European relations in West Africa involved more cooperation than competition in the early centuries of contact, since the opening of the Atlantic trade did not involve supplanting Muslim commercial power along the coast as it did in the Indian Ocean. Nor did the Europeans directly confront large Muslim states, since most of the rulers of the coastal regions were non-Muslims. Over time, however, European commercial activity certainly influenced the Muslim empires in the interior adversely, for their ships diverted gold which might have entered trans-Saharan networks. The political fragmentation associated with the decline of the Mali and Songhai empires actually benefited coastal Muslim merchants who dealt in war captives and sold them to European traders at the coast. Thus, mutual interests in trade shaped relations between Muslims and Europeans along the West African coast.

The dramatic expansion of the trans-Atlantic trade raises questions about Muslim involvement in slavery and the slave trade. All interpretations of the *sharia* prohibited the faithful from enslaving other Muslims. Capturing and owning non-Muslims was acceptable, and Muslims sometimes justified the practice as an effort to convert slaves to Islam. In northern Africa and southwestern Asia, Muslims used African, Asian, and European slaves as domestic servants, manual laborers, and soldiers. The trade in African slaves displaced millions of Africans over a thousand-year span.[6] By the sixteenth century, the patterns of the trans-Saharan slave trade so worried the Timbuktu scholar Ahmad Baba that he argued against the tradition that black Africans were cursed, as descendants of Ham, to serve as slaves of Semitic-speaking peoples.

Plate 20. The cattle and camel market at Kassala, Sudan.
Photo courtesy United Nations/TW/gf.

Ahmad Baba proposed instead a religious geography of West Africa which identified Muslim areas where enslavement should be prohibited. The protection that Muslim identity ostensibly provided probably worked as an incentive to conversion in regions where Muslim merchants sold slaves to Europeans at the coast. For example, some historians argue that the Fulbe peoples of Senegambia asserted their Muslim identity and fought several *jihads* in the eighteenth century to establish lands where Muslims could live without fear of enslavement. Sometimes Muslim slave traders themselves were caught up in the escalating violence of the times, sold to European slavers, and arrived in the Americas; the case of Ayuba Suleyman Diallo of the Fulbe state of Bundu is one such instance, which concluded with Ayuba's return to Africa.[7] Existing data are speculative. However, Muslims probably did not constitute a high proportion of slaves transported to the Americas, for most Muslims kept to the *sharia* prohibitions and sent non-Muslims into slavery.

Elaborations of Islam: Sufism and African Societies

Sufism is an orientation within Islam which emphasizes the personal search for mystical meaning. Sufis perform elaborate rituals in order to experience unification with ultimate reality. The dances of the "whirling dervishes" of Turkey are but one of many manifestations of this orientation; more widespread is the rhythmic and continuous repetition of special prayers. Some refer to the Sufi search as "spiritual athleticism," and this allusion is apt insofar as Sufi rituals often test the physical endurance of practitioners. Precedents for this mystical searching are evident in Muhammad's life, and in the assertions of God's immanence: "Wherever one turns, there is the Face of God" (Qur'an II: 109). Historians of religion suggest that pre-Islamic Persian practices may have mixed with Arabian traditions to produce Sufism as it emerged in the ninth century. While some Sufis integrated their spiritual quest with serious study of Muslim law, others saw in their mystical insights an alternative to the legalism often associated with the *sharia*. In some contexts Muslims have argued that Sufism is an unacceptable innovation and have accused its practitioners of establishing a cult of personal devotion to Sufi leaders. For many, however, Sufism has been an avenue to a faith which they practice with great vigor and sincerity.

The core Sufi relationship is the individual bond between a student and *shaykh* ("master") who expects complete submission to his or her guidance. In the process of study, the *shaykh* reveals efficacious litanies to students, and eager disciples seek to acquire all such religious secrets as well as the *shaykh*'s permission to transmit them to others. The earliest *shaykhs* gained disciples who maintained the movement by creating an organization dedicated to the practices of the founder. Sufism spread throughout the caliphate, but it often was associated with frontier areas, regions such as India, Turkey, and Africa. The close relations between *shaykh* and student provided converts with an intimate context in which to learn the rituals of the faith. Sufi emphasis on the authoritarian *shaykh* also mirrored the patron-client ties of lineage and clan which defined social relations in many rural areas, especially among herding groups. In the Maghrib, where Berber herders formed a sizable and important component of local society, Sufism became so popular that it put an imprint on Muslim practice in the region. Widespread belief in the power of particular *shaykhs* led to the practice of making pilgrimages to the tombs of *shaykhs*, where pilgrims asked the dead to intercede for them before God.

Beginning in the eighteenth century, Sufism became a dynamic force in sub-Saharan Africa. Some scholars speak of "neo-Sufism" to distinguish the movements of the last three hundred years from earlier expressions of Sufism in the Muslim world. What was "new" transcended theological issues, although Sufi *shaykhs* devoted much of their writings to these points. The Sufi movements which gained followers in much of sub-Saharan Africa were led by *shaykhs* who linked the organization to social as well as spiritual concerns. The practice of students' giving gifts to their *shaykhs*, for example, often was transformed into a system for the accumulation and redistribution of wealth by the leader of the movement. Sidi al-Mukhtar al-Kunti, who reinvigorated the Qadiriyya Sufi organization in the central regions of the Sahara during the eighteenth century, was as much a manager of a commercial enterprise as he was a spiritual guide. After his example, other Sufis spread his and other organizations throughout West Africa during the nineteenth century. In the northern areas of the Sudan, Sufi activities were apparent in commercial enclaves by the eighteenth century, but they gained momentum in the nineteenth century after the arrival of Muhammad Uthman al-Mirghani and other disciples of

Ahmad ibn Idris, a Moroccan *shaykh*. Sufi movements proliferated in the region thereafter, in part because the hierarchy helped to organize economic and social relations among members in an era when people moved between Muslim settlements more freely. Similar expansion in the Sufi movement occurred along the Swahili coast under the leadership of numerous Arab and Swahili *shaykhs*.

Sufi *shaykhs* could mobilize followers into political movements, and Sufi leaders were in the forefront of resistance to European expansion at the end of the nineteenth century. Even before, *shaykhs* throughout the savanna lands of West Africa declared military *jihads* against African rulers, inaugurating a century of religious wars. Many of the *jihads* took the form of internal revolts whereby local Muslims challenged the authority of traditional elites. Such was the case in northern Nigeria, where in the early nineteenth century Uthman dan Fodio rallied popular support for a *jihad* against Hausa rulers with the following manifesto, written in Arabic:

> [From] the Commander of the Faithful, Uthman, to all folks. . . . Know then, my brethren . . . that to make war upon the heathen king who will not say "There is no God but Allah" is obligatory by assent, and to take the government from him is obligatory by assent . . . that to make war upon backsliding Muslims who do not owe allegiance to any of the Commanders of the Faithful is obligatory by assent, if they be summoned to give allegiance and they refuse. . . .[8]

Uthman was a member of the Fulbe community which had migrated into the region from Senegambia in a series of movements beginning at least five hundred years ago. Uthman drew upon the grievances of Fulbe herders and Hausa farmers to organize a successful *jihad* in Sokoto, and then supported the efforts of Muslims as the *jihad* spread throughout northern Nigeria. Scholars refer to the political order which emerged under Uthman's successors as the "Sokoto Caliphate." Wars associated with the Sokoto Caliphate produced tens of thousands of captives whom the Muslim elite incorporated into households or on plantations as slaves. The designation of specific ethnic groups as "infidels" and eligible for enslavement engendered cultural resistance in communities neighboring the Sokoto Caliphate. On the other hand, Uthman and his disciples increased membership in their Sufi movement by integrating ethnic groups whom they saw as Muslim. The Sokoto leadership also provided opportunities for greater women's participation in the faith. For example, Nana Asma'u, the daughter of *Shaykh* Uthman dan Fodio, helped to organize activities to inculcate devotion to Islam among Fulbe and Hausa women in the Sokoto Caliphate. Whatever the immediate impact of the numerous nineteenth-century *jihads*, the long-term result was the emergence of overtly practicing Muslim majorities in many regions of the savanna.

European Domination and Muslim Africa

European economic and military domination of Africa shaped the lives of Muslims. In the nineteenth century, as the Industrial Revolution stimulated demand for resources and encouraged Africans to produce "cash crops" or collect products such as wild rubber for sale on world markets, Muslim merchants responded by increasing the numbers of slaves on their farms. Rulers in Egypt and Oman also established African empires to expand export production. Complementing these economic forces was the European conquest of Africa in the late nineteenth century. Many Muslims earned reputations as military resisters, but others sought accommodation with Europeans and maintained vestiges of the old order as they served as intermediaries under colonial rule. European officials tolerated Islam in the twentieth century, allowing Sufis and other Muslims to proselytize, especially in sub-Saharan Africa. Muslims questioned European domination and participated in the nationalist movements which fought for African independence. Still others have been critical of the overall direction of change and call for the creation of Muslim states which follow the *sharia*.

Nineteenth-Century Developments

European demand for resources encouraged rulers to initiate or expand empires in economically attractive areas, while merchants increased their slaveholdings to bolster production. An example of an imperial Muslim state was the Egyptian regime founded by Muhammad Ali, the Ottoman commander who installed his family as Egypt's ruling dynasty. During the nineteenth century, Egypt conquered vast regions in northeast Africa, encouraging slave raiding for the plantation production of export crops such as cotton, indigo, and sugar. Another variation of Muslim imperialism occurred along the East African coast. In the early nineteenth century, Swahili and Omani Arab merchants imported European firearms to expand the ivory trade. These activities increased slave raiding in the interior, and supported the rise of slave plantations along the coast. Sayyid Said, the sultan of Oman at the time of these changes, established Omani political control along the coast and eventually moved his capital from Arabia to Zanzibar Island. This island became the world's principal source of cloves in the nineteenth century. By the end of the century, hundreds of thousands of slaves worked on these coastal plantations. The exclusive nature of coastal Muslim identity continued during this era, as the coastal residents could justify enslaving Africans from the interior in terms of the faith. Whether this slave system was less onerous than plantation slavery in the Americas is a matter of current historical debate. What is clear is that the social cleavages engendered by plantation slavery left their mark on coastal society.

By the late nineteenth century, the era of independent African states was over and European powers divided much of the continent into colonial territories (see chapters 6 and 7). In the "scramble" for Africa, Europeans made alliances with some Muslim elites and claimed their territories without much struggle. The British used a series of economic and political crises in the 1880s to invade Egypt in support of Muhammad Ali's successors, both maintaining the dynasty and gaining control of the state. The sultan at Zanzibar also preserved the Omani position in Zanzibar by agreeing to

British protection of the island and the loss of mainland territories. Muslim dynasties in Morocco and Tunisia also chose such a course after decades of European pressure and intervention into the Maghrib. In the Sokoto Caliphate, members of the political hierarchy negotiated to retain much of the structure of the Muslim state under British colonial rule. Descendants of these Muslim leaders exercised considerable influence well into the second half of the twentieth century; in a few cases they still hold power, such as the ruling family in Morocco.

Muslims also resisted European imperial expansion. European soldiers often returned home with stories of Muslim martyrs who secured a place in Paradise by riding into the fire of their machine guns. These accounts, which speak to the religious zeal of some resisters, represent only one aspect of the struggle. Leaders often were Sufi *shaykhs* who constructed an alternative society for their followers and adopted a range of strategies in order to preserve their autonomy. One strategy was to remain just beyond the immediate range of European firepower and wage a guerrilla war. *Shaykh* Abd al-Qadir pioneered this approach in northern Africa during the middle decades of the nineteenth century. He organized Muslim control over central and southern Algeria as the French first secured the coast in 1830 and then incorporated its hinterland. Abd al-Qadir kept the French at bay by launching intermittent but well-planned raids against European positions. Only with his capture by the French in 1847 did the movement dissipate, but his example inspired numerous Algerian revolts in the decades that followed. Sometimes Muslim leaders directly confronted advancing imperial armies. This was the case in the northern Sudan, where a powerful movement already had arisen to liberate the region from Egyptian colonialism. The founder of the movement was *Shaykh* Muhammad Ahmad, who claimed to be the Mahdi or "guided one" who appeared before the Last Judgment. The Mahdi rallied Sudanese Muslims against the Egyptian colonial regime in the 1880s. His successor, Abdallah, led resistance to European expansion which culminated in the 1898 battle of Omdurman, where twenty thousand Muslims died. Yet another resistance strategy was emigration in conscious emulation of the Prophet Muhammad's departure from Mecca. In West Africa, Ahmad al-Kabir negotiated several treaties with the French, fought them after they broke key provisions, and then migrated toward the east, dying along the route from natural causes. With these examples and numerous others, the heritage of resistance is strong in the living memory of African Muslims.

Twentieth-Century Developments

European military conquest did not prevent the expansion of Islam in twentieth-century sub-Saharan Africa. In areas where Muslims already were a sizable portion of the population, European officials tolerated or even actively encouraged the growth of Sufi movements, especially in cases where they trusted the leaders not to engage in anticolonial activities. The Mouride movement is an example of Sufi expansion under tacit colonial support in Senegal. Its founder, Amadu Bamba

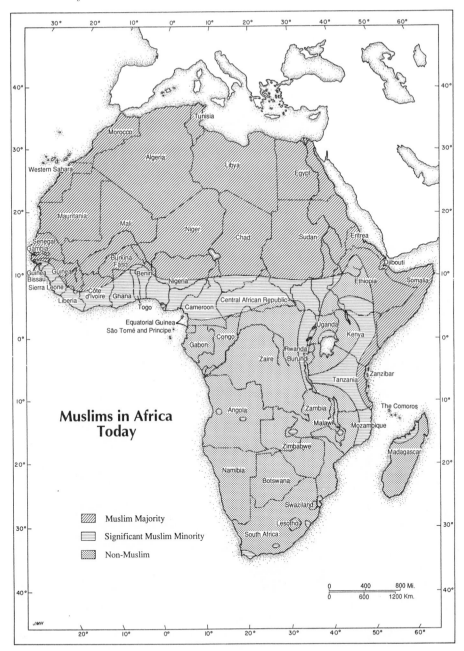

Muslims in Africa Today

Muslim Majority

Significant Muslim Minority

Non-Muslim

MAP 21

Mbacké, was a Qadiriyya *shaykh* who used his organization to incorporate members of Wolof society displaced during the French conquest of Senegal. In an effort to reconstruct society, Bamba stressed the value of agricultural work, and moved his followers into the interior, where they grew peanuts, an important export crop in Senegal. Although the French initially viewed the Mouride movement as a threat and exiled Amadu Bamba from Senegal, they also appreciated the economic dimensions of the Mouride work ethic and peanut harvests. French officials not only allowed Bamba to return to his followers, but cultivated close relations with his successors and even constructed railroads into Mouride areas to facilitate export of this crop. Other Sufi movements expanded their memberships in the twentieth century, although their economic activities and European interests did not always coincide as neatly as in the Mouride case.

The social changes of colonial Africa also expanded Islam in areas where it had not previously existed. In West Africa, the establishment of colonial boundaries and new capitals in the coastal areas encouraged Muslim Africans from the savanna to migrate as workers and merchants. In these new settings, Islam coincided with ethnic boundaries, but the creation of Muslim neighborhoods sometimes led to conversions of coastal populations. The colonial era also brought Muslims from the Indian subcontinent to all regions of sub-Saharan Africa. They proselytized different understandings of the faith and established mosques and schools much in the tradition of Christian missions. In South Africa, tens of thousands of Indian Muslims arrived as both workers and traders in the nineteenth and twentieth centuries. The state allowed them to establish Muslim institutions, through which they not only maintained their faith but questioned the social injustice of the *apartheid* system.

Muslims are divided in their views of African nationalism. In the struggle to win independence, most nationalist parties counted on the support of Muslims, especially those who had received some "Western" education. Muslims in these parties tended not to press for a specific religious agenda, even when they dominated movements, such as in northern Africa. Others were critical of secular nationalism and called for the implementation of the *sharia*. This development, often labeled fundamentalism, gained its first expression in Egypt during the late 1920s with the formation of the Muslim Brotherhood. This movement rejected the secular political order which had emerged under Muhammad Ali's successors during British overrule, and gained followers disaffected by the weakening economy during the Great Depression. Its leaders were not the traditional *ulama*, but a new generation of Egyptians who had roots in other classes. Although the Muslim Brotherhood was outlawed by the Nasser regime in the 1950s, its ideas have inspired other movements in Egypt, including groups which have protested the regimes headed by Anwar Sadat and Hosni Mubarak. Reformist movements have emerged in other states, especially in the Maghrib and the Sudan.

Conclusion

Islam brought about the transformation of African societies. In northern Africa, the arrival of Arab conquerors stimulated a process of conversion to Islam and the Arabization of local populations. South of the Sahara, Arabization is limited, and the expansion of the faith initially was associated with the activities of merchants. In specific regions, new forces produced even greater regional diversity. In particular, the growth of Sufism created organizational opportunities for local initiative. Europeans conquered an African continent in which Muslims were not united politically, economically, or religiously, and the events of the last two hundred years have reinforced local developments. Nonetheless the shared experience of European domination, in combination with the common commitment to a core set of religious texts, provides some Africans with a sense of global Muslim solidarity. Islam's advocates on the continent and elsewhere may well transform such sentiments into a potent political force. Any understanding of Islam's religious message is merely one of many conceivable readings of the central texts and accumulated knowledge of the faith.

NOTES

1. The difficulty in obtaining accurate national population censuses for all regions at the same point in time makes any figure an estimate.

2. In the Muslim calendar, this occurred in 1 A.H., the first year "after the *hjira*" (the emigration to Mecca). Dates used here are from the Christian (Julian/Gregorian) calendar.

3. This savanna region was called *bilad al-Sudan*, "land of the blacks." Scholars refer to the entire savanna zone as "Sudanic Africa," which should not be confused with Sudan, the contemporary state located immediately south of Egypt.

4. Derek Nurse and Thomas Spear, *The Swahili: Reconstructing the History and Language of an African Society, 800–1500* (Philadelphia: University of Philadelphia Press, 1985).

5. Said Hamdun and Noel King, *Ibn Battuta in Black Africa* (Princeton: Princeton University Press, 1994), p. 22.

6. Incomplete sources make a specific figure impossible to set. See Ralph Austen, "The Mediterranean Islamic Slave Trade Out of Africa: A Tentative Census," *Slavery and Abolition* 13 (1992): 214–48, and "The Nineteenth Century Islamic Slave Trade from East Africa (Swahili and Red Sea Coasts): A Tentative Census," *Slavery and Abolition* 9 (1988): 21–44. For an analysis of the slaves' experiences, see J. O. Hunwick, "Black Slaves in the Mediterranean World: Introduction to a Neglected Aspect of the African Diaspora," *Slavery and Abolition* 13 (1992): 5–38.

7. Philip Curtin, ed., *Africa Remembered: Narratives by West Africans from the Era of the Slave Trade* (Madison: University of Wisconsin Press, 1967), pp. 17–59.

8. Uthman dan Fodio, *Wathiqat Ahl al-Sudan*, trans. and ed. A. D. H. Bivar, *Journal of African History* 2 (1961). For Uthman's career, see Mervyn Hiskett, *The Sword of Truth* (New York: Oxford University Press, 1973; Evanston: Northwestern University Press, 1994).

114   A F R I C A

SUGGESTIONS FOR FURTHER READING
Secondary Works

Bravmann, René. *African Islam*. Washington: Smithsonian Institution Press, 1983.
Brenner, Louis, ed. *Muslim Identity and Social Change in Sub-Saharan Africa*. Bloomington: Indiana University Press, 1993.

Anthologies of Source Materials in English Translation

Hanson, John, and David Robinson, trans. and eds. *After the Jihad: The Reign of Ahmad al-Kabir in the Western Sudan*. East Lansing: Michigan State University Press, 1991.
Hopkins, J. F. P., and Nehemia Levtzion, trans. and eds. *Corpus of Early Arabic Sources for West African History*. Cambridge: Cambridge University Press, 1981.
Hunwick, John, trans. and ed. *Sharia in Songhay: The Replies of al-Maghili to Askia al-Haji Muhammed*. Oxford: Oxford University Press, 1985.
Kapteijns, Lidwien, and Jay Spaulding, trans. and eds. *After the Millennium: Diplomatic Correspondence from Wadai and Dar Fur on the Eve of the Colonial Conquest, 1885–1916*. East Lansing: American Studies Center, Michigan State University, 1988.
Mirza, Sarah, and Margaret Strobel, trans. and eds. *Three Swahili Women: Life Histories from Mombasa, Kenya*. Bloomington: Indiana University Press, 1989.

Curtis A. Keim
Africa and Europe before 1900

6 Before the late nineteenth century, Europeans had made little headway in penetrating the African interior. Held back by tropical diseases, geographical obstacles, and African resistance, foreigners who had arrived by way of the Atlantic were largely limited to the continent's fringes. The only major exception was southern Africa. There, a Mediterranean-type climate, a more benign disease environment, and scattered, small-scale societies less able to stop determined settlers had allowed Europeans to advance into the interior. In spite of this apparent minimal contact, foreigners from Europe and from the Americas had a profound impact on Africa's history, through almost five centuries of trade, including the trans-Atlantic slave trade. While historians agree on the essentially destructive nature of this enterprise, there is considerable disagreement over how to measure and interpret the destruction. Some historians believe that the slave trade harmed African societies through "underdeveloping" them and tying them into global markets on disadvantageous terms. This weakness and dependency was to be continued in the colonial period and is still evident today.[1] Some pay less attention to the slave trade and emphasize other factors that shaped precolonial African societies such as environment, technology, social organization, religious beliefs, and individual initiatives (see chapters 4 and 5). These may be related to conditions generated by the slave trade, but they may also be unrelated. Clearly, there was ample room for African creativity and internal dynamism within societies.

External Relations, the Slave Trade, and Its Impact
in West and West Central Africa

The story of African and European interaction began in the early 1400s with voyages sponsored by the Portuguese prince Henry the Navigator, who set himself the life task of bypassing the Arabs who controlled North Africa and establishing direct trade, especially in gold, with the great civilizations of West Africa. This enterprise was made possible by innovations in technology that allowed the Portuguese to venture down the Guinea coast. By 1460, trading ships had arrived at Cape Verde, and soon afterward they reached the Gold Coast (1471), Kongo (1483), and the Cape of Good Hope (1488). In 1497, Vasco da Gama reached the Indian Ocean and the Swahili towns of East Africa, and sailed onward to southern India. These developments, together with Columbus's voyage to the Americas, opened the modern era of European expansion.

The enormously profitable Indian Ocean trade overshadowed the original interest in African gold. While Portugal developed limited trade and settlement at Elmina on the Gold Coast, Kongo, Angola, Mozambique, and Mombasa, its ships mostly bypassed Africa for the Orient. Even when the Dutch, British, and French began to replace Portuguese traders in the mid-1500s, the likelihood seemed great that Africa would continue to be more an obstacle to be circumnavigated en route to the Far East than a destination for Europeans.

This situation changed dramatically with the late-sixteenth-century opening of sugar plantations in South America and the Caribbean. Sugar, and later tobacco, coffee, and cotton, required large amounts of labor. Plantation owners could not meet the demand with native American workers because of their high mortality rates when exposed to European diseases and their prolonged resistance to incorporation into the colonial workforce. European workers also had high mortality rates due to tropical diseases, and their numbers were not sufficient to meet the demand for plantation labor. Africans, on the other hand, had some immunity to tropical diseases, and they also had some resistance to European diseases as a result of ancient contacts across the Sahara Desert and Indian Ocean. Over time a business partnership developed between European traders and African middlemen who delivered slaves captured in the interior.

In the seventeenth, eighteenth, and nineteenth centuries, the slave trade disrupted the lives of millions of Africans. While estimates of the numbers transported to the New World vary widely because of incomplete and inaccurate records, current calculations put the total, including those taken in the fifteenth and sixteenth centuries, at between 10 and 13 million. Of these, about half came from West Africa and half from Central Africa. Nearly half a million were transported to the United States. A continual supply was needed, because once in the Americas, a slave had an average life expectancy of less than ten years.[2]

Millions more Africans died in the process of capture, in caravans taking captives to the coast, in quarantine while waiting for ships, in loading, and in the Atlantic crossing. Estimates of the total loss, including those who arrived in the Americas and those who died in capture or afterward, range from 15 to 20 million. When added to the approximately 7 million slaves taken in the Arab trade to North Africa and the Middle East, the total suggests that the population of sub-Saharan Africa did not grow, and may indeed have declined, during the slave-trade era. On the Atlantic side the severest drain in population came in the eighteenth century, when Africa lost perhaps 10 million people, and in the nineteenth century, when as many as 4 million died or were transported overseas.[3]

Plate 21. An old drawing of Fort Jesus, the Portuguese castle of Mombasa.
From W. F. W. Owen, *Narrative of Voyages to Explore the Shores
of Africa, Arabia and Madagascar,* 1833.
Photo courtesy Lilly Library of Rare Books and Manuscripts, Indiana University.

About two-thirds of the slaves taken to the Americas were men, whom Europeans desired as laborers. Africans were, in any case, often reluctant to sell female slaves because women were highly valued for production and reproduction. Moreover, in African male-dominated societies, slave men were outsiders who could challenge the social order, but women, whether slave or free, were less threatening.[4] As a consequence, Africa kept most of its female captives, and this, together with polygyny, mitigated population losses in the slave trade.

The trade was deadly for Europeans as well as Africans. An estimated half of the white traders on the African coasts died each year, and as many as a fifth of the sailors died on the Atlantic crossings. Yet, for the capitalists and those whites who survived, the profits made the risks worthwhile. In West Africa, Europeans established dozens of factories or trading posts and forts along the coasts. Local rulers granted permission for settlement, collected rent, and furnished supplies of food, firewood, and water. In Central Africa, local rulers followed a free-trade policy and opposed the construction of factories and forts, so white traders had to establish temporary collection points on shore or trade off their ships. An exception was Angola, where the Portuguese government subsidized a small military colony at Luanda to ensure that its traders could compete. Eventually this colony led to a local Euro-African population that competed for trade with metropolitan Portuguese and Brazilians.

Within Africa, African entrepreneurs organized the trade, as was the case, for example, on the Gambia River in the eighteenth century.[5] There, specialist traders

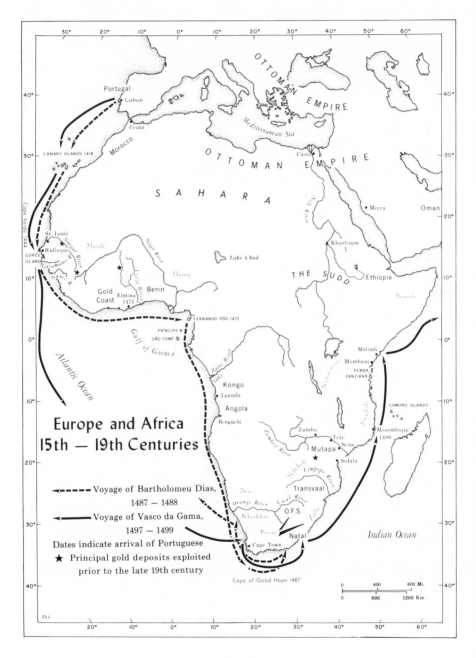

**Europe and Africa
15th — 19th Centuries**

‹---- Voyage of Bartholomeu Dias,
       1487 – 1488

◄── Voyage of Vasco da Gama,
       1497 – 1499

Dates indicate arrival of Portuguese

★ Principal gold deposits exploited
   prior to the late 19th century

MAP 22

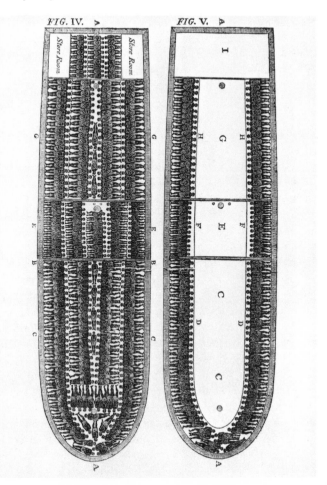

Plate 22. Diagram of a slave ship showing how slaves were transported
across the Atlantic Ocean. From an Abstract of the Evidence delivered
before a select committee of the House of Commons in the Years 1790 and
1791, on the Part of the Petitioners for the Abolition of the Slave Trade.
Photo courtesy of the Lilly Library of Rare Books
and Manuscripts, Indiana University.

traveled inland to the Upper Niger River region, where they purchased slaves who
had been captured in raids and wars, sold during famines, or forfeited as payments of
fines. The traders then assembled their slaves into caravans and marched them toward
the coast. When they reached the headwaters of the Gambia and Senegal rivers, the
traders could select the best market, either the French on the Senegal or the British on
the Gambia. If they chose the Gambia, they could then sell upstream for a quick return

and a lower price, or downstream for a longer trip and a higher price. If they went downstream, the king of Niumi at the mouth of the river regulated the trade through governors he appointed to administer trading towns such as Juffure and Albreda and collect duties from ships. To keep the British from becoming too powerful, the king controlled their access to local supplies and supported a small French trading post.

Ordinary people in the kingdom of Niumi also participated in the Gambia River trade. A British fort, built on a small tidewater island to keep other Europeans out of the river, depended on the local inhabitants to sell food, fuel, and water. On shore, many British traders found it advantageous to marry African or Euro-African women so they could have access to local trade networks and more comfortable surroundings. Some of these women, called *senhoras*, became quite rich because of their business acumen and because they inherited property on the death of their husbands, which happened quite frequently given the high mortality rates among whites from disease. Other local people hosted traders from the interior or used purchased slaves as field hands until slave ships arrived. They also found work loading ships as canoemen, and bred donkeys to transport trade goods inland. Still others sold hides, beeswax, ivory, and gold to Europeans. The situation on the Gambia River demonstrates that the Atlantic slave trade provided new opportunities for social mobility and wealth, although many Africans continued an important trade in other products.

The price for slaves in Africa depended on levels of New World demand and African supply. But price also depended on the quality of slaves offered by Africans, the desirability of the trade goods offered by Europeans, the speed with which traders could buy their cargo, the internal organization of African trading societies, and numerous other factors. The negotiation over the exchange value of lots of slaves for lots of goods was highly competitive, with each side arguing for the high value of their own product and the low value of the others' product. Lists of European trade items included textiles, firearms, gunpowder, flints, hardware, tobacco, liquor, jewelry, paper, crystal, and lace. They also included local products purchased on one part of the African coast and transported to others, as well as local currencies such as cowries, gold, brass, iron, and copper. Most of these trade items were destined for African elites, who used them to display their power, reward followers, and procure more slaves.

Responses to the slave trade varied from society to society, even where they might seem similar, as in the case of centralized state systems. For example, some societies undertook slave raids to profit from European demand, but others sold surplus slaves captured in wars that were unrelated to foreign demands. By the eighteenth century, the heavily centralized Dahomey state, for example, lived for and by the sale of slaves captured in annual raids on neighbors. In contrast, Asante sold slaves captured mostly as a by-product of its empire building. Slaving was not the aim of its wars, even though the sale of slaves often brought Asante more profit than its lucrative gold trade. In nearly all societies engaged in the trade, however, the punishment for crimes such as robbery or witchcraft tended to escalate toward enslavement as the profitable trade progressed. Only a very few states rejected the slave trade in general. The best-known example is Benin, which for much of the slave-trade era forbade the export of male slaves, who were used locally for production and warfare and for conspicuous display of wealth. One eighteenth-century noble was estimated to have owned 10,000 slaves. Benin purchased its guns with the proceeds of a royal monopoly on trade in pepper, ivory, and other products.

A good example of the complex relationship between the external demand for slaves and local conditions was in the western Sudan, the vast grasslands located around the Upper Niger River and extending westward to the Atlantic Ocean.[6] Here, states such as Khasso, Gyaman, Kong, and Segu arose in about 1700 that linked slavery, warfare, and trade. In each state a rural aristocracy employed warriors to capture slaves among surrounding peoples who lived in small-scale political systems. The nobles sold most male captives to urban centers in return for guns and horses, the weapons necessary to build and maintain the state systems. The urban centers acquired the guns by exchanging slaves westward to the Atlantic and the horses by trading slaves northward to the Sahara and North Africa.

The rural nobles and the urban traders also retained many captives in the western Sudan to grow food and produce trade goods. Thus, engaging in the international trade in slaves encouraged elites to increase the number of slaves kept locally and spread the institution in local societies. Slaving was far from the dominant economic activity in the early history of such states, however. Free people still were more numerous and still produced most of the food and manufactured goods. Moreover, slaving was not very profitable because of the high costs involved in maintaining even small armies and in capturing, guarding, and transporting slaves. Thus, rather than completely dominating these societies, the slave trade shaped them over time by allowing the acquisition of guns and horses, which could be used to capture more slaves and control local people.

Gradually, the growing use of slave labor and warfare brought increasing insecurity to the societies of the western Sudan. Evidence of this appears, for example, in the ways that Islam functioned in different societies. By the late eighteenth century, when Islam became a major rallying point for change, Fouta Jalon leaders of *jihads*, or "holy wars," often cast themselves as protectors of free people against enslavement (see chapter 5). In the early nineteenth century, Fouta Jalon leaders were dependent on guns acquired by selling slaves, so they combined holy wars with slave raiding on nonbelievers. By contrast, in nineteenth-century Masina, some religious leaders rallied local slave populations to overthrow their masters and establish new Muslim societies.

In Central Africa, slaving was at the heart of a many-sided competition for wealth and power.[7] Soon after the Portuguese discovered the Kongo kingdom in 1483, traders found that they could profit from slave labor by opening sugar plantations on the islands of São Tomé and Principe. The Portuguese who settled in Kongo and São Tomé tended to marry African women and quickly developed into a Euro-African population with local interests. Thus when Euro-Africans met the Portuguese in Kongo, they were often in conflict. Likewise, within the kingdom of Kongo, there were conflicting interests between the *mani Kongo* (the king), who wanted to centralize Kongo life around his capital, and nobles who had separatist ambitions in the provinces. *Mani Kongo* Afonso I (1506–1543) succeeded in building central power by claiming a monopoly on foreign trade, directing slave traders to the African interior rather than to Kongo itself, and spreading Christianity as a weapon against powerful local priests.

At Afonso's death, however, a series of succession struggles disrupted the trade. Moreover, Kongo was invaded in the 1560s by groups of Jaga, peoples from the interior who apparently had been heavily disrupted by the slave trade. The Portuguese and the Euro-Africans, many of whom were now trading from Luanda to the south, joined forces to help reestablish order so that the slave trade could continue. By the early 1600s, the growth of trade out of Luanda drew southern provinces away from Kongo and gave rise to competing kingdoms such as Kasanje and Matamba. Matamba is especially well known because it was conquered and ruled by a woman, Queen Nzinga. The Kongo kings attempted to keep their land intact against the rising influence of Luanda and the new kingdoms, but the 1665 defeat by the Portuguese and their allies in the Battle of Mbwila meant that the forces of disintegration would finally triumph. Succession struggles and civil war broke Kongo into fragments.

The sequence of events in Kongo was followed in broad outline throughout Central Africa. Dutch, British, French, Brazilian, and Spanish traders competed with the Portuguese here and there along the coast. As European trade spread into new areas, kingdoms such as Kongo, Matamba, and Kasanje benefited at first from their access to the interior, but the opportunities of the slave trade also had bitter consequences. The trade fostered dependence on the cloth, alcohol, firearms, and other European products which became the prestige goods of the region. Such dependence permitted the Europeans to take advantage of conflicts between centralizing rulers and separatist nobles, and between competing kingdoms.

In addition, dependence on European goods forced Africans to prey on their neighbors in order to sustain the supply of slaves. As a result, raiding had to expand farther and farther into the continent, and one society after another fell into the European sphere. West Central Africa was caught up in an eastward-moving wave of violence. In the seventeenth century, slaving states such as Kasanje and Matamba flourished about two hundred miles inland. In the eighteenth century the most violent areas were three and four hundred miles inland. In the first half of the nineteenth century, the Lunda empire, at the center of the continent, grew wealthy on raids and trade.

Behind the wave, within the widening circle of European influence, the violence declined, but the slave trade continued to drain human resources and to impoverish the region. The many poor and powerless had no protection from warlords who extorted taxes, conscripted labor as soldiers or plantation workers, or kidnapped people outright for sale as slaves. In addition, frequent drought and famine spawned groups of marauding bandits who took captives for the trade, and the spread of firearms in the eighteenth century brought new terror to the region.

Some peoples gained a measure of wealth and security by becoming brokers for slaves and other products coming from the interior. But in the turmoil of the era, such groups could usually maintain their position only for brief periods. One increasingly common problem was that African elites became caught in a debt cycle. They depended on imports of cloth, alcohol, and firearms to attract followers. But if they failed to secure enough slaves to pay for the goods, they had to sell some of their own followers in order to keep the goods flowing. This precarious situation could quickly lead to ruin. In a similar fashion, leaders frequently overborrowed trade goods from Europeans and then distributed them to followers who were supposed to repay with local produce or slaves, which they might lack, as in times of drought. Thus even successful groups led a tenuous existence which not only called for exploiting other groups, but also could lead to their being exploited themselves.

The Portuguese also attempted to colonize Mozambique on the southeast coast of Africa. They were first attracted by the gold trade which flowed from the Zimbabwe Plateau in the interior to the town of Sofala on the coast and then northward to Kilwa Island, Arabia, and beyond. In the early sixteenth century, Portuguese expeditions wrested the gold trade from the Swahili and took control of Sofala. They then advanced along the Zambezi River, where they founded military posts at Sena and Tete. High mortality rates from diseases such as malaria, weak support from Lisbon, and resistance from African kingdoms in the interior forced them out of the Zambezi gold trade by 1700, however, and prevented the establishment of a strong settler colony. The few settlers who remained concentrated instead on organizing private fiefdoms. These *prazeros* ("plantation owners") imported guns, organized armies, undertook slave raids, and insinuated themselves in local politics by concluding alliances with local chiefs, marrying their daughters, and extending the Indian Ocean slave trade up the Zambezi toward the Lunda and Kazembe empires. Like the Euro-Africans in Kongo and Angola, the *prazeros* retained a veneer of Portuguese culture, but they were in fact firmly rooted in Africa and African cultures.

While the slave trade clearly had an enormous impact on African societies, particularly those in West and West Central Africa, it is possible to overemphasize its significance in the history of precolonial Africa. As already noted, there were always many powerful non-slave-trade factors such as environment, technology, social organization, and personality operating in African history. Long before the slave trade had begun, historical trends such as larger political units, more intense exploitation of the environment, and increased internal trade were underway, and these continued throughout the slave-trading era. Only some of this movement can be attributed to European contact, for even peoples who were largely unaffected by the trade, such as the forest societies of Central Africa, continued these trends. Likewise, Africa's internal production and commerce were consistently much larger than its external trade. In many societies, social order also proved to be resilient in the face of the destruction of the slave trade. Family order and cooperation continued to sustain individuals, while larger political units had a measure of legitimacy and a continuing ability to accommodate peoples of different origins.

Paradoxically, the European influence, which increased economic opportunities, introduced new food crops from the New World such as corn and manioc, and brought new intellectual and technological contacts with the Atlantic world, allowed some Africans to prosper even at the height of the slave trade. In the face of the massive disruption and death caused by the trade, however, such development offered little recompense.

The Nineteenth Century

If slavery was profitable to Europeans, why did they end it? One reason is that the Enlightenment of the eighteenth century caused Europeans to think differently about the world. Just as the Americans and French rallied around the ideas of liberty and equality in 1776 and 1789, so too a few Europeans, principally British, began to campaign against slavery on moral grounds. Another reason is that the Industrial Revolution made way for a new economic role for Africa. Growing manufacturing interests desired larger African markets as well as cheap and plentiful African raw materials such as palm and peanut oils, rubber, beeswax, ivory, gum, and coffee. But the violence of the slave trade hindered both trade and production of nonslave products. Thus increasingly powerful industrialists began to demand an end to the slave trade.

It took more than a century to stamp out the Atlantic slave trade. The first British abolitionist act in 1772 banned slavery only in Great Britain. In 1807, Britain forbade its citizens to trade in slaves, and in 1833 it outlawed slavery in all British colonies except India. Under pressure from Britain, the other major slaving countries pledged one by one to prohibit the slave trade. The trade was halted, however, only when Britain and France began serious naval enforcement of their abolitionist policy and when emancipation in the Americas ended the demand for slaves. The Arab slave trade came to an end in the 1880s and 1890s, generally as a result of the European conquest of Africa.

The decline of the slave trade was paralleled by a dramatic rise in "legitimate" or commodity trade between Europe and Africa (see also chapter 10). A sharp increase in prices for African products caused many Africans to turn to production for export. Likewise, as the slave trade declined and the commodity trade grew, Europeans also changed the way they did business in tropical Africa. Most significant, they established a number of small but permanent colonies along the coasts to facilitate trade, to resettle slaves seized from illegal slavers, and sometimes even to establish plantations. These colonies, in such places as the Lower Senegal River, Sierra Leone, the Gold Coast, Lagos, and Gabon, eventually became toeholds for the colonization of the whole continent.

In addition to new trade and new colonies, the nineteenth century brought a growing curiosity about the interior of the continent. This curiosity, associated with the ongoing Scientific Revolution, led to dozens of expeditions and so-called discoveries of African peoples and places. The first modern European expedition into the interior of Africa is often considered the 1795–97 trip of Mungo Park up the Gambia River to the Upper Niger River. He was privately sponsored by British middle-class professionals who had recently founded the Africa Association, dedicated to exploration. Park witnessed firsthand the slaving of West Africa, but he praised Africans for their civility and generosity. Following Park, a growing stream of explorers entered the continent to investigate geographic problems such as the course of the Niger River and the sources of the Nile and Zaire rivers.

Not all trips into the continent had purely scientific motives, of course. David

Livingstone sought to map Central Africa so that missionaries and traders could eventually "civilize" the interior. Macgregor Laird founded the African Inland Commercial Company in 1832 and sent expeditions up the Niger River to search for trading opportunities. By the 1880s, Europeans had mapped most major physical features and visited important population centers in Africa. Even though many gaps remained, this geographic knowledge greatly encouraged and facilitated European conquest at the end of the century.

A further nineteenth-century change in Europe's relationship with Africa came through the modern mission movement. This movement, mostly Protestant during the first half of the century, is associated with the rise of the European middle class. The Moravian Brethren sent missionaries to the Khoikhoi people of South Africa as early as 1737, and established there permanently in 1793. Larger and more influential, the London Missionary Society, the Church Missionary Society, the Wesleyan Methodist Missionary Society, and many other Protestant missions had their beginnings in the early nineteenth century. London Missionary Society missionaries arrived in South Africa in 1801, and Church Missionary Society missionaries began in Sierra Leone in 1804. Modern Catholic activity began in the last half of the century, when missionary orders such as the Holy Ghost Fathers, the White Fathers, and the Sisters of St. Joseph of Cluny established themselves in many parts of Africa.

Missionaries played a significant role in spreading European influence. They not only worked to convert Africans within the borders of the new colonies, but they often pushed the frontier of contact well beyond administered zones, introduced Western education, and taught European values. One example of how this happened is the life of Samuel Adjai Crowther. In 1821, at the age of twelve, Crowther was rescued from a slave ship and taken to Sierra Leone, where he was educated by the Church Missionary Society. Returning as a missionary to his Yoruba people in 1843, he evangelized widely beyond the territory then claimed by or receptive to Europeans. In 1864, the Anglican Church consecrated Crowther as bishop of the Niger territory, and he worked successfully until the 1880s, when he was increasingly pushed aside by white missionaries. Crowther died in 1891.

The life of Livingstone, the most famous of all nineteenth-century missionaries, also shows how missionary activity helped to spread European influence. Livingstone, who began his African career in 1841 at a London Missionary Society station on South Africa's Cape frontier, became as much an explorer as a missionary. He traveled throughout Central Africa, and his books and letters excited Europeans with the possibility of spreading "Christianity and commerce" in Africa. In 1871, when Livingstone had not been heard from for several years, the American Henry Morton Stanley led a search expedition that found him at Ujiji on Lake Tanganyika. While Livingstone hardly considered himself lost, since he traveled on paths frequented by slave and ivory traders, he was desperately short of supplies and in ill health. The fame which Stanley gained as a result of this "rescue" is evidence of how Livingstone's dream of opening Africa to the West resonated in Europe and the United States. When Livingstone died in 1873, he was so famous that his body was carried back to England and buried in Westminster Abbey.

The nineteenth century brought numerous technological advances which allowed Europeans to expand into the interior and changed their relationships with local people.[8] The most important of these were firearms, medicine, and transportation. In firearms, there was the invention or widespread adoption of rifled barrels, breech-loaders, brass cartridges, smokeless powder, and interchangeable steel parts, which produced guns that were relatively accurate, powerful, fast, inconspicuous, durable, and cheap. By the 1880s, the resulting "gun gap" allowed Europeans to conquer practically any African state with relative ease and safety.

Medical advances dramatically reduced the mortality rate of Europeans in the tropics. Most significant was the discovery of quinine's effectiveness against malaria in the 1850s. Death rates dropped from near 50 percent per year in 1800 to below 10 percent by 1880. While still much higher than Europe's 1 to 2 percent, the lowered mortality rate in Africa encouraged many more Europeans to consider working in the continent. The growing use of steamboats after 1830 and the opening of the Suez Canal in 1859 also made the supply of provisions and troops to Africa faster and more reliable. More important, the steamboat turned Africa's lakes and rivers into highways and quickened the pace of exploration and trade. Laird, Livingstone, and many others used small steamboats to trade and explore in the interior, and this practice was well established by the 1880s.

In West Africa the end of European demand for slaves and the switch to exclusively nonslave, or "legitimate," commerce often caused transformation in local societies since it required reorganizing political and economic systems. For example, Asante continued to exchange gold for guns to maintain its imperial power. Dahomey, on the other hand, responded by intensifying local use of domestic slaves in order to produce exportable crops such as palm oil. However, its plantations, which employed slave labor, proved unable to compete with independent producers to the east along the Niger coast, and the state fell into decline. In most African societies powerful men had become accustomed to slaveholding, so that the end of the external trade did not end domestic slavery. Internal abolition generally awaited the colonial era.

In West Central Africa, the new production and export patterns of the nineteenth century also brought transformations. As the slave trade declined, European demand for industrial raw materials such as beeswax and rubber increased. Likewise, the growing European middle classes developed an appetite for ivory, used for luxury products such as billiard balls and piano keys. The search for these forest products had much the same effect on African societies as the search for slaves had in earlier years. For example, the Chokwe people, who at the beginning of the century were rough hunters under the domination of the Lunda, began to specialize in wax and ivory trading. These frugal people invested their profits in captive women purchased from slavers and in firearms, so that as the nineteenth century progressed, their numbers and power increased. By the 1870s Chokwe were employed as hunters and soldiers by Lunda nobles, who were contending for power in the wake of the violent slaving wave that had swept the center of the continent in the first half of the century. By the 1880s the Chokwe had left their Lunda employers and were raiding Lunda on their own. Their attacks brought the final dissolution of the Lunda empire.

Plate 23. Unloading surf boats at Accra Harbor.
Photo courtesy United Nations/TW/vmb.

Closer to the West Central African coast, warlords shifted from exporting slaves to employing them in the hunt for ivory, wax, rubber, woods, feathers, and other forest products. Many leaders also began to put slaves to work on plantations, where they produced sugar, cotton, coffee, and especially palm oil for export to Europe. New leaders emerged to take advantage of the new opportunities, while kings and chiefs who remained exclusively attached to the slave trade fell.

In the nineteenth-century substitution of commodity trade for the slave trade, it is noteworthy that European-African relations continued to be based primarily on commerce. Tropical Africa still exported its low-priced raw materials in return for higher-priced European manufactured goods. In fact, the new trade patterns, European exploration, missions, technological advances, and other outside factors are evidence of intensification of European influence on and exploitation of the continent. It is tempting to focus on such outside influences in any assessment of the history of nineteenth-century Africa, because it is easy to see it merely as a prelude to colonialism. As with the slave-trade era, however, assessment should balance outside and local factors. Nineteenth-century developments were also shaped by many significant changes within Africa, which resulted not from external factors but from purely African events and influences.

Southern Africa

In contrast to the rest of the continent, where the European impact came mostly as a result of trade, societies in southern Africa experienced the European presence more profoundly through settlers who demanded land and labor. The intrusion began in 1652, when the Dutch East Indies Company built a supply station at the Cape of Good Hope for ships on their way to Asia. Soon ex-employees and other immigrants moved into the interior as independent wine and wheat farmers, and in the more arid hinterland as pastoralists. These settlers, known first as Boers and then as Afrikaners, were a self-reliant frontier people who as Calvinists believed they were predestined by God to claim the land, water, people, and other resources of the Cape.

As the Boers spread into the Cape, they decimated the Khoikhoi herders they encountered. The Khoikhoi died of diseases brought by the Europeans, especially smallpox, or were defeated in wars in spite of fierce resistance. By 1800, these populations had been either forced into the far interior or absorbed into the so-called Coloured group, a mixed-race people at the Cape which included slaves and other subservient groups. When the settlers reached the Great Fish River at the eastern boundary of the Cape in the mid-1700s, they met the Nguni-speaking peoples, especially the Xhosa. The Xhosa were better organized than the Khoikhoi and put up even more resistance. After a century of intermittent wars over grazing lands and water, however, they too had lost most of their resources and much of their social cohesion.

Further impetus to Boer expansion in the interior came from the British takeover of the Cape in the early nineteenth century. The British presence deeply disrupted Boer society. For example, British missionaries and others influenced by liberal ideas at home sought to liberate the large slave population used by the white settlers. The introduction of English language and laws infringed on Boer cultural and political independence, and the intrusion of British capitalism threatened Boer traders and farmers. The Boers most resented Britain's abolition of slavery in 1833. Anger over the British actions plus opportunities for land acquisition in the interior precipitated the "Great Trek," a movement of Boers northward. Nearly 15,000 Boers loaded their covered wagons and occupied lands as far north as the Limpopo River. This was not the single or united movement that the phrase makes it seem, but rather a process that lasted through the 1830s and 1840s, with a great deal of division among the settlers. The British, wishing to limit Boer expansion, planted a colony on the east coast at Natal in 1842.[9]

By the 1860s, therefore, the area that was later to become the country of South Africa already had a deeply entrenched white population divided between four polities. The British claimed the Cape (with a sizable population of Boers who had not trekked northward) and Natal, while the Boer "trekkers" had established two Boer states, the Orange Free State and Transvaal, between the Orange and Limpopo rivers. Life among Africans was deeply disrupted by European settlement. In the eastern Cape, the British had pushed back or incorporated the Xhosa, while increasing numbers of settlers, missionaries, traders, and officials brought changes in

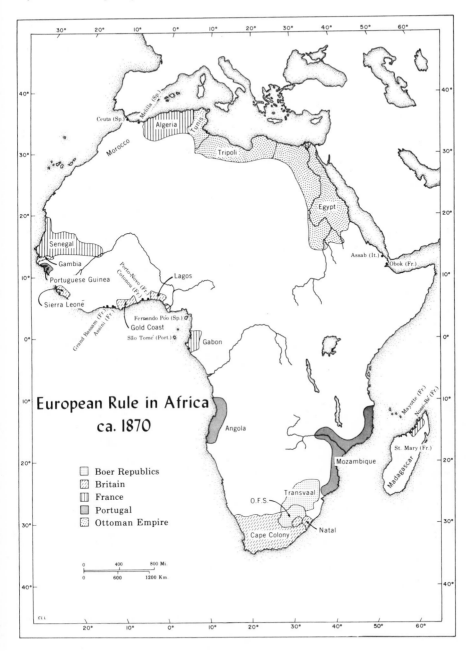

European Rule in Africa
ca. 1870

Boer Republics
Britain
France
Portugal
Ottoman Empire

MAP 23

African life. In Natal, resistance by Africans to menial labor on coastal sugar plantations led to the importation of tens of thousands of Indians as indentured laborers. In the eastern Cape and Natal, the British introduced the earliest measures to control Africans through reserves and passes (identification documents), which eventually became central features of the *apartheid* system. In the northern interior, the trekkers' seizure of land and raids on local populations for labor created further turmoil which had been intensified by the rise of the Zulu kingdom under Shaka and his successors.

The struggle between the Boers and the British continued through the last half of the nineteenth century. British administrators feared the insecurity in the interior, where Boer republics, African states, and frontier settlements clashed regularly, but numerous attempts at military and political solutions failed to bring peace. Indeed, the discovery of diamonds in territory disputed between the Cape and Orange Free State in 1867, and gold in the Transvaal in 1886, brought heightened tensions. The British annexed the diamond fields, but the gold region was in the heart of Boer territory. With gold, the Boers in Transvaal were suddenly wealthy and able to pursue an independent foreign policy. By 1899 growing tensions led to the Anglo-Boer War, a bloody three-year conflict which the Boers lost. But the biggest losers were the black population. A surprisingly generous peace treaty, the benefits of economic cooperation, and a growing sense of a common African threat brought the four European regions together in the Union of South Africa in 1910. Except in Cape Province, Africans received no political rights in the Act of Union. Thus in their conciliation, the two groups of whites united to ignore the needs and demands of the black population.

The Union did not really address the British-Boer tensions either. It ended violent conflict, but the political, economic, and cultural struggle continued. While the Union succeeded because it was supported by moderate Boer leaders who more or less cooperated with the English-speaking business and farming interests, hard-line Boers continued to wage a campaign for the creation of a group consciousness based on racism and nationalism. Through literature, history, theology, and cultural activities they gave birth to a new Boer self-image, symbolized by their renaming themselves "Afrikaners." At the heart of the growing Afrikaner nationalism was the myth that God had chosen the Afrikaner people to dominate black South Africa and that the British had attempted to thwart God's plan. By 1948, hard-line Afrikaner nationalists had sufficient support that they were able to win the South African elections and dominate the white-minority government until 1994 (see chapter 21).

Economically, the period after 1910 was one of significant urbanization and industrialization. The disasters of the Anglo-Boer War as well as cattle disease and drought forced many Afrikaner farmers off their land into towns, while the wealth of gold and diamonds fueled urban economic growth. This economic transformation presented new problems, however, for Africans not only began to buy back farmland from poor whites vacating the rural areas, they also competed for jobs with poor whites and were willing to work in towns for lower wages. The government solution was to limit African economic options just as the Act of Union had limited political options.

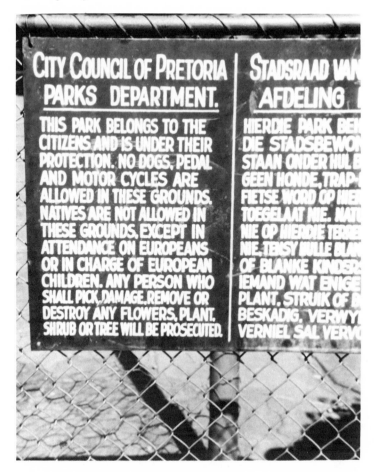

Plate 24. *Apartheid* sign outside a public park in South Africa
which excluded Africans from the grounds.
Photo courtesy United Nations/Boernstein/pas.

A series of laws made it impossible for Africans to compete on fair terms. In 1913, the Natives Land Act limited African land purchases to only 7 percent of South Africa. This land, known as the Reserves, was increased to 13 percent in 1936, but was still far too small to support the African population. As a result, the Reserve land was overused, and a growing number of Africans had to seek employment on white farms and in towns to survive. To save white labor from this influx of Africans, the government enacted laws between 1922 and 1939 that defined a "civilized labor" policy: all high-paying skilled and semiskilled jobs were effectively reserved for whites. At the same time, segregation policies, which were the forerunner of later *apartheid* policies, were introduced. By the mid-1940s, 25 percent of Africans had moved to towns, but they held only menial jobs, lived in segregated townships, and were legally only "temporary sojourners" in urban areas while being denied access to viable farmland.

In the late nineteenth century, some Africans had still been able to mount significant military resistance to white settlement. The Zulu defeat of a British imperial army in 1879 at the Battle of Isandhlwana greatly embarrassed the London government. By about 1900, however, European numbers and weapons were sufficient to put down all armed resistance. The last significant Zulu revolt was the Bambata Rebellion of 1906, which united urban workers with rural peasants in resistance to white power. As the option of armed revolt diminished, Africans turned to other ways of dealing with the European presence. Some ways were self-destructive, such as among the Xhosa, where in 1856–57 the diviner Nonquase convinced thousands of her followers that if they destroyed their cattle and grain, the whites would be swept into the sea. The resulting famine killed up to 20,000 people and forced many to seek work as laborers for Europeans.

Most ways of dealing with oppression and impoverishment were less destructive, however, and highly creative considering the limited opportunities. For example, Africans established thousands of "independent churches" that combined Christianity and traditional religions and emphasized African concerns such as healing, prophesy, salvation, and millennialism. In the last half of the nineteenth century, several thousand Africans entered mission schools such as the London Missionary Society school at Lovedale, and some became teachers, doctors, and lawyers. In 1912, when it became apparent that there would be no political power for blacks in the new Union of South Africa, such middle-class Africans founded the African National Congress in order to lobby for increased opportunities in the white system. In 1919, Clements Kadalie, an immigrant from Nyasaland, started the Industrial and Commercial Workers' Union and led African mine workers to strike. Although whites consistently found ways to stop resistance when it threatened white control, such African efforts at autonomy in the face of colonialism persisted throughout modern South African history.

Conclusion

By the late nineteenth century, South Africa was already deeply colonized, and the rest of Africa was on the brink of conquest and colonization. Europeans had the technology to conquer the continent cheaply. Moreover, by this period they also had compelling motives for conquest, which included nationalist competition; capitalist demands for raw materials, markets, and areas for investment; and scientific and missionary demands for governments to support their ventures. Justification was found in both religious and secular ideologies which perceived Africans as inferior and talked about Europe's "civilizing mission." In the last two decades of the century, European governments became convinced that colonial conquest was in their interest and the partition of the continent was underway.

NOTES

1. See, for example, Walter Rodney, *How Europe Underdeveloped Africa* (Washington, D.C.: Howard University Press, 1974).

2. Philip D. Curtin, *The Atlantic Slave Trade: A Census* (Madison: University of Wisconsin Press, 1969), pp. 265–73; David Henige, "Measuring the Immeasurable: The Atlantic Slave Trade, West African Population and the Pyrrhonian Critic," *Journal of African History* 27, no. 2 (1986): 295–313; Joseph E. Inikori, "Africa in World History: The Export Slave Trade from Africa and the Emergence of the Atlantic Economic Order," in B. A. Ogot, *Africa from the Sixteenth to the Eighteenth Century: General History of Africa, Vol. V* (Paris: UNESCO, 1992), pp. 80–83; Paul E. Lovejoy, "The Volume of the Atlantic Slave Trade: A Synthesis," *Journal of African History* 23, no. 4 (1982): 473–501; Patrick Manning, *Slavery and African Life: Occidental, Oriental, and African Slave Trades* (Cambridge: Cambridge University Press, 1990), pp. 168–76.

3. Paul Lovejoy calculates that at the height of the trade, the ratio of slaves taken from West Africa to those from West Central Africa was about 60:40 in the eighteenth century and 50:50 in the first half of the nineteenth century. Philip Curtin estimates that 399,000 slaves were taken to British North America and 28,000 to Louisiana. See Curtin, *The Atlantic Slave Trade: A Census*, pp. 86–91; Lovejoy, "The Volume of the Atlantic Slave Trade: A Synthesis," pp. 473–501.

4. Claire C. Robertson and Martin A. Klein, eds., *Women and Slavery in Africa* (Madison: University of Wisconsin Press, 1983).

5. Francis Moore, *Travels in the Inland Parts of Africa* (London: Edward Cave, 1738), pp. 42–59, 127–28; Mungo Park, *Travels into the Interior Districts of Africa* (London: W. Bulmer and Co., 1799), pp. 4–30; Philip D. Curtin, *Economic Change in Precolonial Africa* (Madison: University of Wisconsin Press, 1975), pp. 92–127; Donald Wright, "Niumi: The History of a Western Mandinka State through the Eighteenth Century" (Ph.D. dissertation, Indiana University, 1976), pp. 182–87.

6. Martin A. Klein, "The Impact of the Atlantic Slave Trade on the Societies of the Western Sudan," in Joseph E. Inikori and Stanley L. Engerman, eds., *The Atlantic Slave Trade: Effects on Economies, Societies, and Peoples in Africa, the Americas, and Europe* (Durham and London: Duke University Press, 1992), pp. 25–47.

7. Anne Hilton, *The Kingdom of Kongo* (Oxford: Clarendon Press, 1985); Phyllis M. Martin, *The External Trade of the Loango Coast, 1576–1870* (Oxford: Clarendon Press, 1972); Joseph C. Miller, "The Paradoxes of Impoverishment in the Atlantic Zone," in David Birmingham and Phyllis M. Martin, *History of Central Africa*, vol. 1 (New York: Longman, 1983), pp. 118–59; Joseph C. Miller, *Way of Death: Merchant Capitalism and the Angolan Slave Trade, 1730–1830* (Madison: University of Wisconsin Press, 1988).

8. For nineteenth century technological improvements, see especially Daniel R. Headrick, *The Tools of Empire: Technology and European Imperialism in the Nineteenth Century* (Oxford: Oxford University Press, 1981).

9. For recent interpretations of the Great Trek, see Julian Cobbing, "The Mfecane as Alibi: Thoughts on Dithakong and Mbolompo," *Journal of African History* 29 (1988): 487–519; and Norman Etherington, "The Great Trek in Relation to the Mfecane: A Reassessment," *South African Historical Journal* 25 (1991): 3–21.

SUGGESTIONS FOR FURTHER READING

Headrick, Daniel R. *The Tools of Empire: Technology and European Imperialism in the Nineteenth Century*. Oxford: Oxford University Press, 1981.

Inikori, Joseph E., and Stanley L. Engerman, eds. *The Atlantic Slave Trade: Effects on Economies, Societies, and Peoples in Africa, the Americas, and Europe*. Durham and London: Duke University Press, 1992.

Miers, Suzanne, and Richard Roberts, eds. *The End of Slavery in Africa*. Madison: University of Wisconsin Press, 1988.

Moorhouse, Geoffrey. *The Missionaries*. Philadelphia: Lippincott, 1973.

Northrup, David, ed. *The Atlantic Slave Trade*. Lexington, Mass: D. C. Heath and Company, 1994.

Omer-Cooper, J. D. *History of Southern Africa*. 2nd ed. Portsmouth, N.H.: Heinemann, 1994.

Thompson, Leonard. *A History of South Africa*. New Haven: Yale University Press, 1990.

Thornton, John. *Africa and Africans in the Making of the Atlantic World, 1400–1680*. Cambridge: Cambridge University Press, 1990.

Sheldon Gellar
The Colonial Era

7 While often depicted as a progressive and modernizing force, colonialism in fact was based on autocratic and frequently oppressive foreign rule. Ironically, the conquest and partition of the African continent took place at a time when major European powers such as Britain and France were moving toward greater implementation of democratic principles at home.

Although the European occupation of Africa was well under way by 1870, the year 1885 is a useful date to mark the beginning of the colonial era because of the historic importance of the Berlin Conference of 1884–85, which legitimized the "Scramble for Africa" by formally sanctioning the partition of the continent among several European powers. This chapter is primarily concerned with the impact of colonial policies and indigenous responses during the autocratic phases of colonial rule (1885–1945) when Africans had few political and civil rights.

The Partition of Africa and Colonial Conquests

As noted in the previous chapter, the nature of the relationships between Europe and Africa began to change with the abolition of the slave trade and the expansion of commodity exports. The Industrial Revolution spurred Britain and other European countries to intensify their trade with the non-Western world. The requirements of an expanding world capitalist system dominated by the major industrial nations were major factors underlying the subjugation of Africa and other parts of what has come to be known as the developing world.

While superior technological and military strength allowed Europe to conquer and occupy the African continent, the essential causes for colonization were political and economic.[1] Political factors, such as nationalist rivalries and balance of power politics among the leading European nations and a quest for national glory, heightened the desire for colonies. Imperialism was also stimulated by the need of the major industrial powers to acquire and control new markets and sources of raw materials in areas of the globe which Europeans considered economically "backward." In many instances, Africa was not as highly valued as other parts of the world. Britain, for example, was at first more concerned with maintaining and developing its Asian possessions than with acquiring an African empire. Thus, the military intervention and occupation of Egypt in 1882 began primarily as a measure to protect sea routes to the Middle East and Asia by ensuring British control over the Suez Canal.

As the leading military and industrial nation in Europe, Britain obtained the most valuable colonial possessions in Africa. Encouraged by Germany, France also acquired a large number of colonies on the continent, to compensate for the provinces of Alsace and Lorraine, lost to Germany during the Franco-Prussian War of 1870–71. Germany became an imperial power by establishing colonies in German East Africa, South-West Africa, Togo, and Cameroon. However, all these were lost following Germany's defeat in World War I. Portugal, a close ally of Britain and the European nation with the longest historical ties to Africa, acquired more territory in Angola, Mozambique, and Portuguese Guinea. Belgium emerged as a colonial power largely through the efforts of King Leopold II, who established the Congo Free State, which became the Belgian Congo (now Zaire) in 1908. Italy gained colonies in Libya and Somalia, and Spain acquired holdings in the Spanish Sahara and in equatorial Africa. The only two African states to retain their sovereignty during the colonial era were Ethiopia and Liberia, the latter founded in 1821 by freed African American slaves. Even Ethiopia lost its independence for a time in the 1930s when it fell under the domination of Italian fascism.

With the exceptions of Algeria, Senegal, Portuguese enclaves in Angola, Mozambique, and Guinea, and South Africa, where the Afrikaners had pushed inland from the British-controlled Cape Colony to establish their own autonomous republics, most of the continent remained under African control until the last two decades of the nineteenth century.

At the time of the colonial conquest, many African societies were in a state of flux. Morocco, Tunisia, and Egypt in North Africa were Muslim states whose monarchs had begun to modernize their countries before the occupation by France and Britain. In West Africa, Europeans had to deal with highly structured, well-established states such as Dahomey, Asante, and the Mossi empire, as well as numerous Muslim states including the Emirates of Northern Nigeria, Fouta Jalon, and newly created empires built by nineteenth-century Islamic reformers and military leaders such as Umar Tall and Samori Toure. Among the more prominent states in northeast and East Africa were the ancient Christian kingdoms of Ethiopia and Buganda and the Arab sultanate of Zanzibar. As noted in chapter 4, the great diversity of peoples and political units scattered throughout the continent at the time of colonial conquest included not only large-scale states but also smaller chiefdoms and decentralized societies, reflecting different levels of political, social, and economic development.

The military conquest of Africa was precipitated by the terms of the Berlin Conference, which insisted that European powers had to "effectively occupy" a territory before they could claim sovereignty over it. Although Europeans portrayed themselves as liberators, the process of occupation was often violent, conducted by

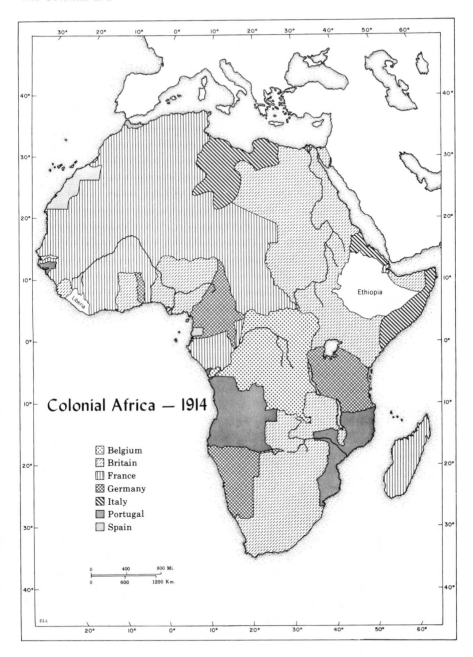

Colonial Africa — 1914

Belgium
Britain
France
Germany
Italy
Portugal
Spain

Liberia

Ethiopia

0   400   800 Mi.
0   600   1200 Km.

MAP 24

mercenaries concerned primarily with enriching themselves and their employers. Perhaps the most notorious case of brutality and greed occurred in the Congo Free State, which came under the personal rule of Léopold II after the Berlin Conference. Under Léopold's rule, the pillaging and abuse of the indigenous populations reached such proportions that the pressure of world opinion obliged him to transfer control of the colony to the Belgian government. With the tacit support of their governments, empire-builders and adventurers such as Cecil Rhodes, George Goldie, and Sir Harry Johnston (all British), Carl Peters (German), and Savorgnan de Brazza (who worked for the French) organized personal armies and expeditions which brought large areas under European rule. France relied primarily upon its regular military forces to carve out a vast empire in West and equatorial Africa and Madagascar, while military conquest was also the principal means used by Germany, Portugal, and Italy in acquiring colonies.

Although resistance to colonial conquest was widespread throughout the continent, Menelik II's success in preserving Ethiopian independence in the face of European imperialism proved to be the exception rather than the rule. Samori Toure organized one of the most spectacular examples of resistance to the imposition of European rule, using guerrilla tactics which delayed the completion of France's occupation of French West Africa for nearly two decades before his defeat and capture in 1898. Armed resistance was also fierce in other Muslim-controlled areas of West Africa, among the desert peoples of the Sahara, the Baoule of the forest areas of Côte d'Ivoire, the Hehe, who kept the Germans at bay for seven years in German East Africa, and the Yao, who fought the Portuguese in Mozambique. After brief periods of resistance, other African states and peoples capitulated, realizing that European technological superiority gave the invaders a decisive edge over conventional African armies, whose tactics and weaponry were ill suited to modern warfare.

However, not all African leaders saw Europeans as enemies. In some instances weaker rulers allied themselves with Europeans to escape the hegemony of more powerful neighbors. Moreover, imperial forces often included large numbers of African troops recruited from conquered territories or provided by African allies. In retrospect, it is clear that the strategy of "divide and conquer," taking advantage of traditional political and ethnic rivalries, proved to be extremely successful in undermining local efforts to form effective alliances for the common purpose of resisting the invader.

The conquest period proved to be a shattering experience for many. Although the imposition of colonial rule eventually led to the abolition of slavery and the establishment of peace, it also meant the end of African political, economic, and cultural autonomy, the transformation of elites and masses alike into colonial subjects with few political and civil rights, foreign economic domination, and the decline and denigration of traditional authority and values.

Colonial Rule and African Responses

Africans responded to colonialism and the accompanying social and economic transformations in a variety of ways. These often led to new ethnic, gender, and class relationships.

Ethnicity continued to be a primary force in shaping identity and expressing social solidarity.[2] In towns, for instance, new ethnic identities emerged where none had existed before. Such was the case with the Bangala of Léopoldville in the Belgian Congo, who had not existed as a distinct rural society in the precolonial period. The explorer-journalist Henry Morton Stanley first gave the name to people living in a string of villages between the Congo and Ubangi rivers. It was then appropriated by workers from that region in order to distinguish themselves from their neighbors in the eyes of whites, who perceived the "Bangala" as industrious and reliable. Subsequently, those migrating to find work in Léopoldville from a large area of the Upper Congo came to be known as the "Bangala," and the language which they spoke, a new *lingua franca*, as Lingala. When political competition intensified in Belgian Congo in the 1950s, the "Bangala" were major rivals of another broad group from the Lower Congo that had developed a politicized ethnicity, the Bakongo. In the Copperbelt towns of Northern Rhodesia (Zambia), a similar process took place as people from the same region but sharing no real sense of common ethnicity took over labels which enhanced their social solidarity in the trying urban conditions experienced under colonial rule. These included the Bemba and Ngoni. Other examples of previously dispersed autonomous communities with linguistic affinities adopting an ethnic identity for social, political, or economic ends can be found all over Africa. In West Africa the Igbo of Nigeria and the Diola of Senegal also exemplify this process. The identity of the Igbo was reinforced when they went to the towns or other regions of Nigeria or abroad to study. Building on their tight ethnic identity, the Igbo organized various self-help voluntary associations and ethnic unions in Lagos and other Nigerian towns and promoted education for their upward mobility. Their ethnic identity became highly politicized and pushed them to play a major role in Nigerian colonial politics. In 1966, ethnic considerations led to a bitter civil war in Nigeria, with the Igbo demanding their own nation-state, Biafra.

In some areas, colonial rule favored one ethnic group over another, thus creating the basis for intense ethnic conflict and competition in late colonial and postcolonial politics. For example, in Guinea, the French favored the Fula over the Mandinka, Susu, and forest societies, and gave Fula aristocrats the best posts in the *chefferies*. Following World War II, Sekou Toure, the Mandinka leader who had led the resistance to French rule in the late nineteenth century, organized an anti-Fula alliance which brought him to power. After independence, hundreds of thousands of Fula fled Guinea as a response to the Toure regime's hostility to this group.

The status of women throughout much of Africa declined under colonialism, as colonial policies often reinforced patriarchal authority.[3] In precolonial Africa, women in some areas had served as chiefs, for example, among the Mende of Sierra Leone; as village leaders, among the Tonga in Northern Rhodesia; and as female officials such as the Iyalode in Yorubaland, who represented women's concerns in male-dominated political councils. Under colonial rule, white officials whose perceptions of female roles were based on their European experience worked almost exclusively through male traditional authorities and ignored female candidates for chiefships in areas where this would have been feasible. For example, in Igboland in Nigeria, where a female counterpart of the male chief (*obi*) existed, only the male *obi* became a salaried official.

Under colonialism, women also saw a decline in their access to land and labor and their share of household income, particularly in the rural areas. Men took control over cash crops and most of the income derived from the sale of their crops. In response, many enterprising women moved to the new towns, where they earned a living as market women, petty traders, and domestics. While some earned enough money to become urban property owners or organized mass-based women's interest groups such as the Lagos Market Women's Association in western Nigeria, others were forced into illegal activities such as prostitution and beer brewing.

Colonial rule also disrupted other precolonial social relations. In Senegal, the defeat of the Wolof states was accompanied by the elimination of the warrior caste, who had to return to the land to make a living. Many of them became followers of Amadou Bamba, the founder of the Mouride Brotherhood in Senegal. Elsewhere in francophone Africa, slaves liberated by the French organized their own villages. On the other hand, the institution of slavery survived in Mauritania and serfdom among the Fula of Fouta Jalon in Guinea.

Many African artisans, such as blacksmiths, jewelers, weavers, woodworkers, and musicians, also saw a decline in their economic status as imported European goods replaced their own products. The destruction of precolonial states undermined formerly wealthy African rulers. The artisans who were previously dependent on them responded by doing more farming or going to the towns, where they often assumed occupations which resembled their former ones. Thus blacksmiths became mechanics. Throughout much of Africa, opportunities for social mobility were few during the colonial era because of the slow pace of economic development. Education was a key factor influencing the transformation of class and gender relations (see chapter 16).

Racial and Cultural Domination under Colonialism

Notwithstanding different patterns of European rule throughout the continent, colonialism was essentially a system of political, economic, and cultural domination forcibly imposed by a technologically advanced foreign minority on an indigenous majority. As a system, colonialism justified itself largely through ideologies which asserted the superiority of the colonizer and the inferiority of the colonized.

Much of the rationale justifying the conquest and colonization of Africa had been based on evolutionary theories of history influenced by the ideas of Darwin, Spencer, Morgan, and Marx. Such theories maintained that societies organized within the

Plate 25. *District Officer on Tour,* a carving by Thomas Ona:
an African's view of a colonial officer.
Photo courtesy Mr. and Mrs. William Bascom, Berkeley, California.

framework of the nation-state and industrial capitalism represented the most advanced human forms of organization. Apologists for European colonialism and imperialism argued that it was the right, indeed the duty, of the "higher" civilizations to conquer the "lower" civilizations in order to bring prosperity and "progress" to all parts of the world. Such claims, often expressed in terms of the "White Man's Burden," or what the French referred to as their "civilizing mission," were reinforced by racial theories which asserted the biological superiority of the "white race."

The dogma of the innate moral inferiority of the indigenous populations was widely shared by many Europeans living in colonial Africa and was used to rationalize the master-servant relationships between Europeans and Africans. The demeaning concept of "the native" implied that Africans, as inferior creatures, were not fit to rule themselves. In his powerful polemic against colonialism, *The Wretched of the Earth,* Frantz Fanon bitterly described the image of "the native" held by the colonizer: "As if to show the totalitarian character of colonial exploitation the settler paints the native as the quintessence of evil. . . .The native is declared insensible to ethics; he represents not only the absence of values, but the negation of value."[4]

The Europeans who came to live and rule in Africa invented new traditions to promote their self-esteem and respectability.[5] White settler farmers who came from lower-middle-class backgrounds perceived themselves as "gentleman farmers" and attempted to imitate the style of the upper classes and aristocracy back home. Colonial administrators also adopted gentlemanly styles, particularly in the British colonies, where colonial officials radiated pride in God, king, and country. The new traditions reflected a feudal, patriarchal ethic rather than the capitalist ethic which had been so instrumental in transforming European social structures.

The Europeans also invented traditions about the unchanging nature of customary Africa. Sometimes these traditions were used to criticize African backwardness and reluctance to modernize. At other times, they were used to praise the "traditional" Africans who knew their place, kept their own customs, and did not aspire to become like Europeans. On the other hand, Africans who sought equal status with Europeans and agitated for political and economic reforms were often viewed as rootless troublemakers who had lost touch with their "tribal" origins.

The racial character of the colonial system was reflected not only in the ideologies of the day but also in colonial social structures. Thus, in most colonies, European officials, businessmen, farmers, and missionaries constituted a privileged ruling caste open only to those of European birth. The principle of racial hierarchy was most developed in South Africa, particularly after 1910, when Britain transferred all of its prerogatives as a colonial power to a white settler minority government. One interesting feature of the colonial caste system was the relatively privileged but ambiguous status of the Euro-Africans, who constituted a small Westernized elite midway between the European rulers and the African masses in the colonial racial hierarchy. In the rare instances when political and civil rights were accorded to "nonwhites," these were generally granted to Euro-Africans such as the Creoles in Sierra Leone, the *métis* in Senegal, and the *mestiços* in Portuguese Africa.

Although the colonial system was often justified in terms of its "civilizing mission," few regimes were willing or able to provide the Western education deemed necessary to transform the "native" into a "civilized" person. Until the end of World War II, education was made available to less than 5 percent of the school-age population. Girls were largely excluded. During the early phases of colonial rule, Catholic and Protestant missions provided the main opportunities for schooling. Whether at government or mission schools, children learned that European culture and civilization were superior and were taught to reject their former religious practices and cultural traditions. The limited education offered to a small minority of Africans did not attempt to make them the equal of the European; it prepared them only to occupy subordinate positions within the colonial system.

While Euro-Africans and educated elites sought political and social equality for themselves, they often regarded the indigenous African masses as backward and not ready for full political and civil rights until they acquired a modicum of Western education and values. Liberal Europeans were willing to grant some rights to *Westernized* Africans. The greatest resistance to African equality came from the relatively large white settler populations of South Africa, Kenya, Southern Rhodesia (Zimbabwe), Portuguese Africa, and Algeria, where relationships between Europeans and Africans most closely approximated the master-slave model depicted by Fanon.

Plate 26. District Commissioner conducts a judicial inquiry in British Cameroons.
Photo courtesy British Information Services.

Metropolitan Policies

The broad outlines of colonial policy were formulated in London, Paris, Brussels, and Lisbon, primarily in terms of the needs of the metropole. Colonial policies were affected more by the political climate at home and by international events than by what was taking place in Africa. Because of France's numerical inferiority in relation to Germany, the French government adopted a colonial policy which treated the African territories as a reservoir of troops for the French army. Germany ceased to be a colonial power not because of revolts in its African colonies but because it was the loser in World War I. During the interwar period (1919–39) the triumph of fascism in Portugal in 1926 perpetuated repressive colonial policies in Portuguese Africa, while the victory of the left-wing Popular Front in France in 1936 led to significant colonial reforms.

Metropolitan governments and public opinion were generally indifferent to colonial matters, which they regarded as less important than domestic issues and foreign policy. Although colonial questions were significant in British politics because of the vast size of the empire, Britain was generally more concerned with events taking place in Asia, such as the rise of Indian independence movements under the leadership of Gandhi and the emergence of Japan as a world power. Smaller European colonial powers such as Belgium and Portugal were more involved with their African possessions than were Britain, France, Italy, and Germany, which were preoccupied with big power politics in Europe. Portugal looked to its African colonies as a means of restoring the grandeur of the past. Despite the fact that Portugal was a fascist state while Belgium was a bourgeois parliamentary democracy with a constitutional monarch, both nations pursued paternalistic colonial policies which stressed the spiritual mission of the colonizer, centralized decision making in the metropole, and denied political representation to both Europeans and Africans in the colonies.

While some commentators on French and British colonial policy have contrasted French "Cartesianism" with British "Empiricism,"[6] these differences may have been overstated. "Cartesianism" implies a uniform approach based on a clear-cut set of rules which are universally applied; yet French colonial policies and practices were far from uniform, since France, like Britain, responded pragmatically to the various political, economic, and cultural realities in different parts of Africa. Thus, French policy in North Africa bore little resemblance to that practiced in Black Africa. In North Africa, the French regarded Algeria as an integral part of the metropole and totally destroyed indigenous political structures. On the other hand, in Tunisia and Morocco, which were governed as protectorates, the French maintained existing political and social structures, particularly in Morocco, where the sultan remained a prominent political figure throughout the colonial period. Colonies in French West and French Equatorial Africa were organized within a highly centralized federal framework headed by a governor-general who supervised and coordinated the activities of the territorial colonial governors. Although France practiced a policy of Direct Rule which insisted upon the legitimacy of only one sovereign authority, that of France, its colonial policy in Black Africa was nonetheless flexible enough to preserve and work through preexisting political structures in territories such as Mauritania, Upper Volta, Chad, and Niger, where the limited French presence necessitated a greater use of indigenous authorities.

Britain's reputation as a "liberal" colonial power was based largely on its policies in West Africa whereby a small number of Africans could vote and participate in modern representative institutions even during the earlier phases of colonial rule. Each British colony in West Africa was divided into a "colony," whose inhabitants were governed by British law and granted political representation in municipal councils, and a "protectorate." Unlike the "colonies" centered on coastal towns such as Bathurst, Freetown, Lagos, and Accra, the "protectorates" in the interior were administered through traditional African leaders and institutions or through newly constituted "native administrations," often organized along ethnic lines and headed by traditional chiefs. The absence of a white settler population and the opportunities for African farmers to be integrated into the colonial export economy on relatively favorable terms made British colonial rule in West Africa less heavy-handed and oppressive than in East and Central Africa, where white settlers expropriated large tracts of communal lands and denied Africans political representation.

The Colonial State

The colonial state in Africa was an overseas extension of the metropolitan state, run by a relatively small number of European colonial administrators whose loyalty was to the metropole. In the name of the metropole, the colonial state exercised sovereignty over often vast territories whose boundaries had been drawn up in Europe. The colonial state was not designed to lay the foundations for the development of a modern African nation-state. It had more modest goals: to maintain law and order, to foster obedience and loyalty to the colonial authorities, and to defend and promote the political and economic interests of the metropole.

The colonial state was autocratic, not democratic. While colonial rule has often been described as a "School for Democracy," this image did not reflect the realities of political life in Africa. Before 1945, less than 1 percent of the African population had full political and civil rights or access to modern democratic institutions. Instead, most Africans were ruled by autocratic bureaucracies with little interest in promoting democratic ideals.

While the establishment of European colonial governments imposed a new political order in Africa, the impact of the colonial state on African societies should not be exaggerated. The European presence in many territories was, in fact, limited to small numbers of administrators, merchants, and missionaries concentrated primarily in the colonial capital and in the major trading centers. In many areas of rural colonial Africa, the people rarely came into direct contact with European officials. As late as the mid-1920s, there was only one British administrator for every 100,000 persons in northern Nigeria. In some parts of Africa, the colonial state was not able to impose its rule permanently and had to rely on periodic military expeditions to "pacify" the area. Thus, in the desert regions of several French colonial territories such as Algeria, Mauritania, Mali, and Niger, the Tuareg and other desert peoples managed to maintain a considerable degree of autonomy because their areas were largely inaccessible and ungovernable.

Because of the small number of European personnel, limited financial resources, and an undeveloped communications infrastructure, the colonial state had to rely heavily upon traditional African rulers, chiefs, and religious authorities to help govern the vast areas and populations under its control. Where the Europeans did not find local rulers, they often created their own chiefs to administer an area or named strangers or people of low social status to fill the role. The French, for example, who had less respect for traditional authority than did the British, would often name an interpreter, a guide, or even a cook as canton chief to replace a local authority when the latter's loyalty to France was in question. The system of Indirect Rule permitted rulers and chiefs to govern certain areas under the careful supervision of the Europeans. The survival of traditional authority did not alter the fact that rulers and chiefs were clearly subordinate to the colonial power structure and could be deposed if they did not follow the dictates of the colonial administration. The ideal chief under the colonial system was loyal, accepted the hegemony of the colonizer, maintained order, collected taxes for the colonial regime, encouraged his people to produce cash

Plate 27. Dar-es-Salaam, 1954, colonial capital of Tanganyika.
Photo courtesy United Nations/V/a/tb.

crops for the export economy, and provided forced labor for public works projects and cheap wage labor for European enterprises.

As long as they complied with the demands of the colonial authorities, traditional rulers and chiefs retained a privileged position within the colonial system. Thus, because of his collaboration with the Belgian colonial administration, a traditional chief such as the father of Moise Tshombe, the leader of the unsuccessful Katanga secession movement after independence and prime minister of Zaire in the early 1960s, could become a millionaire in his own right. In other instances, the colonizer permitted rulers and certain ethnic groups to preserve and even enhance their hegemony over other peoples, as was the case in Rwanda, where the Tutsi continued their domination of the Hutu, a situation that has led to bloody genocidal conflict since independence. Many of the ethnic and regional cleavages which plague contemporary Africa had their roots in the administrative politics of the colonial era, which favored certain traditional authorities, regions, and ethnic groups over others.

The integration of chiefs as subordinate cogs in the colonial bureaucracy, performing unpopular tasks such as collecting taxes and recruiting forced labor, undermined chiefly authority throughout much of colonial Africa. The people came to regard them as agents of the colonizer rather than representatives of African interests. This was particularly true in France's Black African colonies and in the Belgian Congo, where the *chefferies* were clearly creations of the colonial state and had few roots in the African past. On the other hand, indigenous authority tended to persist in colonial areas under indirect rule such as eastern and western Nigeria, where the British successfully modernized traditional authority structures while reinforcing the prestige of chiefly authority.

The colonial state usually relied on educated Africans to run the lower echelons of the colonial bureaucracy as clerks, bookkeepers, and minor officials. With few exceptions, Africans rarely rose to high positions within the administration. Europeans felt no compulsion to Africanize the colonial state, since it was assumed that colonial rule would be more or less permanent.

The army and police force were important components of the colonial state and were used to preserve order. While commanded by European officers, they were composed largely of local recruits. The French and British also used African troops to put down revolts in other parts of their empires or to fight in European wars. The French conscripted tens of thousands of Africans in their West African colonies to fight in World War I and continued to conscript thousands during the interwar period (1919–39), a policy which led many young Africans to flee to nearby English colonies. African soldiers serving in the colonial armies were expected to give their full loyalty and allegiance to the metropole. The British in East Africa, for example, developed elaborate regimental rituals and symbols to cement their troops' loyalty to the British monarchy.

For the masses, the colonial state was a foreign institution which operated according to unfamiliar rules and norms. The official language of the colonial state was a European language unknown to all but a tiny minority of the colonized population. And few European officials spoke any of the indigenous languages. Within a single territory, the administration brought together many different ethnic groups which were obliged to coexist and to live according to the rules of the colonizers, who did little to unite their subjects or to promote nationalist sentiments. On the contrary, they preferred to keep the various groups apart and to prevent any alliances which might be used to challenge their rule.

The limited opportunity that Africans had to Africanize the colonial state before attaining independence, the illegitimacy of the colonial state with the African masses, and its failure to promote a sense of common national identity among the diverse peoples living within the boundaries of the colony were important features of the colonial legacy. All these have contributed to the political instability and fragility of many African nations since independence.

White Settler Politics

White settler politics consisted primarily of efforts by Europeans to perpetuate their political and economic supremacy over colonial populations. In the multiracial societies of Kenya, the Rhodesias, and Tanganyika (Tanzania), white settlers fought to restrict the suffrage of the Asian and Arab populations and to limit their representation in the legislative councils which were set up after World War I. In Kenya, white settlers not only expropriated the best farmlands but also won their battle to prevent Asians from obtaining equal political, economic, and social rights. The white settlers of Southern Rhodesia gained the right to govern themselves in 1923 and used their power to maintain white supremacy. Settler influence on colonial administrative policy was not as great in Nyasaland (Malawi) and Tanganyika, where climatic conditions and fewer economic opportunities attracted much smaller European populations. Despite the presence of significant numbers of settlers, European political life was less intense in Belgian and Portuguese Africa, which had no representative political institutions. Colonial administrators generally had a freer hand in colonies with small European populations.

An unusual blend of democratic and totalitarian politics emerged in South Africa. For the Europeans, there was a highly competitive and democratic form of electoral politics which pitted a predominantly English-speaking party against a predominantly Afrikaans-speaking party; for the so-called Cape Coloureds and the Asians, there was limited political representation and an inferior political, social, and economic status; for Africans, there was almost no representation and, over the years, a steady deterioration of their civil rights. In Algeria, the sizable French population enjoyed all the political prerogatives of metropolitan citizens, including representation in the French parliament, which they used to prevent the passage of colonial reforms aimed at enfranchising Muslims. Ironically, white settler tyranny over the indigenous populations was often greatest in territories such as Algeria, South Africa, Southern Rhodesia, and Kenya, where Europeans insisted on exercising all the rights of citizens living in democratic societies while denying these same rights to Africans. Hence, it was not surprising that African hostility to colonial rule and European domination tended to be most intense in these territories. The Mau Mau rebellion in Kenya, the Algerian revolution, and the wars of national liberation undertaken in Portuguese and southern Africa were, to a large extent, the fruits of the white settler politics of the colonial era.

African Participation in Democratic Politics

Before World War II, the main centers of modern African political activity could be found in colonial protectorates such as Morocco, Tunisia, and Egypt and in West Africa, where colonial policies permitted limited African participation in electoral politics.

In North Africa radical nationalist parties emerged, such as the Neo-Destour Party in Tunisia led by Habib Bourguiba, as well as more tradtionalist nationalist movements which rallied around the banner of Islam in Egypt and Libya or around the persons of the monarch, as in Morocco with Muhammed V. The French harshly repressed North African nationalist movements which challenged French sovereignty, especially in Algeria, which was considered to be an integral part of France.

The British continued to occupy Egypt, despite its nominal independence, until 1936 and intervened frequently to protect pro-British monarchs and governments from being overthrown by nationalist opponents.

Unlike the mass nationalist politics practiced in North Africa, African political activity in West Africa during the colonial era was restricted to a small, educated African elite which was primarily concerned with gaining full rights for educated Africans, increasing the power of representative political bodies in the colony, and widening the scope of African participation in the political process. In British West Africa, educated leaders sought to improve their position by constitutional means. This meant petitioning for more African representation on the legislative councils and demanding less representation by chiefs appointed by the colonial administration or by European officials themselves, who often constituted a majority of the members. The elite of British West Africa resented the system of Indirect Rule practiced in "protectorates," which treated the chiefs as the authentic representatives of the people. The establishment of "native administrations" and the preservation of precolonial entities such as the Emirates of Northern Nigeria often frustrated the aspirations of the new elite to provide leadership in the colony. Yet those with Western education and the chiefs were not always in conflict; blood and marriage ties often bound them together, and some of the chiefs were themselves highly educated by colonial standards. Moreover, the modern elite defended the prerogatives of the chiefs on many occasions, especially on questions concerning the expropriation of communal land by the colonial administration.

African participation in French West Africa was largely confined to Senegal's so-called Four Communes of Dakar, Gorée, Rufisque, and Saint Louis, where they enjoyed the rights and privileges of "citizens." Senegal was the only Black African colony where the French ideal of "assimilation" was actually practiced. The principle of assimilation called for giving the overseas colonial populations the same kind of education and rights extended to the French, representation in metropolitan assemblies, and local political institutions patterned on those found in France. Senegal was perhaps the only colony in tropical Africa during this period in which Africans and Europeans competed and worked together in politics on an equal and integrated basis. Like their counterparts in British West Africa, the African elite of "citizens," led by such men as Blaise Diagne and Galandou Diouf, were more concerned with asserting the rights and prerogatives of the "citizens" in the "Four Communes" than with extending these rights to the "subject" populations of the interior, who constituted more than 95 percent of Senegal's total population. Elsewhere in French West and Equatorial Africa and in Madagascar, Western-educated Africans resented their subject status and sought to gain the same rights enjoyed by Senegal's citizens. Despite France's assimilationist ideals, French colonial officials resisted efforts to increase African participation in democratic institutions and made it extremely difficult for even well-educated African subjects to become naturalized French citizens. It was not surprising that French colonial policy totally excluded African women from participating in electoral politics, since French women in the metropole also did not have the right to vote.

In other parts of colonial Africa, African elites, such as *assimilados* in Portuguese Africa, *evolués* in the Belgian Congo, and the mission-educated in British East and Central Africa, were not permitted to engage in electoral politics. In these territories, Africans learned most of their modern political skills through their activities in various ethnic, cultural, and religious associations.

Although less than 1 percent of the African population directly participated in the limited democratic politics of the colonial era, there were other ways in which the African masses could express their political views. These responses to colonial rules and policies varied from violent rebellions and protest to accommodation and collaboration.

During the early colonial period, rebellions were frequent throughout the continent, often touched off by repressive land, labor, and tax policies. Thus, in South Africa, the Zulus in Natal rebelled in 1906 after the imposition of oppressive poll taxes; in Tanganyika, the Maji-Maji insurrection against German rule in 1905 was put down only after a bitter struggle in which tens of thousands of Africans lost their lives; and in Liberia, the Kru revolted against the black American-Liberian government. With the consolidation of colonial rule, large-scale rebellions became less frequent during the interwar period (1919–39).

In areas where Africans had few formal political outlets to express themselves collectively, political protest was often organized through millennarian religious movements and separatist churches which affirmed African values and world views. Kimbanguism in the Belgian Congo, the Watchtower movement in British Central Africa, the Black Zionist churches in South Africa, and the Muslim Hamallist movement in French Soudan are prominent examples of mass dissatisfaction with European rule expressed in a religious form. On the other hand, Islamic movements often gained more headway when they made their peace with the colonial authorities. Such was the case in Senegal, where the Muslim Brotherhoods thrived (see chapter 5).

Although they were excluded from the political process, African peasants, workers, and women did not remain passive in voicing their sentiments about colonial economic policies and employment practices. Miners in South Africa and Northern Rhodesia, for example, launched illegal strikes to protest low pay and poor working conditions, while the railway workers in West Africa were among the first group of African wage earners to organize trade unions. Asante cocoa farmers initiated the Cocoa Holdup of 1939 to protest the low prices they were getting for their crops. In the rural areas, tax evasion was widespread, particularly among herders, who moved frequently to avoid paying the cattle tax. Market women in Dahomey and Nigeria also rioted to protest against high taxes and harassment by colonial administrators. Africans often expressed their dissatisfaction by voting with their feet and moving across the border into neighboring territories, where they hoped for better conditions which they did not always find.

Despite the unpopularity of colonial rule, most Africans wound up accepting the authority of the colonial state. Indeed, some leaders and societies collaborated very closely with the colonizer in exchange for certain privileges within the colonial system, while others welcomed the colonizer, at least initially, for liberating them from slavery and rule by other ethnic and religious groups. Moreover, many Westernized Africans saw colonialism in Africa as a progressive and "civilizing" force which, despite its many abuses, had eliminated slavery and internecine warfare while providing opportunities for those with modern skills to rise socially and economically regardless of previous low social status.

Africans could also vent their feelings about colonial rule on a personal level, expressing hostility , for example, in popular songs which made fun of the colonizer.[7] Others who identified with the power or the culture of the colonizer wore Western suits and ties and emulated European mannerisms and customs.

The Economics of Colonialism

As an economic system, colonialism bound the peoples of Africa more closely to the international capitalist system in general and to the metropolitan economy in particular. The colonial situation gave the metropole the power to monopolize economic policy and impose a system of "enforced bilateralism." In practical terms, this meant that international trade was generally oriented toward the metropole, that nationals of the metropolitan power controlled the most important sectors of the colonial export economy, and that colonial development policies reflected the interests of metropolitan banks, import-export houses, shipping firms engaged in colonial trade, mining companies which exploited the mineral resources of the colonies, and the white settler population. The colonial system provided the metropole with outlets for its manufactured goods, raw materials for its industries, and tropical products for metropolitan consumers on terms that were advantageous to the colonizers.

Although colonial economic policies clearly stimulated economic growth, this growth was often achieved at the expense of the indigenous populations. From the African point of view, colonial rule meant the expropriation of traditional communal lands, the transformation of many Africans into an uprooted and poorly paid urban and rural proletariat, and a labor system which kept Africans at the bottom of the economic scale and prevented them from effectively competing with European farmers. Economic exploitation, like political oppression, was most pronounced in territories containing relatively large numbers of white settlers in need of cheap African labor.

During the colonial era, the white settler population was primarily concerned with acquiring land and access to cheap labor. Economic exploitation was most systematic in South Africa. There, Europeans took the best land and established a Native Reserve system and an economic "color bar" which forced Africans to work for low wages while legally preventing them from holding the same jobs as whites. Appropriation of vast tracts of land by European settlers was also widespread in Kenya, Southern Rhodesia, Portuguese Africa, the Belgian Congo, and Algeria, and carried out on a smaller scale in Côte d'Ivoire, Tunisia, Libya, and Cameroon. The development of mining and the rapid expansion of plantation agriculture stimulated an enormous

Plate 28. Coal mining, eastern Nigeria, 1956.
Photo courtesy United Nations.

demand for African labor, which was generally supplied from the poorer and usually more densely populated regions in the territory or else imported from neighboring colonies. In most instances, the labor-supplying region had no solid economic base of its own and lacked a source of cash income to pay the taxes levied by the colonial government. Thus, to pay taxes, it was necessary for Africans in Mozambique and Nyasaland, for example, to seek work in the mines of South Africa and on the farms of Southern Rhodesia. In West Africa, Upper Volta became a major reservoir of labor for cocoa plantations in Côte d'Ivoire and the Gold Coast.

The subordinate position of Africans within the colonial economic system was also maintained by discouraging local initiatives which might result in competition for whites in the modern sectors of the colonial economy. Thus, European import-export companies thwarted the development of a modern entrepreneurial class in places such as Senegal by withholding credit from what had been a flourishing class of African traders and middlemen before 1900. European firms and the colonial administration further stifled African competition in the modern sectors of the economy by using nonindigenous groups as middlemen, including the Lebanese in West Africa and the Asians in East Africa. Colonial economic policies also made it difficult for Africans to compete with Europeans in agriculture. Thus, the British in Kenya did not permit African farmers to grow coffee and other cash crops produced by the white settlers, while the French administration in Côte d'Ivoire discriminated against African cocoa producers by offering higher prices to French planters.

In West Africa and Uganda, where colonial policies precluded large-scale European settlement and seizure of African communal lands, rural farmers, though increasingly vulnerable to fluctuating world market conditions, nevertheless enjoyed economic opportunities as producers of cash crops such as cocoa, coffee, cotton, peanuts, and palm oil for European markets. The main beneficiaries of economic growth in the rural areas tended to be notables, chiefs, and religious leaders who could transform their traditional prerogatives over the allocation of communal land and local labor into wealth derived from cash crops.

The development of cash crops had a negative effect on the economic status of women and widened the gap between men and women in many parts of colonial Africa. Male family heads tended to produce the cash crops and to pocket the proceeds from selling them, while women continued to produce the staples for household and local consumption. Colonial economics also adversely affected the status of young males, who often had to serve on forced-labor gangs or leave their village to find work to earn money to pay taxes and the bridewealth. Colonial patterns of development which generally favored coastal areas over the interior and cash crops over food crops widened economic gaps between regions and ethnic groups.

In the urban areas, educated Africans who occupied wage-earning jobs, such as bookkeepers, clerks, civil servants, and school teachers, also profited materially from the patterns of change fostered by the colonizer. On the other hand, for menial laborers working in colonial capitals and mining towns, life was generally harsh and living conditions were difficult. Africans responded to urban life by creating various associations based on ethnicity, place of origin, economic activities, and class. These might take the form of savings associations, burial societies, market women's associations, and craft guilds.

Many regions and territories continued to remain largely untouched by modern economic forces and modes of production, however. This was particularly true of the desert, Sahelian, and forest zones, which lacked modern roads and railways to facilitate the evacuation of tropical products. In territories such as Mauritania and northern Nigeria, precapitalist modes of production and exchange continued to persist as most of the people remained largely outside the colonial economic system. In areas where the colonial economy did not replace traditional African products with European imports, African artisans and merchants continued to supply most of the needs of the local populations in goods and services and to control the traditional long-distance trade in cattle, dried fish, cola nuts, salt bars, and other products.

The colonial situation clearly made it more difficult for Africans to enjoy the full fruits of whatever economic growth took place during this period. However, one should not overstate African economic dependency on the colonizer or understate the ability of Africans to take economic initiatives and to adopt survival strategies which helped them to cope with economic disruptions and to take advantage of new economic opportunities. The diverse patterns of economic development and their consequences for Africa, especially as they relate to the economic problems of the postindependence period, will be discussed further in chapter 19.

Conclusion

The Second World War marked the beginning of the end of the colonial era and its autocratic rule. The war discredited the racist ideologies which had served as the original rationale for European colonization, heightened African aspirations for self-government, and seriously weakened the capacity and the will of the major colonial powers to maintain their overseas empires, thereby setting the stage for the era of political decolonization which was to follow.

NOTES

1. There are two principal contending interpretations of the causes and motivations underlying modern European imperialism. One school of thought, associated with the names of such historians as Brunschwig and Gallagher and Robinson, gives the primacy to political factors, while the other school of thought, associated with such names as Hobson and Lenin, gives the primacy to economic factors. For a useful discussion of these schools of thought and excerpts from their main proponents, see George H. Nadel and Perry Curtis, *Imperialism and Colonialism* (New York: The Macmillan Company, 1964).

2. For an excellent discussion of the development and strengthening of ethnic identity in colonial Africa, see Charles W. Anderson, Fred R. von Mehden, and Crawford Young, *Issues of Political Development*, 2nd ed. (Englewood Cliffs, N.J.: Prentice-Hall, 1974). Also Leroy Vail, ed., *The Creation of Tribalism in Southern Africa* (London: James Currey, 1989).

3. For a thorough discussion of the declining status of women under colonialism, see Jane L. Parpart, "Women and the State in Africa," in Donald Rothchild and Naomi Chazan, eds., *The Precarious Balance: State and Society in Africa* (Boulder, Colo.: Westview Press, 1988), pp. 208–15.

4. Frantz Fanon, *The Wretched of the Earth* (New York: Grove Press Inc., 1968), p. 41.

5. See Terence Ranger, "The Invention of Tradition in Colonial Africa," in Eric Hobsbawm and Terence Ranger, eds., *The Invention of Tradition* (London: Cambridge University Press, 1983), pp. 211–62.

6. See, for example, Thomas Hodgkin's classic *Nationalism in Colonial Africa* (New York: New York University Press, 1957).

7. See Leroy Vail and Landeg White, "Forms of Resistance: Songs and Perceptions of Power in Colonial Mozambique," *American Historical Review* 88, no. 4 (October 1983): 883–919.

SUGGESTIONS FOR FURTHER READING

Balandier, Georges. "The Colonial Situation." In Pierre Van Den Berghe, ed., *Africa: Social Problems of Change and Conflict*, pp. 36–57. San Francisco: Chandler Publishing Company, 1965.

Crowder, Michael. *West Africa under Colonial Rule*. London: Hutchinson, 1968.

Delavignette, Robert. *Freedom and Authority in French West Africa*. London: Cass, 1968.

Gellar, Sheldon. *Structural Changes and Colonial Dependency: Senegal, 1885–1945*. Beverly Hills: Sage, 1976.

Newitt, Malyn. *Portugal in Tropical Africa: The Last Hundred Years*. London: C. Hurst and Company, 1981.

Rotberg, Robert I. *Imperialism, Colonialism and Hunger: East and Central Africa*. Lexington, Mass.: Lexington Books, 1983.

Schmidt, Elizabeth. *Peasants, Traders, and Wives: Shona Women in the History of Zimbabwe, 1870–1939*. London: Heinemann, 1992.

Suret-Canale, Jean. *French Colonialism in Tropical Africa, 1900–1945*. London: C. Hurst and Company, 1971.

Edmond J. Keller
Decolonization, Independence, and the Failure of Politics

8 In 1957 Gold Coast (Ghana) became the first country in sub-Saharan Africa to gain independence from European colonial rule. Over the next thirty-five years the number of independent African states continued to grow until, with the dismantlement of *apartheid* in South Africa, the entire region was under black political rule. After the initial spurt of independence movements, which in most cases led to orderly transitions, the struggle for independence tended to be protracted and violent. For example, the former Portuguese colonies of Angola, Mozambique, and Guinea-Bissau achieved their independence only after more than a decade of armed struggle. The same was the case in Namibia and Zimbabwe, where white settlers fiercely resisted the notion of black majority rule before finally agreeing to a negotiated independence. A war of national liberation was also waged in Eritrea by the Eritrean People's Liberation Front (EPLF), not against European colonialism but against what the Front claimed to be neighboring Ethiopia's denial of the Eritrean peoples' right to self-determination following the demise of Italian colonial rule of the country. In May 1993 Eritrea became independent, and a year later South Africa came under majority rule.

When most African states achieved their independence during the late 1950s and early 1960s, there were great expectations for a bright future. It was assumed that they would develop rapidly, with the help of the more industrialized countries, and fully participate in the world community. Poverty and underdevelopment would be eliminated; the population growth rate and the incidence of disease would be reduced; the benefits of education, safe water, and good health care would be made available to every African citizen. All African leaders had to do was to take control of the political destinies of their countries, and nothing but good would result. But, contrary to such early optimism, the road to self-sustained development in Africa has been long and difficult. Although formal, political colonialism ended, it did not completely disappear. In fact, it was simply transformed into *neocolonialism*, colonialism of a different form. Rather than European interests controlling Africans directly, they came to do so indirectly, mostly through economic relations.

Instead of being characterized by self-sustained development, the first three decades of independence on the continent were marked by the steady exacerbation of underdevelopment, poverty, and inequality. By 1990 the continent's total debt burden stood at $272 billion, or two and a half times what it had been ten years before. This amount was equivalent to 90 percent of Africa's Gross Domestic Product (GDP). Africa's economic crisis cannot be attributed solely to the dependency syndrome. Much of the blame is due to corrupt, inefficient, and sometimes incompetent political leadership. Bad governance and bad policy choices made difficult situations even worse.

Regardless of the source of the continent's problems, there is now little doubt that political independence was not the panacea Kwame Nkrumah assumed it to be when he coined the dictum "Seek ye first the political kingdom and all else will follow" during Ghana's independence struggle. Almost four decades after the independence of Ghana, Africa is still trying to come up with political formulas that satisfy the needs of political democracy and economic development. The reasons why this quest has so far been a failure can be found in the patterns of politics that began in the last days of European colonialism and have continued to unfold to the present day.

Background to Political Independence

A careful examination of the process of decolonization reveals no typical British, French, Portuguese, or Belgian way of granting independence. Although there were similarities in how colonizing powers approached the decolonization process in Africa, there were atypical cases as well. In some instances, special features of certain colonies, whether they were controlled by Britain, France, Belgium, or Portugal, forced them into similar modalities. For example, the movement toward decolonization in Algeria, Angola, Mozambique, Guinea-Bissau, and to a certain extent Kenya, Namibia, Zaire, and Zimbabwe was a much more violent and traumatic process than that in Côte d'Ivoire, Upper Volta (Burkina Faso), Tanzania, or Central African Republic. In the former cases, the presence of European settler interests greatly influenced the nature of the national struggle, while in the latter, settler interests were of little consequence. The character and organizational abilities of certain nationalist leaders also often contributed to important variations.

Before exploring more fully the factors that determined the timing and character of the African independence movement in selected colonies, it would be instructive to briefly examine the historical and intellectual underpinnings of the nationalist period.

World War II was a critical time in African colonial history, a period characterized by events that fundamentally affected the existing relationships between African colonies and their European masters. During the war, the colonies, which in some cases were virtually cut off from their respective metropolitan rulers, were mobilized to play an important role in the war effort. For the first time, the emphasis was mostly upon developing local productive capacities and not just on the extraction of raw

Plate 29. Kwame Nkrumah, the first president of Ghana.
Photo courtesy United Nations/MB/vb.

materials. For example, forced labor was increasingly used in French, Belgian, and British colonies such as Côte d'Ivoire, the Congo, and Kenya, in order to extract record volumes of agricultural and mineral resources. During the war it became difficult to ship raw materials to Europe for processing because of military pressures from Germany. Conversely, it was a problem to ship finished goods from Europe to the colonies to satisfy the consumer demands of white settlers and colonial bureau-. crats. In addition to stressing local economic production, colonial administrations were also responsible for mobilizing their African subjects to provide military and strategic nonmilitary products, such as copper and uranium in the case of the Belgian Congo. Such commodities were not only essential to wage war, they also provided much-needed hard currency for metropolitan state coffers.

Many Africans were also drafted into the armies of the colonizing powers, where they served in various capacities, such as combatants, porters, servants, cooks, and drivers. In many cases, the war experience enabled African soldiers to see another side of their European masters. Rather than being invincible, self-assured, emotionless gods, European soldiers proved to be as human as any African. There were rich and poor Europeans. In the heat of battle they displayed the emotions of fear and apprehension just as all people do. For many African soldiers, the experience of fighting side by side with European soldiers in the war had a tremendous formative impact, expanding their world view and forcing them to question their subject status

Plate 30. Kenya achieves independence, December 1963.
Photo courtesy Ministry of Information and Broadcasting, Kenya.

and the professed benevolence of their European overlords. These Africans gained confidence that they could influence their own destinies if they were willing to take action, make sacrifices, and struggle for what they wanted.

After 1945, a significant number of Africans began to demand more formal education and a fuller role in the economy. This was particularly the case in urban areas. City dwellers, because of their active, instrumental roles as wage laborers in the nascent industrial and manufacturing sectors during the war, had high expectations that their lives would continue to improve once the war was over. At the time, most African schools were still either traditional Koranic schools or Christian mission schools. During the colonial era, formal education was usually only up to the primary level. Africans were generally assumed to need only a basic facility in literacy and numeracy and the ability to communicate in the language of the colonialists. Too much education, it was felt, could result in rising expectations, which in turn might lead to incipient protests, and this was the last thing colonial regimes wanted. Only a few Africans had been fortunate enough to journey to Europe and the United States to pursue advanced education before the war, and it was from this small group that the nationalist leadership emerged. It had not been a conscious policy of any of the colonial powers to educate Africans to fill bureaucratic, technical, or political roles. It was often the determination of individual Africans and their communities that enabled them to seize opportunities to master the ways of their European colonizers and thereby improve their status. Some even went so far as to dream of changing the colonial situation.

The necessities of economic expansion in the colonies during the war dictated the entry of Africans into the market to fill technical roles. Pressures placed on colonial economies to expand served to highlight the paucity of semiskilled, skilled, and professional African workers. Attempts were made in some cases to employ European technicians on private contracts, but this proved to be costly and caused apprehension among Africans over what was viewed as renewed attempts at European entrenchment. Africans in cities who filled these new roles as wage earners represented an emerging social class which began to demand economic opportunities and equity in postwar society. The colonial powers had little choice but to respond positively, training more and more Africans for bureaucratic and technical roles.

Postwar development plans in almost all colonies emphasized a commitment to secondary and university education. Britain trained new African elites mainly in high schools and colleges on the African continent. France, however, trained its African administrators and technocrats in France, and its African teachers were educated most frequently at William Ponty School in Senegal. The demand for economic and political reforms led to increased opportunities for formal education, and this influenced the development of the nationalist movements which emerged after the war.

Educated Africans played an extremely important role in leading their countries to independence. They did so, however, with the support that they were able to elicit from the nascent working class, ex-soldiers, and local chiefs and rulers and their subjects. Individuals such as Kwame Nkrumah of Ghana and Jomo Kenyatta of Kenya, who had gone abroad to study during the war, on occasion came together to exchange ideas about how Africans should relate to the colonial situation. These meetings had a formative impact on the future leaders of the independence struggle. Perhaps the most famous gathering of African intellectuals in the wake of World War II occurred in Manchester, England, in 1945. This was the Fifth Pan-African Congress, chaired by W. E. B. Du Bois, the noted black American Pan-Africanist. Africans from all over the continent and the diaspora attended this conference. The congress was significant because of its timing and the resolutions it adopted. The delegates approved a strongly worded resolution condemning colonialism wherever it existed, and called for various social and economic reforms in the colonies. They also demanded full independence for Black Africa, pledging to pay whatever price was necessary for this right. Significantly, several future African nationalist leaders, including Kenyatta and Nkrumah, were at the congress, and most of the political activity of African nationalists was in London and Paris and not on the continent itself. By the late 1940s, however, these African intellectuals returned home and began to mobilize their people in campaigns for independence. The tactics adopted depended upon local situations, and also on the type of leadership which emerged. In francophone Africa, the pattern was usually for elites to form patron parties and secure political offices which allowed them to represent their territories either at the national level, in the French National Assembly in Paris, or at the federal level, in one of three French territorial assemblies. They used these assemblies to press first for reform and later for independence. In anglophone Africa, mass parties led by charismatic leaders in opposition to the colonial regime were most common.

The timing of African nationalist movements resulted in part from a conscious effort by nationalists to capitalize on opportunities resulting from the unstable international political climate after the war. At the same time the governments of European colonial powers came to be controlled by more liberal, anticolonial elites. Young colonial administrators and missionaries also began to express doubts about the policies their countries had been pursuing. And although decolonization was not part of a well-laid plan for any colonial power, immediately after the war, programs were set in motion which accelerated the rate at which the colonies moved toward self-government. France was confronted with increasing pressures for independence in its colonies in Indochina and North Africa; Britain was being similarly challenged in the Middle East and on the Indian subcontinent. Belgium was racked by internal political turmoil involving liberals and conservatives, clerics and anticlerics; the status of the Belgian Congo was the central issue in these disputes. Throughout Europe, the mood in the immediate postwar period with regard to the colonial experiment was one of reflection and doubt.

African Nationalism and Political Independence

The presence or absence of European settlers in African colonies greatly influenced the rate and pattern of decolonization no matter who was the colonizing power. Where there were no settlers, the colonizing powers looked more favorably on the notion of self-government by Africans; but where there were settlers, the process of decolonization was usually characterized by periods of violent conflict between Africans and Europeans.

The case of the Gold Coast represents a typical example of the British approach to decolonization in the absence of a sizable settler population. The Gold Coast, or Ghana, as it was eventually named, was the first colony in sub-Saharan Africa to secure political independence from Britain. The leader of the Ghanaian independence movement, Kwame Nkrumah, returned home in 1947 after completing his education in the United States and immediately became politically active. At the invitation of older, less educated nationalists, he became the secretary of the United Gold Coast Convention (UGCC). His responsibilities involved organizational activities aimed at securing internal self-government for Africans and eventually independence. Nkrumah was an advocate of nonviolence and civil disobedience. Between 1947 and 1957 he orchestrated what came to be known as the "Positive Action Campaign." In the process the UGCC grew until it had more than five hundred local offices throughout the colony, all capable of mounting local protest.

In the early days, the actions of the UGCC were confined to peaceful demonstrations growing out of specific economic or political grievances, but the organization gradually became more militant, and riots were not uncommon. Perhaps the most significant UGCC-sponsored protest occurred in 1949 in reaction to the high price of commodities sold to Africans in the capital city, Accra. What had started as passive resistance ended in violence and the arrest of the top party leadership, including

Nkrumah. Following this, Nkrumah split with the more conservative elements in the UGCC over strategy and tactics. Refusing to moderate his approach to dealing with the colonial authorities, he was forced to form his own progressive political party, the Convention People's Party (CPP), with the motto "Self-Government Now!"

UGCC moderates tried to work with the colonial administration in fashioning a formula for decolonization. The CPP used this as an opportunity and styled itself as the most legitimate representative of the hopes and aspirations of the Ghanaian people. Nkrumah became a charismatic figure, enriching his reputation as "the Father of African Nationalism" each time he was jailed.

In February 1951, during a period when Nkrumah was incarcerated, general elections, which were to lead to internal self-government, were held, pitting the UGCC against the CPP. Nkrumah's party was the overwhelming victor, outpolling the UGCC by a margin of 90 percent, thus winning thirty-four of the thirty-eight municipal and rural council seats. In securing nine out of every ten votes cast, the CPP demonstrated its numerical strength. The colonial regime had little choice but to ask Nkrumah to form the government that set the stage for the creation of independent Ghana on March 6, 1957.

The process of decolonization in other anglophone countries with few if any European settlers, for example Tanganyika, Nigeria, Uganda, and Cameroon, was similar to the Ghana experience. On the other hand, Kenya, which was characterized by extensive settler involvement, was different. From as early as the turn of the twentieth century, Britain had encouraged settlement in this so-called "White Man's Country" known for its cool and fertile highlands, not unlike the British countryside. Europeans flocked to Kenya between 1904 and the 1950s. As settlers arrived and became entrenched, laws were enacted to protect their rights and to otherwise give them advantage over Africans. Deprived of their land, Africans in ever-increasing numbers were forced onto overcrowded and overcultivated reserves, and a pass system similar to that in South Africa was introduced to regulate population movements.

As early as the 1920s, Africans had attempted to make the relationship with European settlers in Kenya one of partnership, but the trend was consistently toward white dominance and black subordination. Racial discrimination and segregation were legalized. Through labor associations and other types of interest organizations, Africans pressed for fairer treatment, but achieved only limited success.

In the postwar era, political tensions escalated. Government repression and reciprocal African violence grew slowly until eventually, in late 1952, a state of emergency was declared after a series of violent acts attributed to the protest movement called "Mau Mau" by whites but which African fighters called the "Land and Freedom Army." For the next five years the colonial authorities attempted to put down this incipient rebellion. The period of most intense conflict lasted for only two years, but high-intensity government repression and low-intensity guerrilla activities continued for three more. Although this rebellion did not lead to immediate political independence for Kenya, it did set the wheels in motion. In contrast to the situation in South Africa, when the "winds of change" began to blow in the rest of Black Africa, white settlers in Kenya were not strong enough to force Britain to accede to their desire for a white-dominated state. Instead, Britain opted to support nationalists who agreed to protect white rights and to let neocolonial capitalism take root. Under these terms, Kenya eventually achieved independence on December 12, 1963, with Jomo Kenyatta as prime minister.

Southern Rhodesia (Zimbabwe) also had a sizable settler population, but it was much more entrenched and its economic activities were more diversified than was the case in Kenya. This relative strength was translated into action when Rhodesia's settler-based government, under the leadership of Ian Smith, issued a unilateral declaration of independence from British rule in 1965. Subsequently, international sanctions were imposed on the country by Britain, the United States, and other countries as well as the United Nations, in an effort to force the rebellious regime to allow for full African participation in government and politics. The Zimbabwe African National Union (ZANU) and the Zimbabwe African People's Union (ZAPU) launched a war of national liberation against the white minority government, and for more than a decade attempted to bring it down through guerrilla warfare. Over the years, the combination of international economic sanctions and political pressure and African military action caused a deterioration of white Rhodesian solidarity. As the war dragged on in the late 1970s, the British Commonwealth was able to broker a negotiated settlement that resulted in the election of Robert Mugabe as Zimbabwe's first prime minister in 1980.

French colonies in Africa, with the exception of Algeria, were not characterized by substantial European settlement. In Algeria, a national liberation struggle erupted roughly at the same time as did the Mau Mau Rebellion in Kenya. Algerian nationalists were also able to wage a determined guerrilla campaign that forced France in 1962 to abandon its plans to make Algeria its most prized overseas possession.

In other parts of francophone Africa, the pattern of decolonization was quite different. Independence became a real possibility for most French colonies in West and Equatorial Africa when a referendum was held in these territories in 1958. As a result of public disagreement in France over France's role in Algeria, the Fourth Republic collapsed. General Charles de Gaulle, who assumed power in an effort to restore the country's stability, was granted almost dictatorial powers. Among his major priorities was finding a way to silence growing demands from the African colonies for political independence. On September 28, 1958, a referendum was held in which African colonies were asked to vote on whether they wanted to remain a part of the French community. It was felt that most colonies, recognizing their political weakness and economic vulnerability, would opt to remain French. Indeed, only Guinea voted for independence at the time. Over the next two years, however, the other colonies of French Equatorial and West Africa reconsidered their decisions to remain a part of the community, and asked for and were granted independence. Since the francophone African leaders who headed the nationalist movement in the various colonies had participated in local, territorial, and even national politics before independence, they were already steeped in the French brand of politics and government. The French assumed that there was therefore no need for constitutional conventions as had been the case in anglophone Africa.

The Belgian Congo (Zaire) was characterized by significant white settler involve-ment; as a result, Belgium only reluctantly began to contemplate the idea of black majority rule and independence in the late 1950s. Before 1957, Africans were involved in politics only through their association with European political groups that had set up branches in the colony and through ethnic associations.

Belgium practiced a form of pragmatic paternalism, claiming that it dominated Africans only to serve them better. The colonial welfare state was supported by a "Platonic Trinity," which included the colonial bureaucracy, large foreign economic concerns, and the Catholic Church. The state regulated African social behavior; the concessionary companies employed Africans in menial, low-paying jobs; and the missions educated and socialized Africans to accept their subordination. In the postwar era, Belgium began to cultivate a select African bourgeoisie with the intention of creating an indigenous "buffer" class, educated in Belgian culture and supportive of the system. Instead of developing supportive attitudes as the Belgians had hoped for, however, many African elites began to question the contradictions existing in colonial society. They were largely inspired by the nationalist struggles which were being waged in other parts of the continent and elsewhere and by the writings of a young Belgian professor who in 1955 published a proposal for the independence of the Congo, but not until 1985!

African nationalist organizations mushroomed in the latter half of the 1950s. At first these groups had not been political parties, but cultural or ethnic associations. By 1959, on the eve of independence, party activity was at its peak, with more than one hundred separate, predominantly ethnically based political parties concentrated in urban areas. However, only one party, Patrice Lumumba's National Congolese Movement (MNC), approached being a national movement, with a broad base of support. Despite this, the MNC was never able to become a dominant national movement. Independence fever spread too quickly. Belgian efforts to temper African demands led only to violence. In response to these pressures, a conference to discuss the possibility of independence was held in Brussels in January 1960, and six months later, in spite of European settler protest, the independent state of Congo was born. African demands for an end to colonial rule had become irrepressible, and this, coupled with anticolonial sentiment at home, forced Belgium to abandon its colonial experiment. Within the next two years, Belgium left its final two African colonies, Rwanda and Burundi.

The last major European colonies before Zimbabwe to achieve independence were the Portuguese possessions of Guinea-Bissau, Mozambique, Angola, and the islands of São Tomé and Principe. Of all the colonial powers, Portugal had the longest presence in Africa, occupying coastal enclaves as early as the fifteenth century. Until the 1930s, Portuguese colonial policy could best be described as exploitative neglect. Africans were either left alone or forced to work as slaves or contract labor, depending on the exigencies of the moment. Following World War II, Portugal began to become more actively involved in Africa, encouraging European settlement in Angola and Mozambique. However, even where there were few settlers, as in Guinea-Bissau, Africans were kept in a state of near-servitude, with little opportunity for education or socioeconomic advancement.

Plate 31. Political meeting near Cotonou,
Dahomey (Benin), 1964.
Photo courtesy United Nations.

The Portuguese government, which was a dictatorship at home, used the same authoritarian zeal in Africa; but in the colonies, ethnic origin as well as class determined the structure of relationships. Since the colonies were conceived as provinces of Portugal, it was unthinkable that they could be set free. It was this rationale that eventually led Angolan liberation movements to begin armed struggle in 1961, to be followed by similar movements in Guinea-Bissau and in Mozambique, starting in 1962 and 1964 respectively.

The factor in lusophone Africa which seems to have determined the character of the nationalist struggle was not so much the number of white settlers as it was the way in which Portugal perceived its colonies. Since they were seen as mere appendages of the metropole, Portuguese leaders felt justified in spending well over half of the country's annual budget for military purposes, mostly to maintain control of its

African colonies. In the end, the weight of anticolonial public opinion inspired a military coup in Portugal in April 1974, ushering in a reform-minded military regime. The economic as well as the human cost of maintaining the colonies had caused Portuguese society to enter into a period of severe political instability, and this, almost as much as African nationalist military pressure in the various colonies, was important in explaining the timing of Portugal's disengagement from Africa. Guinea-Bissau secured independence in 1974, and Mozambique and Angola in 1975.

Although Eritrea was not a European colony, its people claimed that they were denied the right to self-determination by neighboring Ethiopia, which treated Eritrea as one of its provinces. The ensuing war lasted for thirty years, culminating with the victory of the EPLF on the battlefield in 1991. After a UN-sanctioned referendum, the independent state of Eritrea was born in May 1993.

The Failure of Politics

At independence, the first wave of African states to secure independence from European colonizers were bequeathed political institutions patterned on those of their former colonial masters. There was great expectation among observers that these new African states would simply take the best institutions of Western democracies and use them to form efficient, effective, and equitable models for their own societies. Soon, however, it became apparent that it was not as easy as it had seemed to graft these institutions and patterns of behavior onto Africa. One African state after the other began to reject these forms and to create hybrids of their own. In some places, dominant political parties became single-party systems in the service of authoritarian civilian regimes. In others, competitive party systems were replaced by authoritarian military regimes.

In the 1970s and 1980s, African states were involved in a constant struggle not only to develop their societies, but also to maintain the territorial integrity of the state and to manage or control political conflict. In Africa's quest to achieve these objectives, ideology emerged as a common instrument for manipulating political behavior as well as for organizing society. Initially the trend was toward some variety of "African socialism." The content of these ideologies varied from one state to the next, but all could best be seen as strategies for moving away from the foreign exploitation of the colonial era and for reviving the communal egalitarian elements of the precolonial African past. In this period three main ideological forms predominated: populist socialism, capitalism, and Afro-Marxism.

Populist socialism was based on the assumption that the people in a given country shared common historical and cultural traditions. Precolonial African society was portrayed as having been communal egalitarian and characterized by cooperation and reciprocity among its members. Another important element in this perspective was its radical tone. For instance, Tanzania's *Ujamaa* socialism, the quintessential example of populist socialism, proclaimed war against poverty, rampant capitalism, and neocolonialism. Tanzania was further declared to be committed to the principles of

Plate 32. President Julius Nyerere addressing the
United Nations General Assembly, 1985.
Photo courtesy United Nations.

self-reliance and nonalignment. Julius Nyerere, the architect of *Ujamaa* socialism, proclaimed: "The choice for new nations lies effectively between socialism and capitalism . . . yet having said that . . . there is no real choice. . . . Our present poverty and national weakness make socialism the only real choice for us." Significantly, populist socialism did not look to Marx or Lenin for guidance and a socialist framework, but to some mythicized African past. The aim of the state was to provide the disparate groups in society with a common focus for unity, independence, and cooperation.

African capitalism of the period was a less explicit ideology than either populist socialism or Afro-Marxism. It could be observed mainly at the level of government economic policy. African capitalist states attempted to achieve development by using "neocolonialism as a development strategy." They relied heavily upon foreign aid and foreign private investments to develop their economies. In 1972, for example,

Kenya's president, Jomo Kenyatta, argued: "If we respect ourselves and our *uhuru* (independence), foreign investment will pour in and we will prosper." Whereas populist regimes viewed development as best pursued from the bottom up, capitalist regimes chose the opposite course. Foreign capital and technology were used to promote both industrialization and large-scale agriculture. The capitalist state preached free enterprise, but, as in socialist states, it was heavily involved in directing the economy. Nonalignment was less important to Afro-capitalist states than to populist ones. Although there was a good deal of variation in the success of this strategy, in all cases the main aim was to mobilize capital rather than the populace. Kenya and Côte d'Ivoire were the best examples of the African capitalist strategy.

From the mid-1970s, there emerged yet another ideological strand in Africa: Afro-Marxism. The states which claimed to adhere to this brand of ideology also claimed to be "scientific" in their socialist orientation. What this meant was open to interpretation, but the states which shared this perspective generally insisted on a materialist interpretation of history, the necessity of class struggle for historical change, and the need for the international unity of all oppressed classes rather than only national unity. Although Afro-Marxist regimes claimed nonalignment, they tended to be aligned mainly with the Soviet Union or with other Eastern Bloc countries or Communist parties. As in the other two types of systems, the state was heavily involved in the economy. In fact, it professed commitment to a centrally planned economy and state control of the means of production, distribution, and exchange. Ethiopia, Mozambique, and Angola were the most clear-cut examples of the Afro-Marxist state.

No matter what the ideological character of African states, there was no magical formula for development, and populist, capitalist, and Afro-Marxist regimes saw their economies falter and stagnate. Each type of regime was forced to compromise its ideology and yield to the dictates of pragmatism.

By the mid-1980s, 60 percent of Africa's countries had come under military rule, and among the remaining civilian regimes, only six, Senegal, Swaziland, Botswana, The Gambia, Mauritius, and Zimbabwe, had competitive party systems. Even where civilian regimes existed, national elections tended not to present voters with clear policy choices. Instead, elections served merely to present the illusion of democracy, and many other aspects of democracy were also compromised over the first three post-independence decades. Violations of human rights became common; official corruption and lack of governmental accountability also came to characterize African politics.

Poverty, underdevelopment, economic dependence, ethnic and class conflict, the absence of democratic practices, fragile political and economic institutions, all proved to be structural obstacles, part and parcel of the legacy of European colonialism. At the same time, there was a "revolution of rising expectations" among the African masses, who wanted to realize all that was promised to them during the struggle for independence. However, the objective conditions were not favorable for such developments, and political leadership in most countries was not sufficiently committed to accountable, transparent, responsible, and effective governance. Con-

Plate 33. Voter registration under United Nations
supervision for Namibia's first free election, 1990.
Photo courtesy United Nations/Milton Grant.

sequently, the trend was away from democracy and toward autocracy. Authoritarian
regimes came to closely control politics, rationalizing their actions in the name of
national unity and the need for political stability as a prerequisite for economic
development. While some observers looked upon this trend as a real tragedy, there
were many who seemed not to be concerned. They rationalized that perhaps what was
needed for Africa to develop rapidly was "developmental dictatorships" that priori-
tized economic growth ahead of participatory democracy (see chapters 17 and 18).

By 1986, Africa not only was a continent in "economic free-fall," and characterized by poor governance, it also was the subject of growing attention for international
donors. Dictatorships had not fostered development, and donors came to feel that
they were "throwing good money after bad." At the same time the African people
themselves began to raise their voices and take action against irresponsible and
unresponsive governments. By the dawn of the 1990s, African governments were
being pressured at home as well as from abroad to liberalize both their politics and

their economies. This convergence of interests and the effects that it had on African political economy can be understood only if we consider changes taking place in the world at large. The Cold War had ended; the superpowers no longer competed ideologically and militarily; and international donors were now demanding economic and political reform as a condition for economic assistance to African countries (see chapters 19 and 20).

With the ending of the Cold War, former patrons are attempting to divest themselves from Africa, and in the process Africa is being threatened with marginalization. This has forced Africa's leaders to begin to reexamine critically their roles in creating the current African predicament and to consider ways of finding African solutions to African problems. In this vein, in 1991, the African Leadership Forum, the OAU, and the United Nations Economic Commission for Africa cosponsored a historic conference at Kampala, Uganda, to discuss the continent's problems. The five hundred conferees agreed that in order for democracy to have a real chance, African leaders would have to come to the realization that, although their countries are sovereign, they are also interdependent. Therefore, the security, stability, and development of every African country affects every other African country. The conference made it clear that the denial of democratic rights and fundamental human rights, and the emphasis by African governments on oppression and militarization, greatly contributed to insecurity in Africa. Military insecurity, then, had a ripple effect, causing insecurity in other social areas.

Pressures from foreign donors for African governments to liberalize both politically and economically have contributed to an opening up of the political process. Ordinary people in many parts of the continent have taken advantage of this window of opportunity and succeeded in forcing authoritarian regimes to reform or be ousted. Whereas in the 1960s and 1970s the political pendulum was swinging in an authoritarian direction, today it seems to be swinging toward democracy. Presently only a handful of military governments exist in Africa, and continuing authoritarian regimes are under constant pressure from outside supporters of political and economic liberalization to open more space for popular participation in all aspects of life. This development has prompted some observers to herald the onset of Africa's "Second Independence." However, it is unclear how deep and durable these changes will be.

SUGGESTIONS FOR FURTHER READING

Chazan, Naomi; Robert Mortimer; John Ravenhill; and Donald Rothchild, eds. *Politics and Society in Contemporary Africa*. Boulder, Colo.: Lynne Rienner, 1992.

Davidson, Basil. *The Black Man's Burden: Africa and the Curse of the Nation-State*. New York: Random House, 1992.

Hodgkin, Thomas. *Nationalism in Colonial Africa*. New York: New York University Press, 1957.

Hyden, Goran, and Michael Bratton, eds. *Governance and Politics in Africa*. Boulder, Colo.: Lynne Rienner, 1992.

Rosberg, Carl, and Robert Jackson. *Personal Rule in Black Africa*. Berkeley: University of California Press, 1982.

Rothchild, Donald, and John Harbeson, eds. *Civil Society and the State in Africa*. Boulder, Colo.: Lynne Rienner, 1994.

Young, Crawford. *Ideology and Development in Africa*. New Haven, Conn.: Yale University Press, 1982.

Zolberg, Aristide. *Creating Political Order*. Chicago: Rand McNally, 1966.

Society and Culture

John C. McCall
Social Organization in Africa

9 In the heat of a December afternoon, the streets of a West African village resound with the call of drums. A towering figure covered with raffia palm leaves and topped with a finely carved wooden head is moving through the village. This is an embodied spirit. It is surrounded by young men dressed in short loincloths, their bodies whitened with chalk. These men wield long switches which keep the gathering crowd at a distance. The spirit sways with the music, and the men sing as they dash to and fro. After a while the spirit troupe disappears into the men's meeting house. Then a group of nearly one hundred women singing in unison begin to march ceremoniously down the street. Each hand waves a white handkerchief in perfect synchrony with the music. All through the day, performances such as these will continue: masquerades, singing, dancing, and every sort of festivity.

This is an *otumo* ceremony performed in a village in Ohafia, Nigeria, as it has been for centuries. It is a rite of passage celebrating the fact that a particular age set has officially gained recognition in the community as full adults. The men and women in the community all belong to age sets made up of those people who are close to them in age. Age-set membership is for life. As people get older, their age set passes through various age grades. The younger grades share various minor civic responsibilities such as keeping paths cleared and cleaning the markets. People look forward to the day that their age set will earn the recognition of *otumo* and pass into the adult grade. To qualify for the ceremony, the age set must complete a significant civic project. These groups tax themselves to generate funds and utilize their own labor to undertake major developments. In Ohafia, age sets have brought electricity to remote villages of the region and have built schools, libraries, and markets. Most complete the *otumo* ceremony when their members are between forty and fifty years of age. Once they have completed the *otumo*, the senior age grades share responsibility for policing the village. When they reach an advanced age they graduate to elder status, and the most distinguished among them assume roles as governors of the community. Rule by elders is a common system of government in village communities throughout Africa. Such societies are sometimes referred to as gerontocratic.

This example of the role of age grades in rural community development provides an excellent starting point for discussion of African social organization because it highlights an important aspect of present-day African society. Western observers often overlook the value of this kind of indigenous social institution to current development concerns in Africa. An assumption that economic development means replacing "traditional" African social systems with "modern" Western ones has led planners to favor the centralized administration of development programs and to ignore the practical efficiency of community-based institutions, which can more accurately identify local needs and are relatively free of the bureaucratic waste and corruption that have plagued projects designed on a Western model. In this respect it is important to realize that "modernization" does not necessarily mean "Westernization." This confusion of terms is largely a product of the fact that the period of global industrialization began at precisely that point in history when the continent of Africa became an object of European colonial domination. Thus, we have come to associate the processes of modernization with Western dominance. It would be interesting to know how Africa would have developed if its social and political institutions had been left intact and if Africa had been able to interact and exchange with the rest of the world on equal terms during this crucial period of history. The fact of colonialism, however, makes this impossible to know.

In this chapter we will examine African social institutions as they operate in the present day and on a community level. To the extent that these institutions are "traditional," they are, nevertheless, part of *modern* Africa. We will see that, in spite of the colonial legacy and postcolonial economic pressures from external interests, African societies remain distinctly "African" in character. On the national level, that is the level of political structure established by colonial rule, the colonial model of social control, with its emphasis on autocracy and military dominance, continues to prevail in many regions of sub-Saharan Africa. However, at the community level indigenous systems of social organization remain very important, though in some cases they have been transformed substantially to meet present-day challenges.

It is difficult to generalize about the practices and structure of African societies because the continent is home to a wide variety of peoples whose lifeways differ greatly. Rural chiefdoms exist side by side with industrial urban areas. The boundaries between these "types" of social organization are conceptual and not practical. In fact, people move freely between rural and urban areas in a constant and fluid manner, and it is inaccurate to characterize them as isolated social systems. Several fundamental factors play important roles in the social organization of most African communities, whether they are rural villages or urban enclaves, and these topics will form the foci of this chapter. They are kinship; social status and occupation; the sexual division of labor and gender-based organizations; and age ranking.

Kinship, Family, and Household

While families are a universal component of all human societies, the notion of

Plate 34. Women in the village of Songo, Burkina Faso, pounding millet.
Photo courtesy United Nations/Ray Witlin.

what constitutes a family is so diverse from one culture to the next that a general definition is difficult to formulate even when limited to Africa. However, certain types of family organization are widespread across the continent. One common characteristic of African family structure is polygyny. A polygynous family consists of one husband and two or more wives and their children. Polygyny creates a different family structure from that of the monogamous families typical in Europe and America, and this is reflected in the terms used to refer to other family members. In English we distinguish our siblings on the basis of their sex, that is, either brother or sister. In many African languages this sexual distinction is unimportant (perhaps because it is so obvious), and terms instead indicate whether your sibling is a child of your mother or of your father by a different wife. Likewise, the African child often has a term for mother and another term to indicate the "little mother" or mother's co-wife. The co-wife relationship is one which has a potential for discord. Friction between co-wives is a common theme in gossip as well as traditional stories and legends. It is a key dramatic element in the Sundiata epic, which recounts the legend of the founding of the kingdom of Mali. However, as with the evil stepmother in Grimms' fairy tales, it would be misguided to assume that this archetype represents the conditions of everyday life. The stories remind us not that co-wives or stepmothers are inherently evil but that this particular relationship is especially vulnerable to conflict. In fact, if a husband is judicious in his treatment of his wives, the polygynous family is usually a cooperative unit, and senior wives often consider junior wives assets rather than rivals.

Plate 35. Woman sweeping her compound, Pizonou, Burkina Faso.
Photo courtesy United Nations/Ray Witlin.

To understand the personal and social dynamics of polygyny, it is important to recognize that in the African context the family is more than a bond between people for the purpose of sexual union and child-rearing. It is an institution for the organization of labor. In this sense the word "family" may be misleading because it often implies the simple institution common in Europe and America which is referred to as the "nuclear family." For this reason, scholars of African society often prefer to use the term "household" to designate a group of people who live together and recognize a common head of household. The household consists of a man, his wives, and their children; but it can also include any number of other relations, adopted children, servants, and, in earlier times, slaves.

Farming and animal husbandry continue to be the most important economic activities in Africa, and most agricultural work is done by household groupings. While different peoples have varying cultural norms regarding what constitutes proper work for men and women, nearly all agricultural peoples employ men, women, and children in the production of food. A man with a large household has a sizable labor force to mobilize. Because of his "wealth in people," he may be able to gain high status within his community. In more industrialized areas of Africa, alternatives to the agricultural life are becoming more available. As both men and women increasingly seek work in commerce, civil service, and education, the logic of polygyny appears less viable, particularly from the women's perspective. Hence, in urban areas monogamous families are becoming more common, and in some cities women are actively advocating the reform of polygynous marriage practices.

Plate 36. Village of Cabrais, Togo.
Photo courtesy United Nations.

Marriage in Africa is often accompanied by the exchange of bridewealth: a gift of money, or in some cases money, goods, and services, from the husband to his new wife's family. Sometimes payments of bridewealth are made during the period of engagement. Wedding ceremonies often consist of a formalized presentation of this wealth or part of it. Many African societies practice some form of arranged marriage, though it is now illegal in some countries.[1] In an arranged marriage, parents make the choice of marriage partners for their children. Often this involves a period of betrothal. This refers to the period after the marriage has been arranged but before the wedding takes place. In Sierra Leone, Kuranko girls are often betrothed when they are infants or even before they are born.[2] Such marriages are frequently arranged in order to cement ties between different families. Nevertheless, even in societies where arranged marriages are customary, people often defy custom and marry on the basis of personal attraction. Comaroff and Roberts recount several such cases from their research among the Tswana in South Africa. In one example a man named Molefe rejected the woman his father had chosen for him and instead began marriage negotiations with the kin of a woman he personally favored named Madubu. When Molefe failed to get Madubu's family to agree to the marriage, they eloped to another village. In spite of these circumstances, Molefe's father eventually chose to recognize Madubu as his daughter-in-law.[3]

Marriage between persons who in English would be classified as cousins is practiced in some African societies. This highlights the fact that the English term "cousin" is a vague term which lumps together a variety of relationships. In most African languages, important distinctions are made between cross-cousins and parallel cousins. The former are the children of siblings of opposite sex, while the latter are the children of siblings of the same sex. In some African societies, marriages between cross-cousins are preferred arrangements, while a marriage between parallel cousins would be forbidden as incestuous. The practice of arranged marriages reflects the fact that marriage in Africa is concerned not only with building a family. It also concerns the construction and maintenance of a larger network of relationships within the community as a whole.

The African family extends, through the practice of polygyny, to include multiple wives and their children. It likewise extends across generations to include elders. Children, particularly sons, are expected to take care of their parents when they become elderly. People strive to have many children and to do what they can to assist them to become successful and wealthy, because these children are their legacy who will care for them in their old age, give them a glorious burial when they die, and keep their memory alive long after they have passed on. Children have considerable reason to honor these wishes, because it is through their parents that they secure rights to property and status in the community.

Traditionally, in most parts of Africa the land used for farming or the houses and land where people live are not considered to "belong" to the people who utilize them. Instead this property is held by a corporate group which claims descent from a common ancestor. In some societies this descent is reckoned through the male line. Your paternal descent group would include all of the children of your father, your father's brothers and their children, and your father's sister, but *not* her children. They would belong to the paternal descent group of *their* father. Other societies, such as the Asante of Ghana, reckon descent through the female line. If you were Asante, your maternal descent group would include all of the children of your mother, your mother's sisters and their children, and your mother's brother, but *not* his children. They would belong to the maternal descent group of *their* mother. In most African communities in which descent plays an important role, either the paternal or the maternal descent group is predominantly responsible for land tenure. In some societies, such as the Ohafia in Nigeria, a double descent system obtains in which both the maternal and paternal components are important. In Ohafia, agricultural land is held by maternal descent groups, while residential property is held by paternal descent groups.

The descent-group system of land tenure assures a continuity of land usage over time. It keeps the property within the community and prevents the monopolization of property by a few wealthy individuals. While people may farm on the land of their descent group, they may not sell it, although sometimes the group may jointly decide to sell land. Access to land is continually negotiated by the elders of the descent group, and this is where the social responsibility to take care of the elderly comes into play. If a person fails to support his father (or mother or mother's brother) in their old age, then it will prove to be a liability when negotiating for access to land. In a community where land is held by maternal descent groups, a man who does not contribute to the support of his aging mother's brother may find himself allotted a small, infertile bit of marginal land to farm. Typically, if he questions his lot, he will be challenged: "Where were you when Papa needed you?" In most cases, descent groups are large configurations which link together many families. While people may profess to be descendants of a single ancestor, it is important to realize that kinship is an idiom which people use to refer to their social ties. It does not always refer to biological descent in the strict sense. In fact, careful investigation will usually reveal that elders retain knowledge of migrations and alliances resulting in ties of fictive kinship which have become naturalized over time.

Since the onset of the colonial period, traditional land tenure practices based on the descent group have been challenged in various ways. In some cases colonial administrators forcibly dismantled traditional systems of collective tenure and instituted private ownership of land. This was the case in many areas of Kenya. This program made it possible for foreign investors to purchase land and establish plantations, but it also led to a process which disenfranchised many people, leaving them landless and dependent on seeking low-paying jobs for their survival. In other regions traditional land-tenure systems have remained intact, but they are continually challenged by new "imported" methods of inheritance. In Nigeria, people who want to circumvent the control of the descent group over the distribution of their property after their death can write a will. Such an act often leads to battles which pit government court against elder court. In situations such as these, the negotiability of cultural "norms" becomes apparent. I once knew a man who had always made a big show of his contempt for traditional culture: he dressed in European clothes, attended the Presbyterian church, and ridiculed those who joined ritual societies and poured libations for their ancestors. However, when he stood to lose his birthright on the basis of his mother's brother's claim that the British system of inheritance was more "civilized," he suddenly became an eloquent spokesman for the importance of honoring tradition.

In precolonial times, descent groups and age grades were usually the primary units of political control in rural communities. At higher levels of social organization, royal lineages established the right to rule kingdoms and states on the basis of their claim to descent from ancestral founders. These various levels of political control combined to form dynamic regional political systems. For example, in the Zambezi River valley, which now marks the border between Zambia and Zimbabwe, kingdoms and chiefdoms formed and re-formed through alliances and confederacies (see chapter 4). At different times centralized states arose to which peripheral kingdoms paid tribute. These power relations were constantly in flux, and polities at various levels constantly fused, split off, and repositioned themselves in relation to the changing political relations in the region through time. Immigrant groups often affiliated themselves as branches of ruling lineages, and sometimes men assumed the throne on the basis of such fictive kinship.[4] This dynamic quality of kin-ordered political organization, typical of many regions, has made scholars less confident of applying labels of "lineage," "tribe," and "ethnic group" in Africa because these identities have proved to be highly fluid in the past. For this reason relations of kinship and ethnic identity are best defined in terms not of fixed characteristics but of how they are historically constructed, manipulated, and employed in social interaction.

Occupation and Social Status

People can be found working in every conceivable occupation in modern Africa. Lawyers and accountants, software programmers and engineers are all increasingly in demand. As in other parts of the world, such highly trained professionals are well paid and enjoy high social status. But professionals in the business and industrial sector represent a small minority of African people. Other types of work have historic roots which extend to the time before the industrial age. These occupations are tied to well-established cultural assumptions about the relationship between occupation and status. As already noted, agricultural work is the most common occupation of people in Africa. Many who pursue other professions also farm. The relative poverty of African nations means that working-class people, teachers, and lower-echelon civil servants need to supplement their salaries in order to guarantee survival. Even for the relatively well off, farming provides a hedge against the vagaries of an unstable economy. There is also a strong popular work ethic associated with farming. When I was in Nigeria, well-to-do people often proudly showed me their small farms and explained that they liked to keep a hand in farming because they derived pleasure from it; they noted that if they did not farm, people would consider them lazy in spite of the fact that they were occupied in other work. Songs and folktales extol the virtues of farming, and a full yam barn or granary is considered to be the definitive mark of wealth. Likewise, in many societies in East Africa where cattle raising is the primary occupation, cattle are the unit by which social status is measured. While women often own their farm produce, items which symbolize high status such as yams and cattle tend to belong to men even when women's labor is responsible for their production and upkeep. Among the Maasai of Kenya, women devote most of their time to tending cattle. When they marry, they are given cows by their husbands, but these animals remain the property of the husband until they are inherited by the woman's sons.

Certain other professions such as blacksmith, musician, and healer have significant cultural associations in Africa. Among the peoples of West Africa who speak languages of the Mande group, blacksmiths, leatherworkers, and praise singers are relegated to a particular social status called *yamakala*. These are the professions that "work with materials," iron, leather, and words respectively. These occupations are hereditary, and people who are born to them must marry others of the same profession. *Yamakala* are considered to be of a lower status than the "noble" or ruling class and, being hereditary, their status is fixed at birth in a manner reminiscent of the caste system in India. The low status of the *yamakala* is made somewhat ambiguous by certain powers which these molders of materials are perceived to have. As the official historians, the praise singers (*jeli*) have a unique relationship to the nobles whose power is based largely on their claim to descent from the royal founders of the Mandinka empire. The tale of Sundiata, which recounts in legendary form these national origins, reminds nobles that it is only through the faithfulness and occult powers of his praise singer that Sundiata wins his rightful position as "the Lion King of Mali." In other African societies, classes are not as clearly differentiated or fixed as in the Mande example. Among the Igbo of Nigeria, social status is more fluid, and

Plate 37. An ironsmith at work in M'Baiki,
Central African Republic.
Photo courtesy United Nations/Garacciolo/b.

ambitious persons may use their talents to acquire power and wealth. While Mande traditional healers are usually poorly paid, Igbo healers who build a reputation can sometimes accumulate great wealth. While some Igbo healers live in modest huts, others drive luxury cars and live in large palaces.

A professional site which is crucial to social mobility in many parts of Africa is the market. The food industry in Africa is not as centralized or industrialized as it is in the United States. Market vendors bring produce from their farms, fresh fish and shellfish, palm products, kola, and other goods to trade at market. The larger markets also include cloth vendors and suppliers of manufactured household goods. At the sprawling urban markets, which often cover several square miles, one can find anything imaginable, from computers, video equipment, and designer jeans to goats and chickens. One striking characteristic of the African market is the absence of "stores" as we know them. The vast inventory of merchandise, which far exceeds the variety of the largest department store or shopping mall, is parceled out in small stalls, each the province of an independent vendor. In most areas of Africa the markets are almost exclusively the domain of women. While profits in the markets tend to be small, marketing is an important route to social mobility for African women, and those who are particularly adept can become quite affluent.

With the expansion of commercial and industrial interests in Africa, the range of professional options has increased for some sectors of society, but the majority of Africans struggle daily to survive in an economically hostile world. Some individuals have been able to use the options provided by external markets to undermine traditional limits. A few Mande musicians have been able to become wealthy as pop stars in spite of the fact that *yamakala* are traditionally poor. No one can help but be impressed by the entrepreneurial spirit of the hundreds of vendors who line the crowded highways of Lagos, Nigeria, during rush hour. These enterprising individuals have turned the daily "slow-go" (traffic jam) into a profitable market for bread, candy, toothbrushes, radios, and countless other items.

In Africa as elsewhere, one's occupation is a key component of one's social status. In regions such as the Mande-speaking areas where occupational status is often ascribed at birth, social and economic mobility is much easier for members of "noble" families. In other cultural areas, a more egalitarian social order obtains, and the children of farmers and blacksmiths are freer to pursue other occupations. The growing industrial and commercial sectors and the increasing need for schoolteachers have provided people with many new strategies for social attainment. While these new jobs have created more opportunities for people to gain wealth and status and have, in some regions, been more open to women than traditional high-status occupations, they have also tended to increase the gap between the rich and the poor in Africa and to further marginalize the farmers, who constitute the vast majority of Africans and who are vital to African economies.

Sex, Gender, and Social Organization

All societies have culturally defined notions of which activities are appropriate for men or women. These notions vary widely. In the Gambia rice is grown primarily by women. In southeastern Nigeria it is considered to be a men's crop. Fulani women gain status by never being seen outside their compound, while Asante women gain status by appearing in elegant dress at public events such as weddings and funerals.[5] While these varying practices are strongly reinforced by custom and ideology, they are not unchanging. We are aware that occupations once virtually closed to women in the United States are now becoming more accessible to them. We should not assume that changes in women's status are unique to the present day or to Western culture. It is clear that at various times in the history of particular societies in Africa, the gendered division of social roles has changed. The Fulani concern for protecting women from the public gaze was introduced to Africa with the diffusion of Islam to sub-Saharan Africa many centuries ago. Many changes in the sexual division of labor came about during the period of European colonialism. When colonial agents installed themselves in the coastal areas of West and Central Africa, they encountered societies where women played a significant role in production. However, they were accustomed to the norms of female domesticity in European societies, and they largely overlooked women when they established colonial systems for the export of local products. This often had deleterious effects upon the status of women in these regions. European Christian mission schools, which were established during the ninteenth century, used various methods to coerce parents to send at least one of their children to school. Many people considered the schools to be a nuisance, and parents often chose to send the child they felt was "least valuable." Sometimes these were girls who were considered by their fathers to be "lazy." Hence, in Ghana and Nigeria, women were among the earliest to enter the professions that required literacy, such as teaching and civil service.

The above examples illustrate that attitudes about which behaviors are appropriate activities for men and women are culturally specific and depend on changing historical circumstances. This makes broad generalizations about gender roles in Africa impossible; however, certain observations can be made. The importance of gender tends to be mediated by other status factors. A male praise singer in Mali is considered to be inferior to a noble woman, though she may find that she is a second-class citizen in relation to her male peers. A distinguished elder Yoruba woman of chiefly descent will be treated with great deference by men and may be able to wield considerable political power. In those societies where women participate actively in the production and marketing of food, it is common for a woman to be primarily responsible for feeding her children, even when her husband is wealthy. This economic autonomy can be seen both as a burden, since the husband is not compelled to provide food for his children, and as independence, since the woman's money is her own and she has the ability to become wealthy. In areas where women's economic autonomy is highly developed, women have been moving into politics and international commerce to a greater extent than in regions where women are more economically dependent on their husbands.

In addition to the gendered division of labor, many other aspects of life in African communities are organized in terms of male and female domains. Perhaps the most notable of these are men's and women's ritual societies. Among the Mende of Sierra Leone, men belong to an organization called Poro, which exercises judicial influence in settling disputes between community members and is concerned with the initiation of young boys into adulthood and Poro membership. Likewise, Mende women belong to an organization called Sande, which initiates young girls into adulthood and maintains a body of secret knowledge regarding ritual objects and medicines which are used to treat the sick. Income earned from healing with Sande medicines becomes the property of the Sande rather than the healer.[6] Both of these ritual organizations maintain ritual objects and masks and other materials, and much of the knowledge associated with these is secret. That is, it is never revealed to uninitiated children or members of the opposite sex. For this reason these organizations are sometimes called "secret societies." These societies represent a level of social organization distinct from the kinship-based organization of the descent group. They create alliances between people from different families while maintaining secrets which separate wife and husband, sister and brother. In this way communities are structured not on the basis of a single principle of organization but in terms of many overlapping and interweaving principles. The end result is the complex web of relationships, alliances, obligations, and prohibitions which give the social organization in African communities coherence as well as flexibility and adaptability.

Age Ranking

This chapter opened with a discussion of age grades in Ohafia, Nigeria. We return now to the importance of age ranking in African communities. Age order is a central component of social organization. Many African languages have terms meaning eldest son, second son, or eldest daughter, for which the English language has no equivalents. African people often wonder how English speakers avoid confusion without such terms, which for them are essential for differentiating important social distinctions. In the African household, elder children are considered structurally superior to younger ones. The Kuranko people say that the elder "owns" or "rules" the younger, and this sentiment is common throughout Africa.[7] Among the Igbo of Nigeria, when meat is divided among family members, the senior male always receives the head, the next eldest the neck, and so on, such that the hierarchy of age is mapped symbolically by the body of the animal itself. Likewise, when men sit in the men's meeting house to discuss matters of importance, they sit in order of age, and food and drink is always presented to the eldest first and then served on down through the ranks. In Ohafia, younger age grades include both men and women. Once they have reached the senior ranks, they enter two separate age-grade societies. The men's society is called Akpan and is responsible for settling legal disputes and policing the village. The women's society is called Ikperikpe and is concerned with controlling and punishing men or women who act in ways considered to be an affront to womanhood. Such offenses could include a husband's mistreatment of his wife, which can include not only physical abuse but also demanding money from her; speaking obscenely to a woman, particularly making reference to her genitals; or any man's knowingly trespassing in the women's bathing area. Such offenders are usually confronted by the women of Ikperikpe, who march with a drum to the door of the person's house demanding an apology and usually the payment of a fine. Ikperikpe is headed by an elder woman who goes by the title of *eze nwami,* "female chief."

The gerontocratic structure of African communities is indicative of a broad conceptualization of human continuity through time. People come into the world as helpless beings without status or authority. These are qualities which they acquire to varying degrees through the enactment of their lives within a community. In the domestic sphere they move through the roles of infant, child, spouse, parent, and grandparent. In the community sphere they pass through successive stages, often ceremonialized as initiation, age grade, or secret society. People who reach an advanced age without falling prey to illness, who have many children, and who succeed in establishing themselves as exemplars of community standards will ultimately become elders in the community. In gerontocratic communities the council of elders has considerable authority, but their "rule" is rarely heavy-handed. They are merely one voice of authority among the many which are continually negotiating the shape of community life.

It is this select group of men and women known as elders who, upon death, will ascend even further to the status of ancestor. As such, they will be honored and remembered, remaining in the world by virtue of the actions of their descendants, who keep their collective memory alive. Many scholars have recognized the importance of ancestors in Africa, and early scholars proposed that "ancestor worship" constituted the religion of Africa. It is now recognized that "worship" is not the appropriate term to describe the relationship between people and their ancestors in Africa. Respect or veneration might be more accurate. The concern with ancestors is indicative of a conceptualization of time which does not limit "reality" to the transitory moment of the present but instead encompasses the past. In this view the social organization of a community extends not only to the social space of the village but also through social time to include predecessors. Ancestors are super-elders; they are of paramount importance because they have ascended through the entire process of status accumulation and have attained a kind of immortality as a result.

The meaning of age in African cultures has been strongly challenged by the rapid social changes of the last century. Colonial administrations often appointed younger men to act as "chiefs" in direct contradiction of traditional practices for establishing leadership. As literacy and fluency in European languages have become more important for success in business and government, younger people educated in colonial and mission schools have often surpassed their elders in gaining positions of authority. As the first generation of postcolonial leaders age, however, there has been (not surprisingly) a growing skepticism toward the "cult of youth" prevalent in Western societies. The struggling economies of African states are not prepared to offer state-funded social security programs to support the elderly, and there is an increased recognition of the practical utility of traditional values regarding a child's obligations to care for his or her parents in their old age. It seems possible that as the generation gap moves beyond the twentieth century, the cultural rupture of the colonial period will give way to a renewed interest in traditional African attitudes toward age.

Conclusion

While African social organization can be discussed in terms of different types of structured relationships between individuals and groups, it is also dynamic, adaptive, and historically situated. While African communities have been radically affected by colonial dominance, usually negatively, and by subsequent postcolonial political and economic relations, the process of cultural change is never a simple matter of "Westernization." African people and communities appraise, incorporate, modify, or reject non-African practices on their own terms. In doing so they redefine these practices in terms of an African idiom of meaning.

In Ohafia, where the age-grade ceremony which introduces this chapter is still alive and relevant, people have also embraced European forms of education as a valued goal. Children are encouraged to do well in school, and kinspeople will invest a large percentage of their scarce financial resources to send a promising student to college abroad. While schools have been in this region for only about eighty years, people do not consider this enthusiasm for education to be an indication of westernization. On the contrary, it is considered to be evidence of a continuing ethic of achievement which is said to have characterized the Ohafia people from time immemorial. The "traditional" quality of the achievement is captured in the celebration given to men who return home having completed advanced degrees. The university graduate can expect to return home to a performance of music, dance, and singing which is identical to that performed a century ago for warriors returning successfully from battle. Thus, the attainment of status signified by a university degree is made meaningful and characteristic of traditional values by being linked, ceremonially and symbolically, to the achievements of ancestors long ago.

While African social organization can be shown to be changing and is demonstrably influenced by the West, it also remains distinctly African in character. This tendency toward change and cultural incorporation is not new. The current transformation of African societies merely represents the most recent chapter in a long history of interactions with other cultures both African and non-African. Nevertheless, the colonial era left an indelible mark on Africa, and the nations originally formed for colonizing purposes are still struggling to reestablish themselves on stable social grounds. As the world becomes increasingly international, it is vital for those Western agents involved in negotiating the political and economic future of African nations to recognize that the culturally specific character of African social organization is not an artifact of the past but a vital cultural resource that has the power to consolidate community identity and mobilize community action in modern Africa.

NOTES

1. Alma Gottlieb, *Under the Kapok Tree* (Bloomington: Indiana University Press, 1992), p. 72.

2. Michael Jackson, *The Kuranko: Dimensions of Social Reality in a West African Society* (London: C. Hurst and Company, 1977), p. 95.

3. John Comaroff and Simon Roberts, *Rules and Processes: The Cultural Logic and Dispute in an African Context* (Chicago: University of Chicago Press, 1981), pp. 140–49.

4. Chet S. Lancaster, "Political Structure and Ethnicity in an Immigrant Society: The Goba of the Zambezi." In *The African Frontier: The Reproduction of Traditional African Societies*, ed. Igor Kopytoff (Bloomington: Indiana University Press, 1989).

5. Daniéle Kintz, "Formal Men, Informal Women: How the Fulani Support Their Anthropologists," *Anthropology Today* 5, no. 6 (Royal Anthropological Institute, 1989).

6. Carol P. MacCormack, "Women and Symbolic Systems: Biological Events and Cultural Control," *SIGNS: Journal of Women in Culture and Society* 3, no. 1 (1977): 93–100.

7. Jackson, *The Kuranko*, p. 151.

SUGGESTIONS FOR FURTHER READING

Apter, Andrew. *Black Critics and Kings: The Hermeneutics of Power in Yoruba Society.* Chicago: University of Chicago Press, 1992.

Boddy, Janice. *Wombs and Alien Spirits: Women, Men and the Zar Cult in Northern Sudan.* Madison: University of Wisconsin Press, 1989.

Comaroff, John, and Simon Roberts. *Rules and Processes: The Cultural Logic and Dispute in an African Context.* Chicago: University of Chicago Press, 1981.

Gottlieb, Alma. *Under the Kapok Tree.* Bloomington: Indiana University Press, 1992.

Jackson, Michael. *The Kuranko: Dimensions of Social Reality in a West African Society.* London: C. Hurst and Company, 1977.

Oppong, Christine, ed. *Female and Male in West Africa.* London: George Allen and Unwin, 1983.

Ottenberg, Simon. *Leadership and Authority in an African Society: The Afikpo Village Group.* Seattle: University of Washington Press, 1971.

Shostzak, Marjorie. *Nisa: The Life and Words of a !Kung Woman.* New York: Vintage Books, 1983.

Mahir Şaul
Economic Life in African Villages and Towns

10 In the many towns and villages of Africa, most people earn their living in small-scale enterprises in which they and their family supply most of the work and the necessary funds. The complicated patterns of collaboration and competition in the communities, the relations between spouses and relatives, the political system, and variation in the natural environment make it difficult for uninformed outsiders to understand why people do things one way and not another. This chapter looks at examples of economic strategies in African daily life and considers changes that have taken place over time as people responded to local and foreign incentives. The sectors of economic life to be discussed are not dominated by commercial banking and large-scale industrial technology. This does not mean, however, that they exist in isolation from national and international economic trends. Even in the distant past, African societies had continuous relations with other regions of the world. In some parts of the continent the most fundamental features of economic life were shaped by these exchanges. This is evident in the case of commercial enterprise, and it is also true of food production.

Food Production

Farming and herding are the occupations of the large majority of people in Africa. In recent years in many countries, rural producers have adopted new technologies such as plows, tractors, and chemical fertilizers, but people still also use the simple, yet effective, tools which they learned to handle in their early youth. Often the primary aim of food production is to satisfy the subsistence needs of the household. This is not because people are committed to the principle of self-sufficiency, but because it is unprofitable, risky, or socially unwise to depend on purchased supplies under current market conditions and community organizations. Where circumstances have changed, producers have been able to grow a substantial surplus for sale, in addition to what they needed for their own consumption. There are large areas of rural prosperity. National statistics for some countries are depressing, but these are not always good indicators of ordinary people's living standards (see chapters 19 and 20).[1] An important element preventing rural deterioration in many of these places is that villages are able to retain control of the land, sometimes assisted by customary structures that put land under the ritual and economic care of kinship groups.[2]

Besides property arrangements, the nature of rural subsistence activity depends on natural resources such as soil characteristics and moisture conditions. The single most important of these is the amount of rainfall. Africa has some of the wettest and driest regions on earth. The amount of rainfall varies roughly with latitude, because the continent has no major mountain ranges. Climate and vegetation maps of Africa show parallel bands stretching in an east-west direction (see maps 12, 13, and 14). Around the equator is the zone that receives the largest amount of precipitation, with the dense vegetation of the tropical rain forest with its giant trees and closed canopy. As one moves away from the equator toward the north or the south, the amount of precipitation declines. The landscape turns first into thick woodlands interspersed with herbs and grasses, then to more spacious woodlands with shorter trees and more grasses, then to grasslands with occasional trees, and finally to steppe-like grasslands with annual grasses and denuded patches, and woody species of short, thorny varieties.

This general pattern is modified by the few volcanic highland areas in East Africa, Rwanda and Burundi, and Cameroon, and the special conditions of coastlines and major lakes. In East Africa an uninterrupted zone of dry grasslands connects the northern savanna to that of the south. In West Africa along the coast, a narrow strip of tropical forest extends to the north toward Guinea. Beyond the dry grasslands one reaches arid zones, the Sahara Desert in the north and the Kalahari Desert in the south. Beyond these deserts, along the Mediterranean coast in the north and around the Cape in the south, there are zones of temperate climate and vegetation.

Deserts cover a large part of Africa and rule out certain lifestyles encountered on the grasslands. There is little in common between desert populations. In the Sahara, the Tuaregs, the mysterious heroes of many romantic European novels and films, were camel nomads who constituted a highly stratified and martial society controlling the long distance trans-Saharan trade. They ruled over small subjugated populations who engaged in farming in places where this was possible but never unified around a strong political center. In the colonial period their land was incorporated into nation-states governed from capital cities located at great distances, in the savanna region or on the Mediterranean coast, and they are now citizens of these states, although in recent years some have participated, albeit unsuccessfully, in major secessionist movements.

The near-desert region in the Horn of Africa is inhabited mostly by the much more egalitarian Somali herders of camels, sheep, goats, and cattle. Small Somali groups consisting of related herd owners move year-round to take advantage of the availability of water and grazing. Their high mobility is reflected, as in other nomadic groups, in their houses, which are made of easily transportable material. Their dromedary camels are hardy, wide-ranging animals. They are grazed by young men in herds of a hundred or more animals far away from where the rest of the family lives. Flocks of sheep and goats, in contrast, are kept in the hamlets where the women and the head of the family live. These hamlets include a few families headed by men who are relatives and who subsist on the milk of the herds. The composition of both hamlets and camel camps changes from year to year.

At the opposite end of the continent, the Kalahari Desert in southern Africa is home to a small, dispersed population, known as the San, who until a few decades ago spent their lives in small groups of families, including ten to fifteen people, living off the resources of a circumscribed area by gathering plants and hunting game. Many excellent studies have been conducted among these people. The reason for this lavish scholarly attention is the conviction that the San may have preserved features of social organization and economy that were characteristic of our common distant ancestors living in the African grasslands. Today few people would question that the San represent a mode of subsistence and a civilization sharply contrasting with the agricultural and industrial societies found elsewhere, but the view that they offer a direct window to the distant past of humanity is called into question. Some authors argue that their mode of subsistence is due to their being pushed into inhospitable areas by the more powerful herding and farming populations surrounding them. With the new technological possibilities for digging wells, these populations are now encroaching on the San habitat, and forcing them to become hired herders or farm workers, and some San themselves have started to raise cattle. Recent war conditions in southern Africa have quickened the pace of change. In the 1970s and 1980s, as the South-West African People's Organization (SWAPO) intensified its war for the independence of Namibia, South African forces moved into the region and started to recruit San and to relocate the civilians into camps, contributing to the near-disappearance of hunting and gathering as a mode of existence in the Kalahari.

Most Africans live in the open woodlands or the semi-arid grasslands that are situated between the equatorial forest and the deserts. In most of this savanna and steppe region, the year is divided into a rainy season (corresponding to the summer of the temperate zone) and a dry season. The equatorial grasslands of East Africa have a different pattern, with two shorter rainy seasons separated by a prolonged dry spell. There is a dramatic change in landscape from one season to the other. Toward the end of the dry season, the stream beds dry up, herbs and grasses wither, and areas where trees are not numerous start to look superficially like a dusty desert. With the first major rains, dust is washed off tree leaves, dormant seeds sprout, perennials revive, rivers start flowing, pools of standing water appear, and within days the landscape regains a luxurious tropical cast. This seasonal contrast frames savanna agriculture.

Our stereotypical view of a farm is a crop field behind the house and a barn with cows, horses, and other animals next to it. This, of course, is no longer true in the industrial farming of North America. Nor was it ever widespread in Africa. Part of the reason is the inherent conflict between the rhythms of work necessary for tending cattle and those of grain farming. In Africa fodder crops are rare, and livestock must forage for themselves. The animals have to be taken to distant pastures, and in some seasons this has to be supplemented by pollarding trees to bring leaves to them. In the farming season food and water are abundant, but the herds have to be driven more carefully to avoid damage to growing crops. Furthermore, the best places for cattle are not the most suitable for agriculture. Areas with a brief rainy season have the most nutritious annual grasses and are also healthier for the animals, because one of the most devastating animal diseases, trypanosomiasis or sleeping sickness, is carried by a black fly called tsetse which occurs in wet and wooded environments.

Savanna Herders

For these and other reasons, some groups have historically specialized in herding, while others engage exclusively or primarily in agriculture (see map 25). In northeast and East Africa most pastoralist groups speak related languages and share many features of culture and social organization. Most East African pastoralists keep cattle, sheep, and goats. In the past, many pastoral groups subjugated the agricultural populations with whom they came into contact. This political legacy was reinforced during the colonial period, leading to conflicts that were aggravated by other factors after independence, as the most recent tragic confrontations in Rwanda demonstrate.

The Jie are a Nilotic pastoralist group living in the harsh semi-arid uplands of Uganda. The care and protection of cattle is the business of men who move cattle camps at least four or five times a year in irregular movements. Early in the rainy season, milk supplies are at their peak and the herds are near the homesteads. Then they are driven to temporary pastures where rains arrive late. As the dry season sets in, the animals are moved westward where more water is available. When surface water dries up, camps are compelled to converge on one or another of the half-dozen permanent watering places. Pasture lands are entirely communal, and every herd owner decides where to take his animals on the basis of his own judgment of environmental conditions. The only exception is the intense public disapproval of overusing the permanent pastures by keeping the herds on them when temporary grazing is available elsewhere.

The herd belongs to the house, generally a set of full brothers living under the acknowledged leadership of the eldest, in a homestead which is a series of enclosed yards constituting a rough circle. Each of these yards belongs to a woman married to one of the men, and to her children. Most of the cattle are divided among these women, who use the milk of the animals to feed themselves and their children. When the last one of the original brothers dies, the homestead is split. The full brother sets in each yard, who by now are married and have their own children, establish their own separate homesteads. They inherit the animals that were allocated to their mother.

As among other East African pastoralists, transfers of livestock are important for the Jie in starting and maintaining social relationships, and marriages cannot be established without such transfers. The groom's house puts together about fifty cattle and one hundred head of small stock and sends them to the bride's homestead. Slightly less than half of these are taken by the head from the yards of the homestead. The rest are contributed by the groom's father's friends, with whom he has special relations of reciprocal exchange.

Plate 38. Young herder with cattle, Ethiopia.
Photo courtesy United Nations.

For their diet the Jie, like other cattle-owning groups in the region, depend largely on the milk, blood, and occasionally the meat of their animals; they use the hides for clothing and to manufacture containers and other objects. They also consume grains and vegetables. Women work fields near the homestead, and small informal parties of co-wives and neighbors cooperate in the work of digging up each other's fields to produce sorghum and millet, tobacco, peanuts, and gourds. Each wife stores the produce of her own field in large granary baskets in her own courtyard and uses it to feed herself, her children, and her husband. Some of it she may give to kinswomen in need, or barter, or use to brew beer for sale. Men trade animal products, small stock, or male calves with neighboring agricultural populations to obtain grain.[3]

In West Africa, pastoralists all belong to the same large ethnolinguistic population scattered throughout the region. They are variously referred to as Fulbe, Fulani, or Peul, and they constitute the majority in the semi-arid Sahel grasslands bordering the Sahara. The most important economic unit is the family, which is often small because many Fulbe men have only one wife, and very few have more than two. This group has its separate homestead, which includes a corral for its own herd. The man decides seasonal movements, daily pasturing and watering, and veterinary care, and his sons are the herdsmen. In the dry season, as the zone infested by tsetse flies shrinks, the animals are moved south to take advantage of the grass of more humid areas. In the rainy season, when the tsetse zone expands with increasing moisture, they are taken back north.

The herd of a man derives from animals entrusted to him by his father. He gradually acquires more control over them, and when he is married he starts considering them his. When a father has married off his last son, all of his cattle have passed into the hands of his sons. The herd of each family has at least one stock bull and a complement of cows, heifers, calves, and pack oxen; they spend the daytime grazing apart from other similar herds, and are watered separately. These highly independent families engage in limited cooperation. Married sons set up their homestead near their father's. Related herd owners ensure that each household has sufficient stock. If a man's herd has been depleted by bovine disease or theft, he expects gifts of animals from his patrilineal relatives. Milking and selling the milk is the job of women. The Fulbe family has been described as a herd-owning and milk-selling enterprise.[4] The income is used to buy grain, which has an important place in the Fulbe diet. Fulbe pastoralists also develop other symbiotic relations with neighboring farming populations. Many Fulbe herds include animals belonging to prosperous farmers, kept for them in return for milk and other remunerations. Farmers also contract with herd owners to pen their animals on harvested croplands to fertilize them.

In search of better pastures or better markets for their milk and animals, small Fulbe groups sometimes engage in migratory movements that take them far away from their area of origin. It seems that the Fulbe started their migratory drift more than five hundred years ago from the westernmost part of the Sahel, moving further and further toward the east. In the nineteenth century, Fulbe expansion was energized by conversion to Islam, and religious fervor led to the conquest states of Masina (in what is now northern Mali) and Sokoto (in what is now northern Nigeria) (see chapter 5). They also advanced by peaceful means, reaching territories in Sudan and Ethiopia.

Current conditions and modern veterinary care have allowed Fulbe groups to emigrate to new ecological zones. In the 1970s a serious drought in the Sahel forced some herders to permanently move to the south. The governments of Côte d'Ivoire and Ghana wanted to reduce their dependency on imported meat and encouraged Fulbe herd owners to immigrate, which resulted in the presence of a sizable Fulbe population in the wooded savanna south of the Sahel.

The Farming Household

Agriculture is by far the principal occupation of the largest number of people in rural Africa, and it is often carried out by small groups of people related to each other. As among herders, in the farming communities one finds a division of labor that assigns specific tasks to gender and age groups and determines the contributions of each member of the household to the joint ventures. This division of labor can be sharply defined or it can be flexible. There are also conventions as to how the agricultural produce is to be stored and used, and who decides how much will be sold or exchanged, and what is considered personal as opposed to collective resources.

A farming household often consists of spouses and children, but can also include elder parents, adult brothers and sisters, more distant relatives, and even unrelated strangers who, in one way or another, have become attached to it. In many parts of Africa there is limited sharing between spouses, and especially when the household is large, it is often split into smaller groups for specific purposes. For example, in polygynous households, wives and their children, or married sons who have their own small families constitute distinct sets within the larger unit. In order to illustrate the possible arrangements between the members of a large farm unit, let us take the example of an imaginary group living somewhere in the West African savanna, represented in Figure 6.

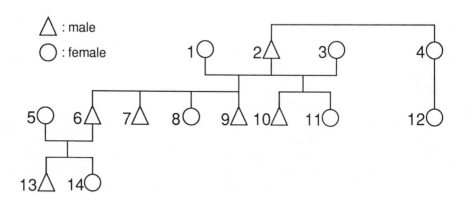

Figure 6. A Farming Household

This group is led by a brother (Person 2) and a sister (Person 4), who are its most senior members, and its primary economic activity is to grow corn, sorghum, and legumes in two main fields located five and six miles from the village. Each working day of the rainy season, all the men of the household go to work in one of these fields from dawn until three o'clock in the afternoon, according to a schedule determined by the elder (2). His two wives (1) and (3) and his daughter-in-law (5) stay a little longer in the compound to put the sleeping rooms in order, clean the yard, and fetch water. After that, two of the women and their daughters go to join the workers at the farm while the third one stays behind to cook a meal that is taken at midday to those working at the farm. The elder sister (4) normally stays in the village except at planting and harvesting time, when she joins the rest of the women of the compound in the fields. Other days of the year she takes care of her peanut garden near the village, brews beer in her courtyard, and prepares condiments for sale with the help of her unmarried daughter (12). She earns enough from all of this to contribute some purchased grain to the budget of the household where she shares the meals.

Occasionally the head of the farming group (2) invites other villagers to help him on his farm in order to finish an urgent task such as weeding. On such days the working party is compensated by an especially generous meal, with plenty of meat or fish and refreshments prepared by the women with ingredients provided by him.

The three women (1, 3, and 5) take turns preparing the evening meal, so that each day when they finish working in the main field, one of them has to return promptly to the compound to fetch firewood, wash and pound the grain, and cook. The wives (1 and 3) each have a personal peanut garden which they work with the help of their children, and where they go to put in a few hours of work before sunset when they are not on cooking duty. The married son (6) in turn has a small personal field of sorghum where he goes after work in the main field, with his older son (13) and his wife when she is not preparing food. One day a week is a rest day, and when they are not attending the weekly market or socializing with friends, the co-wives (1 and 3) and the son (6) and his family are free to spend these days, too, in their personal parcels. The women (1 and 3) each also have a small patch of vegetables near the compound, which they tend on the days in which they stay in the village. The young wife (5) has a few plants of tomato, okra, and sorrel in the border of her husband's personal field.

The head of the household (2) spends most of his afternoons in his small but carefully tended and manured tobacco patch near the village. In this patch he has also planted a special variety of sweet corn, which matures early and is intended for roasting and eating on the cob. He also has chickens and a few goats, for which he has to find fodder in the rainy season when they are confined to the compound.

After the harvest, the grain and beans of the two main fields are sun-dried on a platform, threshed, and transported to the village by the three women (1, 3, and 5), to be stored in two large granaries. The head (2) gives a little of this grain to his wives as harvest gifts. The rest he distributes to them and to his daughter-in-law in weekly rations throughout the year to prepare the daily meals. If the harvest is average or better, he sells some of it to buy tools, clothes for himself, and gifts for his wives, and to have pocket money. He also sells part of the tobacco he grows. The small animals he raises can be sold in an emergency, but they are mostly intended to be sacrificed and eaten during religious festivals. The peanuts of the personal gardens of wives 1 and 3 are stored in their rooms in large pots. They use these and the vegetables they harvest to prepare the relish on the days they are responsible for the meal. Some of it is sold to buy other condiments or clothing for their children. On their trips to and from the fields and on their free days, the women also gather a large number of edible tree leaves and fruits and vegetables that grow in the wild. These too are used mostly to prepare the relish, but some are sold for cash.

The married son (6) harvests the sorghum of his personal field separately. He gives some of it to his wife so that she can supplement her condiments on the days she cooks for the whole household. The rest of the sorghum he sells for personal income. In the dry season he makes a small vegetable garden in the dry river bed, watered from a shallow well with the help of his wife and children. At the end of the season he takes these vegetables on his bicycle for sale in a nearby town. He gives some of the money to his father as a gift and keeps the rest for himself.

People in this household also work for others. Once or twice a year the head (2) takes his wives and his children to help in the weeding or the harvesting of a large field that belongs to a more senior cousin who is considered the leader of the larger kinship group. Two or three times during the farming season, the wives (1 and 3) separately ask permission to help in the farm work of their respective sisters who live elsewhere in the village. The daughter-in-law (5) joins her mother for farm work a few times a year or to help her in brewing beer. The sons (7 and 10) belong to rotating work groups with some of their age mates and participate twice a week in the work of these groups, which are hosted in turn on the farms of each of the parents. They also take a leave from their father to help their maternal uncle and to work in the peanut parcels of their fiancées' mothers. The women in the household receive gifts from their mother and brothers, and the head (2) receives, once a year, a money gift from another married son who lives in the city.

This example shows the complicated relations of sharing and separation that exist between the members of a household, their nearby relatives, and fellow villagers. Elsewhere on the continent the respective tasks of men and women, elders and juniors are different from what is described here. In many parts of more heavily wooded Central Africa, the contribution of men to agriculture is limited to cutting the trees when a new field site is to be cleared. Most of the remaining work of planting, weeding, and day-to-day tending of crops and harvesting is carried out by women. This does not mean that the women can always dispose of the harvest of these gardens as they see fit, because production can still be considered a joint venture and the crops may be stored and distributed for consumption under the supervision of elderly men. Anthropologists have pointed out that these variant definitions of the complementary roles of men and women are in some instances linked to deep-seated beliefs and cosmological ideas. When circumstances change, however, these expectations also may change, and the division of labor may take new forms.

A study describes how this can happen by contrasting the ways in which Yoruba communities of southern Nigeria and the Beti of Cameroon adapted to the introduction of cocoa as an export crop.[5] The Yoruba and the Beti farmed in similar ways, using the same type of technology, but the respective roles of men and women in agriculture were different. In the past, among the Beti, most garden work was done by women, who were associated with all activities involving manipulating the earth. Among the Yoruba, who had a greater occupational diversity, women helped with planting, harvesting, and transport of the produce, but they spent more time in manufacturing pottery, soap, and mats, ginning, carding, and spinning cotton, weaving it into cloth and dyeing it, making beer, and trading their goods in the local market.

When cocoa cultivation was introduced, it became men's work in both areas by changing older patterns of collaboration between spouses. Among the Beti, men cleared additional new fields to plant cocoa trees. Women tended the young trees as an integral part of their work in forest fields. As cocoa plantations expanded and reached maturity, they started absorbing more of the men's time, and in order to maintain self-sufficiency, the production of food shifted to new crops and was shouldered almost exclusively by women. Among the Yoruba, cocoa cultivation started as an extension of men's greater role in agriculture. Women participated in the harvest, processing, and transport as they did for food crops, but for many other tasks, in both food fields and cocoa plantations, Yoruba men had to rely on hired outside workers. Men who produced cocoa also had to cut down their food production and rely more and more on purchases made in the market. This was possible because Yoruba women were already active in processing and trading activities, but it also opened up further opportunities for occupational diversity among women.

Thus, both Beti and Yoruba experienced increasing gender specialization of rural occupation after the introduction of cocoa by intensifying already existing differences. This happened in contrasting ways, and even though Yoruba women ended up having a greater diversity of options, in both places men retained control of the crop with greater returns and increased average income relative to that of women.

Techniques of Agriculture

Africans use a bewildering variety of agricultural techniques, and only a few can be discussed here. In many parts of the continent, farmers use a location as a farm for only a limited number of seasons, then start a new field somewhere else. Many years later the first spot can be farmed again, by a member of the same kinship group or by somebody else. The ratio of number of years of cultivation to number of years of subsequent nontillage, which depends on soil and moisture conditions as well as the abundance of land, indicates the intensity with which the territory is used.[6]

In Central and East Africa it is common to find an extensive pattern. One technique is to clear a large area in the woodlands by lopping the branches of big trees and cutting the smaller trees at chest height. All of these branches and trunks are carried into the middle of the clearing, where they are stacked to form a circle covering about an acre. At the end of the dry season, when the wood and leaves are completely dry, this stack is burned. On the resulting patch of ash, rich in minerals, the first year finger millet (*Eleusine*) is sown. In the second year, after the stubble of the previous millet crop is burned, the patch is usually planted with peanuts. In the third year the garden is often piled into mounds to grow beans intermixed with other crops such as corn, cowpeas, gourds, pumpkins, and sweet potatoes. These mounds are usually cleaned and used for another crop of beans. Sometimes they are broken and spread to form a seedbed for a second millet crop. The crop sequence varies in every region and from one farmer to the next. Three or four years later the site is abandoned. Spontaneous grasses and eventually trees invade the original farm. If left unused long enough, the place can revert to the state in which it was found before the first clearing, and the exact location of the earlier farm is forgotten.[7]

This type of farming is known as *citemene* (from a Bemba word meaning "shifting cultivation"). One encounters it, for obvious reasons, only where the population lives in dispersed hamlets and compounds, with a density of less than twenty-five persons per square mile. When it is expertly done, *citemene* farming brings great returns from effort on relatively poor soil with simple tools.

In most other parts of the African savanna, people practice a more intensive system that can support a higher population density. Farmers use a field site for five or six years and then leave it to lie fallow for ten or fifteen years. Kinship groups permanently control specific tracts of farmland, and the locations of previous farms on them are well remembered. In the scholarly literature this type of agriculture is called by various names such as recurrent cultivation, rotational bush fallow, or land rotation cultivation. One of the main differences with *citemene* is that when a new field is opened, the farmer cuts and burns the woody vegetation of only the portion that is to be sown, and since new fields are opened with less frequency, dependence on ash as fertilizer is less important.

The primary tools of this type of agriculture are hand-held hoes, forged in different sizes and shapes depending on the task for which they are intended. They are usually fitted with a short handle of about twenty-five inches, and the worker uses them in a bending position. Initial land preparation and weeding usually involve scraping a thin layer of soil rather than deep hoeing, but this is sometimes accompanied by the building of mounds or ridges. In places such as southern Nigeria, hoe agriculture with long fallow periods can support population densities as high as six hundred persons per square mile.

The most important cereals of Africa are varieties of sorghum and pearl or bulrush millet (*Pennisetum*), gramineous plants with many local varieties that look somewhat like a corn plant with no cobs on the stem but instead a head full of grain at the top in place of tassels. Corn is the most common secondary crop. It is the staple in Angola and Zimbabwe. Zambia and Malawi export large quantities of it in certain years. There are some African grains which are prominent in one region but not cultivated anywhere else. For example, in the midlands of Ethiopia there is teff, which is universally favored for the famous flat breads of that country, and in West Africa there is fonio (*Digitaria exilis*). Rice is a staple in limited parts of coastal West Africa south of the Gambia River, in Guinea and Guinea-Bissau, parts of Liberia, Sierra Leone, and western Côte d'Ivoire. This area has been described as an old "rice civilization,"

Plate 39. Women farmers at work in the Mbeya Region of Tanzania.
Photo courtesy United Nations/B. Wolff(J).

and the "redskin" varieties found there were probably locally domesticated. Asian swamp rice is the staple of Madagascar, where it was introduced by Malay peoples who immigrated to this island several centuries ago.

When a new grain farm is to be opened on fallow land, the location is usually selected at the height of the previous rainy season, when the vegetation is luxuriant. The farmer decides the potential of the spot by the quality of the soil, the abundance of certain grasses and trees that are known to indicate fertility, and other signs such as the presence of insect and animal life. Trees and big shrubs are cut before the end of the rainy season. After harvesting his crops, the farmer returns to the new field to clear the smaller vegetation. At the end of the dry season, this dry matter is burned around the large stumps. In many places this arduous work is achieved by teams of young workers including fifteen to twenty men, usually relatives and fellow villagers invited for the task and rewarded with refreshments or a big meal.

The preparation of the soil surface before planting depends on the type of soil, the crop to be planted, and the availability of labor. If the newly opened area was heavily wooded, there are not many grasses and the ground does not need to be hoed before sowing. If it was open grassland, the heaviest task is ridding the field of the strong perennial grasses. In some places light ridges are built before the first planting, and in hilly areas people build ridges around contour lines to retain water and reduce erosion.

A typical farm has a mixture of crops. Where the primary crops are grains, legumes such as beans and cowpeas are important secondary crops. These plants have varying demands on soil nutrients, and also take advantage of the different soil depths and drainage provided by the mounds and ridges. In many places different varieties of grain are sown together in a random pattern, or in alternating rows, or in pockets. After the first heavy rains, farmers resow the patches where the plantings fail to come out, often replacing them with different varieties that have a shorter growing season. Other crops are planted in succession, generally legumes and vegetables following the grains, to spread the labor of planting and enable especially favored crops to become well established before other members of the mixture compete for nutrients. The borders of a field are marked with rows of tall plants such as roselle or okra as a kind of temporary hedge.

The sequence of planting reveals food preferences as well as the labor relations within the household and the village, as previously discussed. In the savanna, joint household fields are planted first, before women and dependent men are allowed to start working on their personal parcels. Everywhere the beginning and end of the agricultural season, the planting and harvesting of major crops, are marked by religious ceremonies which ensure fertility at the same time as they reproduce the cosmic order and the social structure of the community.

In successive years grain farmers try different crops and varieties to maximize the yield of the soil. For example, in western Burkina Faso, a new farm site cleared late in the rainy season in a wooded area is often quickly broadcast with sesame, not only to harvest the seeds that yield the valued cooking oil, but also to cover the ground and keep the soil free of grasses until millet is planted the next year. Different varieties of millet and sorghum alternate in successive years. Cotton is now planted in pure stands, on the advice of government extension services. Each year the cotton parcel is in a new location where there were cereals before, so that it becomes part of the rotation. The last year before leaving a field to lie fallow, farmers sow fonio as a final crop. Some abandoned grain farms near the village are reclaimed a few years later by women for personal peanut parcels, because they are free of large, bushy vegetation that is difficult to clear.

One of the most original and unusual aspects of West African multicropping patterns involves the use of economically useful trees. When farmers of the West African savanna clear a new farm site, they spare some of these trees, which gives fields the appearance of an orchard. A large tree may be saved to provide shade for work breaks and meals, but others are preserved for their fruits. The two most valuable are the shea or karite tree (*Butyrospermum parkii*) and the locust bean or nere tree (*Parkia biglobosa*). The shea produces a pale green fruit with a sweet flesh and a nut the size and shape of a pecan. Women extract a solid oil used for cooking and other purposes. Shea is also an export commodity used in the chocolate and cosmetic industries. The locust tree produces ten-inch-long black pods packed with an edible sweet yellow powder and soybean-size black seeds. Women transform these seeds into a condiment that is the indispensable ingredient of West African sauces and gives to many marketplaces their characteristic strong aroma. Locust seeds are one of the most highly valued rural products of West Africa and are traded between countries from Sierra Leone to Nigeria. Thus, both of these tree crops generate large flows of income, most of it earned by women.

In the regions of transition from the equatorial forest to the grasslands, agriculture is based on the cultivation of root crops (see map 25). Yams are one of the most important of these. A yam is a giant tuber that grows up to twelve inches long and four inches in diameter (what is sold as canned yams in American grocery stores is in fact sweet potato, which is a different plant). Its white flesh is often boiled and pounded into a tasty paste with a slightly elastic texture, eaten with a highly flavored meat and vegetable or fish relish.

Yams are usually grown in large mounds, the pride and joy of young farmers who build them with hoes where this type of agriculture is common. In northern Ghana, in Dagomba country, once the garden is hoed off and the vegetation collected and burned, young men build mounds two to three feet high and four or five feet wide at the base. This is a laborious process, but it is said that a man normally makes one hundred to two hundred such mounds. Small "seed" tubers are planted in the sides of the mounds in the dry month of January, and a mulch of dry grass covered with earth is placed on each mound. The Dagomba have a number of yam varieties, and different varieties are used on different soils and for early or late maturity. Early yams are lifted in August, and the later harvest may be taken at leisure from September until the middle of the dry season. Before this harvest, in June or July, a late variety of millet and secondary crops such as okra and calabashes are planted between the mounds. Most gardens have an outer row of manioc or pigeon pea. Among the Tiv people of central Nigeria, men make the mounds with large hoes and women plant the seed yams in the top of the mound with a digging stick. When the yams have been planted men and women plant in the bottom of the mounds other crops such as manioc, beans, corn, and various greens. Some mounds can contain as many as twenty different types of plants.[8]

Another important crop is manioc, also called cassava. Like corn, manioc is a plant of New World origin, and its introduction into Africa within the last four hundred years has revolutionized food production in certain parts of the continent. Manioc is a woody plant propagated from cuttings that develop into thin, straight, three- or four-foot-long stems topped with a crown of deep green leaves. In the ground the plant develops several starchy roots that look somewhat like horseradish and which spread out from the stem in the pattern of a star. In North America, manioc is known as tapioca flour, which is used to make puddings and pie fillings. As a crop, manioc has unusual characteristics. It is a long-maturing crop, harvested a year or eighteen months after planting. Thus it does not cause harvesting bottlenecks because it can be stored in the ground and dug out as it is needed. Some of the many different varieties, called bitter manioc, contain cyanide, which has to be removed by leaching and drying, adding considerably to the processing time spent by women. Unlike grains, manioc is often sold in local markets in this already processed form. Of all the known domesticated plants, manioc is the one that produces the greatest number of calories for a given area and for the effort. In parts of Africa, such as the Luapula Valley of

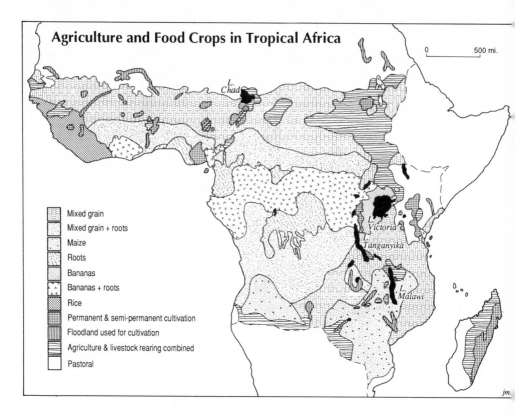

Agriculture and Food Crops in Tropical Africa

0   500 mi.

L. Chad

L. Victoria

L. Tanganyika

L. Malawi

Mixed grain
Mixed grain + roots
Maize
Roots
Bananas
Bananas + roots
Rice
Permanent & semi-permanent cultivation
Floodland used for cultivation
Agriculture & livestock rearing combined
Pastoral

jm

MAP 25

Zaire, its cultivation has made possible great population densities and stable, large villages. Manioc is also the principal crop in the great forest region of the Zaire River basin. In other places it is an important subsidiary crop grown mostly by dependent members of the household for their personal profit. It has been maintained that one day manioc will become a critical crop for the planet as global agricultural resources shrink relative to the population. The other side of the coin is that the manioc root is almost purely starch. Where it is the staple diet, for those who cannot afford to complement it with other foods such as meat or fish, it can cause dietary deficiencies. This disadvantage is somewhat compensated for in that the leaves of the plant are a rich source of vitamins and can be eaten as a vegetable.

Another highly productive plant is the banana, common in East and Central Africa and the forested parts of West Africa. The plant is a tree-like perennial herb which flourishes on strong, rich volcanic soils. Under suitable conditions of temperature and moisture, it will yield fruit for many years without replanting, and without tillage or manuring of any kind. In parts of Uganda, twenty tons of fruit per acre is considered low; this can be got without too much difficulty, allowing the farmers time to grow other cash crops. Of the numerous cultivated varieties, most belong to the plantain (*Musa paradisiaca*) species and are cooked before eating. Others are eaten fresh as fruit or are brewed, often in combination with grains, into alcoholic beverages.

Some special environments allow unusual forms of farming. One of the most amazing is the highly intensive shallot gardens of the Anlo farmers of the densely settled coastal district of southeastern Ghana, established on the poor sandy soils of the narrow ridge between the ocean and the lagoon. Because of the orientation of the coast against the winds, this is one of the driest locations in Ghana, but this is offset by a high water table, and the crops can be watered from shallow wells dug in the gardens. The regime is extremely demanding of labor. The beds have to be rebuilt frequently by carting sand to raise their level, and they are enriched with large quantities of bat droppings, cow dung, fish manure, and now chemical fertilizers. In addition to family workers, shallot farmers hire outsiders. There are three shallot seasons a year, yielding an average of four to eight tons of dried shallots per acre per year; in between, the beds are sown with other vegetables such as tomatoes, peppers, and beans. Presently the shallot industry caters to the demand of the metropolitan coastal zone that extends without interruption from Abidjan to Lomé, but its origins predate this urban development; shallot trading was well established before 1900.

Trade

Apart from local trade, some parts of Africa have had for centuries networks of professional traders connecting different ecological zones (see chapters 4, 5, and 6). East Africa was part of the merchant world of the Indian Ocean, connecting it to India, the Arabian Peninsula, and the rest of the world. In West Africa some of the goods reaching the Sahara Desert and North Africa originated in the remote forest region. One of these forest commodities was the kola nut, an aromatic seed the size of a chestnut which is chewed as a stimulant, as it contains caffeine and theobromine. Pharmacists in Europe invented tonic beverages using an extract of it, from which later developed some of our popular carbonated drinks. Long-distance trade also included gold and manufactured goods.

In some places villagers were deeply suspicious of trade activity and tried to control its disruptive potential by forbidding individuals from taking part in it.[9] In the West Volta region of Burkina Faso, trade was conducted by heads of large kinship groups who exchanged the shea nuts and locust beans collected by women for cloth and manufactured goods stored as treasures and displayed in ceremonies. Village-level exchanges consisted mostly of long-term ties with casted professional groups who produced iron tools and pottery in return for grain and other foods, or the barter of some household production by women for dried fish or condiments brought by itinerant professional women traders.

One way for elders heading large groupings to limit involvement in trade was to control the supply of goods that could be used as currency. In precolonial times, brass rods, cloth, and gold and commodities such as iron forged in the form of hoes, spears, or bars were in circulation as money. For many farming groups, these valuable goods were given away in large quantities only as bridewealth, as animals were among pastoralists. One of the important historical currencies of West Africa was the cowry.

Plate 40. Outdoor market, Mopti, Mali.
Photo courtesy United Nations/A. Rozberg.

Cowries are peanut-sized shells that come from sea mollusks found only in the Maldive archipelago of the Indian Ocean. They have been used as jewelry and as a medium of exchange in many other parts of the Old World and must have first come to West Africa through the trans-Saharan trade. It was especially after the sixteenth century, with the opening of the great sea routes, however, that they became abundant, because European merchants started to transport shiploads of them in order to finance their imports from the region. Thus the zone of circulation of cowrie shells gradually widened from the coast toward the interior.[10] Elders hoarded such valuables for economic and social transactions, and because they alone were capable of mobilizing the numbers of people necessary to manufacture these expensive goods, they had a near-monopoly on currencies. When in the colonial period young people discovered that they could earn wages and buy coveted imported items to substitute for the older valuables in marriage transactions, the old guard in many village communities tried with limited success to stop the trend by declaring that it was against custom to replace the old bridewealth goods with colonial notes or imported goods purchased in the cities.

The use of cowries as currencies was only one of several new developments introduced by the ocean trade. As was noted in chapter 6, along the coast of West and West Central Africa, European merchants dealt from their ships or from small forts that they built on the coast. Some coastal inhabitants became middlemen in commerce, hiring out their canoes or growing crops to feed the inhabitants of the forts. Wage earners, employed in the ports and factories, made their appearance. In West Africa a new elite surrounded by servants emerged, often of mixed European and African parentage. They equipped their own miniature forts with guns and sent their children to study in Europe. New towns grew not only in the Gulf of Benin, connected by the ocean to Europe and the New World, but also on the edge of the forested region and the drier grasslands as extensions and relay points of the sea trade.

Between 1820 and 1850, trade between West Africa and western Europe increased tremendously, as the export of humans, ivory, wax, gum, and indigo declined, replaced primarily by oils and secondarily hardwood timber, hides, and rice. The imports were metals and hardware, liquor, salt, cotton textiles, powder, and munitions. European merchants moved from shore and river factories to stores in the interior. The driving force for this transition was the rising demand in England and France for soap, candles, industrial lubricants, and cooking oils for the growing urban working class. Palm-oil exports reached tens of thousands of tons in the second half of the nineteenth century, mostly to England, constituting one of the amazing episodes of recent economic history. In places such as Togo and Dahomey, the old African merchants who could no longer find a market for slaves in the Atlantic trade put them to work to gather the kernels and process them.

The French traded peanuts from the savanna region of Senegambia, where they were early colonizers. Since the growing of peanuts required little skill, traditional hierarchies of soldiers and chiefs chose it as an easy way to earn money to shore up their shattered prestige and put freed slaves to work. People would come to the coast from as far away as six hundred miles or more in the interior, ask the chiefs for permission to cultivate plots of land for one or more years, and sell the produce to the European merchant or his trader.

Eventually, with growing competition from plantations in southern Asia and soybean farms in the U.S., West Africa lost its near-monopoly in the supply of oil. This was replaced, however, by the production of other cash crops such as cocoa, which African peasant farmers introduced in southern Nigeria and the Gold Coast in the 1880s. In the Gold Coast, migrants started moving north from the coast and purchased land in the forest region to plant cocoa, with money they made selling oil palm kernels and rubber. Other kin came to settle, both to help the original settler and to establish their own farm on the portion of the land that had not been planted. Thus, what started with an individual purchase agreement ended up looking like a kinship estate. Others established groups or clubs with friends, known as companies, to acquire tracts of land which were then divided into strips. The immigrant growers hired contractors to build bridges and roads to evacuate their crops, and some of them invested in trucks and became transporters as well. Local people who controlled access to forest land also joined in this lucrative industry. Indigenous chiefs became prominent cocoa farmers. They also produced food crops for their own needs. Migrants started coming from the savanna in the north, seeking employment in these plantations on a seasonal or year-round basis.[11] Ghana became the world leader in cocoa exports before the First World War, and accounted for two-fifths of total world production at the time of its independence in 1957.

Growing links with the world economy under imposed colonial rule had varying effects on different groups constituting society. In West Africa the local princes and merchant elites of the Gulf of Benin and of Senegambia lost their commercial advantages in the competition with the European merchant houses that came to dominate the import/export trade. Since many of them had received European educations, they played a role in the administration of the colony, and in the mid-twentieth century they were among the leaders in nationalist movements that ended the colonial period (see chapters 7 and 8). Elsewhere manufacturing activities such as iron smelting came to an end, weaving lost its significance, and most of Africa became a supplier of agricultural or mineral raw materials and a purchaser of manufactured goods.

Growing trade links, the increasing volume and circulation of currency, and the growth of metropolitan centers also created new trades and possibilities of advancement for previously disadvantaged groups, such as some casted groups, youths with no authority in the kinship and household organization, and women. The record on all these is mixed (see chapter 16). The growth of large colonial cities and of mining centers created an expanding urban market for foodstuffs that stimulated production of grains and root crops. In places where women already had personal autonomy within the farm household, some of them found a broader scope for establishing their own businesses in cities and towns, where new complementarities emerged between men and women.[12]

One example is the irrigated vegetable gardens that spring up near every city early in the dry season. These gardens, usually established on dried-up watercourses, are well manured and require a lot of work. The banks of West African rivers that go through major cities such as Bamako are full of permanent gardens and fruit-tree groves, sometimes worked by hired hands. Further away from the city, grain farmers in villages make vegetable gardens encircled with a hedge of thorns and shrubs as protection against theft, with domestic animals left to roam about in the dry season. Those who can afford it buy a pump to water the garden and also spend relatively large sums on mulching material and manure to condition the soil. Groves of introduced fruit varieties, such as mangoes and citrus, are an even more important source of income where they do well. The perishable nature of fruits and vegetables imposes special constraints on their trade and distribution. They are usually purchased, transported, and retailed, not by the large national grain merchants but by a different set of traders, including a large proportion of women. In certain areas of West Africa, men who have gardens share the proceeds with their wives, who do the marketing.

Women in towns generally engage in retail trade, market cooking (ranging from street-corner sellers to restaurant-bars employing several people), and beer brewing.[13] Even in places such as the city of Kano in northern Nigeria, where local Muslim norms demand the seclusion of wives in their homes, some women have turned this into an advantage by using their free time to establish flourishing businesses in their homes, using their sons and daughters as retail agents.[14]

Conclusion

A popular perception of Africa has been that people conduct their lives in blind conformity with old customs and traditions. As this chapter has demonstrated, nothing could be further from the truth. When there have been opportunities to better their lives, many Africans have responded with great ingenuity. They have built productive export economies and they have increased food production at home by following, but also modifying and adapting, older patterns of social organization. Even under unfavorable conditions such as political instability, mismanagement of national economies, and adverse world economic trends (see chapters 19 and 20), many Africans continue to devise personal or local strategies to support themselves and their families, as they have always done.

NOTES

1. See, for example, Janet MacGaffey, *The Real Economy of Zaire: The Contribution of Smuggling and Other Unofficial Activities to National Wealth* (Philadelphia: University of Pennsylvania Press, 1910).

2. For landholding patterns and changes in Africa, see T. J. Bassett and D. Crummey, eds., *Land in African Agrarian Systems* (Madison: University of Wisconsin Press, 1993); S. P. Reyna and R. E. Downs, eds., *Land and Society in Contemporary Africa* (Hanover: University of New England Press, 1988); D. Biebuyck, ed., *African Agrarian Systems* (Oxford: Oxford University Press, 1963).

3. P. H. Gulliver, *The Family Herds* (London: Routledge and Kegan Paul, Ltd., 1955).

4. Derrick J. Stenning, *Savannah Nomads* (London: Oxford University Press for International African Institute, 1959).

5. Jane Guyer, "Food, Cocoa, and the Division of Labour by Sex in Two West African Societies," *Comparative Studies in Society and History* 22 (1980): 355–73.

6. W. B. Morgan, "Peasant Agriculture in Tropical Africa," in M. F. Thomas and G. H. Whittington, eds., *Environment and Land Use in Africa* (London: Methuen and Co., 1969), pp. 241–72.

7. William Allan, *The African Husbandman* (New York: Barnes and Noble, Inc., 1965).

8. Paul Bohannan, *Tiv Farm and Settlement* (London: Her Majesty's Stationery Office, 1954).

9. See, for example, for the Luo of Kenya: Parker Shipton, *Bitter Money: Cultural Economy and Some African Meanings of Forbidden Commodities*, American Ethnological Society Monograph Series, no. 1, 1989.

10. Marion Johnson, "The Cowrie Currencies of West Africa," *Journal of African History* 11 (1970): 17–49 and 331–53.

11. The local organization of cocoa production has been described in rich ethnographic studies by Polly Hill (*Migrant Cocoa Farmers of Southern Ghana* [Cambridge: Cambridge University Press, 1963]), Marguerite Dupire ("Planteurs autochtones et étrangers en Basse-Côte d'Ivoire orientale," *Etudes Eburnéenes* 8 [Abidjan, 1960]), and Sara Berry (*Cocoa, Custom and Socioeconomic Change in Rural West Africa* [Oxford: Oxford University Press, 1975]).

12. Phoebe Oteenberg, "The Changing Economic Position of Women among the Afikpo Ibo," in W. R. Bascom and M. Herskovits, eds., *Continuity and Change in African Cultures* (Chicago: University of Chicago Press, 1959); M. Peil, "Female Roles in West African Towns," in J. Goody, ed., *Changing Social Structure in Ghana* (London: International African Institute, 1975).

13. Mahir Şaul, "Beer, Sorghum, and Women: Production for the Market in Rural Upper Volta," *Africa* 51 (1981): 746–64.

14. Dorothy Remy, "Underdevelopment and the Experience of Women: A Nigerian Case Study," in R. R. Reiter, ed., *Toward an Anthropology of Women* (New York: Monthly Review Press, 1975); Enid Schildkrout, "Dependence and Autonomy: The Economic Activities of Secluded Hausa Women in Kano, Nigeria," in E. G. Bay, ed., *Women and Work in Africa* (Boulder, Colo: Westview Press, 1982).

SUGGESTIONS FOR FURTHER READING

Allan, William. *The African Husbandman*. New York: Barnes and Noble, Inc., 1965.

Guyer, I. Jane. "Household and Community in African Studies." *African Studies Review* 24 (1981): 87–137.

Hart, Keith. *The Political Economy of West African Agriculture*. Cambridge: Cambridge University Press, 1982.

Hill, Polly. *Rural Hausa: A Village and a Setting*. Cambridge: Cambridge University Press, 1972.

Lee, Richard B. *The !Kung San: Men, Women and Work in a Foraging Society*. Cambridge: Cambridge University Press, 1979.

Mandala, Elias C. *Work and Control in a Peasant Economy: A History of the Lower Tchiri Valley in Malawi, 1859–1960*. Madison: University of Wisconsin Press, 1990.

Meillassoux, Claude, ed. *The Development of Indigenous Trade and Markets in West Africa*. London: Oxford University Press for the International African Institute, 1971.

Netting, Robert M. *Hill Farmers of Nigeria: Cultural Ecology of the Kofyar of the Jos Plateau*. Seattle: University of Washington Press, 1968.

Ivan Karp
African Systems
of Thought

11

Africa has been perceived by some Westerners as a continent of peoples whose customs and manners are incomprehensible. Others, however, have argued that the thoughts of Africans are intelligible because their world and their perception of it are no different from our own. Most scholars usually try to steer an even course between the twin dangers of assuming that other peoples' beliefs are simply unintelligible to outsiders and that, at some level, all cultures are the same. The topic "African Systems of Thought" is studied by anthropologists, folklorists, historians, and specialists in comparative religions. Their task is not easy. It is somewhat akin to that of the historian who tries to discover what meaning to attribute to the actions and thoughts of the people of another time. A further complication arises because the languages, social organization, history, and environments of Africa are so different from our own. These differences are intensified by prevailing attitudes about other cultures. Westerners tend to think that technological achievements have given them command and control of the world and that all other societies should emulate them. When social scientists write in this way, it is called "modernization theory."

One final obstacle in the path of understanding the belief systems of African cultures is that it is very difficult to make generalizations about the continent. Both the highest and the lowest divorce rates in societies of the world are found there; the forms of political organization range from informal patterns of leadership in hunting and gathering bands to divine kings and bureaucratic states. The country of Tanzania alone has more than eighty different languages. African ways of making a living range from hunting and gathering, through complex agricultural systems using irrigation, to highly specialized craft industries. If such variations can be found in the "objective" circumstances of language, politics, social organization, and modes of livelihood, how different must be the products of the imagination, the ways that Africans have developed of understanding and thinking about their world and their lives?

This chapter will not try to make specific generalizations about the nature of African systems of thought that can be applied to all or even most African cultures. Instead it will use what has been called the "case study method," which looks at different circumstances and attempts to understand how Africans have tried to make sense out of their experience of nature and its vicissitudes, how the social organizations through which people relate to each other operate, and what kinds of problems societies pose for their members. This will finally lead to an examination of the theories about the world that Africans have developed both to explain their experience of nature and human existence and to express their feelings about that experience. This complex of thought and feeling is referred to as "African systems of thought" because scholars attempt to understand both the practical and the theoretical in African lives, including the recipes Africans have developed for living and the images through which they interpret their lives.

Attitudes to the World: What People Have in Common

There is nothing particularly new about trying to understand African systems of thought. The effort is one that the very first explorers made in Africa, often with mixed results. It is important to make that effort, however, because it represents the beginning of a dialogue which involves trying to think the thoughts other people think, and in their own language. Only thus can we begin to speak to each other.

One of the first to try to do this was the famous Scots medical missionary and explorer David Livingstone, who spent his adult life traveling throughout Central Africa. He is popularly known as the subject of Henry Stanley's relief expedition and the object of the famous inquiry "Dr. Livingstone, I presume?" He wrote wonderful books and diaries describing his explorations and experiences. In one of them he describes an encounter with what many Westerners might call a "witch doctor," probably of the "Bakwain" people of Malawi, whose task it was to heal the ill and bring the rain. In the most honest and revealing fashion, Livingstone exposes his own assumptions about the nature of African systems of thought and tells how his African colleague challenged them.

> *Medical Doctor.* Hail, friend! How very many medicines you have about you this morning! Why, you have every medicine in the country here.
> *Rain Doctor.* Very true, my friend; and I ought; for the whole country needs the rain which I am making.
> *M.D.* So you really believe that you can command the clouds? I think that can be done by God alone.
> *R.D.* We both believe the very same thing. It is God that makes the rain, but I pray to him by means of these medicines, and, the rain coming, of course it is then mine. It was I who made it for Bakwains for many years, when they were at Shokuane; through my wisdom, too, their women become fat and shining. Ask them; they will tell you the same as I do.
> *M.D.* But we are distinctly told in the parting words of our Savior that we can pray to God acceptably in His name alone, and not by means of medicines.
> *R.D.* Truly! but God told *us* differently. He made black men first, and did not love us as he did the white men. He made you beautiful, and gave you clothing, and guns, and

gunpowder, and horses, and wagons, and many other things about which we know nothing. But towards us he had no heart. He gave us nothing except the Assegai, and cattle, and rain-making; and he did not give us hearts like yours. We never love each other. Other tribes place medicines about our country to prevent the rain, so that we may be dispersed by hunger, and go to them, and augment their power. We must dissolve their charms by our medicines. God has given us one little thing which you know nothing of. He has given us the knowledge of certain medicines by which we can make rain. We do not despise those things which you possess, though we are ignorant of them. *We* don't understand your book, yet we don't despise it. *You* ought not to despise our little knowledge, though you are ignorant of it.

M.D. I don't despise what I am ignorant of; I only think you are mistaken in saying that you have medicines which can influence the rain at all.

R.D. That's just the way people speak when they talk on a subject of which they have no knowledge. When we first opened our eyes, we found our forefathers making rain, and we follow in their footsteps. You, who send to Kuruman for corn, and irrigate your garden, may do without rain; *we* cannot manage in that way. If we had not rain, the cattle would have no pasture, the cows give no milk, our children become lean and die, our wives run away to other tribes who do make rain and have corn, and the whole tribe become dispersed and lost; our fire would go out.

M.D. I quite agree with you as to the value of the rain; but you cannot charm the clouds by medicines. You wait till you see the clouds come, then you use your medicines, and take the credit which belongs to God only.

R.D. I use my medicines, and you employ yours; we are both doctors, and doctors are not deceivers. You give a patient medicine. Sometimes God is pleased to heal him by means of your medicine; sometimes not—he dies. When he is cured, you take the credit of what God does, I do the same. Sometimes God grants us rain, sometimes not. When he does, we take the credit of the charm. When a patient dies, you don't give up trust in your medicine, neither do I when rain fails. If you wish me to leave off my medicines, why continue your own?

M.D. I give medicine to living creatures within my reach, and can see the effects, though no cure follows; you pretend to charm the clouds, which are so far above us that your medicines never reach them. The clouds usually lie in one direction and your smoke goes in another. God alone can command the clouds. Only try and wait patiently; God will give us rain without your medicines.

R.D. Mahala-ma-kapa-a-a! Well, I always thought white men were wise till this morning. Who ever thought of making trial of starvation? Is death pleasant, then?

M.D. Could you make it rain on one spot and not on another?

R.D. I wouldn't think of trying. I like to see the whole country green, and all the people glad; the women clapping their hands, and giving me their ornaments for thankfulness, and lullilooing for joy.

M.D. I think you deceive both them and yourself.

R.D. Well, then, there is a pair of us (meaning both are rogues).

(Taken from M. Gluckman, Introduction to *The Allocation of Responsibility*, pp. xvii–xix)

What conclusions can be drawn from this exchange about the nature of African systems of thought, about their parallels with and differences from our own? The first lesson is that it is necessary to be very careful about how we compare other people with ourselves. It is conventional to think of non-Western societies as lacking in the advanced scientific knowledge that is so characteristic of recent Western intellectual history. But who are we talking about when we make such assertions? Surely most Westerners know as little about the workings of their computers as most Africans know about the forces that control the divination process to which they frequently have recourse. The knowledge of how things work is not something essential to everyday life, it is something we take on faith. All societies have experts who are credited with knowledge and the capacity to alter forces that seem beyond the control of ordinary people. This is the point at which valid comparisons between African systems of thought and Western modes of thinking can be made. What is important is that we understand how specialists and lay people in any society attempt to manage the world when it seems to be careening out of control, when misfortune intervenes adversely to affect expectations and desires.

Under consideration here is not the difference between scientific and nonscientific cultures, although a widespread Western belief is that science can solve all problems. Any consideration of such moral issues as the abuse of the environment and the termination of the life support of someone who has undergone brain death shows that science, or technology, always tends to create new unsolvable problems once it solves old ones. Instead, a careful comparison of African and Western cultures shows that they share in common spheres of concern with the limits on the controls people can hold over their social and natural environment and with how they can reassert control or influence their worlds. In both Western cultures and African cultures this set of questions and problems includes technology, morality, and belief. Hence the issues go beyond religion and areas of technology such as medicine and include questions about the nature of knowledge, moral issues such as who is to blame for what has gone wrong, and reflections about the ultimate ends often manifested in religious belief. Thus, the covering term "African systems of thought" is more appropriate for a discussion of such issues than is the more restricted idea of "African religions."

These are the questions and problems that animated the debate between Livingstone and the rain doctor presented above. Both were concerned with healing the ill, or at least consoling them. Both desired a social environment in which people behaved morally to each other and in which they could predict the forces of nature, and *both believed they had their science to help them in their goals.*

Are African systems of thought scientific, and what does it mean to say so? A very distinguished physicist and philosopher of science, Michael Polanyi, once compared witchcraft beliefs among the Azande of the Sudan to modern science and arrived at this surprising conclusion: "The process of selecting facts for our attention is indeed the same in science as among the Azande."[1] The process by which the cause for some misfortune is identified among the Azande has its Western parallels in the discovery of causes in science laboratories. An anthropologist who studied the Azande between 1926 and 1930, E. E. Evans-Pritchard, showed them to be very acute at testing hypotheses about the attribution of misfortunes ranging from illness and disease to disasters in the manufacture of crafts. They did this through their oracles, mystical entities that could find out the sources of events which ordinary people could not know. One such entity was the poison oracle, in which poison was administered to a chicken and a question put to it, such as "Why does my child have one illness after another? Is it because so-and-so is bewitching her/him?" If the chicken died, the answer was yes, and if it lived, the answer was no. Before the question was posed, a nonsense question was asked of the poison oracle, such as "Will I fly in the sky today?" The Azande believed that people do not fly in the sky unaided, so if the answer was yes, they knew something was wrong with the poison.

Those familiar with high-school science will be reminded here of hypothesis testing. This was precisely what the Azande did (and do) about their poison. If it showed itself to be ineffective, then the Azande knew it had been polluted, much as we believe that chemicals or medicines no longer work because of age or contamination. Both the Azande and the scientist usually throw out their contaminated substances and begin all over again. The great conclusion of Evans-Pritchard's pioneering study of this African system of thought was that differences between the Azande and Westerners were not differences in logic or thinking capacity. The Azande and other Africans reason much as people everywhere do. They also govern their lives with a mixture of skepticism and belief, and they have the same ambivalent and helplessly dependent faith in their specialists, their doctors.

Attitudes to the World: How People Differ

What are the differences, then? Anthropologists and other specialists who study African systems of thought cannot answer this question so easily, for a number of reasons. First, the comparisons that have been made are too often between Western specialists and African lay people. Only recently have whole systems begun to be compared. Second, parts of African systems of thought, such as witchcraft and sorcery or spirit possession, have been studied, but not the whole process of how people made sense of and managed their misfortunes. Third, and most important, Western systems of thought and practice are not subjected to the same scrutiny as are African systems, because Western systems have become commonplace to us. African thought, however, seems exotic to Western observers, because it is so different from their own. In the Western world of science and technology, it is no longer considered relevant to consult specialists about hidden reasons for such human disasters as catastrophic illness. In practice Western medical specialists are asked to comfort and explain as well as to heal, but they may not be as effective in these tasks as African practitioners are.

There are some differences which seem to emerge from a comparison, however, and these help to demonstrate how African systems of thought vary from place to place. Certainly one significant difference is a matter of emphasis. In African societies the causes of misfortune are often and usually related to personal circumstances and less to such impersonal agencies as "chance." This does not demonstrate that Africans have no idea of natural causation, as was so often asserted by early visitors and observers. Again, the Azande provide a good example. Evans-Pritchard explains that the Azande are skilled potters, famed for the elaborate pottery they make. When an Azande potter discovers that a series of pots have broken when fired in his kiln, an effort is made to find out what has gone wrong with the technological process. For example, perhaps some stones have been mixed with the clay. Only when no natural cause is readily discernible will the potter think about supernatural and personal causes, such as the actions of witches. Thus, while we might attribute misfortune in the absence of natural causes to such impersonal causes as "chance" or "bad luck," the Azande look to the actions of other, malevolent humans. These malevolent humans are motivated by greed and have within them, the Azande believe, a witchcraft substance, called *mangu*, which allows them to act supernaturally on other humans.

Of course, many people in the modern world believe in witches as well, but for the Azande all deaths are attributed to the actions of witches, or of sorcerers, who have no *mangu* but can manipulate poisons. The Azande consult their oracles to find out who these malevolent creatures are and what remedies exist against their actions. Not all societies of Africa are witch-ridden, however, and other personal causes of misfortune can be found in different African cultures at different times. Historians and anthropologists have only recently shown, for example, that beliefs in the power of witches can change within a society. Just as there have been witch crazes in Europe, so there are witch-hunts in African societies. At some points in time people believed that witches were rife among them, while at other points they thought that, while witches might exist, they were far more prevalent in other places. A major task for the historian or the anthropologist interested in African systems of thought is to find ways of understanding and explaining this variation.

Anthropologists and historians also describe the varieties of supernatural phenomena which are part of the unseen world of African cultures, such as witches and sorcerers, ghosts and shades of the dead, ancestral and nature spirits. They attempt to explain how these entities relate to one another and how Africans interpret their experience of the supernatural world and their place in it. Since this mix can vary from time to time and place to place, it is not really possible to generalize. What may be true for East African pastoralists may not apply to peoples such as the Yoruba, who live in large towns and have complex forms of political organization such as sacred kingship.

Another major contrast is the degree to which Western systems of thought emphasize technology. In recent history, belief in an all-powerful technology has been central to Western optimism and to the idea of progress. This attitude persists, although questions are now being raised as to whether technology does in fact affect our environment for the better. African systems of thought, on the other hand, tend to show a concern for the control of people, not the environment; there is a personalistic quality about African ways of imagining the world. Anthropologist Mary Douglas asserts that for Africans, it is a "practical interest in living and not an academic interest in metaphysics which has produced these beliefs." "Technological problems," she tells us, "have been more or less settled for generations past."[2] This should not be taken to mean that Africans are unconcerned with the very conditions of their existence. They do have ideas of natural causation. Anyone who knows about the periodic and increasingly severe droughts that plague Africa will realize that it would be sheer madness to believe that Africans are unconcerned with controlling their environment. The dialogue between Dr. Livingstone and the rain doctor shows a real interest in regularizing the natural forces through which people gain their living and reproduce their societies. The failure of rains can lead to starvation and death for people who are immediately dependent on the produce of the land and on herds of animals.

Africans do not expect to alter the conditions of their lives by changing the environment through technological change. They have a real and immediate sense of the effect that the environment can bring about. African rituals and beliefs are filled with images of natural forces. For example, African divine kings are intimately associated with the course of nature. The Shilluk of Sudan assert that their king must die if he becomes imperfect or senile. While no one knows for sure whether the Shilluk have ever killed their king, it is clear that they believe that his failing health dramatically affects the course of nature in the most unfortunate way.[3]

This view of the world does not include the ability to alter nature. The best that may be hoped for is to influence the effects of nature in particular instances. With regard to African systems of thought, there are two important conclusions to be drawn from the attitudes about nature and technology that they manifest. First, there is an acute awareness of the effects of the environment on people. In most African societies, as in much of the world where medical care is unavailable, the rate of infant mortality in the first year can approach 50 percent. The Iteso of Kenya have special naming systems for children born to a mother after an infant has died. These children have special rituals associated with them, and they are named after the intrusive animals and plants of the forest and plains who invade Iteso homes and destroy their crops and animals. Thus children can be called *etyang* ("animal"), *emoto* ("hyena"), or *emodo* ("striga weed," a weed that is impossible to eradicate and which destroys fields of grain). More than half of all Iteso have names like these. People can tell you that they name their children this way in order to ward off the very destructive forces that killed their other children and endanger their livelihood and lives.[4]

This does not indicate, however, that the Iteso or other Africans think they can change nature itself. To think so would be foolish in light of the limited means at their disposal for controlling their environment. They do believe, however, that they can influence how the environment affects them, because they believe that the effect of the environment on particular lives is conditioned by the actions of other people, particularly evil people such as witches and sorcerers. Thus, Africans see their problems as deriving from their failure to control not technology but other people. Such control involves an attempt to identify other peoples' intentions and dispositions. What is it about them or their world that makes them do the things to others that they do? This is a dual issue. It is a problem of indigenous psychology, the theory held by the people of a society of what motivates and moves people. It is also a problem of moral and ethical judgments; it addresses questions of good and evil. Africans are involved in the task of identifying people who are unredeemable as well as the features that make them so.

Finally, this world view also addresses questions of fate, seeking answers to the question "Why me?" This is the stuff out of which Africans fashion their systems of thought. The remainder of this chapter will consider different solutions from very different settings. The emphasis throughout will be on African ideas of how the environment can be controlled through the control of people.

How People Try to Control Their Social Environments

The Tallensi of Ghana are an agricultural people who earn their living through growing, and sometimes selling, foodstuffs. The major inputs in their agricultural production are land and labor. They live in local communities organized around a core of members of the same patrilineage. The people who compose the lineage hold their land jointly, not individually, support one another in everyday life, and provide essential personnel for the performance of the rituals that occur during life crises as well as in worship for their ancestors. Tallensi households are organized around a household head, his married sons and their wives and children, and his unmarried children. In Tallensi society, men are defined as jural minors so long as their fathers remain alive. Thus a man may be a middle-aged adult with grown children and still be a child in the eyes of the larger society. What does this state of affairs actually entail? What does it mean to be a jural minor?

For the Tallensi it indicates a number of things. Lineages, not individuals, own land. Rights to use this land are allocated through the senior living male of a lineage segment. For a middle-aged Tallensi, this person could easily be his father or, if his father is dead, his father's younger brother. Since the Tallensi can have polygynous marriages, it is possible for the father's younger brother to be younger than the son. Thus seniority is a matter of kinship position and not relative age. Only after all the males of the father's generation have passed away are the men of the next generation allowed to assume their full place in society.

Among the Tallensi, fathers age and sons grow impatient waiting to be full members of society and to realize their full potential. Sometimes the sons align themselves with other groups in the society to realize their goal of independence. When this happens, illness or some other form of misfortune can strike. The case of Pu-Eng-Yii, described by Meyer Fortes, the ethnographer of the Tallensi, illustrates this point. Pu-Eng-Yii was succeeding financially by associating himself with another lineage when he was hit by a truck in an accident. When diviners were consulted, it was discovered that the ancestors of his lineage were angry at his failure to perform rituals for them, and he was forced to give up what Fortes calls his "commercial advantage" and return to live under the control of his lineage kin. This case illustrates the implications of the lack of full jural status in Tallensi society. To be a jural minor means being unable to perform rituals for the ancestors and having to have someone else intercede with them on your behalf. In the case of Pu-Eng-Yii, the senior members of the lineage whose demands he was ignoring were the only persons who could intercede on his behalf with the ancestors.[5]

Herein is the paradox of Tallensi society. It is a social world in which privilege is given to seniority, as is common throughout Africa. At the same time, the seniors are dependent on their juniors. They need them to do the agricultural and household tasks which they can no longer perform. Even though Tallensi society has no formal legal sanctions for senior members of lineages to invoke when they are in need, they do have the backing of the cult of the ancestors to help them recruit and control junior members of their lineage. Not only is access to capital goods controlled by the lineage, but Tallensi beliefs about and efforts to control misfortune in the world put all Tallensi under the control of their ancestors. Among the Tallensi the ancestors, rather than witches, are generally regarded as the agents of misfortune. The Tallensi believe in witches but are one of those African societies who think of them as unimportant in their lives.

What must be stressed here is the element of social control. In societies small in scale, such as the Tallensi, social relations are "multiplex," that is, they tend to have many strands to them. The adult male's father is not only his father, he is also the head of the household in which the adult son lives, the manager of the family estate through which the son makes a living, and, finally, the head of the cult of the ancestors. All of these strands thus come together in a single relationship. The result is that senior Tallensi are able to exercise considerable control over their juniors. The autonomy available to many Tallensi is limited by the complex and intense nature of their social relationships. This is the very model of the small-scale society, and perhaps is responsible for the tensions that are so characteristic of it.

The Barotse (or Lozi) of Zambia have a song that expresses the paradox of social relations in a small-scale society:

> He who kills me, who will it be but my kinsman?
> He who succours me, who will it be but my kinsman?[6]

The people with whom an individual comes into conflict are the same people who are bound by ties of kinship to offer aid in a crisis. These conflicting strands are characteristic of social relations in small-scale societies. Ideas about good and evil usually develop around these sources of tension and control. It is not surprising, therefore, that in many African societies the person most often identified as a witch is also kin. Senior elders do not always escape accusation. Among the Gisu of Uganda, the elder is most often thought to be a witch. Gisu society is short of land and has a very high population density. Although somewhat like the Tallensi in social structure, the Gisu's cult of the ancestors is not used to control the actions of younger men. Instead, young men are often accused of theft and disrespect. Among the Gisu that is a very bad crime, which shows that the person who commits it is a "bad lot," not fit to live in society. Chronic thieves are often killed on the grounds that their character is so flawed that they are unredeemably evil. But it is senior men who get the young accused of thievery. After a life of doing so much damage to others, these men tend to be accused of witchcraft. Among the Gisu the same emotional quality (*lirima*) that marks the character of a thief makes a witch as well. The Gisu see both witches and thieves as having such an excess of this disposition that they are ultimately uncontrollable. Hence, ideas about the makeup of persons are also part of African systems of thought and can differ from our own. In the case of the Gisu there is no distinction, as might be drawn by Westerners, between secular and supernatural crimes. Paradoxically, a career of controlling others can put that person into the category of being so evil as to be uncontrollable.[7] This is also true for the Tiv of Nigeria, who have periodic witch-hunts, in which elders are accused of being witches and of killing off their juniors. These witch-hunts have been called "extra-processual events" because they opened up positions of authority in a nonstandardized manner.[8]

The absence of autonomy in small-scale societies is not always or entirely a disadvantage. The opposite of the multiplex rural relationship is the "simplex" urban one in which two people have no knowledge of each other. This type of relationship has a great deal of autonomy associated with it. A characteristic feature of such a relationship is that the parties involved have no expectation of future interaction or any knowledge of the other person. Under such circumstances people can do what they like to each other without much fear of retaliation, especially when their actions are unobserved and there is no means of tracing an offender. Thus "simplex" behavior is often uncontrolled. The problem is that when autonomy is associated with no control at all, it can also carry with it fear. This is one of the reasons that urban environments are often believed to be so frightening. The persons one meets are unknown and unknowable, hence uncontrollable. What happens in situations such as these is that people develop ways of explaining and predicting their urban experience. In America this has been related to the emphasis on ethnic characterizations. To label people "Jews," "Blacks," or "Anglos" is to give them characters and personalities and to stereotype them in the absence of any direct personal knowledge. American society is characterized by a high rate of social and spatial mobility, by relatively unimportant kinship relations, and by the expectation that many friendships will not last. As a result, many social relationships tend to be simplex and are defined in stereotypic terms.

In African urban settings, ideas about the causes of misfortune are changing. In urban Zambia, for example, misfortune is now less often attributed to the action of witches than it would be in the rural setting from which the people come. Resource to witchcraft as an explanation implies that the evildoer can be reached and is known.[9] Personal agents are no longer found to be the cause of illness. Thus Africans' ideas about the nature of their fate are also related to the social setting in which people find themselves.

This is true not only of occult beliefs such as witchcraft. Many of the entities often described as "tribes" are the creation of the colonial period. Many of the societies who now call themselves by one name did not previously exist. The Abaluyia people of Kenya, for example, were a mixture of ethnic groups speaking mutually unintelligible languages, having origins from different parts of East Africa, and with many different customs. After the establishment of the "Kenya colony," Christian missionaries among these people decided to use only one of their languages as a standard. As the Abaluyia moved to the European-owned farms of the Kenya highlands as labor migrants or to live in cities, they found themselves associating on the basis of common origins and beginning to think of themselves as one people. This became the basis for a colonial political party, the Kenya African Democratic Union. Now there is an Abaluyia literature, an Abaluyia culture, and in many urban and national settings, an Abaluyia sense of identity.

Kenya is in fact now composed of many peoples whose collective identity is recent. They think of themselves as one people in some settings and as a different people in others. Thus in a western Kenya setting in which Abaluyia identity is irrelevant, those Abaluyia who also call themselves Babukusu regard themselves as very different from the Abaluyia who call themselves Wanga. The development of new forms of identity has also had a parallel in the development of new ideas about the nature of persons called "Abaluyia," "Kikuyu," "Swahili," and so on. A young man in Nairobi recently described to the author all the character traits of the Kenyan "tribes" to which he did not belong. His stereotyping included such unattractive features as "cowardice," "dishonesty," and "unreliability." In this respect some aspects of African systems of thought, especially in an urban context, are becoming increasingly like those found in Western society.

Conclusion

What this overview has attempted to show is that African systems of thought are intimately related to how Africans experience their world, and to the means they formulate to understand and control it. In this sense African systems of thought are both theoretical and practical. The systems of belief and of knowledge found in African societies are not based on metaphysical speculations divorced from everyday life. Yet African knowledge cannot be reduced to the codification of common sense. African systems of thought include a speculative element in their practical orientation; they explain *and* provide recipes for action. Nor are African systems of thought irrelevant for people living beyond their local communities. In universities and in black townships, in local cult groups, in churches, and in departments of philosophy, Africans are often engaged in the task of making sense of their current position and future predicaments. If they do not find their inherited wisdom adequate for managing the complexities of the contemporary scene, they have also found that the wisdom of the West posits solutions that fit badly with the problems they face.

Individuals such as spiritual leaders, artists specializing in the knowledge of oral traditions, and community elders have always been the repositories and the formulators of African systems of thought. In addition, new figures, such as novelists, scholars, and political leaders, will add their contribution. A major change has been the emergence of a body of specialists who see themselves as the self-conscious critics and formulators of African systems of thought. The social role of African intellectuals and artists is now of importance both at home and in an international setting. Perhaps a major change in African systems of thought is the degree to which they may become part of the continuing dialogue between Africans and the West.

NOTES

1. Cited in Max Gluckman's introduction to *The Allocation of Responsibility* (Manchester: Manchester University Press, 1972), p. xvi.

2. Mary Douglas, *Purity and Danger* (London: Routledge and Kegan Paul, 1966), pp. 89, 91.

3. E. E. Evans-Pritchard, *The Divine Kingship of the Shilluk of the Nilotic Sudan* (Cambridge: Cambridge University Press, 1958), and W. Arens, "The Divine Kingship of the Shilluk: A Contemporary Evaluation," *Ethos* (1979): 168–81.

4. Ivan and Patricia Karp, "Living with the Spirits of the Dead," in *African Therapeutic Systems*, ed. D. M. Warren et al. (Boston: Crossroads Press, 1979).

5. Meyer Fortes, *Oedipus and Job in West African Religions* (Cambridge: Cambridge University Press, 1985).

6. Max Gluckman, "Moral Crises: Magical and Secular Solutions," in *The Allocation of Responsibility* (Manchester: Manchester University Press, 1972), p. 5.

7. Suzette Heald, "The Making of Men," *Africa* 52 (1982): 15–35, and "The Killing of Witches and Thieves," *Man* (1986).

8. Paul Bohannan, "Extra-processual Events in Tiv Political Institutions," in Simon and Phoebe Ottenberg, eds., *Cultures and Societies of Africa* (New York: Random House, 1960).

9. J. Clyde Mitchell, "The Meaning of Misfortune for Urban Africans," in M. Fortes and G. Dieterlen, eds., *African Systems of Thought* (London: International African Institute, 1967).

SUGGESTIONS FOR FURTHER READING

Douglas, Mary. *Purity and Danger*. London: Routledge and Kegan Paul, 1966.

Evans-Pritchard, E. E. *Witchcraft, Oracles and Magic among the Azande*. Oxford: Clarendon Press, 1937.

Fortes, Meyer. *Oedipus and Job in West African Religion*. [1959] Cambridge: Cambridge University Press, 1985.

Gluckman, Max, ed. *The Allocation of Responsibility*. Manchester: Manchester University Press, 1972.

Heald, Suzette. "The Making of Men." *Africa* 52 (1982): 15–35.

Karp, Ivan, and Charles Bird, eds. *Explorations in African Systems of Thought*. Bloomington: Indiana University Press, 1980.

Karp, Ivan, and Patricia Karp. "Living with the Spirits of the Dead." In D. M. Warren et al., eds., *African Therapeutic Systems*. Boston: Crossroads Press, 1979.

Mitchell, J. Clyde. "The Meaning of Misfortune for Urban Africans." In M. Fortes and G. Dieterlen, eds., *African Systems of Thought*. London: International African Institute, 1965.

Patrick R. McNaughton and Diane Pelrine
African Art

12 To many viewers, African art seems full of paradoxes. It plays many important roles in the lives of individuals and the activities of societies. Yet it is often used only on specific occasions, and so is far less visible than the paintings and sculptures that Westerners can see in museums or urban public spaces. Much African art is sculpture made of wood, but frequently it is made of clay, cloth, or even basketry, materials that are associated with craft in the West. While much African art takes the form of stationary sculptures, shrines, and other types of buildings, very frequently it takes the form of masks, masquerade costumes, staffs, fly whisks, or ceremonial wands that are all intended to be seen in very active contexts of motion and dance. Often, too, these artworks can be experienced fully only when they are accompanied by musical ensembles such as xylophones and drums, guitars and harps, flutes and horns, and female and male singers. African art is often characterized as practical and functional, but it also has refined aesthetic principles, which many Africans use to evaluate it. Finally, much African art is dedicated to portraying and interacting with spiritual beings and properties. Thus, to study African art is also to experience new situations and new points of view.

Westerners have collected and studied African art for many centuries. One of the earliest examples brought to Europe arrived before 1650 (plate 41), and Louis XIV (1643–1715) had a modest collection of West African sculpture, as did various other European rulers, business persons, and travelers. By the beginning of the twentieth century, much African art had reached Europe, and it strongly influenced art history, beginning with German Expressionism and Cubism.

The study of African art has changed drastically over time. For centuries, Europeans viewed it as the exotic production of strange societies, which did not warrant much explanation. Not until the twentieth century was it seen to reflect aspects of African social, spiritual, and political organization, although the basis for contextual information was minimal. As the twentieth century progressed, especially since the 1960s, art historians and anthropologists have developed increasingly sophisticated approaches to learning about and understanding African art's subtleties and complexities. Now, a growing body of work by scholars from Africa and elsewhere is revealing the many ways that individuals and groups use art to create better lives for themselves, their families, their political affiliates, and their communities.

Many scholars divide African art broadly into traditional and contemporary, though they disagree about the exact definition of each. "Traditional" generally refers to art, such as masks or ancestor figures, used in local contexts that existed before colonialism, while "contemporary" refers to art that is believed to be based to a large extent on Western influences. Contemporary art includes tourist art, objects for sale to travelers looking for mementos of their time spent abroad. It also encompasses popular art, a primarily urban art that includes business signs, decorated public transportation, murals, and smaller paintings that consist of popular imagery such as local market scenes, exotic animals, and foreign characters such as Mickey Mouse and Michael Jackson (see chapter 14). Finally, "contemporary" includes fine art made by those who have received Western art training and who create for an international art market.

However, it is somewhat misleading to label some art "traditional" and other art "contemporary." Art is used in many different African settings that relate to the social, political, economic, and spiritual situations that engage people. These situations have always been in flux, as new states and empires evolved, as new trade relations and products developed, as local religions adopted new practices or beliefs, and as people moved to new areas to make better lives for themselves. African art has always been changing in response to these varying situations. Many "contemporary" artworks use "traditional" subjects or styles, drawing upon the beliefs and activities that character-ize people's social or spiritual lives. At the same time, many "traditional" artworks are also contemporary because they play upon and influence the ever-changing situations that people encounter in daily life.

For example, in small towns around the countryside in many parts of Africa today, masquerades with elaborate costumes and carved wooden masks are performed for ceremonies of social and religious institutions. Such activities may have taken place for many centuries, but the masks and costumes change, the intent of the ceremonies is transformed, and the people bring their personal situations into play as they participate in and interpret the festivities (see chapter 9). In large urban centers, painters and sculptors who make art to sell to foreigners or the local elite may seem inspired by Western approaches and materials, but they also partake deeply of their own culture's ideas and points of view.

Most foreign collectors have always favored masks and figures. These come primarily from two large regions: the area around the Niger and Benue rivers in West Africa and the Zaire River basin in Central Africa. But nonfigural arts are the primary visual art traditions for many African peoples, particularly those of eastern and southern Africa. The Maasai, a pastoral people who live in Kenya and Tanzania, for example, do not make masks or figures for their own use; however, they are known worldwide for their beautiful and innovative beaded jewelry (plate 42). In addition to dress and body decoration, the nonfigural arts include furniture, such as stools and neckrests, other household objects, including ceramic vessels and baskets, and even weapons—things which the West often places in the category of "crafts." These arts are also found in the areas that produce figural sculpture, creating a rich, complex array of visual traditions in many parts of the continent. In fact, for most people, nonfigural arts are far more common and seen far more frequently than masks and figures, which may be viewed only on certain occasions or by particular people.

Style and Ethnicity

African art is most often classified according to its style or appearance. Throughout much of the scholarly literature, specific styles are associated with particular ethnic groups. Elaborate scarification carved in relief on a figure's face, neck, and body, for example, is one element of the sculptural style that is associated with the Lulua of Zaire (plate 43). But many ethnic groups, such as the Igbo in Nigeria and the Bamana in Mali, make art in more than one style, which may differ substantially from one another. In addition, ethnic boundaries are often not clear, and this is true not just around the margins of the territory the group inhabits. Frequently, groups simply share large portions of their space with other groups, and a great deal of interaction takes place, from friendships and intermarriage to complementary use of land through farming and grazing and joint business ventures. The arts of people who live in such situations can reflect all this interaction, so that it is often difficult and sometimes impossible to know the ethnic origins of a particular artwork. Furthermore, artists from one ethnic group sometimes create artworks for others, making the origins of artworks even less clear.

Foreign scholars frequently give ethnicity too much credit for determining people's thoughts and actions. Ethnic groups in Africa are certainly important, and in some parts of the continent they are a major component of people's identity. But in many more areas of Africa, ethnic affiliation is not as important as the networks of clans that constitute ethnic groups or the networks of clans and ethnic groups that constitute cultures. Ethnicity is also flexible and sometimes ambiguous. People can change ethnic affiliations, and sometimes even claim to be members of different ethnic groups for different social and professional situations.

Art is no more stuck in ethnicity than are people. Because people frequently travel, and long-distance commerce and expansionistic politics are so much a part of African history, the forms, ideas, and functions of art are often highly mobile and interactive. Numerous ethnic groups share many types of art, and often the appearance and functions of specific examples are very similar. Figural sculptures with medicinal attachments are a good example. These figures range from Nigeria and Cameroon across Zaire and into Angola to the south and Tanzania to the east (plate 44). The huge horizontal masks, found from the Atlantic Ocean in Guinea to central Nigeria near Lake Chad, are another excellent example (plate 45). In each case a single kind of art traverses thousands of miles.

Ownership of artworks is sometimes complex. In some cases, individual owner-ship is clearly apparent. In Mali, for instance, carved wooden door locks secure people's private rooms. They are often sculpted into abstract animals or people, and some owners interpret the images as special, sometimes magical characters in the history of their clans. Elsewhere, though, an object may be owned by a family or clan instead of an individual. Along the Swahili coast of East Africa, Zaramo girls are given abstract miniature female figures during the period of seclusion that marks their initiation into womanhood. When not in use, such a figure is kept by a senior woman on the paternal side of the family. She does not own the figure, but rather holds it in trust as an important family heirloom. In still other cases, religious or social associations or even entire communities "own" artworks, with priests or leaders in charge of their safekeeping. Such is the case, for example, with large Kongo power figures (plate 46), which belonged to whole communities. Like smaller ones which were owned individually, the large ones served as mediators between the physical and spiritual worlds.

Materials and Techniques

Wood is clearly the medium most often associated with African art. It is carved into a variety of objects, from utilitarian stools, neckrests, and containers to the more familiar masks and figures. To Westerners accustomed to art that was created to be permanent, wood may seem to be a poor choice of material, given the climate and insects in most of Africa. With few exceptions, however, objects were not meant to last indefinitely. Instead, their making was grounded in a belief that renewal was to be not only expected but also desired.

Among many peoples, particular kinds of wood are customarily chosen for carving certain objects. For example, the Mijikenda of Kenya use certain termite-resistant acacia trees to make anthropomorphic posts. These posts commemorate important deceased male relatives and are placed in the ground, exposed to the elements, until they fall down and decay. Among the Lulua of Zaire, figures associated with fertility (plate 43) are made from a tree considered both sacred and symbolic of beauty.

The traditional tool of the African carver is the adze, an implement that differs from the axe in having its blade perpendicular, rather than parallel, to the handle. Although this tool seems awkward to foreigners, in the hands of a practiced carver, forms can be blocked out and refined with amazing speed. After carving, some objects are painted. Originally, locally made vegetal and mineral pigments were used, though today factory-made enamel paint is often preferred for its brilliant color and greater permanence.

Though wood is the material most often used, an equally important material for traditional artists is iron. A blacksmith's work is sometimes an end in itself, as with Bamana and Dogon blacksmiths, who are known for their beautiful iron lamps and staffs, for example. More often, however, their products enable other things to be done: fields to be farmed with iron hoes, wood to be carved with iron-bladed tools. In the hands of a master smith, even these seemingly mundane implements can attain a beauty of form and workmanship that places them above the ordinary.

Other metals, particularly gold and copper-based alloys, are prestige materials:

their use generally signifies wealth or importance in the religious or political sphere. This was the case, for instance, in the West African kingdom of Benin, where brass was the prerogative of royalty, and altars honoring deceased kings displayed brass sculpture, such as commemorative heads (plate 47).

Elephant ivory, which was carved into horns, whistles (plate 48), jewelry, containers, and charms, was also a prestige material. In many parts of the continent, the elephant, because of its strength and power, was associated with leadership, making objects carved from tusks especially appropriate insignia of political power.

Traditional African art in clay includes not only bowls, pots, and other vessels, which are sometimes decorated with sculptural anthropomorphic forms, but also freestanding figures. Like metal, it is nonperishable, and terra-cotta figures from Nok, Nigeria (plate 49), are the oldest sculptural tradition that has been discovered south of the Sahara. Most ceramics are more utilitarian vessels, however, formed by hand, using coil and slab methods; the pottery wheel was not used in sub-Saharan Africa until missionaries and colonials brought it to some areas with the hopes of developing small-scale industry. As plastic and enamel containers have become widely available, pottery making has decreased in many areas.

Cloth is woven from local cotton, wool, and silk, and from imported fibers, such as rayon. Most fabric is strip-woven; that is, strips of cloth, ranging from a few inches to two feet in width, are woven on a loom and then sewn together to make a large rectangle. Woven patterns (plate 50), painting, stamping, resist dyeing, embroidery, and appliqué are all used to make African cloth among the most beautiful, complex, and colorful in the world. Factory cloth, made all over the continent, is also popular. Printed images may commemorate special occasions and, particularly in East Africa, often include proverbs, combining verbal and visual arts.

Unlike Western artists, African sculptors have not used stone extensively. We can identify only about half a dozen areas (in Nigeria, Sierra Leone, Guinea, Zaire, Zimbabwe, and Ethiopia) where stone sculpture was carved in quantity. None of those traditions continues to the present day. However, in at least one of these areas, Zimbabwe, stone carving has been successfully revived for the art and tourist markets.

Traditional arts are predominantly three-dimensional, so we find relatively few examples of painting. The Dogon of Mali paint sacred symbols on rock which are said to encapsulate important aspects of their ethos, as do Sukuma associations of snake handlers and snakebite curers in Tanzania, and other groups across the continent. Stunning designs are painted on the facades of homes from Burkina Faso to Cameroon and South Africa. Aside from decorating sculpture, however, paint, sometimes in elaborate patterns, is commonly used to decorate the human body, not only for beauty but also to indicate important social and spiritual transitions.

Artists

In sub-Saharan Africa, certain media and techniques are associated, at least traditionally, with each gender. Metalworking and carving, whether in wood, ivory, or stone, are the domains of men in virtually all societies. One exception is among the

Turkana of Kenya, where women make wooden cooking and serving pots that are among the most elegant bowl forms in the world. Pottery is generally considered a woman's art, and in some societies, the potters are most likely to be the wives of blacksmiths. Again, of course, there are exceptions, such as among certain groups in eastern Nigeria, where women make pots for food and water, while men make anthropomorphic ritual vessels used in divination and healing.

Weaving is practiced by men or women, depending upon the area and the loom type. In parts of West Africa, men weave very long, narrow strips of cloth on horizontal looms (plate 51), while women in the same areas use broader vertical looms to make much wider panels of cloth (plate 52). In Central Africa, however, men weave raffia cloth on a vertical loom, while in Madagascar, off the coast of East Africa, women use horizontal backstrap looms.

Whatever their gender, African artists, like artists worldwide, undergo training and are recognized in their chosen fields. This statement belies a common stereotype about African art, which is completely false, as are so many stereotypes: namely, that the objects on display in museums were made by anonymous, untutored men and women. Rather than reflecting anything about the true situation in Africa, this stereotype tells us more about Western prejudices and misconceptions.

First, most traditional African art is anonymous outside the continent only because collectors did not consider it important to record the artists' names. In most cases within the African setting, artists are remembered, in the case of both ritual objects, such as shrine figures, and utilitarian objects such as stools. The work of a specific artist may also be recognized beyond village boundaries. Truly great artists can develop such reputations that people travel great distances to acquire objects made by them.

Second, the myth of the untutored artist may fit very nicely with romantic Western ideas about the "noble savage," but a careful examination of the objects reveals a sophisticated understanding of materials, techniques, and composition. In many cases, training is informal, carried out in the context of everyday activities. Until recently, for example, Zaramo women in Tanzania were expected, as part of their household duties, to plait the baskets and mats needed by their families for daily living. Basketry was a skill, along with cooking and housekeeping, that girls learned from their mothers or other female relatives, and those who excelled became known for their fine work.

In other cases, training is a formal apprenticeship, sometimes lasting several years. Among the Bamana, for example, blacksmiths are also the woodcarvers, and smithing is a hereditary occupation. By the time a young boy officially begins his apprenticeship, he will already have spent many hours at his father's forge, observing and performing small tasks. His formal apprenticeship may last as long as seven or eight years, as he learns first to work the bellows, then to carve wood, and finally to forge iron.

For most artists, creating art is not a full-time occupation. All over the continent, most people earn their livelihoods through farming, and artists are no exception. Instead, carving, smithing, pottery making, and weaving are all seen as ways to supplement a family's income. Of course, famous artists may be able to earn enough money to make it worthwhile for other family members to shoulder additional farming responsibilities, leaving the artists free to devote more time to their art.

Artists may build up stocks of utilitarian objects, which they sell from their homes or take to market, but masks, figures, and the most prestigious utilitarian objects are likely to be made on individual order. Clients may explain in detail what they want, they may specify the type of object and leave the details up to the artist, or artist and client may negotiate the specifics of a commission.

Art and History

The older the art, the harder it is to know very much about it. This is particularly true for Africa, where many art forms are highly perishable, written documentation is infrequent, and archaeology is an expensive undertaking, not always considered as important as a country's other pressing problems. Thus, our knowledge of ancient African art is patchy and incomplete.

The oldest known arts are paintings and engravings on the walls of caves and shelters in what is now the Sahara Desert and in southern Africa (see chapters 3 and 4). The Saharan paintings have been dated from the mid-sixth millennium B.C. to the first millennium B.C.; those from southwestern Africa may be much older. These are marvelous images of animals and scenes of hunting and spiritual or social ceremonies. The Saharan paintings also record the coming of the horse and camel to the continent, as well as the ancient use of masks. These paintings are generally considered to reflect beliefs about the world, but there is very little evidence to elaborate further.

Architecture must also be included among the arts for which a long history is evident. In southern Africa between A.D. 1000 and 1500, the civilization now known as Great Zimbabwe developed complex networks of production and trade, a ruling elite, and a complex and beautifully constructed system of stone block architecture, which was used to create several regional centers. Remains of city and mosque architecture, cut from coral masonry blocks and dating from the same time or earlier, are also found along the East African Swahili coast. Also from around the same time, or possibly earlier, are Ethiopian Christian churches. They were created by beginning on top of flat rock and painstakingly carving down and into the stone to create intricate facades, interiors, and large moatlike spaces around the four sides.

West Africa is best known for its clay brick architecture. The Songhai empire spawned some remarkable examples, including the thick, sinuous-walled mosque at Tendirma, dated to A.D. 1497, and the massive tomb of Askia Muhammed, who ruled from A.D. 1493 to 1529. This monument contrasts solid, interacting geometric shapes with huge, irregular timbers that emerge horizontally from the clay surface to serve simultaneously as structural reinforcement and permanent scaffolding. The famous Sankore mosque of Timbuktu and a beautiful mosque in Katsina, Nigeria, may also date from the 1500s. One of the advantages of clay brick architecture is that it can be abandoned and allowed to crumble slowly back into earth, or it can be regularly refurbished to last almost indefinitely.

The oldest sculpture we know from Africa is also made of clay, and dates from 500 B.C. to A.D. 500 (plate 49). It comes from northern Nigeria, from a society (or societies—our knowledge is incomplete) scholars have dubbed the Nok culture, after a town where much of the sculpture was found. The makers were well versed in iron technology and were probably involved in large-scale commerce and political enterprises. Aspects of the sculpture, particularly the large bundles of beads represented on many figures, suggest that some of the sculpture represented leaders.

The relative simplicity of Nok terra-cottas contrasts sharply with the elaborate metalwork dating to the ninth century A.D. at the site of Igbo Ukwu in southeastern Nigeria. There, large quantities of remarkable cast brass sculpture were found in a shrine and a burial. Apparently made by the ancestors of today's Igbo people, many of these pieces, which included animals, human heads, and replicas of objects such as shells and calabashes, were thickly textured with detail. It is believed that this art was dedicated to the workings of a complex, widespread, and powerful spiritual-political organization.

Leadership in ancient Nigeria seems to have been an effective combination of statecraft and spiritual capabilities, in which art played a prominent role. South of the Nok area and west of Igbo Ukwu, a complex, loose, and constantly competing confederacy of city-states grounded in commerce and expansionistic ambition emerged as early as the late first millennium B.C. The self-proclaimed hub of these polities was Ife, which between the eleventh and fifteenth centuries A.D. sponsored spectacular leadership arts in clay and brass. In shrines, terra-cotta heads, quite possibly representing actual leaders, were an extremely subtle combination of naturalism and idealized abstraction (plate 53). Brass casters, using expert technique and the same approach to realism, made life-size and nearly life-size portrait heads of leaders that were used in burial ceremonies (plate 54). Clay animals and clay and brass figures of leaders and highly abstract iron staffs were also used in intricate networks of ritual and ceremony for the enhancement of the state.

Later, in the same general area, the kingdom of Benin flourished from the fifteenth century until the British defeated it in 1897. Benin art shows us how rich and multifaceted art in service of the state can be. In addition to the commemorative heads (plate 47) that we have already noted, brass was also cast into animals, figures of court officials, and ancestral bells and staffs. These were set on altars dedicated to maintaining the passage of knowledge, power, and authority through generations of leaders. In addition, walls of the royal palace were covered with brass plaques (plate 55) containing in their imagery spiritual, historical, and procedural information about the state. Extremely elaborate beaded regalia topped with brass and ivory ornaments was reserved for leaders. Much Benin art, pillaged after Britain's attack, was auctioned in Europe, and it played an important role in opening the eyes of Western artists to the power of African creativity.

Because of historical events such as the British looting of Benin, and much archaeology, the ancient arts of Nigeria have been the most extensively studied.

Plate 41. Divination tray collected at Ardra (Porto-Novo) before 1650. Wood.
City Museum, Ulm, Germany.
Photo courtesy Ulmer Museum.

Plate 42. Maasai woman with an
accumulation of jewelry.
Photo courtesy C. Zagourski.

Plate 43. Standing figure. Lulua, Zaire. 19th century. Wood. H. 17 in.
Wielgus Collection, Indiana University Art Museum.
Photo by Michael Cavanagh and Kevin Montague.

Plate 44. Power figure, Songye, Zaire. Wood, iron, fiber, cowrie shells, snakeskin, hair, incrustation. H. 12 1/2 in. Wielgus Collection, Indiana University Art Museum.
Photo by Michael Cavanagh and Kevin Montague.

Plate 45. Komo mask, Bamana, Mali. Wood, horns, quills, feathers, fiber, animal hair, incrustation. L. 27 in. Indiana University Art Museum.
Photo by Michael Cavanagh and Kevin Montague.

Plate 46. Power figure, Kongo, Zaire. Wood, iron, pigment. H. 40 1/2 in. Indiana University Art Museum.
Photo by Michael Cavanagh and Kevin Montague.

Plate 47.
    Commemorative head,
    Kingdom of Benin, Nigeria.
    Middle period (16th–17th century).
    Brass. H. 11 1/4 in.
    Indiana University Art Museum.
    Photo by Michael Cavanagh and
    Kevin Montague.

Plate 48.
    Whistle, Pende, Zaire. 19th century.
    Ivory. H. 4 1/2 in.
    Grunwald collection.
    Photo by Michael Cavanagh and
    Kevin Montague.

Plate 49. Figure of a kneeling man, Nok culture, Nigeria. Late first millennium B.C.
Clay. H. 4 1/8 in. Jos Museum, Nigeria.
Photo courtesy Bernard Fagg.

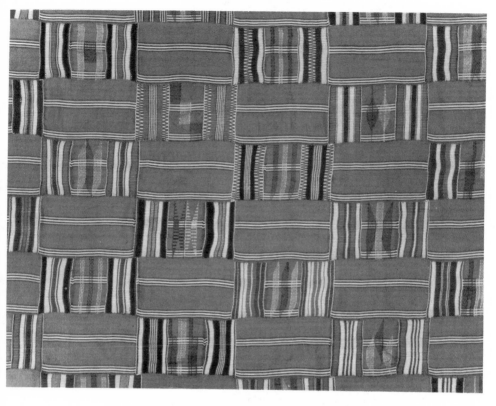

Plate 50. *Kente* cloth (detail), Asante, Ghana. Cotton, silk.
Indiana University Art Museum.
Photo by Michael Cavanagh and Kevin Montague.

Plate 51. Men's looms.
Photo courtesy Archives,
Museum der Basler Mission,
Basel, Switzerland.

Plate 52. Women's loom,
Okene, Nigeria.
Photo courtesy Roy Sieber.

Plate 53. Fragmentary head, Ife, Nigeria. 12th–15th century.
Clay. H. 6 in. Brooklyn Museum, lent by the Guennol Collection.
Photo courtesy Brooklyn Museum.

Plate 54. Figure of a king, Ita Yemoo, Ife, Nigeria. 14th–15th century.
Brass. H. 18 5/8 in. Museum of Ife Antiquities, Nigeria.
Photo courtesy of Museum of African Art, Eliot Elisofon Archives, Washington, D.C.

Plate 55. Plaque depicting a king with attendants, Kingdom of Benin, Nigeria.
Middle period (16th–17th century). Michael C. Rockefeller Memorial Collection,
Metropolitan Museum of Art, New York.
Photo courtesy Metropolitan Museum of Art.

Plate 56. Equestrian figure, Jenne
culture, Mali. 1645 +/- 165
(thermoluminescent dating).
Clay, pigment. H. 9 1/2 in.
Indiana University
Art Museum.
Photo by Michael Cavanagh and
Kevin Montague.

Plate 57. Afro-Portuguese saltcellar,
Sherbo, Sierra Leone. 16th
century. Ivory. H. 12 in. White
Collection, Seattle
Art Museum.
Photo courtesy Cleveland
Museum of Art.

Plate 58. Staff for Esu cult, Yoruba, Nigeria. Wood, leather, cowrie shells, brass, bone.
H. 19 3/4 in. (without shells). Wielgus Collection, Indiana University Art Museum.
Photo by Michael Cavanagh and Kevin Montague.

Plate 59. Mask for the Sande society,
Mende, Sierra Leone. Wood.
H. 15 in. Private Collection.
Photo by Ken Strothman.

Plate 60. Sidi Ballo's bird masquerade, Bamana, Mali.
Photo by Patrick McNaughton.

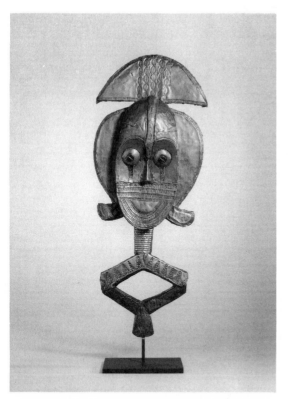

Plate 61. Reliquary figure, Kota,
Gabon. Wood, brass,
copper, iron. H. 22 5/8 in.
Grunwald Collection.
Photo by Michael Cavanagh
and Kevin Montague.

Plate 62. The Golden Stool, Asante,
Ghana. Gold. Archives,
Museum der Basler Mission,
Basel, Switzerland.

Plate 63. Chief sword-bearer to the
Asantehene holding
two state swords.
Photo by Martha Ehrlich.

Plate 64. Initiation mask in the form of
a shark head, Bidjogo,
Bissagos Islands, Guinea-Bissau.
Wood, pigment, fiber. L. 13 in.
Indiana University Art Museum.
Photo by Michael Cavanagh and
Kevin Montague.

Plate 65. Staff (detail), Kongo, Zaire.
Wood, brass. H. 47 3/4 in.
Indiana University Art Museum.
Photo by Michael Cavanagh and
Kevin Montague.

Plate 66. Figure for the Bwami society, Lega, Zaire.
Wood, shell, resin. H. 11 1/2 in. Wielgus Collection.
Photo by Raymond Wielgus.

Plate 67. Youth association masquerade, Bamana, Mali.
Photo by Patrick McNaughton.

Findings from other parts of the continent suggest, however, that while these arts were spectacular, they certainly were not unique.

In Mali's great Middle Delta region of the Niger River, for example, an icono-graphically complex array of terra-cotta figures (plate 56) came to the attention of the outside world in the mid-twentieth century. Usually dated to the twelfth or thirteenth century, the figures have been unearthed in large numbers and sold to Europe and North America for half a century, but precious few have been encountered in systematic archaeological excavations. Information about them is, therefore, ex-tremely limited. Most depict individuals, couples, and snakes and may have served on ancestor shrines or as household guardians against flooding.

In the region of present-day Sierra Leone and Guinea, stone figures of animals, people, and human heads, in a variety of styles, were being made when Portuguese explorers and traders first arrived on the Atlantic coast in the fifteenth century; perhaps they had been carved for centuries before that, too. Surviving Portuguese records do not indicate how these sculptures were used, but local peoples interpret them as ancestral and place them in family shrines or set them in fields to enhance farming.

The Portuguese were so taken with this sculpture that they commissioned local artists to work in ivory instead of stone, resulting in the earliest African tourist art, now known as Afro-Portuguese ivories, which were made until the mid-sixteenth century. Though carved into European-type objects such as spoons, saltcellars (plate 57), decorative hunters' horns, and pyxes, their style is clearly African.

Art and the Spiritual

Much African art involves beings and forces that Westerners call supernatural, but that most Africans see as a very powerful and less visible part of the natural world. People's beliefs vary, so many individuals say these beings and forces are metaphori-cal, or symbolic, or just ways to think about their experiences, while others believe firmly that they exist, and a sizable number say they personally interact with them.

This less visible world is hierarchically arranged, and in some societies this hierarchy is determined by human accessibility. Many people believe that at the top is a creator god, who may be somewhat remote or disinterested in human beings. Often, a second level of deities is much more involved with people. Formal associa-tions, with priests and art, engage these deities to enhance human life.

Such an arrangement is found among the Yoruba of Nigeria and the Republic of Benin, who have a pantheon that includes hundreds of deities (orisa), and who often use artworks in cults devoted to them. In some cases, attributes associate an artwork with a particular deity (plate 58). Esu, an orisa who is both messenger and trickster, for example, embodies concepts of contrast, provocation, and contradiction. He helps people by carrying their offerings to the other gods and spirits. At the same time, though, he has a provocative nature, causing misfortune and havoc to those who he feels do not make appropriate sacrifices, properly acknowledge his powers, or follow

Yoruba moral standards. Sculpture dedicated to him may depict a distinctive long-tailed hairdo, associated with unrestrained sexuality and troublesome social behavior, as well as a whistle or flute, a reference to his role as herald. The whiteness of the cowrie shells attached to some Esu figures contrasts with the darkness of the wood, a visual restatement of the oppositions that are part of the deity's character. Further, as a former medium of exchange, cowries remind viewers of the disagreements that money can engender, as well as the generosity of the devotee.

Wilderness spirits, creatures that live in the waters and wild spaces around cities and towns, are next in the supernatural hierarchy. Tremendous variety typifies their world. Some are believed to live individually; others are organized into invisible counterparts of human society. Spirits may be ugly, nasty, capricious, beautiful, or helpful, and some can be many or all of those things, depending on their moods or how people approach them. Many people establish intimate relationships with spirits that are mutually beneficial. For example, a person may give offerings to a spirit, and receive in exchange the ability to divine the future. People in these spiritual relationships often use artworks, especially masks and figures, to embody the spirits and put them to work.

Such is the case in coastal West Africa, among Mende, Bassa, Gola, and Vai women who belong to an association called Sande. Members of Sande initiate young girls into adulthood; train them to be good mothers, wives, and citizens; and teach them the intricacies of social and spiritual life. The society also provides older members an infrastructure of beliefs and activities that connects to aspects of broader community life, offering women significant amounts of power and authority. During association ceremonies, members dance wearing beautiful jet-black helmet masks (plate 59) that represent wilderness spirits with whom the individual mask owners have established intimate and beneficial relationships. The masks are considered to be the epitome of beauty, which reflects upon the nature of the spirit and also upon the accomplishment and capacity of the woman who owns the mask.

Ancestor spirits are also very important in African art and life. Like people worldwide, most Africans feel a great loss when their relatives die and welcome an institutionalized way to cherish their memory. In addition, many believe that, upon death, the knowledge and experience that a person accumulates in life are taken with the deceased's spiritual essence into the less visible realms, where the forces of the universe and other spirits exert their powers over the living. Many Africans believe they can communicate with their ancestors and, through respect and appropriate offerings, have some influence in the less visible world.

The Yoruba, for example, wear fantastic costumes of boldly colored, multilayered fabric appliqué panels, which fan out horizontally when dancers spin during a masquerade called Egungun. These masquerades represent the spirits of kings, town founders, and good leaders, who are believed to return to the world of the living to subdue malevolent sorcery, to hear disputes, and to uphold the moral fiber of people and communities.

Ancestor references can be less direct but very influential. Mande people, for example, use large, abstract, and often colorful bird masquerades for long evenings of pleasant entertainment. One famous performer, Sidi Ballo, gave his masquerade (plate 60) the praise name of an ancestor said to have played a dominant role as a strategist, diplomat, and military leader in the founding of the enormous Mali empire. This invokes the glories of Mande history through the ancestors who created it and inspires young people to aspire to greatness and productivity in their own lives.

In Gabon and Congo, Kota people both honored their ancestors and appealed for their protection with copper- and brass-covered wooden abstract figures (plate 61). The metal made the sculptures more valuable and more beautiful, thereby pleasing the spirits. These sculptures were set in baskets that held relics of a clan's ancestors, particularly bones. A town's clan reliquaries were kept together in a shrine enclosure, which was part of a community cult.

Another aspect of African spirituality involves the accumulation and activation of energies and forces, often through the vehicles of artworks. These forces are part of the less visible world and are variously described as the energy that makes the universe possible, the force behind all activities, and the power that allows and constitutes organic life. Many people believe these powers to be terrible, even evil. Others believe them to be awesome and dangerous, but manageable. Most people agree that a person must have special, often extensive training to manage these forces. Such trained individuals are the cult priests, the herbal doctors, and the divination experts of African societies, as well as the independent sorcerers, who invoke their power to benefit or harm others.

In West Africa, many masks are designed to possess these powers. Good examples are masks belonging to the Mande Komo associations (plate 45) that are believed by many people in Mali to be the most powerful things on earth. The masks are believed to have the power to destroy antisocial sorcerers and protect communities from malevolent wilderness spirits. Mask owners are Komo leaders, who, like the Mende Sande mask owners, also have close relationships with wilderness spirits.

Komo masks, designed to rest horizontally over a dancer's head, depict the energies they embody. Their mouths and feathers represent the deep knowledge of the world possessed by hyenas and birds. Their horns suggest wilderness and the raw energies that abound there. The murky coatings of sacrificial materials add power and suggest the ambiguity and indeterminate, secret nature of the energies at work in the mask.

Across Central Africa, figures with all sorts of attachments, such as mirrors, horns, nails, shells, beads, and herbal medicines, also harness power to do the bidding of individuals and groups. Among the peoples who use them are the Kongo (plate 46), Bete, Teke, Kuba, and Songye (plate 44). The figures are generally managed by ritual experts, who know herbal, organic, and inorganic substances and how to assemble them to harness the energies in the invisible world. These figures can be part of cults, used by individual experts, or sold to clients. They vary in size, gesture, and attachments, according to the powers they are supposed to harness and the activities they are supposed to help people undertake. Some cure illnesses, others block misfortune, and still others seek and defeat the unpleasant people who try to inflict misfortune on others.

Art and Leadership

As in the arts of Ife and Benin, many African art forms are used to proclaim, aggrandize, and enhance the capacities of leaders. The Asante in Ghana provide excellent examples of these arts. In the late 1600s a priest named Okomfo Anakye and a local leader named Osei Tutu are believed to have assembled a handful of small states into the powerful Asante empire, in part by expanding an important kind of symbolism and art form into a mandate for leadership. Osei Tutu was a very successful military leader, who carved out an empire. But to galvanize the people, his compatriot the priest is said to have caused a marvelous Golden Stool to descend from the sky and land on the knees of Tutu.

Most people in central and southern Ghana place tremendous importance on stools. They are given as gifts and incorporated into many of life's important events, such as when a child first begins to crawl or when a couple marry. The souls of the deceased are believed to inhabit their stools, and people turn their own stools on their sides when they get up, so someone else's soul will not occupy them. The Golden Stool was said by the priest to contain the soul of the nation and all of its citizens. It symbolized both their unity and the right of their king to lead them.

In addition to the Golden Stool (plate 62), Asante royal arts today include spectacular arrays of regalia such as state swords with large golden decorations in the form of animals, each of which is associated with proverbs and stories that become royal messages (plate 63). Asante kings have professional linguists, people who interpret and embellish speech, and these officials carry carved wooden staffs covered in gold leaf. On the tops of the staffs are gold-covered images, which also tell stories and become royal messages. Many state officials wear three- to four-inch disks of gold that symbolize the purification of the king's soul, while the king wears golden ornaments, such as rings and bracelets, and even sandals covered with the precious metal. Exquisitely woven and intricate cloths called kente (plate 50) are also worn, while cloth umbrellas with gold finials punctuate the presence of leaders and protect them from the sun. All of this splendor, with messages attached, asserts that Asante leaders possess the social, economic, and spiritual clout needed to run their state.

Art and Initiation

In Africa, artworks play important roles in initiations, the ceremonies that mark a change in status, position, or role for an individual or group. In most traditional African societies, nearly every person participates in at least one initiation: that which marks the transition from childhood to adulthood. In addition, initiations may mark the acceptance of certain roles or positions within a society. For example, rulers or priests may be initiated when they assume office. Finally, men and women may be initiated if they choose to join voluntary associations, organizations found throughout Africa that are dedicated to particular causes or ideals.

In the Bissagos Islands off the coast of Guinea, boys undergo a two-part initiation which includes masquerade. At certain stages, the boys wear masks depicting ferocious and predatory sea creatures (plate 64), emphasizing the fact that they are at the height of their physical prowess and strength but as yet do not have the knowledge and wisdom necessary for success as adults in the civilized world. In other parts of Africa, masks may be part of ceremonies which present information a boy must acquire to be considered an adult, or masks may represent a monster, which devours the boys and allows them to be reborn as men.

When he assumes office, a Kongo chief undergoes an elaborate initiation. This includes a period of seclusion and an ordeal intended to ascertain the approval of spiritual forces and their willingness to confer some of their powers on the new chief. After successful completion of the ordeal, the chief is given a staff (plate 65), a sword, a bonnet, bracelets, a leopard skin, and a buffalo-hair whisk as symbols of his leadership. The staff, which in former times was often intricately carved, is seen as a special symbol of spiritual approval.

Unlike the Kongo, the Lega of eastern Zaire do not have a centralized political authority. Leadership is provided by a council of elders drawn from the Bwami association, a complex, multilevel institution that is dedicated to the development of moral behavior and to which most Lega men and many women belong. Advancement within the society is based on a series of payments and demonstrations of knowledge about Lega culture and the Bwami society appropriate to each rank. An initiate learns the necessary information from a variety of sources, including proverbs, songs, and the manipulation of different objects, both natural and human-made. For some levels, these objects include wooden and ivory figures (plate 66) and masks as well as nonfigural objects, which an initiate may acquire and display. Thus, artworks become objects for education as well as emblems of rank and status.

The Complexities of Art

Art sometimes appears simple, but it is always composed of intricate layers of human imagination and social activity. Within a community, traditional African art has as its base shared beliefs about the nature of social and spiritual worlds. People use artworks in particular settings, which generally emphasize particular ideas and activities. But much more is very often going on.

In Mali, for example, youth association masquerades (plate 67) help communities celebrate agricultural labor. Many characters are portrayed in the masquerades: historical and mythical figures, contemporary leaders, elders, hunters, village person-alities, and foreigners. Some performers use these characters to demonstrate their social knowledge. Others use them to make critical, satirical commentaries on the inconsistencies and foibles of people's beliefs and behavior. Still others perform just for the fun of it, or because it is expected. Audience members interpret what they see according to their experiences and interests. They may, for example, interpret a character to make a point or assert a position in social relationships, such as a marriage, or business negotiations, such as a big purchase at the local market. Thus, within the framework of commonly held beliefs, the people using initiation masks, or other African art forms, can and do put their own interpretations on the artworks and the events.

Aesthetics, a neglected and too often misunderstood aspect of the arts of Africa, are another part of what makes African art complex. Some Americans and Europeans still believe that African art is purely functional and that neither its makers nor its users consider principles of form or composition to be important. That is simply wrong, as an examination of many of the artworks in this chapter shows. Most scholars have not explored aesthetics in their research, but the few that have find aesthetic considerations to be alive and well, though not always easy for foreigners to discover.

Even in creations such as Komo masks (plate 45), which Americans and Europeans often find ugly, aesthetic principles are at work. In Komo masks the amorphous surfaces, the harsh juxtapositioning of horns, feathers, and quills, the huge mouths, and the overall sense of crawling, messy, but horrific presence are designed to suggest the powers of nature that skilled experts can harness and put to use.

On the other hand, artworks that outsiders generally find attractive may well be appreciated for different reasons by the people who made them. On Mende masks (plate 59), the arrangements of facial features, complex coiffures, broad foreheads, partially closed eyes, and small, delicate mouths depict ideals of beauty to which Mende women aspire, and which flow into broader community ideas about social responsibility, mature, intelligent behavior, and morality.

Aesthetics thus are strategies that move from artworks to the greater world of thoughts and actions. Societies use well-designed and skillfully executed art to acquire some influence on what people think and how they behave.

Be they kente cloths, Egungun masquerades, Kota reliquary figures, or Mende helmet masks, African artworks are supposed to inspire ideas and emotions, attract attention, and impress people. Their compositions are designed for impact and effect, and their articulation of symbols and images is intended to make the viewer pause and to generate a response.

SUGGESTIONS FOR FURTHER READING

D'Azevedo, Warren L., ed. *The Traditional Artist in African Societies*. Bloomington: Indiana University Press, 1989.

Denyer, Susan. *African Traditional Architecture: An Historical and Geographical Perspective*. New York: Africana Publishing Company, 1978.

Picton, John, and John Mack. *African Textiles*. London: British Museum Publications, 1979; reprint ed., New York: Harper and Row, 1989.

Sieber, Roy. *African Furniture and Household Objects*. Bloomington: Indiana University Press, 1980.

Sieber, Roy, and Roslyn Adele Walker. *African Art in the Cycle of Life*. Washington, D.C.: Smithsonian Institution Press, 1987.

Thompson, Robert Farris. *African Art in Motion: Icon and Art in the Katherine Coryton White Collection.* Los Angeles: University of California Press, 1974.

Vogel, Susan. *Africa Explores: 20th Century African Art.* New York and Munich: Center for African Art and Prestel, 1991.

Willett, Frank. *African Art: An Introduction.* Rev. ed. London: Thames and Hudson, 1993.

Ruth M. Stone
African Music Performed

13 African peoples make and listen to music that is intimately bound to the visual and dramatic arts as well as the larger fabric of daily life. Highlife singers promote candidates for political office, for example. As Kofi Busia campaigned for the presidency of Ghana in 1970, a musical warning was piped from a roving van about the political activities of Kwame Nkrumah, a former leader of the country.

> Before it rains, the wind precedes.
> I told you but you did not listen.
> Before it rains, the wind precedes.
> I told you but you did not listen.[1]

Special dancers in Benin kingship rituals in Nigeria clear the path for the heir apparent singing,

> Dark like lightening rain!
> It clears for the Oba![2]

Griots, professional praise and criticism singers, convey messages for their rulers as they have since before the time of Sundiata (1230–1255), the first emperor of Mali.

Performers of *domeisia*, narrative songs of the Mende people of Sierra Leone, fashion words, song, and gesture for evening entertainment. Women improvise a comfortable call-and-response pattern as they bend over to hoe the soil for rice planting and sing the songs of work. Elsewhere, a "money-bus" driver plays a tape in his tape player, and the lyrics of Bob Marley and the sounds of reggae rise in the urban bustle. The assistant runs alongside the accelerating bus and then hops on board through the still open door, jogging a dance to the ambient sound. The members of the East and Central African Apostolic Church of John Maranke invoke the presence of the Holy Spirit with songs. In all of these settings music is integrated into life, and though diversity throughout Africa is apparent, some common elements penetrate the myriad of details.

African performance stands apart from that in the West because it is clearly part of the fabric of life. Music, as Africans view it, is not a thing of beauty to be admired in isolation. Rather, it exists only as woven into the larger textile that also combines games, dance, words, drama, and visual art. A. M. Ipoku, director of the Ghana Dance Ensemble, expressed the idea that dance and music should be so closely connected that one "can see the music and hear the dance."[3] Or as a chief in Cameroon expressed it, "The dancer must listen to the drum. When he is *really* listening, he creates within himself an echo of the drum, then he has started really to dance."[4] The lyrics of a Zairean song sum it up: "I sing: I think."[5]

The words that mean "performance" or "event," whether the *pele* of the Kpelle or *lipapali* of the Basotho, are applied not only to music making, dancing, and speaking but also to children's games and sports. Music also exists as a part of a larger world, a world brought to Africans through radio, television, and tape recorders and naturally incorporated into local music. It is not unusual to find traditional drums playing with electric guitar and other electronically amplified instruments, even as songs are sung in the indigenous languages.

The streams of influence within and beyond Africa have spawned popular music forms such as the East African *beni* and West African highlife, drawing upon brass band music; the Congolese *soukous*, echoing soul and disco music; the Nigerian *juju* and its later offshoot *fuji*, which early on incorporated electric guitar and banjo but later only percussion instruments; and the South African *makwaya*, bringing together European vocal harmonies and ragtime elements with Xhosa rhythms. African composers, among them Akin Euba, Fela Sowande, and Lazarus Ekweme, move easily between the various streams, incorporating Western art music elements with popular music and indigenous forms, binding these influences in individual compositions.

A description of an event from northern Ghana shows the meshing of different media into a larger occasion:

> Dagomba funerals are spectacles. The final funeral of an important or well-loved man or woman can draw several thousand people as participants and spectators. Small-scale traders also come to do business, setting up their tables to sell cigarettes, coffee, tea, bread, fruits, and other commodities to the milling crowds. Spread out over a large area, all types of musical groups form their circles. In several large circles, relatives and friends dance to the music of dondons and gongons. The fiddlers are also there. After a session in the later afternoon, people rest and begin reassembling between nine and ten o'clock in the evening. By that time, several Simpa groups have already begun playing. Two or three Atikatika groups also arrive and find their positions, and by eleven o'clock the funeral is in full swing. After midnight more groups come to dance Baamaya or other special dances like Jera or Bila, though the latter are not common. Baamaya dancers dress outlandishly, with bells tied to their feet and waists, wearing headdresses and waving fans. The dance is wonderful and strenuous: while gongons, flutes, and a dondon play the rhythms of Baamaya, the dancers move around their circle, twisting their waists continuously until the funeral closes at dawn.[6]

Plate 68. Slit drum, Yaoundé, Cameroon.
Photo courtesy Helena Hale.

Early Accounts of African Music

Early travelers to Africa commented on performances which they heard, though they did not always find them pleasing. Father Denis de Carli on a journey through Kongo in 1666–67 remarked, "This harmony is grateful at a distance, but harsh and ungrateful near at hand, the beating of so many Sticks causing a great Confusion."[7] The Benin bronzes of Nigeria that were cast from approximately 1550 to 1650 display scenes with instruments. There are reliefs of a slit-drum, a struck single bell, a double bell, a clapper bell, a pellet bell, a calabash rattle, a rattle staff, an hourglass drum, several kinds of single-headed drums, a multiple bow-lute, an end-blown flute, and a side-blown trumpet.

African peoples maintain lively oral traditions about where music originated. The Vai of Liberia tell of a king who was defeated and shown the way to travel to the underwater world. He and his subjects enjoyed a fine life, and their celebrations can still be heard on a quiet night. But when humans hear them play, it is a sign of an upcoming death.

Many instruments, the Kpelle maintain, come from encounters with animals in the forest in the distant past. The goblet drum, *feli*, for example, originated with the chimpanzee. A hunter in the forest, the story goes, watched chimpanzees beating their chests and got the idea to make a drum, and the animals even showed him how to hollow out a log for the body of the drum. Back in town the hunter shared his idea, and the goblet drum was created. The idea for side-blown horns derived from a story of the *tuu-tuu* birds observed by some women fishing in a creek. The women returned to town and approached the chief to help them capture the lovely sound of the birds: "What can we do [to record the sound]? The chief kept sitting, he kept sitting. He said, 'go into town and quickly kill two cows.' They then returned to where the *tuu-tuu* were responding. When the *tuu-tuu* sang they imitated them [on the cow horns]."[8] In this manner the sound was not only imitated, but captured to be played again and again.

African Music and Sound

Sound in Africa is everywhere noticed, admired, and shaped. Bus drivers take pride in horns that play tunes. Postal workers in Ghana cancel stamps in a deliberate rhythm. Sound in African music imitates many things: the sounds of nature, of birds, of spirits. Virtually everything is subject to portrayal in sound, and all of these voices combine in the music event.

Sound becomes a medium for other senses as well. Consider the plight of the women in this song text:

> Our fellow young women, I raised my eyes to the sky, I lowered them.
> My tears fell *gata-gata* like corn from an old corn farm.[9]

Gata-gata imitates not only the audible dropping but the visual glimpsing of the tears rolling down her face and falling to the ground in full drops. Singers depict visual beauty. They sing about the smooth, shiny blackness of a well-carved bowl with a thin exterior wall that the hero's wife carves in a Kpelle epic.

Timbre, or tone color, that shading of sound which makes a trumpet sound different from a flute, a metal gong from a drum, matters a great deal to many Africans. The West, however, lacks the basic vocabulary to describe timbre, and staff notation only crudely indicates anything about it. Africans appear to pay much closer attention to this.

In the 1930s, ethnomusicologist George Herzog made some early cylinder phonographic recordings and discovered that among the Jabo of southeastern Liberia, musical sounds are "large" and "small"; the large sounds are found in the lower register of pitch, and the small sounds are in the upper register. They refer to birds that live near each other and respond to one another's call. The Kpelle of central Liberia talk about sound in similar ways. When they refer to large voices and small voices, they are commenting not only about pitch but about tone color as well. They think of a large voice as resonant and hollow, "voice swallowed," while a small voice is more penetrating and less resonant, "voice coming out."

Since instruments for Africans are humanlike, it is not surprising that the sounds of instruments are often considered "voices." In Western usage, for example, the low-

Plate 69. Royal drummers in chief's procession, Ghana.
Photo courtesy Mike Warren.

pitched string of a frame-zither may serve as the voice of the mother, and a higher-pitched string as the voice of the child. Two closely pitched strings may be called brother and sister strings. The Lugbara of Uganda name the five strings of the lyre with status terms for women. The Shona of Zimbabwe name the manuals of the *mbira* "the old men's voices" for the lowest register, "the young men's voices" for the middle register, and "the women's voices" for the highest register. They go further to describe individual keys: "mad person, put in a stable position, the lion, swaying of a person going into trance, to stir up, big drum, and mortar, with the names showing something about how the key works in the music."

Africans combine many varieties of pitches. In Western terms they use many kinds of scales, including pentatonic, or five tones to the octave, and heptatonic, or seven tones to the octave. The distance between the tones is highly variable, which demonstrates that Africans are not limited in their selection of musical tones. They have a great tonal assortment, and their music cannot be considered "primitive," as some earlier scholars proposed. Some have suggested, for example, that where a five-tone scale exists, people have not yet evolved to a seven-tone scale. They argue that the large spaces within the scale are "gaps" to be filled in with the "missing" two notes at a later time in cultural evolution. But this is clearly not the case, since the two types of scales coexist in Africa.

Musical notation in much of Africa is heard rather than written. Musicians make mnemonic phrases their guide to playing. A pattern of mnemonic phrases that is found in many parts of Africa and that serves as a partial guide to the other musicians is referred to as a time line. The well-known 12/8 pattern that is repeated by an instrument throughout a song, particularly in West Africa, is verbalized as "Kong kong ko-lo, kong kolo," or "ko ko ko yo, ko ko yo," the sound conveying first, timing or rhythm, and second, something of the tone color. In Western terms, the pattern can be represented with a simple notation where an *x* represents a sound made on an instrument and a . implies silence or sustained sound.

Time Line

12	x	·	x	·	x	x	·	x	·	x	x	·
8	kong		kong		ko-	lo		kong		ko-	lo	

The other drum parts in an ensemble will each have their patterns to play with their own phrases, "Ku-gu," "ku-gu," or "I-za-pa-ni-pa-ti." Even the master drummer who is changing and building his song knows his motifs by verbal patterns.

The vowels *u* and *o* indicate timbres of dark sounds and pitches of the lower register, while *i* and *a* are brighter sounds in the upper register. Language in this way becomes an important base for understanding music and its organization and order in Africa. The Mandinka drummer in the Gambia stresses tone color, for, "in view of the importance of timbre in the drumming technique, one may conclude that his abilities are at least in part attributable to learning each rhythm as a pattern of timbres produced by four basic strokes on the drum."[10]

The drum part for the Lenjengo recreational dance is played on the *kutiridingo* drum, a conical-shaped instrument struck with one stick and one hand as follows:

6/8	kum		ba	din		da
	K	·	B	D	·	d

Kum is played with an open hand that bounces off the drumhead. *Ba* is a damped stroke produced when the fingers hit the head and press it to lessen the vibration. *Din* is an open stick stroke. *Da* is a damped stick stroke. Thus a palette of timbres as well as rhythms can be spoken in the syllables.

Some African languages are tone languages, and these present interesting possibilities for music. In these languages each syllable or phoneme is assigned a relative pitch. It is important to speak with the correct pitch, for a different pitch may drastically alter the meaning of the word. In some music, the pattern of the musical pitches follows closely the speech pitch. In many cases, however, considerable variation results. When instruments reproduce speech pitches, instrumental signaling takes place, a phenomenon that has fascinated observers, who have referred to "talking drums." The drums play patterns of pitches that are understood to comment on actions of the Yoruba chief, the playing of a subordinate drummer, or the generosity of a host. The phrases that are communicated in musical signaling are often proverbs and obscure expressions. This provides a context to clarify the

Plate 70. Trumpeters and drummers in Independence Day parade,
the old city of Birni, Niger.
Photo courtesy Jamie Thompson.

message. Contrary to the popular view that everyone understands signaling easily, research shows that in many areas this esoteric communication is understood only by specialists and people with special training. Signaling is still used as a means to communicate within musical ensembles, particularly messages not meant for the entire audience.

African Music and Time

Musical sounds are deftly organized against each other in a conflicting vitality. The power also shows in quiet ways in a scene one morning following an all-night ceremony for ancestral spirits. Hakurotwo Mude, an *mbira* player, looked in the distance and played quietly, oblivious to the young son who placed a hand on his father's shoulder.

As Mude played the *mbira* his eyes became clouded. Tears welled up and fell silently down his cheeks. It was some time before anyone noticed what was happening. Finally Mude's father-in-law walked over and knelt down before him. Careful not to interfere with the playing of the *mbira*, the old man pulled a handkerchief out of his pocket and blotted up the tears on Mude's cheeks. Tears flowed so steadily that the old

Plate 71. Performing on an ivory horn, Liberia.
Photo courtesy Ruth Stone.

man saw it was to no avail. He stood up and silently motioned to all the other villagers seated around to follow him into the large kitchen where the *bira* had previously been held. So as not to embarrass Mude, we left him to his music and his tears.[11]

As scholars try to untangle how such rhythms are created, it has become increasingly clear that the basis is less linear than it is mosaic. The delight in conflict, in clash of parts, draws from a different source of order than does much Western music.

African rhythms can also be thought of on different levels. In a West African ensemble, there are various strata of rhythms, and they range from simple to more complex. The simpler ones tend to be those that are supporting parts; the more complex are the solo roles played by the master drummer. The Ewe ensembles in Ghana have the highest-pitched instruments playing in the supporting roles and the lowest-pitched instruments playing in the solo roles, quite the opposite from many Western ensembles. There are at least four levels:

(1) relatively simple repeating patterns:
drums, rattles, sometimes gongs
(2) less simple and usually repeating patterns:
intermediate supporting instruments, drums
(3) simple and usually repeating pattern:
basic supporting instrument, gong
(4) complex and often varying pattern:
master drummer, drum.

Africans often think of performance in a transactional sense. As with two people pulling at either end of a rope in a tug of war, rather than two people simply standing alone, one part rarely exists without the other. To understand one part, we must see how it balances with another. Two xylophone players in southeast Africa sit opposite one another, and both share in playing the same instrument. One has the responsibility of starting the performance, the other responds. Similarly, an *mbira* player of Zimbabwe designates one part he plays as "*kushaura* (to lead the peace)" and the other part as "*kutsinhira* (to exchange parts of a song)."[12]

In a different sense, the ubiquitous call-and-response form of African music is transactional. A soloist gives the call and the chorus replies. Though the parts may overlap and form a neat dovetail so that no space between the two is obvious, the solo holds license to vary while the chorus gives never-changing support. In this way the Kpelle speak of the singer "raising the song" and the chorus "agreeing underneath the song." An hourglass drummer has problems playing his part alone, even though the beats of his part cross with the second drum. The drummer complains that he cannot "hear" his part without the second drum playing, and he expresses the idea that drums converse much as singers do.

Africans take the notion of transaction beyond the call and response, for they delight in even more segmentation and fragmentation out of which to later create a togetherness. In hocket, a number of musicians play one or two notes each that all combine to make a single melody. The Kpelle horn ensembles, those groups traditionally attached to the chiefs, delight in this idea. Six horns combine their brief motifs to make a unit of music. The Kpelle hocket vocally in bush-clearing songs, where the voices interlock with great precision. The Shona of Zimbabwe interlock panpipe sounds with voice and syllables and add leg- and hand-rattle accompaniment.

Performers

To be an adult person in many African societies means learning to perform with some degree of proficiency in song and dance. Music is not just something special but something social, and to be a social being is to know about performance. Many groups have apprenticeship systems for young people where a talented boy or girl will receive individual tutelage. Young people also immerse themselves in the rich environment of performances in their town. There is also the special training that might be given in the secret societies, those places and times of spearation from the village, where musical training is one of the areas emphasized. All initiates, neverthe-less, are expected to show a certain skill in music. And when the initiates emerge at the end of seclusion, they will publicly demonstrate their special skills at a commu-nity festivity.

The people vital to a music event are first of all the performers: singers, dancers, storytellers, actors, and instrumentalists. And as in the *domeisia* narrative event, one individual may assume simultaneously the roles of storyteller, actor, and singer. Aside from the performers, those who are usually thought of as the makers of music, there are the receivers and shapers of music, the audience, who matter no less than the performers, since they are judges of the performance. They praise, in the form of token gifts or speeches, and criticize, in the form of finely honed allusion. The town chief in Gbeyilataa, Liberia, offers a praise speech as he calls a halt to the music-making. Stepping into the circle, he exults,

> All of you, thank you, thank you.
> My name is Taa-tii.
> I come from Bonotaa.
> My mother is Goma, my father's name is Leepolu.
> I bring some water to soak the drum head.

The audience laughs at his reference to the cane-juice liquor he hands to the musicians, for it will wet not the drum skin but the skin of their tongues.

Ancestors and tutelary spirits must also be counted as participants in events. For though their presence may be known to a few select insiders, they are surrogate performers who influence and most often enhance the music. Ancestors appear as spirits of deceased players who are called to attend the event. An *mbira* player sings "Gbono-kpate wee" as he invites the late player of that name to attend. And the audience knows that Gbono-kpate has arrived when a high-pitched "Oo," sung by the soloist, is heard in response. Tutelary spirits that are attached in a very private relationship to virtuoso performers attend events to help their clients excel. This relationship may be dangerous indeed, for fine playing exacts a high cost from a player that may include life itself.

Even instruments, those tools of a performer the West often regards as objects, take on a quasi-human quality in some African events. Instruments are extensions of the player, and they can become more or less human depending upon their particular role. Some instruments exhibit this idea clearly, with humanoid features carved and fashioned on them: the head and face of a woman at the end of a Mangbetu harp, the waist rings and feet of a woman at the base of a goblet drum, an *mbira* built on the stomach of a carved wooden figure of a person with arms uplifted.

In conversation about instruments, people mention the ear, the body, the waist, and so on. The master drummer of Gbeyilataa calls his drum Gomaa, "Share-with-me," a female name suggesting one with some beauty and personal vitality. Other musi-cians offer sacrifices to their instruments, to please them and protect the bond between player and instrument, given their part-human, part-spirit nature. The way

Plate 72. Nuru Bari, Fulani *griot,* Ouagadougou,
Burkina Faso.
Photo courtesy Nora Roy.

they are regarded as living beings puts them along a continuum that moves easily from the human to other worlds.

Instruments That Are Struck and Blown

Africans categorize instruments in unique ways, not exactly the string, woodwind, brass, percussion divisions of the Western orchestra or even the ethnomusicological appellations of chordophone, aerophone, membranophone, and idiophone. The Kpelle, the Vai, and the Dan of the Guinea Coast see all instruments as either struck, such as Western string and percussion, or blown, such as brass and woodwind. The term for struck, *ngale*, in Kpelle means literally to break as a millet stalk breaks.

Thus the act of plucking a string, just as surely as bending a drum head through striking, is *ngale*.

Africa is known for its rich variety in instruments. If only drums are taken into account, there are goblet, hourglass, conical, barrel, cylindrical, and frame (tambourine) types, ranging in size from small hand-held drums to those that require large stands to support them or several men to carry them in procession. These instruments sound as "voices" of penetrating tone colors and pitches, not simply rhythms. Their character is much more fully developed than that of drums in the usual Western music conception. The *entenga* tuned drum ensembles of the kings in Uganda, the processional drums carried on horseback in northern Nigeria, the ritual drums laid horizontally on platforms in coastal West Africa, and the hourglass drum of West Africa that plays, glides, and slides off pitch as the player presses the thongs connecting the heads and tightening the skins with lightning velocity, all these are examples of African drums.

String instruments, those often slighted and sometimes forgotten performers of African music, are unexpected with their subtle and often quiet voices. Perhaps the best-known is the *kora*, the harp-lute which is the personal extension of the West African *griot*, the itinerant praise singer, historian, and social commentator of Mali, Senegal, and the Mande region in general. Equally important are the multiple-bow lute, frame-zither, musical bow, harp, lyre, and lute. The haunting sound of the whispered song of East Africa accompanied by the low, resonant, string bass–like sounds of the trough zither is hard to forget. More than one person has observed that in areas of Arabic and Islamic influence, there is a more concentrated use of strings.

The *mbira*, or *sansa*, as it is known in other areas, with its plucked metal tongues, is a versatile instrument. It is often played at a healing event for the Shona of Zimbabwe: "As the music becomes more intense and more participants enter into the performance, the suspense mounts. No one knows just when the possession of the medium (or mediums) will occur, or, at times, whom the spirits will possess. The spirits sometimes choose unsuspecting participants as their hosts."[13] Rattles of all kinds, both container and those with a bead network on the outside, join ensembles. Clapperless bells struck with a stick are important, often setting the time line of the ensemble. Hollowed-out logs are slit "drums" played alone or in ensemble. The variety of struck, plucked, and shaken instruments stretches the imagination. And because sound is more important than appearance, a struck beer bottle will often replace a struck boat-shaped iron.

Many African peoples associate the sound of the blown instruments, such as flutes, whistles, and horns, with voices of spirits. The spirit of the Kpelle Poro secret society is realized through globe-shaped pottery whistles.

The horns, which often appear in ensembles, are associated with the courts of kings and chiefs. They accompany the ruler and sometimes are played exclusively for his entourage. Horns come in many sizes and shapes, and are made of wood, cow horn, ivory, or metal. In Liberia for the 1976 inauguration of President William Tolbert, a Kpelle paramount chief sent his ensemble of six ivory trumpets trimmed in leopard skin and his trumpeters to honor the national leader. In the Asante area of

Plate 73. Influence of new technology on listening
and playing music, Liberia.
Photo courtesy Ruth Stone.

Ghana, local chiefs historically kept short horns while paramount chiefs were permitted long trumpet ensembles.

The Babenzele of the forest region of Central Africa play a breathy flute that leaps from the low to the high register and back again. They alternate from flute to voice, and the singing tone is scarcely different to the ear from that of the flute, so similar is the sound they strive to achieve. Other peoples play flutes, singly or in groups. Some famous ensembles include the royal flute and drum players of the countries of Benin.

The Feeling of Music

Describing the emotions stirred by music is a difficult task because words fall

Plate 74. Mural in local bar, Liberia.
Photo courtesy Ruth Stone.

short. We are just beginning to learn about the affective aspect, which for some people is even more important than are the mechanics of music, the mere nuts and bolts. For many Africans, singing and playing moves them to do unusual things, calms them if they are overwrought with grief, and stirs them to dance if they are apathetic. These special qualities, which go beyond the ordinary, the Kpelle say, characterize a performance after the ensemble is playing smoothly and things are going well. Sometimes the audience is clued that a special feeling is to appear as the singer sings: "Put your ear to my singing song, As I am singing it, I am opening its net." And then gems of feeling appear, condensed bits of meaning, metaphors perhaps, of the entire song. They may be embedded in the song names given to the performer:

Bird-that-is-in-flight
Cassava-snake-in-the-thicket
Insect-infesting-small-rice-buds
Big-big-sacrifice

They may be in the way master drummer Kao gets that special sound from his instrument in Gbeyilataa:

If your hands are light, you can play the goblet drum completely. But if your hands aren't light, if I show you all those goblet drum voices, you won't know it for one cent.

The *sang* (proverbs, patterns) are in your stomach. When it becomes your wisdom, and it rises into all your fingers and they know it, then you play all those *sang* with them.

The power of the music can change the way people feel. Ge-weli-wula, a blacksmith and ritual specialist, describes this transformative power.

What I know about song, it came from sadness. . . . Even if you cry, you do everything, you must perform. . . . The man is performing, the inside of his heart has cooled. If your heart hurts, you can't sit quietly, again. But before you sit quietly, you must sing.[14]

African Music in Perspective

Music on the African continent today is expressed through a dazzling variety of events, instruments, costumes, and forms. Though from all evidence African music has always changed, some kinds of music have changed more rapidly than others as peoples have mingled their musics in interesting ways. The oral history, though not the present practice, of the people of Gbeyilataa in Kpelle country indicates that the harp-lute of the Mande *griots* was played by one of the court musicians. This is not surprising given the role of many Mande as traders to the Kpelle area. The Beni dance and drill teams of East Africa played European brass band instruments, adapting Western music and creatively blending local elements. These groups, flourishing from the 1890s to the 1960s, on one occasion drew this comment from an observer: "They dance about four abreast and burlesque with extravagant airs the British army officer—doing it of course in dance form and keeping time with the music."[15]

On a broader scale, a number of countries today support troupes that select local dances and songs and present them on a Western-type stage. The performance is adjusted to a theater audience. When the National Dance Troupe of Guinea performs in New York at the Brooklyn Academy of Music, included in one portion of their repertoire is a modified ceremony from the Poro secret society. In many ensembles, national culture is emphasized and local differences are minimized. Peter Adegboyega Badejo's opera *Asa Ibile Yoruba* (The Ways of the Land of the Yoruba) premiered in Schoenberg Hall on the campus of the University of California at Los Angeles before an enthusiastic Western audience. At a local level, many schools in Africa have brought in performers to teach young children traditional styles, even in the context of a Western education. At school graduations these troupes exhibit the newly reincorporated skills of earlier music. Thus, the integration of the arts of African life continues. The music of Africa performed represents a vitality, a mosaic in motion, a balance of the arts and everyday life. Through music people can reorder their feelings and live life with renewed vigor.

NOTES

1. Owusu Brempong, "Akan Highlife in Ghana: Songs of Cultural Transition," ms., 1984.

2. Joseph Nevadomsky, "Kingship Succession Rituals in Benin 2: The Big Things," *African Arts* 17, no. 2 (1984): 41–47, 90.

3. Barbara L. Hampton, "Music and Ritual Symbolism in the Ga Funeral," *Yearbook for Traditional Music* 14 (1984): 75–105.

4. Robert F. Thompson, *African Art in Motion: Icon and Act* (Los Angeles: University of California Press, 1974).

5. Johannes Fabian, "Popular Culture in Africa: Findings and Conjectures," *Africa* 48, no. 4 (1978): 315–34.

6. John M. Chernoff, *African Rhythm and African Sensibility* (Chicago: University of Chicago Press, 1979).

7. Michael Angelo and Denis de Carli, "A Curious and Exact Account of a Voyage to Congo in the Years 1666 and 1667," in *A Collection of Voyages and Travels,* ed. A. and J. Churchill, 4 vols. (London, 1704).

8. Ruth M. Stone, *Let the Inside Be Sweet: The Interpretation of Music Event among the Kpelle of Liberia* (Bloomington: Indiana University Press, 1982).

9. Ibid.

10. Roderick Knight, "Mandinka Drumming," *African Arts* 7 (1974): 25–35.

11. Paul Berliner, *The Soul of Mbira* (Berkeley: University of California Press, 1978).

12. Ibid.

13. Ibid.

14. Stone, *Let the Inside Be Sweet.*

15. Arthur M. Jones, "African Music: The *Mganda* Dance," *African Studies* 4, no. 4 (1945).

SUGGESTIONS FOR FURTHER READING

Bebey, Francis. *African Music: A People's Art.* Translated by Josephine Bennett. Westport, Conn.: Lawrence Hill, 1975.

Blacking, John. *Venda Children's Songs.* Johannesburg: Witwatersrand University Press, 1967.

Coplan, David. *In Township Tonight! South Africa's Black City Music and Theatre.* Johannesburg: Ravan Press, 1985.

Erlmann, Veit. *African Stars: Studies in South African Performance.* Chicago: University of Chicago Press, 1991.

Merriam, Alan P. *African Music in Perspective.* New York: Garland, 1982.

Nketia, J. H. Kwabena. *The Music of Africa.* New York: Norton, 1975.

Stone, Ruth M. *Dried Millet Breaking: Time, Words, and Song in the Woi Epic of the Kpelle.* Bloomington: Indiana University Press, 1988.

Waterman, Christopher. *Jùjú: A Social History and Ethnography of an African Popular Music.* Chicago: University of Chicago Press, 1990.

Dele Jegede
Popular Culture
in Urban Africa

14 Popular culture in Africa offers us a means of understanding the dynamics of social and cultural change. One striking feature of African cultures concerns the close interrelationship of art and life. In a continent where festivals often involve active communal participation in public spaces, and where spontaneous oral poetry, dance, and music are fused into a spectacular event involving drummers, masquerades, acolytes, and a strong chorus of participants, the great age of such events is evident. The question remains, however, of the extent to which their scope, form, and content have been influenced by urban growth in the twentieth century.

Although urban settlements in Africa date back many centuries, even millennia, recent decades have been remarkable for the unprecedented rapid growth in the number and size of cities on the continent. In the mid-sixties, the decade in which most African nations gained their independence from colonial rulers, there were 63 cities which either were capitals or had a population of more than 100,000. At this time, too, only 20 percent of Africans lived in urban centers. In 1985, the number of cities with more than 100,000 in population had risen to 109, while 31 percent lived in urban centers. It has been estimated that by the year 2000, about 40 percent of Africans will live in cities.[1] From Cape Coast to Cairo, Dakar to Dar-es-Salaam, from Lubumbashi to Lagos, towns have thus become a place for the negotiation and regeneration of popular culture, the battleground for the contemplation and assimilation of foreign values and practices, and an arena for the initiation of social change. Popular culture can include adaptations that have occurred in such traditional domains as religion, theater, art, and music, and also in newer forms of expression such as the mass media and the cinema, two important agents of social change. In this regard, contemporary Africa is a kaleidoscope of cultures and a vibrant pastiche of values which variously reflect efforts at adaptation, indigenization, appropriation, and synthesis.

Religion

In discussing religion, it is customary to identify traditional African religions, Islam, and Christianity as the three major belief systems of the continent. Compared with Islam and Christianity, traditional African religions may appear to be in decline. Given the well-established organizational structure of Islam and Christianity, their age-long efforts at proselytization, entrenchment, and consolidation, their importance as facilitators of Arabic and Western cultures, as well as their tacit or wholesale recognition by modern African governments, the multitude of religious practices indigenous to the peoples of Africa may seem to have lost their relevance and be doomed to extinction. The rapid, sometimes torrential pace of development in urban Africa, where traditional shrines have often disappeared in the wake of modern projects, seems to lend credence to this view. A careful appraisal of the situation, however, suggests that such a view is misleading because it fails to recognize that traditional African religions and practices permeate every facet of life, from the cradle to the grave, preceding the birth of individuals, influencing their lifestyle and world view, and playing a role upon their death. The kinship system and an enduring nexus of communal interdependency also influence the interface between religious pluralism and modernity, adaptation and rejection, eclecticism and syncretism in urban Africa.

A map of religions in Africa which graphically compartmentalizes the three religious streams may look crisp and beautiful. But it does not adequately demonstrate that the predominance of either Christianity or Islam in one region does not imply the demise of African systems of thought in that region. On the contrary, the acceptance of these two dominant religions is not unrelated to the extent to which both have been grafted onto indigenous systems of thought, becoming so intertwined in the process that, in the view of many Africans, professing one religion and believing in another is not inconsistent. This belief is codified by the Yoruba in the following song:

We shall celebrate our community rites	Awa o soro ile wa o
We shall celebrate our community rites	Awa o soro ile wa o
Christianity does not . . . You got it!	Igbagbo ko pe . . . O ye e
Christianity does not so forbid	Igbagbo ko pe kawa ma soro
We shall celebrate our community rites.	Awa o soro ile wa o

Here, we may consider a number of scenarios. In Nigeria, a university professor seeking promotion may not hesitate to supplement his Christian or Islamic devotions with a visit to the diviner, who consults with his oracle and advises that a sacrifice be offered to some supernatural forces believed to have mediatory powers to positively affect the outcome. A legal practitioner and respected member of the society is at once active at church and at the lodge of a local "reformed" fraternity, considered by devout Christians as a euphemism for a secret society. On purchasing a car, an urban Yoruba business executive first takes a "traditional" insurance policy: he seeks protection from the wrath of Ogun, the god of iron, by summoning community elders to pour libation and ask for ancestral guidance. The car is then taken to the local church, where the minister is implored to bless it. A young Christian couple anxious to have a child seek help from the traditional healer, who also doubles as an *imam* at the local mosque.

These situations exemplify various attempts at resolving the conflict or contradictions which are apparent in the culturally fluid environments of urban Africa. Additionally, they tend to confirm John Mbiti's thesis that traditional African religion is inextricably interwoven with life, and not a learned or acquired faith to which weekly recourse is taken, in the mosque on Fridays by Muslims, or in the church on Sundays by Christians.[2] The university professor, the lawyer, the business executive, and the young couple in these scenarios support Mbiti's findings that traditional African religions remain deeply embedded in the individual's psyche. In times of crisis, these dormant religious instincts predominate, and where they cannot be publicly accommodated, they are embraced in secret. Urban settings act in this regard both as catalysts for religious crisis and as avenues for their resolution. First, urbanization creates an artificial boundary between urban dwellers and their roots and forces them to devise mechanisms for balancing the exigencies of modern living with allegiance to traditional practices. Second, the need to find support networks in urban centers may sometimes result in membership in new religious organizations. Third, because urban dwellers maintain a strong link with their ancestral roots regardless of how successful they are or how long they have lived in their new station, they often look forward to returning home during their community's annual rituals and festivals to pledge loyalty to their ancestors and participate in the ceremonies of renewal and regeneration.

Examples of such ceremonies abound in several parts of Africa. For example, in Cape Coast, central Ghana, the Oguaa-Afahye festival among the Fante, which is often celebrated in the month of August, attracts home people from the region and their friends from various parts of the country.[3] The festivities are usually presided over by the paramount ruler of the town, the Ohene, who, resplendent in his regalia, is borne aloft in his palanquin, surrounded by an equally gorgeously dressed retinue. Although ancestor worship is central to this agricultural festival, and the celebration of the spirit of renewal and regeneration involves the pouring of libation by priests and priestesses, the event has increasingly become a national spectacle and the focal point for political socialization. Government functionaries and members of the diplomatic corps are usually invited as guests to the grand occasion, where *asafo* companies, carrying huge flags and dressed in colorful outfits, attempt to outperform each other.

The Oguaa-Afahye festival is representative of similar festivals which are celebrated in other parts of southern Ghana. To watch any of these festivals is to be awed by the dazzling power of human creativity and the impressive interrelationship of the arts. It is usually a breathtaking event in which ecstasy provides the energy that shapes poetry, music, color, sculpture, costume, dance, and drama into one vibrant extravaganza. A colorfully bedecked mass of humanity in transit from one arena to another becomes a gracious moving theater, a living exhibition of total art. Human beings become kinetic art forms, judging by the way in which they adorn themselves, and the frenzied or rhythmic flow that characterizes their performances. Such festivals alert us to the fluid nature of the boundaries between popular and high art, particularly in urban Africa. They also demonstrate that there are no contradictions in the minds of Africans who profess one religion and believe in another. Some members of the *asafo* groups who participate in the series of cultural enactments such as ancestor worship, war dances, lavish display of ornaments and visual arts, profuse body decorations, and colorful costuming, will also be church members.

There is yet another dimension to religious expression in urban Africa. It concerns the evolution of indigenous churches which, perhaps because of their largely adaptive, integrative, or synthetic nature, have continued to enjoy remarkable congregational growth. By mixing popular cultural elements with important aspects of Christian belief, some churches have emerged to redefine Christianity and popularize a new liturgy. This is referred to by some people as religious syncretism. An example is the Harrist Movement in Côte d'Ivoire, which was established in 1913 by William Wade Harris, a Liberian who, having been inspired by the Bible, trekked to neighboring Côte d'Ivoire in search of converts. In addition to the Bible, Harris took with him on his journey a gourd rattle and two women, with whom he sang and danced at each conversion session. Music and dance thus became an important tool of proselytization.[4] In addition to this there was a new mode of dress: a long white robe and a small hat that contrasted with a black neck scarf and black bands which crisscrossed at the chest. Harris's success was phenomenal, extending beyond Côte d'Ivoire to Ghana. But it was the adaptive nature of his movement that guaranteed its success. First, unlike colonial missionaries, Harris accommodated polygyny, which was an essential part of African family structure. Second, the organizational structure of his church was modeled on the traditional social structure, in which age differentiation and role playing were critical. When singing and dancing were added to this, what emerged was a new religious order.

Today, an impressive number of these syncretic churches have sprung up in urban Africa, inspired not only by popular elements from traditional cultures and the orthodox Christian liturgy, but also by the needs of townspeople and the dictates of modern life. Many of these churches are founded or led by women. The Aladura movement in Nigeria remains one of the best examples in this category. Here, Aladura (which in Yoruba literally translates to "owner of prayer" or "the one who prays") is used as a generic classificatory title in the same way most Yoruba have come to use it, for the numerous churches, including the Church of the Lord (Aladura), the Celestial Church of Christ, and the Cherubim and Seraphim Society, which have emerged within and outside of Nigeria. The first of these churches, the Cherubim and Seraphim Society and the Church of the Lord, were established among the Yoruba in Lagos and Abeokuta in 1925. In urban centers, Aladura churches have mushroomed in an assortment of forms. While some of them have been established as part-time "ventures" by employees in the public or private sectors of the economy, others, such as those at the Lagos beach, have been "founded" by full-time spiritual leaders who cater to the needs of tourists in improvised sheds that are rebuilt as fast as city council bulldozers mow them down.

Plate 75. Member of Aladura sect, Nigeria.
Photo courtesy Dele Jegede.

Praying remains the hallmark of the Aladura. In urban centers, churches have continued to command a strong followership, composed mainly of youngsters and women who are attracted as much by the colorful outfits as by the frenzied dancing and rigorous clapping sessions. It is not uncommon in some of these praying and dancing sessions for a member of the congregation to become possessed by the Holy Spirit, to shake uncontrollably and speak in "tongues," that is, in a language incomprehensible to all but the tutored and the select among them. In such sessions, visions of things to come are expected to be revealed. In addition to the integration of aspects of indigenous culture into the liturgy, such as the Yoruba belief in the existence of malevolent, supernatural forces and the power of ritual enactments, the expansion and popularity of the Aladura movement stem from its pragmatic approach to problems confronting its members.

Through visions that may be revealed during regular or special prayer sessions, or through private consultation with the *alagba* or the prophet-shepherd, not only are

Plate 76. Aladura church sign, Nigeria.
Photo courtesy Dele Jegede.

problems identified, but solutions are also prescribed. Herein lies one of the distinct features of the new religion: the ability to empathize with individuals, and to show concern in personal matters. In urban areas, where individuals may be left to their own devices and confronted with waves of familial, financial, and other socioeconomic problems, the Aladura church becomes a surrogate extended family. Whereas orthodox Christianity is calendrical and mass-oriented, Aladura is more intimately concerned with using the spiritual medium to assist its members in achieving marital, financial, professional, and social success.

Theater

The theatrical fervor with which the members of the Aladura movement conduct their services is a link with popular theater. It is necessary to begin consideration of

Plate 77. New Messenger Apostolic Church,
Soweto, South Africa.
Photo courtesy United Nations/151668/DB.

popular theater in urban Africa with a note of caution. The sense in which the concept of theater is used here transcends the narrow confines of the formalistic tradition of Western classical theater, with its dependence on the proscenium and a penchant for scripted presentations which are vigorously rehearsed, very tightly programmed, and clinically executed. While contemporary dramaturgy in Africa has been influenced by Western theatrical traditions, popular theater derives its energy from taking generous liberties, from constant adaptation and improvisation, eclecticism, and audience participation. Indeed, a liberal definition of theater might lead to the conclusion that much of urban Africa is a vast living theater.

For example, in a city such as Lagos, where perennial traffic congestion has defied the ingenuity of a succession of military and civilian administrators, catching public transport could be both traumatic and funny. The popular commuter buses in Lagos are known as *molu e,* a Yoruba derivation of the injunction "mold it," which is itself an attribute of the no-nonsense stance of the rude and irreverent bus conductors, who are always ready to do battle with recalcitrant or smart commuters and "mold" their faces into shapeless mounds. The *molu e* bus is the modern edition of the wooden mini truck, *bole k'aja,* which in Yoruba translates to "come down and let us fight." It is not unusual to become drenched in a *molu e* during a downpour when the battered roof leaks while the decrepit floor lets in a flood. To take a ride in a *molu e* is to witness unrehearsed drama. The bus itself, which is certified to carry no more than twenty-five passengers, ends up with twice that number. There are many more passengers standing than seated. The mechanic with his heavily soiled uniform challenges the bank clerk for a seat, using the latter's necktie to pull him back; the market woman with a basket of pepper straps one child securely to her back and pushes the older one into the bus before rushing to force her basket into the bus through a forest of legs. She loses one shoe to the encounter, as the gangling ten-year-old conductor issues the "go on machine" order to the driver, who himself is stripped to his waist, soaked in his own sweat in the ninety-degree tropical heat. As the *molu e* speeds down the busy lane, an itinerant salesman who is perched on the doorstep clears his throat and launches into ribaldry spiced with prayers for potential Muslim and Christian customers. In the end, he announces what he calls the greatest medical discovery of all time for the cure of two hundred ailments (*awogba arun*), from premenstrual pains to barrenness, from gonorrhea to insomnia. At the next stop, the salesman alights, the bus moves on, and the drama continues. This vignette brings us once again to our theme concerning the intimate relationship between art and life in Africa, a relationship which becomes accentuated in urban centers.

Of course, not all of popular theater is unscripted and unrehearsed. Indeed, this is a field of specialists, from actors and actresses to dancers, drummers, and a host of others with special skills. Many of these artists have persisted in their chosen career in spite of the cynicism and the negative image of the theater artist that society harbors. Two broad categories of theater artists have emerged across the continent, both of which have been inspired by the Western tradition. The first is the company of professional artists who built their own talents on the initial exposure received through missionary school dramatic activities or youth or club associations. The second group comprises theater artists who received their education in formal academic institutions, or are associated with college-based theater companies.

The evolution of popular theater in the mid-thirties in Lubumbashi, Zaire, demonstrates that Catholic missions, in alliance with a mining company, were instrumental in promoting theater as a means of channeling the energy of urban youths toward a productive end.[5] The youngsters soon outgrew acting in short humorous sketches in the Boy Scouts and singing in the Girl Guides, and mission-inspired plays in French gave way to improvised theater in Swahili. In 1957, the first major production by Kisimba and Mufwankolo received the patronage of the expatriate community and other colonial interests in Lubumbashi. With the success attained by this production, the development of professional popular theater in Zaire was well under way. This Lubumbashi situation is paradigmatic of popular theater in Africa. In Nigeria, for example, the doyen of popular theater, the late Hubert Ogunde, who quit his job as a policeman in the mid-forties to establish his own theater group, was inspired by the concept of theater as popularized by missionary school biblical enactments and concerts. Others such as Oyin Adejobi and the late Kola Ogunmola have created a new culture of popular entertainment which combines modern stage lighting, props, and decor with improvisation and audience participation. The late Duro Ladipo extended the frontiers of this category to engaging heights with his adaptation of Yoruba epics and historical tragedies such as *Oba Koso* and *Moremi*, both of which drew huge audiences at home and abroad in the sixties.

During this period when the winds of change swept across Africa and many countries secured their independence from colonial powers, popular theater developed into a powerful medium of social entertainment and education, a medium of slapstick humor and ethnic jokes, social satire and scathing political moralization. Unlike conventional Western theater, which relies mainly on the language of the colonizer, popular theater speaks the language—slang, effete mannerisms, and all—of the person on the street and the neighbor next door. It communicates with the struggling urban worker and satirizes the boss/bossed relationship that townspeople are only too familiar with. Audiences are addressed directly, and their spontaneous side comments and unrehearsed interjections may actually be woven into the fabric of the play. In Nigeria, the Yoruba have elevated this genre to new heights. A group of popular comedians has emerged in the last three decades, pioneered by Moses Olaiya, who is popularly known as Baba Sala, unquestionably the most hilarious character. The trademark of Baba Sala's Alawada Group is a cross between buffoonery and sauciness. Baba Sala's appearance often evokes animated laughter in his audience, even before he puts on his act. He performs in an outrageous costume—he straps on a polka-dot eighteen-inch cardboard bowtie, adorns his wrist with an enormous watch, dons an oversize coat over his Yoruba danshiki, and constantly puffs at a harmless wooden pipe.

The second group of artists, those who are academically trained, have begun to experiment with certain elements which are believed to have guaranteed the popularity of the likes of Mufwankolo, Ogunde, and Baba Sala. Increasingly, local languages, pidgin, Creole, and other variants are being used. An emerging trend in this type of theater is to use performance as a didactic platform to inculcate in the audience social or political awareness, or to inspire them to support a particular project or embrace a viewpoint. For example, early in 1994, in Johannesburg, South Africa, the Performing Arts Company of the Windybrow Arts Center (PACT) presented *Katakata for Sofahead*. Written in pidgin by Segun Oyekunle and directed by Walter Chakela, *Katakata* is about the experiences of inmates in a prison, and about the social environment that sustains poverty.[6] For South African actors, the challenge that *Katakata* presented was at once linguistic and social. While it demonstrates the possibility of the emergence of a popular Pan-African language, it also shows that urban centers across the continent share a number of things in common, including a culture of poverty. Two other examples are commissioned drama written by Western-trained professional theater artists. The first comes from Uganda, where Rose Mbowa's play *Mother Uganda and Her Children* was first performed at Makerere University in 1987. Since then, it has been taken to other international festivals. The play affirms Uganda's ethnic diversity and celebrates its multicultural traditions through a panoply of songs, dances, mime, and music, carefully selected from the various ethnic groups.[7] The second example is a play which was produced for UNESCO by the Nigerian playwright Bode Osanyin as part of the campaign to popularize family planning among the people. In this play, *Ayitale, the Fruits That Crushed the Trunk,* which was taken to the rural populations in Igbogbo near Lagos, Osanyin depicts the pathetic plight of a poor woman who is married to a bicycle repairer. Because the couple found family planning a crazy and strange idea, it was quickly abandoned. In the process of having her eleventh child, however, the woman died.

These commissioned plays are few and far between, however, and no matter their appeal to popular sympathy, they often do not compare favorably, in spontaneity, improvisation, and adaptation, with less-endowed grassroots theaters. In Uganda today, there is a renaissance of dramatic clubs which, although less financially viable and technically supported than Rose Mbowa and Bode Osanyin, play no less relevant a role. Every Saturday in the poorest districts of Kampala, theater groups perform improvised social comedy laced with political commentaries to packed houses. The demand for popular theater in Uganda has been ascribed to the fact that other than soccer, theater is one of the few sources of entertainment available to urban audiences.

The Mass Media: The Cinema and the Press

Metropolitan centers in Africa are a showcase for the display of modern technology and channels for propagating a myriad of ideas. The advent of the print media promoted a culture of information dissemination and consumption at the same time that it stimulated the curiosity of the urban worker. Newspaper kiosks emerged on street corners, supplemented by professional vendors who, on foot or bicycles, gave a new bent to the town crier's oral poetry. Equally influential is the ubiquitous transistor radio, which has endeared itself to people from all walks of life, from the farmer to the factory worker, all of whom have learned to order their daily schedule according to certain key programs such as the local news. In addition to the radio's easy portability, certain programs, especially those in the local language, have a wide appeal. The other important influential medium of dissemination is television. Since it made its debut in Nigeria in 1959, television has gradually become the essential companion of the urban worker. Its hold on urban audiences is immense, especially in the area of entertainment, where foreign music programs, soap operas, sports, and action movies are a source of fascination and acculturation for millions of Africans. In Kenya, for example, viewers are constantly fed on KTN such programs as "L.A. Law," "Royal Rumble" (Wrestling), "Road Runner," "Neighbors," "Larry King Live," and a host of American movies and musicals, including country and rap music. In most African cities, television antennas are being supplemented with satellite dishes which have become emblematic of the rising middle class. The growth of television in Africa has been enhanced by local programming, especially drama in indigenous languages. Local programs which explore the mystery of mythological or supernatural existence, or portray the stresses and mischievousness inherent in polygynous marriages, usually hold audiences spellbound, especially where such programs are serialized. Thus, this seemingly innocuous modern device has become one of the most influential agents of social change. Certainly it is the most popular and most accessible medium of cheap entertainment for the urban dweller.

The arrival of television in Africa was preceded by the cinema, however. In the hands of imperialist administrators, the cinema was an effective weapon for the propagation and entrenchment of Western ideology. In anglophone, lusophone, and francophone Africa, the cinema was used in varying degrees by colonial powers as an educational and propaganda tool. Its importance today as a medium for the presentation and contemplation of intra-African cultural and political issues as well as its relevance to a growing number of popular artists was probably not anticipated by those who introduced it. The development of the basic infrastructure on which the emergence of African cinema was based dates back to the colonial period, and cannot be divorced from the Eurocentric arrogance that colored Euro-African relations at this period. In the English-speaking countries, the cinema industry owed its origin in 1935 to the establishment by Britain of the Bantu Educational Cinema Experiment in Tanzania, which was the precursor of the Colonial Film Unit a few years later.[8] The situation in the Belgian Congo in the mid-thirties was similar to that in British colonies. A Film and Photo Bureau was established by Belgium soon after the Second World War, in 1947, which produced films for local consumption. In addition to this, Catholic missions in this region also established film production centers for the propagation of religious doctrines. When anglophone countries became free of colonial domination, only Ghana and Nigeria found it expedient to sustain the activities of their film units, while the activities of the colonial and missionary film units ceased as soon as Zaire became independent in 1960. The lusophone countries of Guinea-Bissau, Mozambique, and Angola fared much worse: there were no enduring structural facilities to inherit from Portugal. Today, it is in francophone Africa that a vibrant cinema culture exists, arising from the strong cultural, political, and economic relationship which exists between France and French-speaking African countries. Such a relationship did not come about until the 1960s, after several of its colonies had attained independence. This was the period when the French Ministry of Cooperation decided to commit human and financial resources to the creation of the Consortium Audio-visual International (CIA), in order to assist former colonies to develop a strong cinema industry.

Thus, the importance of cinema as a medium for social change remains strong throughout the continent. Since independence, the relentless pace of transformation which has affected several spheres of life has touched the cinema. Gone is the mobile cinema, a colonial feature of towns and villages in English- and French-speaking areas. The arrival in a town of the mobile cinema unit was a sure invitation to the people, who would excitedly abandon their evening chores and troop after the vehicle. Such excitement was no less intense in rural areas, where the entry of the mobile cinema unit generated clouds of dust, and children scampered after the unit in ecstatic screams. The loud music blaring from their huge speakers was often interrupted by a public invitation to the evening's show at the town square.

At the cinemas which have sprung up in urban centers, Indian and American films are the staple menu, interspersed with occasional European films. In cities, a popular culture has thus evolved, nurtured by the gunslinging antics and dangerous car chases of American film heroes. Equally, Indian films, regardless of the criticisms that these have drawn from the elite and the academics, continue to draw a substantial following from an appreciative crowd of urban workers. But the situation is changing. The number of African filmmakers is growing, although they continue to operate under difficult circumstances. Pioneer filmmakers such as Ousmane Sembene of Senegal and Ola Balogun of Nigeria continue to explore and exploit the relevance of the film in contemporary Africa. Like several other Western media and processes, the film has become a tool for countermanding stereotypical views and assumptions about the continent. For urban Africans who patronize this medium, there is a sense of fulfillment and self-congratulation in watching a film that is made by Africans for Africans. In the last three decades, the continent has witnessed the establishment of organizations which are devoted to the promotion of an African film industry and which can also effectively mobilize Africans and influence political ideology. In addition to the existence of film institutes, for example in Burkina Faso, Zimbabwe, Kenya, Ghana, and Nigeria, there has been since 1969 the Festival Panafricain du Cinema de Ouagadougou (FESPACO), whose annual film festivals have become perhaps Africa's most spectacular cultural jamboree. For example, the 1993 FESPACO attracted more than 130 films and drew a strong international audience of actors, actresses, directors, and audiences. When this is viewed against the situation in Nigeria, where there is a growing interest in local film production, leading to the first Nigerian Film Festival, which was held in Lagos in 1992, it becomes apparent that the importance of cinema as an agent of cultural change and a disseminator of popular culture cannot be underestimated.

In the hands of theater artists, the cinema offers enormous advantages over live theater. As has been realized by a number of Yoruba theater groups, the cinema presents immense opportunities to reach thousands of people at different venues simultaneously. This provides a welcome relief from the rigors of traveling from one point to another, with all the risks and uncertainties that are involved. Moreover, the technology evokes the same response patterns among Africans as it does among any other people worldwide. It elevates the commonplace to the sublime and makes heroes out of simple folks and actors. For many urban workers who have been brought up on a diet of American and Indian films, seeing elements of their own culture, listening to dialogue and folksongs in their mother tongue, and even seeing familiar streets or landmarks on the big screen are an unforgettable thrill. It is this phenomenon that explains the growing popularity of indigenous films, regardless of the quality of the production.

The press is yet another dimension of popular culture in urban Africa. As in other parts of the world, the press is an important tool of communication, social mobilization, and cultural change. Those who control the press have access to power and are in a position to influence public opinion and political developments. The enormous power of the press in Africa has led to the intense interest of various African governments in controlling press ownership. In several instances, other organs of communication such as the radio and television are under government control, and where they are not, the relationship between officials and private enterpreneurship is inevitably one of suspicion. Press censorship is commonplace, especially in African countries where military dictatorships are in power, or one-party political systems have been entrenched.

Most of Africa's nationalist fighters of the precolonial era, for example, Kwame Nkrumah of Ghana, Nnamidi Azikiwe and Obafemi Awolowo, both of Nigeria, Patrice Lumumba of Congo, and Jomo Kenyatta of Kenya, effectively utilized the press in their campaigns for national independence. Today, while the significance of politics remains unquestionable, publishers have realized that in addition to political issues and ideologies, they must also sell newspapers. This path has led to the introduction of features which are meant to generate revenue, captivate a new following, and maintain existing readership levels. Newspapers have attempted to meet this imperative in two ways: through their obituary columns and through the use of cartoons.

Among Nigerians, paid obituary advertisements have been developed to an art. Because advertisement rates for obituaries are the highest, taking out a full-page ad to announce the passing away of a loved one or the thirtieth anniversary of the death of a grandparent is generally regarded as socially prestigious. This is not unexpected in a country where it is easier to obtain loans for expensive burial ceremonies than to send a child to college. Such advertisements are used to legitimize claims to political influence, since the advertiser makes it a point of thanking an endless list of political personages for sympathies expressed or implied. Obituaries also provide advertisers with the chance to let their imaginary enemies know that the worst is over. After the good deeds of the deceased have been extolled, and after he or she has been sent to sit at the right hand of the Lord, a long list of successors, which may include some who are already dead, is then published with an appropriate photograph or artwork.

While obituaries bring in revenue for newspapers, cartoons generate readership and sustain interest. In the turbulent political environment which prevails in many African countries today, political cartoons are a sure means of bringing smiles to the faces of the marginalized and overwhelmed urban worker. In a few deft brush strokes, the cartoonist invents scenarios that become metaphors for social or political situations. Subject matters are not limited to politics, however. For example, the *Daily Nation* of Kenya, in its January 10, 1994, issue, published a cartoon by Gado which depicts an embattled Michael Jackson sitting on the bare floor with his hands and outstretched legs tied by several tapes on which allegations of child abuse and child molestation are printed. Before the April 1994 elections in South Africa, in which Nelson Mandela emerged as the nation's first black president, a turbulent situation provoked by the antagonistic stand of Mangosuthu Buthelezi and his Inkatha Freedom Party was captured by Gado in the February 3, 1994, edition of the *Daily Nation*.

In this cartoon Buthelezi emerges from nowhere, spear drawn, to puncture the soccer ball with which Mandela and Frederick de Klerk are playing. Favorite subjects of cartoonists include military dictatorships, corruption, the tension in the educational sector, and, inevitably, the state of the economy. There are also cartoons which are targeted at urban workers: cartoons which depict or parody the anguish and predicament of the urban poor while taking swipes at elites.

Music

Urban dwellers delight in immersing themselves, especially on special occasions, in the exhilaration and uproarious jollity that music brings. On a Saturday evening in a typical beer parlor or "people's hotel," the combination of music and locally brewed millet beer, palm wine, or a combination of any of these creates an intoxicating *joie de vivre*. The range and styles of popular music produced in Africa are as varied as the people who produce them, and the audiences for whom they are produced. In general, popular music is characterized by adaptation, innovation, eclecticism, and synthesis. Instances of these abound; *juju* and *fuji* music from Nigeria, Zairian *soukous*, South African *mbaqanga*, and *mbalax* from Senegal variously owe their origin to aspects of traditional African culture, from naming ceremonies to observances of the Muslim Ramadan festival and from court music to circumcision rites. The key point in our consideration of popular music in urban Africa has been aptly summarized: "Everywhere there is mixture, collision and collusion. Africa 'impacts' on the West; the West on Africa."[9] This observation sufficiently underlines the tradition of give and take, of continuity and change, innovation and adaptation, which are central to the evolution of popular music and indeed popular culture in urban Africa. The electronic guitar, synthesized bass and drums, computerized organs, amplified wind instruments, and a variety of modern musical gadgets are adapted and fused with an array of traditional African musical instruments. African stringed instruments which have been incorporated into pop music include the *xalam* and the *kora*, which are common among West African *jalis* or *griots*, while traditional percussion instruments include the *sekere* (gourds of portable sizes which are strung with cowry shells, seeds, or beads) and the hourglass talking drum, known as *gangan* in Nigeria and *tama* in Senegal. All of these are complemented by an assortment of other instruments such as the *balafon* wooden xylophone common in Mali, Guinea, and Senegal, and thumb pianos such as the *mbira*, a favored instrument among Zimbabwean pop artists.

The human body is also a musical instrument. The process of making music in traditional Africa involves using the body to produce sound that accentuates or complements rhythm. The waist, arms, wrists, legs, and ankles are fully utilized in aid of percussion since they are adorned with small stringed bells and rattles which produce jingling sounds as the body moves to the rhythm and the legs hit the ground. In many instances, music and dance are inseparable. In such situations, the drums and the dancers are simultaneously engaged in a call-and-response dialogue, with movements, gestures, and the tempo of the dance dictated by the drums. This call-and-refrain pattern, between the soloist and the chorus, in songs or instrumentals, is a popular feature of modern pop music in Africa. For example, one of Africa's most celebrated pop artists, the irrepressible Fela Anikulapo-Kuti, employs the call-and-refrain style in almost all of his work in a seemingly inexhaustible fashion.

Popular music is not confined to specialists. There are occasions, such as campaign rallies, political demonstrations, or soccer matches, when the crowd bursts into songs composed spontaneously to meet the mood. What the audience is celebrating on such occasions is the spirit of the event, rather than the musical performance. Soccer is undoubtedly the form of entertainment that draws the largest crowds in urban Africa. Over the years, keen rivalries between local and national teams have found expression in the formation of supporters' clubs, whose primary objective is to provide support for their teams and to generate excitement for the game. At major intra-African games, such as the African Cup or Nations Cup, drummers who also double as singers can be seen along the sidelines, literally drumming up support for their respective teams. Such drumming, which is usually ferocious and insistent, generally continues nonstop during the ninety-minute game. A variety of percussion instruments, such as the hourglass talking and conga drums, slit and iron gongs, portable xylophones, as well as horns, are also employed. At the end of a particularly testy national or international match that the home team has finally won, a Lagos crowd at the National Stadium may burst out in a boisterous and frenzied chorus:

Baba ti bawa se	The Lord has done it for us
Baba ti bawa se o	Yes, the Lord has done it for us
Ohun to njawa laya	That which has been a nightmare for us
Baba ti bawa se	The Lord has done it for us

Or simply, "O se . . . o se o . . . o se o . . . o se baba": thank you, thank you, thank you, Lord.

In numerous cultures all over the world, music has always had a grip on youth. The situation in urban Africa is no different in this respect. The difference lies in the variety of musical expressions that are available to them, including the West and the African diaspora. One of the distinct features of popular music among the young people is the frequency with which musical events are organized in urban areas. In turn, this results in the synthesis of foreign and indigenous musical mannerisms and encourages the proliferation of amateur pop groups whose activities further spread the gospel of popular music. The latest rave among African youths is reggae, which has its origin in Jamaica. Jamaican reggae is steeped in the Rastafarian philosophy, which affirms the belief of Jamaicans in the sacredness of Ethiopian civilization and the profoundness of its religious ancestry. Rastafarianism, or Ethiopianism, which was bolstered by the political and religious activism of Marcus Garvey in the 1920s, led to the deification of Ras Tafari, the late Haile Selassie I, who ascended the throne in Ethiopia in 1930. Rastafarians combine their ascetic brand of music with a public persona that commands attention: dreadlocks and a head covering of green, yellow, black, and red colors (known as a tam) are standard insignia.

Clearly, the musical outlook and social orientation of today's youth in urban Africa differ considerably from those of the preceding decades. The generation which savored the rock music of Elvis and the Beatles, or post–World War II highlife music from Ghana's E. T. Mensah to Nigeria's Victor Olaiya, is content today to wax nostalgic by listening to some of the hits that defined the early post-independence period on vinyl. The glamour and allure that such American stars as James Brown and Isaac Hayes held for African youths now belongs to the past, just as Michael Jackson's domination of the pop scene is no longer total or unquestionable, thanks to MTV, which continues to beam to urban Africa a variety of new talents, including Hammer, Janet Jackson, Toni Braxton, Snoop Doggy Dogg, and Whitney Houston, among a long list of others. The influence which these artists exert on young Africans transcends the new fad of staying perpetually tuned in through "Walkmans"; it also touches on such other departments as fashion and attitudes. A visit to a local disco session will easily confirm the extent to which urban Africa has been permeated by Americanism.

This does not mean, however, that local popular music is subservient to or completely dominated by foreign pop culture. There are, in fact, some local idols who have exported their brand of African popular music abroad, to Europe and America, where their style continues to influence a new generation of admirers. This continues the give-and-take paradigm. In the early 1970s, London was agog over the exhilarating polyrhythmic sounds created by Osibisa, a band which was formed by a group of London-based black musicians led by Teddy Osei, a Ghanaian. Osibisa's success signaled the entry into the international market of many other Africa-based pop musicians, including two of Nigeria's most popular *juju* musicians, Ebenezer Obey and King Sunny Ade. The latter enjoys tremendous popularity and acceptance in Nigeria, and has had considerable success abroad, arising from his association with Island Records, which successfully organized his European and American tour in 1983. A review by London's *Guardian* newspaper provides a useful insight into the distinctions between European and African popular music:

> Sunny Ade . . . functions less as a star performer than as a conductor orchestrating a series of musical dialogues. [His] show offered a marked contrast with western song structure and our notions of musical climax. Although the set was divided into songs of varying mood and tempo one had the impression it was all part of the same fabric. Each number ended abruptly—in mid sentence as it were—yet without any feeling of discontinuity. They could have all started at any point and played for ever. Their skills and joyful dedication had the effect of making the panorama of English rock music look jaded and trite.[10]

A consideration of popular music would not be complete without a mention of the relevance of Miriam Makeba from South Africa and Fela Anikulapo-Kuti, Nigeria's "enfant terrible," to political developments in Africa. These are two of the most important icons of popular music, both of whom have demonstrated that popular music can indeed be used both as a means of social mobilization and as a political weapon to combat oppression and dictatorship. The institutionalization of *apartheid* in South Africa resulted in the attempted suppression of popular music, a situation which forced many South African artists, such as Dudu Pukwana, Lucky Ranku, and Miriam Makeba, into exile. The musical career of Miriam Makeba, who is generally regarded as Africa's foremost female vocalist, dates back to the fifties in South Africa. During the British tour of *King Kong*, a black opera in which she played the lead role, Makeba went into exile in the United States to pursue her career, becoming one of the strongest anti-*apartheid* crusaders. Fela Anikulapo-Kuti, on the other hand, is based in Nigeria. However, he has experienced government intimidation at the hands of military officers on account of his ceaseless criticism of government policies. His "Kalakuta Republic" home was burned down in broad daylight in 1977 by "unknown" soldiers, while in 1984 he was jailed by yet another military government. The cumulative impact of this has endeared him to millions of Nigerian youths in addition to bolstering his strident anti-establishment posture. His music is his greatest weapon, and he employs it to tell the government what the urban masses and the marginalized workers know but are afraid to verbalize.

Art

With regard to popular art, certain generalizations can safely be made. First, this art is reflective of the caring and interdependent system of interactions which characterizes urban life in Africa. Second, popular art reveals the creative resourcefulness of a people who are being constantly challenged by the perennial influx of Western culture to adapt and innovate without compromising the salient philosophical principles which inform social relations. Third, popular art is, to some extent, on a continuum with traditional arts of Africa in the extent to which both are the physical objectification of an African world view. Both of these art forms reveal an art that is functional and decorative, an art that mirrors and celebrates life, that assists us in constructing the tempo and nature of change over a period of time. Popular art draws its strength from the basic need of people to express themselves and earn a living. Its existence can thus be found in aesthetics and economics or a combination of the two. Popular art manifests itself in several spheres of human endeavor. Its impact is everywhere, from tourist-related events to architecture, from mural designs to fashion. It is sometimes difficult to draw the line between "popular" art and that category which scholars generally refer to as "traditional" art, by which is often implied an art that is worthy of being displayed in Western museums.

The fusion of these so-called distinct art forms is shown in the impact of tourism on popular art, and the incorporation of non-African items or icons into African art, a phenomenon which dates back to the fifteenth century, when Benin artists carved some ivory utensils for visiting Portuguese sailors. Much of what is today regarded as exemplary pieces of "traditional" African art was used originally in the context of popular art. Popular art is perhaps among the initial sources of attraction for the first-time traveler in Africa. In the airport lounge, the hotel foyer, or any of the tourist centers in the city, an assortment of artworks are usually available at reasonable prices. These range from carvings of varying sizes to landscape paintings, from portable drums to beaded staffs. The manufacture of fakes and forgeries for an unsuspecting clientele has become a thriving industry because of the economic returns it offers. Because it is inexpensive and mass-produced, popular art indeed serves the needs of urban dwellers, who cannot afford the usually expensive and often cerebral intellectual art done by elite artists.

Tourism has become an industry which demonstrates the resourcefulness of Africans at capitalizing upon their relationship with curious clients. Rites and rituals which are normally performed on special occasions are now routinely staged for the benefit of tourists and television crews. Paul Lane's work among the Dogon of Mali, for example, shows that tourist officials arrange the staging and directing of dances normally performed as part of funeral rites for the pleasure and convenience of tourists.[11] In the course of such transformations, new forms of popular art emerge. As local materials become difficult to obtain or as imported substitutes become more readily available, innovation takes over, leading to the birth of, say, new costumes for old masquerades. Some of the accouterments of various masquerades constitute a study in appropriation and adaptation. Masqueraders, who are generally revered because they are considered sacred and are believed to be reincarnated ancestors, are now known to wear Nike shoes. Frequently, libations are poured not with local brew but with the best whiskey; some will even specify by name "White Horse" or "Seaman's Schnapps."

In architecture, the twin concepts of adaptation and appropriation define urban and rural landscapes across the continent. The murals on the adobe architecture of the northern belt of Africa combine arabesque and geometric motifs with abstract depictions of bicycles, airplanes, and agricultural implements. In South Africa, this same tendency to incorporate foreign elements is characteristic of the wall murals of the Ndebele people, who have established an impressive visual vocabulary that includes such items as airplanes, buses, clocks, trains, and electric bulbs. Because of their durability and variety of colors, synthetic paints have superseded locally produced earth colors in the design of murals. In urban centers, mural design is only one in a repertoire of designs that the popular artist is capable of executing. In addition to painting larger-than-life pictures of popular figures, such as military rulers and popular musicians, on the walls of his studio, the sign writer/muralist also executes commissioned paintings, usually of provocative women or musicians, on the walls of hotels or beer halls.

Some of the best examples that showcase the popular artist's sense of humor and the combination of aphorisms with fanciful decorativeness are the trucks or luxury buses which are a regular sight on African roads. In Ghana and Nigeria, to cite just two examples, popular artists have turned truck decoration into an engaging exercise. Beautifully painted signs are drawn from proverbs, individual experiences, the Bible, or any catchwords that may be in currency among the people. A journeyman driver who has finally bought a dilapidated bus may have it repainted, with phrases such as "The reward of patient" [sic] and "Where's Yours?" painted on either side. While the signs give reminders of some truisms such as "Sea never dry" and "God's case no appeal," they also ask the reader not to forget that "The world is a market," and to

Plate 78. *Coronation* (1983), an oil painting by Kenneth Ideh.
Photo courtesy Dele Jegede.

"Remember six feet." This last phrase is meant to emphasize the fact that death is an equalizer, and that regardless of how powerful or rich the deceased, a grave will measure only six feet, just like that of the poor that the person may have oppressed.

The popular artist also gives a glimpse of popular fashion. Hairdressers' salons and barbershops regularly display painted or drawn collections of the various hairstyles that they specialize in. For women there are two distinct areas of specialization. One is the Westernized style, which requires some familiarization with the use of hair dryers and hair-care products, while the other is the traditional plaiting and weaving style. The popular artist faithfully illustrates the numerous hairstyles that are available from these two categories, making it easier for clients to choose for themselves. Traditional hairstyling is sometimes created simply for aesthetic reasons or for the commemoration of significant local events. In Nigeria during the early 1970s, the completion of the second bridge linking the Lagos mainland with the island led to the creation of a complex hairstyle that was branded Eko Bridge, while the Second World Black and African Festival of Arts and Culture, which Nigeria hosted early in 1977, inspired yet another hairstyle, which was christened FESTAC, the acronym for this international event.

In the world of fashion, Africans pay considerable attention to the head. In addition to hairstyling, there are also a variety of types of headgear for women and

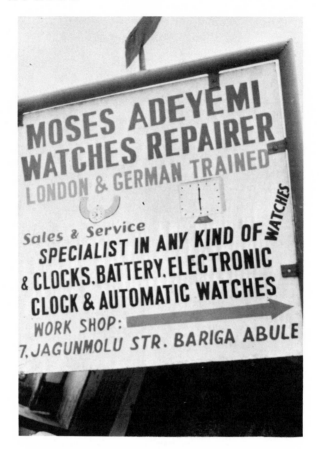

Plate 79. Advertising, Lagos style.
Photo courtesy Dele Jegede.

caps for men, many of which, like hairstyles, derive their names from sources that include events and personalities. Taken in their totality, hairstyling, fashion, and textiles are cultural determinants. They project a group or individual aesthetic, a religious or social outlook. A casual glance often provides the perceptive observer a sufficient indication of the event for which people are dressed, the social class to which they belong, and the ethnic group or, at international forums, the country that they come from. Among the various peoples of West Africa, there is a wide variety of hand-woven cloths, many of which are produced from imported silk yarns, which come in an assortment of brilliant colors. Among the Asante of Ghana, the kente cloth, which is woven on the men's horizontal strip loom, is emblematic of grandeur. Although the wearing of kente is no longer the prerogative of the royalty in Ghana, it nevertheless retains its link with preeminence and distinction, as has been exemplified by the special attachment that African Americans have for it in the United States.

Above all in urban Africa, youth, through their fashion, show the influence of a myriad of factors, including taste, music, peer pressure, and the sociopolitical climate. Of course, the influence of Euro-American culture is apparent in what the youths wear, from college T shirts to faded jeans; from hi-tops to boys' earrings and necklaces. At more formal occasions, Western wear is likely to yield to African fashion. Women have a variety of styles to choose from, depending on the occasion. Among West African women in general, a short blouse, sleeveless, short-sleeved, or with large, medium, or long sleeves, is worn over a generous wraparound, usually of the same material. A second but smaller wraparound may be used over the first. This is complemented with headgear, the volume and style of which depend on the seriousness of the occasion. Men generally wear modernized drawstring breeches with an embroidered caftan on top. At other times, a big blouse or tunic may be worn under a much bigger, more voluminous, and fully embroidered *riga* or *agbada*. In almost all instances, formal wear is incomplete without a cap. The materials from which these dresses are made may be imported or locally made factory cloth. The economic downturn in many African countries has provoked an upsurge in hand-printed textiles, particularly the tie-dye genre, for which many countries in West Africa, including Nigeria, Côte d'Ivoire, Burkina Faso, and Senegal, are noted.

Conclusion

The conclusion that we draw from the foregoing demonstrates the interrelation-ship of the arts especially in urban Africa and the fluid, sometimes imperceptible boundaries that separate popular culture from high or elitist tastes and indulgences. Although Africa remains a continent in a perpetual state of animated flux, it has also demonstrated its capacity to judiciously sift and synthesize, to adapt and create in a way that underlines the resilience of African culture. Urban centers all over the continent are undoubtedly a cultural caldron, and there is no reason to suggest that the inventiveness and adaptive resources of urban Africans will not be carried over into the twenty-first century.

NOTES

1. For a comprehensive view of urbanism in modern Africa, see the following sources: Richard E. Stren and Rodney E. White, eds., *African Cities in Crisis* (Boulder, Colo., and San Francisco: Westview Press, 1989); Margaret Peil and Pius O. Sada, *African Urban Society* (New York: John Wiley and Sons, 1984); Donald George Morrison et al., *Black Africa: A Comparative Handbook*, 2nd ed. (New York: Irvington Publishers, 1989).

2. John S. Mbiti, *African Religions and Philosophy* (New York: Anchor Books Doubleday and Co., Inc., 1969), pp. 1–7.

3. My appreciation goes to Ebenezer Dadson, Stella Wachira, and Zikpi Olivia for sharing with me their knowledge of Ghanaian and Kenyan popular culture. An additional useful source which may be consulted with regard to festivals in Ghana is *The Arts of Ghana*, by Herbert M. Cole and Doran H. Ross (Los Angeles: The Museum of Cultural History, University of California, 1977).

4. Sheila S. Walker, "Women in the Harrist Movement," in Bennetta Jules-Rosette, ed., *The New Religions of Africa* (Norwood, N.J.: Ablex Publishing Corp., 1979), pp. 87–97.

5. For a compelling and detailed reading of the evolution of popular theater in the Shaba region of Zaire, see Johannes Fabian, *Power and Performance: Ethnographic Explorations through Proverbial Wisdom and Theater in Shaba, Zaire* (Madison: University of Wisconsin Press, 1990).

6. Chris Dunton, "Slapstick in Johannesburg," *West Africa*, 18–24 April 1994, pp. 690–91.

7. Eckhard Breitinger, "Agitprop for a Better World: Development Theater—A Political Grassroots Theatre Movement," in Raoul Granqvist, ed., *Signs and Signals: Popular Culture in Africa* (Stockholm: UMEA, 1990), pp. 93–120.

8. For a comprehensive overview of the evolution of the cinema industry in colonial and postcolonial Africa, see Manthia Diawara's *African Cinema* (Bloomington: Indiana University Press, 1992). My discussion of the cinema in Africa has drawn heavily from this excellent source.

9. Chris Stapleton and Chris May, *African Rock: The Pop Music of a Continent* (New York: Dutton, 1990), p. 5.

10. Quoted from John Collins, *West African Pop Roots* (Philadelphia: Temple University Press, 1992), p. 91.

11. Paul J. Lane, "Tourism and Social Change among the Dogon," *African Arts* 21, no. 4 (1988): 66–69, 92.

SUGGESTIONS FOR FURTHER READING

Cole, Herbert M., and Doran H. Ross. *The Arts of Ghana*. Los Angeles: Museum of Cultural History, 1977.

Diawara, Manthia. *African Cinema*. Bloomington: Indiana University Press, 1992.

Fabian, Johannes. *Power and Performance: Ethnographic Explorations through Proverbial Wisdom and Theater in Shaba, Zaire*. Madison: University of Wisconsin Press, 1990.

Jegede, Dele. "Popular Culture and Popular Music: The Nigerian Experience." *Presence Africaine* 144, no. 4 (1987): 59–72.

Mbiti, John. *African Religions and Philosophy*. Portsmouth, N.H.: Heinemann, 1990.

Stapleton, Chris, and Chris May. *African Rock: The Pop Music of a Continent*. New York: Dutton, 1990.

Vogel, Susan. *Africa Explores: 20th Century African Art*. New York: The Center for African Art, 1991.

African Arts and *West Africa* are two additional sources in which articles on various aspects of popular arts in Africa can be found.

Eileen Julien
African Literature

"Truth depends not only on who listens but on who speaks."
                                        —Birago Diop
"Always something new from Africa."
                                        —Rabelais

15 When most Americans and Europeans use the expression "African literature," what they mean is poetry, plays, and narrative written by Africans in English and French, and perhaps Portuguese. This chapter will focus primarily on these texts, sometimes referred to as "Euro-African," which are particularly accessible to Americans because of language and shared recent history. But it is not possible to speak or write of African literature as homogeneous or coherent, any more than this claim can be made for the varied texts that constitute European literature.[1] Africa is a vast continent, consisting of more than fifty nations and several hundred languages and ethnic groups. And despite many cultural similarities across the continent and a virtually ubiquitous history of imperialism and neocolonialism, there are many African experiences and many verbal expressions of them. Moreover, to see what we are calling African literature in proper perspective is to recognize from the outset both that it is a gendered body of work and that it represents but a fraction of the verbal arts in Africa. There is a vast production of African-language literature and oral traditions, which is largely unknown and ignored by those outside the continent.

Indeed, verbal artistic traditions, literary as well as oral, are ancient in Africa. Centuries before European colonialism and the introduction of European languages, there were bards and storytellers, scribes, poets, and writers in languages such as Kiswahili and Amharic. Many of those traditions adapt and live on in various guises today, and the African writers who will be considered in this chapter draw on these indigenous oral and written traditions as well as those of Europe, the Americas, and Asia.

Understanding of African literature has changed tremendously in the last twenty years, because of several important developments: the ever-increasing numbers of women writers, greater awareness of written and oral production in national languages (such as Yoruba, Poular, and Zulu), and greater critical attention to factors such as the politics of publishing and African literature's multiple audiences. These developments coincide with and have, in fact, helped produce a general shift in literary sensibility away from literature as pure *text*, the dominant paradigm for many years, to literature as an act between parties located within historical, socioeconomic and other contexts. Fiction, plays, and poetry by women from around the continent have been singularly important because they "complicate" the meaning of works by their literary forefathers, bringing those works into sharper relief, forcing us to see their limits as well as their merits.

There are many ways to divide the terrain of literature written by Africans. These approaches reflect the fact that the continent is home to many different peoples and cultural practices, political and physical geographies, local and nonlocal languages. Thus we routinely divide African literature by *region* (West Africa, East Africa, North Africa, Central Africa, southern Africa, each of which is more or less distinctive environmentally and historically), by *ethnicity* (the Mande, for example, live across the region now divided by the states of Guinea, Senegal, Côte d'Ivoire, and Mali), or by *nationality* (a heritage of nineteenth-century European literary practice, whose merit in the African context is sometimes debated, and which privileges the force of national history and identity as opposed to ethnic or "African" determinants).

African literature is also often categorized by *language* of expression (anglophone, francophone, Hausa, Swahili, etc.) or *genre* (poetry, proverb, narrative, drama, essay), or some combination of these. The field may also be examined in terms of *themes* or *generations*. These many approaches suggest not only the diversity and complexity of life on the African continent but also the stuff of which literature is made: language, aesthetic and literary traditions, culture and history, sociopolitical reality.

This chapter, then, is divided into three parts. The first part focuses on selected themes and trends of African literature. The second briefly describes several contemporary debates surrounding this literature and challenges and prospects facing African writers and readers of African texts. Some reference will be made to oral traditions and literature in national languages. The third part of this chapter includes a discussion of selected authors and their works.

Themes and Trends

African literature is vast and varied, but there are two impulses or currents in African creative works of which we might make special note: the reclaiming of voice and subjectivity and the critique of abusive power.

Colonialism and Self-Representation

In the 1950s and 1960s, as nations around the continent moved more or less slowly to achieve decolonization, many Africans took up the pen. There were indeed African creative writers, as well as essayists and polemicists, who wrote in European languages well before this time. But it is in this vast, concerted literary practice of midcentury that the moment of acceleration of contemporary African literature can be situated.

African narrative and poetry, in the era immediately preceding and following formal declarations of independence, were born, for the most part, in protest against history and myths constructed in conjunction with the colonial enterprise. Writers struggled to correct false images, to rewrite fictionally and poetically the history of precolonial and colonial Africa, and to affirm African perspectives. The implicit or explicit urge to challenge the premises of colonialism was often realized in autobiography or pseudo-autobiography, describing the journey the writers themselves had made, away from home to other shores and back again. African intellectuals and writers felt keenly that "the truth," as Birago Diop had put it, "depends also on *who* speaks."

In 1958, Chinua Achebe published *Things Fall Apart*. Characterized by a language rich in proverbs and images of agrarian life, this novel and his later *Arrow of God* portray the complex, delicately balanced social ecology of Igbo village life as it confronts colonial power. Achebe's protagonists are flawed but dignified men whose interactions with British emissaries are fatal or tragic. Achebe, like other writers of those years, wrote in response to denigrating mythologies and representations of Africans by nineteenth- and twentieth-century British and European writers such as Joyce Cary, James Conrad, Jules Verne, and Pierre Loti, to show, as Achebe put it, that the African past was not one long night of savagery before the coming of Europe.

Similar processes occurred, and still occur, within other traditions around the continent. The condemnation of colonial domination and the determination to bear witness are more urgent in the Portuguese-language poetry of Agostinho Neto and the fiction of José Luandino Vieira, because of Angola's long war of liberation. Ngugi wa Thiong'o's novels (*Weep Not, Child*, 1964; *The River Between*, 1965; and *A Grain of Wheat*, 1967) explore the many facets of individual Kenyan lives within the context of colonialism: their experiences of education, excision, religious conflict, collective struggle, and the cost of resistance. *A Grain of Wheat* suggests, moreover, the coalescing of lives and forces in the making of historical events.

In his *Death and the King's Horsemen* (1975), Wole Soyinka makes the colonial setting incidental, a mere catalyst, in what is the metaphysical crisis of a flawed character, who is nonetheless the agent of his destiny and of history. Elesin, who must die in order to follow the deceased king to "the other side," sees in the intervention of the British colonial authority a chance to stay his death and indulge his passion for life and love. Through every theatrical means—drum, chanted poetry, gesture, and dance, as well as script—Soyinka suggests the majesty, the social significance, and the great personal cost and honor of Elesin's task, and then the magnitude of his failure.

A particular strain and manifestation of anticolonialist poetry is the French-language tradition known as *négritude*. It was in Paris of the 1930s, in the climate of modernism, surrealism, and jazz, that the idea of négritude arose. African and West Indian students, who were French colonial subjects, had come to the capital to complete their education. Products of colonial schools and assimilationist policies that sought to make Frenchmen of them, they had been taught to reject their African cultures of origin and to emulate the culture of the French. Having experienced a far greater depth of alienation than those Africans schooled under British colonialism, they now felt the need to affirm those cultures from which they had been alienated, and they sought the means, both intellectual and literary, to rehabilitate African civilizations in Africa and the New World. The poetry of *négritude* grew out of this need to reaffirm "African values" and an African identity.

In 1948, Léopold Sédar Senghor published *Anthologie de la nouvelle poésie nègre et malgache* (Anthology of New Black and Malagasy Poetry), in which he assembled the work of French-speaking Caribbean and African poets, each of whom had "returned to the source," composing poems out of the matrix of African culture. The tone and themes of *négritude* poetry vary from poet to poet. Birago Diop's majestic "Souffles" (best translated perhaps as "Spirits") seems to emanate self-assuredly from West African oral traditions and village culture, as it affirms traditional beliefs in the cyclical nature of life and in the ever-abiding presence of the ancestors. David Diop, on the other hand, vehemently and passionately denounces slavery and colonial domination.

There are two Africas in many *négritude* poems: a utopian, pastoral Africa of precolonial times and a victimized, suffering Africa of colonialism. In both instances, Africa is often represented metaphorically as female, as in Senghor's "Black Woman" or David Diop's "To an African Woman." *Négritude* poems tend also to juxtapose an Africa characterized by the communion of humankind and nature and a Europe characterized by the fragmentation and discord of life. Thus, Senghor, in "Prayer to the Masks," for example, emphasizes the complementarity of "Africa" and "Europe," but in so doing he ironically lends credence to notions of their supposed essential difference, a difference that then forms the basis of judgements of inferiority and superiority:

> Let us answer "present" at the rebirth of the World
> As white flour cannot rise without the leaven.
> Who else will teach rhythm to the world
> Deadened by machines and cannons?
> Who will sound the shout of joy at daybreak to wake orphans and the dead?
> Tell me, who will bring back the memory of life
> To the man of gutted hopes?
> They call us men of cotton, coffee, and oil
> They call us men of death.
> But we are men of dance, whose feet get stronger
> As we pound upon firm ground.[2]

The anticolonial tradition within French-language literature thus often stressed the cultural dilemma of the *assimilé* or contrasted two essentially different worlds. Camara Laye's narrative of childhood in Guinea, *The Dark Child*, is another example. Written under difficult conditions, when Laye was an auto worker in France, the narrative nostalgically constructs home as an idyllic space in which the figure of the mother, nature, and the joys and virtues of village life are fused. Cheikh

Hamidou Kane of Senegal, in a philosophical, semi-autobiographical narrative, *Ambiguous Adventure*, adds to these contrasting paradigms of "Africa" and "the West" yet another layer of opposition: the spiritual transcendence of ascetic Islam and the numbing preoccupation with material well-being, characteristic for him, of Africa and the West respectively.

But not all anticolonialist writers within the French tradition practiced confessional narrative, stressing such oppositions. Sembène's epic novel of the 1948 railway strike in French West Africa, *God's Bits of Wood*, is a powerful anticolonialist fiction that moves beyond the opposition between two static moments or sets of values ("tradition" and "modernity" or "good" authentic ways and "bad" alien ones). Moreover, Sembène conceives of change not as the tragic and fatal undoing of cultural identity but as a means of achieving a more just society or as an inevitable process which is stressful but redeemed, perhaps, by its rewards. Thus, in Sembène's novel, the Bambara and Wolof abandon divisive definitions of identity based on ethnic group and caste and forge a larger and more powerful identification based on class. Under Sembène's pen, urban work and technology are disentangled from divisive ideologies, and the strike forces women and men to realize that the supposedly private and feminine sphere of the kitchen and the public, masculine, and political sphere of the railroad are inextricably bound in one and the same space of deprivation and injustice.

There is also a tradition of anticolonialist satire in both English and French. Okot p'Bitek's *Song of Lawino* heaps ridicule on the would-be *assimilé*, while Ferdinand Oyono's *Houseboy* and *The Old Man and the Medal* and Mongo Béti's *The Poor Christ of Bomba* offer scathing portraits of the hypocritical and mediocre French colonial masters who are would-be bearers of "Civilization."

The Logic of Power, Wealth, and Capital

The critique of foreign domination under colonialism and the concomitant, urgent issue of identity are often constructed as a conflict between the assimilation of "Western" ways and an African authenticity, and they are often articulated in realist narratives. With the advent of formal independence little by little throughout the continent, these issues gradually cede center stage to the disillusionment of independence and the critique of abusive power and corruption. This critique was never absent from African literatures. It is fictionalized and unveiled even in Achebe's novels at midcentury. But the critique of postindependence regimes is accomplished in part by a change in literary form, which Ngugi wa Thiong'o suggests in his controversial essay *Decolonising the Mind* (1986):

> How does a writer, a novelist, shock his readers by telling them that these [heads of state who collaborate with imperialist powers] are neo-slaves when they themselves, the neo-slaves, are openly announcing the fact on the rooftops? How do you shock your readers by pointing out that these are mass murderers, looters, robbers, thieves, when

they, the perpetrators of these anti-people crimes, are not even attempting to hide the fact? When in some cases they are actually and proudly celebrating their massacre of children, and the theft and robbery of the nation? How do you satirise their utterances and claims when their own words beat all fictional exaggerations?

Within the last fifteen years, then, the literary landscape has been strewn with quite stunning fictions of failure, as Africans grapple with the new abuses of neocolonial regimes and seemingly inexorable global processes. The Congolese writer Sony Labou Tansi, like his compatriot Henri Lopès, has given us compelling portraits of dictatorship. Labou Tansi's comic and nearly delirious fables (*L'Etat honteux* and *La vie et demie*) expose not only the corruption and savagery of these dictators but their frailty and insecurity. Ngugi's fictions (*Petals of Blood, Devil on the Cross,* and *Matigari*) signal the greed for wealth and power unleashed by "independence" and the betrayal of Kenyan peasants and workers by leaders who collaborate with international capitalism, when they do not vie with it. These fictions cross over into the absurd and turn away from the realism that characterizes many first-generation narratives focused on colonialism. As Ngugi has suggested, writers invent new forms commensurate with the new and deeply troubling reality.

Revisions

The *négritude* poets defended the humanity of those whose humanity had been denied on the basis of race, a step that was unquestionably necessary, but what this quite often meant was an idealization of a precolonial past and the affirmation of an African or racial essence. Traits that were held to be "naturally" African—such as love of nature, rhythm, spirituality—that had been negatively valued, were now seen as positive. These particular representations of African identity and a racial or Pan-African nation came and continue to come under attack by African intellectuals and writers, most notably Wole Soyinka (*Myth, Literature and the African World,* 1976) and, in sustained arguments, by Marcien Towa (*Léopold Sédar Senghor: négritude ou servitude?,* 1971) and Stanislas Adotévi (*Négritude et négrologues,* 1972). Likewise, literary sequels to and revisions of this perspective abound.

Yambo Ouologuem's *Bound to Violence* is a chronicle of a fictional dynasty that is corrupt, barbarous, and politically astute, a fitting adversary, then, for the newly arrived French colonials. Ouologuem negates *négritude*'s claim of precolonial goodness but seems rather to assert an inherent African violence.

A still more important sequel to or revision of these early representations is the writing by women which has developed rapidly in recent years. What was missing, of course, in the early chorus of voices denouncing the arrogance and violence of the various forms of colonialism were female voices. As recent writing by women makes clear, gender gives writing a particular cast. The "first generation" of male writers critique the imperial and colonial project for its racism and oppression, but they nonetheless (and not unlike the European objects of their critique) portray these matters as they pertain to men, and they formulate a vision of independence or of utopias in which women are either goddesses, such as muses and idealized mothers, or mere helpmates.

In 1981, Mariama Bâ's epistolary novel *So Long a Letter* rocked the literary landscape. At the death of her husband, Ramatoulaye writes a "long letter" to her divorced friend Aïssatou, now residing with her sons in the United States. Through the experience of writing, the heroine Ramatoulaye comes to terms with her own independence, having been betrayed by her husband of many years, who took as a second wife the girlfriend of their daughter.

Ouologuem's *Bound to Violence* had already questioned the premises of black nationalism and of a "pure" time before colonialism. Bâ's novel made clear that the nationalism and independence that these (by now) celebrated male writers had been defending were by and large patriarchal: women were symbols of the nation or, at best, helpmates of man, who alone would reap the real fruits of independence. In Bâ's novel, which is imbued with its own prejudices, we nonetheless see a conflation of class biases, male vanity, and female complicity in the practice of polygyny. In this novel and her posthumous *Scarlet Song*, which describes the stakes and constraints in interracial or, more precisely, cross-cultural marriages, one can infer the gender biases of these early notions of nation and identity.

As with the French-language literatures of Africa, a powerful force in English-language literature is the emergence of women writers, who have filled the silences surrounding women's lives. Flora Nwapa's *Efuru* (1966) suggests the tension between women's desires and the strictures of womanhood in the same era that male writers seemed to portray as the nearly golden age before colonialism. She concludes her novel with this haunting passage:

> Efuru slept soundly that night. She dreamt of the woman of the lake, her beauty, her long hair and her riches. She had lived for ages at the bottom of the lake. She was as old as the lake itself. She was happy, she was wealthy. She was beautiful. She gave women beauty and wealth but she had no child. She had never experienced the joy of motherhood. Why then did the women worship her?

Ama Ata Aidoo, in her early collection of short stories and sketches *No Sweetness Here* (1971), gives voice to women's concerns as they face problems of urbanization and Westernization: standards of beauty, the absence of husbands and fathers, prostitution, clashing values and expectations. In her most recent novel, *Changes* (1992), Aidoo explores the meaning of friendship, love, marriage, and family for young women in contemporary West Africa.

Bessie Head's fictions of village life in rural Botswana lay bare the mystifications of race, gender, and a patriarchal God. In a most moving scene in *When Rain Clouds Gather* (1969), for example, titular authority and might give way to the moral force of ordinary people. The mean-spirited and reactionary rural Botswana chief is disarmed by the sheer presence of the villagers who have come purposefully to sit in his yard and wait for him to come out and face them. They make no threats of violence, but he knows they will no longer tolerate his excesses, that he is effectively divested of power. If for Sembène social transformation proceeds from the material world of the workplace and of the kitchen, that is, from the outside in, for Head this transformation proceeds from the heart and spirit, from the inside out: it is personal and collective spiritual strength that enables the transformation of the external social order.

More recently, Tsitsi Dangarembga's *Nervous Conditions* (1988), like Ken Bugul's *The Abandoned Baobab* (1982), is a rebellious young woman's account of coming of age, of the journey from countryside to city. Bugul's fierce and ambiguous autobiographical narrative traces the heroine's hellish road from her Senegalese village to Brussels, while Dangarembga's young Tambu struggles against the racism of colonial Rhodesia, the deprivations of her class, and the male privilege of brother, father, and uncle. Women who survive, who provide, who circumvent patriarchy, are the heroines of this story.

Many of the established writers continue to write with new perspectives or in new ways. Achebe's recent novel *Anthills of the Savannah* (1987), for example, is a "dialogic" narrative, set in the city of Lagos; it interweaves several perspectives and several registers of language, the voices of women and men, professional and popular classes.

Les Soleils des indépendances (1968; *The Suns of Independence*, 1981), the first novel of Ivoirian novelist Ahmadou Kourouma, was a momentous event in the French-language tradition, because of both its nearly creolized, Malinke-inspired French and its exploration of the relationship between masculinity and nation, as embodied in its protagonist, the noble Fama, dispossessed by colonialism and the ensuing independence. Kourouma has since published *Monné outrages défis* (1990; *Monnew*, 1993). Set in the colonial period, this novel also examines the new life of a chief become unwitting collaborator or puppet. But through its formal experimentation, the novel approaches the colonial reality with freshness and insight into the complexity of African responses, failure, and complicity as well as into the power of language, voice, and media.

With regard to formal experimentation, there has been interesting use made of the detective or mystery story, or, more generally, of teleological endings in Ngugi's *Petals of Blood* (1977) and *Devil on the Cross*, translated from the Gikuyu (1982), in Boris Diop's *Le Temps de Tamango* (1981), and in Sembène's *Le Dernier de l'empire* (1981; *The Last of the Empire*, 1983). For some theorists of the nineteenth-century European detective novel, the teleological ending suggests the ability of the reading subject to reorder facts, to rewrite history and thereby create a sense of power to shape destiny. That interpretation might offer some insight into the current popularity of the genre in Senegal, Nigeria, and Kenya.

Another significant development in the practice of African literature is the ever more frequent marriage of text to media and performance, enabling writers to gain wider local audiences for their works. Thus, although cinema is not without its own constraints and contradictions, Sembène has turned to telling his stories through film (*La Noire de . . .* , 1966; *Mandabi*, 1968; *Emitaï*, 1971; *Xala*, 1974; *Ceddo*, 1977;

Camp de Thiaroye, 1987; *Guelowaar*, 1993). Ngugi wa Thiong'o has turned to theater and co-authored two plays, *I Will Marry When I Want* and *The Trial of Dedan Kimathi*. The greater local impact of these media and of national languages is evident when films are censored and playwrights arrested. Radio and television are also great popularizers, but since they are controlled by the state in most cases, there is a built-in process of censorship. "Popular" fiction, such as the the many pamphlets available at Nigeria's Onitsha market, appeals to an urban, minimally schooled audience. Written in European and local languages, it is often moralizing and didactic. Newspapers, which may or may not be state-owned, also provide important outlets for both writers and their critics.

At the same time that writers are engaged by local issues and traditions, they also have had vital exchanges and intertextual relationships with writers from other African cultures and from other continents, those from Europe and North America as well as from Asia and Latin America. It was in the former Soviet Union that Ousmane Sembène received his training as a filmmaker. Whether by "influence" or affinity, African writers such as Sony Labou Tansi and Ben Okri use narrative techniques akin to the "magical realism" of Colombian writer García Márquez. Likewise, for most of this century there has been a literary and cultural tradition shared by African, African American, and Caribbean writers. As early as the 1920s, Senghor and Aimé Césaire of Martinique read and admired the African American writers of the Harlem Renaissance. It was the literary project and achievements of these writers that inspired Senghor's and Césaire's early poetry and cultural theorizing. Now, at century's end, the transatlantic dialogue is still more spirited, with African writers and intellectuals coming frequently to the American side, and American and Caribbean writers and intellectuals of African descent, such as Maryse Condé of Guadeloupe, crossing over to the African side and contributing to Africa's ongoing discourse on itself.

Debates, Challenges, and Prospects

Of course, the consensus has always been that literature in Africa is deeply political. Part of its politicality may, of course, be in the eye of the Western beholder, who often has been trained to see art and aesthetics as apolitical. But, indeed, many African texts are explicitly political.[3]

An important debate in African literary circles focuses, then, on the implications and consequences of writing in national or now Africanized European languages. Ngugi has been in the forefront of a campaign for African literatures in African languages. For him, this would seem to be a matter both of the irrelevance of the European language to "authentic" experience and of the audience for whom the author writes. If African writers and intellectuals want to address Africans, most of whom are not literate in European languages, then writers should write, this argument runs, in the languages and aesthetic traditions of those African populations. This shift in audience will also affect what writers say, the perspectives they offer, and will foster the growth of African languages and literatures.

This debate has been divisive for African writers, many of whom feel at home in European languages. In addition, there are many forces, foreign publishers and (paying) readerships, and still lower literacy rates in national than in European languages, militating against the use of African languages. But there are indeed many thriving African-language literatures, such as those in Yoruba, Swahili, Poular, and Zulu, and these will continue to grow. With the ever-increasing legitimacy of these literatures, through school and university curricula, and new interest by publishing houses, the controversies surrounding European-language literatures are likely to subside.

An equally important debate in African literary circles, as in African studies generally, is the very meaning of the term "African." For some, Africa is either racially or culturally defined, and they often look toward the past, "original," that is, precolonial, Africa to locate the signs of African authenticity. Those who hold this view may equate certain forms, such as proverbs and tales, or types of language, such as colloquial or creolized French or English, as the pure expressions of Africa and those to which writers of European language texts should aspire or which they should emulate.[4]

For others, such as philosophers Anthony Appiah and V. Y. Mudimbe, these supposedly pure, authentic forms and the notion of "traditional times" are illusory. So, too, for the Arabic-language writer Tayeb el Salih of Sudan, who holds that Africa has always been syncretic.

This debate has serious repercussions. To champion a narrow African authenticity based on some arbitrarily chosen moment of the past is probably to exclude the work of white South Africans. It is to exclude much of the work of a writer such as Wole Soyinka, whose work is syncretic, embodying Yoruba and multicultural elements. Indeed, Soyinka's *Death and the King's Horseman* makes this point explicitly: there is no contradiction in being African and being "universal."

Perhaps this is an appropriate moment, then, to note that the literature of North Africa has not been included in this chapter. This is less a matter of principle than it is the consequence of the nineteenth century's compartmentalization of the continent into "black" (sub-Saharan) Africa and "Arab" (north) Africa. To have been able to study the literatures of Africa at all is a recent phenomenon, and it is more recent still that the literatures to the north and south of the Sahara are read and taught side by side. The reconciliation of Africa to itself is one of the challenges facing African writers and peoples today: to overcome the topographical/cultural division of North African/ Arab and sub-Saharan/black, on the one hand, and, on the other, given the new South African ideal of a "nonracial" society, to reconsider the role of race in a definition of African identity.

Thus the circumstances in which African novels, plays, and poetry are produced, many of them the legacy of colonialism, are as important to our understanding of African literature as are the style and images of the texts we read. Many factors give African writing its character and at the same time impinge on its development. One of the terrible, ironic testimonies to the vitality of African literature, to its resolute denunciation of all forms of domination, is the fact that writers—Kofi Awoonor,

Mongo Béti, Bessie Head, Dennis Brutus, Nuruddin Farah, Jack Mapanje, Ngugi wa Thiong'o, and Wole Soyinka, to name some of the most prominent—are routinely censored and forced into exile, when they are not incarcerated and tortured. African writers often wander, teach, and write on foreign shores because they cannot do so at home.

Within Africa, college students in a former French colony such as Côte d'Ivoire may, in fact, never read Ngugi of Kenya, either because of francocentric and anglocentric educational legacies, or because they cannot afford to buy books, were books available. American students have far greater access to African literature than do most African students.

Books by African writers are likewise more likely to be published and marketed in Paris and London than in Dakar or Lagos; or those published in major overseas capitals are more likely to garner international acclaim. African books are also more plentiful in university libraries in Europe and the United States, and scholars outside of Africa are more likely to review and critique those books in the prominent and widely read periodicals, newspapers, and publications of the West.

All these factors come between the reader and the lines on the page when one picks up a book of "African literature." To insist on such categories of literature and to contextualize it in this way is also to recognize that our understanding of the field has shifted in the last few years. We are far more conscious of the ways in which the factors outlined above are present *in texts*, of the ways in which new texts *revise* the meaning of their antecedents, and the fact that the literary act is a function of the *reader* as well as of the writer and what is written.

Selected Authors and Titles in African Literature

English-Language Literatures: West Africa

Nigeria, Africa's most populous nation and home of the University of Ibadan, has been a particularly important site of English-language literature. In 1958, Chinua Achebe published what has become to date the most widely read African novel, *Things Fall Apart*. Achebe retells the initial moment of colonialism, the encounter between the Igbo and the British, from the perspective of the colonized. In this novel and in *Arrow of God* (1964), which treats a later moment of the colonial period, he constructs an African voice and subject, denied by the literature of empire and colonialism. His *No Longer at Ease* (1960), *Man of the People* (1966), and recent *Anthills of the Savannah* (1987) focus on the corruption and contradictions of life in the post-independence era. Achebe is also an essayist and short-story writer.

Nigeria's 1986 Nobel laureate for literature, Wole Soyinka, is especially known as a playwright and poet, although he has written several novels (*The Interpreters*, 1965; *Season of Anomy*, 1973), memoirs (*The Man Died*, 1972; *Aké*, 1981; *Isara*, 1989), and essays (*Myth, Literature, and the African World*, 1976; *Art, Dialogue, and Outrage*, 1988). His plays range from the popular *The Lion and the Jewel* (1963) and *Trials of*

Brother Jero (1963) to the dense and sophisticated *A Dance of the Forests* (1963), *The Road* (1965), *Madmen and Specialists* (1971), to *Death and the King's Horseman* (1975), which ranges in tone from slapstick to dirge. His collections of poetry include *Idanre* (1967), *Shuttle in the Crypt* (1971), *Ogun Abibiman* (1976), and *Mandela's Earth and Other Poems* (1988). Soyinka's work is rooted in Yoruba mythology and aesthetics and in Nigerian history, both current and past. It explores a range of experiences and is articulated in a brilliant, poetic language revealing an extraordi- nary command of English and of world literature.

Buchi Emecheta and Flora Nwapa have challenged or modified our understanding of Nigerian history and society with works that consciously introduce feminist perspectives. Nwapa's *Efuru* (1966) was the first novel to be published by a woman writer in Nigeria. Emecheta is the author of several novels and has now created her own publishing house in London, where she resides. Her most acclaimed novel to date is *The Joys of Motherhood* (1979), which examines marriage and the family in the village and colonial city from a woman's perspective.

Amos Tutuola's *The Palm-Wine Drinkard* made a singular impression when it was published in London in 1952. Tutuola's adventurous tale and hero are virtually lifted from the repertoire of Yoruba oral traditions and placed on the page in effective but non-"literary" English. The combination of rich imagination and untutored language gives the work a freshness and originality that garnered critical acclaim and stirred a great many debates about African writers and writing.

Ben Okri's *The Famished Road* (1991), winner of the Booker Prize, is the story of a spirit child, an *abiku*, born to poor Nigerian parents and is, in some sense, a postmodern descendant of Tutuola's narrative.

Other prominent Nigerian writers include playwright Femi Osofisan, who has well over fifty stage and television plays to his credit, including *The Chattering and the Song* (1977) and *Once upon Four Robbers* (1991); poet and playwright John Pepper Clark, who has also edited and transcribed the Ijaw epic *The Ozidi Saga* (1977); the syncretic, modernist poet Christopher Okigbo (*Labyrinths with Paths of Thunder*, 1971); and neotraditional poet Niyi Osundare (*The Eye of the Earth*, 1986), winner of the Commonwealth poetry prize and the Japanese-sponsored NOMA Award, given each year to "the best" book published in Africa.

Ghana's premier novelist is Ayi Kwei Armah. His earliest fiction, *The Beautyful Ones Are Not Yet Born* (1968), is set in the last days of Nkrumah's regime. In this novel of disillusionment and alienation, a railway clerk, "the man," makes his way in a greedy and corrupt world. In later novels, *Fragments* (1970), *Why Are We So Blest?* (1972), *Two Thousand Seasons* (1973), and *The Healers* (1978), Armah's fiction moves from this focus on the personal experience of disillusionment to historical and allegorical analyses of African failure to resist Arab and European conquerors.

Ama Ata Aidoo is a playwright (*Dilemma of a Ghost*, 1971; *Anowa*, 1980), short- story writer (*No Sweetness Here*, 1971) and novelist (*Our Sister Killjoy*, 1966; *Changes—A Love Story*, 1991). In each of these genres, Aidoo, who has an extraor- dinary ear (and pen) for dialogue, renders the dynamism and complexity of women's experiences in rapidly changing societies.

Other distinguished Ghanaian writers include the poets Kofi Awoonor (*Night of My Blood*, 1985; *This Earth, My Brother*, 1971) and Kofi Anyidoho (*Elegy for the Revolution*, 1978; *Ancestral Logic & Caribbean Blues*, 1993) and playwright Efua Sutherland (*Edufa*, 1969; *The Marriage of Anansewa*, 1980).

English-Language Literatures: East Africa

East Africa has produced several remarkable English-language writers. The talent and vision of Somalia's Nuruddin Farah have come to international attention only relatively recently. He has written a series of striking novels (*From a Crooked Rib*, 1970; *A Naked Needle*, 1976; *Sweet and Sour Milk*, 1979; *Sardines*, 1981; and *Maps*, 1986) whose female protagonists bring into sharp focus issues of gender and nationalism.

Ngugi wa Thiong'o of Kenya has had a long and important literary career. His early trilogy of lyrical novels (*Weep Not, Child*, 1964; *The River Between*, 1965; and *A Grain of Wheat*, 1967) are set in the days of the Emergency, Mau Mau, and the period immediately preceding Kenyan independence in 1963. Through the portrait of intersecting, individual lives, Ngugi explores the ethical, religious, and social dilemmas of those times. In his later fiction, *Petals of Blood* (1977), *Devil on the Cross* (1982), and *Matigari* (1987), he attacks the savage greed of the neocolonialist elites. Ngugi has been a practicing playwright as well and has also co-authored several important plays (*The Trial of Dedan Kimathi*, with Micere Mugo, 1976, and *I Will Marry When I Want*, co-authored in Kikuyu with Ngugi wa Mirii, 1982).

Okot p'Bitek of Uganda, in a satiric poem, *Song of Lawino* (1966), translated from Acoli and modeled on songs of the oral tradition, uses the persona of a scorned wife to attack indiscriminate assimilation of Western ways. *Song of Ocol* (1970) is p'Bitek's husbandly reply.

Taban lo Liyong, also of Uganda, is the author of *Fixions and Other Stories* (1969) and a great many other original collections of poems, proverbs, and tales. Jack Mapanje of Malawi is likewise a respected poet (*Of Chameleons and Gods*, 1981).

English-Language Literatures: Southern Africa

Zimbabwe has recently become an important hub of literary activity. A group of talented young novelists have risen to international prominence. Chenjerai Hove's *Bones* (1988), winner of the 1989 NOMA award, and Shimmer Chindoya's *Harvest of Thorns* (1989) are literary testimonies to Zimbabwe's war of liberation. Tsitsi Dangarembga's *Nervous Conditions* (1988) is the story of women's resistance and resignation before the double bondage of settler colonialism and patriarchy, while Dambudzo Marechera's collection of short fiction *The House of Hunger* (1978), winner of the 1979 Guardian Fiction Prize, tells, in near verbal delirium, of the brutalization and violence of black life in a Zimbabwean township.

South Africa, like Zimbabwe and Kenya with their history of settler communities, has produced significant English-language literature for more than a century. Between 1948 and 1994, in the context of legislated *apartheid*, English-language literature in South Africa was written both by white South Africans of British and Afrikaner descent, and by black South Africans and those of mixed descent. South African literature is one of the richest and most complex on the continent.

Liberal, white South African writing came to international attention in 1948 with Alan Paton's sentimental and paternalistic *Cry, the Beloved Country*. Prominent white South African writers of recent years include poet and novelist Breyten Breytenbach (*In Africa Even the Flies Are Happy*, 1978; *True Confessions of an Albino Terrorist*, 1984; *Memory of Snow and of Dust*, 1990), J. M. Coetzee (*Waiting for the Barbarians*, 1980; *Life and Times of Michael K.*, 1983; *Foe*, 1986), and André Brink (*A Dry White Season*, 1979).

Nadine Gordimer, the Nobel laureate of 1991, is also a writer of fiction. To date she has published eleven novels and nearly as many collections of short stories. Her most recent fictions include the novels *Burger's Daughter* (1979), *July's People* (1981), *A Sport of Nature* (1987), *My Son's Story* (1990), and *None to Accompany Me* (1994), a first post-*apartheid* work, and the collection of short fiction *Jump and Other Stories* (1991). One of the unique strengths of Gordimer's fiction is its sustained probing of racial and gender identities through incidents, objects, and her characters' very own voices. In particular, she deconstructs whiteness and masculinity (and their opposites) as natural attributes.

Athol Fugard, the white South African playwright, has been a highly visible presence in New York theater circles for many years. Among his plays are *Boesman and Lena* (1969), *Master Harold and the Boys* (1982), *A Lesson from Aloes* (1981), and *Sizwe Bansi Is Dead,* co-authored with John Kani and Winston Ntshona (1976). Fugard's plays are spare dramas of survivors, those who cope with lives entangled and nearly wasted in the snares of *apartheid*.

While liberal white South Africans, by and large, have expressed the guilt, fear, alienation, and general malaise of the white minority living under *apartheid*, black and black-identified South African writers have written of the deprivation, injustices, violence, and anger suffered by the black majority. Their narratives are often set in the cities and townships.

Among the earliest narratives of black life under *apartheid* are autobiographical novels set in urban South Africa, *Mine Boy* (1946) and *Tell Freedom* (1954) by Peter Abrahams, and *Down Second Avenue* (1959) by Ezekiel Mphalele. The alienation of life in the slums of *apartheid* is also the subject of Alex LaGuma's naturalist fictions *A Walk in the Night* (1967) and *In the Fog of the Season's End* (1972). More recently, Mbulelo Mzamane's *Mzala* (1980) and *Children of Soweto* (1981) have stressed the resilience of black South Africans.

Bessie Head is one of the best-known South African writers among Western feminists. An exile to rural Botswana, she authored several novels, including *When Rain Clouds Gather* (1968), *Maru* (1971), *A Question of Power* (1974), and a collection of short stories, *The Collector of Treasures* (1977).

In the category of fiction, South Africans have made particular use and developed particular talents for the short story, among them Richard Rive, James Matthews, and Miriam Tlali. Many novelists also, such as LaGuma, Head, and Mzamane, have practiced the short story.

Yet poetry has been a singularly important medium for black South Africans who reside in the townships. Oswald Mtshali's *Sounds of a Cowhide Drum* (1971) and *Fireflames* (1980), Sipho Sepamla's *Hurry Up to It!* (1975), *The Blues Is You in Me* (1976), and *The Soweto I Love* (1977), and Mongane Wally Serote's *Yakhal'inkomo* (1972) and *No Baby Must Weep* (1975) are all forged in the crucible of black urban life in South Africa. Of South African exiles residing in the U.S., the poet Dennis Brutus is surely the best-known in Europe and America. Brutus's poetry (*Sirens, Knuckles and Boots*, 1963; *Letters to Martha*, 1969; *Stubborn Hope*, 1978) is poised between an unrelenting naturalism, in which life in prison, in urban slums, or in exile has been narrowed, caged, trivialized, and demeaned, and a painful, tenacious desire for life as it might be, that space of imagination, possibility, energy, and renewal.

We wait now to see the literature of the new South Africa.

French-Language Traditions

The writers who have been most important for French-language traditions have come from the West African countries of Senegal, Cameroon, Guinea, Côte d'Ivoire, and Mali, and from the Central African nation of Congo. Senegal was home to several of the poets of *négritude* to whom we referred in the first section of the chapter: David Diop (*Coups de pilon*, 1961; *Hammer Blows*, 1993), Birago Diop (*Leurres et lueurs*, 1960; *Les Contes d'Amadou Koumba*, 1947, *Tales of Amadou Koumba*, 1966), and Léopold Sédar Senghor, future president of Senegal (*Chants d'ombre*, 1945; *Hosties noires*, 1948; *Ethiopiques*, 1956; *Nocturnes*, 1961; and *Lettres d'hivernage*, 1973; all translated in Melvin Dixon's *Léopold Sédar Senghor: The Collected Poetry*).

Senegal also has a rich tradition of novels in French. Cheikh Hamidou Kane's *L'Aventure ambiguë* (1961; *Ambiguous Adventure*, 1969), a novel of coming of age and the journey north, is now a classic of French-language literature in Africa. Aminata Sow Fall is the author of several novels, including the provocative *La Grève des battu* (1979; *The Beggars' Strike*, 1981). Boubacar Boris Diop has also authored several novels, among them the political mystery *Le Temps de Tamango* (1982). Mariama Bâ is an important feminist writer (*Une si longue lettre*, 1979, *So Long a Letter*, 1981; *Un chant écarlate*, 1981, *Scarlet Song*, 1985), and Ken Bugul has written a woman's account of going to Europe in *Le Baobab fou* (1983; *The Abandoned Baobab*, 1991). Ousmane Sembène has been a powerful artistic voice for African self-determination, both as a novelist (*Le Docker noir*, 1956, The Black Dockworker, 1987; *O pays, mon beau peuple*, 1957; *Les Bouts de bois de Dieu*, 1960, *God's Bits of Wood*, 1970; *Le Mandat*, 1966, *The Money Order*, 1972; *Xala*, 1973; and *Le Dernier de l'empire*, 1981, *The Last of the Empire*, 1983) and filmmaker.

Guinea is the home of novelist Camara Laye, whose tender, nostalgic *L'Enfant noir* (1953; *The Dark Child*, 1954) is one of the best-known French-language texts outside of Africa. The younger generation of talented Guinean novelists includes Alioum Fantouré (*Le Cercle des Tropiques*, 1972), William Sassine (*Wirriyami*, 1976; *Le Jeune Homme de sable*, 1979), and Tierno Monenembo (*Les Crapauds-brousse*, 1979). Djibril Tamsir Niane has produced a version of the Mande epic of Sundiata, *Soundjata ou l'épopée mandingue* (1960; *Sundiata: An Epic of Old Mali*, 1965), as has Camara Laye, *Maître de la parole* (1978; *Guardian of the Word*, 1980).

Two major writers from Mali are Amadou Hampâté Bâ and Yambo Ouologuem. Hampâté Bâ, the editor and transcriber of several Poular narratives, is the author of *L'Etrange Destin de Wangrin* (1973; *The Fortunes of Wangrin*, 1987), an account of French colonialism as experienced by an enterprising interpreter. Ouologuem's *Le devoir de violence* (1968; *Bound to Violence*, 1973) is an innovative, iconoclastic novel, a chronicle of a fictional precolonial dynasty.

Bernard Dadié of Côte d'Ivoire has been a prolific playwright, the author of serious plays (*Béatrice du Congo*, 1970) as well as numerous comedies and satires (*Monsieur Thogo-Gnini*, 1970; *Papassidi maître-escroc*, 1975; *Mhoi-Ceul*, 1979). Dadié has also published traditional tales, short fiction, and satirical accounts of life in New York, Paris, and Rome. Ahmadou Kourouma, also of Côte d'Ivoire, is the author of *Les Soleils des indépendances* (1968; *The Suns of Independence*, 1981) and of *Monnè, outrages, défis* (1990; *Monnew*, 1993), novels whose originality of language lends still greater power to their stories of colonial and postcolonial disinheritance.

Cameroon is home to two novelists who have provided the francophone tradition with its most satirical portraits of the French: Ferdinand Oyono (*Une vie de boy*, 1956, *Houseboy*, 1966; *Le vieux nègre et la médaille*, 1956, *The Old Man and the Medal*, 1969) and Mongo Béti (*Le Pauvre Christ de Bomba*, 1956, *The Poor Christ of Bomba*, 1971; *Mission terminée*, 1957, *Mission to Kala*, 1964). Béti's later novels focus on the mediocrity and failure of post-independence Cameroon (*Remember Ruben*, 1974; *Perpétue ou l'habitude du malheur*, 1974). René Philombe is another well-known Cameroonian writer. He has authored plays, poetry, and short fiction (*Lettres de ma cambuse*, 1965; *Les époux célibataires*, 1971; *Petites gouttes de chant pour créer l'homme*, 1977; *Africapolis*, 1978). More recently, Cameroonian writer Werewere Liking has brought new energy and vision to stage productions both in French and in African languages, with the use of puppets and the revitalization of ritual theater (*Une nouvelle terre*, 1980). Her fictions *Orphée Dafric* (African Orpheus, 1981) and *Elle sera de jaspe et de corail* (1983) which she calls "song-novels," abandon traditional and static generic boundaries as well.

French-language literature in Africa has been immensely enriched by the contributions of Congolese writers. Among the poets are Jean-Baptiste Tati-Loutard (*Poèmes de la mer*, 1968; *Les Normes du temps*, 1974; *La Tradition du songe*, 1985) and Tchicaya U Tam'si (*Le Mauvais Sang*, 1955; *Feu de brousse*, 1957; *A triche coeur*, 1958). Both have written fiction as well: Tati-Loutard has written short stories (*Chroniques congolaises*, 1974; *Nouvelles chroniques congolaises*, 1980); U Tam'si wrote two novels, *Les Cancrelats* (1980) and *Les Phalènes* (1984).

Henri Lopès began his career as a writer of short stories or vignettes (*Tribaliques*, 1971, *Tribaliks*, 1987), and has gone on to write both political satire (*Le Pleurer-Rire*, 1982, *The Laughing Cry*, 1987) and quasi-autobiographical fiction (*Le Chercheur d'Afriques*, 1990). Sylvain Bemba is both a novelist (*Rêves portatifs*, 1979; *Le soleil est parti à M'Pemba*, 1982) and playwright (*L'Enfer, c'est Orféo*, 1969; *Une eau dormante*, 1975; *Un foutu monde pour un blanchisseur trop honnête*, 1977). Likewise, Sony Labou Tansi writes both plays (*Conscience de tracteur*, 1979; *La Parenthèse de sang*, 1981) and novels (*La vie et demie*, 1979; *L'Anté-peuple*, 1983; *Les Sept Solitudes de Lorsa Lopez*, 1985), which dissect the neocolonial reality.

Portuguese-Language Literatures

It is not surprising that there have been fewer Portuguese-language writers than English- or French-language writers; only five African states were formerly colonies of Portugal: Cape Verde, Guinea-Bissau, São Tomé and Principe, Angola, and Mozambique. Moreover, these writers have been little known outside the lusophone countries of Africa, Portugal, and Brazil. They are at last coming to the attention of a wider audience.

There are significant parallels between the anticolonial impulse of lusophone writing and that of anglophone and francophone literatures, but lusophone literature is distinctive nonetheless for a number of reasons. Many Portuguese who immigrated to Portugal's African colonies were poor and thus found themselves living among African peoples in the suburbs of major cities. A large *mestiço* population resulted. This racial contact and mixing has been significant in the development of lusophone African literatures and has thus always posed a challenge to the notion of "race" as a defining feature of African identity. In addition, unlike their anglophone and francophone counterparts, lusophone writers who have grown up in such urban areas tend to have little direct experience of African-language oral traditions.

Among the celebrated Portuguese-language writers of Africa are Baltasar Lopes of Cape Verde, Luis Bernardo Honwana of Mozambique, José Luandino Vieira of Angola, and Agostinho Neto, poet, activist, and first president of independent Angola. Baltasar Lopes, a pioneer of Cape Verdean literature, has written in many forms, from poetry to novel to essay. His 1947 novel *Chinquinho* is the child's story of home, schooling, and leavetaking so characteristic of African and Caribbean writers. As such, the novel portrays humble lives and the hardships of Cape Verdean life. Luis Bernardo Honwana is a journalist whose literary reputation rests on a single, remarkable collection of short narratives. The title story of Honwana's *Nos matamos o cão tinhoso* (1964; *We Killed Mangy-Dog*, 1969) is typical of his subject and style: it is an eloquent allegorical tale about masculinity, the origins of violence, and, not incidentally, the brutalizing effects of colonialism. Vieira's *A Vida Verdadeira de Domingos Xavier* (1974; *The Real Life of Domingos Xavier*, 1978, published first in French in 1971, when Vieira was incarcerated) is an account of arrest, imprisonment, and torture, an inspiring testimony to the bravery and faith of the Angolan people under Portuguese repression. Neto's collection of poems *Sagrada Esperanca* (1974; *Sacred Hope*, 1974) likewise portrays the humiliation of colonial domination and expresses hope for justice and dignity.

NOTES

1. The cultural unity of Africa continues to generate considerable debate. For an affirmation of such unity, see Cheikh Anta Diop, *The Cultural Unity of Black Africa* (1959; reprint, Chicago: Third World Press, 1978), and Clinton Jean, *Behind the Eurocentric Veil: The Search for African Realities* (Amherst: University of Massachusetts Press, 1992); for an opposing view, see Anthony Appiah, *In My Father's House* (New York: Oxford University Press, 1992), and V. Y. Mudimbe, *The Invention of Africa* (1988).

2. Melvin Dixon, trans., *Léopold Sédar Senghor: The Collected Poetry* (Charlottesville: University Press of Virginia, 1991).

3. See Fredric Jameson's "Third World Literature in the Era of Multinational Capitalism," *Social Text* 15 (1986): 65–88, and Ahmad Aijaz's rejoinder, "Jameson's Rhetoric of Otherness and the 'National Allegory,'" *Social Text* 17 (1987): 3–27, for arguments about the political nature of postcolonial literature.

4. See Chinweiger, Onwuchekwa Jemie, and Ihechukwu Madubuike, *Toward the Decolonization of African Literature* (Washington, D.C.: Howard University Press, 1983), vol. 1.

SUGGESTIONS FOR FURTHER READING

Burness, Donald, ed. *Critical Perspectives on Lusophone Literature from Africa*. Washington, D.C.: Three Continents Press, 1981.

Gérard, Albert. *African Language Literatures: An Introduction to the Literary History of Sub-Saharan Africa*. Washington, D.C.: Three Continents Press, 1980.

Okpewho, Isidore. *African Oral Literature*. Bloomington: Indiana University Press, 1992.

Research in African Literatures (a quarterly journal).

Rouch, Alain, and Gérard Clavreuil. *Littératures nationales d'écriture française*. Paris: Bordas, 1987.

Soyinka, Wole. *Poems of Black Africa*. London: Secker and Warburg, 1975.

Zell, Hans M.; Carol Bundy; and Virginia Coulon, eds. *A New Reader's Guide to African Literature*. New York: Africana Publishing Company, 1983.

Claire Robertson
Social Change in Contemporary Africa

How could he understand that the [Kikuyu] people [of
Kenya] did not want to move backwards, that the ridges
no longer desired their isolation? How could he know that
the forces that drove people to yearn for a better day
tomorrow, that now gave a new awareness to the people,
were like demons, sweeping the whole country . . . from
one horizon touching the sea to the other horizon touching
the water?[1]

16

Change is the predominant aspect of contemporary African
life for rural and urban dwellers. In this chapter the focus will
be on two types of change: class formation, that is, the
exaggeration of inequality, and change in gender relations.
These processes are intertwined in many cases. With the disappearance or modification of deeply rooted customs and the proliferation of Western-type education,
African life, especially in towns, is taking on aspects familiar to Western readers. But
it is dangerous to assume that "Westernization" is taking place, for social change has
assumed particularly African aspects, while economic change significantly differs
from that experienced in Western countries.

Historical Background to Contemporary Social Change

The West industrialized over a relatively long period of time beginning in the
eighteenth century, after it had already increased its agricultural productivity considerably, and used emigration to rid itself of excess population. This process of
industrialization was developed and controlled by Europeans, who then used their
sophisticated technology to conquer most of the rest of the world in the nineteenth
century. Even before conquest, which took place in most areas in the late nineteenth
century, some areas of Africa had been extensively involved in Western trade,
although on African terms. One motivation for conquest was to shift the terms of trade
to favor Europeans. Thus, other world areas were incorporated into a European-

dominated economic system. Africa, a continent with ancient and extensive Arab and Asian contacts and numerous cultures, was conquered by Europeans despite valiant opposition, and its economic development was subordinated to European needs. Similarly, its social development was distorted by European conquest to suit European purposes; it soon became evident to Africans that high status under colonialism involved choosing to accept the domination of European culture in everything from dress to religion and schooling.

In the early years of European rule, the social impact of colonialism was moderate. Before World War I most efforts were expended in simply establishing control over the vast new areas of conquest, whether this meant fighting pitched battles or making political deals with local rulers. Along with colonial government came the missionaries, whose presence in some areas prior to conquest had encouraged that conquest. If they found their progress in making converts impeded on occasion, they sometimes promoted political control to put them in a better position to succeed. Thus, the missionaries played a critical role in perpetuating the idea of the "white man's burden" as a justification for European conquest. After conquest Protestant and Catholic missionaries had the important functions of providing some schooling and health care. The colonial governments took very little responsibility for the social welfare of the conquered until after World War II. All colonies were supposed to be at least self-supporting and at best profitable; thus it was generally left to the private sector to provide social services.

In providing Western-style education to relatively few Africans, the missionaries sowed the seeds of revolutionary change by altering both values and the means of access to power. In precolonial societies power and status were determined by age, family position, and ability, and in many societies by gender. Thus, the elders of any given group, a village, a clan, a town, a lineage, had political power to make decisions and administer law for that group, in some areas subject to centralized monarchy, in others independently. This power tended to be limited by popular consensus; often there were not large differences in the distribution of wealth from family to family. The advent of European rule was to change all that, although this was not immediately evident. Thus, some rulers, when urged by missionaries to send their children to school, sent the children of their slaves instead, considering that education was unimportant and that they could more easily control low-status educated persons. But in order to obtain even low positions in the colonial administration, Africans had to have a Western-style education. After World War I it was evident to all that the Europeans had prevailed and that the struggle for power was henceforth to be within the new system. Between the wars the power of those precolonial gerontocracies that had survived the initial conquest was undermined by the newly educated Africans, who organized themselves into political parties, trade unions, and other voluntary associations, some with international connections such as the YMCA and the Boy Scouts.

After World War II the pace of change accelerated, with unprecedented increases in urban populations. Africa had precolonial ancient cities, most of which were commercial centers for trade crossing the Sahara, the Mediterranean, the Indian

Plate 80. A Senegalese family in their home, Dakar.
Photo courtesy United Nations/CH/jr.

Ocean, or the Atlantic. With colonialism, old centers expanded and new ones were founded as administrative or mining centers. The colonial presence created new opportunities for wage work or self-employment: clerks, carpenters, masons, domestic servants, porters, miners, and others were needed, jobs most frequently filled by men. In the towns, efforts were made to provide clean piped water, sewers, electricity, cemeteries, schools, paved roads, and other amenities customary for Europeans, and later extended to some African quarters. Segregation was often maintained, both before World War I and after. Nonetheless, the possibilities for wider opportunities and a higher standard of living were evident. The profits from agriculture were invested in the towns; agricultural work was more arduous and less profitable than urban wage work. Unsurprisingly, many towns became cities, and many cities doubled their populations from 1930 to 1945, again from 1945 to 1960, and tripled or quadrupled them from 1960 to 1980 or 1990.

Disparities of wealth and privilege of a scale unknown in precolonial Africa became common, especially after independence, when Africans took over the highest governmental positions. Many functionaries earned salaries and benefits from subsidized housing and transport. These privileges had been initiated by the colonialists to entice Europeans to "hardship" posts and were carried over after independence, thus making towns even more obviously the seats of privilege. In some cities with a segregated colonial tradition, class instead of racial segregation prevailed, as Africans moved into formerly European quarters. But if the towns often exhibited glitter, most urban migrants were not becoming rich and powerful.

Rather, they came from poverty with food grown in the villages, to poverty without food in the towns. And they had new, higher expectations about sending their children to school so that they might move up the social scale. In a novel by the Nigerian writer Buchi Emecheta, a woman migrant to Lagos, Nigeria, expresses town tension well: "Everything was costing her money, money she did not have. Adim's schoolwork began to suffer and the boy was losing weight. It was true what they said, she thought, that if you don't have children the longing for them will kill you, and if you do, the worrying over them will."[2]

The towns presented both a challenge and a threat to many migrants, who often lived with no amenities, crowded into shantytowns similar to those of Rio de Janeiro or Bangkok. Population density was often twenty or more persons per room in shacks built of scraps of zinc, mud, or even cardboard. The migrants' high expectations were often unfulfilled. What they found instead was a growing struggle to feed their children, with women often playing the strongest role in these efforts, a precolonial responsibility that continued. If the migrants could walk among fashionable hotels and high-rises, it was only by expending the time and effort to get there from their marginal locations, and this few could afford to do. If they could look up to the few famous, successful people, they could also look sideways at most of their compatriots, whose struggle was debilitating in a game whose rules had changed. The old rules of the village no longer applied. If they did not realize that themselves, their children born in the towns soon made it very evident to them.

Urban Structural Change and Gender Roles

One of the most important areas in life where change became evident was marriage. This change involved both the increasing importance of the marriage ceremony for status purposes, and a decline in its incidence. Before colonialism, and even now in some villages, marriages were largely an arranged affair between two lineages. In most cultures funerals and births were celebrated more prominently than marriages because they symbolized lineage continuity. The overall good of the families was considered to be more important in making a marriage than the desires of the two individuals involved. Marriage took place for three basic reasons: political alliance, especially for the influential; procreation, to perpetuate the lineage; and the addition of women's labor to the family work group. Polygyny[3] was useful for men economically since wealth depended on the amount of labor a person controlled. Land was not usually privately owned, but rather communally held so that people owned its produce only. This means that the more labor a person controlled, the more land could be worked, and the higher the returns. Women did and do most of the routine agricultural labor in Africa—weeding, planting, and harvesting, especially of food crops. There are, of course, exceptions to this rule in some areas, but it generally holds. Recent studies have shown that, even in societies which are called "pastoralist" and "hunter-gatherer" by anthropologists, it is women's agricultural or gathering activities which provide most of the society's subsistence needs. Thus, attracting and keeping women's labor is still essential in rural areas, and marriage is an excellent mechanism for doing so. The great economic value of women is often indicated in the giving of bridewealth, gifts or money from the family of the groom to that of the bride. The exchange that seals the marriage goes in the opposite direction from that which prevailed in old upper-class European or Chinese societies, where dowry was in some sense a compensation to an upper-class man for taking on an economically unproductive upper-class woman.

In towns, things change drastically. The elders may be back in the village. The wages that young men earn may allow them to arrange their own marriages because they do not have to rely on their relatives' pooled resources for bridewealth. But even bridewealth may become obsolete as couples make their own marriages, consensual unions with few formalities. Interethnic marriages have become common in many places because of urban heterogeneity. Thus, a Nigerian Igbo father reacts to his daughter's plan to marry a Yoruba:

> Yoruba elder: "You cannot prevent a girl from marrying anybody she likes."
> Father: "We don't do so in my town. I will choose husbands for all my girls. They are too young to know their own minds."
> Elder: "Look, this is Lagos, not your town or your village."[4]

Poverty inhibits polygyny, which becomes less attractive when women's labor loses value in town, where expensive educational qualifications are important for getting well-paid jobs. Women will still be largely responsible for feeding their families, but they can no longer grow the food. In fact, in town the whole family situation changes radically for both sexes. If in the rural areas men and women perform separate but complementary tasks in agriculture, immersed in family work groups with men clearing and harvesting, in town the spheres of the sexes become more separated. Men generally get more formal education than women, which means that the world of wage labor is in most countries overwhelmingly male. Ninety percent or more of the wage laborers are often men. To fulfill their economic responsibilities, most women have two avenues: self-employment in low-profit activities, or marriage to a financially dependable man, preferably upwardly mobile. A very few women are white-collar professionals, such as lawyers and doctors; more elite women are nurses, secretaries, and teachers, earning substantially less than men. But women do not generally depend on men for their support; most couples do not pool property in marriage. Thus, women have both the advantage of economic autonomy in controlling their own earnings and the disadvantage of low earnings and lack of access to male wages. They *must* work outside the home, just as they do not usually see remaining unwed as a choice.

Women in towns may trade, selling everything from hardware or clothing to prepared foods, Africa's "fast foods," such as porridge, fried bananas, stew, and rice. In some areas, especially West Africa, women traders have carried out most of the retail trade in essential commodities for as long as we have any recorded history. In

Plate 81. A young boy riding a
homemade wooden scooter.
Photo courtesy United Nations/BZ/me.

others, such as Mozambique, Zaire, and Zambia, the necessity of earning money imposed by urban living has made trade a new activity. Another possibility is represented by the impact of new urbanization in central Kenya, which transformed the older patterns of women's trade. Other common urban female occupations are low-level clerical work, domestic service (especially in South Africa), factory work in the few industrialized areas, prostitution (without pimps, so the women keep their own earnings), and hairdressing and sewing for those who can afford the training. Women's crafts have largely been displaced by competition from imports, but a few survive on a small scale: spinning, weaving, dyeing, soapmaking, and potting.

Women may try to overcome their disadvantages by forming an advantageous alliance, whether formalized by marriage or not. Sometimes marriage is not appealing, because of the loss of autonomy involved (men may insist on taking charge of women's earnings), or because of its lack of security, since there is no communal property and a fairly high divorce rate. Thus, women spend their lives doing the

Plate 82. Outdoor nursery, Maputo, Mozambique.
Photo courtesy United Nations/Ray Wittin.

domestic work and raising their children (tasks seldom shared in any major way by men), working in the neighborhoods where they live, and socializing primarily with other women of the same class who are neighbors or relatives. An old tradition in some areas, which has spread and taken on vitality in new cities, is the formation of women's groups for various purposes: shared savings and/or purchases, work groups, church groups, etc. Even in elite marriages, spouses do not commonly socialize much with other couples. Sex segregation is the prevailing pattern in play as well as in work.

Men's lives in cities are more often affected by wage work. They may take public transportation to work in an office, a factory, or a small business, lunch with male co-workers, relieve the work routine with shared jokes, and after work go to bars to socialize with other men and "good-time girls," who are a variety of prostitute, or attend meetings of fraternal organizations, family associations, unions, professional organizations, and so on. Such organizations have proliferated in towns, somewhat replacing the stronger family links of the villages. In male and female urban budgets, more of men's earnings go for savings, investment, dues, entertainment, and transport, while women's largest expenditures are on food and school fees for the children. Sex segregation is thus exaggerated in towns as life becomes more complex for everyone.

Consider the different role expectations for men and women indicated in the following letter and reply from a Ghanaian newspaper's equivalent of the Ann Landers column (only Nana, in this case, is male).

Dear Nana,

I am a boy of 22. About a year ago I found my true love. We were very much in love and planned to marry. Fortunately for us I put her in the family way. I now plan to take a four-year course which will lead me to a better paid job as my present salary is low. Unfortunately, my parents are too poor to look after her for four years. The girl has told me that her parents will not be happy if they have to look after her for four years.

I am now confused and worried. What should I do since I am eager to do the course?

Edwards

Reply: Before you start the course I suggest you persuade your wife to go into business so that she can support herself until you come out of school. Why doesn't she sell cooked food? It doesn't need much capital . . . but it can be very profitable. A farm [for her to work] in addition to that will solve all your problems. It is a good idea for you to go back to school so talk to your wife to go into business as soon as possible.[5]

The obvious expectations here are that she will provide daily support while he goes ahead to better himself for future benefit. Premarital pregnancy is viewed favorably, though it is inconvenient, and Nana blurs the distinction between the status of girlfriend and wife. It is likely that if this couple remains together, she will still be expected to support herself after he begins earning again.

From the other side of the continent, Nairobi, Kenya, come different perspectives on contemporary marriage, played out in the forum of women's magazines, which are read by elite and subelite women, such as secretaries and nurses. The *Woman's Mirror* of October 1987 carried an article by Marjorie Kavuma worthy of any 1950s U.S. magazine catering to future housewives. Entitled "How to Recognize Mr. Right," it advised women to cook, clean, bring up children, refrain from nagging, and listen to their husbands. Women were not to argue with their husbands and were to be faithful to them. "It would be a splendid idea," Ms. Kavuma said, "to turn a blind eye, even if there are positive signs of straying on the part of the man," which could be avoided by the wife creating a romantic atmosphere. But "men are delicate creatures," she said, who would not respect an unfaithful woman. Above all, she advised, "You are the 'speaker' of your own house, which is a very good portfolio, so you should refrain from becoming 'Managing Director.'"[6] Thus, instead of concentrating upon desirable characteristics of a prospective husband, Kavuma adjured women to make themselves desirable by being domestic, subordinate, and passive except in encouraging sexual attraction, and by tolerating a double standard.

As if in rebuttal, Jane Were, in an article in *Viva* entitled "The Ideal Wife: Is She an Imbecile?", sharply attacked such notions. She complained that women's health suffers from too much childbearing, that wife-beating was condoned by Parliament, that male alcoholism was a big problem causing poverty, and that husbands expected wives either to give them their earnings or to support the family completely. "The ideal wife," she said, "has been taught that she may not own anything on her own, including her ownself." She ended by questioning the whole institution of marriage. "How many unmarried girls today want to join the ranks of ideal wives? Perhaps the gradually increasing number of young girls/women who are opting to remain single parents out of their own choice is a timely indicator to this question."[7] Were's voice rings as the more authentic indicator of current trends: fewer urban women and men are marrying; more marriages are ending in divorce; more female-headed households are being established as women have children in any case; and more women are looking to women's groups for help rather than to weakened lineage families or husbands. Class differentiation means that more of the urban population is poor, while the stresses imposed by poverty often weaken marriages. One response from more educated women has been to ask, like Were, "If marriage is so restrictive for women, and men so impossibly demanding and abusive, then why should we marry?"

Just as marriage changes in town, other customs do also. Puberty rites, which had great importance for both boys and girls in declaring their maturity and marriage-ability, usually disappear, perhaps as an undesirable vestige of the elders' authority. Rituals celebrating birth and death continue, of course, but may become more elaborate as occasions for demonstration of conspicuous consumption among the socially ambitious. West African urban newspapers are full of prominent funeral notices which catalogue the accomplishments of the deceased and their relatives, and invite all comers to the funeral. In West Africa, funerals still are more than celebrations of death—they also celebrate the continuation of life; it is important that many surviving relatives attend to show the ongoing strength of the lineage family. Families spend as much as possible to make the funeral lavish; such a funeral is often attended by a procession of friends dressed in identical clothes as an expression of unity, a church singing group, and a band. In fact, the greater importance of funerals than of marriage ceremonies in many areas indicates that links between blood relatives are more important than conjugal links in defining the African family, a very different tradition from that found in the Euro-American nuclear family.

Funerals also contribute to the exotic appearance of African cities. Such processions, the multicolored houses, and the open-air markets give a colorful impression, as do the slogans painted on many trucks and buses. But above all there are the people, women with babies tied to their backs, carrying headloads of food to sell, or firewood, and wearing long, bright cotton clothes; the men in traditional embroidered or woven robes or European dress; and everywhere the children, well dressed and scrupulously clean in starched school uniforms, doing business for their parents, or pitifully starving. No wonder that the infinite variety and activity of the towns make rural life indeed seem dull to many people.

Rural Change

Meanwhile, the rural areas have not remained encased in immutable tradition. The impact of the world capitalist economy is felt even in the most remote areas, often not beneficially, however, since the profits of "development" usually go to urban dwellers or abroad. Relatively little is invested in agriculture, and there is a constant siphoning off of male labor to towns. More recently, women too have been escaping an increasingly burdensome agricultural workload by going to town. Formal education furthers this process by preparing young people for wage jobs not available in the

Plate 83. Science class, Teachers' Training College, Lagos, Nigeria.
Photo courtesy United Nations.

countryside. Although town life is difficult, it is also more stimulating and has more potential rewards that attract the ambitious. The colonialists in some areas tried to stem urban migration by imposing controls that prohibited women and persons other than workers from migrating to town. This was the case in South Africa, Zaire, Zambia, and Zimbabwe. Except in South Africa, where totalitarian control enforced them until recently, such efforts failed and ceased with independence. Thus, there is a rapidly emerging continent-wide pattern of villages inhabited by a disproportionate number of women, children, and old people. Whereas colonial migration often entailed eventual return to the village on long visits or permanently, the contemporary pattern more often involves a final exodus from the villages, a finality promoted by increasing landlessness. This creates both permanent urban populations and depopulated villages.

More of the farmwork is therefore left to women, who must fill in for absent men. In some cases, as in Botswana and Lesotho, where migrant men work in South African mines for years on end, male control is such that the absentees continue to make decisions about planting and harvesting, thus making agriculture even more fragile. More often women simply must cope with a larger workload without much capital input or agricultural extension training. Without significant mechanization, women often spend twelve hours a day in various forms of economically necessary labor.[8] The profits from agriculture go disproportionately to men, who control the growth and sale of export crops and who may not invest in agriculture. Older women

Plate 84. Women taking sewing lessons, Damara,
Central African Republic.
Photo courtesy United Nations/Carolyn H. W. Redenius.

in rural areas bear disproportionate responsibility both for agricultural labor and for childcare when their daughters leave for town, their grandchildren staying on the farm. Gender, then, has become a primary determinant of access to power and authority, with rural women becoming the poorest of the poor, a peasantry who receive little of the fruits of their labor. African agriculture has suffered in consequence, especially the growing of food crops, which is largely the responsibility of women. Since 1960 there has been a fall in food production in many countries as land was converted to cash crop production.

As society is changing, then, African patterns are emerging that are different from those in Western societies, in everything from conjugal relations to agricultural work. There is a great deal of poverty by Western standards; in most countries those with a comfortable standard of living constitute less than 5 percent of the population. This in turn means that social forms must adapt to those conditions, which were not always so extreme. Marriage has become less formal in terms of arrangement for most people, and perhaps more fragile. Consensual unions may be less stable than arranged marriages because of the changing whims of the partners, and because of the reduced interest of the lineages in keeping the marriage going, since the lineages no longer mediate disputes. At the same time, the urban situation imposes new and more difficult conditions. The increased necessity for earning cash, the heterogeneity of the population, and the possibilities for anonymity all weaken social controls.

> The news that Adaku had . . . become a public woman spread throughout Lagos like wildfire. Ibuza men gloried in the unfaithfulness of women: "Leave them for ten minutes, they turn into something else." Many people put the blame on Lagos itself; they said it was a fast town which could corrupt the most innocent of girls.[9]

Groups which were subordinate in the village challenged that subordination in town; the young defied the old, the women the men. If women became less controlled by men in some ways, their economic dependence on men often increased, which meant that making an advantageous liaison became a prime strategy for women to improve their status. In some areas, however, the disadvantages for women entailed by marriage have caused them to shun it in favor of temporary liaisons or complete independence from men, even if poverty is a result. But even in the villages things have changed; those seeking upward social mobility receive formal education and leave for the towns if they can. Farming subsidizes urban development and has become largely unprofitable. A number of issues, then, must be addressed if Africa is to prosper.

Critical Issues

The chief manifestation of the many problems facing African societies today is increasing socioeconomic inequality, both worldwide and at home. Thus, while Western businesses strain to convince more people that they need useless luxury goods, because the market for necessities is glutted, African countries are generally becoming poorer. There has been a long-term decline in the prices of raw materials relative to those for manufactured goods, due partly to monopolistic controls by international corporations. Even so, many African countries do not have quantities of valuable raw materials to sell. Industrialization efforts are hindered by competition from wealthier countries and control by foreign-dominated corporations. It would probably be in everyone's best long-term interests to remedy the international unequal distribution of wealth. The potential market represented by the 90 percent of the world's population who are poor staggers the imagination. But short-term narrow interests tend to dominate economic planning by governments and businesses who might be able to help.

Plate 85. A typical "shantytown."
Photo courtesy United Nations/BZ/ara.

Inequality within African countries is also on the rise. Relatively few people have profited from "development"; often it is those who skim off part of the exported profits. If governments spend more than 20 percent of their budgets providing Western-type education to more people than ever before, there are also more people than ever before, so that the proportion of literates in the population rises very slowly. In any case, the contraction of most economies does not provide jobs for many who leave school. Those who manage to join the elite remain a tiny minority who are in a better position to ensure elite status for their children. In many African cities, much of the construction is going on in the wealthy suburbs. For wealthy families, connections with poorer relatives are becoming more distant in both time and space, reducing their cooperation and help for the less fortunate. Economic cooperation, in particular, seems more characteristic of poor people, who must cooperate to survive. In both rural and urban areas such cooperation is often extensive, indeed a primary characteristic of the social order. Yet it is extremely arduous, difficult, and above all necessary, for the margin between life and death is small.

The average life expectancy in Africa has risen more slowly than elsewhere and mostly remains in the fifties. Western medicine has made tremendous advances, but it cannot cure poverty and malnutrition, the root cause of many diseases. Probably because of these conditions, AIDS has had a more dramatic impact on Africa than elsewhere. A recent estimate placed the death rate in Zambia from AIDS at *one-third* of the population, mostly concentrated in the most economically productive age groups of men and women. This catastrophe overtaking many African countries dwarfs even those of the recurrent droughts and famines. The 1983 drought and famine affected most of sub-Saharan Africa and caused a huge mortality (one estimate, not the highest, was that 30 million children died in a three-month period in 1983 alone). But climatic conditions alone do not explain such figures. Overpopulation, farming of marginal land, poor soils, lack of capital inputs into agriculture, the conversion to export rather than food crops, and the disadvantages faced by women farmers have been offered as explanations for the drastic mortality. Nothing indicates more grotesquely the burgeoning international inequality than this African situation in the face of enormous U.S. grain surpluses.

Overpopulation is a problem directly connected to African poverty. Better health care has improved the long-term African infant mortality rate. However, contrary to the expectations of population experts, African birth rates have not generally declined but remain steady at an average of about six children per woman (in Kenya it is more than eight, the highest in the world). A good explanation for this apparent anomaly lies once again in a consideration of women's situation. Historically, and in the present, birth rates tend to decline permanently when people have become better off and their expectations for their children have risen. Urban African elites follow this pattern and have fewer children, but they are not numerous enough to have a big statistical impact. Urbanization itself plays a role in reducing family size, since urban children are more of a financial liability than rural children, who perform necessary labor when agriculture is not mechanized. But in Africa both urban and rural children perform necessary labor for their mothers, who often cannot afford to hire workers to help with the twelve-hour day. Perhaps even more important, children are the sole support for most old people in the absence of pensions and social security. Some men may not want to have many children, because they have pensions, wage jobs are scarce, and higher education is expensive, but uneducated women and men will generally still want as many children as possible to help with the labor-intensive work and for security in their old age. Such people are still in the majority. Thus, the continuing high birth rate in Africa is understandable, even without considering all the customary reasons associated with the importance of perpetuating the lineage.

If urban/rural differences are one striking aspect of internal socioeconomic differentiation in Africa, the overrewarding of white-collar work and burgeoning of the governmental bureaucracy are its primary symptoms. Thus, "success" is easiest to achieve in salaried government work rather than in private entrepreneurial activities, a tradition bequeathed by the colonialists, who discouraged African businesses by economic disincentives. The best option for many civil servants, however, is to use their government job as a sinecure and, at the same time, put energy into private ventures, which are made more profitable by the advantages of the government position. Such corruption has diminished government effectiveness considerably.

There are also problems with the educational systems, which are often still

Plate 86. Collecting water at a public fountain, Lomé, Togo.
Photo courtesy United Nations/B. Wolff.

oriented toward producing government civil servants. If American universities began a strong tradition of agricultural research and training in the mid-nineteenth century, African universities largely remain in the more theoretical European tradition. A contempt for manual labor and practical applications sometimes impedes productive activities, another hindrance to improving agriculture. From the 1960s to the 1980s, however, reforms were instituted in several countries to make education more suited to African conditions and expressive of African cultures; because of a lack of funds, such progress is necessarily slow. There is also continuing discrimination against women, especially in access to higher education.

A last aspect of socioeconomic inequality, then, is the disadvantaging of women. Increasingly, being poor means being female, a phenomenon with drastic implications for African societies, affecting everything from seemingly uncontrolled population growth to lack of investment in agriculture. A striking manifestation of the socioeconomic differentiation between the sexes is the increasingly segregated spheres of women and men, which have in turn reduced mutual understanding and contributed to women becoming scapegoats. In Zaire, Zambia, and Zimbabwe they have been accused of corrupting society's morals; in Ghana and Nigeria they were blamed for the countries' many economic ills. Arrests of women on flimsy pretexts have even been accompanied by executions in a few cases.

Conclusions

The overriding theme here, then, is division, the exaggerating of social and economic differences due to the spread of capitalism and the experience of hard times. The intense pace of change has made things all the more difficult for Africans, who have had to accommodate not only to economic domination and subordination, but to unprecedented poverty in the face of unprecedented wealth in the industrialized world. The shocks imposed by this situation have severely tested African ingenuity, tolerance, and flexibility, and placed great strain on social systems. Most of these social systems have shown themselves to be capable of great adaptation to change, but the exaggeration of social differences is making that adaptation more difficult. The cracks are showing, not only between the sexes and the rich and the poor, as has been shown here, but also between religious and ethnic groups. Islam has spread at a rapid rate, and Christianity has lost the enforcement provided by colonialism; most schools are now secular or Koranic. Parts of Africa have been swept up in growing Islamic fundamentalism. In northern Nigeria in the 1980s, a whole quarter of a town was destroyed by government troops in crushing a rebellion led by the charismatic leader of an Islamic sect. In Zimbabwe, majority rule required immediate resolution of a two-way ethnic rivalry which, as so often was the case, was exacerbated by colonialism and submerged in the liberation struggle. To their credit, African countries have not generally succumbed to divisiveness with the ferocity of Yugoslavia (with the exceptions of Rwanda, Sudan, and Somalia), despite their artificial origins as states. Nonetheless, wars characterized by starvation of hapless civilian populations are becoming more common in Africa. Such problems have deep roots; their solutions require tolerance, well-developed understanding, and a willingness to change further. African peoples are working on that understanding, but it takes time to mold one nation out of many cultures, languages, religions, classes, and interest groups, and sufficient leisure to develop it. For many the struggle to survive, which subordinates all other concerns, allows neither time nor leisure for anything else. Class formation and socioeconomic differentiation, then, exacerbate other differences and impede their resolution.

Remedies for the many problems will entail even more radical change, not least in social structure. The processes of democratizing decision making and redistributing wealth must be undertaken as quickly as possible to redress the balance between wealthy and poor, women and men, African and industrialized countries. Ultimately, the concentration of wealth in a few hands worldwide and in Africa will harm everyone, so it is only enlightened self-interest to develop mechanisms for equality. It is possible that Africans will find strength in egalitarian precolonial traditions to carry into the future. Given the large external and internal obstacles to be overcome, only by massive cooperative efforts using every ounce of their strength and vitality will Africans be able to overcome differences and develop new strategies for success.

NOTES

1. Ngugi wa Thiong'o, *The River Between* (London: Heinemann Educational Books Ltd., 1973), p. 166.

2. Buchi Emecheta, *The Joys of Motherhood* (London: Heinemann, 1979), p. 212.

3. "Polygyny" is the precise term for a man having more than one wife at a time; "polygamy" refers to any sort of multiple-spouse marital arrangement and includes polyandry, which was not practiced in Africa so far as we know.

4. Emecheta, *Joys*, p. 210.

5. *Daily Mirror* (Accra), no. 1270, December 9, 1977, p. 5.

6. *Woman's Mirror* (Nairobi), October 1987, pp. 10–11.

7. *Viva* (Nairobi), September 1987, pp. 24–28.

8. In contrast, time studies often show that rural men put in five to seven hours.

9. Emecheta, *Joys*, p. 170.

SUGGESTIONS FOR FURTHER READING

Aidoo, Agnes Akosua. "Women and Food Security: The Opportunity for Africa." *Development* 2, no. 3 (1980): 56–62.

Chazan, Naomi; Robert Mortimer; John Ravenhill; and Donald Rothchild. *Politics and Society in Contemporary Africa.* Boulder, Colo.: Lynne Rienner, 1988.

Dangarembga, Tsitsi. *Nervous Conditions.* Seattle: Seal Press, 1988.

Hay, Jean, and Sharon Stichter, eds. *African Women South of the Sahara.* New York: Longman, 1984.

Iliffe, John. *The African Poor.* Cambridge: Cambridge University Press, 1987.

Ndegwa, P.; L. P. Mureithi; and R. H. Green, eds. *Development Options for Africa in the 1980s and Beyond.* Nairobi: Oxford University Press, 1985.

Robertson, Claire. *Sharing the Same Bowl: A Socioeconomic History of Women and Class in Accra, Ghana.* Bloomington: Indiana University Press, 1984.

Schmidt, Elizabeth. *Peasants, Traders, and Wives: Shona Women in the History of Zimbabwe, 1870–1939.* Portsmouth, N.H.: Heinemann, 1992.

Takyiwaa Manuh
Law and Society in Contemporary Africa

17 It is nine o'clock in the morning, and Kofi M. and his lawyer are making their way to the High Court in Kumasi, Ghana. Kofi is followed by his sisters and nephews, who are all dressed in black. As they enter the courtroom they see Madam K., the widow of Kofi's deceased brother Mensah, and her four children, one of whom is holding the briefcase of the young female lawyer who is representing them and who works for the Legal Aid Bureau of the Women Lawyers' Association. No courtesies are exchanged between Kofi M., Madam K., and their entourage, and they all take their seats as the clerk pounds the gavel for the court to rise. The judge enters, and the clerk shuffles his papers and begins to call out the list of cases for the day. When the first case is called, the lawyers and the defendant are not present, and as the plaintiff finally stands up, the judge tells the clerk to adjourn the case for another month. The plaintiff is still standing when the next case is called, and the clerk hurriedly explains to him in Twi to return to court with his lawyer the following month.

After about an hour, the clerk announces the case of *Kofi M. and Others v. Madam K.*, and the plaintiffs and defendant stand up as their lawyers approach the bench. The attorneys speak in low tones to the judge and go back to their seats. The judge reads his ruling in English. He has decided that, in terms of the new law on succession, Madam K. and her children are entitled to the government pension and the house built by the late Mr. M., while the cocoa farms left by the deceased are deemed to be family property, to be distributed in accordance with the principles of Asante customary law. Members of each party grumble after hearing the judge's ruling, and as they leave the courtroom, the clerk shouts, "Order in the court."

At the eastern end of town, across from the palace of the Asantehene, five women are making their way to the Ohemaa's[1] house to attend a summons they have received. They are yam traders who have refused to adhere to the new prices fixed by their commodity queen,[2] who has now filed a complaint against them before the Ohemaa. When they arrive, the Ohemaa herself is not present, but court is being held, and her chief female attendant and a number of her linguists are present.

When their case is called, the commodity queen energetically states her case and threatens the traders with expulsion from the market should they fail to adhere to the new prices she has announced. The presiding elders call on the recalcitrant traders, who hesitantly begin to state their case. They explain that they are small traders who buy from middlewomen in the market. According to them, these middlewomen have refused to reduce the prices at which they give them their goods. In addition, they have to pay newly announced market rates to the municipal council controlling the market, and if they sold at the rates set by the commodity queen, they would make no margins and would have to stop trading. This would in turn jeopardize their efforts at maintaining their households.

After some discussion and more questioning of the commodity queen by the panel members, they recommend that a meeting be called of all the traders in the market to reopen the issue and to solicit the viewpoints of the different categories of traders. They are asked to reappear before the court in a month to inform the elders of the outcome of the negotiations.

The two scenarios presented capture some of the elements of legal pluralism in contemporary African societies. They also reflect some of the issues that are being debated as well as the different forums open for the resolution of conflict. Legal pluralism has been defined as the "situation in which two or more legal systems coexist in the same social system." A more legalistic or "juristic" view of legal pluralism defines it as a legal system in which the ruler "commands different bodies of law for different groups of the population varying by ethnicity, religion, nationality or geography."[3] It has been noted that this situation creates a range of legal problems, including the need to decide when a subgroup's law applies to particular transactions or conflict, to what group particular individuals belong, how a person can change which law is applicable to him or her, and choice of rules for issues between people of different groups. There may also be very different ways of thinking about the nature of evidence and the meaning of judging. All these problems were confronted in colonial Africa, and the manner of their resolutions continues to bedevil contemporary African states.

Laws provided the framework for incorporating precolonial African societies into the colonial framework, and in many places, lawyers and other educated elites became the intermediaries between the colonial governments and the peoples who were exposed to their political domination. But the rules introduced to extend the powers of the state can sometimes be turned against it, and lawyers were also early leaders of African nationalism against colonial domination. In their capacity as intermediaries with foreign capital, they were also closely associated with local economic interests created through the accumulation of surplus from trade and commodity crop production in rural areas. Thus, in their dual role, lawyers put the external legal traditions to service in pursuing domestic interests, at the same time that they were modifying indigenous traditions of customary law to suit the requirements of external penetration.[4] This interplay of the indigenous and the acquired and the roles of various intermediaries account for both the problems and the potentials in the relationship of law and society in Africa. The relationship is not merely one of subordination and dominance, but one of choice, manipulation, negotiation, and ultimately a new synthesis. This is evident in the manner in which laws, structures, and institutions inherited from the colonial past have been dealt with; the place of customary law in the legal systems of several African states; and ongoing experimentations with constitutional forms and attempts to formulate distinctive African conceptions of rights and institutions. The results may not often be satisfactory, but the process is necessary so that African states and peoples can engage in the dynamic process of creating secure societies which are based on their own concepts of law and order.

The Situation of Legal Plurality

All over Africa, the legal systems established in the colonial period are still in place to varying degrees. These structures were imposed on preexisting indigenous legal institutions which were customary and based largely on unwritten laws. Precolonial legal systems were characterized by their informality, nonbureaucratization, and the flexibility and adaptability in their rules, with decisions aimed more at reconciliation and neighborliness than at a strictly legal determination of right and wrong. Thus the validity and enforceability of a decision depended very much on the fairness embodied in decisions which also reflected societal values. This is not to suggest that these systems were necessarily simple and did not attain the status of law. Detailed investigations of the legal systems of various African groups undertaken by anthropologists such as Rattray on the Asante of Ghana, Bohannan on the Tiv of northern Nigeria, and Gluckman on the Lozi of southern Zambia brought out both the sophistication of particular systems and the existence of distinctive legal notions and concepts, as well as the variability among systems.

But whatever their adequacy for the needs of different African societies, these legal systems changed fundamentally toward the end of the nineteenth century as one European power after another extended its jurisdiction around Africa. In this process, law was crucial in legitimizing change. Through various legal forms, colonies were established, protectorates declared, and lands annexed in furtherance of imperial designs. While relations between several states and imperial powers had existed for well more than a century before formal colonialism (see chapter 6), and some irregular jurisdiction had developed in coastal areas such as Senegal, the Gold Coast, and Angola, the last quarter of the nineteenth century witnessed profound transformations in this relationship as the British, French, Portuguese, Belgians, and Spanish carved out territories for themselves over most of Africa (see map 24). Using the formula of a general law,[5] elements of metropolitan legal systems were selectively introduced to the colonies or protectorates, at the same time as there was restricted application of "native law and custom" or customary law, where these were held not "repugnant to natural justice, equity, good conscience," or did not run counter to the demands of colonial administration. In the French colonies, customary law was applicable only if it was compatible with notions of French civilization. And in many places, Islamic law was simply assumed to be a form of customary law applicable to Muslims.

These general laws were based on English common and statute law for British colonies in West and East Africa, Roman-Dutch law as modified by British- and South African–inspired legislation for Zimbabwe and southern Africa (South Africa, Lesotho, Botswana, and Swaziland), and civil law in the Portuguese, Belgian, Spanish, and French African colonies. When statutory reform occured in the metropoles, these were sometimes imported, depending on the existence of provisions in local legislation allowing for this, but otherwise the reforms had to be specifically adopted. This had the effect of leaving several African countries with laws which had been repealed and were no longer valid in the country of origin.

The creation of these legal systems in the newly acquired territories has been explained as necessary in order to provide the essential framework of law and order, with a special emphasis on criminal law and procedure; regulate the personal and proprietary relationships of non-Africans, with each other and with Africans; establish legal structures for the development of the territory; and allow those Africans who wished by reason of their education or their functions to move in general or particular transactions and relationships out of customary law and into a Western-law system.

In all cases, the new colonial government assumed all criminal jurisdiction, abolishing customary criminal laws, and denying to chiefs and local powerholders their former powers of arrest, imprisonment, and executions. In their place, criminal codes and statutes were introduced detailing technical offenses, and evidence in criminal cases was based on the English common law or French civil law in respective colonies. These codes were fairly interchangeable among colonies, so, for example, laws originally drafted for Australia, Jamaica, or India found their way to British colonies in Africa.

While customary law was excluded in criminal cases, in many places it governed transactions concerning marriage, succession, contracts, and land transfers where these were between Africans, and court systems were set up administering different systems of laws to different classes of persons. Marriage and family relations were to be governed by the personal law or customary law in the case of Africans. But in all the British colonies, a system of monogamous marriage was introduced for educated or Christian "natives." This had a major effect on their legal status and gave rights of succession to property to spouses and children which were not generally recognized in customary law. At the same time it denied such rights to the majority of women and their children.

Matters of inheritance or death were generally left to customary law, which would appoint a successor from among the family to take the place of the deceased to fulfill obligations toward his wives and children. But it was also possible for persons normally subject to customary law to make written wills in accordance with English law. This had the effect of depriving customary heirs of property which would normally have come to them and produced severe tensions between the extended family and the surviving spouse and his or her offspring.

In the case of contracts, legislation and judicial decisions allowed Africans normally subject to customary law to take themselves or their property out of the customary legal process through agreements or transactions made in accordance with noncustomary law. Thus, Africans subject to customary law could deal with their land by way of English law conveyances, they could enter into a contract of employment, and they could buy and sell goods or incur a debt, all in accordance with English law.

With regard to torts, which is the area of law dealing with legal wrongs such as defamation and negligence which do not arise from breaches of agreements, it was hard to know what law was to govern the transaction, and colonial practice was to refer the matter to the law of the parties. Thus defamation between two Africans in British colonies would generally be decided by the customary law, and by English law in cases between non-Africans. In cases involving Africans and non-Africans, the convention was to apply English law.

The needs and demands of colonial development meant that more and more, English or French law affected the lives of the majority of Africans as commercial legal principles were extended to govern contracts for the sale of goods and property, and colonial master and servant regulations were made to govern employment. In new mining industries and cash-crop production for export, European legal systems were used to mold a cooperative labor force. However, colonial peoples were remarkably tenacious in the face of superior or overarching power. Thus, in some areas, while judicial powers were taken from chiefs, people continued to take their cases to them for settlement under an escape clause that allowed chiefs, like ordinary people, to arbitrate cases where there was voluntary submission. As a strategy of avoidance of the Native Authority courts, which were seen as administrators of colonial laws, this can be interpreted as an attempt by Africans to maintain some autonomy in their private affairs. Even when the right to grant or manage their lands was taken from colonial subjects, as in the Concessions Ordinances introduced in the Gold Coast, various stratagems were devised to ensure that chiefs continued to be involved in land allocation and to receive some revenues from it. Thus, colonized peoples were not passive in the face of overwhelming power, but sought ways to maintain some autonomy and create space for independent action.

Customary Law

An important issue concerned the customary law that was allowed to continue subject to its compatibility with British or French notions of justice. It has been argued that this customary law was not necessarily the same as what scholars or the people themselves called their customary law. First of all, customary law when applied in courts was regarded as "foreign" law. This had to be "proved" in a manner similar to the system applied under European law. This meant calling expert witnesses until the rule had attained sufficient notoriety. Once proved, these rules were relied on by courts in other decisions because of the system of judicial precedent, and even where mistakes had occurred as to the actual content of a rule of customary law, it could continue to be relied upon, and even be incorporated into legislation. Thus there was often a divergence between what the people themselves regarded as their customary laws, which were often fluid and adaptable rules, and what emerged from the declarations of judges and courts. These court-declared formulations have been referred to as "judicial customary law" or "lawyers' law."[6] An example relating to the alienation of land will serve to illustrate the point.

Under the customary law of several African groups, land was considered to belong to communities or families and was rarely sold except in cases of extreme necessity. When land was eventually sold, the community or family tried to recover the alienated land by buying it back when more favorable circumstances arose. However, it was also possible to allow others to use land for a period and to recover it later so that the title was not lost. Under the impetus of colonial rule and the economic and social changes initiated, sales of group land were increasingly recognized even where they did not meet the permissible circumstances, and eventually the rule was arrived at that land could be sold by the holder at will. Similarly, customary law rules against alienation of individual land away from the family were compromised or ignored as individuals were permitted through the formula of a will to alienate substantial portions of land.

This "lawyers' law" was in effect the creation of a new type of "customary law" even though the courts appeared to be applying existing customary law. This was similar to the theory and practice of Indirect Rule (see chapter 7), and the "native courts" set up under it, for example, bore little resemblance to the traditional institutions which they gradually replaced, and the new customary norms they enforced were eventually not customary norms of conduct. This process of law creation was appropriate to the development of market capitalism, with elements of continuity maintained to prevent costly social upheaval.

These new powers of creation of customary norms which were reserved to the colonial state or recognized by African elders in the native courts particularly affected the rights and freedom of action of women and young men. The existing flexibility in marriage, labor arrangements, and property relations was removed, and more rigid formulations of what constituted African marriage, the duties of wives, and their access to land and other resources emerged.

Independence and After

After African countries achieved their independence, they had a range of choices in respect to their legal systems and the multiplicity of courts and laws that were applied. The Nigerian approach is fairly representative of the choices made. In general, the native courts were replaced by local, magistrates', or customary law courts; the judicial system was integrated, with the courts applying both the "general laws" and customary law; the final appeals system was revised, with the cessation of appeals to the Judicial Committee of the Privy Council for the former British colonies; and there was movement toward Africanization of the judiciary, which had been made up almost exclusively of white judges. This period also saw a flurry of activity aimed at reforming and "modernizing" laws. The system of a plurality of legal orders was seen as a problem, and legal expert A. N. Allott summed up these concerns as follows: "The new African governments . . . must i) modernize their legal systems in line with current economic and social needs, ii) replace the plurality of legal systems with a single national law, and at the same time will have to make them more genuinely African."[7]

Under the "Restatement of African Law" project, attempts were made in some cases to write down the "native customs" of different groups in each country, as a first step toward unification. Other attempts concerned the harmonization and eventual integration of customary law into general law. But restatement was not unlike what had happened under colonial rule. For example, a Tanzanian attempt at restatement in the 1960s produced rules which in many instances varied considerably with the local practice, but the declarations were accepted by the district councils and were promulgated as rules of law binding upon the courts.

By and large, customary law was seen as counterdevelopmental and unsuited to the tasks of nation building and modernization. This ignored the fact that what was termed customary law was not static. It had undergone major changes during the period of colonial rule and contributed to the adjustment of African communities to socioeconomic change, as Africans selectively adapted elements of English or French law in their own transactions or modified particular African forms for transferring property. In fact, customary law possessed a sufficient legal repertoire which is highly adaptable to changing conditions and is not an impediment to development.

The "development assistance" that was directed to the new states by American and European governments and international agencies also included assistance for the development of new legal institutions to "protect individual freedoms, expand citizen participation in decision-making, enhance social equality and increase the capacity of all citizens rationally to control events and shape social life."[8] But the reforms in the laws which were introduced failed to have the desired effect of creating a framework for the prosperity of individual citizens or leading to the development of more democratic institutions. For instance, attempts to reform the land law in several states to permit individual ownership and registration of land led in many cases to social inequality as the rights of women and smallholders were ignored and registration was found to have an ambiguous relationship to increased productivity. Reforms in family law were not always successful or seen as desirable and sometimes introduced concepts regarded as alien to the majority of the population, as, for instance, in the treatment of illegitimacy. Under the laws of various African groups, a child was legitimate once it had been acknowledged by its progenitor, but state laws sometimes produced the situation where a child was legitimate under one system of laws and illegitimate under another. Different systems of customary law also facilitated divorce once there was proof of irreconcilable breakdown, but new divorce procedures were sometimes cumbersome, while the marriage laws often did not recognize irregular unions, thus denying protection to women and children.

Constitutions and Constitutionalism

At independence, African countries inherited constitutional structures and arrangements modeled on those of the departing colonial power. In the main, these constitutions were based on doctrines of separation of powers among the executive, the legislature, and the judiciary, with judges possessing the power to review administrative and executive action and to pronounce on their conformity with the constitution. Some constitutions also contained a Bill of Rights under which basic human freedoms were guaranteed. But the efficacy of such a bill depends on the degree of independence enjoyed by the judiciary in their enforcement of rights, and to date the record of most African states has been one of judicial failures or acquiescence, and, with few exceptions such as Botswana and Zimbabwe, judicial review has not been an important instrument of government control. At the same time, the setting up of special administrative tribunals as instruments of government to try political and economic offenses removed them from the judicial scrutiny of the courts. Only a few judges were willing to go beyond a narrow interpretation of the law to question the legality of such acts.

A few years after independence, many of these constitutions were amended or abandoned as unworkable as new states worked to transform the internal and external conditions which perpetuated the poverty and underdevelopment of their societies. In many cases, opposition was regarded as a luxury that new states could not afford, and criticism or dissent was seen as undermining the immense task of nation building and as tantamount to treason. Preventive detention laws, which authorized imprisonment without trial for indefinite periods, were widely used.

The first twenty-five years after independence witnessed deep constitutional experimentation, as various forms of "guided" democracies, one-party democracies, no-party democracies, and "developmental dictatorships" under the military were instituted (see chapter 18). These arrangements cut across doctrinaire beliefs. Thus, countries such as Côte d'Ivoire and Kenya, both of which pursued open-door capitalist models of economic development, were one-party states, along with Tanzania, which espoused African socialism and economic planning. The different models were justified as reflecting African models of government which aimed at consensus building, facilitating nation building, and welding previously disunited ethnicities into one nation, and as necessary for economic development.

Almost without exception, these forms led to varieties of personal rule which left little room for the development of genuine pluralism in political life. What was also remarkable about these experimentations was that in their haste to modernize, few African states saw the wisdom of building constitutions which borrowed from existing traditional institutions. These better reflect African conceptions of the accountability of rulers to the ruled, provide against arbitrary rule, and are accepted by the majority of the population where they exist. While modern governments have come and gone, in many countries traditional political authority and institutions have shown a tenacity even in the face of governmental attempts to curb their power. This is an important point to keep in mind in the present period, when many African states reconsider new directions for their societies and for relations between ruler and ruled, either because their citizens demand it or because it has become conditional for assistance from the World Bank, the International Monetary Fund, and Western governments. These conditions were stated by Douglas Hurd, the British Foreign and Commonwealth Secretary: "Countries that tend towards pluralism, public accountability, respect for the rule of law, human rights, market principles should be encouraged. . . . Governments which persist with repressive policies, corrupt management, wasteful discredited economic systems should not expect us to support their folly with scarce aid resources, which could be better used elsewhere."[9]

This is what has become known as good governance, with the constitutional order seen as central to the securing of human rights, multiparty systems, fair and internationally supervised elections, strong and independent judiciaries, and efficient and responsible administration based on the foundations of effective constitutions and laws. But it has been pointed out that discussions of constitutionalism in Africa often proceed without reference to the economic and social conditions prevailing in particular countries. As a result, the constitutional documents that are fashioned do not reflect existing social cleavages, and many groups and interests have been left unprotected. Thus typically, African constitutional thinking and practice have not recognized the necessity to protect the interests of the peasantry, women, or ethnic and religious minorities. And governments have been overthrown by the military even where they have been based on elaborate constitutions with checks and balances; careful distribution of powers between the executive, legislature, and judiciary; protection of the independence of judges; and where the judiciary was the guardian of the constitution. The picture is thus more complicated than that suggested by the advocates of good governance. It is clear that enduring systems of constitutional authority will need to pay more attention to social processes in Africa and borrow from some of the principles and practices of traditional institutions, and other popular associations.

Human Rights and Development in Africa

African countries are members of the United Nations and subscribe to the provisions of its charter advocating respect for and promotion of human rights. They also recognize the 1948 Universal Declaration on Human Rights and other international conventions dealing with the protection and promotion of human rights. Furthermore, the constitutions of various countries also contain provisions on human rights. Yet the continent has witnessed massive violations of such agreements in the treatment of both nationals and nonnationals, such as the massacre of Hutus in Burundi in 1973, the mass murders in Uganda during the regime of Idi Amin (1971–79), in Central African Republic under Jean-Bedel Bokassa (1966–79), and in Equatorial Guinea under Macías Nguema (1969–79). In the recent past, there have also been massive abuses in Sudan, Liberia, Somalia, and Rwanda. In addition there has been the regular use of detention without trial in several countries, as well as the denial of political choice and restrictions on freedom of association. Yet the judicial systems in many cases have not been able to secure adequate protection for individuals faced with state oppression, and until recently there were few African nongovernmental organizations (NGOs) reporting on and documenting the violations of human rights. Thus, it has seemed that the pressure for respect for human rights has come from outside the continent as foreign governments and human rights organizations such as Amnesty International, Human Rights Watch (Africa), and the International Commission of Jurists have drawn attention to the problem. African countries, and principally the Organization of African Unity (the OAU), have also been seen in the untenable situation of keeping mute over events in each other's countries because of the OAU Charter's principle of noninterference in the internal affairs of member states. At the same time, they were able regularly to condemn South Africa for its racist and *apartheid* practices because it denied the principle of self-determination to the majority of its citizens. But it is significant that after the ousters of Amin, Bokassa, and Nguema in 1979, the OAU set about preparing a charter for the protection of human rights within member states with the assistance of the United Nations, and in June 1981, the African Charter on Human and Peoples' Rights, or the Banjul Charter, as it is known, was adopted unanimously by the OAU. It came into force in October 1986 and has been ratified by forty of the OAU's fifty-one member states.

The Banjul Charter draws heavily on prior international human rights documents, in particular the Universal Declaration of Human Rights and the International Covenants on Civil and Political Rights (1966) and Economic, Social and Cultural Rights (1976). It is also an attempt at putting forward a distinctly African conception of human rights which recognizes not only civil, political, economic, social, and cultural rights, but also the collective rights and duties of "peoples." Article 61 of the charter also includes African customs and practice insofar as they represent binding legal rules as a subsidiary means of determining the applicable legal principles.

The Banjul Charter has been subject to much criticism by both African and non-African commentators, with criticisms leveled at what are known as "clawback clauses" in the charter that confine its protections to rights as they are defined in national legislation, and the nonincorporation of charter norms into domestic legislation.[10] And unlike other regional systems of human rights protection, there is no court set up under the charter. The main body charged with the promotion of the provisions of the charter is the African Commission on Human and Peoples' Rights. It is a fact-finding and conciliatory body with no decision-making powers, and it is seen as too dependent on the OAU, whose member states it is meant to police.

While the functioning of the commission has brought out a number of defects inherent in the charter and the weakness of indigenous human rights organizations, the very existence of such a body must be seen as an advance toward an ongoing elaboration by Africans themselves of what they consider appropriate norms for securing personal freedoms and enlarging the space for political and social action. Only in this way can such norms hope to gain wide social acceptability and be considered worthy of protection by individuals and groups in society.

Women and the Law

Closely related to the issue of human rights are the rights of women in the different African legal systems. African women have been depicted in Western texts as powerless and oppressed by various systems of customary law, but as we have seen, these customary laws themselves were constructions, leading to a situation described by one scholar as "neither customary nor legal."[11] Precolonial African societies manifested a variety of attitudes and practices toward women, with women possessing political, religious, and social power in some systems and having little or no formal power in others. In many societies also, the spheres of men and women were regarded as separate and complementary. However, under colonialism, all these systems were overlaid with Western conceptions, and significant alterations occurred. One of these areas was in marriage and family law, where new laws were passed which introduced a new form of marriage to a minority of women, and gave them rights of succession with regard to the estate of a deceased husband. These marriages, based on a European model of monogamy and close companionate ties, aimed at the creation of a nuclear family. In many cases, there were deep ambiguities in these relationships for women, who were vulnerable because of the differences in expectations for men and women. Educated Nigerian women, for example, caught in the conflict generated by Christian monogamous marriages, relied on their kin and avoided the use of colonial and, one may add, modern-day state courts to resolve their disputes.[12] It has also led to the abandonment by women of the ideal of a "housewife" who is maintained by her husband, and many educated women resumed the active economic roles that African societies expect of women generally (see chapter 16).

For the majority of women, customary law continued to be the operative law in their marriage and family relations, and the rigidities introduced in customary law under colonialism worked to produce many inequities. Thus, even as women's labor became important in the production of cash crops such as tea, coffee, and cocoa, they were denied shares in the proceeds, under the fiction that it was the duty of wives to make labor contributions to husbands without remuneration. This led to tensions in family relationships, and to demands by women to be given shares of proceeds. Women increasingly resorted to courts to try to enforce their rights, or in the absence of that, to divorce and migration.

Migrations of both men and women to town, their separation from kin, and the stresses of town life also led to cases of domestic violence, desertion, abandonment, divorce, and lack of support. All these issues have formed part of women's concerns about the law. The inefficacy of attempts by social welfare agencies, churches, and kin have led in the contemporary period to the formation of women's groups, and specifically to organizations of women lawyers such as the one representing Madam K. at the beginning of the chapter, as a means of dealing with the inequities suffered by women in family, local and national systems.

The activities of women's groups have been helped by international developments such as the United Nations Decade for Women and the formulation of the Convention on the Elimination of all forms of Discrimination Against Women (CEDAW). This convention has been ratified by a number of African countries, but it has not found its way into national legislation, although some countries have introduced reforms in the succession rights of women which conform to the provisions of the convention. The African Charter on Human and Peoples' Rights also makes mention of women's rights but does not elaborate them, and limits them to their conformity with African customs and practices.

Currently, the major movement with respect to women's rights is the Women in Law and Development in Africa (WILDAF), which has groups in several West, East, and southern African countries. Its activities focus on law reform, the popularization of the law, legal literacy, and paralegal training for women as a means of "empowering" them to take control of their lives. It has set up legal aid centers where advice and counseling are offered, and when necessary, legal counsel is provided for court appearances. Women come to the centers seeking advice or action concerning child support, domestic violence, divorce, and property issues, and many of these centers appear to enjoy the support of the states where they operate. The centers are confined to urban areas, and many have yet to reach the majority of African women who live in rural areas.

Conclusion

This chapter has focused on the situation of legal pluralism in contemporary African states, and the particular resolutions of the problems it has engendered. Colonial rulers imposed foreign conceptions of order on distinct African notions of ordering their societies. These impositions led in some cases to an ouster of previously existing situations, as in the criminal law, while in others, a coexistence of forms emerged. At the same time, Africans were not passive in the face of these developments. As with the lawyers described at the beginning of the chapter, there was a clear conception of different interests.

The collaboration that resulted led lawyers and other educated elites to gain some measure of power. But there was also resistance, as the lawyers turned the acquired legal traditions on their head and used them ultimately to undermine colonial rule. Similarly, ordinary people were not passive, and went along with colonial laws when they had to, but they also continued to uphold indigenous legal institutions as they took their cases to chiefs and other traditional power holders. Africans also adapted to changed economic circumstances and demonstrated considerable flexibility in their notions of property holdings and developed new forms where appropriate. In this they were assisted by the colonial courts, which were anxious to develop institutions and practices favorable to the development of capitalist relations.

After independence, many states moved to abolish the various courts which applied different laws and to Africanize the judicial system, but initial attempts at unification largely failed. This reflected some realism on the part of leaders who realized that pluralism was an obvious fact of life in states which had been artificially welded together. This recognition of pluralism was not followed in the political sphere, as government became increasingly centralized and alienated the majority of inhabitants.

Following the failure of many states to realize the hopes of independence and the crises in many African nations, debate is beginning on the relationship between law and the creation of more just and efficient states, and the structures necessary to fulfill these goals. The needs and interests to be protected in such an order, as well as the role of institutions such as the judiciary, human rights groups, and foreign governments and organizations, all need to be discussed. This may ensure that this time around, African states create systems which are firmly grounded in their own histories and experiences, and approximate their own conceptions.

NOTES

1. The *Ohemaa*, translated loosely as "Queen Mother," is usually the sister or aunt of the ruling chief, and reflects the complementarity in Akan lineage principles.

2. There are queens or *ahemaa* for the commodities traded in the markets. They are elected by their peers and act to safeguard the interests of a particular group of traders. Among their functions are representing the traders and acting as spokespersons in negotiations with municipal authorities, settling disputes among traders, and regulating competition from visiting traders from other markets.

3. Sally E. Merry, "Legal Pluralism," *Law and Society Review* 22, no. 5 (1988): 869–96.

4. Robin Luckham, "Imperialism, Law and Structural Dependence: The Ghana Legal Profession," in *Lawyers in the Third World: Comparative and Developmental Perspectives*, ed. C. J. Dias, R. Luckham, D. O. Lynch, and J. C. N. Paul (Uppsala: Scandinavian Institute of African Studies, 1981), p. 93.

5. For the English colonies, general law specified that the laws to be applied were to be based on the common law, the doctrines of equity, and the statutes of general application which were in force in England at the date when the colony obtained a local legislature or the time an order commenced. See Anthony N. Allott, *New Essays in African Law* (London: Butterworths, 1970).

6. A. N. Allott, "What Is to Be Done with African Customary Law," *Journal of African Law* 28, nos. 1 and 2 (1984); G. R. Woodman, "How State Courts Create Customary Law in Ghana and Nigeria," in B. Morse and G. R. Woodman, eds., *Indigenous Law and the State* (Dordrecht: Foris Publications, 1988).

7. A. N. Allott, "The Future of African Law," in H. and L. Kuper, eds., *African Law: Adaptations and Development* (Berkeley: University of California Press, 1965).

8. D. Trubeck and M. Galanter, "Scholars in Self-Estrangement: Some Reflections on the Crisis in Law and Development Studies in the United States," *Law and Society Review* 4 (1974): 1062–1102.

9. Cited in Peter Slinn, "A Fresh Start for Africa? New African Constitutional Perspectives," *Journal of African Law*, special number on Recent Constitutional Developments in Africa (London: SOAS, 1991), p. 3.

10. See Claude Welch, "The African Commission on Human and Peoples' Rights: A Five-Year Report and Assessment," *Human Rights Quarterly* 14 (1991): 43–61.

11. Martin Chanock, "Neither Customary nor Legal: African Customary Law in an Era of Family Law Reform," *International Journal of Law and the Family* 3 (1989): 72–88.

12. Kristin Mann, "Women's Rights in Law and Practice: Marriage and Dispute Settlement in Colonial Lagos," in M. Hay and M. Wright, eds., *African Women and the Law: Historical Perspectives* (Boston: Boston University Press, 1982).

SUGGESTIONS FOR FURTHER READING

Adelman, S., and Abdul Paliwala, eds. *Law and Crisis in the Third World*. London: Hans Zell, 1993.

Allott, A. N., and G. R. Woodman, eds. *People's Law and State Law: The Bellagio Papers.* Dordrecht: Foris Publications, 1985.

Amissah, Austin N. "Constitutionalism and Law in Africa." In D. Ronen, ed., *Democracy and Pluralism in Africa*, pp. 41–51. Boulder, Colo.: Lynne Rienner Publishers, 1986.

Cohen, Ronald; Goran Hyden; and Winston P. Nagen. *Human Rights and Governance in Africa*. Gainesville: University Press of Florida, 1993.

Hay, M., and M. Wright, eds. *African Women and the Law: Historical Perspectives*. Boston: Boston University Press, 1982.

Morse, B., and G. R. Woodman, eds. *Indigenous Law and the State*. Dordrecht: Foris Publications, 1988.

"Recent Constitutional Developments in Africa." Special number, *Journal of African Law* 35, nos. 1 and 2 (1991). London: School of Oriental and African Studies.

Stewart, Julie, and Alice Armstrong, eds. *The Legal Situation of Women in Southern Africa*. Harare: University of Zimbabwe Publications, 1990.

Economics and Politics

N. Brian Winchester
African Politics since Independence

18 African independence was accompanied by great optimism and great expectations. There was a widely held belief that the former colonies would make a quick and easy transition to representative democracy guided by democratic constitutions, multiparty systems, and other Western liberal institutions that had been put in place during the latter stages of decolonization by the departing European colonial powers. Most expectations, however, proved to be unrealistic, and the optimism was short-lived.

Within a few years, many of the newly independent African states moved from a multiparty system to a one-party state and, subsequently, to military rule. In most cases, the introduction of democratic institutions just prior to independence was a case of "too little, too late"; colonialism's real legacy, after all, was authoritarian rule, and the assumption that political empowerment would result in rapid and total decolonization ignored the countervailing power of economic dependency and neocolonialism.

Furthermore, since their political boundaries were artificial, and most of their people were united neither by a common historical experience nor by linguistic affinity or a shared cultural heritage, most African states had rather tenuous claims to nationhood. Typically, while a sense of community often existed at the local or regional level, allegiance to an "alien" national political system either did not exist or was just beginning to develop. Precolonial political life in many cases had been relatively decentralized, and the imposition of an artificial, corporate identity during the colonial period more often exacerbated ethnic and regional rivalries than provided the foundation for future political identity. In the end, history, geography, and political realities seem to have conspired to indenture these nascent states. An observer of Africa's transition to independence summed up the situation when he noted that the newly independent states were "governed by insecure regimes uneasily in control of unsettled societies."[1]

It thus seems all the more remarkable that colonial political divisions created solely to serve European interests survived African independence intact. Equally remarkable is the fact that the majority of African states achieved independence with little or no violence. Where independence was accompanied by armed struggle, as in Algeria, Kenya, the Portuguese colonies, Zimbabwe, and Namibia, it was attributable to white settler minorities whose intransigence to African demands for majority rule and justice made the resort to violence inevitable. The same was true for the transition to majority rule in South Africa.

The independent states shared a number of immediate and long-term objectives, the first of which was the need to consolidate the state system that they had inherited. From an African point of view, colonial boundaries, no matter how undesirable, were at least internationally recognized, and the alternative—to redraw the political map—would have involved great uncertainty and the risk of precipitating a series of confrontations with rival neighbors. While there were a few notable exceptions, such as the successful renegotiation of the boundary between Cameroon and Nigeria, most demands for changes were resisted, fiercely so in the case of secessionist threats by Katanga province from Zaire (1960–1963), by Biafra from Nigeria (1967–1970), and in the Eritrean and Tigre liberation movements in Ethiopia. It is noteworthy that the charter of the Organization of African Unity (OAU), which governs relations between members, declares that none of the borders existing at independence shall be changed by force, and that each member-state shall respect the others' sovereignty and not interfere in their internal affairs.

Irrespective of their particular domestic political agendas, most states opted for international nonalignment, ostensibly to distance themselves from the obvious dangers of the East-West superpower rivalry. An impression of nonalignment was created by expanding international contacts, acting independently in the international arena, and establishing alliances beyond the orbit of the former colonial power. The great majority of African states, for example, established diplomatic relations with at least some communist bloc countries almost immediately after gaining independence. Nevertheless, most independent nations continued to maintain close ties with their former rulers. Radical and conservative-minded regimes alike sought to ensure survival through pragmatism despite their revolutionary or conservative ideologies. Thus, although these states had become sovereign, independent nations recognized by the international community, the real distribution of power, based on extensive economic linkages, a shared monetary system, military treaties, and bilateral aid, continued to reflect and assert the dramatic inequities of the past. In this was a central contradiction of African independence.

The Concentration of Political Power

Exploiting the accumulated grievances against their former colonial rulers may have initially won votes and created support for the new African governments, but it did little to solve complex monetary, developmental, and social problems, which defied quick, easy solutions. Widespread poverty, illiteracy, and divisive ethnic rivalries persisted. Furthermore, certain African leaders, civil servants, and politicians perpetuated some of the worst aspects of elitism and exploitation characteristic of the colonial period. Under the circumstances, political discontent was inevitable and the integrity and effectiveness of the new political institutions was questioned. Many African politicians, who aimed to stay in power as long as possible in order to implement their independence programs, extended their mandate through extra-constitutional means. Under great pressure to satisfy rising expectations but unable to do so, one African regime after another eliminated formal parliamentary opposition by adopting a one-party system. Members of competing political parties were in some cases co-opted into the ruling party, while in others they had their political activities proscribed or were banned outright. The center of decision making then frequently shifted from the legislature to the central committee of the party, which further aggrandized its power at the expense of any autonomous or representative institutions, such as universities, trade unions, and newspapers. Typically the civil service, the police and armed forces, and the independent judiciary were all brought under closer party control. The identification of the party with the state was often symbolically established where a single political leader assumed the leadership of both the party and the government.

Sensitive to external criticism in particular, one-party regimes went to great lengths to justify the elimination of competitive party politics. They pointed out, for example, that in most cases the nationalist party that led their countries to independence became the majority party or ruling party when power was transferred, and therefore truly represented the will of the people. Mass parties in such countries as Ghana, Kenya, and Tanzania legitimately claimed the support of the great majority of the population. The Parti Democratique de Guinée (PDG), for example, claimed that without the PDG, Guinea would not be independent, and that as a mass party truly representative of the nation, the PDG was Guinea! One-party regimes further argued that the multiple reinforcing crises of poverty, illiteracy, and underdevelopment confronting them at independence were analogous to crises which prompted even established Western democracies such as the United States, Canada, and France to invoke emergency powers and circumscribe democratic practices to combat what they perceived as either an external or an internal threat. For advocating so-called developmental dictatorship, African leaders were simply demanding the same prerogative. They also maintained that a· disciplined, one-party system allowed the limited pool of expertise and resources, typically in short supply in developing countries, to be directed to solving problems, whereas multiple parties were seen as divisive forces which wasted time, resources, and manpower. Put most simply, what they seemed to be saying was that they could not afford the luxury of opposition.

The risks of disintegration attached to multiparty systems were seen to be further increased where party loyalties or voting patterns were reinforced by ethnic, religious, and regional divisions. Since almost every African state has experienced firsthand the divisive effects of extreme ethnic competition, and a majority have had to cope with religious pluralism and regionalism as well, many chose to try to create consensus through the creation of a single-party state. This was accomplished either through electoral victory, through merger, or through coercive means such as intimidation and banning. Kwame Nkrumah's government used "legalized coercion" when it banned the Muslim Association Party, the Northern People's Party, and the Asante-dominated National Liberation Movement in Ghana in the late 1950s, ostensibly to engineer consensus in the midst of the centrifugal effects of Ghana's extreme degree of cultural pluralism.

Events in Ghana foreshadowed the increasing concentration of power by single parties at the expense of other competing parties and other independent and representative institutions in one African state after another. Malawi and Uganda among others, for example, moved quickly after independence to eliminate electoral competition altogether. By the end of the first decade of African independence, only two states, The Gambia and Somalia, had competitive party systems.

Some one-party regimes, such as Kenya, Tanzania, and Zambia, were able to retain a modicum of electoral competition, even where voters were allowed to choose only from among candidates who were themselves members of the single party. The Tanzanian African National Union (TANU) is a good example of such competition. In elections after TANU became the only legal political party in Tanzania in 1964, voters rejected as many as 45 percent of the incumbent members of parliament, and even cabinet ministers became subject to similar public accountability.

On the other hand, in most former French colonies, opposition political parties and electoral competition within the remaining single party were eliminated. For Africa as a whole, this more authoritarian type outnumbered those which sought to preserve competition within the one-party framework. General elections, as a consequence, became plebiscites in which voters cast votes only for or against the one official candidate for each office. Plebiscitary elections serve to generate support for the regime and party, raise national consciousness, and provide the regime with the opportunity to publicize its policies, as well as with a formal mechanism to dispense political patronage by replacing "elected" members, but they rarely offer voters a meaningful choice.

Single-party regimes, regardless of the degree of competitiveness, do not appear to have been any more successful at governing than the multiparty systems which they replaced. Nor do they appear to have been any less susceptible to corruption and maladministration.

Soldier-Politicians Assert Control

The maintenance of an armed force is regarded as a fundamental mark of sovereignty by virtually all states, and since few African states have been involved in serious interstate conflicts, the military have often become preoccupied with internal affairs. This, in turn, has affected their disposition to intervene and made them more sensitive to the opportunities to do so. When a grievance is added to that sense of power, a motive to intervene begins to develop. Where the grievances of civilians and soldiers coincide and military intervention is popularly perceived as a panacea, the disposition to intervene is reinforced. The opportunity to take action is further enhanced where the popularity of the civil authorities is on the decline and they are increasingly dependent upon the military.

Ironically, the one-party state is particularly vulnerable to takeover by the military when the party attempts to strengthen its own position at the expense of trade unions, students, an independent judiciary, and other interest groups. In the Third World the military is acutely aware of its nearly unrestrained power, and the absence of a vigorous civil society as a countervailing force allows it to intervene with little fear of organized opposition.

The history of coups d'état in Africa reveals numerous specific, immediate causes, including any one or a combination of the following: unacceptably high levels of corruption and profiteering, government mismanagement and financial extravagance, the decision by political leaders to stay in power beyond their constitutionally mandated tenure, demands on the military to carry out distasteful policies such as strikebreaking on behalf of politicians, and attempts by civilian government to compromise or reduce the power, budget, or perquisites of the military. Still others see a correlation between the increasing frequency of military intervention and the economic deterioration which has affected most of tropical Africa; that is, where governments have failed to fulfill rising expectations, army takeovers have often followed. The rapid succession of coups d'etat in geographic proximity to one another lends some credence to the "contagion theory," which maintains that each succeeding coup predisposes the military elsewhere to intervene. Finally, power is, of course, desirable in itself, and in some instances the personal ambition of particular military leaders has been sufficient cause for a coup.

While the seizure of power has been relatively easy for Africa's soldiers, the effective exercise of that power has proved to be far more difficult. The problems that beset previous civilian regimes soon test the skills of the new soldier-politicians. It is not surprising, then, that one of the first acts of a new military regime is to co-opt the least tainted civilian politicians and form alliances within the bureaucracy. Ultimately, the military has been no more successful than civilian regimes in reducing ethnic conflict and accommodating diverse religions, in providing the order and stability necessary for political development, or in accelerating economic growth.[2] As one political scientist observed, "A military takeover and rule by officers never constitutes a revolution in Tropical Africa, but rather a limited modification of existing arrangements."[3]

Since independence, a majority of African states have experienced at least one successful coup d'etat, and a majority of those more than one. In addition, it is estimated that as many as several hundred coup attempts failed during the same period. There is great concern that the number and frequency of coups since independence have created a "culture of violence," frustrating the growth of what former President Nyerere of Tanzania once described as "the habit of democracy."

Efforts to Reestablish Political Participation

Political transformations of major significance occurred in many African states in the 1970s (see chapter 8). Five centuries of Portuguese colonialism ended; four military regimes in West Africa relinquished power to civilians, if only for a short time; orderly constitutional succession occurred in Kenya and Botswana after the deaths of the founding fathers of both of these nations; in a number of countries real efforts were made to increase citizen participation in politics; and a protracted guerrilla war ended in Zimbabwe, and, remarkably, the protagonists resolved their differences at the ballot box.

Africa's second wave of independence brought an end to colonial rule in the former

Plate 87. Young soldier of the MPLA, Luanda, Angola.
Photo courtesy United Nations/J. P. Laffont.

Portuguese colonies of Guinea-Bissau (1974), Angola (1975), and Mozambique (1975), and to Portugal's island possessions of São Tomé, Principe, and Cape Verde (1975). With the independence of Zimbabwe in 1980, the liberation of white-minority-ruled Namibia and South Africa remained the final obstacle to Africa's "unfinished revolution."

In Senegal, President Léopold Sédar Senghor lifted the ban on political activity and approved a modified multiparty system in place of the former one-party state. His subsequent decision to step down in favor of Prime Minister Abdou Diouf in January 1981 places Senghor in an exclusive group of African leaders who have relinquished power voluntarily. These include Ahmadou Ahidjo of Cameroon, General Olusegun Obasanjo of Nigeria, Julius Nyerere of Tanzania, Aristides Pereira of Cape Verde, Kenneth Kaunda of Zambia, Hastings Banda of Malawi, and F. W. de Klerk in South Africa.

In a half-dozen other states, predominantly in West Africa, tentative constitutional developments took place which resulted in the return of civilian rule. Military regimes in Upper Volta, Ghana, and Nigeria relinquished power to civilians in 1978–1979 in competitive elections. Democratic, parliamentary systems were tentatively restored in the latter two countries, a striking reversal on a continent far more used to the contagion of coups d'etat. Elections were also held in a number of other countries: in Botswana, President Sir Seretse Khama was elected to a fourth term in an open democratic election; in Côte d'Ivoire and Gabon, for the first time since independence in 1960, citizens were given a greater freedom of choice, if only within the one-party framework. In Côte d'Ivoire, a number of discredited older-generation politicians were, in fact, defeated. Fears that an immediate period of political instability would follow the deaths in the late 1970s of Kenya's president since independence, Jomo Kenyatta, and President Sir Seretse Khama of Botswana were allayed with the constitutional transfer of power in each case. In Kenya, a highly competitive, one-party election was held for the National Assembly in which nearly half the incumbents were defeated. A one-party contest in Mali saw former military ruler Brigadier General Moussa Traore affirmed as the new "civilian" president. The long-term viability of democratic institutions in Africa remained unresolved.

Also in the 1970s, Africa's three worst personal tyrannies came to an end. In April 1979 Idi Amin's eight-year reign of terror in Uganda was ended by a combined force of Tanzanian army units and Ugandan exiles; the predatory regime of Francisco Macias Nguema in Equatorial Guinea was overthrown in August 1979, apparently with Spanish assistance; and in September of the same year, Jean-Bedel Bokassa, self-crowned emperor of the Central African Empire, was deposed by the military with French military support. The three left a common legacy: thousands forced into exile, thousands more murdered, often with the approval and involvement of government officials, and near-bankrupt economies, in large part a result of rampant corruption and gross personal mismanagement.

Economic Decline and Increasing Dependency

Like all developing regions, Africa is heavily dependent on importing goods which it does not produce itself (for example, pharmaceuticals, fertilizer, vehicles, and so-called high-tech items). Most imports must be purchased with foreign exchange, which is earned through exporting domestic products or through investment, development assistance, or loans from outside. Nine out of ten African countries depend on primary commodities for 70 percent or more of their exports. However, prices for such commodities, Africa's main source of foreign exchange, plummeted drastically in the 1980s, costing governments tens of millions of dollars in lost export revenues. At the same time, total external resource flows (development assistance, loans) remained constant or actually declined slightly, forcing countries to borrow even more to compensate for the shortfall.

By the mid-1980s, economic decline had reached near-crisis proportions, with some states, both military- and civilian-ruled, barely able to meet interest payments on loans. International lending agencies, led by the International Monetary Fund (IMF), began to impose conditions on subsequent loans (see chapters 19 and 20). This "conditionality," requiring drastic changes in domestic monetary and fiscal policies, included the removal of agricultural subsidies, increases in the price of staple foods, the reduction of nonfood imports, the freezing of wages, and the devaluation of currencies. Some of the more austere monetary reforms, such as the 90 percent devaluation of the Ghanaian cedi, clearly demonstrated the extent to which the IMF had emerged as one of the most significant influences not only on the economic and political life of many African countries but on domestic politics as well. Critics of the IMF's insistence on a free market approach and its opposition to government intervention into the economy alleged that conditionality was tantamount to a new form of colonialism.

On the other hand, however, African states have seldom been forced into roles as clients of Western or Soviet or some other imperialism. Foreign intervention has often come at the invitation of Africans themselves when interests coincided and provided the excuse to interfere.[4] The competing interests which have kept Chad the pawn in a game dominated by more powerful players during its more than twenty-five-year civil war are one such example. The formation of patron-client relationships was the result of rampant religious, regional, and ideological factionalism within Chad itself, as well as French opportunism; Libyan illusions of expanding the Qaddafi-style Pan-Islamic sphere of influence; Sudanese fears of Libyan expansionist aims; Saudi fears of Qaddafi's Islamic radicalism; and Nigeria's commitment to prevent interference in African politics while enhancing its own growing role in the international arena.

Few regions of Africa better illustrate the capriciousness of ideological commitment than the Horn. Described by some as an example of "revolving door" diplomacy, the changing international alignments involved in the Somali-Ethiopian conflict represented a microcosm of East-West great-power rivalry as it existed before the end of the Cold War. Internal changes in Ethiopia were as much a result of such external forces as they were due to internal pressures. A little more than six months after Ethiopia expelled the U.S. military and broke with the United States in 1974, the Ethiopians were embracing the Soviets. After Soviet expulsion from Sudan and Soviet and Cuban expulsion from Somalia, relations between the United States and those two countries warmed considerably. The result was an extraordinary exchange of clients who simply continued as surrogates for their "new" Cold War allies.

However, with the end of superpower rivalry, the Horn of Africa lost its strategic importance and its military support, and internal forces were able to challenge and upset the prevailing balance of power in both Somalia and Ethiopia in 1991. The twenty-one-year reign of President Mohammed Siad Barre was ended by three clan-based rebel groups whose continuing struggle with each other for power brought Somalia to near-anarchy. With the Soviet pullout and a nearly simultaneous 50 percent decline in the price of its principal export, coffee, a destabilized Ethiopia was unable to further resist the combined assault of the Eritrean and Tigrean liberation movements. President Mengistu Haile Mariam was forced to flee, and Eritrea, after a thirty-year struggle, became independent in 1993.

Popular Revolt and Democratic Renewal

Criticized from within and without for their failure to bring economic well-being and political stability after nearly three decades of mostly authoritarian rule, regime after regime faced escalating demands for democratic reform. By the late 1980s and early 1990s, many of Africa's autocrats were under "assault" by a combination of trade unionists, human rights activists, civil libertarians, students, religious leaders, and others who were emboldened by the success of reformers elsewhere, particularly in Eastern Europe and in southern Africa.

One of the precipitating events occurred in February 1990, when the president of Benin, Mathieu Kérékou, was forced to convene a National Conference to address the country's economic and political crises. Unexpectedly, the delegates, who came largely from the educated and political elite, declared the conference sovereign, suspended the constitution, and dissolved the National Assembly. By the end of the ten-day conference, Kérékou had been stripped of his power, and a former World Bank official, Nicéphore Soglo, had been chosen interim prime minister. Subsequently, Benin's first democratic election in seventeen years reconfirmed the conference's choice of Soglo to run the country. Widely reported and analyzed, democratization in Benin became a model of political reform, and the National Conference emerged as the mechanism of choice for regime change in nearly a dozen francophone African countries alone, with strong support from French president François Mitterrand.[5] In the short space of two to three years, more than half of sub-Saharan Africa's governments were forced to respond to growing pressure for democratic reform "from the streets" and from external donors. The trend toward political liberalization may be widespread, but it remains fragile and incomplete. For every apparent success (Mali, Zambia, Malawi), there have been as many outright failures (Zaire, Nigeria, Togo, Gabon) or stalemates (Madagascar) caused by incumbents manipulating or simply ignoring conference or election outcomes. In an ironic lesson, Kenyans voted almost 2 to 1 for change in an election in 1993, but autocratic incumbent president Daniel arap Moi prevailed with 36.7 percent of the vote simply because the opposition was split.

In perhaps the most bitter irony of all, as Africa finally made significant concessions to democratic reform demanded by the West, the end of superpower rivalry has "orphaned" or marginalized many governments such as in Angola and Zaire, among others, where foreign assistance has diminished and they can no longer command the attention they once did.

The Specter of Anarchy

Somalia, Liberia, and Rwanda, among others, represent a nightmarish paradox: at the same time that authoritarian rule is giving way to democracy in much of Africa, it looks as if elsewhere in Africa authoritarianism may be degenerating into anarchy.[6] In these three tragic cases, the accelerating collapse of authority is being likened to a violent, political implosion which leaves a vacuum then filled by warlords, urban mafias, and undisciplined young "warriors" with automatic weapons. Violence becomes the princi-

Plate 88. Billboard celebrating national independence, Windhoek, Namibia, 1990.
Photo courtesy United Nations/J. Isaac.

pal means of security, with predictable results. Those without security who have fled for their lives reached and then surpassed 5 million in the 1990s, one-third of the world's total refugees.

In several countries, more and more people competing for fewer and fewer resources reduces life to a struggle for sheer survival. Scarcities of water, land, food, and other necessities continue to inflame historical enmities, further exacerbated by the proliferation of weapons, which are the legacy of Cold War confrontations. A terrifying descent toward anarchy is not inevitable, however. Uganda and Mozambique, only recently on the brink of anarchy themselves, offer cautious optimism that even desperate situations can be turned around. Proposed solutions all call for some form of external intervention or assistance, including military action, economic reconstruction, and debt forgiveness. One of the more thought-provoking and controversial proposals calls for the reconfiguration of Africa from fifty countries to no more than fourteen or fifteen. Based on the assumption that the geographic, demographic, and political decisions made at the Berlin Conference in 1884–85 contributed to the failure of the postcolonial state, Africa, it is argued, must now create new states more in conformity with cultural homogeneity, ethnic similarities, economic viability, and political-historical factors.[7]

Conclusion

South Africa's nonracial, democratic election in April 1994 not only was a historic first for that country's black majority, but also signaled the removal of the final obstacle to Africa's total liberation. On the other hand, growing foreign influence, exemplified by aggressive French economic and military intervention in more than twenty African countries and by International Monetary Fund and World Bank conditionality, represents, according to some critics, a form of neocolonialism imposed on the continent. Indeed, there are more expatriates in some parts of Africa today maintaining that historic dependency than were there during the colonial period.

By the end of the first decade of independence, the weakness of most African economies and political institutions was already apparent. In the 1970s, the ongoing search for effective and responsive political institutions was complicated by a widespread drought of historic proportions and the worst recession in forty years. Mismanagement and corruption exacerbated the already deteriorating situation. By the mid-1980s, the World Bank and the Economic Commission for Africa confirmed widespread economic decline and correctly predicted a period of even greater economic impoverishment. This and the fact that the continent continued to be an arena for great-power politics contributed to widespread political instability. Though the coup d'etat became the most predictable mechanism for regime change, preference for civilian government over military rule remains an article of faith. An exiled Nigerian lawyer, discussing the fifth Nigerian coup, maintained that it was "far better to have a shabby democracy in which people have some say in the running of things than a shabby military regime in which they have none."[8] Thus, while authoritarian political systems outnumbered democratic states during the first three decades after independence, many of these same states have subsequently experimented with participatory democracy again. The African experience suggests that participatory democracy is an idea that dies hard.

Africa's politicians, soldier-politicians, administrators, bureaucrats, and others have directed a period of political and institutional experimentation which will no doubt continue for the foreseeable future. The years of experimentation are reflected in the range of regime ideologies, from the doctrinaire Marxism-Leninism of Congo to the foreign-dominated corporate capitalism of such places as Gabon, and in the now familiar cycle of multiparty states, single-party rule, military intervention, and the return to participatory democracy. (For a further discussion of regime ideologies, see chapter 8.) In retrospect, while independence has not fulfilled the promise of individual freedom or met the expectations of most Africans, thirty-five years is not a very long time for newly independent countries as disadvantaged as most of those in Africa to have developed effective and responsive political and economic institutions. Furthermore, it should not be forgotten that America's early history was characterized by the forcible expulsion of more than eighty thousand British loyalists, the near-monopoly of executive and legislative powers by early administrations, a severely restricted political franchise, and slavery.[9]

As the twentieth century comes to a close, ethnic, religious, regional, and ideological factionalism, as well as external interference, continue to severely restrict the range of available political choices. As a result, some countries will make pragmatic accommodations with external economic and political interests and will likely be able to buy a certain measure of stability, others will continue to be plagued with instability, while a few will suffer instances of near-total systemic breakdown and anarchy.

NOTES

1. Dennis Austin, *Politics in Africa*, 2nd ed. (Hanover and London: The University Press of New England, 1984), p. 27.

2. See J. Gus Liebenow, "The Military Factor in Africa," in Gwendolen M. Carter and Patrick O'Meara, eds., *African Independence: The First Twenty-Five Years* (Bloomington: Indiana University Press, 1985).

3. Aristide Zolberg, "Military Rule and Political Development in Tropical Africa," in J. van Doorn, ed., *Military Profession and Military Regimes* (The Hague: Mouton, 1969).

4. Colin Legum, "Annual Survey," in *Africa Contemporary Record* 1980–81, vol. xiii (London: Africana Publishing Company), p. 500.

5. Pearl T. Robinson, "Democratization: Understanding the Relationship between Regime Change and the Culture of Politics," *African Studies Review* 37, no. 1 (April 1994).

6. Aristide Zolberg, "The Specter of Anarchy," *Dissent*, Summer 1992, pp. 303–11.

7. Makau wa Mutua, "Redrawing the Map along African Lines," *Boston Globe*, September 22, 1994.

8. Interview quoted in *Time*, January 16, 1984, p. 25.

9. J. Gus Liebenow, "Africa: Four Crises of Political Development," in *American Universities Field Staff Omnibus Report* 29 (1979): 19.

SUGGESTIONS FOR FURTHER READING

Carter, Gwendolen M., and Patrick O'Meara, eds. *African Independence: The First Twenty-Five Years*. Bloomington: Indiana University Press, 1985.

Hyden, Goren, and Michael Bratton, eds. *Governance and Politics in Africa*. Boulder, Colo.: Lynne Rienner, 1992.

Johnson, Thomas H.; Robert O. Slater; and Pat McGowan. "Explaining African Military Coups d'Etat, 1960–82." *American Political Science Review* 78, no. 3 (September 1984).

Liebenow, J. Gus. *African Politics: Crises and Challenges*. Bloomington: Indiana University Press, 1986.

Rosberg, Carl, and Robert Jackson. *Personal Rule in Black Africa*. Berkeley: University of California Press, 1980.

Rothchild, Donald, and Naomi Chazan, eds. *Precarious Balance: State and Society in Africa*. Boulder Colo.: Westview Press, 1988.

Tordoff, William. *Government and Politics in Africa*. Bloomington: Indiana University Press, 1993.

Young, Crawford. "Politics in Africa." In Gabriel A. Almond and G. Bingham Powell, Jr., eds., *Comparative Politics Today*. Boston and Toronto: Little, Brown and Company, 1984.

Sara Berry
Economic Change in Contemporary Africa

19

Economic Performance in Africa, 1945–1990

At the end of World War II, most Africans were still subject to European colonial rule and seemed likely to remain so, if not indefinitely, then at least for a considerable time. Over the next twenty years, however, decolonization proceeded at an unexpectedly rapid rate. By 1965, European regimes remained in power only in Guinea-Bissau and southern Africa. There Angola, Mozambique, and Rhodesia were still colonies, and Namibia was effectively ruled by South Africa, which, though not a colony, was tightly controlled by a white minority regime committed to permanent racial segregation and the total disenfranchisement of blacks. Elsewhere on the continent, Africans' euphoria at gaining control of their own governments was reflected in and reinforced by the belief that political power meant economic power as well. Politicians and people alike viewed independence as the beginning of an era in which Africans would not only control their economies but also enjoy the fruits of their own labor and natural resources which, under colonial rule, had been appropriated by foreign firms and colonial regimes.

At the time of independence, the economic optimism of newly installed African regimes and their constituents was not without foundation. During the colonial period, total output and the volume of commercial activity increased substantially in most African colonies. In fact, the growth of African exports of foodstuffs and raw materials began in response to changing world market conditions well before the imposition of direct European rule at the end of the nineteenth century. In chapter 7 it was noted that European powers established colonial rule in Africa partly to protect an already expanding volume of trade and investment. Although in some areas colonial administrations sought actively to induce or coerce Africans to produce more crops and minerals for European markets, on balance their effect on African economic growth was limited. In terms of economic policy, for example, colonial governments sought to secure a favorable environment for the operation of private enterprise, but left it to the companies themselves to determine where and how to exploit Africa's productive potential. In eastern and southern Africa, Europeans acquired direct control of arable land and of forest and mineral resources, and most of the primary products exported from these areas were produced by European-owned concerns. Nearly three-fourths of private European capital invested in sub-Saharan Africa went to the major mineral-exporting regions: the Union of South Africa, South-West Africa, Northern and Southern Rhodesia, and the Belgian Congo.[1] Colonial administrations permitted white farmers in East and Central Africa to occupy some of the best agricultural land. They facilitated a steady supply of cheap labor to these farms, for example, limiting opportunities for Africans to sell their own agricultural produce on the world market, or by raising taxes in order to force them to seek wage employment. Where so-called economic incentives proved inadequate, colonial governments resorted to forced labor and mandatory resettlement of Africans in "reserved areas" in order to clear additional land for European cultivation. Under these forced circumstances, neither European nor African farmers were likely to devote much energy to increasing yields or labor productivity on their farms. The exploitation of forest reserves was carried out without regard for conservation, and in some cases literally at the point of a gun, as on the rubber and palm concessions granted by colonial governments to private firms in the French and Belgian Congo.[2]

In West Africa, on the other hand, Europeans invested primarily in trade rather than in the actual production of export goods. Apart from occasional ventures into mining, especially in the Gold Coast and Sierra Leone, Europeans left the cultivation and extraction of export commodities to Africans and concentrated instead on controlling the export-import trade. Thus, the growth of agricultural production for export, which began well before the colonial period, was largely due to African initiative and enterprise. The establishment of colonial rule facilitated the growth of export production by bringing to an end the wars which had flared among a number of West African peoples for much of the nineteenth century, and by constructing railways into the interior. For example, the construction of a railway to northern Nigeria from the coast stimulated peanut and cotton production for the world market. The railways did not, however, serve as the basis for an expanding internal transportation network, since they were built only between areas of cash-crop production and major ports (see map 8). Moreover, every effort was made to finance railways and other public works out of colonial revenues rather than from the imperial treasury. Indeed, most British colonies actually benefited Britain by exporting more to it annually than they bought there in return.

Whatever the means used, particular colonial peoples were induced to expand export production, and the basic economic result was the same throughout Africa. Colonial economies devoted an increasing proportion of their land, labor, and capital to producing foodstuffs and raw materials for the world market. The consequences of this increasing specialization in agricultural and mineral production for export have been debated extensively by scholars and political leaders. Some have emphasized the enterprise and ingenuity displayed by African producers in adapting to changing world market opportunities and in expanding production for export. Others have pointed to Africa's growing dependence on foreign capital and uncertain world markets as evidence that, because of this pattern of specialization, Africa has fallen further and further behind wealthy industrialized economies in productive capacity and material well-being. Both arguments have an element of truth. Individual Africans have adopted new methods of production and invested in increased productive capacity in a variety of circumstances. In West Africa, farmers opened up new areas for cultivation of tree and arable crops for the market. Their incomes helped to stimulate domestic production and trade in foodstuffs and other commodities, and many invested in trade, transport, housing, and such public facilities as schools, clinics, and market stalls. They also paid school fees for their children and other young relatives, thus contributing to the growth of an educated labor force. Even in areas, such as Kenya or the Rhodesias, where African farmers were excluded from the best arable land and sometimes were forced to sell their crops at prices well below those paid to European farmers, Africans managed to produce growing supplies of food crops for sale during the 1920s and 1930s.[3]

During the international depression of the 1930s, the export-oriented economies of colonial Africa suffered declining trade, income, and employment. Levels of trade, production, and income remained low throughout World War II, both because of wartime controls on consumption in Europe and because of the extreme shortage of shipping for maritime commerce. As the world economy recovered after the war, however, African export prospects improved dramatically. European shipping and trade controls were relaxed; American savings were applied to the task of rebuilding Europe's shattered economies; and the rapid growth of demand in industrialized countries led to soaring world prices for foodstuffs and raw materials. At the same time, European firms developed a renewed interest in exploiting African resources and markets. Between 1947 and 1958, the French government invested twice as much in French West Africa, mostly for public construction, as it had from 1903 to 1946, and this inflow of capital was accompanied by a substantial migration of skilled French workers seeking employment in Africa.[4] In British colonies, officials embarked on new programs to expand public services, especially education, and induce Africans to manage their farms and natural resources more productively.

The effects of late colonial development programs were not always productive. In Tanganyika, northern Nigeria, and The Gambia, for example, government experiments with large-scale, mechanized agricultural production proved to be costly failures. In addition, to the extent that schemes for improving African farming involved increased official demands on Africans' labor or controls over African farmers' own uses of land and labor, they provoked resistance rather than increased output, and contributed to the rise of anticolonialist movements.[5] However, the costs and failures of late colonial development efforts were juxtaposed with overall growth of trade and income. Buoyed by steadily rising export sales, agriculture, trade, and manufacturing all tended to expand throughout the 1950s, fueling a revolution of rising expectations among African peoples and their leaders on the eve of independence.

During the 1960s, however, it became increasingly clear that the road to prosperity was likely to prove long and difficult. Africans' expectation of rapid increases in national income and their own standards of living had been fueled in the late 1940s

Plate 89. A sewing room at a fiber factory in Kumasi, Ghana.
Photo courtesy United Nations/PJ/jb.

and early 1950s by unusually favorable world market conditions for many of Africa's principal export commodities. As the industrial nations recovered from World War II, global demand for primary commodities soared, and the boom was prolonged by industrial countries' stockpiling of raw materials during the Korean War. For a decade after 1945, Africans sold both agricultural and mineral products abroad in rising quantities and on increasingly favorable terms. By the mid-1950s, however, world prices of many of Africa's principal exports began a steady decline which lasted through the 1960s. In consequence, African countries' earnings of foreign exchange, and hence their capacity to import, stagnated or declined. African politicians, who had come to power promising rapid economic development, began their regimes by launching ambitious programs of public investment in industry, infrastructure, and social services. These programs absorbed large amounts of government revenue and foreign exchange. Expenditures on imports soon outstripped export earnings, and it proved difficult to raise tax revenues at the same rate as government expenditures. Domestic programs suffered setbacks (often compounded by official inexperience in managing state enterprises or complex programs of public development); domestic borrowing to cover budget deficits proved inflationary; and foreign creditors demanded high rates of interest on loans to cover rising import bills. These difficulties provoked and were compounded by rapid urban growth, mounting unemployment, wasteful public expenditure, and increasingly obvious inequalities in wealth and living standards. By the late 1960s, few African economies had achieved the gains in output and income anticipated at the time of independence, and some, such as Ghana, Zambia, and Zaire, were in crisis. The disappointments of what had been heralded as Africa's first "development decade" certainly contributed to the military coups and political conflicts which swept across Africa in the late 1960s (see chapters 8 and 18).

Nevertheless, at the beginning of the 1970s, both African and foreign observers remained optimistic about Africa's economic position and long-term prospects. The difficulties of the first development decade touched off intense debates over African development strategy, debates often informed as much by ideology as by evidence. Opinions ranged from the view that unless African regimes took complete control of their own economies, African peoples were doomed to poverty and underdevelopment because of their peripheral position in the global economy, to the belief that Africa could develop only if African governments abandoned their attempts to shield their economies from world market forces.[6] Others warned that African governments were misallocating the resources at their disposal by expanding bureaucracies rather than productive investment, relying too heavily on traditional export crops, building more schools and clinics than they could afford to staff, and allowing urban growth and rural emigration to proceed at socially disruptive rates.[7] However, most regarded Africa's economic situation as basically sound, if underdeveloped, and economic problems as manageable through the better design and more effective implementation of government policy.

By the early 1980s, cautious optimism gave way to an increasingly pessimistic view of Africa's past development and future prospects. Many African economies, weakened during the 1970s by oil price shocks, drought, or civil war, began to suffer declining standards of living. The rate of growth of gross domestic product (GDP) in sub-Saharan Africa fell from 4.2 percent per annum in the period 1965–1980, to only 2.1 percent in the years 1980–1990, while agricultural production, long the mainstay of African economic output and the source of livelihood for the majority of the population, hovered around 2 percent per annum. Over the same period, average population growth rose from 2.7 percent in 1965–1980, to 3.1 percent per annum from 1980 to 1990. Thus, both agricultural output and GDP per capita declined throughout the 1980s. On the national level, basic services declined, including essential infrastructure such as roads and communications, and some governments found it increasingly difficult to pay their employees or buy fuel and spare parts for official vehicles, or to function on a day-to-day basis. For many households, life centered around daily struggles to find, far less buy, such necessities as food, fuel, and water. Even earlier economic "successes," such as Kenya, Côte d'Ivoire, and Cameroon, experienced declining output and investment and growing poverty, hunger and unrest. And in Ethiopia, Sudan, Mozambique, Liberia, and Rwanda, recurrent periods of drought and escalating military conflict devastated local economies and uprooted thousands of people, producing floods of refugees whose desperate needs placed unbearable strains on scarce resources in neighboring countries.[8]

From the early 1970s, Africans' capacity to cope with economic decline and political turmoil was further eroded by an increasingly unfavorable international

Plate 90. Diamond mine, Namibia.
Photo courtesy United Nations.

environment. Private foreign investment, never very large in Africa to begin with, declined sharply after 1980 in the face of global recession and growing foreign anxieties about Africa's own economic decline and political instability. And by the end of the decade, official funds were increasingly diverted to assist the economic restructuring of former communist countries in eastern Europe and the Soviet Union. Thus, by the mid-1980s, most African economies were caught in a double bind of falling per capita incomes and production at home, and spiraling foreign debts. From 1985 to 1990, sub-Saharan Africa paid out more, in interest and debt repayment, to the IMF and the World Bank combined than it received from them in the form of grants and loans.[9]

Sources of African Economic Change

The sharp deterioration of economic conditions may, in many African countries, be dated from 1973. This was a watershed year in which soaring prices of petroleum were perhaps the most dramatic sign of structural change in the global economy as a whole. In addition to the emergence of the Organization of Petroleum Exporting Countries (OPEC) as an international cartel of enormous power, U.S. dominance of world markets for both agricultural and industrial commodities was challenged by

Plate 91. Miners returning from their shift, Zimbabwe.
Photo courtesy United Nations/lb.

the rising strength of other nations, such as Japan, and of multinational conglomerates. Industrialized nations placed increasing emphasis on the export of technology and intermediate goods, rather than finished manufactures, to less developed economies; and some of the latter, notably in East and Southeast Asia, embarked on periods of sustained economic growth and diversification which brought rising prosperity to their own peoples but left poorer African economies even further behind in the competition for world markets and international capital.

Even more significant than changing global patterns of production and trade were concurrent changes in the structure of international financial markets. In most countries, fixed exchange rates gave way to floating ones, and the volume of international capital movements grew astronomically, dwarfing international trade in goods and services.[10] An important consequence was that national economies became increasingly interdependent, and governments' ability to control the performance of their own economies or shield them from the vicissitudes of global markets was fundamentally eroded.

For Africa, these changes heralded a new era of hardship.[11] Rising oil prices led to rapidly increasing balance-of-payments deficits, as Africans struggled to maintain their imports of crucial petroleum products, such as gasoline and fertilizer. Foreign banks preferred to lend to relatively industrialized economies in Asia and Latin America, and many African governments were forced to impose severe restrictions on imports to try to contain their balance-of-payments deficits. Individual Africans proved adept at evading these restrictions, and their ingenuity served to disrupt rather than strengthen the fabric of domestic economic activity. Those with access to government power used it to monopolize restricted imports and foreign exchange, often enriching themselves at the expense of their less powerful compatriots. Faced with rising costs, unstable prices, or outright lack of consumer goods and productive inputs, ordinary people either abandoned productive activity, leaving farms or workshops to join the growing pool of un- or underemployed jobseekers in cities and commercialized farming areas, or tried to stretch their limited energies and resources over several income-seeking activities. For most, however, neither petty wage or self-employment nor diversification led to increased incomes, while both patterns of individual response contributed to the further disorganization of local systems of production and exchange.[12]

As many African economies plunged further into economic crisis and political turmoil in the 1980s, international debates over African development veered sharply to the right. In 1981, a controversial report by the World Bank inaugurated a new phase in relations between African governments and the international donor community (see chapter 20). Official optimism over Africa's long-term prospects for development gave way to widespread criticism of past trends and policies and grim prognoses for the future. Criticism centered on African governments' economic policies and practices. Abandoning the earlier view that governments must play a leading role in promoting economic development, economists and officials alike attributed the majority of Africa's economic woes to overspending, excessive government regulation of economic activity, and gross mismanagement of public resources and development policies alike.

Hailed by the mid-1980s as a "new consensus,"[13] these arguments became the blueprint for a concerted campaign, led by the International Monetary Fund (IMF) and the World Bank, to effect sweeping changes in African governments' economic policies and practices. African governments were urged to reduce or eliminate controls on foreign trade and payments, devalue their currencies, dismantle domestic price controls, decrease government spending and employment, and divest themselves of productive assets and enterprises. The IMF and the World Bank added pressure to persuasion, making both short-term balance-of-payments credits and long-term development loans "conditional" on governments' adoption of these "structural adjustment policies."

Sudden reductions in government spending and employment led to contractions in overall levels of income and employment, and structural adjustment programs hit hard African economies already weakened by the crises of the 1970s. Devaluation led to sharp declines in real income, especially for urban populations dependent on imports for such basic necessities as food and fuel. In Tanzania, for example, the purchasing power of urban workers' wages fell 50 percent between 1980 and 1984; in Ghana, urban incomes fell by 40 percent in the same period.[14] Trade liberalization policies had the advantage of dismantling costly and largely ineffective controls, but African producers were ill equipped to cope with increased competition from cheap foreign goods. Divestment of government property often meant simply that assets and enterprises were transferred to members of governing elites as private individuals. A decade after structural adjustment reforms were launched, little progress has been made either in reducing African economies' foreign debts or in expanding and diversifying their productive capacities, let alone improving living standards for the vast majority of people.

Observers do not agree on the reasons for these developments. Some critics have argued that the whole structural adjustment policy package was a cynical effort to marshal economic analysis to generate profitable trade and investment opportunities for wealthy, industrialized countries and multinational corporations. Others have questioned its impact, arguing that African governments downsized their public sectors and dismantled unworkable economic controls in the 1980s out of sheer necessity, rather than because of arm-twisting by the IMF and the World Bank. Both arguments have a measure of truth, but neither takes us very far in understanding the dynamics of Africa's economic decline or charting a course for the future.

Part of the problem lies in the methods of research and analysis used to gain such understanding. Rejecting arguments based on racial or cultural stereotypes, and mindful of the limitations of aggregate data on African economic performance, many scholars have preferred to study economic change in Africa at the micro level. Local studies show clearly that Africans' distinctive cultural traditions rarely inhibit them from seeking or enjoying material wealth when they have the opportunity to do so, and therefore, that African underdevelopment cannot be attributed to Africans' lack of initiative or indifference to economic gain. Indeed, not only do Africans respond to economic incentives, but they do so with as much understanding of their economic environment, as much awareness of the unpredictability of environmental and economic conditions, and as much concern for the future as producers in any other part of the world. Africans' technical knowledge sometimes surpasses that of foreign experts brought in to advise them, and their resilience in the face of recent crises and deprivations is eloquent testimony to their resourcefulness and adaptability.

For the student of African economic development, there are valuable lessons to be drawn from this literature—for example, that the design of appropriate technologies, incentives, and agendas for African development must proceed through a dialogue between local actors and scientifically trained experts, rather than being simply imposed by the latter. Another lesson which is often drawn from the microliterature is less valuable, however, and can be positively misleading. Clearly, most Africans

Plate 92. General view of Kariba dam, Zambia/Zimbabwe.
Photo courtesy United Nations/pf,ARA.

are poor not by choice but by circumstance, and individual initiative alone will not produce economic development for all. But it does not follow that Africa's economic problems are simply the result of bad government. It is true that some African regimes are corrupt, inept, or oppressive; that early development programs were too ambitious, especially in their presumption that newly created African governments could manage economic resources effectively; that ongoing struggles over power in nations which were arbitrarily created by colonial rulers have sapped the energy and resources of many African governments and their opponents. But as the achievements of newly industrializing economies in Asia have shown, those regimes which govern least are not necessarily best for economic development.

Nor is there a single set of policies which guarantees successful economic performance. African governments have, for example, been advised repeatedly to give priority to agricultural expansion, both to generate export revenues and to lay a foundation for sustained and equitable development at home. But this argument requires qualification. First, it is not clear that agricultural stagnation, brought about by misguided government policies, has been the only or even the major source of deteriorating export earnings, rising food imports, and mounting foreign debts. Countries which derive most of their foreign exchange from mineral exports have suffered even greater instability and more unbalanced patterns of growth than those which rely principally on agricultural exports. Moreover, gains from increased production of export crops have frequently been negated by unfavorable shifts in world market prices or trading conditions and hence are not invariably productive of economic growth.

Increased agricultural production for domestic use does not guarantee balanced or equitable economic growth, either. The Green Revolution has often led to increased expenditures on imported inputs and exacerbated economic inequality.[15] Farmers who wish to adopt the new technology must often specialize in producing for the market, or go into debt, in order to acquire money to buy the necessary inputs. In doing so, they incur costs which may prove too much to cope with when market prices fall or bad weather reduces output. Some of the most successful cases of agricultural expansion in Africa have occurred through foreign investment in or government subsidization of large-scale farms, for example, in Kenya, Malawi, Zimbabwe, and Côte d'Ivoire. Sometimes, in these cases, increased output has been achieved at the cost of reduced living standards for smaller producers. In other cases, large foreign- or government-sponsored agricultural schemes have proved as wasteful, unproductive, and damaging to future development as the most ill-advised schemes of import-substituting industrialization.[16]

These examples underscore the obvious point that economic development does not arise from any one form of economic activity, but depends on the interrelations among sectors of production. They also suggest that the success of any strategy of development depends not only on how it is conceived, but also on how it is carried out. Agriculture, industry, and services are all important to the development process, and growth can occur in a variety of ways: in large firms or small ones; through dramatic technological breakthroughs or gradual, adaptive changes; through price incentives or direct subsidies. More generally, as African development experience shows, the process of economic development tends to create new problems as well as resolve old ones. Accelerated development creates new supply bottlenecks to be broken, new opportunities and assets to be struggled for, and new issues of distribution and control of wealth, to be negotiated or fought over among different social groups. How these problems are faced, with what results, depends not only on producers' ability to calculate costs and returns to alternative activities, but also on who controls the acquisition and management of productive resources, the uses of output and income, and the determination of terms of exchange. To understand the sources and implications of African economic performance, we need to look at relations of power as well as of property, production, and price.

Power, Accumulation, and Instability:
African Economic Underdevelopment in Historical Perspective

Under colonial rule, Africans were subjected not only to European demands for goods, land, and labor, but also to European strategies of colonial government and administration. These strategies, like the economic interests they sought to promote, were not always mutually consistent.[17] In establishing and consolidating their power over African peoples, colonial officials both altered and reinforced existing rules and practices with respect to the pursuit of gain, the preservation of social order, and the mediation of conflicts over control of goods and productive resources. They wished, of course, to protect European economic interests in Africa, but they also recognized that they lacked the money and labor to carry out radical programs of economic restructuring or contain explosive reactions to them. In German Tanganyika, Mozambique, the Belgian Congo, or Southern Rhodesia, European attempts to force Africans to grow cotton, gather wild rubber, or mine coal proved costly and unproductive.[18] Similarly, bloody "pacification campaigns" in Kenya, Côte d'Ivoire, and southeastern Nigeria gained their instigators tenuous control, at best, over African labor and goods.[19] However, colonial authorities often deliberately protected traditional leaders and political systems, finding it expedient to rule indirectly through existing systems of government, and to profit from existing trade networks and farming systems rather than incur the expense and risks of creating new ones.

Colonial efforts to govern and profit through "customary" African institutions and practices were reflected in every aspect of colonial society. In agriculture, European firms were encouraged to purchase marketable crops from African farmers and traders, except in colonies such as Kenya and Southern Rhodesia, where they gave preference to crops grown by European settlers. Colonial officials also took measures to promote African production of domestic food crops, both to keep down the cost of wage labor and to prevent social unrest. In administration, chiefs and elders who were prepared to cooperate with colonial authorities were confirmed in office, and sometimes given new duties or small salaries in exchange for their assistance in the task of colonial administration. In addition, colonial officials tended to define administrative jurisdictions to coincide with what they conceived to be "traditional" social and cultural units, both to maintain continuity in local practices and to forestall revolt by preserving or strengthening ethnic divisions among their colonial subjects. For simplicity and economy, they also left the settlement of many civil disputes to indigenous authorities, to settle on "customary" grounds. In practice, however, since neither "traditional" social units nor "customary" rules and practices were static or uncontested, colonial officials' efforts to build a stable social and administrative order on traditional foundations often had the opposite effect. They promoted confusion and sometimes conflict over which rules applied in some situations and who had the authority to enforce them.[20]

Under the resulting hybrid systems of government and administration, Africans could neither rely on tradition nor dispense with it (see chapters 17 and 18). Access to property, labor, administrative office, and the protection of the colonial state was mediated through chiefs, elders, and family heads according to "custom"; yet, because local authorities were now part of a larger colonial system, they exercised old roles and prerogatives in new ways.[21] Men and women wielded influence within the colonial order in proportion to their willingness to collaborate with the colonial regime, their facility with European languages, or their ability to persuade or coerce their kinfolk or subjects to satisfy European demands for labor and taxes. At the same time, however, colonial officials looked with suspicion on those who demonstrated too great an ability to command a popular following or debate the merits of colonial rule in the colonizers' own language. In these circumstances, Africans sought opportunity or redress through both traditional and colonial channels. A farmer, for example, might use cash to acquire arable land or livestock, but then have to defend his or her right to use and enjoy them in customary courts, where decisions were based on the reputations of witnesses rather than on the terms of market transactions. Entrepreneurs might draw on the assistance of relatives in launching a business, only to find themselves pressured to spend the proceeds on meeting customary obligations to kin.

In these circumstances, the issue was not that "traditional" obligations and values undermined people's desire or ability to produce, plan, innovate, or invest, but that access to the means of production and power depended on negotiating customary as well as colonial rules and social relations. Colonial administrations neither froze African societies into unchanging traditional molds nor replaced them with European imports, but rather provoked debate, sometimes conflict, over their meanings and their relevance to economic and political practice. Hence, Africans found it necessary or expedient to invest in relations of patronage and obligation along both customary and colonial lines in order to acquire property, mobilize labor, manage productive activity, and gain access to profitable opportunities. As a result, much of Africa's wealth not appropriated by foreigners was used to feed, educate, entertain, and honor kinsmen, clients, chiefs, and Western-trained functionaries, as well as to expand directly productive activity.

If Africans' propensity to invest in relations of patronage and obligation grew out of the hybrid character of colonial economic and political practice, it was reinforced by African governments' own efforts to accelerate economic development and consolidate their power after independence. To gain office, African politicians frequently invoked traditional loyalties based on kinship, culture, and traditions of origin, as well as shared political agendas and beliefs; to remain in office, they used scarce public resources to create jobs, build amenities, or award inflated state contracts to their supporters, rather than to expand productive capacity. In addition, the more actively African regimes sought to manage their economies and stabilize their power, the more likely they were to provoke political rivalry and social unrest, and hence to invest in the means of social control.

As the performance of African economies deteriorated, not only did popular criticism of African ruling classes increase, but it became more difficult for leaders to retain power by declaring their commitment to particular principles or strategies of government. Whatever the intrinsic merits of their position, their inability to produce the promised results invited skepticism, while their comparatively privileged life-styles betokened a widening gulf between their own interests and those of the mass of their compatriots. To retain power, many African leaders have resorted to increasing repression, military force, or the manipulation of ties of descent, ethnicity, or religious belief. This, in turn, has encouraged ordinary people to cherish such ties, as potential channels of access to power and privilege, while seeking relief from economic privations and official harassment by flouting or evading the law. Social turmoil and ethnic and religious conflict are products as well as sources of uneven development and economic decline.

The seeming intractability of Africa's economic and political problems gave rise, in the 1980s and 1990s, to widespread efforts by international agencies and foreign governments to effect programs of economic and political reform. In the 1980s, structural adjustment programs tied foreign aid to economic liberalization; in the 1990s, official grants and loans were also made conditional on African governments' willingness to replace authoritarian rule with multiparty democracies. While the goals of such reforms are widely shared, within Africa as well as outside, it is not clear that imposed solutions have not created more problems than they have solved. Economic and political conditionality have arguably contributed to some of the worst upheavals of recent times, including Rwanda's. At the same time, the dismantling of *apartheid* and establishment of a government based on universal suffrage in South Africa testifies eloquently to Africans' potential for self-directed political transformation. The very complexity of ongoing struggles for power and privilege, and their importance for the pursuit of economic opportunity and the management of economic resources, means that sustained development will come about only if Africans play the leading role in transforming their own economies.

NOTES

1. S. H. Frankel, *Capital Investment in Africa* (London: Oxford University Press, 1938), p. 214.

2. C. Coquery-Vidrovitch, *Le Congo au temps des grandes compagnies concessionaires, 1891–1930* (Paris: Mouton, 1972), pp. 180–83; R. Harms, "The End of Red Rubber: A Reassessment," *Journal of African History* 16, no. 1 (1975).

3. See, e.g., G. Kitching, *Class and Economic Change in Kenya* (New Haven: Yale University Press, 1980); R. E. Baldwin, *Economic Development and Export Growth: A Study of Northern Rhodesia, 1920–1960* (Berkeley: University of California Press, 1966), pp. 163–64; P. Moseley, *The Settler Economies* (Cambridge: Cambridge University Press, 1983).

4. E. J. Berg, "The Economic Basis of Political Choice in French West Africa," *American Political Science Review* 54, no. 2 (June 1960): 394–95.

5. For a discussion of these issues, see S. Berry, *No Condition Is Permanent: The Social Dynamics of Agrarian Change in Sub-Saharan Africa* (Madison: University of Wisconsin Press, 1993), chap. 3.

6. The first view was elaborated by, *inter alia*, S. Amin, *Unequal Development* (New York: Monthly Review Press, 1976); W. Rodney, *How Europe Underdeveloped Africa* (London: Bogle L'Ouverture, 1972); and I. Wallerstein, "The Three Stages of African Involvement in the World Economy," in P. Gutkind and I. Wallerstein, eds., *The Political Economy of Contemporary Africa* (Beverly Hills: Sage, 1976). Advocates of the open-door approach included D. T. Healey, "Development Policy: New Thinking about an Interpretation," *Journal of Economic Literature* 10, no. 3 (September 1972); and S. Acharya, *Two Studies of Development in Sub-Saharan Africa* (Washington, D.C.: World Bank, 1975).

7. See, e.g., ILO, *Employment, Incomes and Equality in Kenya* (Geneva: ILO, 1972); M. Todaro, *Economic Development in the Third World*, 5th ed. (New York: Longman, 1994).

8. Data cited in this paragraph are taken from World Bank, *World Development Report, 1992* (Washington, D.C.: World Bank).

9. G. K. Helleiner, "The IMF, The World Bank and Africa's Adjustment and External Debt Problems: An Unofficial View," *World Development* 20, no. 6 (1992).

10. G. E. Schuh, "The New Macroeconomics of Food and Agricultural Policy," in C. Eicher and J. Staatz, eds., *Agricultural Development in the Third World*, 2nd ed. (Baltimore: Johns Hopkins University Press, 1990).

11. For discussion of the overall impact on Africa of global economic change in the 1970s, see World Bank, *Accelerated Development in Sub-Saharan Africa* (Washington, D.C.: World Bank, 1981); Organization for African Unity, *Lagos Plan of Action* (Lagos: OAU, 1978); U.S. Department of Agriculture, *Food Problems and Prospects in Sub-Saharan Africa* (Washington, D.C.: USDA, 1981).

12. N. Chazan, *An Anatomy of Ghanaian Politics: Managing Political Recession, 1969–1982* (Boulder, Colo.: Westview, 1983); M. Cowen, "Commodity Production in Kenya's Central Province," in J. Heyer, P. Roberts, and G. Williams, *Rural Development in Tropical Africa* (New York: St. Martin's Press, 1981), and "The Commercialization of Food Production in Kenya after 1945," in R. Rotberg, ed., *Imperialism, Colonialism, and Hunger: East and Central Africa* (Lexington, Mass.: D. C. Heath, 1983); A. Shepherd, "Agrarian Change in Northern Ghana: Public Investment, Capitalist Farming and Famine," in Heyer, Roberts, and Williams, *Rural Development in Tropical Africa.*

13. See, e.g., R. Berg and J. Whitaker, *Strategies for African Development* (Berkeley and Los Angeles: University of California Press, 1986).

14. World Bank, *Financing Adjustment with Growth in Sub-Saharan Africa* (Washington, D.C.: World Bank, 1986).

15. For some differing assessments of the Green Revolution, see Peter B. R. Hazell and C. Ramasamy, eds., *The Green Revolution Reconsidered* (Baltimore: Johns Hopkins University Press, 1991); and Vandana Sharma, *The Violence of the Green Revolution* (London: Zed Books, 1991).

16. See, e.g., P. Little and M. Watts, eds., *Living under Contract: Contract Farming and Agrarian Transformation in Sub-Saharan Africa* (Madison: University of Wisconsin Press, 1994); A. B. Ayako and D. Glover, "Contract Farming and Smallholder Outgrower Schemes in Eastern and Southern Africa," *Eastern Africa Economic Review*, special issue (1989).

17. For a seminal discussion of the contradictions of colonial policy in Africa, see two articles by J. Lonsdale and B. Berman—"Coping with the Contradictions: The Development of the Colonial State in Kenya, 1895–1914," *Journal of African History* 20, no. 4 (1979), and "Crises of Accumulation, Coercion and the Colonial State: The Development of the Labor Control System in Kenya, 1919–1939," *Canadian Journal of African Studies* 14, no. 1 (1980).

18. J. Iliffe, *A Modern History of Tanzania* (Cambridge: Cambridge University Press, 1979); R. Harms, *River of Wealth, River of Sorrow* (New Haven: Yale University Press, 1981); C. van Onselen, *Chibaro: African Mine Labour in Southern Rhodesia, 1900–1933* (Johannesburg: Ravan, 1980).

19. W. Ofonagoro, *Trade and Imperialism in Southern Nigeria* (New York: Nok, 1979); J. Forbes Munro, *Colonial Rule and the Kamba* (Oxford: Clarendon Press, 1975); T. Weiskel, *French Colonial Rule and the Baule Peoples* (Oxford: Clarendon Press, 1980).

20. See, e.g., I. Sutton, "Law, Chieftaincy and Conflict in Colonial Ghana: The Ada Case," *African Affairs* 83, no. 330 (1984); S. Berry, "Hegemony on a Shoestring: Indirect Rule and Access to Agricultural Land," *Africa* 62, no. 3 (1992).

21. These themes are discussed and illustrated in numerous case studies of particular African societies under colonial rule. See, e.g., J. Forbes Munro, *Colonial Rule and the Kamba* (Oxford: Clarendon Press, 1975); W. Beinart, *The Political Economy of Pondoland* (Cambridge: Cambridge University Press, 1982); J. D. Y. Peel, *Ijeshas and Nigerians* (Cambridge: Cambridge University Press, 1983).

SUGGESTIONS FOR FURTHER READING

Berg, Robert, and Jennifer Whitaker. *Strategies for African Development*. Berkeley and Los Angeles: University of California Press, 1986.

Berry, Sara. *Fathers Work for Their Sons: Accumulation, Mobility and Class Formation in an Extended Yoruba Community*. Berkeley and Los Angeles: University of California Press, 1985.

Callaghy, Thomas, and John Ravenhill. *Hemmed In: Responses to Africa's Economic Decline*. New York: Columbia University Press, 1993.

Gibbon, Peter. "A Failed Agenda? African Agriculture under Structural Adjustment, with Special Reference to Kenya and Ghana." *Journal of Peasant Studies* 20 (1992): 50–96.

Helleiner, Gerald. "The IMF, the World Bank and Africa's Adjustment and External Debt Problems: An Unofficial View." *World Development* 20 (1992): 779–92.

Himmelstrand, Ulf. *African Perspectives on Development: Controversies, Dilemmas and Openings*. Nairobi: EAEP; Dar-es-Salaam: Mkuki na Nyota; Kampala: Fountain; New York: St. Martin's; London: James Currey, 1994.

Little, Peter D., and Michael J. Watts. *Living under Contract: Contract Farming and Agrarian Transformation in Sub-Saharan Africa*. Madison: University of Wisconsin Press, 1994.

Onimode, Bade. *A Political Economy of the African Crisis*. London and Atlantic Highlands, N.J.: Zed Books, with the Institute for African Alternatives, 1988.

Richard Stryker and
Stephen N. Ndegwa
The African
Development Crisis

20 Sub-Saharan Africa,[1] a vast region comprising over fifty
independent countries with a population surpassing 500
million people, has long been the "least developed" area of
the world, with the lowest levels of industrialization, life
expectancy, nutrition, literacy, access to medical care, and safe water supplies, and
the highest rates of population growth and infant, child, and overall mortality. The
end of colonial rule and the achievement of political independence in the 1960s for
most countries in the region ushered in a wave of optimism about development
prospects, but this was soon overwhelmed by harsh economic realities, many of
which were legacies of colonial domination.

African economies grew slowly in the 1960s and 1970s, but at a pace well below
that of other developing areas. Then, while the global recession of the early 1980s had
severe consequences for all regions, the African decline was the most precipitous and
longest-lasting, persisting into the 1990s. By some estimates, real average income
levels have regressed to the level of the early 1960s. Economic projections to the year
2000 remain gloomy, with almost no per capita gain forecast. Consequently, the
social and economic gaps separating Africa from all other world regions continue to
widen and, most tragically, the absolute quality of life has deteriorated for many
Africans over a generation.

Comparisons with the high-income countries of North America, Western Europe,
and Japan are hardly appropriate. The total economic output of sub-Saharan Africa is
less than that of Austria, a nation of 8 million people; if one includes the Republic of
South Africa, the total approaches that of Australia or South Korea. A more useful
perspective on Africa's plight can be gained by examining its relative position within
what used to be called the "Third World" (see table 4).

At one end of the spectrum, much attention has been focused on the Newly
Industrializing Countries (NICs) of East Asia, such as South Korea and Taiwan,
which followed Japan in rapid export-oriented manufactured growth from the 1970s,
raising dramatically the incomes and quality of life of their populations. Even more
sudden has been the economic surge of China, which has the fastest-growing

Table 4

Sub-Saharan Africa in Comparative Perspective[2]

	Year	All LDC's	SSA	SSA+ SoAf	South Asia	East Asia	Latin Am
Pop: mils	1992	4,610	503	543	1,178	1,689	453
Pop Growth	1980-92	1.9%	3.1%	3.0%	2.2%	1.6%	2.0%
GNP p/c	1992	$1040	$350	$530	$310	$760	$2,690
GNP p/c Growth	1960-70	3.3%	0.6%	...	1.4%	3.6%	2.5%
	1970-80	3.0	0.9	...	1.1	4.6	3.1
	1980-92	0.9	-1.2	-0.8%	3.0	6.1	-0.2
Projected	1990-00	2.9	0.3	...	3.1	5.7	2.2
Agricul Growth	1980-92	3.1%	...	1.7%	3.3%	4.4%	2.0%
Industrial Growth	1980-92	3.6%	...	1.2%	6.4%	9.4%	1.3%
Life Exp	1960	46 yrs	40	43	43	47	56
	1992	64	51	52	60	68	68
Literacy	1970	46%	27%	...	31%	...	73%
	1990	64%	50	...	45	76%	85
IMR	1960	136	151	...	147	128	108
	1992	65	104	99	85	39	44
Pop w/ Safe Water	1990 all (rural)	72% 65	... ...	44% 37	80% 78	71% 65	80% 57
Pop per Physician	1990	4,810	23540	19690	2,930	6,170	1,180
Daily p/c Calories	1965 1989	2,108 2,523	2,074 2,122	... ...	1,992 2,215	1,939 2,617	2,445 2,721
Pop. Below Pov Line	1985 1990 2000	30.5% 29.7 24.1	47.6% 47.8 49.7	... ...	51.8% 49.0 36.9	13.2% 11.3 4.2	22.4% 25.5 24.9

LDCs: Less Developed Countries; SSA+SoAF: Sub-Saharan Africa+South Africa; GNP p/c: Gross National
Product per capita; IMR: Infant Mortality Rate per 1000 live births.

economy in the world since 1980, and which already had far better human development indicators than Africa.

More surprising, South Asia, dominated by India, which traditionally has had a slow growth rate, with the largest number of poor people in any single country, has far surpassed Africa economically in the past couple of decades. There have been glimpses of an Indian "economic miracle," and the World Bank refers to "the development saga of South Asia." All quality-of-life measures in South Asia are rising, and its poverty rate has fallen below that of Africa for the first time. Projections to the end of the 1990s show major reductions in poverty in South Asia and all other less developed regions, except for Africa. Of the forty to fifty poorest countries in the world, three-quarters are now located in sub-Saharan Africa.

Across East and South Asia, average incomes are projected to increase three- to fivefold between 1990 and 2030, while they double or triple in Latin America. But in sub-Saharan Africa, prospects are for only modest rises, almost invisible in global perspective. The gaps between Africa and the rest of the world are becoming a chasm. As an insightful former president of Nigeria remarked, "Contrasting all this [that is happening elsewhere] with what is taking place in Africa, it is difficult to believe that we inhabit the same historical time."[3]

International concern that regions of sub-Saharan Africa faced a developmental crisis first emerged at the outset of the 1980s. A series of influential World Bank reports have provided the dominant tone since.[4] In 1981, the "Berg Report" argued that "the [African] record is grim and it is no exaggeration to talk of crisis." A 1984 report was even gloomier: "No list of economic or financial statistics can convey the human misery spreading in sub-Saharan Africa." The tone of the 1986 report was slightly more optimistic, but "there is little cause to celebrate. . . . For the first time since World War II, a whole region has suffered retrogression over a generation. . . . If present trends continue, the human disaster of [famines in] 1983–84 in sub-Saharan Africa will return to haunt the world community."

The most comprehensive report to date was issued in 1989, lamenting that "sub-Saharan Africa as a whole has now witnessed almost a decade of falling per capita incomes, increasing hunger, and accelerating ecological degradation. The earlier progress made in social development is now being eroded. Overall Africans are almost as poor today as they were 30 years ago." The latest World Bank Africa report, published in 1994, reaffirms the depth of the crisis but insists that "Africa's poor record over the past twenty years is no reason for undue pessimism about its future." The major reason for this renewed hope is evidence that an ever larger number of African governments are pursuing "structural adjustment" programs of economic reform and budgetary austerity.

Dimensions of the African Development Crisis

Obviously, the African crisis has many dimensions. For many African countries, the news headlines seem to be horror stories of disease, war, and famine, and in many instances these have indeed been daily life experience for millions of people. Many of the earlier advances in health care have been reversed as a result of cuts in social spending and widening social disorder. Newly resistant strains of malaria have appeared, along with the old diseases which afflict mostly children (diarrhea, cholera, parasitic infections), and the new plague of AIDS, which is ravaging youthful populations. Indeed, by the mid-1990s, Africa had almost two-thirds of the world's

HIV-positive people and three-quarters of the cumulative global deaths from AIDS. The fastest growth of HIV infections over the coming decade will be in Asia, but Africa's share of the world's AIDS deaths will still be about 60 percent in the year 2000.[5]

Over the past couple of decades, civil wars have devastated certain countries, including Rwanda, Burundi, Somalia, Liberia, Sudan, Ethiopia, Mozambique, and Angola. These conflicts derive from ethnic, religious, and other communal cleavages; but such "cultural pluralism," which characterizes virtually all African nations, does not erupt into violence necessarily or spontaneously. Rather, communal conflict comes about as a consequence of manipulation by political demagogues, in and out of government, who exploit real and imagined grievances or fears in order to mobilize supporters and gain political advantage.

The resulting casualties number in the hundreds of thousands since the mid-1970s, but that is only part of the cost. Much social life, economic activity, and the bases for future political trust and cooperation have been undermined or disrupted. Although they are limited to specific regions of the continent, Africa has by far the largest number and highest proportion of refugees in the world today. Driven from their homes, fields, and jobs, these millions of refugees are the poorest and most vulnerable people of all, and the least able to contribute productively.[6]

The same countries which have suffered armed conflicts have also been among the major sites of recurrent famines over the past quarter-century. The number of deaths caused by famine during this period is even greater than that resulting from warfare, but the calamities are closely related. Indeed, food has been used as a weapon of war through burning and mining of fields and the diversion of food surpluses and aid from areas in need controlled by opponents. Famine has also resulted from severe droughts in the past couple of decades, especially in southern Africa and the Sahel, though "nature" is rarely responsible solely or directly. Government policies, past and present, colonial and national, which have, for example, neglected food crops and ignored the environmental consequences of much "development," must be brought into any explanation. So must be the decisions of many individuals and companies seeking private gain or simply pursuing short-term survival strategies at the expense of the longer-term viability of the land, water, and forests.[7]

The economic regression experienced over the past generation is not, however, limited to areas of war and famine; nor can the widespread agricultural and industrial decline be fully explained by these events. Since Africa is still a largely agrarian region, falling agricultural productivity affects all other sectors of the economy. Two-thirds of the labor force remains employed in agriculture, and 70 percent of the population lives in rural areas. Agricultural products account for about one-third of total economic output and of total exports.

In this context, it is disastrous that agriculture in general and food production in particular has grown more slowly than population for the past thirty years, causing a deterioration in per capita terms with the trend worsening over time. Low and declining levels of domestic food production have been offset only partially by rapidly rising food imports. Africa has become by far the largest per capita importer

Plate 93. Famine victims, Ethiopia, 1984.
Photo courtesy United Nations/John Isaac.

of food globally and, as well, the largest per capita recipient of food aid. Nothing symbolizes more dramatically the changing statuses of Africa and India than the latter's donations of food aid to assist African famine victims during the 1980s. Average daily calorie supply in Africa, the most fundamental measure of well-being, has hovered around 90 to 93 percent of minimal nutrition requirements over the past decade, 12 to 14 percent below the comparable figure for less-developed countries as a whole, and 6 to 9 percent below the average for previously famished India and South Asia.

Agricultural exports have also stagnated or declined in most African countries, reducing the region's share of world markets for its traditional commodities, especially coffee, cocoa, cotton, groundnuts, and timber. The proportion of global exports from Africa shrank from about 2.5 percent in 1970 to less than 1.2 percent by the early 1990s, reflecting the region's marginalization within the world economy. Africa's share of the world's primary commodity markets (excluding oil) has fallen from 7 percent to about 3 percent over the past two decades. Since most African countries rely on one to three commodity exports for much of their foreign exchange, declining output of these crops weakens their entire economies and reduces their financial capacity to import needed goods.

Since Africa is the least industrialized region of the world, it must import the bulk of the machinery and equipment used in local production, as well as a substantial portion of its consumer-manufactured goods. These categories account for more than three-quarters of Africa's imports, and the total approaches 90 percent if food is

Plate 94. Women displaced by war at a makeshift settlement, Eritrea, 1993.
Photo courtesy United Nations/M. Grant.

included. By contrast, only 10 percent of the region's total exports are manufactured goods. African industry grew fairly rapidly in the 1960s, but from a very small base. Subsequently, there has been widespread "deindustrialization": the share of manufacturing in total output and the proportion of the labor force in manufacturing has stagnated or declined in most countries.

Among Africa's industrial sectors, only mining, especially petroleum production, continued to grow over much of the past two decades, though falling prices in the 1980s discouraged exploration and production slowed. Several oil-based economies, including the biggest, Nigeria, have suffered the most dramatic economic declines since 1980. The same fate has befallen a number of the largest mineral exporters, notably Zaire and Zambia, among the world's leading copper and cobalt sources. On the other hand, Botswana has prospered throughout the African crisis on the basis of progressively expanded mineral exports.

Questions of commodity prices and exports force attention to the larger world economic context in which the African crisis has unfolded. With few exceptions, African economies are extremely small and based upon the production and export of a handful of primary commodities with minimal industrial processing. This size and dependency is, of course, a result of colonial domination, reinforced by a world economic order which has severely constrained growth opportunities for the "last and least" seeking to develop. A historical and global perspective is essential to any understanding of Africa's exceptional vulnerability to external forces beyond its control.

These forces include the region's terms of trade, the relative prices received for its (mostly commodity) exports compared with the prices paid for its (mostly manufactured) imports. Relative prices have deteriorated sharply for Africa over most of the period marking its crisis, reducing the purchasing power of its exports. The terms of trade vary a great deal, to be sure, depending upon particular commodities and upon the specific years compared; but about 25 percent of the purchasing power of the exports of sub-Saharan Africa as a whole was lost over the 1980s. The global recession of the early 1980s caused new postwar lows for African commodity prices, but even lower levels were reached in 1986–87, followed by yet further declines in prices for several key African commodities such as cocoa and coffee.

Terms of trade reflect only one aspect of Africa's international vulnerability. The explosion of the region's external debt is a consequence of the economic crisis that has, in turn, resulted in a deepening of that crisis. The total sub-Saharan debt surpassed $180 billion by the early 1990s; it was less than $10 billion twenty years earlier. The debt is now larger than the region's total economic output and four times the total value of its exports. Servicing this debt absorbs more than 20 percent of all African export earnings each year, a cost four times larger than annual expenditures on health and education. But these payments constitute not much more than half of the scheduled obligations, as the majority of countries have fallen far behind, requiring recurrent reschedulings and deferrals of payments. African debt crises numbered more than 120 by 1990, involving some two-thirds of the region's countries and providing the trigger for the imposition of structural adjustment programs by the World Bank and IMF.[8]

Serious as these varied economic problems are, the African development crisis is not just a matter of economics. Africa has the highest rate of population growth in the world over the past two decades and will continue to average about 3 percent annual increases throughout the 1990s. The reason for this rapid growth is that African death rates, though still the highest in the world, have been dramatically reduced over the past thirty years, but their fertility rates, also by far the highest in the world, have remained at very high levels. African fertility rates declined only from 6.6 to 6.4 births per woman of child-bearing age between 1970 and the early 1990s. By comparison, fertility rates in South Asia fell from 6.0 to 4.2 and in Latin America from 5.2 to 3.1 over the same period. Consequently, the population of sub-Saharan Africa doubled between the mid-1960s and mid-1980s and will double again between the early 1990s and 2010.

The social and economic costs of such rapid growth are devastating: rising pressures on land and other resources, rising employment competition, and ratios of youthful dependents to those of working age. It will be ever more difficult to meet even minimum consumption needs of more people for education, health care, and other necessities of both individual and national development without reductions in population growth. The great dilemma, however, is that children are the most valuable and reliable investments of most poor families, who lack sufficient private assets or access to social security to provide for their own economic security. Children can supply important household and family labor services, often offsetting child-raising expenses at an early age. Their potential income and security contributions to a poor family over time are major factors motivating parents to have large families. This represents a rational calculation of costs and benefits, as large poor families have more actual and potential resources and more alternatives than do small poor families. On the other hand, rapid population growth, mostly among the poor, increases the amount of labor relative to the amount of land and capital, increasing competition for available wage-labor opportunities. Consequently, wage levels have often not kept up with inflation.[9]

High rates of population growth also have a heavy impact upon the environment. Environmental concerns have received increasing attention in Africa, especially as a result of evidence of escalating desertification and deforestation, which exacerbates the consequences of recurrent droughts. Tropical African soils are generally fragile, and the pressures of rapid population growth and intensified economic exploitation are causing widespread ecological damage, as well as contributing to reduced agricultural yields. Arable land per person is declining, and in many areas, fallow periods are no longer sufficient to restore soil fertility. There has been wholesale invasion of the dense forest zones, where indiscriminate felling to clear land for cultivation, combined with exploitation of timber for commercial purposes, has severely depleted the tropical forests. People and their livestock are also moving into ever more marginal environments, spreading erosion and turning grasslands into arid zones. In recent years, environmental problems have been compounded by some industrial countries which have tried "to dump their toxic waste in Africa."[10]

Intertwined with and underlying many of these components of the African crisis are powerful political forces. Political instability and misgovernment in all its forms, from military intervention, repressive rule, and massive corruption to the widespread civil warfare discussed above, have become endemic in Africa. Generalized political instability means that governments are often unable to exercise effective control over their territories and peoples. African states are "soft" in that they have unusually limited capacity to design and implement policies which could begin to transform the severe conditions of underdevelopment which typify Africa. Some are mere clients of external powers, others are in receivership to their creditors, and many are as lacking in domestic legitimacy as in administrative capability. Such states are typically "hard," however, in responding to criticism or opposition, violently silencing political challenges. "Personal rule" tends to be arbitrary and uncertain, coercive and corrupt, in contrast to institutionalized and constitutional rule. It has roots in both indigenous and colonial rule in Africa and has been the dominant form of government over the past generation.

Finally, the World Bank and other international institutions have stressed that above and beyond all of these other factors, the most fundamental, or at least most tractable, cause of the African crisis is the systematic policy biases of African governments. These biases can be summarized as "statism": excessive government intervention to control and regulate agriculture and other areas of the economy so as to extract financial surpluses for government consumption and expansion. The specific policies at issue are numerous and complex, involving a multitude of ways in which African governments have interfered with market forces, causing waste, poor use of resources, loss of incentives, and slower economic growth. Among the many causes of Africa's decline, it is these public policies which are the almost exclusive focus of structural adjustment programs.

Variations across Africa

Before turning to the dynamics of structural adjustment, it is essential to note some of the developmental variations across contemporary Africa, given the popular image of an undifferentiated African crisis. Certainly the overall picture is dismal, but there are important diversities in conditions and in developmental progress across countries and from one local area to another. The major findings of rural field research in the 1970s and early 1980s, for example, were not that food production was generally falling, but that "agricultural performance in Africa has varied a great deal, from one crop and area to another, and for a variety of reasons."[11] Over the past decade, the range of variation and the number of exceptions to the negative trends have declined; but African development is still characterized by much more diversity than is commonly recognized.

Africa, even the sub-Saharan region, was never homogeneous except from afar. Over the past generation, significant economic, social, and political variations among countries have appeared. To be sure, only a few have sustained rates of economic growth above 6 percent for more than twenty years, and they are all very small (Botswana, Lesotho, Mauritius), but that is an exacting standard in any region apart from East Asia. A considerably larger number achieved 5 percent or better growth rates during 1965–80, including Côte d'Ivoire, Burundi, Malawi, Zimbabwe, Nigeria, Kenya, Congo, and Gabon. None of these was able to continue that pace into the 1980s and 1990s, although a couple maintained moderate growth thereafter, while the others declined precipitously. On the other hand, some previously stagnant economies rebounded over the past decade and moved or are moving in the 1990s toward moderate growth (Ghana, Tanzania, Chad, Uganda). Unfortunately, there are also many cases of nearly continuous stagnation or decline over a long period, including Zaire, Zambia, Somalia, Ethiopia, Madagascar, Mozambique, Sierra Leone, Niger, Senegal, and Benin.

Similar contrasts can be pointed to with respect to average daily calorie supplies, which range from more than 2,500 in Côte d'Ivoire, Congo, and a few others, to less than 1,700 in Ethiopia and Mozambique. Virtually all young girls attend primary school in Zimbabwe, Botswana, Lesotho, Kenya, and Cameroon, in comparison to only 10 percent in Somalia and 20 percent in Mali and Niger. Total adult literacy is more than 70 percent in Madagascar, Zambia, Zaire, Botswana, and possibly Tanzania, while it is less than 25 percent in Sierra Leone, Guinea, Somalia, Burkina Faso, and Benin.

The range of Africa's developmental diversity was significantly expanded in 1994, it should be added, as the Republic of South Africa made its monumental

Plate 95. Women building a road in Lesotho.
Photo courtesy United Nations/Muldoon/jr.

transition from an alien pariah state to a fully democratic African nation (see chapter 21). With a per capita income surpassing $2,600 (more than seven times higher than the average for the rest of the region), a life expectancy of sixty-three years (more than ten years higher), a daily calorie supply of more than 3,100 (1,000 calories above the average), near-universal primary schooling, and an important industrial infra-structure, South Africa presents a new African development profile of great potential. The major qualification, of course, concerns the country's enormous racial inequalities, which will not be easily or quickly reduced.

South Africa is not the only African country with extreme inequalities. Measures of income inequality in Africa are generally higher than in Asia and similar to those in Latin America. Consequently, there is little uniformity in the distribution of miseries and benefits across the social and geographic segments of most countries.

Increasing disparities in life chances among citizens of Kenya, Botswana, or Senegal are as characteristic of contemporary Africa as are the widening gaps between countries in the region and between Africa and the rest of the world.

Structural Adjustment

By 1980, the extent of the African crisis had prompted a new paradigm in development policy for the region, articulated and underwritten by the World Bank and the International Monetary Fund (IMF). The Bank and IMF, the two largest aid donors to Africa, are perforce the most influential actors in shaping development and aid policy for the continent. By conditioning much-needed development aid and debt rescheduling agreements on a set of reforms, the two international financial institutions have been able to mandate fundamental restructuring of African economies. Other leading donors, such as the United States, Britain, France, and Germany, have acted in concert with the Bank and IMF through consultative groups and have withheld bilateral development aid from countries that reject or renege on Bank and IMF conditions. Since 1981, when the Bank and IMF began offering conditional financing, nearly all the countries in sub-Saharan Africa have had little choice but to subscribe to the reform programs widely known as structural adjustment programs (SAPs).[12] Not all countries have been adjusting for that long, however, since each negotiates its own package of reforms, a process that is invariably staggered over a period of years. Moreover, some countries adopted or started implementing adjustment programs late in the decade, while others interrupted them because of political instability or pursued their own "home-grown" reform programs until recently.

Structural adjustment programs grew out of the World Bank's prognosis in the early 1980s of the sources of economic decline in Africa, which it identified as: structural factors such as history, politics, geography, and climate; external factors, especially the disadvantaged position of African economies in the international marketplace; and deficient domestic policies, especially those relating to exchange rates, agriculture, and the government's role in the economy. The Bank's prescriptions, however, focused solely on the third set of factors: the domestic policies of African states. The core elements of structural adjustment programs have therefore targeted agricultural policies, macroeconomic policies, and the government's role in the economy.

Rejuvenating the agricultural sector has been a core concern of structural adjustment programs, with emphasis placed on raising producer prices and improving the agrarian infrastructure. The focus on price reform stems largely from the fact that African governments have traditionally underpaid farmers by depressing food prices for the benefit of urban dwellers, whom they see as their primary supporters, and by withholding a large portion of the world market prices for export crops through exchange controls, price setting by marketing boards, and other forms of indirect and direct taxation. Low producer prices and overtaxation therefore undermined farmers' incentives for greater production. Structural adjustment programs have mandated the abolishing of price controls through government agricultural marketing boards, liberalizing exchange rates, and allowing farmers to earn a larger share of world prices for their exports. Governments have also been required to revamp agrarian infrastructure, such as roads and extension services, and to reduce excessive and inefficient government interference in markets for inputs such as fertilizer and seeds, and in credit schemes.

Two fundamental ideas undergird reform in macroeconomic policy: freeing markets from state interference and instituting strict discipline in monetary and fiscal policies. "Unleashing" markets has entailed considerable state withdrawal from direct participation in economic activity or indirect control of such activity. This has been achieved through complete privatization, restructuring, or demonopolization of state corporations such as mines, airlines, banks, and agricultural marketing and export boards. African governments have also been forced to withdraw price controls, limit wage-setting practices, and withdraw or rationalize subsidies on commodities and industrial and agricultural inputs.

Fiscal discipline has been emphasized through trimming budget deficits and reducing the long-term dependence on external deficit financing which contributes to increased debt. To achieve balanced budgets, African governments have been forced to reduce public expenditure through reduction of the public wage bill by cutting the size of the civil service, selling off loss-making public enterprises, and instituting "cost-sharing" measures such as user fees for services that government continues to provide to the public, including education and health care. Monetary policy has focused primarily on liberalizing the exchange rate by devaluing overvalued currencies. The resulting lower exchange rates mean that African goods fetch lower prices abroad and can thus be more competitive in the world market. In order to further promote exports, trade reforms have been mandated in tandem with currency devaluations. These have included the rationalization of tariffs, the removal of export and import restrictions, and the relaxation of foreign exchange controls used to ration scarce foreign exchange.

The Record

After more than a decade as the sole development choice available to African countries, the implementation of structural adjustment programs remains uneven and the results mixed and contentious. The economic record is a mixed bag of positive growth and better macroeconomic policies for some countries, and continued decline and policy failure for others. Structural adjustment policies have also entailed great social and political costs and have been severely criticized by African governments, continental organizations, some international agencies, and the general public in Africa.[13] The results of adjustment have been uneven and difficult to compare across countries, given differences in the length of time each country has been implementing austerity measures, the previous state of the economy, and political factors impinging on successful implementation. Across the three targeted sectors of agriculture, macroeconomic policy, and the public sector, the implementation and success of adjustment policies has been equally uneven. Some progress has come in improving agricultural and macroeconomic policies, but less success has accrued to efforts to "unleash" markets and reduce government regulation of the economy. Special difficulties have plagued attempts to streamline fiscal and monetary policies and to privatize state enterprises.[14]

One can get a better picture of how structural adjustment has affected development in Africa by considering four questions that relate to the central elements of the African crisis: economic growth, agriculture, the public sector, and the poor.

Has adjustment produced sustainable economic growth? The unevenness of the adjustment record in Africa is underscored by the fact that among the adjusting countries that the World Bank studied over the adjustment period (1981–86 and 1987–91), the annual rate of economic growth increased for half but declined for the other half. The Bank argues that better macroeconomic policies are substantially responsible for this growth, which is likely to be sustained by such a supportive policy environment. Critics emphasize external factors, however, to explain both the increase and the decline in African economic growth in the adjustment period. Thus, generous flows of external aid for adjusting countries explain the positive results, while deteriorating terms of trade for exports account for the decline.

Both these arguments have substance, both have wrinkles. Given that policy reforms require time to take effect and that external financial flows accrue almost immediately upon a government's commitment to policy reform, it is safe to assume that external factors, especially aid flows, have a substantial impact on economic growth. However, as the Bank points out, external transfers do not explain all improvements achieved. For instance, despite declining external transfers, Nigeria registered a positive change in per capita GDP growth of 7 percent over the adjustment period. A reasonable conclusion would be that both adjustment in macroeconomic policies and external factors such as terms of trade and external finance matter in explaining the recorded economic turnarounds of faithfully adjusting countries.

How has agriculture fared? Overall, the agricultural sector has improved in some important ways, although unevenly. Of twenty-seven adjusting countries for which data were available, ten increased real prices paid to farmers for agricultural exports despite declines in world market prices; nine others increased local producer prices to offset declining export earnings for farmers because of local currency devaluations. In the remaining eight countries, governments were unable to offset the cumulative effects of local currency devaluations and falling world prices, leading to an overall decline in producer prices.

On the other hand, as a result of adjustment programs, seventeen adjusting countries reduced the tax burden on agricultural producers. Most achieved this through reform of agricultural markets, for example, by eliminating agricultural marketing boards (Nigeria), linking producer prices to world market prices (Kenya), or demonopolizing marketing boards by allowing private competition (Tanzania). Have these changes increased incentives for farmers to produce more? This is difficult to establish, as data presently available show increased yields for one or two crops, usually leading exports, that have fetched the highest prices. Yields for food crops have not registered a noticeable increase.

How has the public sector fared? Public sector reform has focused primarily on reducing the bloated civil service, reducing the wage bill it consumes, and increasing its efficiency. Adjusting countries have attempted to achieve these results through retrenchment, voluntary early retirement programs, hiring freezes, and abolishing job guarantees for university graduates. Even so, only a few have managed to reduce the civil service by more than 5 percent, though more than half of the adjusting countries reduced their wage bill as a proportion of the GDP between 1985 and 1991. A telling reason for the slow progress of civil service reform is the fact that the civil service continues to be an instrument of patronage to reward regime supporters. In general, countries have stopped hiring or retrenching at the lower echelons of the civil service, but not at the high-salaried levels, thus ballooning the wage bill despite retrenchments. Moreover, recently introduced democratic politics have derailed potential gains because of pork-barreling: for instance, in Congo and Ghana, the wage bill increased by 60 percent and 80 percent, respectively, as a consequence of electioneering.

Another important element of public sector reform involves divesting from public enterprises, so-called parastatals, which have been parasites on public coffers and grossly inefficient. Public enterprises include all conceivable activities from agencies dominating buying and selling in critical sectors, to agriculture, telecommunications, airlines, banks, and insurance companies, to mundane wholesale and distribution outlets. These enterprises provide lucrative positions with which incumbent governments reward supporters as well as general employment. Similar to efforts to reduce the size of the civil service, getting African governments to divest from these public enterprises has been especially difficult because of their political import. Between 1986 and 1992, only five countries had divested from more than 40 percent of their parastatals. These five also had the fewest state-owned enterprises, numbering one hundred or less. Countries with more than two hundred parastatals, such as Kenya and Tanzania, had divested from less than 10 percent of their public enterprises. In Ghana, eleven out of twenty-one enterprises "privatized" in 1991 had reverted back to government control by 1992. Given such slow progress in privatizing public enterprises, their ills have persisted: inefficiency, government subsidies to cover losses, deficits, and political patronage.

How have the poor fared? The short- and medium-term effects of structural adjustment policies on the poor have been the most contentious. In its latest report, the Bank attempts to deflect criticism that structural adjustment has hurt the poor by posing a counterfactual: would the poor have benefited from less or no adjustment? Given that 70 percent of Africa's population is rural, the Bank points to turnarounds in economic growth and, particularly, better prices for agricultural output as clear indicators of the benefits of adjustment to the poor.

Critics argue that structural adjustment programs have further impoverished the rural poor and the working class. For instance, liberalizing markets, withdrawing subsidies, and devaluing local currencies have pushed food prices higher, while salary freezes and retrenchment have undermined people's abilities to cushion these effects. Pressure on governments to balance budgets and maintain fiscal discipline has entailed cutting back on social expenditures. The resulting cutbacks and the imposition of user fees for health and educational services provided by the government have been a major burden on the poor and have resulted in declining quality of life, poorer health, and higher mortality rates. Patients face user fees for a widening range of basic services, including child immunizations and AIDS tests.

As a result of criticism of the adverse effects of austerity measures on the poor, the Bank and other donors have instituted funding programs since 1985 meant to cushion the effects of adjustment on vulnerable groups. The establishment of a Social Dimensions of Adjustment (SDA) unit indicates the Bank's recognition of the adverse social effects of adjustment and the need to make funding available for programs to mitigate these effects. SDA projects are meant to generate employment or income-generating activities and to provide support for basic social services that have deteriorated because of the withdrawal of government support. These programs have already been implemented in more than a dozen countries. Some of the activities supported include retraining schemes, temporary jobs, and credit facilities for laid-off civil servants and unemployed graduates. Support for basic social services includes the rehabilitation of primary health care and educational facilities, training for health workers, provision of essential medicines or teaching aids, and, in a few cases, constructing primary schools.

The Future of Structural Adjustment

The record of structural adjustment has revealed the intractability of the development crisis in Africa. Confronted by slow progress and criticisms of the ineffectiveness of structural adjustment programs, the Bank and the IMF have "adjusted" their own views, albeit very slowly.[15] Structural adjustment is now seen as a long-term process rather than the short-term intervention it was thought to be at the outset. Moreover, the general development crisis requires a multidimensional solution with coordinated interventions in different sectors of development rather than a single focus on the economic realm. This thinking represents the current movement in structural adjustment as articulated by the World Bank in its major 1989 report. Adjustment programs now seek to address social and political factors that impinge on economic performance either directly or indirectly and in the short and long term. To the previously succinct list of macroeconomic reforms that formed the core of adjustment programs, an ever-expanding list of noneconomic factors and variables requiring attention for Africa's eventual recovery has been added. For example, renewed emphasis is placed on poverty reduction, meeting basic human needs, grassroots participation, and democratic governance as necessary and supportive conditions for sustainable recovery to emerge.

While the evolution of structural adjustment programs over the last decade may respond to some dimensions of the development crisis in Africa, two sets of factors continue to constrain development: external factors (especially dependent econo- mies, declining terms of trade, and growing debt) and structural factors (such as history, politics, geography, and climate). External factors present special difficulties for economic recovery in Africa. With increasing debt for which additional revenues from increased trade and economic activity must go to servicing costs, declining terms of trade for primary products, and limited aid, the possibilities for sustainable recovery in Africa seem slight. While international donors view these external factors as "surmountable obstacles," they are very high. The debt burden, for example, is a two-edged sword: if governments choose to devote funds to servicing their debts, they forgo investing in their economies to push growth; and if they do not service debts, they risk losing new funding and foreign investors. Discussions of Africa's debt do not usually broach the possibility of debt forgiveness, and structural adjust- ment programs do not go beyond a concern that countries service their debts as a way of reducing them or seek IMF credit and debt rescheduling to buy time.

Few of the structural factors can be reversed by African policy actions. However, the changing face of politics in Africa can be partly linked to donor pressure on incumbent regimes to adopt more pluralistic political systems, especially after the fall of the Soviet Bloc. Nevertheless, the preponderance of political instability in Africa, in spite of and sometimes because of newly introduced democratic politics, under- mines hope for recovery, at least in the short term. For countries such as Rwanda, Angola, Liberia, and Mozambique, embroiled in or emerging from particularly devastating civil wars, any prospects for social development and economic growth necessarily rest on a fragile political rapprochement.

Democracy and Development

As was seen in chapter18, by the early 1990s, a wave of fundamental political change was sweeping through sub-Saharan African countries, causing the toppling of authoritarian regimes and the setting up of democratic governments, or at least important steps toward this goal. The impetus to democratize came from both internal grassroots pressures and national oppositions as well as external pressures, especially from donor governments which have increasingly conditioned development aid on democratic reforms. The case of Kenya illustrates the political conditionalities that external donors have placed on African governments and their effects on political change. Throughout 1990–91, the single-party government resisted strong internal pressures from opposition groups, churches, and grassroots organizations to allow opposition parties. However, in November 1991, the major western donors to Kenya met in Paris and agreed to suspend development aid to the Kenyan government until it allowed political pluralism. The following month the Kenyan government amended the constitution to legalize opposition parties; but it was not until multiparty elections were held in 1992 that a substantial amount of aid was released. In subsequent negotiations with its major donors, Kenya's performance on political pluralism has featured prominently alongside questions of economic reform prior to the release of promised development aid.

Political liberalization in Africa provides both opportunities and problems for efforts toward economic reform and development. Political pluralism provides opportunities for organized publics to demand better governance from their rulers by pressing for more accountability and the rule of law, as well as allowing public participation in policy processes, especially important to legitimate difficult economic reforms. On the other hand, particular obstacles to specific economic reforms could arise within the new political space: groups whose status is undermined by economic reform programs have more latitude to undermine reforms through dissent. For example, labor unions demand higher wages to offset price increases, while civil servants or large-scale farmers may negotiate for less radical reforms.[16] Moreover, electoral politics may exacerbate corruption and patronage, as Nigeria's experiments with democracy have shown.

The linking of development and democracy is reflected not only in recent conditions attached to development finance by Western donors, but also in the development programs they have pursued since the early 1990s which view economic and political democracy as preconditions for sustainable development. Economic democracy refers to greater private participation in economic activities without undue government control, while political democracy emphasizes issues of government accountability to citizens. While the former is addressed by structural adjustment programs, the latter has been targeted by "governance" projects, such as those initiated by the U.S. Agency for International Development since 1991. USAID and other donors have funded projects to monitor human rights, enhance the independence of the media and the judiciary, and support civil society organizations that can articulate public concerns, participate in policy processes, and ultimately demand accountability from governments. Many of these programs have also funded election-related activities such as voter registration, voter education, and observing transition elections. In short, development agencies have embraced the linking of democracy and development as a route to recovery in Africa.

Africa's Future: Tempered Hope

For many, Africa's development crisis appears to be an apocalyptic amalgam of economic decline, human distress, recurrent famine, tyranny, and incessant civil wars. All this seems to leave little room for optimism. Despite more than thirty years of self-government and the pursuit of development, this general view sees African countries as spiraling further into desperation. Many of those who would like to project some hope find little room for it. One such writer noted, "For the moment, African glory lies around a historical bend of the river in some unseeable future."[17] Others even less sanguine see Africa as "becoming the symbol of worldwide demographic, environmental, and societal stress, in which criminal anarchy emerges as the real 'strategic' danger."[18]

In fact, there is room for optimism, and it is based not on naive romanticism but on discernible and promising movements "on the ground" that suggest progress toward sustainable development. A first basis for tempered optimism is the variation in performance among African countries discussed above. Attention is spotlighted on the "basket cases" to the near-exclusion of those cases with promising returns on reform. For example, while Mozambique's economy is crippled by negative growth, a debt four times its annual GNP, and minefields instead of cornfields, in neighboring Botswana the economy grew at 10.1 percent per year during 1980–1992, a rate three times that of the United States. Botswana also boasts a functional democracy with broad grassroots participation in policy processes and a light debt at 16 percent of annual GNP. Similarly, while countries such as Kenya and Côte d'Ivoire, earlier star performers, have backpedaled on reforms, others such as Tanzania and Ghana, earlier development pariahs, are systematically implementing reform programs with pay-offs such as increased development aid, investment, and institutional recovery.

A second basis for tempered hope for Africa's recovery lies in the recent move toward political liberalization and democratization, much of it driven by Africans themselves in demanding accountability from their governments. The emergence of strong grassroots organizations, an independent media, political parties, and an active civil society has provided channels for articulating citizens' preferences, mobilizing for political action, and ultimately holding governments and political elites account-able through competitive elections. Authoritarian and corrupt governments that have long subsisted on repressed populations now find it increasingly difficult to survive the performance and accountability conditions demanded by both citizens and the international community, especially aid donors.

Third, as noted earlier, discussions of Africa's potential must now also take into account the Republic of South Africa, whose democratic transition to majority rule, level of industrialization, and relatively high social indicators not only raise the statistical averages for the region but, more important, provide a model, even a powerful force, for progressive change on the continent. The future of Africa is not yet written. If much of its recent past seems sobering, contemporary developments do provide new bases for hope.

NOTES

1. As used here, "sub-Saharan Africa" does not include the Republic of South Africa unless explicitly indicated. The region of sub-Saharan Africa is usually referred to in the text simply as "Africa"; where necessary, it is distinguished from "continental Africa."

2. Sources: World Bank, *World Development Reports* (Oxford University Press, 1992, 1993, 1994), Appendix Tables; UNICEF, *State of the World's Children* (Oxford University Press, 1993, 1994), Appendix Tables. These reports are also the primary sources for data throughout this chapter unless otherwise noted.

3. General Olusegun Obasanjo, quoted in John A. Marcum, "Africa: A Continent Adrift," *Foreign Affairs* 68, no. 1 (1988–89): 177.

4. The World Bank reports referred to are *Accelerated Development in Sub-Saharan Africa*

(1981); *Sub-Saharan Africa: Progress Report on Development Prospects and Programs* (1983); *Toward Sustained Development in Sub-Saharan Africa* (1984); *Financing Adjustment with Growth in Sub-Saharan Africa, 1986–90* (1986); *Sub-Saharan Africa: From Crisis to Sustainable Growth* (1989); and *Adjustment in Africa* (1994).

5. John Darnton, "Lost Decade Drains Africa's Vitality," *New York Times*, June 19, 1994; "AIDS in the Year 2000," *New York Times*, June 28, 1994.

6. John Darnton, "Refugee Crisis That Never Ends," *New York Times*, August 8, 1994.

7. See Amartya Sen, *Poverty and Famines* (New York: Oxford University Press, 1981).

8. John Ravenhill, "A Second Decade of Adjustment," in Thomas Callaghy and John Ravenhill, eds., *Hemmed In: Responses to Africa's Economic Decline* (New York: Columbia University Press, 1993), pp. 31–32; World Bank, *Sub-Saharan Africa: From Crisis to Sustainable Growth*, pp. 20–21; and John Darnton, "In Decolonized, Destitute Africa Bankers are the New Overlords," *New York Times*, June 20, 1994.

9. William Murdoch, *The Poverty of Nations* (Baltimore: Johns Hopkins University Press, 1980), is an excellent introduction to issues of population and development. On African population problems, see World Bank, *Population Growth and Policies in Sub-Saharan Africa* (World Bank, 1986).

10. World Bank, *Sub-Saharan Africa: From Crisis to Sustainable Growth*, p. 22. Also see the World Bank's World Development Report, 1992, which focuses upon "Development and the Environment."

11. Sara Berry, "The Food Crisis and Agrarian Change in Africa," *African Studies Review* 27, no. 2 (1984): 62–63.

12. The actual number of countries implementing SAPs varies at any given moment. The most recent World Bank report on adjustment studied twenty-nine countries that have been implementing a reform program since 1981. In some cases, reform programs have collapsed following the outbreak of civil war, such as in Liberia and Rwanda.

13. See Economic Commission for Africa (ECA), *African Alternative Framework to Structural Adjustment Programs for Socio-Economic Recovery and Transformation* (Addis Ababa, 1989); UNICEF, *Adjustment with a Human Face*, 2 vols. (New York: Oxford University Press, 1987); and Julius E. Nyangoro and Timothy Shaw, eds., *Beyond Structural Adjustment: The Political Economy of Sustainable Democratic Development* (Westport, Conn.: Praeger Publishers, 1991).

14. This section draws upon *World Bank: Adjustment in Africa* (1994); Jeffrey Herbst, "The Politics of Sustained Agricultural Reform in Africa," in Callaghy and Ravenhill, *Hemmed In*, pp. 332–56; Mamadou Dia, "A Governance Approach to Civil Service Reform in Sub-Saharan Africa," technical paper 225 (World Bank, 1993); SDA Steering Committee, "The Social Dimensions of Adjustment Programs" (World Bank, 1993); and Alexandre Marc, Carol Graham, and Mark Schacter, "Social Action Programs and Social Funds: A Review of Design and Implementation in Sub-Saharan Africa," technical note 9 (World Bank, 1993).

15. See John Ravenhill, "A Second Decade of Adjustment," and David Gordon, "Debt, Conditionality and Reform," both in Callaghy and Ravenhill, *Hemmed In*.

16. See USAID, *Economic Reform in Africa's New Era of Political Liberalization* (Washington, D.C., 1993); and USAID, *Growth Renewed, Hope Rekindled* (Washington, D.C., 1993).

17. Lance Morrow, *Time*, September 7, 1992, pp. 41–46.

18. Robert Kaplan, "The Coming Anarchy," *Atlantic Monthly*, February 1994, pp. 44–76.

SUGGESTIONS FOR FURTHER READING

Callaghy, Thomas, and John Ravenhill, eds. *Hemmed In: Responses to Africa's Economic Decline*. New York: Columbia University Press, 1993.

Chazan, Naomi, et al. *Politics and Society in Contemporary Africa*. 2nd ed. Boulder, Colo.: Lynne Rienner, 1992.

Nanda, Ved, et al., eds. *World Debt and the Human Condition: Structural Adjustment and the Right to Development*. Westport, Conn.: Greenwood Press, 1993.

Nyangoro, Julius, and Timothy Shaw, eds. *Beyond Structural Adjustment*. Westport, Conn.: Praeger, 1992.

Sandbrook, Richard. *The Politics of Africa's Economic Recovery*. Cambridge: Cambridge University Press, 1993.

Sen, Amartya. *Poverty and Famines*. New York: Oxford University Press, 1981.

Widner, Jennifer, ed. *Economic Change and Political Liberalization in Sub-Saharan Africa*. Baltimore: Johns Hopkins University Press, 1994.

World Bank. *Accelerated Development in Sub-Saharan Africa*. Washington, D.C.: World Bank 1981.

—-. *Sub-Saharan Africa: From Crisis to Sustainable Growth*. Washington, D.C.: World Bank, 1989.

C. R. D. Halisi and
Patrick O'Meara
South Africa

21 With the electoral victory of the National Party (NP) in 1948, the guiding principle of public policy in South Africa became the legal entrenchment of white privilege and racial domination. The National Party created a harsh and intrusive security system and expanded unequal and separate education, job reservation, and residential segregation. In the space of a few years, *apartheid* (an Afrikaans term for "separation") legislation sought to reconstruct South African society solely on the basis of race distinctions, but in a manner that had profound implications for class structure as well. *Apartheid* laws determined who could vote, who could receive an education, and whom one could marry. They also established a racial register of the entire population, prohibited sexual intercourse between the races, and racially restricted ownership of land, property, and businesses. To preserve white supremacy the rule of law was abrogated, including such fundamental rights as protection against search without a warrant and detention without trial.

The Emergence of *Apartheid* and Black Resistance

In a society where whites represented less than 17 percent of the population, the National Party government considered it essential to control the movement of black people for political, economic, and logistical reasons through the so-called pass laws, which restricted and controlled access to white areas. The control of the movement of blacks to the cities began long before *apartheid* legislation was instituted; indeed, as early as 1809, a pass law was introduced in the Cape Province. From 1952 onward, however, the pass laws became a cornerstone of repression, with extensive harassment of blacks by the police and courts. In 1954 black women as well as black men were required to carry these passes or identity books, which provided details of their residential and employment status. Those who remained in urban areas for more than seventy-two hours without a pass were subject to imprisonment, and millions were arrested for such violations. As was clearly demonstrated by mass resistance against

Plate 96. A view of Johannesburg, the largest city in South Africa.
Photo courtesy United Nations/Frank/nj.

these pass laws, the black population and a small number of white supporters began to mobilize against racial restrictions by the *apartheid* state, which reacted by placing harsher limitations on freedom of movement, association, and assembly. In order to control and intimidate opponents further, the government enacted extensive security legislation, including the Suppression of Communism Act of 1950 (in which "communism" was so broadly defined as to be a weapon against any opponent of the regime), the Riotous Assemblies Act of 1956, the Unlawful Organizations Act of 1960, the General Laws Amendment Act of 1962 (the so-called sabotage act), and the Terrorism Act of 1967.

More than just a system of racial repression, *apartheid* was designed to prevent black economic competition and to ensure the supply of cheap black labor to farms, mines, and industry. As a labor strategy, legislation sought to cheapen the cost of black labor while co-opting white workers and their unions, thus blurring the distinction between racial domination and class exploitation and greatly affecting the future political role of black trade unions.

Africans were barred from skilled mining jobs with the passage of the Mine and Works Act in 1911. Prior to the implementation of *apartheid*, white workers had also gained economic advantages stemming from the entrenchment of racial privileges, especially in the gold-mining industry (see chapter 6). The Industrial Conciliation Act of 1924 excluded blacks from being designated as employees. Since they were simply considered "native labor," white workers now had exclusive access to better training and higher wages. This so-called civilized labor policy of the 1920s was designed to protect unskilled whites from black competition, and in 1932, the Native Service Contract Act made breach of contract by African farm and mine workers a criminal offense.

Central to the economic exploitation of black workers was the legally mandated absence of black trade unions and the right of collective bargaining. Such restrictions on black trade-union activity resulted in low wages and exclusion of blacks from health, training, and unemployment benefits. Although stay-aways, illegal boycotts, and wildcat strikes punctuated labor relations for several decades, black trade unions began to assert themselves to an unprecedented degree in the 1970s. This led to a decade of confrontation between black labor, white capital, and the *apartheid* regime.

By 1981, African trade unions had won the right to be officially registered, to have access to the mechanisms of collective bargaining, and to conduct legal strikes; the unions also challenged the long-standing tradition of allocating skilled jobs on the basis of race. Largely because of the dependence of the South African economy on skilled, semiskilled, and unskilled black labor, trade unions were strategically placed to become a major political force. Furthermore, the simultaneous denial of industrial and political rights to black workers ensured that trade unions would emerge as a powerful component of the liberation movement.

At the center of *apartheid* was territorial segregation, which eventually took the form of the so-called homeland policy (see map 26). The myth that Africans did not belong to South Africa, but rather to separate "homelands" or "bantustans," was a key factor in the harshest form of black worker exploitation—the migrant labor system. The absence of husbands and fathers for long periods had a disastrous effect on family life, and inadequate wages and poor living conditions in the homelands produced health and nutritional problems and high infant mortality.

Furthermore, the myth of separate territories was used to deny the African majority citizenship rights throughout the country. Laws originally passed in 1913 and 1936 legalized the creation of reserves for Africans and ultimately restricted their ownership of land and property to 13 percent of the country. However, with passage of the 1951 Bantu Authorities Act, which designated specific territories for Africans on an ethnic basis, and the 1959 Bantu Self-Government Act, which granted these areas "self-government," *apartheid* ideologues sought to transcend mere negative perceptions of territorial segregation and give *apartheid* policy a "positive" political content. By claiming to have established "self-governing homelands" in which Africans could vote and participate in "their own" political process, the government hoped to deflect black opposition at home and international criticism abroad. The homeland policy accomplished neither goal. Black South Africans saw "separate development," as this policy was sometimes termed, as a balkanization of their real homeland, all of South Africa, and as a further erosion of their rights.

The economics of the homeland policy, like its politics, was also based on a myth:

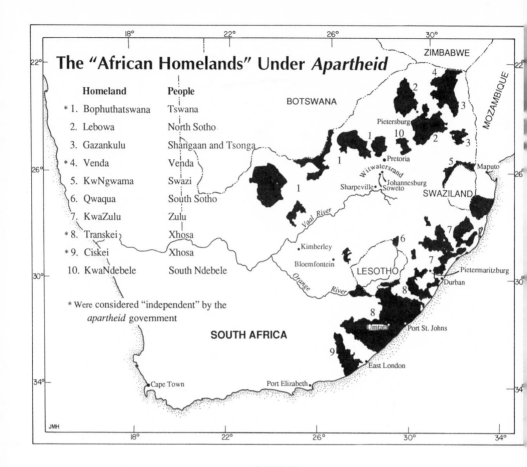

The "African Homelands" Under *Apartheid*

Homeland	People
* 1. Bophuthatswana	Tswana
2. Lebowa	North Sotho
3. Gazankulu	Shangaan and Tsonga
* 4. Venda	Venda
5. KwNgwama	Swazi
6. Qwaqua	South Sotho
7. KwaZulu	Zulu
* 8. Transkei	Xhosa
* 9. Ciskei	Xhosa
10. KwaNdebele	South Ndebele

* Were considered "independent" by the
  apartheid government

MAP 26

that migrant laborers could be paid survival wages because women in the homelands augmented their incomes by agricultural production. However, econometric studies show that as early as the 1920s, agriculture in the homelands was incapable of sustaining the black population in these areas. Since most wage earners tried to find ways to leave to find work in the cities or on white-owned farms, the homeland population had a disproportionate number of women, old people, and the very young.

With the largest portion of their budget coming from Pretoria, these homelands were neither economically viable nor politically independent. As a result, in 1976, the Transkei, the first of four homelands to be granted complete independence, did not receive diplomatic recognition from any country other than South Africa. In addition to the Transkei, Bophuthatswana (1977), Venda (1979), and the Ciskei (1981) were granted so-called independence. Ironically, in the Transkei and Ciskei, leaders were overthrown by military coups d'etat.

At least half the African population permanently lived in cities and had few, if any, ties with the homelands. Since they were denied rights in places where they actually lived, urban Africans were particularly enraged by so-called homeland indepen-

Plate 97. Kwazulu, one of South Africa's ten former "homelands."
Photo courtesy United Nations/Muldoon/pas.

dence. Moreover, black and white taxpayers were forced to foot the bill for the fiasco. In the "homelands," a well-subsidized political elite and bureaucracy presided over extremely high levels of poverty and underdevelopment, and in reality, homeland bureaucracies, police, and security establishments were part of the South African state.

However, as the collapse of the Bophuthatswana government in 1994 graphically demonstrated, opposition existed even within the bureaucracies of these mini-states. Black liberation movements clearly understood that *apartheid* policymakers conceived of homeland elites and ethnic institutions as an alternative to militant African nationalism. However, to varying degrees, black leaders also realized that ethnic identity, while manipulated by the white government, could not be ignored as a fact of political life. It is therefore not surprising that liberation movements such as the African National Congress (ANC) and the Pan Africanist Congress (PAC) enjoyed covert support in these areas. During the 1994 election, the ANC won large majorities in all former homelands except Kwazulu. After the election, the new ANC-led government was faced with the difficult task of reintegrating homeland educational, police, military, and social service administrations into the new South Africa. The new government also has the perhaps more difficult task of adjudicating a large number of land claims by individuals and communities that have been victims of forced removals.

Although not forced into homelands, so-called Coloureds (people of mixed racial descent, who make up about 10 percent of the population) and Asians (predominantly

Plate 98. Barrack-like quarters for African gold miners near Johannesburg.
Photo courtesy United Nations/Pendl/db.

Indians, who first came to South Africa in the second half of the nineteenth century as indentured workers on sugar plantations in Natal Province and now constitute about 3 percent of the population) were victimized by the repressive policies of the white regime and also suffered from forced residential relocation by the government.

Black Resistance

In 1912, a black leadership began to galvanize around what was to become the African National Congress. Despite decades of white intransigence to demands for justice and equality, black opposition was nonviolent for nearly fifty years, consisting of protests and petitions to the government. During the 1940s, the younger and more militant leadership of the ANC's Youth League gradually gained control of the parent body. In cooperation with the Indian Congress and whites generally associated with the Communist Party, the ANC launched the 1952 Defiance Against Unjust Laws Campaign. In this campaign *apartheid* laws were deliberately broken. After several months of civil disobedience and eight thousand arrests, rioting broke out in a number of cities and resulted in considerable property damage and forty deaths. In 1956, three African women were killed when thousands of women confronted the police because of their inclusion under recently amended pass laws.

By repeatedly foreclosing the possibility of peaceful change and insisting on racial repression, the government ensured that African nationalists would inevitably resort to armed resistance. With respect to armed struggle, many historians have pointed out that the ANC's views on nonviolence lagged behind black mass opinion. The tactics of liberation changed dramatically after March 21, 1960, when white police opened fire on a mass demonstration organized by the Pan Africanist Congress at a police station in the African township of Sharpeville. The PAC, under the leadership of Robert Sobukwe, had broken away from the ANC in 1959 because it wanted a more exclusively African-based strategy of protest. In contrast, the ANC had begun to move increasingly in the direction of forming alliances which cut across race lines and included the anti-*apartheid* South African Communist Party.

The Sharpeville massacre, in which sixty-seven PAC-led protestors were killed and hundreds wounded, resulted in demonstrations and thousands of additional arrests all over the country. In the face of government repression, black nationalists increasingly considered civil disobedience and conventional nonviolent tactics to be ineffective. In 1961, some members of the ANC and the South African Communist Party organized Umkhonto We Sizwe (Spear of the Nation) to conduct an armed struggle against the regime. From its inception, this ANC military wing disavowed terrorism and attacks on white civilians, preferring acts of sabotage against symbolic targets, the economic infrastructure, and the police and military. At the same time, the PAC initiated Poqo (meaning "pure"), which was inclined more toward a strategy of political violence that included direct attacks on whites.

With the government's banning of both the ANC and the PAC in April 1960, African nationalist movements began to develop underground and exile operations. Before police raided the Umkhonto headquarters in the Johannesburg suburb of Rivonia in 1963, the organization was responsible for numerous acts of sabotage. Many top leaders were imprisoned, including Nelson Mandela, the single most prominent symbol of resistance among opponents of *apartheid*. Subsequently, South Africa entered more than a decade of enforced calm.

During what appeared to be a period of lull, student groups and the black trade unions were gaining in strength and effectiveness. The 1973 wildcat strikes in the coastal city of Durban, involving more than 100,000 workers, initiated a revitalized phase of black trade unionism, community activism, and resistance. Up until this time, government repression of unions, such as the South African Congress of Trade Unions (SACTU), had largely contained the political clout of black workers, although a decade earlier, SACTU had organized more than 50,000 black workers and played an important political role in the ANC's Congress Alliance, a multiracial grouping of anti-*apartheid* organizations.

Just as the Durban Strikes signaled the emergence of a new generation of militant workers, the Soweto Rebellion thrust radical black students and youth to the forefront of liberation politics. In Soweto (short for the Southwestern Townships of Johannesburg) on June 16, 1976, thousands of African high-school students demonstrated against a government ruling requiring that half of all school subjects be taught in Afrikaans, which was seen as the language of oppression and domination.

The National Party's educational policy was a source of continuing bitterness among black South Africans. In 1954, Dr. H. J. Verwoerd, then minister of native affairs and later to become prime minister, summed up the NP's attitude toward black education: "There is no place for him [the Bantu] in the European community above the level of certain forms of labour. . . . For that reason it is of no avail for him to receive a training which has as its aim absorption in the European community" (*Hansard*, The South African Senate, 7 June 1954). The government's attitude toward black education was reflected in the funds allocated for education. For example, in 1969–70 more than 300 million rands was spent for the education of 1.1 million whites and roughly 50 million rands for 5.8 million Africans. While the precipitating incident concerned instruction in Afrikaans, the intensity and duration of the Soweto uprising can be best explained as the result of accumulated grievances over a long period of time. The Soweto uprisings led to an undetermined number of African schoolchildren being killed or wounded during the first several days, as rioting and confrontations between youth and police spread throughout the country. Over the next few months, at least one thousand were killed, and many thousands more wounded and arrested.

During the late 1960s, educational inequities on segregated college campuses had already sparked the growth of the South African Student's Organization (SASO), the harbinger of the Black Consciousness Movement. Influenced by Black Power and Black Theology in the United States, writings on African socialism, and Frantz Fanon's black revolutionary sociology, Black Consciousness philosophy was an attempt by a younger generation of intellectuals and activists to rethink and revitalize the black nationalist tradition. This dynamic youth movement found an articulate popularizer of its message in Steve Biko, whose death at the hands of security police, while in detention in September 1977, caused yet another round of protests, violence, further repression, and the banning of most Black Consciousness organizations. However, in contrast to the respite after the government crackdown of the 1960s, black political confrontation with the *apartheid* state escalated in the 1980s.

Animated by a new revolutionary fervor, high-school students formed the South African Student's Movement (SASM), which became a fertile ground for recruitment into various liberation movements. Thousands of SASM youth and others left South Africa to join the exiled liberation movements in such African countries as Zambia and Tanzania, while others remained in the country to work underground. Ten years after the 1976 Soweto uprising, the ANC army had grown to more than ten thousand combatants stationed at its exile bases, and numerous cells operated inside the country. The exodus of young militants in search of military training under the auspices of either the ANC or the PAC was so great that not all could be accommodated. The ANC, which recruited the vast majority of these youth, began to establish a more viable underground operation and to encourage many to remain at home to organize mass support. With assistance primarily from the former Soviet Union, the military wing of the movement was able to carry on a low-grade guerrilla war against Pretoria, which increased in intensity over time. That the ANC had become a factor in internal politics was dramatized by the number of bombings of economic targets and assassinations of collaborators and informers, and by the frequency of political trials involving ANC militants.

On the diplomatic front, the ANC expanded its contacts with foreign governments and organizations such as the United Nations in an ongoing effort to encourage the international community to take more stringent measures against Pretoria. Also, through their respective networks of international contacts, the churches, the trade unions, and the student movement contributed to the growth of anti-*apartheid* sentiment internationally. The South African government, on the other hand, spent millions of dollars in its attempt to influence world opinion and took seriously the need to counter ANC activities abroad.

The 1970s made it apparent that with respect both to the economic boom and to relative political tranquility, the 1960s had been the exception rather than the rule. The government's policy had succeeded in radicalizing a younger generation of blacks. The proliferation of militant worker and youth organizations during this period was a clear indication that banning the nationalist movements had made black resistance more determined. Although they too faced discrimination, the *apartheid* system granted Indians and Coloureds a higher social status, limited political privileges, and better government services. Nonetheless, many Asians and so-called Coloureds, began to refer to themselves as "black" rather than accept state-imposed racial classifications. In addition, a new generation of radical white students and faculty on English-speaking campuses made a contribution to trade union, education, and community organization. The struggles of the 1970s forced the government to experiment with a number of cosmetic reforms, which only set the stage for the next round of confrontation with *apartheid*.

Deepening Confrontation of the 1980s

In May 1983, Prime Minister P. W. Botha introduced a constitutional amendment that provided for three racially separate parliamentary chambers for whites, Indians, and Coloureds, in which they would deal separately with matters affecting their respective groups. While the new tricameral parliament gave the appearance of power sharing, real political power remained in white hands. Under the new constitution, the real locus of power was with the state president, the President's Council, and the white chamber of the parliament, which alone dealt with "national" issues.

The office of the prime minister was abolished by the new constitution, and P. W. Botha became South Africa's first executive president on September 14, 1984. Until then the presidency had been largely ceremonial. The next day Botha announced a cabinet, which for the first time in the country's history included one Coloured and one Indian member. The Reverend Allan Hendrickse, leader of the Labor Party, and Amichand Rajbansi, of the National People's Party, were appointed to the cabinet but were given ministries without portfolio. Most important, the tricameral legislature made no provision for the majority of South Africa's population classified as African, who could not stand as candidates or vote. In his 1986 speech on the occasion of the opening of the third session of Parliament, President Botha saw the constitution as "a new beginning," but for black South Africans it was nothing more than a cosmetic change and yet another attempt to undermine the gains of the black opposition.

The government's efforts to co-opt Indians and Coloureds via the new constitution did not go unchallenged in these two communities. In 1983, the United Democratic Front was established within the country. The UDF, which pulled together a large number of diverse groups and trade unions opposed to the new constitution, did little to hide its sympathy for the ANC. Indeed, the imprisoned Nelson Mandela was one of its patrons, and it hailed the ANC's Freedom Charter as the blueprint for a new South Africa. Offering the more militant Azanian Manifesto as an alternative to the Freedom Charter, another movement, the National Front, which was a much smaller federation of Black Consciousness–oriented unions and community organizations, also campaigned strongly against the new constitution.

While the new constitution had the general support of the whites, who had voted in favor of the changes in November 1983, it had only minimal support from the Indians and Coloureds. In organizing opposition to the referendum to ratify the constitution, the UDF launched a national boycott, which was a clear rejection of the constitution and an indication of the strength of the new UDF coalition of anti-*apartheid* groups. The legitimacy the government sought was undermined by the 77 percent of the eligible Coloured voters and 80 percent of eligible Asian voters who boycotted the elections. Africans, who constituted 73 percent of the population, were excluded from voting since no constitutional provision had been made for them.

Botha had unwisely decided to restructure racial domination constitutionally at a time when the majority of black townships were faced with chronic unemployment, inadequate housing, and staggering rates of crime. In effect, the new constitution accomplished the exact opposite of what the white government had intended, since it precipitated a crisis of unprecedented magnitude and duration.

From September 1984 onward, violence erupted in black townships in the Pretoria-Witwatersrand-Vereeniging (PWV) area, the largest metropolitan complex in the country, and hundreds of people were killed or injured. Although angered by the reassertion of white supremacy in the new constitutional order, protestors also expressed a host of local grievances such as rent increases, inferior schools, and the imposition of unpopular, hand-picked local authorities in the townships. During this period, the ANC called on blacks to make South Africa ungovernable. The Defense Force was used in domestic affairs to suppress resistance on an even greater scale than during the Soweto Uprising. In October, 7,000 police and Defense Force troops conducted house-to-house searches in different townships that resulted in the arrests of more than 350 persons. As the incidence of violence increased and the death toll approached 1,000, the South African government declared a state of emergency in July 1985.

The state of emergency, the first since Sharpeville in 1960, gave police and the army even wider powers of detention without warrant or trial and extensive rights of search and seizure, as well as providing the security forces with full indemnity from all legal claims arising from their actions. The immediate detention of several hundred black political, religious, labor, and educational leaders served only to incite greater violence. Ironically, the declaration of the state of emergency was a clear

Plate 99. Funeral of those killed in anti-*apartheid* demonstration,
Uitenhage, South Africa, 1985.
Photo courtesy United Nations.

indication that the police were losing control of the African townships, within which most of the violence was confined. The targets of popular rage were frequently those who were believed to be collaborating with the *apartheid* system. Black policemen, by then approximately 40 percent of the force, urban councillors, and suspected informers were often stoned or burned to death by a technique known as "necklacing," in which a tire, doused with gasoline, was placed around the victim's neck and ignited. Black police, who had once lived peacefully in the townships, had to be placed in isolated barracks. Continued violence, labor unrest, and school boycotts led to the reimposition of the second and more draconian state of emergency one year later, which demonstrated the government's determination not to give in to escalating internal dissent or international criticism and growing support for sanctions. The eventual restoration of "law and order" through widespread arrests and detention resulted in 24,000 arrests and hundreds killed.

Limited Political Reforms

The failed attempt of the new constitution highlighted the fact that the South African government was unable to promote collaboration within the established institutional framework, and this deepened its crisis of legitimacy. At a time when black South Africans demanded a nonracial democracy, President Botha was prepared only to justify reforms in the context of a counterinsurgency program. This was made evident by the expanded political role for the military and the even more ominous State Security Council (SSC) a high-level government body made up predominantly of military elites whose expanded role in political policy was ostensibly to counter a total "communist" onslaught against South Africa with a "total nation strategy," that is, the coordination of all resources of the state against the forces of opposition to white domination.

By often using the military as a counterweight against the National Party, Botha initiated a limited agenda of nondemocratic reforms from above. The first state of emergency was ended in spring 1986. At this point, the intent of the government was to repeal a number of *apartheid* laws such as restrictions on blacks' freedom of movement, residence, and citizenship without endangering continued white control. Even before the imposition of the 1985 state of emergency, the prohibitions against racially mixed political parties and interracial marriages had been repealed. Restaurants and hotels were permitted, though not required, to serve blacks. The minister of constitutional development and planning was empowered to open central business districts to businesses of all racial groups, and black South Africans could, for the first time, acquire ownership rights to property in a larger number of designated areas. Finally, the old system of influx control with its hated pass books was abolished and replaced by a new system of identity documents for both blacks and whites. However, trespass laws and housing and work permits were still available to the government in order to control the movement of blacks. These continuing restrictions underscored the fact that full freedom of movement could not be achieved until the entire edifice of *apartheid* legislation was abolished.

The most significant reform of the period was the result of efforts by government and business to come to terms with the growing power of the independent black trade union movement. The legalization of black trade unions by the white government in 1981 reflected a combination of factors: the rapid expansion of labor organization and activity, a recognition on the part of the business community that the inclusion of black workers in collective bargaining was inevitable, and the failure of the white government to suppress the demands of black labor.

These attempts to reform *apartheid* were opposed by different segments of the population for different reasons. Right-wing whites felt that the government was going too far, white liberals felt that the reforms did not go far enough, and blacks did not want *apartheid* reformed, they wanted it abolished. However, even the limited changes that had been made caused increasing numbers of alarmed whites to shift their allegiance to right-wing political groups. While most Afrikaners continued to support the ruling National Party, right-wing factions, including the Conservative Party (CP) and the Herstigte Nasionale Party (HNP), grew in strength. The CP, which broke away from the NP in 1982, became the official opposition in the white parliament. On the far right, the Afrikaner Resistance Movement (AWB), led by Eugene TerreBlanche, openly advocated the use of political violence as a means to maintain white supremacy.

The political turmoil inside the country simultaneously helped to precipitate and was, in part, caused by South Africa's declining position in the world economy. More than a decade of protest and the worsening internal political crisis adversely affected the high rates of growth that characterized the 1960s boom period. The cost of repression at home and of military operations in southern Africa designed to protect *apartheid* placed considerable fiscal pressure on the economy. The combination of mounting internal and international pressure compromised South Africa's standing as an attractive arena for foreign investment. President Botha's unwillingness to abolish *apartheid* laws, his refusal to openly engage in dialogue with legitimate black leaders, and his often heavy-handed responses to protest undermined his claims of being a reformer. The government was able to maintain an uneasy semblance of stability only by renewing the existing state of emergency, banning or curtailing a number of black political and labor organizations, and stifling press freedoms. Despite stringent controls, there were national strikes, boycotts, protests by church leaders, and acts of sabotage and bombings organized primarily by the ANC.

By the 1980s, Western governments began to view economic sanctions as a serious option, and in the United States pressure for sanctions came from a wide range of constituencies. International bankers refused to lend new money to the government or to renew existing loans, and many international corporations withdrew for either financial or political reasons or both. In 1986, over the veto of President Ronald Reagan, the United States Congress passed the Comprehensive Anti-Apartheid Act. This legislation prohibited new bank loans, the sale of nuclear power equipment and technology, the export of computers to government agencies, the sale of South African Krugerrand gold coins, and landing rights for South African Airways. Similar measures were taken by the European Economic Community (EEC) and the Commonwealth. South Africa's currency, the rand, fell to its lowest level ever, and the government reintroduced strict exchange control regulations to avoid a drain on its foreign exchange resources.

The Demise of *Apartheid* and the Rise of Democratic Negotiations

After suffering a mild stroke in January 1989, President P. W. Botha relinquished the leadership of the National Party the following month. He was succeeded by the minister of national education, F. W. de Klerk, who had been leader of the National Party in the Transvaal province since 1982.

Early in September, the ruling NP won a national election, as it had done in every election since 1948. Despite losses to both the right-wing Conservative Party and the more liberal Democratic Party, de Klerk, who was elected president, interpreted the combined votes for his party and the DP as a mandate for reform. Most white South Africans saw him as a pragmatist and expected him to expand the limited reforms that had been instituted by Botha. Although Botha had been the first Afrikaner political leader to alert whites to the need to "adapt or die," de Klerk came to the historic realization that political restructuring could be accomplished only through some form of power sharing as a means to accommodate black political demands. The collapse of the Soviet Union made it possible for de Klerk to deemphasize the threat of a "communist onslaught" which had been so central to Botha's strategy and, more generally, National Party ideology.

Clearly, de Klerk intended to continue with the policy of limited reforms while realizing that they had to be on different levels. First, at the level of government, he moved to reclaim control of reform policy from the security establishment. At a second level, he sought to expand channels of communication, initiated by Botha with black leaders, most notably with Nelson Mandela. Soon after taking up office, de Klerk permitted multiracial anti-*apartheid* demonstrations and, like Botha, met with important black church leaders. These meetings seemed to suggest that de Klerk, unlike Botha, was prepared to take preliminary steps toward negotiating fundamental change. His release of eight of South Africa's most prominent black political prisoners at the end of 1989, including Walter Sisulu, former secretary general of the ANC, and the subsequent release of Nelson Mandela and the unbanning of the ANC in February 1990 were seen as creating a climate in which "talks about talks" could occur. By making these moves, de Klerk acknowledged that he was ready to meet the conditions for lifting international sanctions and to introduce the reforms required by the international community and the black opposition to end South Africa's economic and political isolation. He had been brought to his advocacy of power sharing through a number of factors, including South Africa's continuing economic crisis exacerbated by the effects of international sanctions. Given the bleak prospects for the country's political and economic future, it had become apparent to the National Party leadership that there was no better time to begin talks with legitimate African leaders. While many blacks welcomed these moves, they remained suspicious about de Klerk's commitment to the implementation of an acceptable democratic order.

At the same time, the ANC and the NP leadership tacitly recognized that a growing culture of violence had developed in South Africa, which various black interests as well as the police, the security establishment, and the military often manipulated, but which none totally controlled. At the center of most of the political violence within black communities was the hostility between the ANC and the Zulu-based Inkatha Freedom Party. But even this deep-seated political rivalry was influenced by a number of factors that fueled the overall culture of violence, such as high unemployment (more than 50 percent in most places), ethnic divisions, warlordism, the blurring of boundaries between criminality and politics, and class divisions between migrant workers and permanent residents in townships.

Within this context, a series of preliminary meetings were begun. As a result, all parties made a commitment to work to create a peaceful and stable climate for negotiations, including the granting of amnesty to agents of both the government and the black liberation movement. At the end of June 1993, a compromise was reported between the South African government and the ANC at the multiparty negotiations taking place in Johannesburg. Negotiations toward the country's first truly nonracial democratic election began in early 1994, but the level of violence continued unabated. In Natal province and the eastern Transvaal, levels of violence reached staggering proportions. Deaths caused by political violence exceeded 15,000 in 1994.

While white South Africans considered power sharing a big step, blacks really had a transfer of power in mind. Coming to terms with these two contrasting images would prove central to the negotiation process. In fact, perhaps the best way to interpret the complex and often frustrating maneuvering that took place at the Convention for a Democratic South Africa (CODESA) between December 1991 and May 1992 is to see it as a process of working out a compromise between the ANC and the NP on the mechanisms of transferring and sharing power. Although many South Africans viewed CODESA as a case of "motion without movement," and despite the fact that the talks stalled on two occasions, a number of important working groups grappled with crucial issues such as the role of a constituent assembly, the character of interim government, ratification of the new constitution, and a host of other questions regarding the nature of the election and the transition to democracy. The multiparty meetings that followed CODESA set April 27, 1994, as the date for South Africa's first democratic nonracial election. At the same time, negotiators completed work on a draft interim constitution which was subsequently ratified by a special session of parliament. In September 1993, the White Parliament and the Indian and so-called Coloured parliaments voted themselves out of existence, and the government agreed to share power with a Transitional Executive Council (TEC) in the months leading up to the election. With the advent of the TEC, for the first time in South African history, prominent black South Africans were given a direct role in national decisions. Finally, in November 1993, President de Klerk, Nelson Mandela, and eighteen other leaders agreed to an interim constitution for the governing of South Africa until a final constitution could be written.

Despite violent efforts by right-wing extremists to derail the electoral process, often in alliance with the Inkatha Party, the election, which began on April 27, was marked by an extremely large and enthusiastic voter turnout and by minimal violence, and as a consequence the Independent Electoral Committee declared the election "substantially free and fair." The African National Congress won a solid victory of 63 percent of the nearly 20 million votes cast, but short of the two-thirds majority that would have given it the power to write the new constitution on its own without having to negotiate with other parties. The National Party won 20 percent of the votes, and only two other parties were able to win the 5 percent minimum for a cabinet seat in the coalition government, Chief Buthelezi's Inkatha Freedom Party (IFP) and the Freedom Front, a coalition of white conservative groups. The ANC won outright majorities in seven of the nine provinces. In the Western Cape region, the ANC conceded defeat to the National Party, which won the support of the majority of the so-called Coloured vote primarily because it had played on Coloured fears of domination by the ANC. In KwaZulu/Natal the IFP won a decisive victory over the ANC. The Pan Africanist Congress and the liberal Democratic Party made surprisingly poor showings, gaining less than 1.5 per cent of the national vote.

Nelson Mandela was elected president of the new Government of National Unity by the National Assembly. One deputy president, Thabo Mbeki, was chosen by the president, and the other, F. W. de Klerk, the former president, came from the National Party, which finished second in the election. The elected National Assembly, in which the ANC holds 252 seats out of a total of 400, must write a permanent constitution by

Plate 100. Nelson Mandela with Thabo Mbeki and F. W. de Klerk
after special parliamentary session, 1994.
Photo courtesy *Cape Argus.*

April 1999 and make all new laws. The Senate, whose concurrence is needed for passage of legislation, consists of ninety members, ten from each province, chosen on a proportional basis by the provincial lawmakers. An eleven-member Supreme Court, similar to that of the United States, will have the power to interpret the interim constitution. It will decide if laws passed by the Parliament adhere to the new Bill of Rights and to the constitutional principles determined in the multiparty negotiations.

The nine new provinces—Northern Transvaal, North West, PWV, Eastern Transvaal, Orange Free State, KwaZulu/Natal, Northern Cape, Eastern Cape, and Western Cape—elected provincial legislatures based on proportional representation. They will have the power to adopt their own constitutions but will not be able to override the federal government. Each has a prime minister and an executive council. At the local level, towns and cities now have one administration and a single tax base for all. As stated above, the new Government of National Unity will rule for a five-year transition period, during which time the terrible legacy of *apartheid* must be addressed and full democratic rights and freedoms established.

Conclusion

Although *apartheid* legislation has finally been repealed, South Africa remains a country of extreme contradictions. In the townships, rural slums, and squatter settlements, unemployment has reached astronomical levels. The new government faces the enormous challenge of reforming virtually every social, economic, and political institution. The lifting of sanctions and the promise of a new constitutional arrangement greatly increase the chances for an improvement in South Africa's economic conditions, especially since it is now eligible for support from a host of national and international donors including the International Monetary Fund (IMF) and the World Bank. Clearly there is interest on the part of many international companies to reinvest in South Africa. On his trips abroad, Nelson Mandela has made efforts to assure investors that their investments would be safe from government expropriation and that they would be able to repatriate dividends and profits. He has also promised that in the future, tax incentives would be provided to facilitate investments.

With the successful completion of South Africa's first democratic election, the restructuring of the economy, most notably redistribution of economic benefits, better housing and health care, and significantly improved employment and educational opportunities, has rapidly become the major problem facing Mandela's government of national unity. Such problems must be addressed if discontent among black youth, massive crime, and township violence are to be tackled. The ANC understands the centrality of restructuring the economy and has moved quickly to enunciate its economic vision for the new South Africa through its Reconstruction and Development Program. While ambitious, this plan makes it clear that the ANC seeks to encourage economic investment within the framework of greater social, political, and workplace democracy. The majority of parties that participated in the election recognized that a viable political solution is crucial in coming to terms with the nation's economic woes. In this respect, the political transition to a more democratic order has been rightly hailed by the international community as a historic event. For most observers, despite the serious inequalities that remain, South Africa represents an example of old enemies acknowledging that they must resolve their conflicts in order to ensure the future political and economic advancement of their nation.

SUGGESTIONS FOR FURTHER READING

ANC. *The Reconstruction and Development Program: A Policy Framework.* Johannesburg: ANC, 1994.

Friedman, Steven, ed. *The Long Journey: South Africa's Quest for a Negotiated Settlement.* Johannesburg: Ravan, 1993.

Gerhard, Gail M. *Black Power in South Africa: The Evolution of an Ideology.* Berkeley: University of California Press, 1978.

Kane-Berman, John Stuart. *Political Violence in South Africa.* Johannesburg: South African Institute of Race Relations, 1993.

Mandela, Nelson. *Nelson Mandela Speaks: Forging a Democratic Nonracial South Africa.* New York: Pathfinder, 1993.

Marks, Shula, and Stanley Trapido, eds. *The Politics of Race, Class and Nationalism in Twentieth Century South Africa.* New York: Longman, 1987.

Pityana, N. Barney, ed. *Bounds of Possibility: The Legacy of Steve Biko and Black Consciousness.* Cape Town: David Philip; London, New York: Zed, 1992.

Reynolds, Andrew, ed. *Election 94: South Africa.* New York: St. Martin's Press, 1994.

Nancy J. Schmidt
Africana Resources for Undergraduates: A Bibliographic Essay

Contents

Introduction
General Overviews
Geography
History, Including Archaeology
Society, Including Anthropology, Sociology, and Women's Studies
Religion and Philosophy
Economy
Politics and International Relations
Art
Music
Literature, Including Folklore
South Africa
Materials Published in Africa
Audiovisual Resources
Computer Resources

Introduction

Although courses on Africa have been part of the undergraduate curriculum in American colleges and universities for more than three decades, it is surprising how few materials have been written specifically for undergraduates. The resources included in this essay were written for undergraduates or are relatively accessible to them. The focus is on resources in English published or reissued since 1980, which cover the whole continent or sub-Saharan Africa, rather than individual countries. It is beyond the scope of this essay to provide resources specific to Africa's more than fifty nation-states. However, resources on South Africa have been included, since a chapter on South Africa is included in this volume.

This essay is addressed to undergraduate students, librarians who select materials for undergraduate collections, and faculty who teach undergraduate courses. Accurate, up-to-date materials which could form a core collection for undergraduate libraries have been selected for inclusion in the essay. Sections on audiovisual and computer resources have been included, since they are as essential to curricula on Africa in the 1990s as are print resources.

The essay is arranged in subject sections which generally correspond to academic disciplines in the social sciences and humanities included in the undergraduate curriculum. However, a hallmark of much research and writing on Africa is that it is interdisciplinary or multidisciplinary. Thus, resources on most subjects will be found in more than one section. Journals and reference materials are described in the appropriate subject sections. Journals are referred to again in the section on computer resources, without being described.

General Overviews

Given the size of the continent, it is not surprising that there are few works which attempt to synthesize information for the whole region. However, several works that are broad in scope provide useful general background on the continent.

The Africa That Never Was (Prospect Heights, Ill.: Waveland Press, 1992), by Dorothy Hammond and Alta Jablow, was first published in 1970. This is a study of how literary stereotypes of Africa developed in Britain from the sixteenth through the nineteenth centuries. It is even more relevant in the 1990s than when it was first written because of the current interest in mixed genres, and the distinction between and blurring of fact and fiction. This work provides background for both social science and humanities writing about Africa.

The first edition of *Through African Eyes* (New York: Cite Books, vol. 1, 1988; vol. 2, 1994), edited and with introductions by Leon Clark, was a highly successful collection of readings written by Africans and expressing African viewpoints published in 1969. It has been extensively revised and published in two volumes. Volume 1, *The Past and Road to Independence*, includes essays and excerpts from fiction and poetry in four sections: the African past, the coming of the European, the colonial experience, and the rise of nationalism. Volume 2, *The Present—Tradition and Change*, was scheduled for publication in December 1994.

Understanding Contemporary Africa (Boulder, Colo.: Lynne Rienner, 1992), edited by April A. Gordon and Donald L. Gordon, is written especially for persons with little previous knowledge of Africa. It provides background for understanding the realities of Africa in the 1990s, taking a multidisciplinary approach to major issues and institutions, with one chapter on South Africa. The emphasis is on the present and the near future.

Two interdisciplinary journals which are basic for African Studies and include both essays and book reviews are *Africa* and the *African Studies Review*. *Africa: Journal of the International African Institute* (Manchester: Manchester University

Press) has been published quarterly since 1928. It began as a journal for anthropology and linguistics but has been interdisciplinary, with an emphasis on the social sciences, since the 1970s. It still includes more anthropological articles than does the *African Studies Review* (Atlanta: African Studies Association), which has been published quarterly since 1958. In the 1980s a series of major reviews of contemporary research appeared in the *African Studies Review*, which includes more articles on the arts than does *Africa*.

For general reference, the *Political and Economic Encyclopedia of Africa* (Detroit: Gale Research, 1993), by Guy Arnold, gives information on fifty-four countries, including historical, cultural, geographical, political, and economic background, major leaders, and statistical information on such topics as population, trade, education, birth rate, life expectancy, and imports and exports. General information on international organizations, political parties, and a range of topics such as debt, health, and guerrilla movements also is included.

Geography

The Changing Geography of Africa (New York: Oxford University Press, 1993), by A. T. Grove, is written especially for secondary school and college students. It covers the physical and cultural geography of the continent thematically from the prehistoric period to the present and includes numerous diagrams and maps. The physical environment, ecology, pests and diseases, traditional lifeways, and history are covered as general background. Development during the colonial period and since independence, including mineral extraction, water resources, agriculture, and industrialization, as well as population, migration, and urbanization are discussed.

Tropical Africa (New York: Routledge, 1994), by Tony Binns, is a concise text included in a series on Third World Development which covers forty-three continental and island states. The environment, population, and rural and urban communities in historical perspective are discussed, and short case studies on the Gambia, Kenya, Mali, Burkina Faso, Nigeria, Sierra Leone, Tanzania, Ghana, Zimbabwe, and ECOWAS (the Economic Community of West African States) are included.

Contemporary Africa: Development, Culture and the State (New York: Longman, 1986), by Morag Bell, focuses on the political geography of sub-Saharan Africa, examining both macro factors such as subcontinent, nation, and region, and micro factors such as community and household. Development since the colonial period is related to a range of factors of interest to geographers, including population, migration, foreign investment, spatial planning, development planning, and regional cooperation, among others. Most examples are from English-speaking Africa.

Lloyd Timberlake provides an overview of environmental problems in the continent in *Africa in Crisis* (London: Earthscan, 1988). He takes an activist stance and focuses on issues that make the newspaper headlines, such as drought, famine, and overpopulation, as well as on other fundamental problems such as the loss of forests and the misuse of soil and water, and relates them to their social and political causes.

Cities in sub-Saharan Africa, excluding southern Africa, are the focus of *The African City* (New York: Africana, 1983), by Anthony O'Connor. He provides an overview of their distribution, rural-urban migration, ethnic groups, economy, residential patterns, housing, rural-urban relationships, and national urban systems, with an emphasis on the period from independence to the early 1980s.

Since there is no recent atlas with large detailed maps which focuses on the continent, recent world atlases should be consulted. For example, *The Times Atlas of the World* (London: Times Books, 1993) includes detailed maps, with two or three African countries shown per page. The gazetteer includes major cities, towns, and natural features.

Africa Today: An Atlas of Reproducible Pages (Wellesley, Mass.: World Eagle, 1994), which is updated every few years, provides a collection of maps in the public domain that cover historical, economic, social, and political data for the continent, and the most recent 8 1/2" x 11" CIA map for each African country. The CIA maps are less detailed than those in *The Times Atlas of the World. Africa Today* is a useful resource for teaching, as well as quick reference.

History, Including Archaeology

There are more general works written on African history than on most other subjects. *African Archaeology* (New York: Cambridge University Press, 1993), by David W. Phillipson, provides a summary and interpretation of data from the first appearance of humans until written history becomes a primary resource. The focus is on economic development and general lifestyle, rather than on the definition and succession of archaeological industries. The emergence of human beings, early toolmaking and other skills, regional diversification, the beginning and development of permanent settlements, farming, ironmaking, and other craft skills are discussed. Graham Connah's *African Civilizations* (New York: Cambridge University Press, 1987) is more narrowly focused on an archaeological perspective on precolonial cities and states in sub-Saharan Africa. He synthesizes data available to the early 1980s and discusses it by region. Archaeological concepts and types of evidence used also are discussed.

A History of the African People (Prospect Heights, Ill.: Waveland Press, 1992), by Robert W. July, now in its fourth edition, is a chronological, thematic history that aims to synthesize data and explain the past. It is divided into four major sections on ancient Africa, the period of modern state building and colonization, colonial Africa, and independent Africa. Within each section, chapters are arranged regionally and thematically, with discussion of such topics as state building, trade, population changes, and religion. There is more focus on cultural history than in most other comprehensive histories, with a final chapter on cultural independence in which such topics as *négritude*, the African personality, ecology, free trade, and democracy are discussed.

Africa since 1800 (New York: Cambridge University Press, 1994), by Roland Oliver and Anthony Atmore, is a standard narrative history of the continent now in its fourth edition. Africa is discussed regionally within three major time periods: precolonial, colonial, and since independence. It has been substantially updated since the third edition to include new perspectives of the precolonial period and reflect changes since the end of the Cold War. Numerous maps are included.

Decolonization in Africa (New York: Longman, 1983), by John D. Hargreaves, is written for students and general readers and focuses on the period from the 1930s up to the early 1960s. It covers the continent and is divided into chapters on historical periods, each of which is subdivided into sections on regional differences and other significant factors. It summarizes much primary material which will not be available in most undergraduate libraries.

In *The African Experience* (London: Weidenfeld and Nicolson, 1991), Roland Oliver provides an overview of African history from prehistoric times to the present, taking a chronological and thematic approach and dealing with themes of importance for the continent as a whole. It draws on data from *The Cambridge History of Africa* and the *UNESCO General History of Africa*, but is written for the general reader and avoids the use of specialized terminology and the many details included in these two compendia.

For significantly more detailed coverage than is included in the sources mentioned above, there are two multivolume compendia of essays by African and Africanist historians which cover the period from early prehistoric times to the early independence period in eight volumes. Although much the same data are covered in both compendia, the approach differs. *The Cambridge History of Africa* (New York: Cambridge University Press, 1975–86) follows standard historiography and includes bibliographic essays in each volume related to the major topics covered in the volume. The *UNESCO General History of Africa* (Berkeley: University of California Press, 1981–92) takes a cultural historical approach. Since it aims to take a revisionist approach, a substantial part of the first volume is devoted to methodology, explaining the interdisciplinary nature of the research upon which it is based. Both compendia are recommended for any undergraduate library which can afford to collect on African history in depth.

One aspect of the revisionist approach taken in the *UNESCO General History of Africa* which has attracted considerable attention in the U.S. in recent years is Afrocentrism. The basic historical work from which the Afrocentric approach is derived is Cheikh Anta Diop's *The African Origin of Civilization: Myth or Reality* (New York: Lawrence Hill, 1974), in which Diop, a Senegalese scholar, discusses black African contributions to Egyptian civilization and the relationship between Egyptian and sub-Saharan African cultures. This work was first published in French in 1965, was translated into English in 1974, and is still in print. In *Afrocentricity* (Trenton, N.J.: Africa World Press, 1988), Molefe Asante discusses the ideas of Diop and other selected African authors to a Pan-African or Afrocentric perspective of American and world culture, while in *The Afrocentric Idea* (Philadelphia: Temple University Press, 1987) Asante provides a general summary of the conceptual background (historical, cultural, and philosophical) of Afrocentrism and its relevance to the African-American context.

The *Journal of African Civilization* (New Brunswick, N.J.: Transaction Publishers), published annually or biannually since 1979, takes an Afrocentric approach in showing the contributions of Africans to world civilization. Most of the volumes focus on single topics such as Cheikh Anta Diop, Egypt revisited, the African presence in early Europe, and black women in antiquity. Two highly respected quarterly journals which represent mainstream scholarship and include articles and book reviews are the *Journal of African History* (New York: Cambridge University Press, 1960-), which includes articles on archaeology, and the *International Journal of African Historical Studies* (Boston: African Studies Center, Boston University, 1968-).

For reference, the *Historical Atlas of Africa* (New York: Cambridge University Press, 1985), edited by Michael Crowder and J. F. Ade Ajayi, covers seventy-two topics from the prehistoric period to the 1980s. For each topic there is one or more maps of high cartographic standard, one or more photographs, and a short authoritative essay on the events, processes (such as migrations or growth of states), or tabulations (such as distribution of prehistoric sites or rainfall) depicted. A detailed index includes all the names on the maps. *The New Atlas of African History* (New York: Simon and Schuster, 1991), by G. S. P. Freeman-Grenville, covers the prehistoric period to 1990 in 103 maps, with sixty-three pages of commentary. The maps cover fewer topics and are less detailed than those in the *Historical Atlas of Africa*, although some maps focus on more specific historical events.

Society, Including Anthropology, Sociology, and Women's Studies

Since anthropology was the first discipline to study African societies, there is a wealth of anthropological material on Africa written since the end of the nineteenth century compared to most other disciplines. In the 1960s and 1970s, case studies of African societies were written especially for undergraduates to supplement earlier essays that had long been used in the absence of textbooks. In recent years anthropological studies have become quite specialized, and few general societal overviews like those characteristic of the early twentieth century have been written. However, a significant number of materials that describe African societies in the 1950s, 1960s, and occasionally earlier are still in print.

Peoples of Africa (Prospect Heights, Ill.: Waveland Press, 1988), edited by James L. Gibbs, was first published in 1965 and is still in print, since no recent collection of general case studies has been published. This collection of fifteen essays provides short descriptions of economic, social, and political organization and values of some of the best-known ethnic groups in sub-Saharan Africa in the mid-twentieth century: the Igbo, Tiriki, Ganda, Hausa, Jie, Kpelle, Kung, Mbuti, Somali, Fulani, Rwanda, Suku, Swazi, Tiv, and Yoruba.

In the 1960s and 1970s, Holt, Rinehart and Winston published a series of case studies of African societies especially for undergraduates, which in around one hundred pages covered the same topics as the essays in the Gibbs volume, plus providing historical background and a discussion of change. A few of these case studies are still in print, including Victor Uchendu's *The Igbo of Southeast Nigeria* (1965).

Waveland Press has reprinted some of the Holt, Rinehart and Winston case studies, to which the authors have added a chapter discussing changes since the case study was first written. These reprints include *The Swazi: A South African Kingdom* (1986), by Hilda Kuper; *The Yoruba of Southwestern Nigeria* (1984), by William Bascom; *The Kanuri of Borno* (1987), by Ronald Cohen; *The Barabaig: East African Cattle-herders* (1985), by George J. Klima; and *The Qemant: A Pagan-Hebraic Peasantry of Ethiopia* (1984), by Frederick C. Gamst. Waveland Press also has published new case studies for undergraduates, including *Mandinko: The Ethnography of a West African Holy Land* (1987), by Matt Schaffer and Christine Cooper, and *Nubian Ethnographies* (1991), by Elizabeth Fernea, Robert Fernea, and Aleya Rouchdy.

Several older collections of essays which were written before materials for undergraduates were prepared deal with a specific facet of culture, and these have been reprinted. *African Political Systems* (New York: Kegan Paul, 1987), edited by Myer Fortes and E. E. Evans-Pritchard, was first published in 1940 to provide examples of the diversity of political systems in sub-Saharan Africa. The essays describe political organization and leadership among the Zulu, Ngwato (Tswana), Bemba, Ankole, Kede, Kavirondo, Tallensi, and Nuer. *African Systems of Kinship and Marriage* (New York: Kegan Paul, 1987), edited by A. R. Radcliffe-Brown and Daryll Forde, was published in 1950 to provide a general view of the nature of kinship and its implications in sub-Saharan Africa in the colonial/pre-independence period. The essays discuss the Swazi, Nyakyusa, Tswana, Lozi, Zulu, Central Bantu of Zaire and Zambia, Ashanti, Yako, Nyaro, and Nuer.

The new People of Africa Series of case studies is appropriate for undergraduates. It takes an interdisciplinary approach, focusing on archaeology, history, and anthropology, to discussing African ethnic groups in their historical and cultural contexts. The first volume, *The Shona and Their Neighbors* (Cambridge, Mass.: Blackwell, 1994), by David Beach, traces the history of the Shona from prehistoric times to the present, in rural and urban settings, including Harare, Zimbabwe, and describes their economic, social, political, and religious life and thought and their relationship to the neighbors, especially the Ndebele. Future volumes will be on the Berbers, Maasai, Ethiopians, Swahili, and other major ethnic groups of the continent.

Some works which combine ethnographic and personal accounts of African societies are appropriate for undergraduates. Elizabeth Marshall Thomas wrote *The Harmless People* (New York: Vintage, 1989) in 1958, providing an empathetic portrayal of the San (also known as the Bushmen) of Botswana and Namibia. It combines a nontechnical description of San culture and depictions of individuals the author knew. A final chapter briefly describes how life had changed for those San the author knew who were still alive in 1986 and 1987. A series of films by John Marshall, discussed in the audiovisual section of this essay, depicts some of the people described in *The Harmless People*. *In the Shadow of the Sacred Grove* (New York: Vintage, 1989), written by Carol Spindel, is an empathetic account of the Senufo of Côte d'Ivoire in the 1980s, which describes both the author's experiences during fieldwork and the village surroundings in which the Senufo live. This contemporary, humanistic account depicts one West African society more holistically than most contemporary ethnographies written by anthropologists.

Life histories by anthropologists provide an understanding of the role of individuals in their societies, and sometimes also an understanding of the relationship of anthropologists to the people they study. *Nisa: The Life and Words of a !Kung Woman* (New York: Viking, 1983) covers Nisa's life from childhood to middle age as told to Marjorie Shostak. It is a detailed and empathetic account of Nisa's life, with an introduction and epilogue by Shostak about the fieldwork related to the collection of the biography. *Bambo Jordan: An Anthropological Narrative* (Prospect Heights, Ill.: Waveland Press, 1994), by Bruce T. Williams, tells the story of Jordan's life, especially his relationship to Williams during his fieldwork in Malawi in the 1960s and 1970s. Told in narrative and dialogue, which contributes to the characterization of Jordan and Williams, the narrative also depicts the colonial legacy and status inequality in Malawi, and the relative poverty of Malawi compared to the great wealth of the U.S.

Although not written especially for undergraduates, *Social Conditions in Sub-Saharan Africa* (Basingstoke: Macmillan, 1990), by Roy A. Carr-Hill, presents important background for understanding social and economic issues. Carr-Hill, a sociologist, discusses how information is produced from available data covering such topics as how statistics take on a life of their own, how governments and international agencies use dubious statistics to make points, and the limits of quantification. He discusses methods of collection, provides summaries of available statistics, and suggests ways to improve data collection topically (e.g., food, fuel, water, health, education) and thematically (industrialization, modernization, urbanization, refugees, war, and destabilization).

The study of African women is a relatively recent focus for social scientists and is highly interdisciplinary. *African Women South of the Sahara* (New York: Longman, 1984), edited by Margaret Jean Hay and Sharon Stichter, includes eleven essays divided into three sections on women in the economy, society and culture, and politics and policy, which discuss women in rural and urban contexts, in literature and art. A new edition is being prepared. *Women and Class in Africa* (New York: Africana, 1986), edited by Claire Robertson and Iris Berger, includes fourteen essays on sub-Saharan Africa from Marxist and feminist perspectives using theories from the social sciences and history. The essays are grouped into three sections on women's access to critical resources (social, economic, educational), dependence vs. autonomy (economic, social, political), and female solidarity or class action. Most of the case studies are from English-speaking Africa, which is also true of those in *Women and the State in Africa* (Boulder, Colo.: Lynne Rienner, 1989), edited by Jane L. Parpart and Kathleen A. Staudt. The ten essays deal with women's roles in the economy, development, urban life, and land resettlement in the colonial and postcolonial periods. The essays in these volumes and special issues of journals such as "Women, Family, State, and Economy in Africa," *Signs* 16, no. 4 (1991), can be used to supplement more general works in the social sciences and history.

Short life histories of women such as those in *Three Swahili Women* (Bloomington: Indiana University Press, 1989), edited by Sarah Mirza and Margaret Strobel, and *Life Histories of African Women* (Atlantic Highlands, N.J.: Ashland Press, 1987), edited by Patricia Romero, also can be used as supplements to more general works. The Swahili biographies are from women who lived in Mombasa, Kenya, and cover the period 1890 to 1975, while the seven biographies collected from women in sub-Saharan Africa by Romero are about life in the colonial period, and are of interest for folklore and anthropology, as well as history.

Religion and Philosophy

Discussions of religion are frequently included in anthropological works, historical accounts of the spread of Islam and Christianity, and discussions of the arts which are created in religious contexts. Although there are many books on African theology in specific contexts, there are relatively few that discuss African religion in general. Books on philosophy are less common, since academic interest in the field is more recent. Very few books on African philosophy are easily accessible to undergraduates, since they assume detailed cultural and sometimes linguistic knowledge.

John Mbiti has written two books that provide introductions for undergraduates to the basic concepts of religion and philosophy in sub-Saharan Africa. *Introduction to African Religion* (Portsmouth, N.H.: Heinemann, 1991) is the second edition of a highly successful work first published in 1975, which places religion in its historical and cultural contexts. Although Christianity and Islam are discussed briefly, the focus is on major concepts and practices of indigenous religions related to the nature of god, spirits, and the universe, the origin of humans, rituals related to birth, marriage, and death, agriculture and other social activities, religious objects, leaders, and morals. *African Religion and Philosophy* (Portsmouth, N.H.: Heinemann, 1990) provides an introduction to the major issues of African religion and philosophy and their interrelation. It covers concepts of time, the nature of God and other supernatural beings, concepts of the person, kinship and ethnic groups, birth, marriage, and death, concepts of justice and evil, Christianity, Islam, and other religions, and provides examples primarily from English-speaking Africa.

African Philosophy in Search of Identity (Bloomington: Indiana University Press, 1994), by D. A. Masolo, is a clearly written historical overview of the ideas of major scholars and criticism of their work written for persons who are not familiar with specific works of African philosophy. It is more detailed and covers ideas and philosophers not included in Mbiti's *African Religion and Philosophy*. *African Philosophy in Search of Identity* is the most recent volume in the African Systems of Thought series, which exemplifies the interdisciplinary nature of studies of philosophy and religion. Contributing authors to the series include anthropologists, philosophers, historians, a political scientist, and a linguist. The subjects of the books in the series range from detailed discussions of philosophy, religion, and divination, to the relationship between mythology and indigenous states and modern prophets in Zaire. Most of the other volumes in the series are quite specialized for undergraduates.

Economy

Most recent works on the African economy deal with development. The World Bank's *World Development Report 1991* (Washington, D.C.: World Bank, 1991) focuses on "The Challenges of Development." It provides a solid introduction to development economics, including theories and policy approaches, which is accessible to undergraduates. It includes examples from countries worldwide, including African countries, and thirty-three tables on development indicators, that cover African and other nations worldwide.

Sub-Saharan Africa: From Crisis to Sustainable Growth (Washington, D.C.: World Bank, 1989) reviews economic development since independence and discusses the kinds of economic changes that will be needed to improve living standards and achieve food security and full employment by 2020. It provides a broad economic overview of the subcontinent with numerous tables that compare countries from 1960 to the mid-1980s. This is one of the most important general studies by the World Bank and is influencing current directions in economic assistance.

Goran Hyden's *No Short Cuts to Progress* (Berkeley: University of California Press, 1983) discusses concepts of development, provides an overview of the management of African development since independence, takes a critical perspective of the contexts of African development, and looks at the challenges of development and the lack of real progress. It discusses such topics as governance, policymaking, administration, decentralization, parastatals, nongovernmental organizations, building local capacity, and the need for change by donor agencies and African governments.

Rural Development in Tropical Africa (New York: St. Martin's Press, 1980), edited by Judith Heyer, Pepe Roberts, and Gavin Williams, provides an overview of rural development theory and practice and discusses why government-organized and foreign-financed projects often fail. It provides case studies on Kenya, Tanzania, Sudan, Ghana, Nigeria, Niger, and Senegal.

Markets and States in Tropical Africa (Berkeley: University of California Press, 1981), by Robert H. Bates, discusses agricultural politics in sub-Saharan Africa, providing examples primarily from English-speaking Africa. It discusses the relationship between agriculture, government policy (especially government intervention in markets for agricultural commodities), and the fate of peasants in the development process.

African Cities in Crisis (Boulder, Colo.: Westview Press, 1989), edited by Richard E. Stern and Rodney R. White, combines economics and politics in analyzing rapid urban growth. The ten essays discuss rapid urban growth especially in the 1970s due to migration from rural areas, covering such topics as environmental and economic factors, the administration of urban services, and urban local government. Case studies on Nigeria, Côte d'Ivoire, Zaire, Senegal, Tanzania, Sudan, and Kenya are provided in a comparative empirical framework relevant for policy studies.

Politics and International Relations

The focus of most recent political writing is on politics since independence and on the role of Africa in the world arena in the 1990s and beyond. A unique work by a historian points to a dimension of politics usually ignored by political scientists. In *An African Voice* (Durham, N.C.: Duke University Press, 1987), Robert W. July discusses the role of the humanities in African independence, focusing on the ideas of African humanists surrounding independence. It discusses oral and written literature, the visual arts, theater, dance, education, and concepts of the African personality in the two decades after World War II, providing insight into locally relevant background that is rarely the concern of political scientists.

Two recently revised textbooks take different approaches in giving an overview of African politics. *Government and Politics in Africa* (Bloomington: Indiana University Press, 1993), by William Tordoff, takes a topical approach, providing an overview of African politics from independence to mid-1991, with sections on nationalism and the transfer of power, state and society, political parties, administration, the military, and revolutionary movements and regimes in Mozambique, Angola, Guinea-Bissau, Zimbabwe, Tanzania, Guinea, Congo, Somalia, and Ethiopia. It includes a list of changes in country names. *Politics and Society in Contemporary Africa* (Boulder, Colo.: Lynne Rienner, 1992), by Naomi Chazan et al., uses a political interaction framework and places Africa in the context of global structure and priorities in recent years. It is divided into four parts on political structure, political process, political economy, and international relations within Africa and the world at large, and provides examples from the continent. South Africa is the only country which has a single chapter. Information on rulers since independence and political parties for each country is provided in an appendix.

Two collections of essays which provide political surveys of the first twenty-five years of independence take different approaches and complement each other. *African Independence: The First Twenty-Five Years* (Bloomington: Indiana University Press, 1985), edited by Gwendolen Carter and Patrick O'Meara, takes a thematic approach, covering topics such as the legacy of colonialism, ethnic relations, regionalism, the military, urban growth, relations with major powers and the United Nations, and ideology. It also includes a short bibliography of books arranged by topic and country, most of which are appropriate for undergraduates. In contrast, *Politics and Government in African States, 1960–1985* (Stanford: Hoover Institution Press, 1986), edited by Peter Duignan and Robert Jackson, takes a geographic approach covering sub-Saharan Africa. Essays focus on regions such as francophone West Africa, lusophone Africa, and the Horn of Africa, or countries such as Nigeria and Ghana, Zaire and Cameroon, and South Africa. Although not all countries of the subcontinent are covered, those which have been of most interest in the United States are included.

Other collections of essays focus on recent political changes and topics of current political interest. *Democracy in Developing Countries,* vol. 2: *Africa* (Boulder,

Colo.: Lynne Rienner, 1988), edited by Larry Diamond, Juan J. Linz, and Seymour Martin Lipset, is part of a four-volume series that takes a multidisciplinary approach (historical, social, economic, political, cultural, and international) to selected countries. Six case studies, of Nigeria, Ghana, Senegal, Botswana, Zimbabwe, and Uganda, review the political history of the countries since independence and discuss factors related to the future persistence of democracy. An introductory chapter discusses general factors related to democratic success and failure in sub-Saharan Africa.

The essays in *Governance and Politics in Africa* (Boulder, Colo.: Lynne Rienner, 1992), edited by Goran Hyden and Michael Bratton, attempt to put current reforms in the context of how selected countries have been governed since independence. There is a general discussion of governance and three regime types: experiments with democracy, populist and military, and one-party states. The case studies are of Senegal, Botswana, Nigeria, Ghana, Burkina Faso, Niger, Kenya, Rwanda, Tanzania, and Zaire.

Two collections of essays examine diverse aspects of Africa in world politics in the 1990s. *Africa in World Politics* (Boulder, Colo.: Westview, 1991), edited by John W. Harbeson and Donald Rothchild, examines the changing position of Africa in international relations in the post–Cold War world and identifies new issues and opportunities that may emerge. The fifteen essays are divided into four sections on the determinants of Africa's international relations, international conflict areas in Africa (South Africa, the Horn, Libya), Africa and the powers (Europe, Middle East, Russia, U.S.), and the management of interstate conflict. The nine essays in *Africa in World Politics: Into the 1990s* (New York: St. Martin's Press, 1989), edited by Ralph I. Onwuka and Timothy M. Shaw, discuss the nonaligned movement, the Organization of African Unity, the Soviet-based Council for Mutual Economic Assistance, the Economic Organization of West African States, regionalism, foreign military intervention, the Angolan struggle, and francophone exclusivity and interdependence. The introduction argues for new approaches, and the conclusion is on the political economy of Africa from 1960 to 1985.

Book-length case studies of politics in many African states have been published since 1980 in the Profiles of Nations of Contemporary Africa series (Boulder, Colo.: Westview) and the Marxist Regimes series (New York: Pinter). The volumes in these two series cover the period since independence but provide relevant historical background from the colonial period.

For reference, *Political Leaders of Contemporary Africa South of the Sahara* (Westport, Conn.: Greenwood Press, 1992), edited by Harvey Glickman, provides detailed discussions of fifty-four major political leaders since 1945 which provide far more information than either general or Africa-focused biographical directories. This biographical dictionary is also valuable as a collection of essays on persons who have had influence on African politics beyond their own countries. *African Political Facts since 1945* (New York: Facts on File, 1991), compiled by Chris Cook and David Killingray, provides a short chronology of major events for the continent 1945–1990, and information for each country on such topics as governors, heads of state and major ministers, constitution and parliamentary structure, political parties, major treaties, wars and coups, and a comparison of population at selected dates from the 1940s to 1980s. There is a section of short biographies, but no criteria are provided for selection. Nor are sources provided for statistical information.

American newspapers which provide significant coverage of African news are discussed in the section on computer resources. Many libraries subscribe to the weekly *Facts on File* (New York: Facts on File, 1940-), which provides short news summaries primarily from English-speaking Africa and on trouble spots. Longer news summaries with somewhat broader coverage are included in the "Update" section of *Africa Report* (New York: African American Institute), America's longest-lived news magazine on Africa, which has been published bimonthly since 1956. *Africa Report* also includes articles on political, economic, social, and occasionally cultural events of the continent. For more frequent coverage, the weekly *West Africa* (London: West Africa Publishing Company, 1917-) provides reports on major events outside West Africa and more detailed coverage for West African countries. *Transafrica Forum* (New York: Transafrica Forum, 1982-) is a quarterly journal that focuses on current U.S. policy toward Africa.

Art

The African arts were studied by anthropologists before they became of interest to art historians and other scholars. Contemporary contextual studies of the African arts are highly interdisciplinary, and the arts are frequently studied in combination, even though one of them may be the focus.

African Art in Cultural Perspective: An Introduction (New York: W. W. Norton, 1973), by William Bascom, an anthropologist, is still in print after more than twenty years. It focuses primarily on sculpture in sub-Saharan Africa, is organized by country and region, focusing on a few ethnic groups in each, and is illustrated by more than one hundred black and white photographs. *African Art* (New York: Thames and Hudson, 1993), by Frank Willett, an art historian, is a revision of the 1971 edition which provides an introduction to the art, architecture, and sculpture of the continent. Methods for studying African art are discussed, art from prehistoric rock painting to contemporary art influenced by European art is surveyed, and black and white and a few color photographs illustrate the works discussed.

Art and Society in Africa (New York: Longman, 1980), by Robert Brain, provides a functional discussion of sub-Saharan African art in relation to its major social roles in hunting, herding, agriculture, trade, government and social control, religion, women's activities, and entertainment, with numerous illustrations. The essays in *The Traditional Artist in African Societies* (Bloomington: Indiana University Press, 1989), edited by Warren d'Azevedo, were first published in 1974 and are still basic to the study of art and music in the field, aesthetics, the training and performance of individual artists, and audience responses to the arts. Descriptive examples are provided for the Yoruba, Akan, Anang, Hausa, Marghi, Fang, Chokwe, Basongye, and Gola who live in western and Central Africa.

The first survey of contemporary African art in Western media and tourist art of sub-Saharan Africa, *African Art: The Years since 1920* (New York: De Capo Press, 1989), by Marshall Mount, was first published in 1973. It discusses anglophone and francophone schools of art, as well as artists who are independent of these schools, and relates the "new" art to "traditional" art and mission-inspired styles. More than seventy artists are included, and there are more than one hundred black and white photographs.

Although exhibit catalogues are specialized, some are especially appropriate for undergraduates because of their interdisciplinary focus. For example, *African Art in the Cycle of Life* (Washington, D.C.: Smithsonian Institution Press, 1987), by Roy Sieber and Roslyn Adele Walker, focuses on sculpture in sub-Saharan Africa but provides a general overview of the study of African art in the introduction. Works of art are discussed in relation to the continuity in family and social groups, transitions (such as initiation), governance, status, security (such as divination and curing), display, death, and reincarnation. Numerous photographs show both individual works and contexts of use.

Icons, Ideals and Power in the Art of Africa (Washington, D.C.: Smithsonian Institution Press, 1989), by Herbert M. Cole, includes both "traditional" and contemporary art in relation to selected forms, e.g., naturalistic and abstract, and themes: male-female couples, mother and child, warriors, mounted leaders, and strangers, including Europeans and nonlocal Africans. The artworks are related to social, political, religious, and historical contexts and illustrated with numerous photographs. *I Am Not Myself: The Art of African Masquerade* (Los Angeles: Museum of Cultural History, University of California, 1985), edited by Herbert M. Cole, provides examples of masquerades in fourteen ethnic groups to show the diversity of contexts in which masks are used in sub-Saharan Africa. The introduction discusses hypotheses about the origins of masking, styles, the relationship to the supernatural, audiences, and masks as mediators. Each of the case studies discusses masks in the context of performance, religion, and other relevant ideas. The illustrations show both masks and their contexts of use.

African Arts (Los Angeles: African Studies Center, UCLA), published quarterly since 1967, began as a journal for nonspecialists but has become more academic over the years. It covers both "traditional" and contemporary art, has numerous articles on art in context, and contains excellent photographs, many in color. Contributors reflect the interdisciplinary scope of the study of the African arts. Long book reviews and reviews of exhibits are included in addition to articles.

Music

In recent years there has been an increasing interest in the popular as well as ethnic music of Africa. *African Music: A People's Art* (New York: Lawrence Hill, 1975), by Francis Bebey, is still in print. Written for the nonspecialist, it provides a general introduction to sub-Saharan African "traditional" music and its communal nature.

Contexts in which music is performed, roles of musicians in their communities, musical instruments and how they are played, and general characteristics of musical compositions are discussed. There are numerous black and white photographs. The discography is now quite out of date. *African Rhythm and African Sensibility* (Chicago: University of Chicago Press, 1981), by John Miller Chernoff, first published in 1979, also continues to be a standard introduction for nonspecialists to the general characteristics of music in sub-Saharan Africa and how music fits into African cultures. The author cites many examples from his own fieldwork.

Breakout: Profiles of African Rhythm (Chicago: University of Chicago Press, 1992), by Gary Stewart, includes profiles of fourteen musicians of popular hits in Zaire, Ghana, Nigeria, and Sierra Leone. Their musical styles and the social, economic, and political conditions of the urban areas in which they perform are discussed. A discography of their major works is included. *Sweet Mother: Modern African Music* (Chicago: University of Chicago Press, 1991), by William Bender, was first published in German in 1985 and is based on interviews and scholarly and journalistic sources. Written with enthusiasm to interest nonspecialists in contemporary popular music in sub-Saharan Africa, it focuses on regionally based musical styles, although it is neither comprehensive nor authoritative. The musicians' accounts of their goals and activities are of particular interest. A discography is included.

Literature, Including Folklore

The publication of African literature in all genres continues to grow at a rapid pace, and the criticism of African literature is becoming both more specialized and theoretically diverse. Although many presses have published works of African literature, Heinemann has published the most volumes which are available in the U.S.

The Heinemann African Writers Series of some three hundred volumes is a major source for African literature, including fiction, poetry, and drama, written in English and translated from French, Portuguese, and Arabic into English. Works of two of Africa's three Nobel laureates, Nadine Gordimer and Naguib Mahfouz, are represented in the series. Wole Soyinka is the only African writer in English with a worldwide reputation whose works are not represented. The series includes works by such pioneer writers as Chinua Achebe, Ayi Kwei Armah, Mongo Beti, Okot p'Bitek, Bessie Head, Ngugi wa Thiong'o, Flora Nwapa, Sembene Ousmane, and Leopold Senghor, as well as by younger writers including Shimmer Chinyoda, Mia Couto, Chenjerai Hove, Tanure Ojaide, Ben Okri, Sipho Sepamala, and Tiyambe Zeleza, among many others.

In addition to more than two hundred literary works by individual authors, the Heinemann African Writers Series also includes anthologies of prose, poetry, and drama, representing the continent or regions of Africa. For example, there are two volumes of literature by women, both edited by Charlotte H. Bruner, *Unwinding Threads* (1983) and *African Women's Writing* (1993). Short stories from the continent, arranged by region, are found in *Contemporary African Short Stories* (1992), edited by Chinua Achebe and C. L. Innes, while only South African authors are represented in *The Heinemann Book of South African Short Stories* (1994), edited by Dennis Hinson and Martin Trump. Contemporary South African poets are represented in *Poets to the People* (1980), edited by Barry Fineberg, while well-known poets who write in English, French, and Portuguese are represented in *A New Book of African Verse* (1984), and only French-language poets, translated into English, are included in *French African Verse* (1992). These latter two volumes are edited by John Reed and Clive Wake. In contrast, *Poems of Black Africa* (1975), edited by Wole Soyinka, includes 371 poems written in English, French, and Portuguese and from the oral tradition. Eight radio plays from the BBC African Theatre Series are included in *African Theatre* (1973), edited by Gwyneth Henderson, while four radio plays are included in *South African People's Plays* (1981), with an introduction about performances in South Africa by Robert Mshengu Kavanagh.

The Heinemann African Writers Series also includes more than a dozen nonfiction volumes of political interest, including such works as Jomo Kenyatta's classic ethnography of the Gikuyu, *Facing Mount Kenya* (1979, first published in 1938), Kenneth Kaunda's biography, *Zambia Shall Be Free* (1962), Kwame Nkrumah's critique of the early independence period, *Neo-Colonialism: The Last Stage of Imperialism* (1968), and Steve Biko's statement on Black Consciousness in South Africa, *I Write What I Like* (1978).

A complete list of the volumes in the Heinemann African Writers Series which are still in print is available from the U.S. office (361 Hanover St., Portsmouth, NH 03801-3912).

Gerald Moore's *Twelve African Writers* (Bloomington: Indiana University Press, 1980) includes criticism and brief biographical information on some of the best-known writers in English and French of the pioneer generation of writers: Leopold Senghor, Ezekiel Mphahlele, Sembene Ousmane, Camara Laye, Alex La Guma, Chinua Achebe, Tchicaya U Tams'i, Okot p'Bitek, Mongo Beti, Wole Soyinka, Kofi Awoonor, and Ngugi wa Thiong'o. Some of these authors, including Leopold Senghor, Ezekiel Mphahlele, Camara Laye, and Wole Soyinka, as well as others not included in Moore's volume, are the subject of volumes in the Twayne World Authors Series (New York: Twayne Publishers), which provides general introductions to the works of well-known authors.

Two general volumes of criticism which take different approaches and have been widely influential since 1980 are *The African Experience in Literature and Ideology* (Bloomington: Indiana University Press, 1990), by Abiola Irele, and *Toward the Decolonization of African Literature* (Washington, D.C.: Howard University Press, 1983), by Chinweizu, Onwuchekwa Jemie, and Ihechukwu Madubuike. Irele's volume, first published in 1981, covers the study of African literature, the nature of criticism, the question of whether to write in African or European languages, *négritude*, Pan-Africanism, and essays on authors of fiction in French and three Nigerian authors who use the Yoruba tradition in different ways: D. O. Fagunwa, Amos Tutuola, and Wole Soyinka. The volume by Chinweizu et al., first published in

Nigeria in 1980, criticizes the approaches to criticism of African literature taken up to 1980 and argues for a more Afrocentric and less Eurocentric approach to the writing and study of African literatures.

The most recent attempt to provide a history of African written literature in one volume is *A History of Twentieth Century African Literatures* (Lincoln: University of Nebraska Press, 1993), edited by Oyekan Owomoyela, a collection of essays on literature in English, French, and Portuguese, covering fiction, poetry and theater, African-language literatures, women writers, the question of language, and publishing. Although the essays vary in scope and depth, the volume provides an introduction to major themes and well-known authors.

For reference, *A New Reader's Guide to African Literature* (New York: Africana, 1983), edited by Hans M. Zell, Carol Bundy, and Virginia Coulon, is the most comprehensive one-volume reference work that covers African literature written in European languages and oral literature selectively. Works of literature with brief annotations are listed by country, biographical information and a summary of criticism are provided for nearly one hundred of the best-known writers, and a list of major literature journals with brief descriptions of their content are included. There are no plans for updating this work in the near future. *Twentieth-Century Caribbean and Black African Writers* (Detroit: Gale Research, 1st series 1992, 2nd series 1993), edited by Bernth Lindfors and Reinhard Sander, includes detailed biographies and summaries of criticism for forty-one of the best-known African authors who write in English. The assessments of these authors are longer and more up-to-date than those in *A New Reader's Guide to African Literature*, and include longer bibliographies of critical works.

Research in African Literatures (Bloomington: Indiana University Press), published quarterly since 1970, covers both oral and written literature. It is the leading journal in the field, which includes critical essays, bibliographies, and reviews of works about the literature of the continent in European and African languages. *African Literature Today* (Trenton, N.J.: Africa World Press) is currently an annual available on subscription, or separately by the volume. Each volume includes essays on a single topic, for example, the question of language (African or European) (1990), oral and written poetry (1988), women (1987), recent trends in the novel (1983), and myth and history (1980).

Several collections of oral literature present material in different contexts. *African Folktales* (New York: Pantheon, 1983), selected and retold by Roger D. Abrahams, is an attempt to provide a representative collection of oral narratives from sub-Saharan Africa. An introduction discusses the contexts in which the narratives are told. The narratives are divided into five topical sections: tales of wonder, stories to discuss and argue about, trickster tales to entertain, epics, and making a way through life. The retellings reflect different narrative styles of the original narrators.

The African Storyteller (Dubuque, Iowa: Kendall Hunt Publishing Co., 1990), compiled by Harold Scheub, includes sixty oral narratives divided into four sections according to the types of characters: gods, tricksters, heroes, and men and women. More than half of the narratives are in the latter section. Thirty-five countries are represented; all but four narratives are from sub-Saharan Africa. The narratives, which are identified by country and ethnic group, are written in a variety of styles, reflecting the original sources in which they were published. Several photographs of storytellers are included.

Geoffrey Parrinder's *African Mythology* (New York: Peter Bedrick Books, 1986), first written in 1967 and revised in 1982, provides a general overview of the content and context of sub-Saharan African mythology and is illustrated with photographs of art related to the materials discussed. Summaries of legends and animal tales are included, as well as summaries of myths related to creation, birth, death, and supernatural beings with beneficial and harmful powers.

South Africa

So many books are being published on South Africa that it is difficult to select only a few to recommend. Those mentioned in this section provide basic historical background on the country and the momentous changes which have been taking place since 1990.

A History of South Africa (New Haven: Yale University Press, 1990), by Leonard Thompson, begins with the significance of the prehistoric period for contemporary South African perspectives, then focuses on the seventeenth century to 1989, covering five major periods: 1652–1870, 1870–1910, 1910–1948, 1948–1978, and 1979–1989. It presents balanced coverage of all racial groups and includes a chronology of major historical events.

Apartheid in South Africa (New York: Cambridge University Press, 1990), by David M. Smith, is a short (86-page) basic, general introduction to the history, development, and social, economic, and political impact of *apartheid*, intended for persons unfamiliar with South Africa. It provides background for the period before Nelson Mandela was released from prison in .1990, which initiated significant changes that are still in process.

Apartheid in Transition (Boulder, Colo.: Westview, 1987), by Anthony Lemon, is a more detailed work that provides brief historical background from the peopling of South Africa to 1948, the ideology of *apartheid*, rural and urban economy, population and urbanization, Indians and Coloureds, constitutional alternatives, and internal and external forces for change. Like Thompson, Lemon provides balanced coverage of all racial groups. A more journalistic account by Allister Sparks, *The Mind of South Africa* (New York: Knopf, 1990), gives a historical overview of *apartheid*, covering its major facets and capturing the essence of events since 1948. It is useful for persons unfamiliar with the history of South Africa and details of recent events there.

A History of the ANC: South Africa Belongs to Us (Bloomington: Indiana University Press, 1989), by Francis Meli, a member of the ANC National Executive Committee, covers the period from 1912 to 1987, with chapters on sources of inspiration, the formative period (1912–1919), influence of workers' organizations (1919–1928), fundamental changes (1930–1949), defiance and new strategies (1949–

1960), armed resistance (1961–1969), and its reemergence since 1969, including Black Consciousness, workers' action, Soweto, and the ANC. A chronology of South African history as it pertains to the ANC, the Freedom Charter, and lists of ANC presidents and secretary generals are included.

Nelson Mandela Speaks (New York: Pathfinder Press, 1993) includes thirty-one speeches given primarily to mass rallies in South Africa between Mandela's release from prison on February 11, 1990, and July 10, 1993, on goals for the future and problems that need to be solved. A chronology of events from 1990 to July 1993 and a glossary of persons and groups involved in the transition to democracy are included along with photographs of events from the period. Mandela's life from childhood to 1989 is described by Fatima Meer, a sociologist who knows Mandela and the South African situation well, in *Higher Than Hope: The Authorized Biography of Nelson Mandela* (New York: Harper Collins, 1991).

Waiting: The Whites of South Africa (New York: Random House, 1985), by Vincent Crapanzano, provides perspectives of individuals on being white in *apartheid* society. It includes personal narratives by a variety of white men and women, with background and commentary by Crapanzano. An anthology of short stories, poems, and plays by well-known black and white writers, *Ourselves in Southern Africa* (New York: St. Martin's Press, 1989), compiled by Robin Malan, gives personalized perspectives arranged by topic: speaking of ourselves, children growing up, the country, the city, on the trains, encounters with police, and inside jail. The authors are from Zimbabwe, Botswana, and Swaziland as well as South Africa.

Major Political Events in South Africa (New York: Facts on File, 1991), by Eileen Riley, will be useful if libraries lack in-depth sources on South Africa. It includes a chronology from 1948 to 1990, with one to three paragraphs for each date, and thirty very short biographies of politically prominent blacks and whites.

Materials Published in Africa

It is now relatively easy to acquire materials from some thirty major publishers in English-speaking Africa from the African Books Collective (The Jam Factory, 27 Park End Street, Oxford OX1 1HU, England), which publishes a quarterly annotated catalogue, bills libraries in dollars, and encourages individuals to charge purchases to their Visa or Master Card.

A variety of books are available, from popular general-interest material such as cookbooks, to scholarly books in science and technology. Some of the books are appropriate for undergraduates, although few focus on Africa as a whole. For example, among works of literature are *The Other Woman* (Nairobi: East African Educational Publishers, 1992), a collection of short stories by Grace Ogot, one of Kenya's best-known women writers, *Breakfast of Sjamboks* (Harare: Zimbabwe Publishing House, 1987), a collection of poetry about the civil war in Mozambique by Luckas Mkuti, and *The Singing Anthill: Ogoni Folk Tales* (Port Harcourt: Saros International, 1991), a collection of tortoise tales by Ken Saro-Wiwa, a well-known

Nigerian writer. *Life in Stone: Zimbabwean Sculpture* (Harare: Baobab Books, 1992), by Oliver Sultan, is an illustrated volume about contemporary Zimbabwean stonecarving, while *Making Music: Musical Instruments in Zimbabwe Past and Present* (Harare: Baobab Books, 1992), by Claire Jones, describes and depicts musical instruments, as well as providing instructions on how to make and play them.

Works of social science appropriate for undergraduates include Kole Omotoso's work of "faction," *Just before Dawn* (Ibadan: Spectrum Books, 1985), which covers one hundred years of Nigerian political history and has been cited for providing a profound understanding of it. An introduction to contemporary social life in Ghana is provided in *Tradition and Change in Ghana. An Introduction to Sociology* (Legon: Ghana Universities Press, 1993) by G. K. Nukunya, while thirty-four Zimbabwean women tell their life stories in *Independence Is Not Only for One Sex* (Harare: Zimbabwe Publishing House, 1987), a volume illustrated with photographs, compiled by Kathy Bond-Stewart.

Audiovisual Resources

Africa on Film and Videotape, 1960–1981 (East Lansing: African Studies Center, Michigan State University, 1982), compiled by David Wiley, continues to be the best single source for selecting audiovisual materials for classroom use, although it is now quite dated. It includes detailed descriptions of the content of nearly eight hundred audiovisual materials, evaluations of the content by Africans and Africanist scholars, suggestions for classroom use, and overall evaluation of both content and technical factors on a five-point scale from poor to excellent. This valuable compendium is now being updated, with an anticipated completion date of 1998.

Some feature films and docudramas by African filmmakers are now available for rental and sale in the U.S. by California Newsreel (149 Ninth Street #420, San Francisco, CA 94103). It has a *Library of African Cinema* accompanied by guides for classroom use which include brief information about the videos, the countries in which they are made, and filmmakers, as well as general suggestions for use of the videos in the classroom.

For more information about some of the best-known African filmmakers, *Twenty-five Black African Filmmakers* (New York: Greenwood Press, 1988), by Françoise Pfaff, provides biographical information and descriptive and critical information about the filmmakers and their films. Reviews of films by African filmmakers can be found in some of the same U.S. newspapers that have relatively comprehensive coverage of news about Africa, including the *Christian Science Monitor*, *Los Angeles Times*, *New York Times*, and *Washington Post*.

The Africans (Washington, D.C.: Annenberg/CPB Project, 1986), a nine-part television series by PBS narrated by Ali Mazrui, provides a historical, cultural, and political overview of the continent within the framework of the triple heritage of African traditions, Westernization, and Islam. The series was designed as an educational unit supported by two books. *The Africans: A Triple Heritage* (New York:

Little Brown, 1987), by Ali A. Mazrui, includes a chapter related to each of the films, plus a general introduction and conclusion. It is attractively illustrated and can stand on its own as "an" African perspective on the relation between the African heritage, Islam, and Westernization in the colonial and independence periods. *The Africans: A Reader* (New York: Praeger, 1986), edited by Ali A. Mazrui and Toby Kleban Levine, includes short readings of fiction and nonfiction that support ideas expressed in the narration for the films. The readings are divided into four sections, on indigenous Africa; the triple heritage in historical, anthropological, political, fictional and journalistic perspectives; connections between North and sub-Saharan Africa; and Africa and African-American connections.

Africa: A Voyage of Discovery (Chicago: Home Vision, 1984) is a television series of eight programs prepared by Basil Davidson that first appeared on British television. It covers the continent chronologically and thematically from the precolonial period to the present. Basil Davidson is the author of numerous historical works. His *Modern Africa: A Social and Political History* (New York: Longman, 1989 or 1994 edition) provides background related to more than half the films. It focuses on the twentieth century and is divided into four sections covering the partition of Africa up to 1930, the colonial period from 1930 to 1945, the rise and success of nationalism, and problems and progress since independence.

The San Series of films by John Marshall, most of which have printed study guides, are available for rental and sale from Documentary Educational Resources (101 Morse Street, Watertown, MA 02172). The series includes two long and more than a dozen short films about the daily life of the San of Botswana and Namibia on such topics as hunting, games, curing, and interpersonal relations. Book-length material related to the film series is mentioned in this essay in the section on anthropology. The Documentary Educational Resources catalogue includes detailed descriptions of all of the films on Africa which DER distributes.

Audiovisual materials on Africa can be identified in the *Educational Film & Video Locator* (New York: Bowker, 1990) and *The Video Source Book* (Detorit: Gale Research, 1994), but these general sources provide neither detailed descriptions nor evaluations as do the African-focused sources mentioned above.

Computer Resources

When the previous edition of this volume was published in 1986, the CD ROM periodical indexes which are now taken for granted in libraries had only recently been developed. There are no CD ROM indexes which focus exclusively on Africa, and most of the general subject-focused indexes give only a superficial coverage of Africa. For in-depth research on Africa, currently available CD ROM indexes provide only a small beginning for research, and a variety of print indexes must be used in order to cover periodical articles published in and about Africa.

For undergraduate libraries, the best CD ROM indexes to use are the *Expanded Academic Index*, because it provides access to African-focused journals which undergraduate libraries are most likely to include in their collections, and the *National Newspaper Index*, which covers five U.S. newspapers with relatively extensive coverage of Africa. The African-focused journals among the 960 in the *Expanded Academic Index* are *Africa Report, Africa Today, African Affairs, African Arts, African Studies Review, International Journal of African Historical Studies, Journal of Asian and African Studies,* and *Research in African Literatures.* In addition, there are other journals in this index which regularly include articles on Africa, such as *American Anthropologist* and *World Literature Today.* The five newspapers covered by the *National Newspaper Index*—the *Christian Science Monitor, Los Angeles Times, New York Times, Wall Street Journal,* and *Washington Post*—are among the U.S. newspapers with the most extensive regular coverage of African news.

The files for the *Expanded Academic Index* begin in 1987, while those for the *National Newspaper Index* begin in 1982. Both are updated monthly. These indexes can be searched by author, title, keyword, and modified Library of Congress subject headings. The latter also are used in the print indexes, which must be used for materials published before the coverage of the CD ROM indexes: the *Humanities Index, Social Sciences Index,* and *Readers' Guide to Periodical Literature* (all produced by the H. W. Wilson Company, New York), which are available in most undergraduate libraries. A full-text version of the *Expanded Academic Index* became available in early 1995 which includes four hundred of the journals covered by the current CD ROM index. Among the African-focused journals listed above, only *Africa Report, Africa Today, African Affairs, Journal of African History,* and *Research in African Literatures* will be included in the full-text product.

INDEX

Abaluyia (Kenya), 220–21
The Abandoned Baobab (Bugul), 302, 309
Abdallah (Mahdi), 110
Abd al-Qadir, 110
Abrahams, Peter, 308
Accelerated Development in Sub-Saharan Africa: An Agenda for Action (World Bank, 1981), 44
Achebe, Chinua, 297, 299, 302, 305, 428
Acheulean phase, of Stone Age, 53, 57–58, 59
Act of Union (South Africa), 130
Ade, King Sunny, 288
Adejobi, Oyin, 281
Adotévi, Stanislas, 300
Aesthetics, of African art, 255
Afonso I (1506–1543), 121–22
Africa: size, diversity, and division of, 4–6; in world perspective, 6–7. *See also* Central Africa; East Africa; Geography; North 'Africa; Southern Africa; West Africa; individual countries and ethnic groups; specific topic headings
African-Americans, African heritage of, 6
African Charter on Human and Peoples' Rights (Banjul Charter), 339, 341
African National Congress (ANC), 132, 399, 400–403, 404, 408, 409, 411
African Studies, resources for: general overview of, xiii–xiv, 414–15; geography, 415–16; history and archaeology, 416–18; social sciences and anthropology, 418–21; religion and philosophy, 421; economics, 422; politics and international relations, 423–25; art, 425–26; music, 426–27; literature and folklore, 427–30; South Africa, 430–31; materials published in Africa, 431–32; computer resources, 433–34
Afrikaner Resistance Movement (AWB), 406
Afrikaners (South Africa), 128. *See also* Boers
Afrocentricity: and early civilizations of North Africa, 79; as revisionist approach to history, 417
Afro-Marxism, 168
Age: social organization and, 186–87; belief systems and, 218–19
Agriculture: environment and climatic patterns, 28, 30, 31–32; women's labor in, 28, 177, 316–17; in Later Stone Age, 62; origins and spread of, 64–67; Iron Age in sub-Saharan Africa, 71; and early civilizations of North Africa, 79; precolonial history of West Africa, 81–82; precolonial history of Bantu-speakers, 87, 88; economics of colonialism, 151, 152, 153, 370; social organization and,
178, 196–99; as primary and secondary occupation, 182; economics of village life, 190–93; techniques of, 199–205; women's labor in, 316–17; social change in rural areas, 322–23; crisis in economic development and, 368–69, 378–79; decline in exports, 379; structural adjustment programs and, 385–86, 387–88. *See also* Crops; Food production; Pastoralism
Ahidjo, Ahmadou, 352
Ahmad al-Kabir, 110
Ahmad Baba, 105–106
Ahmad ibn Ibrahim of Adal, 104
Ahmad ibn Idris, 108
Aidoo, Ama Ata, 301, 306
AIDS (acquired immunodeficiency syndrome), 42–43, 325–26, 377–78
Aksum. *See* Axumite kingdom
Aladura movement (Nigeria), 276–78
Algeria: Islam and French colonialism, 110; French colonial policies in, 144; white settler politics in, 148; national liberation struggle in, 148, 163
Allott, A. N., 336
Ambiguous Adventure (Kane), 299
Amin, Idi, 338, 353
Amnesty International, 339
Ancestor spirits, 251–52
Anglo-Boer War, 130
Angola: civil war, 5, 352; Portuguese colonialism, 117; independence in, 156, 164–66; Afro-Marxist regime, 168. *See also* Kongo
Anikulapo-Kuti, Fela, 288, 289
Anthills of the Savannah (Achebe), 302, 305
Anthologie de la nouvelle poésie nègre et malgache (Senghor), 298
Anthropology, resources on, 418–21
Anyidoho, Kofi, 307
Apartheid, in South Africa: end of, 3, 407–11; history of, 130–32, 142, 395–403; and popular music, 288–89; literature and, 308; emergence of and black resistance to, 395–403
Appiah, Anthony, 304
Arabs: written sources for precolonial African history, 74; Arabization of North Africa, 100–101; Islam and Arabization in sub-Saharan Africa, 113. *See also* Islam
Archaeology: as source of precolonial African history, 77; resources on, 416. *See also* Prehistory
Architecture: as art form, 229–30; popular culture and, 290
Armah, Ayi Kwei, 306

Arrow of God (Achebe), 297, 305

Art, African: rock art of Later Stone Age, 62–63; study of, 223–25; style and ethnicity, 225–26; materials and techniques of, 226–27; history and, 229–30, 250; examples of, 231–49; spirituality and, 250–52; political leadership and, 253; initiation rites and, 253–54; complexities of, 254–55; and popular culture, 289–93; resources on, 425–26. *See also* Artists

Artisans, decline in economic status under colonialism, 140. *See also* Basketry; Fabric; Metalworking

Artists: belief systems and social role of, 221; media and techniques of art, 227–29

Asante (Ghana): early history of, 86; slave trade, 120; matrilineal descent groups, 180; art of, 245, 246, 253; music of, 268–69

Ashanti. *See* Asante

Askia Muhammed, 229

Assyria, 69

Aterian phase, of Stone Age, 59

Audiovisual resources, for African Studies, 432–33

Australopithecus species, 52

Authoritarianism: postindependence governments and, 168–70; one-party regimes and, 350; collapse of and anarchy, 355–56. *See also* Military

Authority, patterns of in precolonial period, 94–95. *See also* Authoritarianism

L'Aventure amibguë (Kane), 309

Awolowo, Obafemi, 285

Awoonor, Kofi, 304, 307

Axumite kingdom, 69, 73, 80

Ayuba Suleyman Diallo, 106

Azande (Sudan), 214–15, 215–16

Azanian Manifesto, 404

Azikiwe, Nnamidi, 285

Bâ, Amadou Hampâté, 310

Bâ, Mariama, 301, 309

Babenzele (Central Africa), 269

Badejo, Peter Adegboyega, 271

Bakongo (Angola, Congo, Zaire), 139

Balogun, Ola, 284

Bamana (Mali), 225, 234, 244, 249

Bamba, Amadu, 110, 112, 140

Bambata Rebellion (1906), 132

Bananas, 87, 204

Banda, Hastings, 352

Bangala (Zaire), 139

Banjul Charter, 339

Bantu Authorities Act (1951), 397

Bantu language group, and precolonial African history, 86–94

Bantu Self-Government Act (1959), 397

Le Baobab fou (Bugul), 302, 309

Baoule (Côte d'Ivoire), 138

Barley, 65, 66, 67, 80

Barotse (Zambia), 219

Barre, Mohammed Siad, 354

Basketry, 228

The Beautyful Ones Are Not Yet Born (Armah), 306

Belgian Congo. *See* Zaire

Belgium: European partition of Africa, 136; colonial policies of, 144; and independence struggle in Zaire, 164

Belief systems, African: commonalities in, 212–15; differences in, 215–18; social organization and, 218–21. *See also* Culture; Religion; Spirituality

Bemba (Zambia), 90, 139

Bemba, Sylvain, 311

Benin: precolonial history of, 70, 86; slave trade and, 120–21; art and history of, 230, 235, 241; art and spirituality in, 250–51

Berbers: conversion to Islam, 100; and Sufism, 107

Berlin Conference of 1884–85, 135, 136

Beti (Cameroon), 198–99

Béti, Mongo, 299, 305, 310

Biafra, 139

Biko, Steve, 428

Bissagos Islands (Guinea-Bissau), 247, 254

Black Consciousness Movement, 402

Black Zionist Church, 150

The Blues Is You in Me (Sepamla), 309

Boers (South Africa), 128, 130. *See also* Afrikaners

Boesman and Lena (Fugard), 308

Bokassa, Jean-Bedel, 338, 339, 353

Bones (Hove), 307

Bophuthatswana, 398, 399

Botany, as historical reconstruction method, 77–78. *See also* Agriculture; Environment

Botha, P. W., 403–404, 406

Botswana: mineral exports of, 380; economic growth in, 392

Bound to Violence (Ouologuem), 300, 301, 310

Bourguiba, Habib, 148

Breytenbach, Breyten, 308

Bridewealth, 179, 205, 207, 317

Brink, André, 308

Brutus, Dennis, 305, 309

Bugul, Ken, 302, 309

Burger's Daughter (Gordimer), 308

Burkina Faso: agriculture in, 177, 202; international trade, 205

Busia, Kofi, 257

Buthelezi, Mangosuthu, 285–86

Bwami association, 254

Cameroon: pastoralism, 22; renegotiation of boundary with Nigeria, 348; tropical rain forest, 27. *See also* Beti

Les Cancrelats (U Tam'si), 310
Capitalism: and neocolonialism in postinde-
   pendence period, 167–68; social change
   and, 328
Capitals, of African countries, 19
Cartoons, political, 285–86
Cassava. *See* Manioc
Catholic Church, nineteenth-century missionaries, 125. *See also* Christianity
CD-ROM indexes, 433–34
Censorship, of media, 285, 303
Central Africa: division between North Africa
   and, 5; slave trade in, 6, 115–23, 124, 126–
   27; physiographic structure and early
   European contact, 26; Stone Age in, 59, 61;
   agriculture and prehistory of, 66, 71;
   precolonial history of, 86–90; Islam, trade,
   and social change in, 102–106; Islam and
   Arabization in, 113; European expansion
   into, 124–26; democratic politics under
   colonialism, 150; colonialism and social
   organization, 176; precolonial status of
   women, 185; agricultural techniques in,
   199–200; art and artists of, 227–29, 252;
   literacy in, 383. *See also* Babenzele;
   Chokwe people; Economics; specific
   countries
Central African Republic, 338, 353
Césaire, Aimé, 303
Chad: agriculture, 31; civil war in, 354
Changes (Aidoo), 301
The Chattering and the Song (Osofisan), 306
Children of Soweto (Mzamane), 308
China, economic development in, 375–76
Chindoya, Shimmer, 307
Chinquinho (Neto), 311
Chokwe people (Angola), 126
Christianity: early development of in northern
   Africa, 69–70; and Islam, 98; Coptic in
   Egypt, 100; nineteenth-century missionar-
   ies in interior of Africa, 125; gender and
   social organization, 185; and traditional
   African religions, 274–75, 276; social
   impact of missionaries, 314
Chronology, oral traditions as historical source,
   76–77
Cinema: popular culture and, 283–84; African
   literature and, 302–303
Ciskei, 398
Citemene farming, 200
Civil wars, development crisis and, 378
Clark, John Pepper, 306
Class: and racism under colonialism, 141–42;
   occupation and, 182–84; and racial segre-
   gation in urban areas, 315–16. *See also*
   Social change
Climate: development and patterns of, 22–33,
   36; prehistoric of Sahara Desert, 65

Clothing, popular culture and, 293
Cocoa, 150, 153, 199, 207, 208, 379, 381
Coetzee, J. M., 308
Cold War, impact of on Africa, 170
A Collector of Treasures (Head), 308
Colonialism, European: and levels of diversity
   in Africa, 4; interaction of Europe and
   Africa, 6–7; impact of on development, 43–
   44, 361, 369–72; Islam and, 108–13; early
   years of, 115–16; expansion of into interior
   of Africa, 124–27; and South Africa in
   nineteenth century, 128–32; partition of
   Africa, 135–38; African responses to, 139–
   40; racial and cultural domination under,
   140–44, 314; metropolitan policies of, 143–
   44; white settler politics under, 147–50;
   African participation in politics during,
   148–51; economics of, 151–53; social
   organization and, 176, 185, 187–88, 314;
   land tenure and, 181; international trade
   and, 206–208; cinema and, 283; as theme
   in African literature, 296–99; and legal
   systems, 331–35; political legacy of, 347–
   48. *See also* Decolonization; Neocolonial-
   ism; specific countries
Comprehensive Anti-Apartheid Act (1986), 407
Computer resources, for African Studies,
   433–34
Condé, Maryse, 303
Congo Free State, 138. *See also* Zaire
Conservative Party (South Africa), 406
Constitutions, legal systems and, 337–38
Contract law, 333–34
Convention for a Democratic South Africa
   (CODESA), 409
Convention on the Elimination of all forms of
   Discrimination Against Women (CEDAW),
   340–41
Convention People's Party (CPP), 162
Coptic Christianity, in Egypt, 100
Corn, 6, 28, 31, 65
Côte d'Ivoire: capitalist strategy of develop-
   ment in, 168; Fulbe herders in, 195; reli-
   gion and popular culture of, 276; constitu-
   tion of, 337; democratic elections in, 353;
   development crisis in, 392. *See also* Baoule
Cotton, 153, 202, 370, 379
Cowry shells, as currency, 205–207
Crafts and craftsmen. *See* Art; Artisans; Artists
Creole culture, emergence of on eastern coast,
   103
Criminal law, 333
Crops, 6, 28, 31, 65, 66, 67, 68, 69, 80, 81, 87,
   112, 123, 124, 127, 150, 153, 196, 197,
   198, 199, 200–201, 202–205, 207, 208,
   323, 370, 379, 381. *See also* Agriculture;
   Food production; individual crops
Crowther, Samuel Adjai, 125

Cry, the Beloved Country (Paton), 308
Culture: European domination under colonialism, 140–44, 314. *See also* Belief systems; Popular culture
Currency, cowry as, 205–207
Customary law, 334–35

Dadié, Bernard, 310
Dagomba (Ghana), 203, 258
Dahomey: early history of, 86; slave trade and, 120, 126
Daily Nation (Kenya), 285–86
Dakar, Senegal, 315
A Dance of the Forests (Soyinka), 306
Dangarembga, Tsitsi, 302, 307
Dar-es-Salaam, Tanganyika, 146
The Dark Child (Laye), 298
Death and the King's Horsemen (Soyinka), 297, 304, 306
Decolonization: background to political independence, 157–61; African nationalism and political independence, 161–66; and failure of politics, 166–70; African literature and, 296–97. *See also* Neocolonialism
de Gaulle, Charles, 163
Deindustrialization, development crisis and, 380
de Klerk, F. W., 352, 407–11
Democracy, development crisis and, 390–91
Le Dernier de l'empire (Sembène), 302
Desertification, and agriculture in West Africa, 31–33, 36. *See also* Droughts; Famines
Detention laws, 337
Development: African crisis of, 3, 44, 375–83; geographical pattern of, 13–21; climatic patterns and, 22–33, 36; impact of colonialism and postcolonialism on, 43–44; social organization and modernization, 176; and legal system, 338–39; variations across Africa, 383–85; structural adjustment programs and, 385–90; politics and, 390–91; future of, 391–92. *See also* Economics
Devil on the Cross (Ngugi wa Thiong'o), 302, 307
Le devoir de violence (Ouologuem), 300, 301, 310
Dhows (sailing vessels), 104
Diagne, Blaise, 149
Dias, Bartholomeu, 118
Diola (Senegal), 139
Diop, Birago, 297, 298
Diop, Boubacar Boris, 302, 309
Diop, David, 298, 309
Diouf, Abdou, 352
Diouf, Galandou, 149
Divorce, legal reform and, 336
Djenne. *See* Jenne
DNA, mitochondrial and human evolution, 61
Dogon (Mali), 227, 290
Domeisia (narrative songs), 257, 266

Domestication, of plants and animals, 64–66, 67
Douglas, Mary, 216
Down Second Avenue (Mphalele), 308
Droughts: and desertification in West Africa, 31–32; and famines in sub-Saharan Africa, 326, 378
Drums, African music and, 268
Du Bois, W. E. B., 160
Durban, South Africa, 401
Dutch East Indies Company, 128

East Africa: hominid evolution and habitats of, 52; precolonial history of, 91–94; cattle raising as occupation in, 182; equatorial grasslands and agriculture, 192
Economics: statistics on by country, 15–16; colonialism and, 43–44, 151–53; precolonial history of West Africa, 82; impact of slave trade on West Africa, 122–23, 124; agriculture and, 190–93, 196–99, 199–205; of pastoralism, 193–95; of international trade, 205–209; and postindependence politics, 353–54; status of in postindependence period, 359–64; sources of change, 364–69; underdevelopment in historical perspective, 369–72; international sanctions against South Africa, 407; and future of South Africa, 411–12; resources on, 422. *See also* Development
ECOWAS (Economic Community of West African States), 5, 43
Education: precolonial state support for Muslim, 101; racism and sexism of under colonialism, 142; and postwar independence movements, 159, 160; and social organization, 187, 188; colonialism and social change, 314; socioeconomic inequality and, 326–27; in South Africa, 401–402
Efuru (Nwapa), 301, 306
Egypt: early agriculture in, 66; Iron Age, 69–71; early literate tradition, 73; history of ancient, 79–80; Arab conquest of, 99–100; imperial Muslim state in, 109; Islamic fundamentalism in, 112; British invasion and occupation of, 136, 149
Elders, role of in community, 187
Elephant, ivory as art medium, 227
Eleusine, 28, 31, 200
Elle sera de jaspe et de corail (Liking), 310
Emecheta, Buchi, 306, 316
L'Enfant noir (Laye), 309–10
Ensete, 67
Environment: hominid evolution and, 52; and precolonial process of state formation, 78, 79; precolonial history of southern Africa, 91; and agriculture, 191–92; belief systems and, 217; population growth and, 382; resources on, 415–16

—Geography: and elements of natural, 21–22; physiographic features, climatic patterns, and development, 22–33, 36; population growth and politics, 36, 37; and health issues, 37–43

Eritrea: war of national liberation, 156, 166; independence of, 354; refugees, 380

Esu (deity), 250–51

Ethiopia: early food production in, 67; Ottoman empire and, 104; retention of sovereignty during colonial era, 136, 138; and independence of Eritrea, 156, 166; Afro-Marxist regime in, 168; pastoralism, 194; international relations and conflict with Somalia, 354; famine victims, 379

Ethnicity: diversity of, 4; changes in under colonialism, 139; and belief systems in Kenya, 220–21; styles of art and, 225–26; African literature and, 296; interethnic marriages in urban areas, 317; and constitutionalism in Africa, 338

Europe: written accounts of precolonial Africa, 74; maritime expansion in fifteenth century, 104, 115–16, 118; and end of slavery, 124; expansion into interior of Africa, 124–27. *See also* Colonialism; European Economic Community; Neocolonialism; specific countries

L'Etrange Destin de Wangrin (Bâ), 310

European Economic Community (EEC), 407

Evans-Pritchard, E. E., 214–15, 215–16, 419

Evolution, of *Homo sapiens*, 49, 50–53, 55, 58, 60–61

Exports, 6, 44, 80, 109, 112, 126, 127, 158, 205, 207, 208, 353, 359, 360, 361, 362, 363, 370, 379, 380, 381, 387

Fabric, as art form, 227, 228, 237, 238, 292, 293

Fall, Aminata Sow, 309

Family: social organization and structure of, 176–81; funerals and, 321; legal system and, 333, 336. *See also* Marriage

Famines, development crisis and, 326, 378

The Famished Road (Okri), 306

Fanon, Frantz, 141, 402

Fante (Ghana), 275

Fantouré, Alioum, 310

Farah, Nuruddin, 305, 307

Fashion, popular culture and, 291–92

Fatimids, 101

Festival Panafricain du Cinema de Ouagadougou (FESPACO), 284

Festivals, popular culture and religion, 275–76

Fifth Pan-African Congress (1945), 160

Fireflames (Mtshali), 309

Fixions and Other Stories (Liyong), 307

Flax, 80

Folklore, resources on, 429–30. *See also* Oral tradition

Food production, 178, 182, 190–93, 194, 197–99, 199–205, 383; in prehistoric Africa, 50, 63, 64–67; in early Africa, 80, 81, 86, 87, 153. *See also* Agriculture; Crops

Fortes, Myer, 218, 419

Fouta Jalon, 121

Fragments (Armah), 306

France: neocolonialism and, 7; Muslim resistance to colonialism of, 110; and European partition of Africa, 136, 138; colonial policies of, 143, 144; military conscription of Africans, 147; repression of nationalist movements, 148; and national liberation struggle in Algeria, 163

Franco-Prussian War of 1870–71, 136

Freedom Charter (South Africa), 404

Freedom Front (South Africa), 409

Fula (Guinea), 139

Fulani (Nigeria), 184–85, 195

Fulbe (Nigeria), 108, 195

Funerals: music and, 258; as urban ritual, 321

Gabon, 245, 357

Gama, Vasco da, 116, 118

Gambia, The: size of, 4; women and agriculture, 28, 184; political parties in 1980s, 168, 350; colonialism and agriculture, 361

Gambia River, eighteenth-century slave trade on, 117, 119–20

Garvey, Marcus, 287

Gender: and social organization, 184–86; of artists, 227–28; urban social change and, 316–21. *See also* Women

General Laws Amendment of 1962 (South Africa), 396

Genetics: mitochondrial DNA and common ancestral population, 61; historical reconstruction and, 77–78

Geography, African: location of countries, 11; European and American lack of knowledge of, 10; U.S. compared to, 12, 13; pattern of development in, 13–21; elements of natural environment, 21–22; physiographic features, climatic patterns, and development, 22–34; population, politics, and the environment, 36, 37; environmental elements and health, 37–43; Islamic expansion in North Africa and cultural, 101; and agriculture, 191–92; resources on, 415–16

Germany: and European partition of Africa, 136, 138; colonial policies of, 143

Ghana: early history of, 70, 82, 85–86; Islam and, 102; independence of, 156, 161–62; Fulbe herders in, 195; agriculture in, 205; international trade, 208; art of, 237, 245, 246, 253; music in, 258, 261, 264–65; festivals and popular culture of, 275–76;

popular art in, 290–91; literature of, 306–307; legal system of, 330–31; government suppression of cultural pluralism in, 349; devaluation of currency, 354; fiber factory in, 362; structural adjustment programs and urban poverty, 367; development crisis in, 392. *See also* Asante; Dagomba; Fante; Tallensi

Gisu (Uganda), 219–20

God's Bits of Wood (Sembène), 299

Gordimer, Nadine, 308

Grain crops. *See* Crops

A Grain of Wheat (Ngugi wa Thiong'o), 297

Great Britain: invasion and occupation of Egypt, 109, 149; and end of slavery, 124; colonialism in South Africa, 128, 130–32; and European partition of Africa, 136; colonial policies of, 144

Great Depression (1930s), 361

Green Revolution, 369

La Grève des battu (Kane), 309

Griots, 74, 257, 267

Guinea: ethnic conflict in, 139; decolonization and independence, 163; art and history of, 250; National Dance Troupe, 271; literature of, 309–10; human rights violations in, 338; one-party regime in, 349; overthrow of Nguema in, 353. *See also* Fula

Guinea-Bissau, independence in, 156, 164–66

Gyaman (state of), 121

Haile Selassie I, 287

Hamallist movement, 150

Harlem Renaissance, 303

Harris, William Wade, 276

Harrist Movement (Côte d'Ivoire), 276

Harvest of Thorns (Chindoya), 307

Hausa (Nigeria), 108

Head, Bessie, 301–302, 305, 308

The Healers (Armah), 306

Health: environmental elements of and patterns of development, 37–43; of Europeans in nineteenth-century Africa, 126; and development crisis, 325–26, 377–78. *See also* AIDS; Malaria; Public health

Hehe (Tanzania), 138

Hendrickse, Rev. Allan, 403

Henry the Navigator, 115

Herstigte Nasionale Party (HNP), 406

Herzog, George, 260

History, of Africa: art and, 229–30, 250; background to contemporary social change, 313–16; resources on, 416–18

—Colonialism, European: establishment of, 115–16; expansion of into interior of Africa, 124–27; South Africa in nineteenth century, 128–32; partition of Africa, 135–38; African responses to, 139–40; racial and cultural domination under, 140–44; metropolitan policies, 143–44; colonial state in Africa, 145–47; white settler politics and, 147–50; African participation in politics under, 148–51; economics of, 151–53, 369–72; and international trade, 206–208; social impact of, 314

—Decolonization: as background to political independence, 157–61; African nationalism and political independence, 161–66; and failure of politics, 166–70

—Islam: conquest and social change in North Africa, 70, 80, 99–101; introduction of in Sudanic regions, 85–86; emergence of as world religion, 97–99; trade and social change in sub-Saharan Africa, 102–106; Sufism and African societies, 106–108; and European colonialism, 108–13; and transformation of African societies, 113

—Precolonial: sources for, 73–78; traditions of origin and state formation, 78–79; of North and Northeast Africa, 79–80; of West Africa, 80–86; of Central, eastern, and southern Africa, 86–94; patterns of authority in, 94–95; intergroup relations and external contacts, 95; slave trade and, 115–23; economics of trade, 205–206; ancient cities of, 314–15; status of women, 340; political life, 347

—Prehistory: human evolution, 49, 50–53, 55, 58, 60–61; overview of major developments in, 50; Early Stone Age, 53–58; Middle Stone Age, 59–60; Later Stone Age, 61–64; origins and spread of agriculture, 64–67; Iron Age developments, 67–71

Hittites (Egypt), 68

Homelands policy (South Africa), 397–99

Homo erectus, 52–53, 58

Homo habilis, 52

Homo sapiens, 60–61

Honwana, Luis Bernardo, 311

Houseboy (Oyono), 299

Household: social organization and structure of, 176–81; farming and, 196–99; urban women and female-headed, 320–21

The House of Hunger (Marechera), 307

Hove, Chenjerai, 307

Human evolution, 49, 50–53, 55, 58, 60–61

Human rights, legal systems and, 338–39

Human Rights Watch (Africa), 339

Hunting, in Stone Age, 59–60

Hunting-gathering: as subsistence pattern in Later Stone Age, 61–64; in Iron Age, 71; in contemporary Africa, 192

Hurd, Douglas, 338

Hurry Up to It! (Sepamla), 309

Hutu (Rwanda), 146

Ibo. *See* Igbo
Idanre (Soyinka), 306
Ife culture. *See* Nigeria
Igbo (Nigeria): as example of decentralized
    society, 94–95; ethnic identity of, 139;
    social organization of, 182–83, 186; art of,
    225, 230
Imperialism, Muslim in nineteenth century,
    109–10
Imports, 80, 153, 158, 208, 353, 354, 362, 366,
    367, 369, 378, 379
Independence: background to, 157–61; nation-
    alism and, 161–66; politics of postinde-
    pendence period, 166–70; legal systems
    and, 335–36; expectations versus reality of,
    347–48; economic performance following,
    359–64
India, economic development in, 376, 379
Industrial and Commercial Workers' Union
    (South Africa), 132
Industrial Conciliation Act of 1924, 397
Initiation rites, art and, 253–54. *See also* Rites
    of passage
Inkatha Freedom Party, 408, 409
Intellectuals, belief systems and social role of,
    221
International Commission of Jurists, 339
International Monetary Fund (IMF), 7, 354,
    357, 366–67, 385–90
International relations: strategy of nonalign-
    ment, 348; Somali-Ethiopian conflict and,
    354; resources on, 423–25
Intertropical Convergence Zone (ITCZ), 33,
    34–35, 36
In the Fog of the Season's End (LaGuma), 308
Ipoku, A. M., 258
Iron Age, 67–71
Iron technology, 68–70, 82, 89, 226
Isandhlwana, Battle of (1879), 132
Islam: conquest and social change in North
    Africa, 70, 80, 99–101; introduction of in
    Sudanic regions, 85–86; emergence of as
    world religion, 97–99; trade and social
    change in sub-Saharan Africa, 102–106;
    Sufism and African societies, 106–108; and
    European colonialism, 108–13, 150; and
    transformation of African societies, 113; slave
    trade and, 121; gender and social organiza-
    tion, 185; and traditional African religions,
    274–75; contemporary social change and
    conflict, 328; legal system of, 332
Islamic fundamentalism: origins of, 112; social
    change and conflict, 328
Italy, European partition of Africa, 136, 138
Iteso (Kenya), 217
Ivory, as art medium, 227
I Will Marry When I Want (Ngugi wa
    Thiong'o), 303

Jabo (Liberia), 260
Jakhanke people (Senegal), 102–103
Jenne (Mali), 86, 242. *See also* Songhai empire
Jie (Uganda), 193
Jihad, 98
Johannesburg, South Africa, 281, 396, 401,
    408. *See also* Sharpeville massacre; Soweto
    Rebellion
The Joys of Motherhood (Emecheta), 306
Judaism, 98
July's People (Gordimer), 308
Jump and Other Stories (Gordimer), 308

Kadalie, Clements, 132
Kalahari Desert, 192. *See also* San
Kane, Cheikh Hamidou, 298–99, 309
Kanem-Bornu empire, 82–83
Kani, John, 308
Kano, Nigeria, 8, 9, 26, 27
Kasanje, 122
Kaunda, Kenneth, 352, 428
Kenya: archaeological excavation, 57; early
    food production in, 67; precolonial history
    of, 94; white settler politics in, 148;
    decolonization and independence, 162–63;
    capitalist strategy of development, 168;
    land tenure in, 181; ethnicity and belief
    systems in, 220–21; contemporary marriage
    in, 320–21; constitution of, 337; demo-
    cratic reforms in, 353, 390–91; develop-
    ment crisis in, 392. *See also* Abaluyia;
    Maasai; Mijikenda; Turkana
Kenya Africa Democratic Union, 221
Kenyatta, Jomo, 160, 163, 168, 285, 353, 428
Kérékou, Mathieu, 355
Khalifa, political structure of Muslim com-
    munity, 98
Khama, Sir Seretse, 353
Khasso (state of), 121
Khoikhoi (South Africa), 128
Khoisan-speaking peoples, 67
Kilwa (town of), 104
Kimbanguism, 150
Kinship, social organization and patterns of,
    176–81
Kiswahili language, 103
Kitara (state), 92
Komo (Mali), 234, 252, 255
Kong (state of), 121
Kongo, kingdom of: early history of, 90; slave
    trade in, 121–22; art of, 237, 247, 254. *See
    also* Angola; Zaire
Koran. *See* Qur'an
Kota (Gabon), 252
Kourouma, Ahmadou, 302, 310
Kpelle (Liberia), 259–60, 265, 267, 270, 271
Kru (Liberia), 150
Kush (kingdom), 69, 73, 80

Labor: economics of colonialism, 151–53; gendered division of, 185–86; division of in farming household, 196–99; importance of women's in rural areas, 316–17; *apartheid* and, 396–97

Labor unions: resistance to *apartheid* in South Africa, 132, 397, 406; strikes as resistance to colonialism, 150

Labou Tansi, Sony, 300, 303, 311

Ladipo, Duro, 281

Lagos, Nigeria, 139, 140, 144, 184, 279–80, 287, 322

Lagos Plan of Action (OAU, 1980), 44

LaGuma, Alex, 308

Land tenure: economics of colonialism and, 151, 153; descent group system of, 180–81; customary law and, 335; legal reform and, 336

Lane, Paul, 290

Languages, African: linguistic families of, 13, 14; linguistics as historical source, 77; Bantu origins and migrations, 86; precolonial history of East Africa, 91–92; Islam and Arabic dialects of North Africa, 101; and ethnic identities under colonial rule, 139; colonial administrations and, 147; diversity of in Tanzania, 211; tone languages and music, 262; African literature and, 296, 305–12

Laye, Camara, 298, 309–10

Leakey, Mary and Louis, 53

Lega (Zaire), 254

Legal system: *sharia* and Islamic, 99; legal pluralism, 331, 341–42; colonialism and, 331–35; customary law, 334–35; after independence, 335–36; constitutions and constitutionalism, 337–38; human rights and development, 338–39; women and, 340–41; reform of in South Africa, 411

Leopold II, King, 136, 138

Lesotho, 384

A Lesson from Aloes (Fugard), 308

Liberia: sovereignty during colonial era, 136; rebellions in, 150; music in, 264. *See also* Jabo; Kpelle; Kru; Vai

Life expectancy, 325–26. *See also* Health

Lifestyles, diversity of, 4

Liking, Werewere, 310

The Lion and the Jewel (Soyinka), 305–306

Literacy: early literate traditions as historical sources, 73–74; variations in sub-Saharan Africa, 383

Literature, African: diversity of, 295; study of, 295–96; trends and themes in, 296–303; debates, challenges, and prospects of, 303–305; selected authors and titles by language group, 305–12; resources on, 427–30

Livestock. *See* Domestication; Pastoralism

Livingstone, David, 125, 212–13

Liyong, Taban lo, 307

Lopés, Henri, 300, 311

Louis XIV (1643–1715), 223

Lozi, kingdom of, 90

Luba, kingdom of, 90

Lugbara (Uganda), 261

Lulua (Zaire), 225, 226, 232

Lumumba, Patrice, 164, 285

Lunda empire, 88–89, 122, 126

Lusaka, Zambia, 8

Lwoo (Kenya, Uganda), 92–93

Maasai (Kenya), 94, 182, 224, 231

Maasai Civil Wars, 94

Madmen and Specialists (Soyinka), 306

Mahdi (Sudan), 110

Mai Idris Alooma, 82

Maize. *See* Corn

Maji-Maji insurrection (1905), 150

Makeba, Miriam, 288, 289

Malaria, 38, 126

Malawi, 71, 148, 212, 350

Mali: medieval empire, 70, 82; Islam and, 102; gender roles in, 185; art in, 225–26, 234, 242, 244, 249, 250, 254–55; democratic elections in, 353. *See also* Bamana; Dogon; Jenne; Komo; Mande

Mande (Mali), 182, 184, 251–52, 271

Mandela, Nelson, 3, 401, 404, 408, 409, 411, 431

Mandela's Earth and Other Poems (Soyinka), 306

Manioc, 6, 28, 31, 65, 123, 203–204

Man of the People (Achebe), 305

Mansa Musa, 102

Mapanje, Jack, 305, 307

Maranke, John, 257

Marechera, Dambudzo, 307

Mariam, Mengistu Haile, 354

Markets, social organization and, 183–84. *See also* Trade

Márquez, García, 303

Marriage: social organization and, 179–80; urbanization and social change, 316–21; legal system and, 333, 336. *See also* Family

Maru (Head), 308

Marxism, Afro-Marxist regimes in postindependence period, 168

Masai. *See* Maasai

Masks, as art form, 252, 255. *See also* Komo

Masquerades, art and spirituality, 251, 254–55

Master Harold and the Boys (Fugard), 308

Matamba, kingdom of, 122

Maternal descent groups, 180

Matigari (Ngugi wa Thiong'o), 307

Matthews, James, 309

Mau Mau rebellion, 148, 162

Mauritania, colonial economic system in, 153

Mauritius, 168
Mazrui, Ali A., 433
Mbeki, Thabo, 409, 410
Mbiti, John, 275, 421
Mbowa, Rose, 281–82
Media, popular culture and, 282–86
Mende (Sierra Leone), 185–86, 244, 255, 257
Menelik II, 138
Menes, King (Egypt), 79
Meroe (city-state), 69, 73, 80
Metalworking, as art form, 226–27, 228
Migration: seasonal pattern of in West Africa, 33, 36; traditions of in precolonial history, 78, 79; of Bantu-speakers in sub-Saharan Africa, 87–88; precolonial history of East Africa and, 93–94
Mijikenda (Kenya), 226
Military: colonial states and conscription in Africa, 147, 158; and politics in postindependence Africa, 168, 350–51; regimes and constitutionalism, 338
Millet, 28, 31, 65, 66, 67, 68, 69, 81, 196, 200, 202, 203
Mine and Works Act (1911), 396
Mine Boy (Abrahams), 308
Mining industry, 151–52, 364, 365, 380
Mitterrand, François, 355
Modernization: concept of, 7–8; social organization and, 176
Moi, Daniel arap, 355
Monenembo, Tierno, 310
Monnè outrages défis (Kourouma), 302
Monomotapa, empire of, 90
Mopti, Niger, 83
Moravian Brethren, 125
Morocco: as Muslim state under British rule, 110; French colonial policies in, 144; nationalist movement, 148
Mouride movement, 110, 112
Mozambique: independence in, 156, 164–66; Afro-Marxist regime in, 168; nursery, 319; development crisis in, 392. *See also* Yao
Mphalele, Ezekiel, 308
Mtshali, Oswald, 309
Mude, Hakurotwo, 263–64
Mudimbe, V. Y., 304
Mugabe, Robert, 163
Muhammad (prophet), 97–98
Muhammad Ahmad (Mahdi), 110
Muhammad Ali (Egypt), 109
Muhammad Uthman al-Mirghani, 107
Muhammed V, 148
Murals, as popular art form, 290
Music, African: role of in daily life, 257–58; early accounts of, 259–60; and sound, 260–63; and time, 263–65; performers of, 265–67; instruments in, 267–69; feeling of, 269–71; in perspective, 271; popular culture and, 286–89; resources on, 426–27

Muslim Brotherhood, 112
My Son's Story (Gordimer), 308
Mzala (Mzamane), 308
Mzamane, Mbulelo, 308

Namibia: independence in, 156, 192; free elections, 169; mining industry, 364
Naming systems, 217
Nana Asma'u, 108
Natal: British colonialism in, 128, 130; Zulu rebellion of 1906, 150
National Congolese Movement (MNC), 164
National Dance Troupe of Guinea, 271
Nationalism, African: Muslim views of, 112; Afrikaner in South Africa, 130; before World War II, 148–51; decolonization and political independence, 161–66
National Party (South Africa), 395
Native Lands Act (South Africa), 131
Native Service Contract Act (1932), 397
Ndebele (South Africa), 290
Négritude: African literature and, 297–98; literary themes of, 300
Neocolonialism: continuance of ties with Europe, 7; transformation of colonialism into, 156; and capitalism in postindependence period, 167–68; as theme of African literature, 299–300; and policies of International Monetary Fund and World Bank, 357. *See also* Decolonization; Postcolonialism
Neo-Destour Party, 148
Nervous Conditions (Dangarembga), 302, 307
Netherlands, colonialism in South Africa, 128, 130
Neto, Agostinho, 297, 311, 312
Newspapers: popular culture and, 284–86; literature and, 303
Ngoni (Zambia), 139
Nguema, Francisco Macías, 338, 353
Ngugi wa Thiong'o, 297, 299–300, 302, 303, 305, 307
Niane, Djibril Tamsir, 310
Niger, 83
Nigeria: early history of, 70; civil war in, 139; mining industry, 152; colonial economic system in, 153; social organization in, 175; land tenure in, 181; small-scale farming in, 182, 200; architecture of, 229; art and history of, 230, 235, 236, 239, 240, 241, 243, 250; religion and popular culture in, 276–78; popular theater in, 280–81; government suppression of popular music, 289; popular art in, 290–91; literature of, 305–306; education, 322; Islam and conflict in, 328; legal system of, 335; renegotiation of boundary with Cameroon, 348. *See also* Fulani; Fulbe; Hausa; Igbo; Ohafia; Tiv; Yoruba
Nigerian Film Festival, 284

Nile region, early agriculture in, 66. *See also* Egypt
Niumi, kingdom of, 120
Nkrumah, Kwame, 157, 158, 160, 161–62, 257, 285, 349, 428
No Baby Must Weep (Serote), 309
Nok culture (Nigeria), 68, 230, 236
No Longer at Ease (Achebe), 305
None to Accompany Me (Gordimer), 308
Nongovernmental organizations (NGOs), reports on human rights, 339
Nonquase, 132
Noog, 67
North Africa: division between sub-Saharan Africa and, 5; precolonial history of, 79–80; introduction of Islam and social change in, 99–101; early Islamic trade routes in, 103; national movements before World War II, 148–49; literature of, 304
Nos matamos o cão tinhoso (Honwana), 311
No Sweetness Here (Aidoo), 301
Ntshona, Winston, 308
Nubia, Islamic expansion into, 104
Nuer (Sudan), 94
Nwapa, Flora, 301, 306
Nyerere, Julius, 167, 352
Nzinga (Queen), 122

Obasanjo, Olusegun, 352
Obey, Ebenezer, 288
Obituary advertisements, 285
OCAMM (Organization commune africaine, malgace et mauricienne), 5
Occupation: social organization and, 182–84; art as, 228–29; urban female, 317–19
Oguaa-Afahye festival, 275
Ogun Abibiman (Soyinka), 306
Ogunde, Hubert, 280–81
Ogunmola, Kola, 281
Ohafia (Nigeria), 180
Oil palm, 65, 124, 127, 153
Okigbo, Christopher, 306
Okomfo Anakye, 253
Okri, Ben, 303, 306
Olaiya, Moses, 281
The Old Man and the Medal (Oyono), 299
Oldowan phase, of Stone Age, 53, 55–57, 58
Olduvai Gorge (Tanzania), 53
Oman, Muslim imperialism in, 109–10
Once upon Four Robbers (Osofisan), 306
Onchocerciasis, 38–40
Oral tradition: as sources for precolonial African history, 74–77; collections of oral literature, 429–30
Orange Free State, 128, 130
Organization of African Unity (OAU), 5, 43, 44, 339, 348

Organization of Petroleum Exporting Countries (OPEC), 364
Origins: in oral traditions, 75–76; precolonial history and traditions of, 78–79
Orphée Dafric (Liking), 310
Osanyin, Bode, 282
Osei, Teddy, 288
Osei Tutu, 253
Osibisa (musical group), 288
Osofisan, Femi, 306
Osundare, Niyi, 306
Ottoman empire: expansion into North Africa, 101; and Portuguese in northeastern Africa, 104
Otumo ceremony, 175
Ouologuem, Yambo, 300, 301, 310
Oyekunle, Segun, 281
Oyono, Ferdinand, 299, 310
The Ozidi Saga (Clark), 306

Paleolithic. *See* Stone Age
The Palm-Wine Drinkard (Tutuola), 306
Pan Africanist Congress (PAC), 399, 401, 409
Park, Mungo, 124
Parti Democratique de Guineé (PDG), 349
Pastoralism, 22, 32, 193–95. *See also* Agriculture
Paternal descent groups, 180
Paton, Alan, 308
p'Bitek, Okot, 299, 307
Peanuts, 112, 124, 153, 196, 197, 198, 200
Pereira, Aristides, 352
Performing Arts Company of the Windybrow Arts Center (PACT), 281
Petals of Blood (Ngugi wa Thiong'o), 302, 307
Peul (West Africa), 195
Les Phalènes (U Tam'si), 310
Philombe, René, 310
Phoenicia, 68, 69
Poetry: *négritude* movement, 298; black urban life in South Africa, 309. *See also* Literature; Oral tradition
Polanyi, Michael, 214
Politics: and ethnic identity, 4, 181; and population growth, 36, 37; authority and precolonial, 94–95; of white settlers under colonialism, 147–50; African participation in under colonial rule, 148–51; regimes of postindependence period, 166–70; kinship patterns and, 181; art and, 253; legacy of colonialism, 347; concentration of power, 348–50; military regimes, 350–51; reestablishment of political participation, 351–53; economic decline and, 353–54; popular revolt and democratic renewal, 355; threat of anarchy, 355–56; future of, 357; development crisis and, 382–83, 390–91; resources on, 423–25. *See also* State

Polygyny, social organization and, 177–78, 180
The Poor Christ of Bomba (Béti), 299
Popular culture: music and daily life, 258, 286–89; dynamics of social change and, 273; and religion, 274–78; and theater, 278–82; mass media and, 282–86; art and, 289–93
Population: growth of and patterns of development, 36, 37, 326, 381–82; urbanization and distribution of, 41–42
Portugal: maritime expansion in fifteenth century, 104, 115–16; slave trade and, 121, 123; and European partition of Africa, 136, 138; colonial policies of, 143, 144; decolonization and independence movements, 164–66; and African tourist art, 250, 289; colonies of and concept of race, 311
Postcolonialism, impact of on development, 43–44. *See also* Decolonization; Neocolonialism
Pottery, as art form, 227, 228
Poverty: in postcolonial period, 156, 157; and migrants to urban areas, 316; structural adjustment programs and, 367, 388–89; development crisis and, 377
Precipitation, average annual, 25, 26–27, 191. *See also* Droughts
Prehistory, African: human evolution, 49, 50–53, 55, 58, 60–61; overview of major developments in, 50; Early Stone Age, 53–58; Middle Stone Age, 59–60; Later Stone Age, 61–64; origins and spread of agriculture, 64–67; Iron Age developments, 67–71
Primates, evolution of, 49, 50–53
Prostitution, 318, 319
Public health, policies of African governments on, 42–43. *See also* AIDS; Health
Pukwana, Dudu, 289

A Question of Power (Head), 308
Qur'an, 97, 98, 99

Race, European domination under colonialism, 140–44
Railways, 19, 360
Rainfall. *See* Precipitation
Rain forest, 27, 38
Rajbansi, Amichand, 403
Ranku, Lucky, 289
Rastafarian philosophy, 287
Refugees, civil wars and development crisis, 378
Reggae music, 287
Religion: resistance to *apartheid* in South Africa, 132; and popular culture, 274–78; resources on, 421. *See also* Belief systems; Christianity; Islam; Judaism; Spirituality
Resources, in African Studies: general overview of, 414–15; geography, 415–16;

history and archaeology, 416–18; social sciences and anthropology, 418–21; religion and philosophy, 421; economics, 422; politics and international relations, 423–25; art, 425–26; music, 426–27; literature and folklore, 427–30; South Africa, 430–31; materials published in Africa, 431–32; computer resources, 433–34
Rhodesia, white settler politics in, 148. *See also* Zimbabwe
Rice, 65, 67, 68, 184, 200–201
Riotous Assemblies Act of 1956, 396
Rites of passage, 175–76, 253–54. *See also* Age; Initiation rites
Rive, Richard, 309
River blindness, 38–40
The Road (Soyinka), 306
Rock art, of Later Stone Age, 62–63
Roman empire, 69
Rural areas: "tradition" and "modern" in contemporary Africa, 8; importance of women's labor in, 316–17; social change in, 321–24
Rwanda, 3, 37, 146, 338, 372, 390

Sagrada Esperanca (Neto), 312
Sahara Desert: prehistoric environment of and agriculture in, 65; contemporary lifestyles in, 191; cave art in, 229
Salih, Tayeb el, 304
Samori Toure, 138
San (Botswana, South Africa), 63, 94, 192
Sande association, 185–86, 251
Sassine, William, 310
Scarlet Song (Ouologuem), 301
Scientific Revolution, 124
Sculpture, African art and, 227, 230
Segu (state of), 121
Self-representation, as theme in African literature, 296–99
Sembene, Ousmane, 284, 299, 302–303, 309
Senegal: Sufism in, 110, 112; slave trade in, 119; colonial rule and social relations in, 140; African participation in colonial politics, 149; literature of, 309; political participation in postindependence, 352
Senghor, Léopold Sédar, 298, 309, 352
Sepamla, Sipho, 309
Serote, Mongane Wally, 309
Shaka (Zulu), 91
Shallots, 205
Sharia, Islamic legal system, 99
Sharpeville massacre, 401
Shaykh (Sufism), 107
Shi'a, establishment and early influence of, 101
Shilluk (Sudan), 217
Shona (Zimbabwe), 261, 265, 268

Shuttle in the Crypt (Soyinka), 306
Sidi al-Mukhtar al-Kunti, 107
Sidi Ballo, 252
Sierra Leone: arranged marriages in, 179; art and history of, 242, 244, 250. *See also* Mende
Sisulu, Walter, 408
Sizwe Bansi Is Dead (Fugard, Kani, and Ntshona), 308
Slave trade: and African diaspora, 6; Islamic involvement in, 105–106; historical interpretations of, 115; impact of on West Africa, 115–23; and end of slavery, 124
Sleeping sickness, 38, 193
Sobukwe, Robert, 401
Social change: popular culture and, 273; cinema as medium for, 283–84; historical background to contemporary, 313–16; urban structural change and gender roles, 316–21; in rural areas, 321–24; critical issues in, 324–27; capitalism and increase in socioeconomic inequality, 328. *See also* Social organization
Social Dimensions of Adjustment (SDA—World Bank), 389
Socialism, in postindependence African politics, 166–67
Social organization: impact of colonialism on, 176, 187–88; kinship, family, and household, 176–81; occupation and social status, 182–84; gender and, 184–86; age and, 186–87; of savanna herders, 193–95; of farming households, 196–99; belief systems and, 218–21. *See also* Social change
Sociology, resources in African Studies, 418–21
Soglo, Nicéphore, 355
Sokoto Caliphate, 108, 110
Les Soleils des indépendances (Kourouma), 302, 310
So Long a Letter (Bâ), 301
Somalia, 32, 37, 191, 338, 350, 354, 355
Songhai empire: precolonial history of, 85, 86; Islam and, 102; architecture of, 229
Song of Lawino (p'Bitek), 299, 307
Song of Ocol (p'Bitek), 307
Sorghum, 28, 31, 65, 66, 67, 68, 69, 196, 197, 198, 200, 202
Sounds of a Cowhide Drum (Mtshali), 309
South Africa: end of *apartheid* and inauguration of Mandela, 3, 156, 407–11; immigration of Indian Muslims to, 112; colonialism in nineteenth century, 128–32; establishment of *apartheid*, 142, 395–403; Zulu rebellion of 1906, 150; economic exploitation in, 151; religion, 279; popular theater in, 281; *apartheid* and suppression of popular music in, 288–89; literature of, 308–309; democratic elections in, 357; economic development in, 383–84, 392;

black resistance to *apartheid*, 395–403; deepening confrontation of 1980s, 403–405; limited political reforms in, 405–407; future of, 411–12; resources on, 430–31. *See also* Khoikhoi; Ndebele; San; Tswana; Xhosa; Zulu
South African Communist Party, 401
South African Congress of Trade Unions (SACTU), 401
South African Development Community (SADC), 5
South African Student's Movement (SASM), 402
South African Student's Organization (SASO), 402
Southern Africa: Stone Age in, 53, 55, 62–63; agriculture and prehistory of, 67, 71; precolonial history of, 69–70, 91; colonial history of, 128–32; colonialism and social organization, 176; art and artists, 227–29; literature of, 307–309. *See also* South Africa
South Korea, economic development in, 375
South-West African People's Organization (SWAPO), 192
The Soweto I Love (Sepamla), 309
Soweto Rebellion, 401, 402
Soyinka, Wole, 297, 300, 304, 305–306, 428
Spirituality, art and, 250–52. *See also* Belief systems; Religion
Sport of Nature (Gordimer), 308
Stanley, Henry Morton, 125, 139, 212
State: precolonial history and formation of, 78–79; character of colonial in Africa, 145–47. *See also* Politics
State Security Council (SSC—South Africa), 406
Stone Age, 53–67
Strikes. *See* Labor unions
Structural adjustment programs (IMF and World Bank), 367, 372, 385–90
Sub-Saharan Africa. *See* Central Africa; Southern Africa; West Africa
Sudan: early agriculture in, 66; early Islamic trade routes in, 103; livestock market, 106; Muslim resistance to European colonialism in, 110; slave trade in, 121. *See also* Azande; Shilluk
Suez Canal, 126
Sufism, 106–108, 110, 112, 113
Sukuma (Tanzania), 227
Sundiata epic, 77, 177, 182
Suppression of Communism Act of 1950 (South Africa), 396
Supreme Court (South Africa), 411
Sutherland, Efua, 307
Swahili, precolonial history of, 103–104

Taiwan, economic development in, 375
Tallensi (Ghana), 218–19

Tanganyika: colonial capital of, 146; white settler politics in, 148; resistance to colonialism in, 150; precolonial history of, 181

Tanzania: early food production in, 67; *Ujamaa* socialism in, 166–67; diversity of languages in, 211; legal reform in, 336; constitution of, 337; one-party regime in, 350; structural adjustment programs and urban poverty, 367; development crisis in, 392. *See also* Sukuma; Zaramo

Tanzanian African National Union (TANU), 350

Taro, 28, 31

Tati-Loutard, Jean-Baptiste, 310

Taxation, resistance to colonial rule, 150

Technology, belief systems and, 216–17. *See also* Agriculture

Television, popular culture and, 282–83

Tell Freedom (Abrahams), 308

Le Temps de Tamango (Diop), 302, 309

Terre Blanche, Eugene, 406

Terrorism Act of 1967 (South Africa), 396

Theater, and popular culture, 278–82. *See also* Literature

Things Fall Apart (Achebe), 297, 305

Thiong'o, Ngugi wa, 297, 299–300, 302, 303, 305, 307

Timbuktu, Mali, 8, 86, 102

Tiv (Nigeria), 203, 220

Tlali, Miriam, 309

Togo, 85, 179, 327

Tolbert, William, 268

Tort law, 334

Toure, Sekou, 139

Touregs. *See* Tuaregs

Tourism, impact of on popular art, 289–90

Towa, Marcien, 300

Trade, international: economics of, 205–209; changing global patterns of in 1970s and 1980s, 365–66; development crisis and, 379, 381

Tradition: concept of, 7–8; social organization and, 176; art and, 224, 289

Transitional Executive Council (TEC), 409

Transkei, 398

Transportation, colonial pattern of, 43. *See also* Railways

Transvaal, 128, 130

Traore, Moussa, 353

The Trial of Dedan Kimathi (Ngugi wa Thiong'o), 303

Trials of Brother Jero (Soyinka), 306

Tsetse fly, 28, 31, 38, 193. *See also* Sleeping sickness

Tshombe, Moise, 146

Tswana (Botswana, South Africa), 179

Tuaregs (Sahara), 39, 191

Tunisia: as Muslim state under British rule, 110; French colonial policies in, 144; nationalist movement, 148

Turkana (Kenya), 228

Tutsi (Rwanda), 146

Tutuola, Amos, 306

Two Thousand Seasons (Armah), 306

Uganda: economics of colonialism in, 153; pastoralism in, 193; agriculture in, 204; popular theater in, 281–82; human rights violations in, 338; one-party regime in, 350; end of Amin regime, 353. *See also* Gisu; Jie; Lugbara; Lwoo

Ujamaa socialism, 166–67

Ulama (learned ones), 99

Umkhonto We Sizwe (Spear of the Nation), 401

United Democratic Front (UDF), 404

United Gold Coast Convention (UGCC), 161–62

United Nations: human rights, 338, 339; Decade for Women, 340

United States Agency for International Development, 391

Unlawful Organizations Act of 1960 (South Africa), 396

Urban areas and urbanization: "tradition" and "modern" in contemporary Africa, 8; and population distribution, 41–42; precolonial history of Bantu history, 88–89; in nineteenth-century South Africa, 130; popular culture and, 273, 275, 276; increase of in postwar period, 314–15; social change and gender roles, 316–21; birth rates and overpopulation, 326

U Tam'si, Tchicaya, 310

Uthman dan Fodio, 108

Vai (Liberia), 259

Vegetational zones, 28, 30, 54

Venda, 398

Verwoerd, Dr. H. J., 401–402

A Vida Verdadeira de Domingos Xavier (Vieira), 311–12

Vieira, José Luandino, 311–12

A Walk in the Night (LaGuma), 308

Watchtower movement, 150

Weaving. *See* Fabric

West Africa: pattern of development and climate of, 31–33, 36; early agriculture, 66; precolonial history of, 80–86; history of Muslim-European relations, 105–106; impact of slave trade on, 115–23; British colonial policies, 144; African political activity during colonial era, 149; economics of colonialism, 153; pastoralism, 195; farming households, 196–99; architecture, 229–30; art and spirituality, 252; English-language literature of, 305–307; funerals, 321; military regimes and return of civilian rule, 353

Westernization, social change and, 313
Wheat, 65, 66, 67, 80
When Rain Clouds Gather (Head), 301–302, 308
Why Are We So Blest? (Armah), 306
Wilderness spirits, 251
Witchcraft, belief systems of Azande, 214–15, 216
Women: and authority in precolonial societies, 95; decline in status of under colonialism, 139–40, 340; exclusion from participation in colonial politics, 149; economics of colonialism and, 153; marketing and, 184, 208–209; division of social roles, 184–86; art and spirituality, 251; African literature by, 296, 300–302; importance of labor in rural areas, 316–17; self-employment and economic autonomy in urban areas, 317–19; magazines for, 320–21; discrimination against in education, 327; and constitutionalism in Africa, 338; legal system and, 340–41; resources in Women's Studies, 418–21. *See also* Gender
Women in Law and Development in Africa (WILDAF), 341
Wood, as art medium, 226
World Bank, 7, 357, 366–67, 377, 385–90
World War II, 154, 157–59
The Wretched of the Earth (Fanon), 141

Xhosa (South Africa), 128, 130

Yakhal'inkomo (Serote), 309

Yamakala, social status of, 182
Yams, 6, 28, 31, 65, 67, 68, 87, 203
Yao (Mozambique), 138
Yoruba (Nigeria): early history of, 70; gender roles, 185; agriculture and social organization of, 198–99; art of, 243, 250–51; music and, 262; religion and popular culture, 274–75, 276–78; popular theater, 281

Zaire: precolonial history of, 90; decolonization and independence, 164; art of, 232, 233, 234, 235, 247, 248; popular theater in, 280. *See also* Bakongo; Bangala; Kongo; Lega; Lulua
Zambia: precolonial history of, 71, 181; urban settings and belief systems, 220; AIDS in, 325–26; Kariba dam, 368. *See also* Barotse; Bemba
Zanzibar, Muslim imperialism in, 109–10
Zaramo (Tanzania), 226, 228
Zimbabwe: precolonial history of, 71, 89–90, 181; independence in, 156; decolonization and independence, 163; political parties in 1980s, 168; music in, 265; literature of, 307; ethnicity and conflict in, 328; mining industry, 365; Kariba dam, 368. *See also* Rhodesia; Shona
Zimbabwe African National Union (ZANU), 163
Zimbabwe African People's Union (ZAPU), 163
Zulu (South Africa): precolonial history of, 91; resistance to colonialism, 132, 150. *See also* Inkatha Freedom Party